The Monetary and Financial System

3rd edition

BANKERS WORKBOOK SERIES

ROD APPS BA (Econ), MA (Econ), PhD

DAVID GOACHER BA (Econ), PhD

Revised with additional material by
Geoffrey Lipscombe BSc (Econ), FCIB

Published in association with

Sheffield
Hallam University

First published in 1991
Reprinted 1992
2nd edition 1994
3rd edition 1996

BANKERS BOOKS LIMITED
c/o The Chartered Institute of Bankers
90 Bishopsgate
London EC2N 4AS

CIB Publications are published by The Chartered Institute of Bankers, a non-profit making registered educational charity, and are distributed exclusively by Bankers Books Limited which is a wholly owned subsidiary of The Chartered Institute of Bankers.

The Chartered Institute of Bankers believes that the sources of information upon which the book is based are reliable and has made every effort to ensure the complete accuracy of the text. However, neither the CIB, the author nor any contributor can accept any legal responsibility whatsoever for consequences that may arise from errors or omission or any opinion or advice given.

ISBN 0–85297–414–0

Contents

Introduction

The Concept of the Course

This is a practical workbook written for students studying for banking and finance qualifications and also for practitioners in the financial services who are looking for a practical refresher.

Each unit is divided into sections and contains:

- Learning objectives;
- Clear, concise topic-by-topic coverage;
- Examples and learning activities to reinforce learning, confirm understanding and stimulate thought;
- Often, past examination questions to try for practice;
- Self-assessment questions to test your knowledge, understanding and skills.

Learning activities

Learning activities are provided throughout. These come in a variety of forms. For example, they:

- Test your ability to recall information, your ability to analyse material, or assess whether you have appreciated the full significance of a piece of information.
- Require discussion with colleagues, friends or fellow students.
- Require you to do some research.

Virtually all require you to record something in writing and you should keep your notes/answers for later reference.

Where the activity comprises a series of short questions, a reference is given to the precise part of the preceding text where you can find the answer. For others, where appropriate, a suggested answer/response/solution is given, but often in abbreviated form to help you avoid the temptation of merely reading the 'answer'! You will find our suggestions in the Appendix.

At the end of each unit there are self-assessment questions. These usually comprise a number of short answer questions and multiple-choice questions and, often, a full specimen examination question. The answers to all of these questions are also to be found in the Appendix.

Syllabus

The key sections of the Management and Organisation syllabus are:

- The Properties and Pricing of Financial Assets

- Financial Institutions
- Financial Markets
- Derivative Instruments
- The Regulation of Financial Institutions and Financial Markets
- The Analysis of Interest Rates
- Derivative Instruments
- Monetary Policy
- The Analysis of Exchange Rates
- Derivative Instruments
- Corporate Sector Finances
- Personal Sector Finances and the Housing Market

Your contribution

Although this workbook is designed to stand alone, as with most topics, certain aspects of this subject are constantly changing. Therefore it is very important that you keep up-to-date with these key areas.

We anticipate that you will study this course for one academic year, reading through and studying approximately two units every three weeks. However, note that as topics vary in size and as knowledge tends not to fall into uniform chunks, some units are unavoidably longer than others.

The masculine pronoun 'he' has been used in this workbook to encompass both genders and to avoid the awkwardness of the constant repetition of 'he and/or she'.

Study Guide

Below we offer advice and ideas on studying, revising and approaching examinations.

Studying

As with any examination, there is no substitute for preparation based on an organised and disciplined study plan. You should devise an approach which will enable you to complete this workbook and still leave time for revision of this and any other subject you are taking at the same time. Many candidates find that about six weeks is about the right period of time to leave for revision, enough time to get through the revision material, but not so long that it is no longer fresh in your mind by the time you reach the examination.

This means that you should plan how to get to the last chapter by, say, the end of March for a May sitting or the end of August for an October sitting. This includes not only reading the text, but making notes, working through the student activities and answering any illustrative examination questions which are included.

We offer the following as a starting point for approaching your study.

- *Plan time each week* to study a part of this workbook. Make sure that it is 'quality' study time: let everyone know that you are studying and that you should not be disturbed. If you are at home, unplug your telephone or switch the answerphone on; if you are in the office, put you telephone on 'divert'.

- Set a *clearly defined objective* for each study period. You may simply wish to read through a unit for the first time or perhaps you may want to make some notes on a unit you have already read a couple of times. Don't forget the student activities, self-assessment questions and any examination questions.

- *Review your study plan.* Devise a study checklist and/or timetable so that you can schedule and monitor your progress. Don't panic if you fall behind, but do think how you will make up for lost time.

- Look for *relevant examples* of what you have covered in the 'real' world. If you work for a financial organisation, this should provide them. If you don't, then think about your experiences as an individual bank or building society customer or perhaps about your employer's position as a corporate customer of a bank. Keep an eye on the quality press for reports about banks and building societies and their activities.

Revising

The period which you have earmarked for revision is a very important. Now it is even more important that you plan *time each week for study* and that you set *clear objectives* for each revision session. So ...

- *Make use of a timetable.*

- *Use time sensibly.* How much revision time do you have? Remember that you still need to eat, sleep and fit in some leisure time!

- *How will you allocate the available time between subjects?* What are your weaker subjects? You will need to focus on some topics more than others. You will also need to plan your revision around your learning style. By now, you should know whether, for example, early morning, early evening or late evening is best.

- *Take regular breaks.* Most people find they can absorb more if they attempt to revise for long uninterrupted periods of time. Award yourself a five minute break every hour or so. Go for a stroll or make a cup of coffee, but don't turn the television on!

- *Believe in yourself.* Are you cultivating the right attitude of mind? There is absolutely no reason why you should not pass the exam if you adopt the correct approach. Be confident, you have passed exams before so you can pass this one.

The examination

Passing examinations is half about having the required knowledge, understanding and skills, and half about doing yourself justice in the examination. You must have the right *technique*.

The day of the exam

- Set at least one alarm (or get an alarm call) for a morning exam.

- Have something to eat but don't eat too much; you may feel sleepy if your system is digesting a large meal.
- Don't forget pens, pencils, rulers, erasers and anything else you will need.
- Avoid discussion about the exam with other candidates outside the exam hall.

Tackling the examination paper
First, make sure that you satisfy the examiner's requirements

- *Read the instructions on the front of the exam paper carefully.* Check that the exam format hasn't changed. It is surprising how often examiners' reports remark on the number of students who attempt too few – or too many – questions, or who attempt the wrong number of questions from different parts of the paper. Make sure that you are planning to answer the right number of questions.
- *Read all the questions on the exam paper before you start writing.* Look at the weighting of marks to each part of the question. If part (a) offers only four marks and you can't answer the 12 marks part (b), then don't choose the question.
- *Don't produce irrelevant answers.* Make sure you answer the question set, and not the question you would have preferred to have been set.
- *Produce an answer in the correct format.* The examiner will state the format in which the question should be answered, for example in a report or memorandum. If a question asks for a diagram or an example, give one. If a question does not specifically asks for a diagram or example, but it seems appropriate, give one.

Second, observe the following simple rules to ensure that your script is acceptable to the examiner.

- *Present a tidy paper.* You are a professional and it should always show in the presentation of your work. Candidates may be penalised for poor presentation and so you must make sure that you write legibly, label diagrams clearly and lay out your work professionally. Assistant examiners each have dozens of papers to mark; a badly written scrawl is unlikely to receive the same attention as a neat and well laid out paper.
- *State the obvious.* Many candidates look for complexity which is not required and consequently overlook the obvious. Make basic statements first. Plan your answer and ask yourself whether you have answered the main parts of the question.
- *Use examples.* This will help to demonstrate to the examiner that you keep up-to-date with the subject. There are lots of useful examples scattered through this workbook and you can read about others if you dip into the quality press or take notice of what is happening in your working environment.

Finally, Make sure that you give yourself the opportunity to do yourself justice.

- *Select questions carefully.* Read through the paper once, then quickly jot down any key points against each question in a second read through. Reject those questions against which you have jotted down very little. Select those where you could latch on to 'what the question is about' –

but remember to check carefully that you have got the right end of the stick before putting pen to paper.

- *Plan your attack carefully.* Consider the order in which you are going to tackle questions. It is a good idea to start with your best question to boost your morale and get some easy marks 'in the bag'.

- *Read the question carefully and plan your answer.* Read through the question again very carefully when you come to answer it.

- *Gain the easy marks.* Include the obvious if it answers the question and do not spend unnecessary time producing the perfect answer. As we suggested above, there is nothing wrong with stating the obvious.

- *Avoid getting bogged down in small parts of questions.* If you find a part of a question difficult, get on with the rest of the question. If you are having problems with something the chances are that everyone else is too.

- *Don't leave the exam early.* If you finish early, use your spare time to check and recheck your script.

Don't worry if you feel you have performed badly in the exam. It is likely that the other candidates will have found the exam difficult too. As soon as you get up and leave the exam hall, forget the exam and think about the next – or, if it is the last one, celebrate!

Don't discuss an exam with other candidates. This is particularly the case if you still have other exams to sit. Put it out of your mind until the day of the results. Forget about exams and relax.

Unit 1

The Properties and Pricing of Financial Assets

Objectives

After studying this unit, you should be able to:

- **describe the nature of financial assets, their cash flow and their functions;**

- **identify the characteristics (properties) of financial assets;**

- **understand the nature of money, its characteristics, functions and value;**

- **explain the principles of the pricing of financial assets;**

- **explain what is meant by the price volatility of financial assets;**

- **appreciate the significance of risk and how portfolio diversification can eliminate part of risk.**

---

1 The nature of financial assets, their cash flow and functions

1.1 An asset is a possession or a claim on something or a claim on a person, e.g. a factory, a mortgage, a book debt, or a loan to or a deposit with a third party. Also, it can be a brand, e.g. Pepsi or Black Magic, or goodwill which, in effect, is a business's existing customers and reputation.

1.2 A financial asset can be defined as a claim which is expressed in money, as opposed to a real asset such as a car or a house. Such real assets are termed tangible assets, because they are physical items. However, although investors can touch a financial asset such as a share certificate, the certificate is really only evidence that the holder owns part of a business.

1.3 Financial assets have one similarity with physical assets, in that they both yield income for their owners – interest, profits or dividends for the provider of finance, while the machinery produces output which, in turn, produces sales revenue. Also, the two types of assets are linked because issuing a financial asset is the usual way of becoming the owner of a physical asset, e.g. a hire purchase agreement is issued by the HP company to acquire a lathe. The lathe's cash flow eventually is used, in part, to provide the cash flow for the hire purchase company.

1.4 Financial assets are intangible assets; along with brands and goodwill. However, financial assets are different from these other intangible assets because they are much easier to value, or to price.

1.5 Most financial assets generate a stream of income and other receipts – known as cash flow – for their owners, for example:

- Mortgage/loan – interest, and repayment of principal.

- Company share – half yearly dividends, a rise in share prices (bringing in cash when the share is sold).

- Bond (or gilt edged security) – interest, plus capital repayment on maturity.

- Bill – discount (= excess of maturity value over purchase price).

- Trade debt – eventual payment, plus any interest if specified in contract of sale.

- Bank deposit – most, but not all, pay some interest (in Switzerland, there can be negative interest, i.e. a regular charge for maintaining the account in a very stable currency and for the protection of secrecy under Swiss law).

- Building society deposit – almost invariably this pays interest. However, if the balance falls below £100, some societies do not pay interest.

- Bank note – no interest is paid, although early bank notes did pay interest.

- Coin – no interest paid, although 'clipping' occurred several centuries ago – a sort of illegal cash flow from melting the clippings.

Transfer of ownership

1.6 From the selection of financial assets shown above, you should be able to discern the ways in which ownership is transferred: purchase and sale – shares, bonds, loans (third world debt) and mortgages; exchange for goods (physical assets) or services – deposits, notes, and coin. Legal specialists will spot assignments – of trade debts and life assurance policies – and negotiability – of bills, CDs and bank notes.

1.7 Most of these transfers take place in markets, which we will study, although some may occur 'by private treaty', as with the transfer of shares between members of a private limited company where the articles of association specify that share transfers are to be restricted.

Student Activity 1

For investigation and discussion at work, using personal finance sections of quality newspapers.

1. In what sense is an endowment policy an asset?

2. What are the income streams associated with such policies?

3. Are these streams negative, positive, or both (although not at the same time!).

4. Is there a market in second hand endowment policies?

5. Compare an annuity to a life assurance policy – in what sense is it a mirror image of a policy?

The functions of financial assets

1.8 Financial assets have two main functions, to:

- Transfer funds from people and organisations with surplus funds to those who need funds – usually so that they can purchase tangible assets. Immediately a mortgage should spring to mind.

- Redistribute the risk arising from the flow of funds (e.g. profits) generated by these tangible assets. Thus, a company may be financed partly by shares – with a fluctuating dividend – and by loan stock which has a fixed coupon (rate of interest per £100 of stock). Another example of such a redistribution is the debt/equity structure of a management buy out. We can expand this function into the containment of risk, in ways which we will examine later.

1.9 Other functions include:

- Transferring funds over distances, e.g. investing in the 'Tiger Economies' of SE Asia – and over time. A borrower needs money now whereas a lender usually prefers a steady trickle of money over the period of the loan.

- Aggregating funds from small lenders to larger borrowers: the classic example is a mortgage, which requires about eight retail depositors (lenders) for every borrower. (£50K thus requires 8 people with deposits averaging £6.33K)

- Disaggregating funds, where a bank funds credit card or mortgage lending from the inter-bank market. This, of course, is the opposite of aggregation.

- Displaying price information, to enable firms and householders to take their own decisions in a decentralised economy. In a centralised (or command) economy, such as the former USSR, most decisions were taken for people by the government.

- Creating incentives. Two examples may be given here: lenders may be concerned that business borrowers will overspend and become insolvent, so they try to prevent this inserting restrictive covenants/clauses in the loan agreement. Thus, the lenders restrict the borrower's freedom of action. Another example is the creation of share options to encourage senior managers to be more active in achieving their goals.

Student Activity 2

1. In what ways might financial assets be devised to distribute income unfairly? Should society (i.e. the government) permit this? If not, then how can a fairer distribution be achieved? And, what is a 'fair distribution'?

2. Define a financial asset. *(Paragraph 1.2)*

3. How are such assets transferred? *(Paragraph 1.5)*

4. How are financial assets related to real (physical) assets? *(Paragraph 1.3)*

5. What is meant by the cash flow of a financial asset? *(Paragraph 1.5)*

6. Give three examples of financial assets, and the cash flows which they generate. *(Paragraph 1.5)*

7. What are the major economic functions of financial assets? *(Paragraph 1.8)*

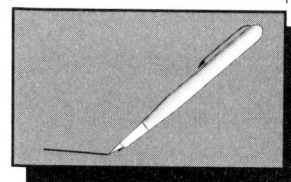

2 The properties (characteristics) of financial assets

2.1 You will probably recall the characteristics of money, summarised by the acronym SPUDRAD. However, here we look at financial assets, which are much broader than money, i.e. money is just one of a large number of financial assets. Accordingly, these characteristics are going to include most of those of money but also some which may be new. Also, some of money's characteristics may be missing.

Student Activity 3

1. When reading the next section, try and think of an acronym that could help you remember (and explain, comment and criticise) these characteristics of financial assets.

2. Go through these characteristics, identifying those which are caused by the nature of the asset and those which result from the nature of the market in which the asset is traded.

2.2 There are many characteristics of financial assets and, for those seeking the acronym, not one begins with a vowel:

- Moneyness;
- Divisibility and denomination;
- Reversibility (into and out of cash);
- Cash flow;
- Term to maturity;
- Convertibility;
- Liquidity;
- 'Return Predictability';
- Complexity;
- Currency;
- Tax Status.

Moneyness

2.3 How close is the asset to money? For instance, a CD is fairly close, being considered 'near money' but an undated gilt – 2.5% Consols or 3.5% War Loan – is not.

Divisibility and denomination

2.4 Loan stock is divisible into penny units, but company shares, e.g. a 25p share, are not. Denomination refers not to currency but to the units of a financial asset which is not divisible. Thus, CDs are issued in units (denominations) of £50,000 or £100,000.

Reversibility (into and out of cash)

2.5 This is akin to liquidity but not exactly the same. If there are plenty of market makers in a share, then it is easy to sell and then buy back. There is a cost, of course, and this is made up of the 'bid-offer spread' or 'touch' on the screen, and commission, stamp duty and other charges. In the USA, these costs are termed 'round-trip costs' or 'reversibility costs' but there is no English term for them. The size of the bid-offer spread will be analysed in Unit 3. The round-trip cost of a bank deposit is, of course, nil – apart from any loss of interest.

Cash flow

2.6 This was mentioned and illustrated in paragraph 1.5 but it is important to appreciate how inflation can eat into the expected cash flow from an asset. Thus, as well as looking at nominal cash flows (returns), analysts and investors examine real returns, i.e. after allowing for anticipated inflation. It is possible to subtract the inflation rate from the nominal interest rate to get a real rate of interest, e.g. $6 - 3 = 3(\%)$. However, at this academic level, it is better to divide, i.e:

$$(1.06/1.03 \times 100) - 100 = 2.913\%$$

In the UK, a number of financial assets are index-linked, so that their real returns rise in line with inflation. Certain gilts are index-linked, in regard to both capital and repayment. The USA is about to issue index-linked Treasury bonds.

Term to maturity

2.7 This characteristic is determined by the nature of the financial asset. Gilts provide a good example of differing maturities – shorts (nought to five years); mediums (5-15 years); longs (over 15 years) and undated. (This classification is from the FT, and covers conventional (i.e. not index-linked) gilts).

Convertibility

2.8 This does not refer to 'cashability' but to the possibility that the asset, by the terms of the contract which created it, may be exchanged for or converted into another financial asset. An example is a convertible loan stock which may, on certain specified dates, be converted into ordinary shares at a stated price.

Liquidity

2.9 You may recall the text book definition from the Foundation Course or the Banking Certificate – exchangeability into cash without delay, cost, loss of capital or interest. This still holds but, at this academic level, the concept of a liquid market needs to be introduced. A market is said to be liquid when assets can be sold on it without their losing much capital value or there being much delay or expense. In UK language, we talk of markets as being either liquid or illiquid; we also use the term 'thin' market to describe an illiquid one. In the USA they use 'thick' rather than 'liquid'. Liquidity can be derived from the market or from the contractual nature of the asset, e.g. a bank deposit, or from a statute (notes and coins defined as legal tender).

'Return predictability'

2.10 This comprises the risk or uncertainty that the cash flow will change in the future. Gilts are the only financial asset in the UK with a certain rate of return (this is not the same as a fixed rate of return). However, inflation can eat into the purchasing power of this guaranteed income stream. Accordingly, the UK government has issued index-linked gilts.

Complexity

2.11 Some financial assets can be split into two, often simpler, assets. An example is a callable bond, when the borrower has the right to redeem the bond before it matures – occasionally the FT publishes lists of numbers of bonds which have been 'drawn' (as in a sort of lottery) for redemption. The value of such an asset is the value of the bond if it went to full maturity, less the value of the borrower's right to redeem it before maturity.

Currency

2.12 Most financial assets are stated to be in one currency, e.g. sterling, but some are issued in a 'currency basket'. An instance is an ECU Treasury bill, which is issued by the Bank of England. An ECU (European Currency Unit) comprises stated amounts of the currencies of the 12 EU states in 1989 and will become the new EU currency, under the name 'Euro', at a date to be decided.

Tax status

2.13 This is a very important characteristic of an asset, because most income flows and some capital gains are subject to tax. However, rates of tax can change annually, while the underlying principles of each country's tax system can also change, although usually less frequently. In the UK, there are assets which are completely free of income tax and capital gains tax, e.g. National Savings Certificates, although they are still subject to inheritance tax. Obviously, the liability of its cash flow to taxation does reduce the attraction of an asset to potential investors who are subject to that tax.

Student Activity 4

1. What is meant by the moneyness of an asset? *(Paragraph 2.3)*

2. Explain why denomination is important if an asset is not divisible. *(Paragraph 2.4)*

3. What is reversibility and what are its costs? *(Paragraph 2.5)*

4. Distinguish between nominal and real yield (cash flow). *(Paragraph 2.6)*

5. Give examples of 'term to maturity' using gilts. *(Paragraph 2.7)*

6. Is convertibility a characteristic given to an asset by the market in which it is traded? *(Paragraph 2.8)*

7. Compare the liquidity of an asset with the liquidity of a market. *(Paragraph 2.9)*

8. Give an example of an asset with a very high 'return predictability'. *(Paragraph 2.10)*

9. Explain what is meant by a 'complex financial asset'. *(Paragraph 2.11)*

10. For which tax do National Savings Certificates have to be considered when assessing the tax liability of a deceased person's estate? *(Paragraph 2.13)*

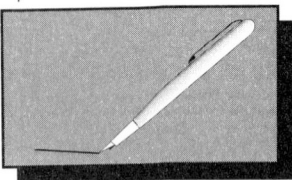

3 Money

Definition

3.1   Money can be defined as any asset which is generally acceptable for the settlement of debts. Two key words are 'asset' and 'acceptable'. Money is not a 'thing' but an asset. Usually it is a financial asset, i.e. a claim on the issuing organisation (bank or government) but it has been commodities. Indeed, in prisons, drugs and tobacco often function as money. Money also is 'acceptable' by people: if people do not like it they will not use it. In the UK today, a £50 note is not as acceptable as a £5 note because of the greater risk of its forgery.

Characteristics of money

3.2   Assets functioning as money have to have eight characteristics, which are parallel to but not exactly the same as those of financial assets in general. Money is universal – within a country – because everybody uses it and welcomes it. This is unlike assets such as bonds or company shares.

3.3   In the Foundation Course there may have been an acronym – SPUDS on a RADiator – to help to memorise these features of money. At this stage, you must use first principles to deduce these characteristics rather than rely on pure memory. Accordingly, these will be discussed in a different order: of possible importance.

Acceptability

3.4   This is the first and greatest characteristic: we all accept notes, coins, bank deposits and building society deposits. However, a possible new form of money, such as an 'electronic wallet', is not yet acceptable and will not be until the technology is available throughout the country to fill it with money from specially adapted telephones and ATMs and to spend it at newsagents, petrol stations etc equipped to download the money from our cards to their computers.

Stability

3.5   Money has been criticised as being 'a financial tape measure made of elastic' because its value (its purchasing power) changes over time – and usually downwards. Countries which have experienced hyperinflation usually have to change their currency, as has occurred in both Argentina and Brazil. Germany has had two new currencies this century – the Rentenmark in 1923 and the Deutsche Mark in 1948 – following two spells of hyperinflation. In the late 1950s, France created the Nouveau Franc, worth 100 of the old francs.

3.6   Another way of coping with the declining value of money (the result of ever-rising prices) is to index-link some financial assets, social security benefits and taxes. In the UK, the usual link is with the general (headline) index of retail prices (RPI).

Scarcity

3.7   'Money doesn't grow on trees' is an old saying, referring to the fact that, in the past, countries have usually chosen precious metals to be their money, i.e. silver and gold ('solid silver', 'as good as gold'). Countries do not choose assets which are in plentiful supply. Today, the Bank of England supervises banks to ensure that they do not lend too much money, while counterfeiting and forgery have long been criminal offences.

Portability

3.8 Originally, this meant 'easy to carry' but today it encompasses 'easy to transfer, in person, or in writing, or by telephone or by electronic means'.

Durability

3.9 Silver and gold were used as money not only because they are scarce but also because they are hard and long lasting; our coinage can last for years. Bank notes are different, however, with a life span of just over a year for a £5 note. For bank and building society deposits, the balances due to customers run on for years, although in practice such 'unclaimed balances' are routinely transferred to head office, for security reasons.

Divisibility

3.10 Most countries use a ratio of 1, 2, 5, 10, 20, 50, 100 ... for their notes and coin, and this is the ratio for the notes and coins of the EU's new Euro. By using such numbers, all amounts can be paid in a currency.

3.11 Most cheques can, of course, be written for amounts in units of one penny, but some bank accounts (usually earning a premium rate of interest) do not permit cheques below (say) £250 to be drawn. Remember, however, that cheques are not money, but merely instructions to transfer a financial asset (a credit balance) or to increase a financial liability (an overdraft or loan) by transferring a financial asset to the payee.

Recognisability

3.12 For ease of day-to-day business, money must be easily recognisable as such. Most of us can recognise notes and coin from many countries but it may be harder to recognise a foreign cheque, payment order or giro transfer.

Uniformity

3.13 This final characteristic is sometimes called homogeneity. All, or nearly all, units must be alike. For instance, a bank deposit should be money whether it is with, say, NatWest or Bank of Scotland.

Student Activity 5

Compare and contrast, by means of a table, the characteristics of (a) financial assets and (b) money. Remember, of course, that money is just a special kind of financial asset.

Functions of money

A medium of exchange

3.14 Before money, when exchange was by barter, goods were exchanged directly for goods. With the use of money, exchange is now indirect: people exchange goods/services, first, into money and then from money into another good or service or into a financial asset (other than money). Money is the medium by which the exchange is completed.

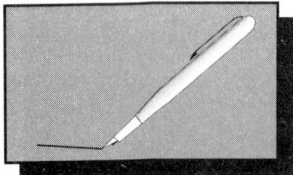

A liquid store of value

3.15   People need to store their assets – in a fridge or freezer or in a bank account. Money permits people to exchange their physical assets and their earnings into money and then to store that money for future exchange back into a physical asset or another financial asset. In paragraph 3.9 we saw that money should be durable, but in paragraph 3.5 we noticed that its stability of value can be poor on occasion.

A standard of deferred payment

3.16   Here, money is being used in legal contracts – for renting a house or shop or for repaying a loan. If money's value is deteriorating, the lender might be able to insist on index-linking the repayments of principal or substituting another currency. Thus, in Israel it was common for the US dollar to be inserted into contracts when the Israeli shekel was depreciating rapidly.

A unit of account

3.17   This function is more than just pricing goods and services in money, but using money as a yardstick for all bookkeeping, budgeting and management. For instance, at present the ECU is used largely as a unit of account for some loans and for budgeting in the European Commission. It certainly is not a liquid store of value and a medium of exchange – but it is likely to be soon, once the single currency is launched.

Measuring the quantity of money

3.18   This topic featured in the Banking Certificate, but it is relevant for monetary policy (Unit 7). In the UK, there are two major measures:

M0

3.19   M0 comprises largely sterling notes and coin in the UK, but outside the Bank of England. It also includes the banks' operational deposits with the Bank of England. M0 is the 'wide monetary base' and sometimes called 'narrow money'.

3.20   Its ratio to GDP (total domestic output) fell until about 1990, because people used less notes and coin after they acquired the 'banking habit'. Since then, however, this ratio (M0's velocity of circulation) has remained fairly constant.

M4

3.21   M4 is a measure of 'broad money' and comprises notes and coin outside the banks and building societies (not just outside the central bank) and sterling bank/building society deposits held in the UK by the personal and corporate sectors.

3.22   Its velocity of circulation swings violently occasionally, largely as a result of changes in bank/building society lending or government borrowing. In the 1980s, it fell as, first, the government borrowed and, later, when the banks and building societies became more generous in their lending. In 1990, the 'brakes were applied' and M4's growth (compared to GDP) declined, with the result that for some years its velocity of circulation has been about 1.19 when compared to GDP. In everyday terms, the total of GDP (output of the domestic economy) is about 120% of M4. (By comparison, GDP is about 33 times the total of M0).

Student Activity 6

Compare and contrast the functions of financial assets used as money with those of all financial assets.

4 Inflation

4.1 Inflation is a general rise in the overall price level, resulting in a general fall in the purchasing power (value) of money. Price indices are used to measure changes in the internal purchasing power of money, i.e. what it buys in the form of goods and services. Exchange rates (see Unit 8) can be used to measure changes in money's external purchasing power. For instance, the exchange rate between the US dollar and sterling indicates changes in how many US dollars can be bought with one pound sterling and, indirectly, what the pound buys in terms of US goods and services.

The problems caused by inflation

4.2 We noted above that inflation could be defined as a 'general fall in the general purchasing power (value) of money'. In consequence, one of the major effects of inflation is the erosion of the real value of money and of the real value of financial assets that are denominated in money terms. (Remember that, in economics, 'real' means 'value in actual goods and services', e.g. real wages.) Cash and certain other assets such as bank deposits that pay no interest are subject to the full eroding effect of inflation on their real value. One of the problems of inflation is therefore that it undermines the ability of money to act as a *store of value*, one of the functions of money identified earlier. When extremely high rates of inflation (known as 'hyperinflation') are experienced, the destruction of the store-of-value function of money becomes so great that people refuse to hold money or to accept it as payment for goods and services, so that it also loses its function as a *medium of exchange*. In these circumstances people revert to the use of barter. Even with quite moderate rates of inflation, however, attempts are made to economise on the volume of cash and non-interest-bearing assets, which leads to a loss of efficiency within the economic system.

4.3 Some compensation for the erosion of real purchasing power caused by inflation may be obtained from the payment of *interest*. If inflation is running at a rate of 8% pa, but 10% pa is obtainable by investing in a particular financial asset, then an individual will, at the end of the period, have received a 2% (10% − 8%) real return on his funds. There are, however, several problems here. *First*, the inflation rate may well be higher than the available interest rate on an investment, so that the individual can only receive a partial compensation for the effects of inflation. This situation of the inflation rate being higher than the interest rate faced investors in the UK for most of the 1970s. *Second*, an interest rate to match or exceed the inflation rate may only be achieved by investing in assets of a very low liquidity. Assets offering a high level of liquidity tend to offer lower interest rates, and so the investor is faced with the choice either of achieving good protection from inflation or of achieving an acceptable level of liquidity. *Third*, the level of inflation will not be known in advance. On the basis of the *current* rate of inflation, an investor may invest in an asset that offers complete protection from inflation, but if there is an *unexpected increase* in the inflation rate, the protection from inflation will be accordingly reduced. *Fourth*, in addition to the risk of unexpected increases in inflation, by investing in a financial asset in order to gain protection from the effects of inflation the individual is then subject to the *default risk* of that asset – the risk that either the interest or the principal, or both, will not be paid when due. *Fifth*, the prevalence of inflation may, by itself, increase the riskiness of financial assets purchased by investors seeking protection from the effects of inflation.

4.4   It is common for many financial assets to suffer declines in their real value in times of inflation. As we have seen, cash and non-interest-bearing bank deposits will inevitably incur falls in their real value due to inflation, but interest-bearing assets may also do so. The majority of bonds issued by the government are issued at a fixed rate of interest, and consequently when the inflation rate rises above that interest rate, real capital losses are incurred by the holders of the bonds. Much of the debt issued by companies is also of a fixed-interest type, and hence the holders of that debt are in the same position. In practice, the major investors in government and corporate fixed-interest debt are pension funds and insurance companies, and hence the members of pension funds and the holders of insurance policies will suffer losses as a result. Although the returns on the investment portfolios of pension funds and insurance companies may rise to some extent in times of inflation, this is invariably insufficient to allow the pension payments and the proceeds of maturing insurance policies to be increased commensurately.

4.5   It is therefore clear that holders of financial assets that are expressed in money terms are likely to be losers in times of inflation. In broad terms, these will be the *lenders* of money in an economy. By contrast, those who gain from inflation will be the *borrowers* in an economy. A government, with a large outstanding debt and a budget deficit which requires borrowing to finance it, is therefore a major beneficiary of inflation. The corporate sector, in so far as it is also a debtor – via its issue of interest-bearing securities and borrowing from banks – will also benefit from inflation. Within the personal sector the major debtors are those with house mortgage loans, who, at least until recently, have seen increases in the value of their homes substantially above the inflation rate; and this has often been at the expense of those individuals with savings in building societies and other mortgage providers.

4.6   The major problem that inflation brings is therefore the r*edistribution of income and wealth* from lenders to borrowers. This redistribution happens in an arbitrary fashion without there being any decision to bring it about. There are also lesser problems associated with inflation, including:

- *Uncertainty*. Inflation introduces uncertainty since in the case of longer-term contracts that are expressed in money terms, the *real* return from any such contract will be affected by future rates of inflation which are, of course, unknown. The response may then be for people and business organisations to *avoid* longer-term contracts and to place emphasis on short-term returns, which may well lower the efficiency and growth rate of the economy.

- *Inflation illusion*. During periods of inflation, there is a tendency for people to *think* that their real purchasing power is falling due to increases in prices, and to forget to consider what is happening to their incomes which, if wages or salaries, are almost invariably rising by a similar rate as inflation.

●   *Costs of changing prices.* The costs of more-frequent changes in price lists, of changing parking meters, payphones and so on, as a consequence of inflation are costs that may be substantial, particularly for certain industries.

●   *Costs of learning prices.* The presence of inflation will cause an individual's knowledge of prices to become out-of-date very quickly. With frequent purchases this will not present a difficulty unless inflation is very rapid; with infrequent purchases, however, an individual will have little idea of an appropriate price, and will have to devote time and effort to re-learning what the appropriate price for that product or service is by surveying the market.

These problems caused by inflation have ensured that inflation has been a cause of concern, and hence to government policies to combat it.

Student Activity 7

1.   How does inflation affect the use of money as a medium of exchange and a store of value?   *(Paragraph 4.2)*

2.   Need money always be a poor store of value? Why?   *(Paragraph 4.3)*

3.   In what sense may borrowers be regarded as the gainers from inflation? *(Paragraph 4.5)*

4.   Assess the major problems caused by inflation.   *(Paragraph 4.6)*

5.   What is likely to happen to the exports, imports, and the exchange rate of a country with a much higher rate of inflation than that of other countries?

5   Discount rates and the value of financial assets

5.1   Most people know something about interest and how it is added to an asset, e.g. a loan, by the owner over a period of time, But discounting is a less familiar concept. However, its everyday meaning of 'something deducted from a price' is very close to the truth. Discounting is deducting an amount from the future (known) value of an asset (a bond or bill) to establish what it is worth today. You may have encountered discounting to obtain a Net Present Value (NPV) in your earlier studies, but to others it may seem very strange.

Discounting
5.2   Discounting, briefly, is the mirror image of charging interest. If we charge interest at 10% pa, compounded annually, on a debt of £1,000, then, in a year's time, the debt will be worth £1100. Discounting approaches the situation from a different standpoint.

5.3   If an asset is worth £1,000 in a year's time, then what is it worth today? The answer is 'less' but there is a need to establish just how much less than £1,000 it is worth today (its 'present value' in technical language). To do this, a discount rate must be used – but 'which one? The brief answer is the one which the market uses for that type of asset but for ease of illustration we will use 10% here.

5.4 Taking the example of £1,000 due in a year's time, and ignoring interest received in the year ahead – in fact, the interest was probably received today so the assumption is justified – we can use 10% as our rate of discount. However, it is not just 'deducting 10% from one grand' to reach the present value, because that results in an answer of £900 which, when interest is charged at 10%, results in a final value of £990 and not £1,000. The calculation is:

$PV = CF/(1+0.10)$ to the power of 1 when we use 10% for a period of one year.

Next the CF (cash flow) of £1,000 is inserted, giving:

$PV = £1,000/1.1 = £909.0909$

Checking back, we multiply £909.0909 by 1.1 to find its value in a year's time, and we get £999.9999 recurring, which is approximately £1,000.

5.5 The next stage is to lengthen the period to two years, with the receipt of interest at 10% at the end of the first year. The formula is:

$PV = CF/(1+r)^n$

where r is the rate of interest and
n is the number of years.

Here r = 10%; n = 2

So, we have for the capital amount

$PV = £1,000/(1 + 0.10)^2 = 1000/1.21 = £826.4463$

However, we must now add in the £100 due in a year's time which, from paragraph 5.4, can be seen to be £90.09090 (the answer shown there divided by 10).

Therefore, by adding the NPV of the interest due in a year's time to the NPV of the capital amount due in two years' time the NPV of the asset is

£826.4463 + 90.90909 = £917.35539

The question 'Why square the bottom half of the fraction? Why not just double it?' should spring to mind. The answer is that interest is compounded (interest on interest) and so the correct procedure is to square, cube and express amounts to a power equal to the number of occasions when discounting occurs.

5.6 The formula can now be expressed for n periods of compounding:

$PV = CF(1)/(1+r)1 + CF(2)/(1+r)^2 + CF(3)/(1+r)^3 ... CF(n)/(1+r)^n$

In period n, the cashflow is likely to be the principal, with no interest. In the intervening years, the cash flow is likely to be just the interest.

Constructing the appropriate discount rate

5.7 This can be divided into several elements:

- The real rate of interest, i.e. ignoring inflation, which is the reward for not spending the amount on consuming goods and services today (RR).

- An inflation premium, to compensate for the expected fall in the purchasing power of the money in which the debt is expressed (IP).

- A default risk premium, which is the reward for accepting the possibility that the borrower may not repay the principal (DP).

- A maturity premium, to reward the lenders for being without their money for a long time (MP).

- A liquidity premium, for investing in an asset which cannot be converted into cash quickly, cheaply and without loss of market value (LP).

- An exchange risk premium (ERP) (if the asset is denominated in a foreign currency) .

To use symbols:

Discount rate = RR + IP + DP + MP + LP + ERP

The inverse relation between price and discount rate

5.8   When the discount rate rises, the price falls. This is a relationship which should be evident when it is remembered that the numerator of the equation is being divided by a larger denominator.

5.9   Another way of considering the relationship is to examine the price of a fixed-interest rate gilt – such as 2.5% Consols. If the approximate interest rate is 2.5% then their price will be 100. If r = 5%, then holders of the asset will sell, to get better rates on other assets at 5%, forcing the price down to 50. At 50, investors will obtain £200 of the asset for £100, yielding them twice £2.50, i.e. £5 per annum.

Basis point

5.10   This is a technical term for 'a one-hundredth of one per cent'. Thus, 25 basis points are the same as 0.25% pa. One hundred basis points equal 1% pa; 200 bp = 2% pa. The letters 'pa' are omitted when basis points are used. The abbreviation is 'bp'.

Price volatility

5.11   The volatility of a financial asset is today regarded as important as its liquidity. However, liquidity is an older concept and hence more widely known and understood. Volatility refers to the sensitivity of an asset to price changes. Volatility can vary over time, and is difficult to forecast, while liquidity does not change to the same degree. In fact, volatility is volatile.

5.12   The factors affecting the volatility of fixed interest rate assets – which have known future cash flows and known future maturity values – include:

- The time to maturity of an asset;

- The asset's coupon;

- The effect of the prevailing level of yields.

The time to maturity of an asset

5.13   In the London gilt-edged market, the time to maturity of an asset gives rise to what is known as the 'pull to maturity': the nearer a gilt gets to maturity the smaller the change in its price, compared to gilts with a longer maturity.

Student Activity 8

Look at the gilt-edged prices in a recent quality newspaper

Write down the price changes shown for short-dated gilts. Write down the price changes shown for long-dated gilts. Notice how much greater are the latter, compared to for the 'shorts'

5.14   The common sense way of appreciating this relationship is to think: if the asset has 18 months to run, then there are only one or two divisions to be made into the maturity value and interest payments; if it has 18 years to run then there are more than 10 times as many divisions to be made – and far more cash flow receipts to be changed. Of course, it is important to remember that the divisor (denominator) is the square of the number of time periods.

The asset's coupon

5.15   If the asset's coupon is high, as with gilts issued in the late 1970s and early 1980s, then the effect of a change in market interest rates will be lower than if the coupon itself were low. The reason for the difference is that, in the formula, the numerator is much larger for the higher coupon stock, while the denominator is the same no matter the size of the coupon.

The effect of the prevailing level of interest rates

5.16   If there is a 100bp rise from 3% to 4% then the effect on asset prices will be much greater than that of a 100bp rise from 15% to 16%. The reason is that, proportionately, the rise from 3% to 4% is much greater (25% up) than from 15% to 16% (6.7% being the rise from a starting point of 15%). In general terms, the denominator in the fraction does not rise as much proportionately in the case of the higher yield.

6   Risk and diversification

6.1   The general public might define 'risk' as 'the chance that something unpleasant might occur': the 'thing' might be disease, accident, fire, flood, explosion, unemployment or death. In finance, however, risk has a more limited meaning: the chance that the result of a transaction may not be what was expected. More strictly, risk can be defined as the chance that the actual return from an investment will be less than the expected return. Although this definition is limited in scope, there are still many types of risk.

Types of risk

6.2   The types of risk are:

- Name or counterparty risk: is the other party in the transaction dependable? If its employees are dishonest or your total exposure to the party is excessive, then there is a risk of the transaction not being honoured.

- *Liquidity risk*: here the counterparty is honest, but illiquid, i.e. its short-term (current) assets are far less than current liabilities.

- *Credit risk*: here the counterparty is liquid but has over-borrowed or lent badly, so that total performing assets are far less than total liabilities. It is insolvent.

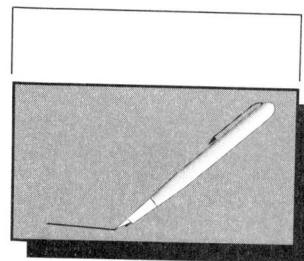

- *Systems risk*: here the clerical/electronic systems break down, causing extra expense. And if it is your systems which have 'crashed', then your net returns from these transactions will be lower.

- *Settlement risk*: here the market settlement system fails, so that cash flows are considerably delayed. Both parties suffer. A notable instance of these delays occurred in 1987, after 'Big Bang' in London.

- *Market risks*: these will be examined in more detail in Units 3 and 4 but one can be mentioned here – the level of interest rates (discount rates) has unexpectedly altered. This will inevitably cause asset prices to change.

- *Legal risk*: here the transaction suddenly encounters legal problems, and these are not necessarily due to having to sue the other party. Much more likely is new legislation or an important judgment in a court – on matters which affect the legal foundation of the transaction or the characteristics of the asset in question.

- *Systemic risk*: this is the financial equivalent of the melt-down of a nuclear reactor. Perhaps the worst example was the near-collapse of the US banking system at the end of 1932, after which the new President began his term of office by declaring a succession of bank holidays. Forty years later, to avoid such a collapse, the Bank of England organised the 'lifeboat' operation with the clearing banks to rescue a large number of distressed smaller banks in 1974. Systemic risk is not the same as either systems risk or systematic risk (which is discussed shortly).

- *Specific risk*: this is the result of particular events or trends or cycles which affect specific industries or trades. Construction, insurance and banking are sectors of the stock market which are well known for pronounced slumps and booms. Another sector at present with a specific risk is biological engineering where many companies do not yet make a profit although their share prices keep on rising, fuelled by news of promising tests of drugs and hopes of profits in the next century.

Diversification and risk

6.3   *Specific risk* can be minimised by the policy of diversification (not 'putting all one's eggs into one basket'). Another way of expressing this concept is 'spreading the risk'. The expectation is that the specific factors will cause some assets (in a portfolio of assets) to rise in value, while others fall.

6.4   In ordinary language, *systematic risk* is general market risk, when prices fall 'across the board'. The technical definition of this type of risk is 'risk which cannot be eliminated by diversification'. It is due to factors such as the business cycle or a change in monetary or fiscal policy.

6.5   Studies have shown that systematic return on a portfolio of assets (or one asset) is proportional to the return on all the assets in that market (market return). The proportion is known as beta (β). The remainder of the portfolio's return (called unsystematic risk) is denoted by epsilon (ε). Thus, if a security has a beta of 1.5 then a 10% market return will result in a 15% return on that security.

6.6   *Risk aversion*: there is a universal assumption in all this analysis that investors on average are risk averse, i.e. they wish to minimise their risk.

Student Activity 9

1. What is meant by 'risk':

    (a) In everyday life;

    (b) With reference to a financial asset?   *(Paragraph 6.1)*

2. What does 'risk averse' mean? Which types of investors are likely to be 'risk averse'?   *(Paragraph 6.6)*

3. How does 'diversification' reduce risk? Express the term in ordinary language?   *(Paragraph 6.3)*

4. Give examples/instances of these types of risk:

    (a) Systemic;

    (b) Specific;

    (c) Systematic.   *(Paragraphs 6.2–4)*

5. Which type(s) of risk can diversification help to minimise? Which risks can't it help to minimise?   *(Paragraphs 6.2 and 6.3)*

6. What is meant by volatility?   *(Paragraph 5.11)*

7. What are the factors affecting the volatility of fixed interest rate assets?   *(Paragraphs 5.12–15)*

8. Explain the relationship between the price of such assets and the rate of interest (discount).   *(Paragraphs 5.8–9)*

9   Explain what is meant by discounting.   *(Paragraphs 5.1–3)*

Summary

Now that you have studied this unit, you should be able to:

-   **describe the nature of financial assets, their cash flow and their functions;**

-   **identify the characteristics (properties) of financial assets;**

-   **understand the nature of money, its characteristics, functions and value;**

-   **explain the principles of the pricing of financial assets;**

-   **explain what is meant by the price volatility of financial assets;**

-   **appreciate the significance of risk and how portfolio diversification can eliminate part of risk.**

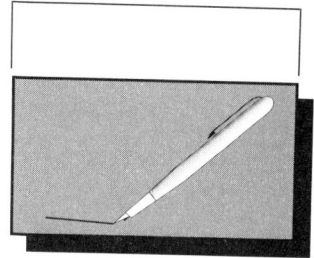

Self-assessment questions

Short-answer questions

1. You are an employee of ICI and a member of the ICI pension fund. Which financial markets are likely to affect you?

2. Distinguish between financial assets and money.

3. What might be the problems for the UK if its annual rate of inflation were to rise from 2.1% (August 1996) to around 5%?

4. Explain how financial assets are valued.

5. 'Financial markets can be very risky.' Elaborate on this statement.

Multiple choice questions

1. The cash flow for the lender in an HP agreement is:
   (a) all interest
   (b) all capital
   (c) Part interest, part capital in fixed proportions
   (d) part interest, part capital in varying proportions
   (e) part interest, part capital, with increasing proportions.

2. The two major functions of financial assets are:
   (a) creating and redistributing risk
   (b) transferring funds from ultimate lenders to borrowers and redistributing risk
   (c) transferring funds from ultimate borrowers to ultimate lenders and redistributing risk
   (d) aggregation of funds and risk assumption
   (e) displaying price information and creating incentives.

3. Volatility is:
   (a) the opposite of liquidity
   (b) the speed at which prices change in a market
   (c) the sensitivity of an asset to price changes
   (d) very high when long-term assets approach their maturity
   (e) an effect of exchange rate changes.

4. Index-linking is a device to protect assets from losing their value as a result of inflation by means of linking their money value to changes in:
   (a) the Index of Retail Prices (RPI)
   (b) interest rates
   (c) exchange rates
   (d) the Index of Retail Prices excluding payments of mortgage interest
   (e) the index of average earnings.

5. If a fire destroyed the back office of your counterparty in the gilts market, then it is an example of:

   (a) specific risk

   (b) counterparty risk

   (c) settlement risk

   (d) systematic risk

   (e) systems risk.

6. Diversification of a portfolio can reduce which type of risk:

   (a) counterparty risk

   (b) systematic risk

   (c) specific risk

   (d) credit risk

   (e) market risk.

Unit 2

Financial Institutions

Objectives

After studying this unit, you should be able to:

- **define and distinguish between financial institutions and financial intermediaries;**

- **explain in outline the role of central banks;**

- **distinguish between banks and building societies;**

- **describe the other deposit-taking financial intermediaries;**

- **compare and contrast deposit-taking and investing financial intermediaries;**

- **examine the roles of insurance companies and pension funds;**

- **understand the differences between unit trusts and investment trusts;**

- **explain what is meant by *bancassurance*.**

1 Financial institutions defined

1.1 Financial institutions are enterprises or organisations which provide services in connection with one or more of the following:

- Financial intermediation, linking ultimate providers of funds with ultimate users and creating new financial assets in the process. This is the most important activity of financial institutions, and its analysis takes up most of this unit.

- Exchanging financial assets on behalf of their customers, i.e. acting as brokers or agents for clients.

- Exchanging financial assets for their own accounts – proprietary dealers, as they are termed.

- Helping create financial assets for their customers, and then selling these assets to others in the market – underwriting new share issues, for example.

- Providing investment advice to others, e.g. to people seeking a personal pension or to firms on mergers and takeovers.

- Fund management – managing the whole or part of a pension fund, for example.

1.2 Some large companies have their own financial subsidiaries. In the UK there is Ford Motor Finance and, of course, Marks & Spencer Financial Services. In the UK also there is the National Savings Bank, which is wholly owned by the Government and where deposits are used by its owner to help finance a budget deficit.

2   Definition of financial intermediation

2.1   Financial intermediation is the process of channelling funds between those who wish to lend or invest and those who wish to borrow or use. Such intermediaries act as principals, creating new financial assets and liabilities. They do not act solely as agents, charging a commission for their services.

2.2   Given that definition, it is important to note that a wide range of financial institutions is engaged in financial intermediation and that this activity is by no means restricted to banking institutions. Any institution standing between the ultimate provider of funds and the ultimate user of funds is engaging in financial intermediation.

2.3   At the same time it is important to remember that many of the services offered by financial institutions are *not* intermediation activities. Financial advisory services provided by many financial institutions, fund management services and advice on takeovers and mergers provided by merchant banks are all examples of non-intermediary services. Also, insurance agents are sometimes called 'intermediaries' but, in reality, they are only agents and not principals who deal in their own name.

2.4   An important distinguishing characteristic of financial intermediation is that new financial assets (discussed in the first unit) and liabilities are created. When money is lent to a financial intermediary the lender holds a claim against that financial intermediary, while if money is borrowed from the financial intermediary, that financial intermediary will be holding a claim against the ultimate borrower. Had the ultimate lender lent directly to the ultimate borrower, only one claim and one liability would have been created; lending through the financial intermediary has resulted in two claims and two liabilities.

2.5   In the case of a bank or building society deposit, the nature of the claims and liabilities created is usually straightforward. The depositor has a claim for a given amount of money, perhaps to be repaid on demand, while the bank has a matching liability to repay a given amount of money. If the bank onlends that deposit it has a claim against the borrower for a given amount of money, perhaps to be repaid (with interest) at a given point in time in the future. The borrower, naturally, has a liability to repay that sum of money with interest on the specified date.

2.6   With other financial intermediaries the nature of the claims and liabilities created may not be so straightforward. An individual who buys a long-term insurance policy, for example, will have a claim against the insurance company for a capital sum at a date in the future or on death if that occurs earlier. The capital sum involved will invariably *not* be for a fixed amount. The insurance company may use the premiums from that policy to purchase a range of different assets, including perhaps ordinary shares in companies (equities), whereby the insurance company will have a claim on the profits earned by the companies involved. The essential point is that not only does financial intermediation involve the creation of additional assets and liabilities, but it may also involve the creation of financial assets and liabilities of a wholly different nature.

3 The requirements from financial intermediation by lenders and providers of finance

3.1 The fact that financial intermediation takes place on a wide scale suggests that both lenders and borrowers have certain requirements that cannot be met by the lender dealing directly with the borrower but that *can* be met by the use of a financial intermediary. We look first at the requirements of lenders.

3.2 The relative importance of the different requirements on the part of the lender will depend on factors such as income, wealth, the existing holdings of financial assets, etc. However, we may identify four areas that will feature in the requirements of any lenders.

- Expected return;
- Risk;
- Liquidity;
- Transactions costs.

Expected return
3.3 Any lender will only engage in lending because of the profit to be gained from doing so. Lenders will, therefore, be seeking a high return on their loaned funds.

Risk
3.4 Lenders will be concerned to gain a high return on their loaned funds while at the same time minimising the risk involved in the lending. As you saw in the previous unit, risk associated with lending money may come in a variety of forms:

Default risk
3.5 This is the risk that the borrower will not repay the sum borrowed or the interest charged when such payments are due. All loans carry a default risk although the extent of the risk will vary. Loans to commercial companies, for example, will carry a higher risk than the negligible default risk associated with securities issued by the UK government.

Risk of capital loss
3.6 This is the risk associated with increases in market interest rates causing a fall in the price of loans made in the form of fixed-coupon marketable securities. This form of lending includes, notably, government securities but also a range of securities issued by companies.

Inflation risk
3.7 This is the risk that unexpected increases in the rate of inflation during the life of the loan will reduce the real value of the sum lent, and of the interest payments, below what was anticipated at the time of the loan.

Portfolio risk

3.8 This is the risk that the initial choice of lending opportunities will prove to be poor, in that some of the alternative opportunities that were rejected will turn out to yield higher returns than those selected.

Liquidity

3.9 A liquid asset was defined in the previous unit as one which can be turned into cash quickly and without capital loss or interest penalty. Most bank deposits are therefore very liquid, but investment in, for example, property is highly illiquid. The liquidity that is required by a lender will depend on a number of factors, including in particular the range of liquidity inherent in other securities held. Other things being equal, however, lenders will wish to have a high level of liquidity in their loans.

Transaction costs

3.10 Lenders will be seeking to keep as low as possible the costs associated with seeking out and taking up lending opportunities. They will also, in the case of marketable securities, be taking into account the costs of selling the securities when they wish to withdraw from the loan. Such transaction costs need to be viewed in broad terms, since they will include not only the fees or commissions associated with the purchase and sale of many assets, but will also include the time and trouble involved in identifying and evaluating lending opportunities.

4   The requirements from financial intermediation by borrowers

4.1 Corresponding to the requirements that *lenders* seek from financial intermediation, *borrowers* will also be seeking to fulfil certain requirements. We may identify five areas that will be of importance to borrowers:

- Interest payable;
- Term of the loan;
- Transaction costs;
- Size of the loan;
- Risk.

Interest payable

4.2 Borrowers will be seeking to minimise the amount of interest that they will pay on their borrowed funds. In this regard, their objectives will be exactly opposite to those of lenders, who will be seeking to maximise the interest return on their loans.

Term of the loan

4.3 An important consideration for borrowers will be the date on which the loan is due to be repaid. In general, borrowers would prefer to have a long period of time before a loan has to be repaid, since this provides them with additional flexibility and reduces the risk of having difficulty in repaying the loan. In this regard also, therefore, the interests of borrower and lender are opposed, since lenders will generally prefer a high level of liquidity.

Transaction costs

4.4   As with the lenders of funds, borrowers will be seeking to minimise the whole range of transactions costs involved in setting up a loan.

Size of loan

4.5   Many borrowers will require relatively large sums of money. This is true of the government, which has in the past required large sums of money to fund its borrowing requirement, and of businesses wishing to fund specific projects, e.g. the Channel Tunnel. It is common, therefore, for the amount of money that a potential borrower wishes to borrow to exceed substantially the amount that any individual lender will wish to lend. Hence, companies may borrow large amounts from a syndicate of banks while some house-owners borrower from another lender by means of a second mortgage.

Risk

4.6   Any borrower will need to be aware of the risks associated with a loan, in particular:

- Difficulties involved in renewing a loan if the original loan is for a shorter period than the total required;

- Difficulties and costs caused by the early recall of a loan, if the conditions of the loan allow for this;

- Finding that, due to changed circumstances, the loan is for a smaller amount than required (and that additional funds are necessary), or that it is larger than required (so that interest is being paid on unnecessary funds);

- Obtaining a loan to commence from the date needed;

- Penalty payments may be incurred if the borrower has to repay a loan earlier than originally agreed.

As a consequence of these risks, any borrower will be seeking to build in several aspects of *flexibility* to the conditions of the loan.

Student Activity 1

1. State the functions of financial institutions.   *(Paragraph 1.1)*

2. Define the term financial intermediation.   *(Paragraph 2.1)*

3. Explain how new financial assets and liabilities are created by the process of financial intermediation.   *(Paragraph 2.4)*

4. Give some examples of assets and liabilities created by the financial intermediation process.   *(Paragraphs 2.5 and 2.6)*

5. List the factors which are likely to be considered by a person contemplating *lending* funds.   *(Paragraphs 3.2–9)*

6. List the factors which are likely to be considered by a person contemplating *borrowing* funds.   *(Paragraphs 4.1–6)*

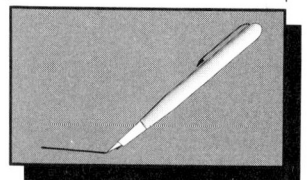

5 Accommodating the needs of lenders and borrowers by financial intermediation

5.1 Plainly, what potential lenders are seeking on one side and what potential borrowers are seeking on the other will create difficulties in matching borrowers and lenders. When a potential lender is brought together with a potential borrower it may be, for example, that the risk the potential lender is prepared to take on is less than the perceived risk involved in lending to that particular borrower. Alternatively, it might be the case that the borrower wishes to borrow for a much longer period of time than the lender is wishing to lend, or that the borrower requires a much larger loan than the lender wishes to provide. The consequence of this is that even if potential borrowers and lenders are brought together on a widespread scale, so that in principle they could arrange a loan directly between themselves, their conflicting objectives are likely to lead to their being unable to agree terms. The result of this, in turn, is that there will be both unsatisfied demand and unsatisfied supply of loans.

5.2 To a limited extent the different objectives of borrowers and lenders may be accommodated through negotiation over the interest rate on the loan. Payment of a high interest rate on the loan might induce a lender to make a loan that is larger, of longer duration or carries a higher perceived risk than is desired. On the other side of the negotiations, the higher interest rate may cause the borrower to reduce the size of the loan or to make it of shorter duration, to bring it into line with what the lender may be offering. In order to avoid paying a higher interest rate the borrower may also be prepared to offer collateral to reduce the risk on the loan, or he may offer greater flexibility with regard to repayment.

5.3 Negotiation over the interest rate *may*, therefore, accommodate the differing objectives of borrowers and lenders in some circumstances. In a great many circumstances, however, it is likely that the differences will be too large for resolution by adjusting the interest rate. In any event, this process assumes that the prospective lenders and borrowers will be brought together in the first place, which may be an unrealistic assumption; with lenders and borrowers distributed throughout the country (or even in different countries), the practical problems associated with bringing the two parties together are immense. In addition, it remains the case that even if the practical problems could be overcome, the *costs* of doing so would substantially reduce the desired volume of borrowing and lending activity. Since that would, for example, leave many businesses short of funds, the result would be a lower level of economic activity within the economy.

5.4 The alternative method of accommodating the needs of lenders and borrowers is by means of financial intermediation. As we have seen, financial intermediation involves channelling funds between the ultimate lender and the ultimate borrower, and as a consequence of this activity it results in four major outcomes:

- Aggregation of savings;
- Pooling of risk;
- Maturity transformation of funds;
- Reduction of transaction costs.

Aggregation of savings

5.5   As we noted earlier, it is common for lenders to wish to lend smaller amounts of money than borrowers commonly wish to borrow. One outcome of financial intermediation, therefore, is that a number of relatively small deposits from ultimate lenders can be aggregated in order to satisfy the needs of potential borrowers. In this way financial intermediation can overcome one of the problems associated with borrowing and lending directly, by providing a system whereby lenders deposit only modest amounts but borrowers may borrow what could constitute very large amounts.

5.6   The reverse process – disaggregat*ion – can occur.* For example, a wholesale lender may not wish to incur the expense of processing a large number of mortgages so it lends, often as a member of a syndicate of banks, to a financial intermediary which has the necessary administrative backup to provide mortgages to the ultimate borrowers. In this way, some hundred mortgages, at an average size of £50,000, could be financed by the mortgage lender borrowing £5m in the wholesale money markets. Disaggregation is also helpful to these mortgage lenders, who can raise finance more quickly in the wholesale markets than in the retail markets, thereby enabling them to increase their share of the mortgage market.

Pooling of risk

5.7   A second problem which we identified as associated with lending and borrowing directly is that the various elements of risk associated with a loan may be too high for the individual lender to accept. This is essentially because the entire risk is borne by the single lender: if the borrower, for example, defaults on the loan then the loss is suffered by the one individual. If, however, the loan to the ultimate borrower is made by a financial intermediary, then that risk is spread over all the depositors with the financial intermediary. In consequence, the risk of any one depositor losing all his funds is substantially reduced, although the risk of losing *some* funds is increased. Note that financial intermediation does not in itself reduce the risk of a loan going into default but that risk is spread over all the depositors with the intermediary.

5.8   In order to see this process more clearly, consider the following simple example. Suppose that on average one in every 10 loans goes into default, with the lender receiving no compensation. Any individual lender (particularly if he has only limited wealth and is only able to make one loan at a time) may find the 10% risk of losing the whole loan too great. If, however, the loan is initially to a financial intermediary which is lending to a large number of different borrowers, the risk of losing the whole of one loan is transformed into the near-certainty of losing 10% of the whole portfolio of loans. For the individual lender, therefore, the risk of losing the whole of the loan is virtually zero, but is replaced by the near-certainty of losing 10%. In principle, the 'law of large numbers' operates, not to *eliminate* risk (since the risk of loans going into default is unaltered), but to *transform* it from the point of view of the individual lender to the financial intermediary. In practice, the default risk will be reflected in the difference between the interest rate paid on deposits and the interest rate charged to borrowers; the differential is used in part to absorb the default losses.

5.9   While the *pooling* of the risk involved with lending is the most important

27

consequence of financial intermediation with regard to risk, note that there may be other consequences.

- The financial intermediary will be able to *diversify* the lending across different types of asset, which an individual may not be able to achieve due to a lack of funds. Hence, losses on one type of asset will be offset by gains on another type, so that the risk is reduced further.

- The financial intermediary is likely to have the *expertise and resources to make a much better evaluation* of the risk involved in lending opportunities than individuals would be able to achieve on their own, and consequently the risk taken by the financial intermediary will be *less than the average risk* involved in all lending opportunities.

- In many cases, the *reserves or shareholders' capital* of the financial intermediary will be available to make up deficiencies in the value of deposits should an unusually high rate of defaults occur.

- When supplemented by certain *guarantees initiated by the government*, the risk to the individual lender is reduced further. However, such protection is never for 100% of the amount, to ensure that investors and depositors avoid the most risky propositions (termed the 'moral hazard' of complete protection).

Maturity transformation of funds

5.10   We have noted that borrowers typically want to borrow for a longer period of time than lenders wish to lend. A major feature of financial intermediaries is that they are able to accommodate these different requirements; in general, the claims on a financial intermediary by the lenders are much more liquid than the claims by the financial intermediary on its borrowers. The classic example of this is provided by a building society, where the majority of the funds are repayable on demand yet the society is able to make loans with an initial maturity of, usually, 25 years. However, not all mortgages run their full 20–25-year term and their average length has been eight to 10 years (when the house is sold and the mortgage loan repaid). While building societies provide an extreme example, the principle is also true of, say, banks where the average period of notice to return deposits is very much less than the average time to maturity of its outstanding loans.

5.11   Financial intermediaries are able to do this by virtue of the 'law of large numbers'. The principle involved is that where there is a large number of lenders, the probability of all of those lenders wishing to withdraw the maximum amount of their deposits at the same time is extremely small. While there will be *individual* depositors who do wish to withdraw the whole of their deposits on a particular day, this will be balanced by new deposits and by the majority of deposits being left untouched. Day-to-day variations in the amount withdrawn relative to the amount deposited can be met by changes in the volume of cash or other liquid assets held, and the intermediary will learn from experience what proportion of total deposits needs to be kept as reserves for this purpose. The majority of funds are, however, available for longer-term loans on which the interest rate chargeable will frequently be higher. In summary, it is clear that the financial intermediary has *transformed the maturity* of the short-term deposits into longer-term loans without sacrificing solvency.

5.12   Note that there are certain prerequisites for this maturity transformation of funds to operate smoothly. In particular:

- The number of individual depositors must actually be large enough for the law of large numbers to apply. If the numbers are low, other things being equal, the intermediary will have to hold a large proportion of deposits as cash or other liquid assets.

- Depositors must have confidence that the intermediary will be able to repay funds when required. If this confidence lapses, then depositors *will* seek to withdraw all their funds at the same time and the law of large numbers collapses.

- In order to keep the proportion of cash and other liquid assets low, the intermediary must be able to acquire funds when random fluctuations cause the ratio to fall below the target. For a building society this might involve raising interest rates to attract savings or borrowing funds on the wholesale money market.

5.13 Certain financial intermediaries (notably wholesale banks) have only a small number of depositors, and hence cannot rely on the law of large numbers in order to create maturity transformation of funds. Such institutions will, however, achieve maturity transformation by means of heavy reliance on obtaining funds as and when required and, perhaps, by accepting a higher level of risk than other institutions.

Reduction of transaction costs

5.14 Given the size of the majority of financial institutions, they are able to benefit from economies of scale in a number of areas. These will include:

- Economies in the administration associated with taking in deposits and making loans, due to these transactions becoming routine.

- Economies in the employment of specialist personnel, since the volume of business will allow such people to be fully employed.

- Economies in the acquisition and interpretation of financial information.

Student Activity 2

1. Even if potential borrowers and lenders can be brought together, they may not be able to arrange loans between themselves. Why?   *(Paragraph 5.1)*

2. What is the role of interest rates in accommodating the needs of borrowers and lenders?   *(Paragraph 5.2)*

3. What is the importance of financial intermediaries' ability to aggregate savings?   *(Paragraph 5.5)*

4. What effect do financial intermediaries have on the risk faced by a lender?   *(Paragraphs 5.6–9)*

5. What is meant by the maturity transformation of funds within the context of financial intermediation?   *(Paragraphs 5.10–11)*

6. What are the prerequisites for the maturity transformation of funds to operate smoothly?   *(Paragraph 5.12)*

7. In what ways do financial intermediaries reduce transaction costs?   *(Paragraph 5.14)*

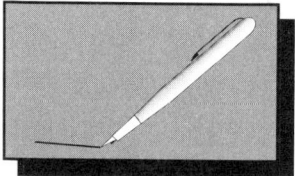

6 The benefits of financial intermediation

6.1 As a recap, it is now appropriate to review the *benefits* that accrue from financial intermediation. We may consider these in terms of the benefits to the *ultimate lender*, to the *ultimate borrower* and to *society as a whole*.

The benefits to the ultimate lender

6.2 These are:

- *Greater liquidity* is generally achieved by lending to a financial intermediary rather than to the ultimate borrower.

- *Less risk is involved*, due to the pooling of risk inherent with financial intermediation, the improved risk assessment that such intermediaries are able to undertake and the portfolio diversification that can frequently be achieved. This reduction in risk may be reflected in guaranteed interest rates on deposits with a financial intermediary.

- *Marketable securities* may be created. Lending to a financial intermediary will normally give rise to greater liquidity than direct lending to the ultimate borrower. However, additional liquidity will be created when the intermediary issues marketable securities in return for deposits. The depositor, instead of waiting until maturity of the security, may sell it in a secondary market to regain the cash.

- A *guaranteed return* may be offered to the lender by a financial intermediary, in contrast to the variable returns more likely to be obtained from lending directly to the ultimate borrower.

- The *lending decision is simplified*, since there are fewer lending opportunities to financial intermediaries than there are to ultimate borrowers. In addition, the assessment of the opportunities for lending to intermediaries is generally a simpler procedure than the individual assessment of the opportunities for lending to ultimate borrowers.

The benefits to the ultimate borrower

6.3 These are:

- Loans will generally be available for a *longer time period* from a financial intermediary than from the ultimate lenders.

- Financial intermediaries will generally be prepared to make loans of *larger amounts* than will ultimate lenders.

- Using financial intermediaries will generally be *cheaper and quicker* than approaching ultimate lenders directly.

- The *interest rate* will generally be *lower* when borrowing from a financial intermediary, compared with borrowing directly from the ultimate lender.

- When borrowing from a financial intermediary, there is a greater likelihood that loans will be *renewed* when required.

The benefits to society as a whole

6.4 Financial intermediation is considered likely to:

- Cause a *more efficient utilisation of funds within an economy*, since the evaluation of lending opportunities will be improved.

- Cause a *higher level of borrowing and lending to be undertaken*, due to the lower risk and costs associated with lending to a financial intermediary.

● Cause an *improvement in the availability of funds to higher-risk ventures*, due to the capability of financial intermediaries to absorb such risk. High-risk ventures are widely considered to be important for creating the basis of future prosperity for an economy.

Student Activity 3

1. What benefits are generated for lenders by the operations of financial intermediaries? *(Paragraph 6.2)*

2. What benefits are generated for borrowers by the operations of financial intermediaries? *(Paragraph 6.3)*

3. What benefits are generated for society as a whole by the operations of financial intermediaries? *(Paragraph 6.4)*

7 The classification of financial intermediaries

7.1 Formerly, UK financial intermediaries were classified according to whether or not their liabilities (their deposits) were included in official measures of the money supply. Because the definitions of money were changed over time, it is now usual to classify financial intermediaries on the basis of the broad nature of their business activities, i.e. deposit-taking and investing, with further subdivisions within these two broad groups.

Deposit-taking financial intermediaries
7.2 These are classified as follows:
    ● *Retail banks.* These are defined by the Bank of England and comprise:
        ○ London clearing banks (including the 'Big Four', TSB Bank, Abbey National, Co-operative Bank, Girobank, and Yorkshire Bank)
        ○ Scottish clearing banks
        ○ Northern Ireland banks
        ○ Banking Department of the Bank of England.
    ● *Wholesale banks*:
        ○ British merchant banks (now often called investment banks);
        ○ Other British banks
        ○ Overseas banks.
    ● *Discount houses*;
    ● *Other deposit-taking institutions*:
        ○ Building societies
        ○ Finance houses
        ○ Credit unions

Investing financial intermediaries
7.3 These include:
    ○ Insurance companies
    ○ Pension funds

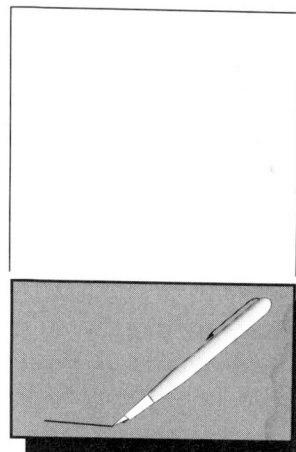

○   Unit trusts

○   Investment trust companies

○   Open-ended investment companies (OEICs)

○   Friendly societies.

8   Financial intermediation as a business activity

8.1   Before leaving the topic of financial intermediation, we should consider the business aspects of the process. In common with any business, financial intermediaries will only undertake an activity if it is profitable to do so, which means that the revenues generated by the activity are greater than the costs. What are the revenues to be derived from financial intermediation and what are the associated costs?

8.2   The *revenues* are the interest payments, dividends and capital gains resulting from the funds which they have lent or used to buy securities.

8.3   The *costs* of financial intermediation arise in three principal areas, the:

- Interest payments or other income flow that has to be allocated to the providers of the funds;

- Operating costs of the institution, which will include salaries and expenses of its employees, rental of buildings and equipment, rates, payment for telecommunications services, VAT and so on. With regard to the retail banks and some building societies, included here will be the costs of operating the money transmission system:

- Losses caused by borrowers of funds going into default with regard to either interest or principal or both.

8.4   Given that Profit = Revenue – Cost, the profit of a deposit-taking financial intermediary may therefore be enhanced by one or more of four ways, by:

- Increasing the margin between the interest rate paid to lenders and the interest rate charged to borrowers;

- Minimising the operating costs of the institution, and striving to increase efficiency, especially in the utilisation of staff which invariably constitutes the largest proportion of costs;

- Minimising the losses due to default, which may justify the employment of specialist staff and techniques in order to assess risk;

- Pursuing profitable activities not requiring the use of depositors' money, e.g. selling insurance policies. Another name for such activities is 'non-funds based products'.

8.5   With regard to the interest rate margin, remember that competitive forces will be important, because if the interest rate on deposits is lowered and that on loans is increased, the intermediary may end up driving business in the direction of its competitors, thereby reducing balance sheet growth and hence profits. Unless the intermediary is able to differentiate its services in some way, so that it can pay a lower interest rate and/or charge a higher interest rate, the interest rate margin will be set by the level of competition within the system. As a consequence, intermediaries will be placing greater emphasis on controlling costs and limiting default losses in order to increase profitability.

8.6   Finally, although this unit has been concerned until now with the nature of financial intermediation, note that many of the services offered by financial intermediaries are *not* intermediary services. Many of them – such as money transmission by the retail banks and building societies – are provided as an adjunct to the intermediary services, either because they are cheap to provide alongside those intermediary services, or because the institution has certain marketing advantages. Frequently these non-intermediary services are provided on a fee basis, and allow the institutions to make better use of some aspect of their resources and expertise.

Student Activity 4

1. Upon what basis are UK financial intermediaries now normally classified?
    (Paragraph 7.1)

2. List the groups of banks included amongst UK retail banks.   *(Paragraph 7.2)*

3. List the groups of institutions included under the heading of other (non-bank) deposit-taking institutions.   *(Paragraph 7.2)*

4. What types of revenues may be derived by a financial intermediation business?
    (Paragraph 8.2)

5. What types of costs are associated with a financial intermediation business?
    (Paragraph 8.3)

9   Central banks and the Bank of England

9.1   Central banks are a particular kind of bank, and there is usually one for each country, responsible for the note issue and for implementing monetary policy. Some central banks are owned by or are under the control of their country's government; others are not. Usually, central banks do not have a broad customer base. The Bank of England, the UK's central bank, retains only a few corporate customers while its private customers are mainly its employees. However, it argues that these accounts give it practical experience of retail banking.

Ownership and organisation of the Bank of England

9.2   The Bank of England is owned by the UK government, having been nationalised in 1946 by the Bank of England Act which gave the Treasury powers to issue directions to it. In turn, the Act gave it powers to issue directions to the other banks in the UK. These powers have never been used. In 1844, the Bank was granted a monopoly of the note issue in England and Wales (note: not in Scotland or Ireland) and divided into two departments:

- Banking Department, which carries on the usual activities of banking – maintaining accounts (mainly for the government, other central banks and retail banks), accepting deposits and trading in the discount and foreign exchange departments. As you will see in section 11, the Banking

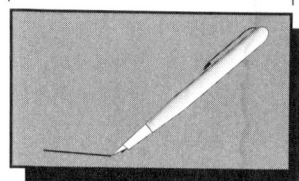

Department is treated as a retail bank for statistical purposes. It is also a member of all sections of the sterling clearings.

- Issue Department, which is responsible for the note issue. The notes are backed by assets, which are mainly government securities (gilts) but which can include commercial bills and Treasury bills. It is not responsible for coins, which are the responsibility of the Royal Mint.

9.3 For many operating purposes, the two departments have been superseded by other organisational structures, but in 1994 the Bank was again divided into two – two wings, one for each of the two main roles it has to play:

- Monetary stability wing;
- Financial stability wing.

Monetary stability wing

9.4 'Monetary stability' is a term not frequently used in the UK. It means stability of:

- Domestic prices (inflation);
- Interest rates;
- Exchange rates.

The wing covers:

- Banking;
- Gilt-edged and money markets, including debt management;
- Foreign exchange;
- Statistics and economic analysis;
- Monetary policy advice;
- The quarterly *Inflation Report* and *Bulletin*.

Its work forms most of Unit 7. The tasks are not covered by any Act of Parliament, unlike the work of the other wing.

Financial stability wing

9.5 This wing is charged with the duty of ensuring that the UK has a strong and stable financial system, and that the risks inevitable in banking and finance are controlled and minimised. The wing covers:

- Supervision of banks in detail;
- Supervision of the wholesale money markets, including gilt-edged, also in detail;
- Payment, settlement and clearing systems, including real time gross settlement (RTGS) and CREST (see Unit 3);
- Business finance, which is the new term for 'industrial liaison';
- Measures to prevent money laundering;
- Registrar's department, which keeps the stockholder registers of the national debt;
- The printing works, which prints bank notes and treasury bills. A number of central banks do not print their own notes: for instance, in Germany notes are printed by the Federal Government printing office.

Many of these functions are covered in greater detail in Unit 5.

9.6   The Bank of England is not a large financial intermediary. It lends to the government and to the discount houses. In the interwar years it did finance a number of distressed industrial companies affected by the depression. Perhaps the note issue is its largest activity (some £20bn worth) as an intermediary. However, there is no doubt that it is the UK's leading financial institution, because it is:

- An intermediary;

- A broker;

- A trader;

- An adviser (to the government and to other banks).

9.7   Its importance is also enhanced as a result of its role as a supervisor, under the Banking Act 1987 and s.43, Financial Services Act 1986. The latter Act requires the Bank to supervise the wholesale money markets.

Relationship with the Government

9.8   The Bank of England is not independent of the UK government. It was, in the 18th and 19th century, but this century has seen the ascendancy of elected politicians, answerable to the House of Commons and, ultimately, to the electorate. The matter came to a head towards the end of the First World War, in a bitter struggle between a dominant Governor and Lloyd George, the Prime Minister. The dispute was over the use of the government's gold and US dollar reserves to buy weapons and ammunition; the government won. In 1920, a notorious eccentric (Sir Montagu Norman) became Governor of the Bank for 24 years, and in 1925 persuaded Winston Churchill, then Chancellor, to return to the gold standard at what proved to be too high a rate of exchange. As a result, UK exports (especially coal) were depressed. By 1946, when the Labour government nationalised the Bank, the Conservative opposition was halfhearted and Churchill did not attend, speak or vote in the debate. Since the mid-1950s, decisions on interest rate changes have been taken by the Chancellor of the Exchequer.

9.9   Independence has become an issue in the 1990s, partly because of the support for it from Nigel Lawson, the Chancellor from 1983 to 1989 and the need for the Bank to be independent of instruction if the UK were to join the Economic and Monetary Union (EMU). If that occurs, the Bank of England will become part of the European System of Central Banks.

9.10   Advocates of greater independence for the Bank of England dislike the political pressures on a Chancellor of the Exchequer to cut interest rates in the run-up to a general election. They argue that stable prices, interest and exchange rates (monetary stability as people on the European mainland term these policy goals) are so important that decisions affecting them should not be taken by politicians. Instead, monetary stability should be taken out of the political arena, as are the principles of the rule of law and the independence of judges. Moreover, supporters of the single currency argue that, when the UK joins (if, indeed, it does) then the Treaty of Maastricht requires that the Bank of England shall be 'free of instruction'.

9.11   Opponents of greater independence cite the very important consequences which changes in monetary policy – which is largely interest rate policy at the present time – on firms and voters. Therefore, the opponents argue, important decisions on matters such as interest rates and exchange rates should be left in the hands of elected politicians who are answerable to the House of Commons and ultimately to the electorate. Underlying this argument is the strong relationship between changes in short-term interest rates caused by the operation of monetary policy and the cost of borrowing on mortgages and business loans. This does not occur on the Continent, where most long-term lending by banks and mortgage lenders is financed by long-term deposits or long-term borrowing.

Other central banks

9.12   Other central banks include:

- Federal Reserve System (USA) – independent;
- Bundesbank (Germany) – independent;
- Bank of France – independent only recently;
- Bank of Japan – not independent.

9.13   The first two are central banks of federal states, so the central banks are organised on a federal basis too. In the USA, there are 12 regional central banks, e.g. Federal Reserve Bank of Chicago, for the 50 states, while in Germany each state has its own central bank which sends delegates to the Federal Bank (Bund = Federal) in Frankfurt. The European Central Bank will be located in Frankfurt, where the European Monetary Institute is working on the plans for a single currency. At present, the Bank of England is a full member of the EMI, as are the central banks of the other 14 members of the EU.

9.14   In 1930, the central banks of the western world formed their own bank, located in Basle, Switzerland and known as the Bank for International Settlements (BIS). Since then, the BIS has grown in membership and in the late summer of 1996 it issued invitations for membership to the central banks of the following countries:

- China;
- India;
- Russia;
- Singapore;
- Brazil;
- Hong Kong;
- Mexico;
- Saudi Arabia;
- Korea (South).

9.15   This list gives an indication of the likely new players in the financial markets of the first decades of the 21st century, when many European countries will be using the euro as their currency. Cynics have commented that the BIS, once primarily a European bank, fears competition from the new European Central Bank and so is aiming to become a truly world bank for central banks.

Student Activity 5

1 What is a central bank? *(Paragraph 9.1)*

2 How is the Bank of England organised to carry out its functions? *(Paragraph 9.3)*

3 What are the functions of the Bank of England? *(Paragraph 9.4–5)*

4 How important is the Bank of England as:

(a) a financial intermediary

(b) a financial institution? *(Paragraph 9.6)*

5 Why did the Bank of England lose its independence this century? *(Paragraph 9.8)*

6 Examine the arguments for and against greater independence for the Bank of England. *(Paragraph 9.9–11)*.

10 Commercial banks

10.1 To some extent, classification of financial institutions is becoming progressively more difficult as the distinctions between them are being blurred, due primarily to changes in the regulatory framework and to competitive forces within the industry. Nevertheless, some classification is necessary for expository purposes, and there is a need to look at each group of financial institutions in turn, in order to attain a better understanding of their activities and their place within the financial system. In doing so, however, always bear in mind the extent to which financial institutions are increasingly offering a range of financial services which were traditionally offered by *separate* institutions.

Retail and wholesale activities of financial institutions

10.2 Before looking at each of the groups of financial institutions in more detail, we must first to ask the question: what is the difference between the retail and wholesale activities of financial institutions?

10.3 The major distinction between retail and wholesale activities undertaken by financial institutions is in the *size of transactions* involved. Retail activities are concerned with deposits and loans that are of relatively low value, and wholesale activities are concerned with high-value deposits and loans. While no hard distinction between retail and wholesale is possible, a transaction of less than £100,000 would usually be regarded as a retail transaction.

10.4 The distinction between retail and wholesale activities also relates to the *type of customer* involved. Predominantly, retail activities of banks will involve taking in deposits from and making loans to personal customers and small businesses. Notwithstanding this, note that *very large* organisations will often also need to make use of the retail financial services offered by banks. For example, if an organisation has a number of retail outlets, it will make use of local branches of banks in order to deposit cash and cheques.

10.5 A third aspect of the distinction between the retail and wholesale activities of financial institutions relates to the *distribution system* for the services provided.

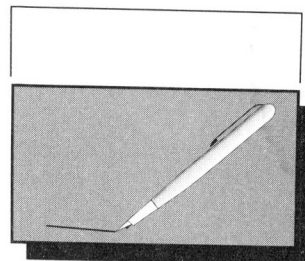

Usually, the provision of retail activities has involved *branch networks* – best typified by the retail banks and by building societies. Although this is the usual format, note that developments in technology, in particular, are enabling many retail financial services to be provided without a branch network, while some institutions – such as unit trusts – have never operated a branch network. Thus, telephone banking has been developed, while some building societies have launched 'postal accounts'. In a few years' time, retail financial services are likely to be widely available on the internet.

10.6 A consequence of retail activities involving transactions of relatively low value is that the *volume* of such transactions will generally be very high. The banks, and increasingly the building societies, are as a consequence partly involved in *money transmission facilities* (such as cheque book accounts, electronic funds transfer and so on) to enable the transfer of funds from one individual or business to another to take place.

10.7 Wholesale activities, being concerned with high-value transactions, typically involve customers that are larger businesses or else other financial institutions. Since these high-value transactions will be of limited *volume*, a branch network to support such activities is unnecessary. Due to the high level of competition found in wholesale markets and due to the lower total costs arising to be gained from dealing with limited numbers of high value transactions, the interest rates on wholesale transactions will generally be market-related rates and will usually be at a much finer margin in comparison to retail transactions.

10.8 Although the distinction between retail and wholesale activities is a useful one, remember that the distinction is in relation to *activities* rather than institutions. Many financial institutions will be engaged in both wholesale and retail activities. The retail banks, for example, are heavily engaged in wholesale activities, both in terms of obtaining funds and in lending. The larger building societies typically obtain a proportion of their funds from wholesale sources. The basis of classification is therefore in terms of an institution's *dominant* activity, rather than on its *exclusive* activity.

Student Activity 6

1. In relation to size of transactions and types of activities, what are the differences between retail and wholesale activities undertaken by financial institutions?
   (Paragraphs 10.3–8)

2. What is the normal form of distribution channel for retail financial services?
   (Paragraph 10.5)

3. For what reasons may wholesale banking activities operate on narrower margins than retail banking activities? *(Paragraph 10.7)*

4. List the broad groups of UK banks. *(Paragraph 10.12)*

11 The retail banks

11.1 As you can see from the list of retail banks in paragraph 7.2, this group comprises a rather diverse set of institutions which vary substantially in terms of *size*.

11.2 Some of the institutions, notably the London clearing banks, have been established as banks for a very long time; others for a relatively short time, one example being the Abbey National which has been a bank only since July 1989, a consequence of its conversion from a mutual building society to plc status. In 1997, Halifax plc will be formed, as the building society becomes a retail bank.

11.3 The scope of the activities of the institutions varies substantially. The largest clearing banks, for example, all have very extensive wholesale activities, while those of the Yorkshire Bank, for instance, are much more limited. Abbey National plc, unsurprisingly in view of the recent conversion from mutual building society status, has activities that are more akin to building societies than to the other banks in the group. (The Banking Department of the Bank of England has a very different set of activities from the other retail banks in the group and was covered in section 9 of this unit.

11.4 Despite these differences, all the institutions offer banking services at a retail level, which involves large numbers of low-value transactions. All the institutions have large branch networks, although in the case of Girobank plc, its branch network consists of post offices rather than being under its direct control.

Services

11.5 Their most important function, which the large branch networks support, is to offer current accounts, the major purpose of which – from the point of view of the account-holder – is that they allow the settlement of debts by means of the transfer of funds from one account to another. To allow these transfers of funds, the retail banks have to provide, in conjunction with the current accounts, domestic payments *services*. To achieve this, they offer cheque payment services (supported by cheque guarantee cards to improve acceptability), bank giro credit facilities, direct debits, standing orders, electronic funds transfer (via the Bankers' Automated Clearing Service, now shortened to BACS) and by the Clearing House Automated Payments System (CHAPS)), together with debit and credit card facilities.

11.6 Although current accounts, and the associated payment mechanisms, represent the most important function of the retail banks, note the wide range of other banking services that they also provide. Directed particularly at *personal customers*, these services include:

- A range of savings accounts;
- Personal loans, both secured and unsecured;
- Mortgage loans;
- Overdraft facilities;
- Automated teller machines (to allow cash dispensing and other banking services out of normal banking hours);

- Home banking by telephone (to allow transactions to be initiated away from branches and outside normal banking hours);

- Travellers' cheques and foreign currencies;

- Advice on taxation and financial matters;

- Executor and trustee facilities;

- 'Private banking' for individuals with incomes of about £35,000 or over and net assets of about £75,000–£100,000 and over.

11.7   Directed particularly at *corporate customers*, the services include:

- Overdraft facilities and loans, ranging from short-term working capital facilities to long-term secured loans;

- Cash management schemes;

- Electronic banking, using electronic data interchange (EDI) techniques;

- Leasing and hire purchase, often through subsidiaries;

- Export and import financing facilities;

- Payroll services;

- International financial transfers;

- Financial management advice.

11.8   Naturally, not all the retail banks will be offering all these services. In particular, some of the retail banks will be concentrating on services to *personal* and small business customers. Furthermore, the activities listed above relate to *banking* services, although the retail banks are increasingly offering a range of 'non-banking' services, including unit trust operations, insurance broking, stockbroking and the provision of personal equity plans. These, together with advice and executor and trustee business (products dating back over half a century) are the non-funds based products mentioned in paragraph 8.4. Profit margins are often higher on such products, the provision of which is not subject to the controls on liquidity and capital adequacy discussed in Unit 5.

Student Activity 7

1. Outline the key characteristics of the retail banks.   *(Paragraph 11.4)*

2. Name 10 different types of services provided by a typical retail bank for its personal customers.   *(Paragraph 11.6)*

3. State 10 different types of services provided by a typical retail bank for its corporate customers.   *(Paragraph 11.7)*

The balance sheets of the retail banks

11.9   An alternative perspective on the operations of retail banks can be obtained from an examination of the aggregate 'balance sheet' for the group. The summary totals for the retail banks as at 30 April 1996 are given in Table 2.1.

Assets
(i) Sterling assets

11.10 Sterling assets represent over 70% of total assets, and hence it is clear that they dominate the business of the retail banks. The components of those

Table 2.1 UK retail banks: summary balance sheet as at 30 April 1996

Assets	£bn	£bn
Sterling		
Cash & balances with Bank of England		4.7
Market loans		95.6
Secured money with discount houses	6.4	
Rest of UK banking sector	62.8	
Certificates of deposit held	17.0	
UK local authorities	0.3	
Overseas	9.2	
Bills		18.9
Treasury bills	7.9	
Eligible bank bills	10.6	
Other	0.4	
Claims under sale and repurchase agreements		9.3
Advances		307.6
UK private sector	303.6	
Others	4.0	
Investments		48.0
Foreign currency		
Market loans and advances		99.3
UK	38.4	
Overseas	60.9	
Bills		2.9
Investments		50.9
Claims under sale and repurchase agreements		8.1
Miscellaneous assets (in sterling and foreign currency)		32.6
Total assets		677.9

Liabilities	£bn	£bn
Sterling		
Notes issued		2.4
Sterling deposits (of which £203bn are sight deposits)		426.8
UK banking sector	51.8	
UK private sector	306.0	
UK public sector	5.1	
Overseas residents	26.5	
Certificates of deposit issued, etc.	37.4	
Liabilities under sale and repurchase agreements		7.9
Foreign currency		
Foreign currency deposits		146.6
UK	41.1	
Overseas residents	83.0	
Certificates of deposit issued, etc.	22.5	
Liabilities under sale and repurchase agreements		6.0
Miscellaneous liabilities (in sterling and foreign currency)		88.2
Total liabilities		677.9

Source: Bank of England Monetary Statistics, Table I.2

sterling assets are as follows.

11.11 *Cash and balances with the Bank of England.* Despite being the most vital asset for the day-to-day operations of the retail banks, the latter manage to keep the total very small. They do so because cash and balances at the Bank of England bring them no income. The balances with the Bank of England are partly operational balances used to meet commitments arising from payments-clearing operations, though they also include the cash ratio balances that all banks are required to hold with the Bank of England as part of the authorities' regulatory provisions. Only the operational balances are liquid assets.

11.12 Market *loans*. At £95.6bn, these represent about 14% of total assets and about 20% of sterling assets, and consequently represent a significant proportion of the retail banks' assets and activities. The 'market' aspect of these loans refers to the fact that they are wholesale loans that are usually made at market-related rates of interest and usually to other banking institutions. The majority of market loans are very liquid, i.e. they have only a short period to maturity, and hence represent an important means of holding interest-bearing assets that are also very liquid as an alternative to holding cash. They form the greater part of the banks' liquid assets.

11.13 *Bills.* Bills total only £18.9bn, representing 2% of total assets and 3.9% of sterling assets. As such, they now constitute only a fairly minor element of the retail banks' business, though their importance has been higher in the past. The largest element of these bills is 'eligible bank bills', so called because they are commercial bills that have been accep*ted* (underwritten) by banks which have eligibility status with the Bank of England. To achieve eligibility status, banks have to meet certain criteria set by the Bank of England, relating to the quality of their acceptance business. The significance of eligible bank bills lies in the fact that they are eligible for re-discounting at the Bank of England. A bill that has been accepted by a bank which does not have eligibility status is a normal, non-eligible bank bill and will be included in this category of bills, along with Treasury bills and local authority bills. With a liquid secondary market in bills, these also represent liquid assets that yield an investment return.

11.14 *Claims under sale and repurchase agreements.* These are a new type of asset, introduced in the discount market on a formal basis to market members in 1993. In 1996, an 'open' repo (as these facilities are known) was introduced to the gilt-edged market. Banking statistics now show repo claims as a separate asset, with repo liabilities also being shown separately. These claims arise where the banks have bought assets (bills or gilts) in sterling from other parties, who must later complete the transactions by buying the assets from the banks with cash. The figures show claims at £9.3 billion and liabilities at £7.9 billion, so that the retail banks have net claims of £1.4 billion, which is small compared to the figure for wholesale banks.

11.15 *Advances.* At £307.6bn, representing 45% of total assets and over 63% of sterling assets, sterling advances clearly represent the most important element of retail banks' assets. Advances constitute the lending made predominantly to the UK private sector, either in the form of overdrafts or loans for fixed periods of time. If the lending is for a fixed period of time, the original maturity may range from a few months to 10 years or more; in the case of mortgage loans, the original maturity is normally for 25 years. The arrangements for the interest rate charged on advances will be either floating (changing with the bank's base rate or the sterling London inter-bank offered rate – LIBOR), or fixed over the duration of the loan, or a hybrid of the two with rates fixed for a certain period of time. In addition, the interest rate charged will vary with the size of the sum borrowed, the creditworthiness of the borrower, the maturity of the loan, the arrangements for repayment, and so on. (For a longer discussion of this point, see section 4, Unit 6.)

11.16 Advances represent the least liquid element of the retail banks' financial assets but also represent the most important source of profit to a retail bank since, subject to competitive forces, the interest margin is greatest on these assets. In order for advances to be profitable, however, the banks need to control the costs of originating and administering the advances and to minimise losses through defaults. Given the lack of liquidity associated with advances, the importance of a substantial proportion of liquid assets – that is, cash, operational balances with the Bank of England, market loans and bills – within the total sterling asset portfolio can be appreciated.

11.17 *Investments.* At £50.9bn, these represent only 7.5% of total assets and just over 10% of sterling assets. The bulk of these investments is accounted for by securities issued by, or guaranteed by, the British government. An important aspect of British government securities is that they are highly marketable and hence the underlying investment can be realised quickly. Their value changes, however, in the opposite direction to changes in interest rates.

(ii) Foreign currency assets

11.18 Table 2.1 shows that foreign currency assets constituted £161bn and therefore about 24% of the total assets of the retail banks. The significance of these figures is that the retail banks are not just dealing in sterling at a retail level, but that almost 25% of their business involves foreign currencies.

11.19 The components of the foreign currency assets are very similar to those for sterling assets. A notable figure is the £99.3bn for market loans and advances to the overseas sector, demonstrating the point that not only is a substantial element of the business of the retail banks expressed in foreign currency, but furthermore a significant element of that is non-domestic in nature. In practice, around 75% of the 'market loans and advances' elements constitutes market loans, and therefore only 25% constitutes advances. Sale and purchase agreements are available in foreign currencies, so there is an entry for claims of £8.1bn.

(iii) Miscellaneous assets

11.20 This figure on the asset side of the balance sheet consists of items such as the retail banks' own branch premises and equipment and the value of cheques that have been credited to customers' accounts but which have not been presented for payment to other banks. Since it includes assets in both sterling and other currencies, it has been excluded from the calculation of the percentages above.

Liabilities

(i) Sterling liabilities

11.21 Sterling liabilities represent £437bn, equivalent to 64.5% of total liabilities. This is slightly lower than the proportion of sterling assets in total assets, but account needs to be taken of the higher proportion of the 'miscellaneous' item on the liabilities side of the balance sheet than the asset side. Moreover, most of these 'miscellaneous liabilities' items will be the banks' sterling capital and reserves.

11.22 *Notes issued.* These constitute £2.4bn and represent the notes that are issued by the Scottish and Northern Ireland banks, which are backed, pound for pound, by notes issued by the Bank of England.

11.23 *Sterling deposits.* These constituted £426.8bn, nearly 63% of total liabilities. Examination of the balance sheet in Table 2.1 reveals that 12% of these deposits emanated from the UK banking sector, nearly 72% from the UK private sector (both individuals and businesses), 1.2% from the public sector and almost 6.1% from overseas residents. In addition, 8.8% of sterling deposits were in the form of certificates of deposit and other short-term paper where the source, in terms of the previous classifications, is unknown. (Sterling certificates of deposit are negotiable bearer securities of fixed term (usually between 28 days and five years), carrying a fixed rate of interest and issued in denominations of £50,000 or more.)

11.24 What the balance sheet does not identify is the maturity structure of these sterling deposits because this is market-sensitive information. In practice, around 50% of sterling deposits are in the form of *sight* deposits repayable on demand, with around 70% of these being interest-bearing. The time deposits have maturities that range from a few days up to several years, and are sourced on both a retail and a wholesale basis. In practice, however, a significant number of the time deposits are repayable on demand (albeit with an interest penalty), and a significant number also have only a short period to maturity. The overall picture facing the retail banks, therefore, is that their sterling liabilities are highly liquid, emphasising their dependence on the 'law of large numbers' to enable them to provide loans and other advances.

11.25 *Liabilities under sale and repurchase agreements.* These arise when a bank has sold assets (bills or gilts) in return for cash under the newly introduced 'repo' facilities described earlier. As part of the contracts, the banks have liabilities to repurchase these bills or gilts at some date in the near future. In this instance, the retail banks' liabilities are slightly less than their claims.

(ii) Foreign currency deposits

11.26 Foreign currency deposits originate primarily in the form of wholesale deposits, with a high proportion, not surprisingly, coming from the overseas sector. Certificates of deposit are also issued in foreign currencies.

(iii) Miscellaneous liabilities

11.27 Constituting £75.6bn, this item represents 14.3% of total liabilities and includes credit balances received but not yet credited to customers' accounts, and standing orders and credit transfers debited to customers' accounts but not transferred to the payee. This miscellaneous liabilities item, however, also includes the important element of shareholders' funds, the vast majority of which are denominated in sterling. Like any business, a bank needs capital backing for its business operations; in addition to the capital required for premises and equipment and for working capital, shareholders' funds are required to cover the possibility of defaults on loans and capital losses on investments. The size of shareholders' funds relative to total assets therefore represents the ability of a bank to absorb losses, and therefore its ability to repay depositors when it does incur losses. (Capital adequacy is covered in Unit 5.) Since it includes liabilities in both sterling and other currencies, the miscellaneous liabilities item has been excluded from the calculation of the percentages above.

Student Activity 8

1. What are eligible bank bills? *(Paragraph 11.13)*

2. What is the significance of eligible bank bills for retail banks? *(Paragraph 1.13)*

3. What is the significance of foreign currency assets for retail banks?
(Paragraphs 11.18–20)

4. Describe the structure of a typical retail bank's liabilities portfolio.
(Paragraphs 11.21–27)

5. Distinguish between claims and liabilities under sale and repurchase agreements.
(Paragraphs 11.14 and 11.25)

The changing environment and activities of the UK retail banks

11.28 The analysis of the activities and of the summary balance sheet of the retail banks in the previous paragraphs provides an overview of what the banks currently *do*, but not of how this has changed over time and is likely to change in the future. This section provides a brief overview of the way in which the environment, and hence the activities, of the retail banks has changed in recent years.

Competition

11.29 The major change in the environment within which the retail banks operate is that it has become much more *competitive*. This has come about not only as a consequence of deregulation within financial markets, but also as a consequence of innovation by participants within those markets. The result of this has been that the domination of the market for banking services by the retail banks in the UK has come under attack. With regard to the market for personal customers, a major source of increased competition has been the building societies which, mainly as a consequence of the changes brought about by the Building Societies Act 1986, have started to offer a much more comprehensive range of banking services including, on a limited basis, personal loans for purposes other than house purchase. It has also been suggested that the general public is now much more financially sophisticated than, say, 10 years ago, so that they are better able to evaluate alternative financial products and are more willing to move funds between different financial institutions to take advantage of better interest rates or other facilities.

Personal customers

11.30 The ability of the retail banks to attract funds from their personal customers was seen to be under threat, and they have responded in a number of ways:

- Instead of offering just the one type of savings account, the 7-day deposit account, a range of savings accounts with competitive interest rates are now offered with, often, improved access to the funds by the customer.

- Improved current account facilities, in the form of interest-bearing current accounts, free banking subject to certain (more generous) criteria, facilities such as automatic overdrafts, and the provision of debit cards.

- Improved the access to current account funds, by means of automated teller machines, longer opening hours and home banking facilities.

- Expanded advertising and marketing to increase customer awareness and to improve the image of the retail banks.

- Purchases of building societies by some banks: Lloyds bought Cheltenham & Gloucester; Abbey National bought National & Provincial and the Bank of Ireland intends to buy Bristol & West.

- Merger – in the autumn of 1996, Lloyds Bank announced its purchase of TSB Bank and they intend to merge the two businesses in perhaps 1998; meanwhile the separate branch networks continue.

Corporate customers

11.31 In the market for corporate customers, the changing environment has also manifested itself primarily in the form of increased competition, brought about again by deregulation. The deregulation of the capital markets has enabled corporate borrowers to raise funds from sources other than banks, while increased competition has extended the range of alternative means of finance available from the capital market and has lowered the cost of such finance relative to bank finance.

11.32 The *response* by the retail banks to the increased competition for corporate customers has taken a number of forms:

- Improvement of existing facilities for corporate customers. Given that the cost of funds lies largely outside a bank's control, however, their ability to improve existing facilities is necessarily limited and is concentrated on increasing the flexibility offered to such customers.

- Greater involvement in the securities markets. For some retail banks this has meant acquiring firms operating as brokers or market-makers within the capital markets, but they have also become increasingly involved in merchant and investment banking via their subsidiaries and directly involved in, for example, managing issues of commercial paper.

- Development of particular segments of the market for corporate customers, and in this respect small- and medium-sized businesses have become the focus of attention, since the ability of such businesses to take advantage of deregulation and increased competition within the capital market is limited by their size.

11.33 For both the market for personal customers and that for corporate customers, an additional response to the changing environment has been a movement away from their financial intermediary services towards the whole range of non-intermediary financial services. These activities do not require the banks to obtain and then onlend funds, allowing the banks to benefit from the interest margin; rather, they generate fees or commissions for the bank concerned, and to some extent are subject to less competition. Many of these activities enable the banks to make more intensive use of their branch networks and hence to lower average costs. They include insurance broking, unit trust operations, stockbroking and estate agency operations. They are sometimes called 'non-funds based products'.

Student Activity 9

1. Examine the importance of the Building Societies Act 1986 for UK retail banks.
   (Paragraph 11.29)

2. It is sometimes suggested that the general public have become more sophisticated in their financial requirements. How might this fact have affected retail banking operations? *(Paragraph 11.30)*

3. Discuss some of the improvements which retail banks have made to their facilities in recent years in order to enhance their position in attracting personal customers. *(Paragraph 11.30)*

4. List some of the ways in which retail banks have attempted to improve their facilities for corporate customers in recent years. *(Paragraph 11.32)*

5. For what reasons might retail banks move into the provision of non-intermediation financial services? *(Paragraph 11.8)*

12 Wholesale banks

12.1 The wholesale banks represent a diverse group of institutions within the UK financial system. They comprise three broad groups:

- British merchant banks;
- Other British banks;
- Overseas banks, which in turn are divided into American, Japanese and 'other overseas banks'.

The balances outstanding of the wholesale banks

12.2 The total size of the wholesale bank sector, at nearly £1205bn is *far larger* than that of the retail bank sector, with assets of nearly £678bn. However, remember that while the retail sector constitutes just 20 different institutions (excluding the Banking Department of the Bank of England), the wholesale sector comprises over 500 institutions, which implies that the *average* size of a wholesale bank is appreciably smaller than that of a retail bank. Moreover, there is a considerable amount of inter-bank transactions in the table; if net figures, i.e. excluding inter-bank business – were shown, then the totals would be smaller.

12.3 The wholesale bank sector as a whole has a *much greater involvement in foreign currency business* than does the retail bank sector. Examination of the balance sheet for the wholesale banks reveals that some 73.8% of the assets of

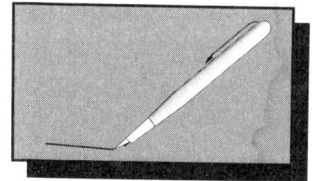

Table 2.2 Wholesale banks in the UK: summary balance sheet as at 30 April 1996

Assets	£bn	£bn
Sterling		
Cash and balances with the Bank of England		0.6
Market loans		93.1
Secured money with discount houses	2.1	
Other UK banks	44.9	
Certificates of deposit held	12.8	
UK local authorities	1.1	
Overseas	32.2	
Bills		1.0
Treasury bills	0.1	
Eligible bank bills	—	
Other	0.9	
Claims under sale and repurchase agreements		16.3
Advances		135.2
UK private sector	122.2	
Others	13.0	
Investments		26.2
Foreign currency		
Market loans and advances		646.7
UK	141.1	
Overseas	505.6	
Bills		8.8
Claims under sale and repurchase agreements		110.4
Investments		123.0
Miscellaneous assets		43.4
Total assets		1204.7

Liabilities	£bn	£bn
Sterling deposits (of which £37.5bn are sight deposits)		244.6
UK banks	61.5	
UK private sector	83.2	
UK public sector	3.7	
Overseas residents	54.4	
Certificates of deposit issued	41.8	
Liabilities under sale and repurchase agreements		11.7
Foreign currency deposits		785.6
UK		139.3
Overseas residents	576.6	
Certificates of deposit issued	69.7	
Liabilities under sale and repurchase agreements		91.5
Miscellaneous liabilities (including capital)		71.3
Total liabilities		1204.7

Source: Bank of England Monetary Statistics, Table I.2

wholesale banks are denominated in foreign currency. Furthermore, over 50% of the liabilities of the wholesale banks were attributable to *overseas* residents, which serves to emphasise the *international* nature of the wholesale banking sector in the UK.

12.4   Given the overwhelmingly wholesale nature of the activities of the banks in this group, *holdings of cash and balances at the Bank of England are extremely small* – some £600m in total, representing 0.05% of total assets. As a further indication of the wholesale nature of the activities, only around 15% of sterling deposits with wholesale banks are sight deposits, the bulk therefore constituting time deposits.

12.5   *Market loans and advances dominate both sterling and foreign currency assets*, with bills and investments, both in sterling and in foreign currencies, constituting only 12.6% of total assets. This is to be expected, given the wholesale nature of their activities, and is consistent with the low proportion of sight deposits within the liability portfolio.

12.6   'Repo' transactions (see paragraphs 11.14 and 11.25) feature prominently in this table. For foreign currency business, repo claims total £110.4bn, approaching the total of investments denominated in foreign currencies.

12.7   In summary, it is clear that the major activity of the wholesale banks is in taking in term deposits and using them to make term loans. Taking this in conjunction with the fact that the transactions are *wholesale* in nature (that is, small numbers of high value transactions) leads to the result that the wholesale banks cannot rely on the 'law of large numbers' to apply. The fact that a large number of *different currencies* are involved compounds this problem.

12.8   Consequently, there has to be a degree of *matching* of assets and liabilities, possibly to a greater extent for maturity terms than in retail banking. The matching will be in terms both of matching the term to maturity of loans and deposits, and of the currency of denomination. The matching will not, however, be perfect: if it were, the bank would in effect be acting as little more than a broker rather than as a bank. A mismatch of either the term to maturity or of the currencies involved will potentially allow the bank to gain higher profits, and hence the choice is frequently between lower risk and higher profits. The riskiness of mismatching is alleviated to some extent by the existence of the inter-bank market, where a bank can obtain funds as and when necessary – at a cost. The risk involved in the mismatching of assets and liabilities lies less, therefore, in the threat to solvency than in the loss to profits that might be incurred as a consequence of adverse interest rate or exchange-rate movements.

Student Activity 10

1. List the main categories of wholesale banks to be found within the UK financial system.   *(Paragraph 12.1)*

2. Taking the wholesale banks as a group, what are the three most important types of assets to be found on their balance sheet?   *(Paragraphs 12.3 and 12.5)*

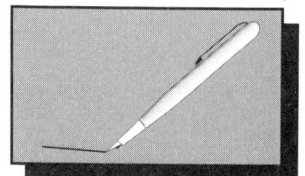

3. For the wholesale banks as a group, what is the most important liability on their balance sheet? *(Paragraph 12.3)*

4. In terms of balance sheet size, how large is the UK wholesale bank sector compared with the retail bank sector? *(Paragraph 12.2)*

5. What is the size of the typical wholesale bank compared with the typical retail bank? *(Paragraph 12.2)*

6. Examine the main characteristics of wholesale banking operations. *(Paragraph 12.7)*

7. Why do wholesale banks match their assets with their liabilities according to maturity? *(Paragraphs 12.7 and 12.8)*

British merchant banks

12.9 The group of wholesale banks called the British merchant banks comprises around 40 institutions, with assets totalling £44.8bn in April 1996. Historically, a major element of their business lay in the 'acceptance' of bills of exchange. This involves the bank in guaranteeing payment of the bill upon maturity to whoever is then holding the bill. The bank receives a fee for fulfilling this underwriting role, and hence acceptances are an early example of a bank providing non-intermediary services. Such acceptances feature on the balance sheets of the accepting bank only as a footnote – contingent liabilities offset by contingent (possible) claims against the drawers if the bills. Once a bill is accepted by a reputable bank it becomes much more marketable, and as a consequence the merchant banks facilitate the use of bills as a significant source of short-term corporate finance.

12.10 The risk involved in accepting bills of exchange is that the debtor may default when the bill matures. As a consequence, the key to running a profitable acceptance activity was being able to evaluate accurately the default risk associated with bills, and to do this the merchant banks had to acquire considerable information and expertise. Subsequently, they found they could use this information and expertise in *other* areas, and as a result the British merchant banks have progressively diversified away from acceptances as the main element of their business. The majority now offer a wide range of banking services to corporate customers so that, in addition to taking in deposits and making loans on a wholesale basis and the acceptance activity, the merchant banks as a group now offer:

- Management and underwriting of capital issues by companies;
- Management consultancy services, especially with regard to financial aspects;
- Advice on mergers and takeovers;
- Fund management services for pension funds, insurance companies, unit and investment trusts;
- Trading in foreign exchange markets;
- Trading in the bullion (gold and silver) markets;
- Trading in the eurocurrency markets;
- Trading in the derivatives markets.

12.11 Like the retail banks, the British merchant banks have also suffered from increased competition within their spheres of activity. Many have perceived themselves to be too small to withstand this competition, especially from institutions abroad, as their activities become increasingly international in character. In addition, the ability to participate in the capital markets has become increasingly attractive to the retail banks. This has meant that many of the merchant banks have become part of larger banking groups, either UK-based or overseas. For other merchant banks the consequence has been a rethinking of their strategy and the basis of future competition, which has led to some of the smaller banks competing on the basis of expertise within specialist market niches. The larger ones are tending to be known as investment banks, derived from their trading in investments, mentioned in the previous unit.

Other British banks

12.12 This group comprises around 150 different institutions, with assets totalling £62bn in April 1996. Given the size of the group, it is not surprising that it constitutes a rather disparate range of institutions. Having said that, a significant proportion of the group's activities are overseas, stemming from the fact that many of these banks originated when the UK was a major colonial power and banks were needed to service the needs of companies and individuals with dealings in the colonies. This need has declined, but banking services are still required within the former colonies and the status of London as a major financial centre has meant that it has been appropriate for these banks to retain their base in Britain.

12.13 Other banks in this group include wholesale banks that provide corporate banking services on a regional basis or that specialise in services to particular industries, and former finance houses that have taken on full banking status.

Overseas banks

12.14 The overseas banks represent the largest group of banks within the UK financial system, totalling around 350. Their dominance in numbers is matched by their assets, totalling almost £1,100bn (about 10 times the size of the British wholesale banks) as at 30 April 1996. They have exhibited very rapid growth since the early 1970s, in terms of both assets and numbers.

12.15 The overseas banks came to London originally to meet the business requirements of firms in their own countries. While they still perform that function, they are now important participants within the eurocurrency markets, and as such facilitate the taking-up of deposits from a wide range of sources and the financing of a wide range of different projects, with their activities no longer particularly related to their home countries. London's status as the major centre of eurocurrency market activity has facilitated this development and made it necessary for a bank of any size, wherever it is based in the world, to have a London office.

12.16 In addition to these wholesale banking activities, many overseas banks have moved into other areas of activity. This has in some cases included retail financial services, and in other cases has, as a consequence of the deregulation of the capital markets, included market-making and stockbroking activities. Some of the overseas banks have become major investment banks.

12.17 The following summary of their balance sheet totals (footings in American parlance) as at 30 April 1996, indicates their relative sizes.

Total asses in the UK	£bn
American banks	159.5
Japanese banks	205.7
Other overseas banks	732.8
Total	1098.0

Student Activity 11

1. What is an 'acceptance'? *(Paragraph 12.9)*

2. List the main areas of activity currently undertaken by British merchant banks. *(Paragraph 12.10)*

3. Why have many British merchant banks felt it necessary to reappraise their strategy in recent years? *(Paragraph 12.11)*

4. What types of activities are undertaken by 'other British banks'? *(Paragraphs 12.11–12)*

5. How important are overseas banks within the UK financial system? *(Paragraphs 12.15–16)*

6. Examine the main types of activities undertaken by the overseas banks in the UK. *(Paragraphs 12.15–16)*

13 The discount houses

13.1 Discount houses are a very special group of banks. They comprise seven institutions which are unique to the UK financial system, and they fulfil three significant functions.

- Their activities are crucial to the Bank of England's monetary policy operations.

- They have an important function in permitting the retail banks, in particular, to adjust their liquidity positions and to smooth flows of funds between banks as a consequence of their payments-clearing operations.

- They are instrumental in providing a mechanism for short-term financing of companies.

Their title of 'discount houses' stems from the fact that they were originally established to purchase bills of exchange at a discount to their maturity value, thereby providing the vendor with immediate funds whilst earning for the house an effective capital gain (yield) upon the asset's maturity.

13.2 The essence of the operations of the discount houses is that they attract short-term wholesale deposits and then use these to make short-term loans and to buy assets with short periods to maturity. The funds used to purchase the short-dated assets are borrowed, mainly, from the UK retail banks. Profits are earned by borrowing money at a lower interest rate than that earned on the assets purchased. This activity would appear to be very straightforward and of low risk, except that the funds they borrow are extremely short-term: the overwhelming majority of these funds are either 'at call' (meaning that the lender can demand them back without notice) or are on an overnight basis. If the lenders find themselves short of cash for whatever reason, they will call in, or not renew, loans to the discount houses, and in so doing are able to adjust their liquidity position quickly and easily. The discount houses then find themselves short of funds and have to pay higher rates in order to maintain their deposit bases – perhaps rates higher than they are earning on their purchases of short-dated assets, so that losses are being incurred. As a consequence, the ability to forecast accurately cash shortages or surpluses within the banking system, and future levels of short-term interest rates, is crucial to the profitability of these institutions.

13.3   It could conceivably be the case that funds are unavailable to the discount houses at almost any interest rate, and under these circumstances their solvency is threatened. This possibility is, however, covered by a unique characteristic of the discount houses: the right to borrow funds directly from the Bank of England (in practice, it is the sale – 'rediscounting' – of suitable assets to the Bank of England). The rate at which the Bank of England acts as a *lender of last resort* to the discount houses is, however, a rate of the *Bank of England*'s choosing, and it is this characteristic of the relationship between the discount houses and the Bank that is the basis of the Bank's ability to influence short-term interest rates throughout the whole of the financial system (see Unit 7).

13.4   The primary activity of the discount houses remains essentially straightforward, however: it is the purchase of short-dated assets by means of borrowed funds. The aggregate balance sheet of the discount houses is correspondingly straightforward; the asset side is dominated by holdings of commercial bills and, in particular, sterling certificates of deposit (CDs). The liability side of the balance sheet is dominated by very short-term borrowing in sterling from UK banks and, to a much lesser extent, other financial institutions.

13.5   The discount houses are collectively responsible for holding very large quantities of commercial bills and sterling CDs, and are responsible for the maintenance of a liquid secondary market in them. Through thc purchase of commercial bills, they allow holders of these bills to realise their funds prior to maturity. As a consequence, the discount houses are important providers of short-term finance to the commercial sector.

13.6   Like all groups of financial institutions, the environment within which the discount houses operate has been changing. Although the Bank of England acknowledges the importance of the discount houses to the financial system in general and the operation of government monetary policy in particular, it has been prepared to allow, and indeed has encouraged, a higher level of competition within the discount market. In 1981 the Bank sought to maintain the privileged position of the discount houses by requiring banks with eligibility status (that is, those banks who were responsible for underwriting – accepting – bills eligible for rediscounting at the Bank of England) to maintain amounts of funds with the discount houses that constituted a certain proportion of their short-term sterling deposit liabilities. This arrangement was phased out during the late 1980s, so that the discount houses no longer had a secure supply of funds and had to compete more openly for them. At the same time, the 'Big Bang' reforms of the Stock Exchange in 1986 allowed more participants into the gilt-edged market, causing a higher level of competition for the discount houses in the area of short-dated gilts. Since the mid-1980s the Bank of England has additionally been prepared to deal directly with institutions *other than* the discount houses. This has been in the form of sale and repurchase agreements (termed Repo agreements) with individual banks and building societies, which has enabled these institutions to manage their liquidity positions by means of direct dealing with the Bank of England rather than at one remove via the discount houses. Since January 1996 these Repo transactions have been shown gross, i.e. both assets and liabilities, in UK banking statistics.

13.7　In 1988 the Bank of England published its intention to extend its dealing relationships *beyond* what at the time constituted the eight discount houses and made clear that it would be prepared to establish dealing relationships with any suitable institution. This move resulted in two additional institutions establishing dealing relationships with the Bank, although only one of these took on full discount house status. However, subsequently two discount houses withdrew from the market.

13.8　Taken together, these developments represent a substantial shift away from the houses' protected position of the past and hence raise questions regarding their future development. While the majority of the institutions have hitherto been prepared to remain involved with the discount market, a number of them have been busy diversifying their activities to reduce their dependence on the discount market. They have, for example, become involved in leasing, in futures business and in the insurance market.

Student Activity 12

1.　State the broad functions of the discount houses.　　　*(Paragraph 13.1)*

2.　What types of deposits dominate discount houses' liabilities portfolios?
　　　　　　　　　　　　　　　　　　　　　　　　(Paragraph 13.2)

3.　What is the major risk faced by discount houses in their intermediation activities?
　　　　　　　　　　　　　　　　　　　　　　　　(Paragraph 13.2)

4.　What special facility is available to the discount houses which helps them to be able to meet substantial demands for withdrawals of funds at very short notice?
　　　　　　　　　　　　　　　　　　　　　　　　(Paragraph 13.3)

5.　What are the most important assets held by the discount houses?
　　　　　　　　　　　　　　　　　　　　　　　　(Paragraph 13.5)

6.　In what way do the discount houses provide short-term funds for the commercial sector?　　　　　　　　　　　　　*(Paragraphs 13.5 and 13.8)*

7.　Examine the main events which have put pressure on discount houses' operations in recent years.　　　　　　　　　　*(Paragraph 13.6)*

8.　How have discount houses tended to react to the pressures which they have faced in recent years?　　　　　　　　　*(Paragraph 13.8)*

14   Building societies

14.1   The primary purpose of building societies has been to provide finance for residential housing, and as such they provide a large proportion of the finance for house purchase within the UK. As a consequence of the need to raise funds to do this, they are also major participants in the market for savings, particularly retail savings. In more recent years, however, they have started to provide a range of other services, to make loans for purposes other than house purchase, and to reduce their dependence on the retail savings market by raising an increasing proportion of their funds from wholesale sources.

The summary balance sheet of the building societies

14.2   Table 2.3 provides the summary balance sheet of the building societies as at 30 April 1996.

Table 2.3 UK building societies: summary balance sheet as at 30 April 1996

Assets	£bn	£bn
Liquid assets		50.7
Notes and coin	0.3	
Sterling bank deposits and CDs		
(certificates of deposit)	28.7	
Bank bills	0.3	
Building society CDs	2.2	
British government stocks	6.2	
Other public sector debt	2.2	
Other	10.8	
Commercial assets		245.0
Class 1	220.8	
Class 2	9.1	
Class 3: individuals	1.4	
other	13.2	
Other assets		4.6
Total assets		300.3
Liabilities	£bn	£bn
Retail shares and deposits		215.0
Wholesale liabilities		54.3
(of which, foreign currency)	(10.6)	
CDs	8.3	
Deposits and commercial paper	23.7	
Syndicated borrowing	3.8	
Bonds	18.5	
Other liabilities and reserves		31.0
Total liabilities		300.3

Source: Bank of England, Monetary Statistics, Table J

14.3 With total assets/liabilities of £300bn, the building societies in the UK constitute a sizeable element of the financial system. In order to put this figure into context, recall Table 2.3 where the total assets/liabilities of the retail banks constituted approximately £668bn. The retail banks were only, therefore, slightly more than twice as large in asset terms as the building societies. However, after these figures were compiled, the National & Provincial Building Society was taken over by Abbey National Plc (a retail bank), so the societies' totals will fall. Moreover, in 1997 four other large societies are planning to become banks, while another is seeking to be taken over by the Bank of Ireland, so that these figures will continue to fall, and the banks' totals will rise by the same amount.

Assets

14.4 The bulk of the assets of building societies are categorised as 'commercial assets', which are divided into three classes: 1, 2 and 3.

- Class 1 assets are loans secured by a first mortgage on owner-occupied residential property, and as at April 1996 represented 90% of all commercial assets. They are the core lending product of the societies.

- Class 2 assets are other loans, secured on property, and these constituted approximately 3.7% of all commercial assets.

- Class 3 assets are loans, both secured and unsecured, that are not covered by Classes 1 and 2, as well as a building society's investments in land and property for residential use and investments in associates. They constituted almost 2.5% of all commercial assets.

14.5 The creation of Class 2 and Class 3 assets by building societies has been allowed only since the relevant provisions of the Building Societies Act 1986 came into force. That Act restricted their creation to the larger building societies (assets of £100m+) and specified that Class 2 assets could not exceed 10%, and Class 3 assets could not exceed 5%, of all commercial assets. These limits were relaxed in 1989 and in 1993 the limit for Class 2 assets was raised to 25% and for Class 3 assets to 15% (with the limit for Classes 2 and 3 together set at 25%). Clearly, the building society sector as a whole is a long way from utilising the limits which were applied at the end of 1993. However, the limits may represent a pointer to the way in which building societies are liable to develop in the future: away from sole dependence on mortgage loans and into a more broadly based retail loans portfolio – the total of £1.4bn for Class 3 loans to individuals is only 10% of the debt outstanding on all credit cards. Furthermore, it is worth noting one implication of the fact that 90% of all commercial assets are Class 1 assets: building societies are involved in very extensive maturity transformation of funds. Building societies are taking in deposits, mainly from retail sources and mainly repayable on demand, and using them to fund loans with an initial maturity of, normally, 25 years. However, the average length of a mortgage is about eight to 10 years.

14.6 At £50.7bn at the end of April 1996, representing nearly 17% of total assets, building societies held a significant amount of *liquid assets*. The summary balance sheet demonstrates that most of these liquid assets were held as sterling bank deposits, but a significant element was also held as British government stock (gilts) and other public sector debt. Given that the bulk of building societies' commercial assets (mortgage loans) are highly illiquid, building societies find it necessary to hold substantial liquid assets to meet variations in the volume of funds withdrawn. Also, it should be noted that gilts do not feature as liquid assets for banks.

Liabilities

14.7   On the liabilities side of the balance sheet, *retail shares and deposits*, at £215bn and constituting nearly 72% of all liabilities, are clearly the building societies' main source of funds. Prior to the early 1980s, retail shares and deposits constituted the *only* source of funds, since the raising of finance from wholesale sources was not permitted. From 1982 onwards, however, under a series of *ad hoc* arrangements, individual building societies were permitted to raise funds from wholesale sources, and these arrangements were formalised in the 1986 Act. By April 1996, as the table demonstrates, wholesale liabilities represented almost 18% of total liabilities, showing a substantial increase in a relatively short period of time. With the limits on wholesale funding being raised in stages to 50%, from the 1986 Act's 20%, the proportion of wholesale funding could be set to rise, thereby reducing still further their dependence on retail funding.

14.8   The wholesale funding takes place in a variety of forms including, notably, CDs, wholesale deposits, bonds and, most recently, foreign currency. Given the flexibility of wholesale funding, this development is allowing the building societies to operate on lower proportions of liquid assets than previously, and allowing their business to be led by lending opportunities rather than by the availability of retail funds.

14.9   The 'other liabilities and reserves' element of the liabilities of the balance sheet serves to emphasise that building societies, by definition, are *mutual* organisations. They are, therefore, owned by their borrowing and lending members and not by shareholders. The implication of this is that there are no 'shareholders' funds' within the balance sheet, and thus a building society cannot raise funds from shareholders. Reserves can only be accumulated by means of making profits, and hence the growth of building societies is constrained by their profitability. More recently, the building societies have been able to issue subordinated debt designed to act as a substitute for accumulated profits, but this facility has tended to be used by only the larger institutions and to a limited extent.

Student Activity 13

1.   What is the primary purpose of building societies?   *(Paragraph 14.1)*

2.   In terms of assets held, how large is the building societies sector relative to the retail banks sector?   *(Paragraph 14.3)*

3.   How are the building societies' assets classified in their accounts?
                                                                                    (Paragraphs 14.4–6)

4.   What is the most important type of asset held by building societies?
                                                                                    (Paragraph 14.4)

5.   Roughly, what proportion of building societies' assets are held in liquid form?
                                                                                    (Paragraph 14.6)

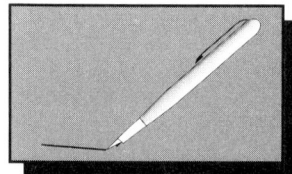

6. Outline the structure of the liabilities as shown in the building societies' summary accounts. *(Paragraph 14.7)*

7. Why might building societies now be able to operate with lower proportions of liquid assets in their portfolios than was formerly the case? *(Paragraph 14.8)*

The changing environment of the building societies

14.10 Two of the significant changes in the environment facing building societies in recent years – the ability to make loans for purposes other than first mortgages, and to make extensive use of wholesale funding – were a consequence of the Building Societies Act 1986 (see above). The 1986 Act gave rise to two other significant changes in the societies' environment, the abilities to:

- Convert from being mutual organisations to public limited companies; and

- Provide a much wider range of financial services.

14.11 In order to convert to a public limited company, a society requires the permission of its members. This permission is defined as a 75% majority amongst the lending members who vote in the ballot on conversion, where this 75% is achieved from a minimum of 20% of the lending members who are entitled to vote. It also requires a simple majority of the borrowing members who exercise their vote and the approval of the Building Societies Commission. This is designed to ensure that members' interests are protected during the conversion process.

14.12 Since a building society that achieves plc status will have shareholders and will no longer be a *mutual* organisation, it cannot be a building society; in practice, it becomes a *bank*, and therefore authorisation from the Bank of England to become a bank is also a necessary part of the process for conversion to plc status.

14.13 Although at the time of writing only two building societies (Abbey National and Cheltenham & Gloucester) have converted to plc status, several of the other large building societies are planning to do so in 1997. In fact, the Cheltenham & Gloucester, as part of the conversion plan, was immediately acquired by Lloyds Bank, and in August 1996 the National & Provincial was taken over by Abbey National. In 1997, Halifax, Woolwich, Alliance & Leicester and the Northern Rock all plan to become plcs (although not necessarily in that order), while Bristol & West proposes to be taken over by Bank of Ireland. Of these societies, only National & Provincial has lost its identity, although the Leeds Permanent was purchased by the Halifax in 1995 as part of its move to a plc, and all the Leeds' branches are now closed or bear the emblem of the Halifax.

14.14 The major *advantage* of conversion to plc status was considered to be freedom from the restrictions of the legislative framework of the building society industry, the 1986 Act. The restrictions which were seen to be particularly harmful to the future prosperity of the building societies were the limits on

- Unsecured lending;

- Lending to corporate and overseas customers;

- The ability to increase capital only by means of retaining profits;

- The ability to take over or merge (apart from paying cash) with other financial institutions in order to add to the range of financial services offered;

- The range of financial services which building societies are permitted to offer;

- The ability to offer profit-sharing schemes in the form of share distributions to their staff.

14.15 By the mid-1990s, however, there was a new reason for the urge to convert to plc status. A number of the largest societies saw conversion as the only way to continue to grow in size, because the housing market was dormant and the banks were gaining a large market share of new mortgage business. Plc status was the route away from a declining/stagnant mortgage market to the expanding markets of financial services.

14.16 Substantial though these constraints may be, the fact that some building societies strenuously assert their opposition to plc status implies that there are *disadvantages* also. These are seen to include the:

- Supervisory requirements of the Bank of England;

- Need to pay dividends to shareholders and the danger of being pressured into short-term responses to strategic issues;

- Possible eventual concentration of shareholdings into the hands of a limited number of investors, with the chance of increased shareholder influence on strategy;

- Possibility of takeover bids; and the

- Adverse impact on the image of a building society that its move away from mutual status would bring.

It has also been suggested that the more competitive environment into which a building society would move upon conversion would raise its operating costs as a consequence of having to recruit appropriately qualified staff.

14.17 The 1986 Act allows societies to:

- Provide a much wider range of financial services;

- Take equity stakes in both general and life insurance companies;

- Take equity stakes in stockbroking firms;

- Establish and manage personal equity plans and unit trusts through associated bodies; and

- Undertake fund management.

14.18 Thus, building societies are able to offer a much more complete set of retail financial services, although it has been argued that this is still too narrow to allow the building societies to compete with banks on an equal footing. Further powers are available for societies to incorporate in their constitutions, after approval by the members at AGMs, and these include insurance and the formation of subsidiaries to lend to small businesses. Some societies now have these powers, but they have yet to enter these new markets.

The position of building societies relative to retail banks

14.19 The rationale for the 1986 Building Societies Act was that the building societies should be allowed to engage in a wider range of financial services, including forms of lending and sources of funds. This was perceived as being necessary because if they were restricted to their original activities they would not be able to compete with other financial institutions and hence their share of the retail financial services market would inevitably decline. The changes brought about by the 1986 Act have caused the majority of building societies to become much more generalised retail financial services organisations.

14.20 However, as we noted above, restrictions remain on what building societies can do, and some of these – particularly the restrictions on the extent of lending other than as Class 1 assets and the extent of wholesale funding – are seen by some as being prejudicial to the future prosperity of building societies.

14.21 As a consequence of the 1986 Act there has been a substantial convergence of the retail banks and the building societies in the field of retail financial services for the personal sector. Several of the larger building societies are members of the clearing house system, offer interest-bearing current accounts, personal loans, overdraft facilities and credit cards, as well as several of the non-banking services permitted under the 1986 Act. One society (the Alliance & Leicester) bought Girobank – although it is highly likely to become a bank itself in 1997. Also, the Cheltenham & Gloucester still operates as a separate entity to that of its owner – Lloyds Bank.

14.22 *Outside* the personal sector, however, this convergence of retail banks and building societies has been very much less. A significant proportion of retail banks' lending is to the corporate sector, compared with only a tiny proportion for building societies. In addition, the retail banks offer a diverse set of services to the corporate sector. The retail banks are also involved in international activities to a substantial degree, whereas the building societies have virtually no involvement.

14.23 Part of the remaining differences between building societies and retail banks is, of course, due to the different regulatory frameworks involved. Given that the convergence of activities of separate institutions over time tends to identify anomalies in the regulatory frameworks, it is likely that increased harmonisation of these frameworks will occur, and that further convergence of activities will result.

Student Activity 14

1. What was the importance of the Building Societies Act 1986 to building societies' lending activities?   *(Paragraph 14.5)*

2. State the advantages to a building society of converting to plc status.
                                                         (Paragraphs 14.14–15)

3. Examine the disadvantages to a building society of converting to plc status.
                                                         (Paragraph 14.16)

4. How did the Building Societies Act 1986 affect the range of financial services which building societies are allowed to offer?   *(Paragraphs 14.15 and 14.17)*

5. List the ways in which building societies have converged with retail banks in recent years. *(Paragraph 14.21)*

6. Describe the areas of activity in which building societies and retail banks are still markedly different. *(Paragraph 14.22)*

15   Other deposit-taking intermediaries

Finance houses

15.1   These are hybrid financial intermediaries, many of them having evolved from hire purchase (HP) companies. HP companies financed themselves by raising share capital, taking deposits from the general public and borrowing from banks. These funds were used to buy assets, which were paid for by companies and people borrowing on 'HP'; after the last payment was made (usually it was £1 more than the others), the ownership of the machine or car passed to the company or individual concerned. Most HP companies later broadened their activities into the products mentioned in the next paragraph and became known as finance houses.

15.2   Today, most finance houses do not accept deposits from the public, although some are owned by retail banks which offer deposits with their finance house subsidiaries as a 'home' for larger sums of money. Moreover, they have moved into other activities, so that their lending activities comprise:

*   Traditional HP business;

*   Factoring of book debts;

*   Leasing – 'small-ticket' business on machinery and equipment of up to say, £50,000 per item;

*   Second mortgage finance for double glazing, conservatories, kitchens, bathrooms and the like.

Credit unions

15.3   These are, in general, very small scale savings and lending societies. Members are usually linked by neighbourhood, religion or employment, with members saving regular amounts each week; interest is paid gross of tax. The other main activity is lending, with a statuary maximum interest rate of 1% per month. Members may borrow up to £5,000 plus another £5,000 providing that they have £5,000 in savings with the union. The membership of a credit union may not exceed 5,000.

15.4   Credit unions are supervised by the Registrar of Friendly Societies, under the Credit Union Act 1979. They are fairly important in Northern Ireland, but are of very limited significance in Great Britain. However, they are more important in Ireland, Canada, USA and Australia. (They are mentioned here only for the sake of completeness.)

16   Investing financial intermediaries

Introduction

16.1   In earlier parts of this unit we concentrated on deposit-taking financial intermediaries which, in general, take deposits and onlend them, rather than buying and selling assets. However, there are exceptions:

- Banks and building societies buy and sell gilts and Treasury bills;
- Banks buy and sell the debts of third world countries (the so-called 'Brady' bonds);
- Investment banks buy and sell assets in the financial markets, rather than take deposits.

16.2 In the final part of this unit, we focus on intermediaries which buy and sell: for them lending and deposit-taking are minor activities. Unfortunately, the market term for them is 'the institutions' and, as was stressed in section 1, they are more than just brokers and agents. Also, they are more than providers of advice.

16.3 The investing intermediaries are dealt with in order of size.

17 Insurance companies

17.1 The assets of all insurance companies are grater than those of pension funds, but for the purposes of the Insurance Companies Act 1982, a distinction is made between the short-term and long-term insurance business of insurance companies. Broadly, short-term business is renewable annually, e.g. house or motor insurance.

17.2 Together, the two 'footings' (balance sheet totals) come to £466bn, much larger than the total for building societies and slightly larger than the £443.5bn for pension funds. When we include the investment trusts and unit trusts, the aggregate size of these 'institutions' exceeds £1,000 bn, most of which are assets located in the UK.

General Insurance

17.3 This comprises insuring such items as:

- Houses – contents and structure;
- Motor vehicles;
- Aviation;
- Marine;
- Public liability;
- Personal accident;
- Unemployment.

17.4 This is usually short-term business, with policies renewable annually and often up-rated annually. However, there are two classes of long-term insurance which are included here, i.e:

- Permanent health insurance – say for 20 years from the age of 30;
- Critical illness – or 'dread disease'- cover.

17.5 Risks in general insurance are spread between people, businesses and over space. However, general insurance is not very profitable, so that premiums

Table 2.4 Insurance companies' assets – short-term funds end of 1994

		£bn	%
Short-term assets		2.1	3.3
Gilts:		12.3	19.9
index linked	0.3		
0–5 years	7.0		
5–15 years	4.7		
over 15 years and undated	0.3		
UK company securities		14.0	22.6
equities	10.1		
other	3.9		
Overseas securities		8.7	14.1
Unit trusts		0.3	0.5
Loans/mortgages in UK		1.3	2.1
UK land, property etc		2.1	3.4
Other (incl. £6.1m for agents' and reinsurance balances)		21.7	34.1
		61.9	100.0

Source: Financial Statistics Table 5.2A

Table 2.5 Insurance companies assets – long-term funds end of 1994

		£bn	%
Short-term assets		13.6	3.4
Gilts:		64.9	16.1
index linked	7.1		
0–5 years	4.3		
5–15 years	31.6		
over 15 years and undated	21.9		
UK company securities		187.8	46.5
equities	159.4		
other	28.4		
Overseas securities		55.0	13.6
Unit trusts		29.6	7.3
Loans/mortgages in UK		7.5	1.8
UK land, property etc		35.9	8.9
Other		9.8	2.4
		404.1	100.0

Source: Financial Statistics Table 5.1A

must be raised to meet claims; thus general insurance companies often rely on their investments to increase their overall profits. Many premiums for house insurance are index-linked, so that they rise in line with the prices of household furniture etc

Life assurance

17.6 Here, the word 'assurance' is used, because death – unlike theft or accident – is a certainty, so that the policy will always be the subject of a claim – except when it has been lost and the deceased's executors are unaware of its existence. There are several main types of life insurance products:

Whole life assurance

17.7 Whole life assurance pays a lump sum at death.

Term assurance

17.8 Term assurance pays a lump sum if death occurs before a date stated in the policy (say) before 20 years of the date of the policy. If death occurs after that date, then nothing is paid because the policy has expired. However, the assured has had the protection for that period. Mortgage protection policies are term life cover

Endowment assurance

16.9 Here the sum assured is payable at a certain date, e.g. 13 October 1998 or prior death.

Annuity

16.10 An annuity is the reverse of an assurance policy which pays a lump sum after a stream of annual or monthly premiums. With an annuity, the purchaser pays a lump sum now, and receives a stream of income payments until his/her death. Joint annuities for husbands and wives or for partners can be bought but they are more expensive because payments will continue until the death of the second survivor. For people's peace of mind – 'what if I die the month after I bought the annuity?' – most annuities can be guaranteed for five years, so that if early death occurs then payments will continue for five years after the date of purchase.

16.11 Prices of annuities – the yield per year per £1,000 spent – depend on the age of the purchaser and current levels of interest rates. The older the buyer and the higher the yields on fixed-interest rate securities, the more income each £1,000 will buy.

Personal pensions

16.12 In 1988 great changes took place in their legal basis. Those pension contracts taken out before July of that year are termed 'retirement annuities' and many of these will continue until their owners purchase special kinds of annuities from which they will draw their pensions. This could continue until 2030 or later.

16.13 Personal pensions replaced the older products and began to be sold in 1988. They are particularly suitable for self-employed people and those workers with no occupational pensions. Most providers of personal pensions are life assurance companies rather than pension funds.

Additional voluntary contributions (AVCs)

16.14 These, before 1988, could be provided by pension funds for their members to 'top up' their pensions to the maximum possible level. Since 1988, new AVCs must be 'money purchase' schemes, usually provided by life assurance companies, rather than allowing members to buy extra years of service for their pension schemes provided by their employers.

Profits

16.15 Apart from term life assurance, holders of whole life, endowment policies and annuities can share in the profits of the company or organisation providing the cover. Traditionally, profits have been declared annually or every three or five years, and added to the sum assured in what are known as reversionary bonuses. These cannot be taken away, so that assurers adopt a very conservative attitude when 'declaring' (announcing) them. A second type of bonus is paid on maturity – the terminal bonus – and this fluctuates in line with conditions in the stock and property markets. In the 1990s, many companies have been reducing their terminal bonuses, while others have even been unable to declare reversionary bonuses at the level of previous years.

16.16 These uncertainties of the trend of profits have caused some companies to cease to sell 'with profits' endowment policies. Instead, they have begun to sell 'unit-linked' endowment policies, which are divided into units whose value fluctuates in line with market trends. In other words, their value can fall, unlike the traditional 'with profits' endowment or whole life policy.

Types of insurance company

16.17 Some companies specialise in life assurance, e.g. Scottish Widows. Others concentrate on general insurance, e.g. Norwich Union (which has a separate life assurance company). Yet other are composite insurers, providing both life and general cover from the same business.

16.18 There is also a very strong 'mutual' element in the industry, with the firms being owned by their policy holders and not their shareholders. Scottish Widows is one of these, as is Standard Life, the largest of the mutuals. Norwich Union is, at present, a mutual but plans to become a plc in 1997 or 1998. Another mutual – Clerical, Medical and General – has been bought by the Halifax Building Society.

Student Activity 15

1. What are the two main types of insurance business, as required by the insurance Companies Act 1982 and what are the approximate sizes of their investment funds? *(Paragraph 17.1 and Tables 2.4 and 2.5)*

2. Compare and contrast the portfolios of gilts held by these two types of insurance companies' funds. *(Tables 2.4 and 2.5)*

3. Distinguish between general insurance and life assurance. *(Paragraphs 17.2–6)*

4. Describe the main products sold by life insurance companies.
   (Paragraphs 17.7–14)

5. What recent change has occurred in 'with profits' life policies? *(Paragraph 17.16)*

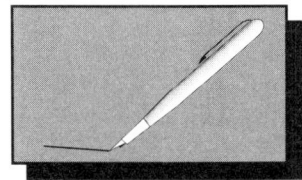

18 Pension funds

18.1   Pensions can be financed in two ways: unfunded or funded.

Unfunded pensions

18.2   Unfunded pensions are, in effect, 'pay as you go' schemes. Examples are the state retirement pension, financed by the National Insurance Contributions of today's workers, and pensions for civil servants, the police service and firefighters. The latter group of pensions is financed by taxation and borrowing. (Because they are not true funds, contributed by the pensioners during the period when they were working, and in which are held identifiable assets, we shall not consider them further.)

Funded pensions

18.3   Funded pensions come in three types:

- Defined benefit schemes;
- Defined contribution schemes; and
- Hybrid schemes.

All have their own funds, with identifiable assets.

Defined benefit schemes

18.4   Defined benefit schemes are the standard schemes of this century. Contributions are made by employees and (usually) by their employees, who earn themselves a benefit (pension, of which part can be taken in a lump sum) of either $1/_{60}$ or $1/_{80}$ of their final salary (or the average of the last three years' salaries) for every year in which contributions are made. Thus, 40 years' service gives a pension of $2/_3$ or $1/_2$ of final salary if the benefit is $1/_{60}$ or $1/_{80}$ respectively. The assumptions are that employees stay in their jobs for a long time and that salary changes are upwards. However, it is now a fact that job changes are more frequent, so transfers have to be made between funds. Second, the 'upward salary' assumption makes it hard for older workers to move to part-time or less remunerative work with their employers as they approach retirement age.

18.5   A severe problem can arise with these schemes if there is a period of substantial inflation (as there was) because the earlier contributions are unable to finance the higher final salaries caused by the inflation. As a result, the employers are required by the trustees of the schemes to make up the contributions and this can be a drain on their profits and cash flows. Moreover, if inflation then slows (as it did), the schemes may become 'over-funded' instead of 'underfunded', so that a 'pensions holiday' is declared. In some funds, the over-funding has allowed employees, as well as employers, to pay lower contribution rates. These 'defined benefit' schemes have been virtually universal in the largest companies and typically are run by trustees advised by merchant banks in their investment decisions. A more common term for them is 'final salary' pensions.

Defined contribution schemes

18.6   Defined contribution schemes are the opposite, in that the contribution percentages rarely change. They build up a fund which is used to buy an annuity when the employee retires. Their other name is a 'money purchase' scheme and, typically, they are provided by life assurance companies for smaller firms. Personal pensions are a type of 'money purchase' pension, as are AVCs taken out after 1988. Recently, some of the retail banks have instituted defined contribution schemes for their new employees; other employers may follow. There is less chance of a money purchase scheme becoming underfunded, because contributions rise in line with inflation, and benefits are not linked to inflation or salaries.

Hybrid schemes

18.7 Hybrid schemes, incorporating features of both the other schemes, have become fairly common in the USA, but were rare in the UK. However, in July 1996, Glaxo-Wellcome introduced the first combined final salary and money purchase scheme offered by a major company in the UK, following a merger of the two companies. Existing employees will have a choice between the two schemes, with an option to swap; new employees will have to join the money purchase scheme, although they can switch into the final salary scheme at the age of 40. The 'sponsors' of the schemes are a merchant bank for the defined benefits scheme and the Equitable Life Assurance Society for the defined contribution scheme.

Table 2.6 Pension funds' assets end of 1994

		£bn	%
Short term assets		16.8	3.8
Gilts:		41.9	9.4
index linked	20.3		
0–5 years	2.1		
5–15 years	15.0		
over 15 years and undated	4.5		
UK company securities		223.1	50.3
equities	219.2		
other	3.9		
Overseas securities		89.0	20.1
Unit trusts		15.8	3.6
Loans/mortgages in UK		0.5	0.1
UK land, property etc		24.4	5.5
Other		32.0	7.2
		443.5	100.0

Source: *Financial Statistics Table 5.1B*

Assets

18.8 The assets of pension funds are distributed in a very similar way to those of the long-term funds of insurance companies. The reason is that they are both 'intermediating' over long periods of time and operating in the same economy – the UK. For this reason, the percentage distributions of assets are shown alongside the money amounts in Tables 2.4–6. One significant difference is the much larger amount of index-linked gilts held by pension funds, when compared to insurance companies. The reason is that pension funds frequently increase their benefits in line with inflation, and the best way of financing this index-linking of liabilities is, of course, to purchase an index-linked asset. At present, insurance companies do not incorporate index-linking in their life products, although some household contents premiums are index-linked.

18.9   Pension funds' assets are usually managed by merchant banks, in their role as fund managers. The assets are owned by trustees. (The prudential regulation of these funds, along with that of other financial intermediaries is considered in Unit 5.)

Student Activity 16

1.   Distinguish between the two ways in which pension schemes are financed.
     (Paragraphs 181–3)

2.   Explain what is a defined benefit scheme and why it is often known as a final salary scheme.   *(Paragraph 18.4)*

3.   Describe how a defined contribution scheme operates.   *(Paragraph 18.6)*

4.   Illustrate, with a UK example, a hybrid pension scheme.   *(Paragraph 18.7)*

5.   Why are employees tending to change their pension schemes?
     (Paragraphs 18.5 –6)

6.   Why do pension funds hold a greater percentage of their assets index-linked gilts than insurance companies?   *(Paragraph 18.8)*

19   Unit trusts

19.1   Unit trusts are long-term investment products sold by managers to investors, often with charges of up to 5% of the purchase price. Investors in unit trusts are usually private people but, from Tables 2.4 and 2.5, it is apparent that insurance companies had £29.9bn invested in unit trusts at the end of 1994. In many cases, these investments were in unit trusts which the companies managed. Managers of unit trusts are specialist companies, such as M & G or Save and Prosper, or banks and insurance companies; they play an active role in selling the units to investors, investing the proceeds and finding the cash to repay investors wishing to withdraw (sell their units back to the managers). In addition, there is always a second financial institution involved in a unit trust – acting as trustee and holding the investments (assets) on behalf of the unit-holders (as investors are called). The advantages of unit trusts are principally that risks are pooled and that specialist managers should enhance investors' returns.

19.2   There are more than 1,400 unit trusts, with one manager sometimes running 10 or more unit trusts. In the USA, managers often permit 'switching' between unit trusts in the same group – known as a 'family of funds'. This term is little used in the UK, where a different practice has evolved – a 'fund of funds', which is a unit trust which invests in a number of other unit trusts, often but not always from the same group. In December 1994, the assets of unit trusts totalled £87bn, but greater sales of units to investors, and rising prices for their investments had increased the value of assets to well over £120bn by April 1996.

19.3 Unit trusts are 'open ended' funds, i.e. if investors buy more units, then the managers issue more units and buy more assets; if investors sell back their units, the managers have to repay the sellers from their cash balances, cancel the units and, possibly, sell some of the long-term investments to top up the short-term assets.

19.4 Unit trust prices are published by the managers, who calculate them from the market values of the shares held by a trust divided by the number of units in existence. Hence, a fall (rise) in the price of a unit is due to a fall (rise) in the prices of the shares which the unit trust owns. At present, managers quote two prices – bid and offer – for their units, but it is planned to introduce single pricing soon.

19.5 The assets of unit trusts are shown below. Note that the short-term borrowings are shown separately, unlike the data for insurance companies and pension funds.

Table 2.7 Unit trusts' assets end of 1994

		£bn
Short term (net)		3.7
gross	5.0	
liabilities	(1.3)	
Investments		
Gilts		1.2
UK equities		45.3
Overseas equities		32.2
Other		4.8
		87.2

Source: Financial Statistics Table 5.1D

20 Investment trusts

20.1 Investment trusts have a similar name to unit trusts, and they also pool investments managed by specialists. However, the similarities end there. Investment trusts are much older – starting in 1868 compared to 1935; they are subject to lower charges and they are 'closed ended' funds. This means that, if people want to buy more of them, and because their quantity is limited then their share prices can rise above the value of the assets they own.

20.2 In brief, investment trusts are limited companies which invest in other limited companies. Most of them are quoted on the stock exchange: there are over 300 investment trusts. Investors buy and sell them through stockbrokers (they buy and sell unit trusts through the managers). In the financial pages, their share prices are shown along with a column showing the percentage premium or discount of the share price to the net average value of a share (NAV).

20.3   Investment trusts can borrow long term so as to invest in more assets, rather than asking the shareholders for more money. However, because the number of shares is fixed (hence their name of 'closed funds'), the share price can vary more sharply than the price of the underlying assets. The price can fall to a discount below the NAV. In fact, this is common with investment trusts.

Table 2.8 Investment trusts' assets end of 1994 (Short-term assets are not shown separately.)

	£bn
Gilts	2.5
UK company securities	16.9
Overseas company securities	19.5
Other	0.7
	39.6

Source: Financial Statistics Table 5.2C

20.4   Many investment trusts specialise in overseas markets, and this accounts for the fact that nearly 50% of their assets are in overseas securities.

20.5   Shortly, the EU will institute a new type of financial intermediary incorporating parts of the concepts of unit trusts and investment trusts. Its official name is likely to be an 'Open Ended Investment Company', with a horrible abbreviation – OEIC! In the UK, the Treasury is likely to permit these OEICs to operate some time in 1997.

21   Changes in financial intermediation

21.1   Two main trends are that:

- Already, in the UK, we can see banks and building societies coming together.

- Non-financial companies, such as British Gas, Marks & Spencer, Virgin and Tesco, are entering the financial services market. At present, Tesco do not provide savings accounts, but NatWest Bank maintain the balances: it is expected that Tesco will soon form its own bank, as has Marks & Spencer.

21.2   *Bancassurance* is a development which began on the continent, involving the grouping of banks and insurance companies. Three types of *bancassurance* can be seen:

- *Linkages*, e.g. Scottish Widows now has its own bank; Direct Line (telephone motor and other insurance) now sells savings accounts and mortgages and has begun to sell its own unit trust.

- *Market interpenetration*: Lloyds Bank bought a controlling interest in Lloyds Abbey Life; Halifax Building Society has taken over Chemical, Medical and General (a mutual insurance company).

- *Co-operative marketing arrangements* – where (say) a building society ties itself to sell the products of one insurance company.

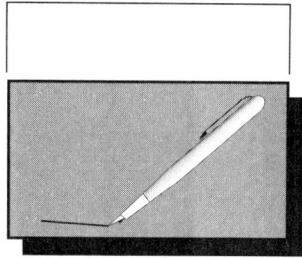

Student Activity 17

1. Describe the principal features of a unit trust. *(Paragraphs 19.1–3)*

2. Explain what is meant by 'open ended'. *(Paragraph 19.2)*

3. Distinguish between the ways in which the prices of unit trusts and investment trusts are determined. *(Paragraphs 19.4 and 20.2)*

4. Outline the principal features of an investment trust. *(Paragraphs 20.1–3)*

5. Compare and contrast the assets held by unit trusts and investment trusts. *(Tables 2.7 and 2.8)*

6. Examine the ways in which bancassurance can occur. *(Paragraph 20.2)*

Summary

Now that you have completed this unit, you should be able to:

- **define and distinguish between financial institutions and financial intermediaries;**

- **explain in outline the role of central banks;**

- **distinguish between banks and building societies;**

- **describe the other deposit-taking financial intermediaries;**

- **compare and contrast deposit-taking and investing financial intermediaries;**

- **examine the roles of insurance companies and pension funds**

- **understand the differences between unit trusts and investment trusts;**

- **explain what is meant by *bancassurance*.**

Self-assessment questions

Short-answer questions

1. What factors are likely to be taken into account by a person contemplating lending money?

2. In what sense might an increase in interest rates bring together borrowers and lenders?

3. A financial intermediary may have liabilities with an average maturity of one month and assets with an average maturity of ten years. How is this institution able to continue in business?

4. List the benefits generated for a borrower by the existence of financial intermediaries.

5. Which groups of banks are included under the heading of wholesale banks?

6. List the main groups of investing financial intermediaries to be found in the UK.

7. In what ways might a financial institution seek to increase the profitability of its intermediation business?

8. What is the normal type of distribution system for retail banking services?

9. Why are interest-rate margins for wholesale transactions often finer than those for retail transactions?

10. List the main domestic payments services provided by a typical retail bank.

11. Do retail banks specialise exclusively in the provision of retail banking services?

12. What is the importance of sterling assets and liabilities to the typical retail bank?

13. In what ways have retail banks responded to the competitive threat posed by other financial intermediaries in respect of their personal customer deposit bases?

14. List the dominant characteristics of the intermediation activities of UK wholesale banks.

15. Within the context of wholesale banking operations, what is meant by the term 'matching'?

16. What are the major functions of the discount houses?

17. How are the discount houses able to operate successfully with around 90% of their liabilities withdrawable at call or overnight?

18. In what ways has the environment faced by the discount houses altered in recent years, and how have they tended to react?

Multiple-choice questions

1. Retail operations of banks normally involve:

   (a) transactions with a minimum size of £500,000

   (b) corporate customers

   (c) primarily personal customers and small businesses

   (d) only sterling denominated activities

   (e) telephoned-based services.

2. By far the largest single element in the assets portfolio of a typical retail bank is:

   (a) sterling advances to the UK private sector

   (b) money market loans to the UK banking sector

   (c) UK private sector deposits

   (d) foreign currency loans to the overseas sector

   (e) claims under sale and repurchase agreements.

3. An eligible bank bill is:

   (a) a commercial bill of exchange purchased by a bank which is authorised by the Bank of England

   (b) A Treasury bill which has been underwritten by an eligible bank

   (c) a commercial bill of exchange which has been accepted by a bank endowed with eligibility status by the Bank of England

   (d) a commercial bill of exchange which has been issued by the Bank of England

   (e) a certificate of deposit which has been purchased by a commercial or industrial company.

4. In terms of balance sheet size, the wholesale banks' sector in the UK is:

   (a) about the same size as the retail banks sector

   (b) less than half the size of the retail banks sector

   (c) much larger than the retail banks sector

   (d) slightly smaller than the size of the European banks based in the UK

   (e) slightly smaller than the size of the Japanese banks based in the UK.

5. The activities of wholesale banks in the UK:

   (a) are dominated by foreign currency business

   (b) relate purely to customers based overseas

   (c) involve no sterling lending to the UK private sector

   (d) are dominated by sterling lending to the UK corporate sector

   (e) are primarily directed at stock exchange transactions.

6. Overseas banks operating in the UK:

   (a) are excluded from participation in capital market activities

   (b) undertake no retail activities

   (c) are major players in the eurocurrency markets

(d) are a relatively insignificant group as compared to British wholesale banks

(e) have been reducing the scale of their activities since the Single European Market (1993).

7. Long-term funds of insurance companies hold most of their gilts in medium-dated stocks because:

(a) short-dated gilts are riskier

(b) in this way they can match a large proportion of their outstanding life policies

(c) there are good opportunities to make profits by switching in and out of these stocks

(d) the Insurance Companies Act 1982 requires 40% of their gilts to be held in this category

(e) both (b) and (c) above.

8. The table for unit trusts, unlike the other three tables, show data for short-term borrowing because:

(a) unit trusts are relatively new institutions and hence have small net assets

(b) unit trusts borrow as part of their investment strategy

(c) unit trusts can have spells when investors, on balance, are selling units back to them, so they need extra short-term assets

(d) some unit trusts are owned by banks, which use them as a source of deposits

(e) unit trusts borrow occasionally to finance take-ups of rights issues and to acquire other unit trusts.

9. Short-term assets are not shown in Table 2.8 for investment trusts because:

(a) they are held with the parent company

(b) they are of little importance because investment trusts are closed funds and hence do not need large short-term assets

(c) they can raise funds easily by borrowing

(d) they do not advertise as much as unit trusts and hence do not receive investors' funds on a daily basis

(e) they can borrow short-term assets from their parent company.

10. An example of financial intermediation is:

(a) the provision of advice on takeover activity by a merchant bank

(b) the purchasing of shares by a stockbroker on behalf of a personal client

(c) the taking of deposits and the making of mortgage loans by a building society

(d) the provision of investment advice by a retail bank

(e) fund management by an investment bank.

11. Financial intermediation benefits lenders by:

    (a) removing all risk associated with lending

    (b) spreading the risk associated with lending over a large number of lenders

    (c) ensuring that funds are lent only to individuals and institutions who will not default.

    (d) raising the rate of interest which they will receive on their funds

    (e) ensuring that the intermediary is supervised by a regulator.

12. Which of the following is *not* included amongst the UK retail banks?

    (a) TSB Bank plc

    (b) The Banking Department of the Bank of England

    (c) Abbey National plc

    (d) National Savings Bank

    (e) Bank of England.

13. Which group amongst the following comprises investing financial intermediaries?

    (a) unit trusts

    (b) finance houses

    (c) building societies

    (d) British merchant (investment) banks

    (e) credit unions.

14. Which of the following is *not* classified as a banking institution?

    (a) TSB Bank plc

    (b) Abbey National plc

    (c) a discount house

    (d) an investment trust company

    (e) Bank of Ireland.

Unit 3

Financial Markets

Objectives

After studying this unit you should be able to:

- state the functions of financial markets;

- classify them and explain what is meant by the EMH;

- subdivide the UK wholesale sterling money markets into their various markets;

- describe the organisation of the London Stock Exchange and the problems which it has faced;

- distinguish between the equity and fixed-income (debt) markets;

- state the reasons for the growth of the eurocurrency markets

- examine the role of financial innovations on the markets and the financial instruments which are traded on them.

1   Introduction

Functions of markets

1.1   Financial markets are where financial assets are traded and they have three functions:

- *Providing price information* about the financial assets traded on them;

- *Offering liquidity* – or, in American, a thick market;

- *Reducing the costs of buying and selling* – comprising:

    ○ search costs – contacting a broker/trader to notify intention of trading, plus the implicit cost of the investor's time;

    ○ information costs, incurred when assessing the relative merits of investment;

    ○ commissions and fees charged by the traders, together with their spreads (between bid and offer prices).

Classifications

1.2   Financial markets may be grouped under several headings.

- Nature of the asset – debt, equity. In general, debt is a type of financial asset which is older than equity.

- Maturity of the asset – money market, capital market.

- Seasoning (age) of the asset – primary markets for brand-new assets, secondary markets for existing (second-hand) assets. Secondary markets may not create new financial assets, but they ensure liquidity, so that owners can exchange their assets and new owners take over from owners who are relinquishing their assets They also enable owners to price assets, even if they do not wish to trade.

- Immediacy of delivery – cash/spot delivery (now), derivative (fixtures/options).

- Organisation of the market – auction, over-the counter (OTC), intermediated (with brokers and dealers).

- Wholesale or retail – wholesale markets deal with large quantities, with trading usually by firms, companies and organisation; retail markets deal with small quantities, with one of the parties being a private individual.

Interrelationships

1.3   Financial markets are not independent entities, but are linked in various ways.

- Although the debt and equity markets are fairly distinct, they are linked by sentiment and economic events, particularly changes in interest rates, as well as by the existence of convertible financial assets. The latter, as indicated in paragraph 2.8 of the first unit, give investors an occasional opportunity to switch from debt to equity of the issuing company.

- There is a continuous gradation of maturity from the money market to the capital market. For example, a medium-term note is a type of financial asset which could be discussed as a form of debt, although later in this unit it appears at the end of the money market section.

- As soon as an asset is issued on the primary market, it becomes 'eligible' for trading in the secondary market. Indeed, unsatisfied investors who did not receive an allotment of the new stock or shares will bid up the price on the secondary market within minutes of the start of trading. This illustrates the need for a primary market not to disturb the secondary market too much.

- Cash and derivative markets are linked in that investors will often sell in the cash or spot market and buy a derivative (or vice versa). Another instance of this link is that, in theory, a foreign exchange deal concluded on a Monday for delivery on the Thursday is a forward deal, whereas it would have been a spot transaction if settlement were on the Wednesday.

- Market segmentation need not be exclusive, because a securities exchange can have an OTC section.

- The distinction between wholesale and retail is, of course, blurred when the sizes of the individual retail transactions become very large.

- Cross-relationships are very important – derivatives are to be found in most wholesale markets, such as money, capital, debt, and equity. Many derivative markets are exchange-based, especially the largest. However, the foreign exchange derivative markets are OTC, as is most of the cash foreign exchange market.

- Finally, the impact of interest rate changes is felt in every financial market.

Market efficiency

1.4   There are three ways in which markets can be said to be efficient:

- *Allocative efficiency*, whereby primary markets allocate funds to new borrowers/users without fees, commissions, discounts etc taking up a large proportion of the total raised.

  The secondary market must be efficient in the following ways:

- *Operational efficiency*, which means a low buy/sell spread and brokerage charges, when compared to the value of the transaction .

- *Informational efficiency*, which refers to the amount of price information and price-sensitive information which is in the hands of the investors and potential investors

Efficient market hypothesis

1.5 The above points are summarised in the efficient market hypothesis (EMH), which is a theory that the public availability of relevant information about the issues of financial assets will lead to a correct pricing of these assets if they are openly and easily traded in properly functioning markets. Most research into this theory has been conducted on stock exchange prices, so the theory applies mainly to stocks and shares. It is discussed at greater length in section 9 of this unit.

Student Activity 1

1. Classify the various types of financial markets. *(Paragraph 1.2)*

2. What roles do they play? *(Paragraph 1.1)*

3. Examine eight links between these various markets. *(Paragraph 1.3)*

4. In what ways can financial markets be said to be 'efficient'? *(Paragraph 1.4)*

5. Explain what is meant by the Efficient Market Hypothesis (EMH). *(Paragraph 1.5)*

2 UK money markets

2.1 The transactions involved in the UK money markets are the *borrowing and lending of short-term wholesale sterling funds*. All the transactions in the UK money markets are denominated in sterling (when in foreign currencies they are classified as transactions in the eurocurrency markets), and 'wholesale' in this context refers to a *minimum* transaction normally set at £50,000, with the *average* size of transaction naturally much higher. It is difficult to be precise about the *short-term* nature of the transactions since this will vary with, amongst other factors, the particular money market under consideration. Nevertheless, the initial maturity ranges from overnight to one year, with the vast majority of the transactions in the UK money markets involving an initial maturity of less than three months. Occasionally, transactions involving initial maturities longer than one year are dealt with in some of the money markets. The transactions may take the form of either conventional borrowing and lending activities on a secured or an unsecured basis, or of issues of short-term securities bought or sold for immediate delivery.

2.2 The City of London has been a major *international* centre for money market transactions since the 1950s. This has come about because of:

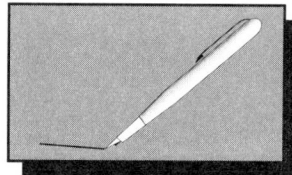

- The relative stability and sophistication of the UK financial system;

- London's long-established reputation as a centre of financial and trading activities;

- The high concentration of powerful financial institutions in London (with many of these institutions originating from abroad); and

- A level of supervision sufficient to promote confidence but not so much as to stifle innovation.

2.3   More recently, the growth of the money markets has been heavily influenced by the rising demand for increasingly sophisticated financial services. Whereas at first much of the growth of the money markets was associated with circum-venting the official restrictions on the more normal banking and credit facilities within the UK, since the early 1970s the growth and development has been associated with demands for new financial services. For example, the:

- Trend towards securitisation of short-term corporate finance needs led to the development of the sterling commercial paper market;

- Demand for new liability management techniques from the banks led to the further development of the inter-bank market;

- Increasing use of wholesale funding by the building societies led to the further development of the inter-bank market.

2.4   The London money markets are normally divided into two parts: the:

- Primary sterling money market;

- Secondary (or parallel) sterling money markets.

The *primary money market* consists of the oldest money market, the *discount market*, which dates back to the early 19th century. The *secondary (parallel) sterling money markets* have only evolved since the 1950s, and in a way that allows the separate identification of seven secondary sterling money markets. We may classify the London money markets as follows, using the term 'parallel' to avoid confusion over the meaning of secondary:

- Primary sterling money market: Discount market
- Parallel sterling money markets: Sterling inter-bank

                                    Sterling certificate of deposit

                                    Sterling commercial paper

                                    Medium-term notes

                                    Inter-company

                                    Local authority

                                    Finance house.

2.5   These eight money markets will be considered in turn in the following sec-tions. Given the existence of substantial inter-market flows of funds, and given the fact that many institutions operate in several of the money markets simultaneously, take care to avoid viewing these eight markets *too* separately.

Student Activity 2

1. What types of transactions take place in money markets? *(Paragraph 2.1)*

2. What are the reasons for London's leading position as an international centre for money market transactions? *(Paragraphs 2.2–3)*

3. What are the component parts of the London money market? *(Paragraph 2.4)*

4. Why might it be incorrect to view individual sterling money markets in isolation? *(Paragraph 2.5)*

3 The discount market

3.1 At the heart of the discount market are the *discount houses*, a set of institutions unique to the UK financial system that were discussed in Unit 2. You will recall that the major function of the discount houses is to buy high-quality short-dated securities (predominantly eligible bank bills, i.e. commercial bills which have been accepted by eligible banks, and short-dated CDs issued by UK banks and building societies, but also Treasury bills and short-dated gilts) at a discount to their maturity value, and to hold these securities until maturity. In order to fulfil this function, the discount houses need to acquire funds and. To fulfil the function *profitably*, they need to acquire those funds at an interest rate lower than that implicit in the securities they hold. The major source of funds to the discount houses is their borrowing from the *clearing banks*, which therefore form the second major set of participants within the discount market, providing the majority of their funds on an overnight or call basis.

3.2 Given that only bills of the highest quality are traded in the discount market, it is only those bills which have been accepted (underwritten) by first-line banking institutions, notably the British merchant banks but also the clearing banks, that would be involved in this discount market activity. Because eligible bank bills have in recent years played a key role in the trading activities in the discount market and upon which the Bank of England has relied for its money market intervention activities, it is the *British merchant banks* which form the third major set of participants within the discount market. The fourth major participant is the *Bank of England*, which has several roles within the operation of the discount market, including:

- Issuing Treasury bills, by tender on a weekly basis;

- Buying and selling short-term securities on its own account, for the purpose of achieving its specific market intervention objectives;

- Acting as lender of last resort, standing ready to provide liquidity to the market when conditions require;

- Supervising the market directly and the participating banking institutions.

The functions of the discount market

3.3 The *functions* of the discount market were examined in the discussion of the discount houses in Unit 2, and were identified as:

- Providing an important method by which the commercial banks may adjust their liquidity positions;

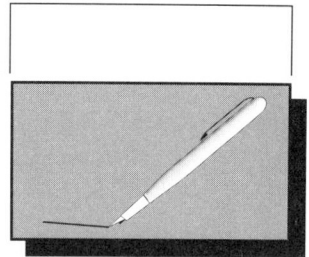

- Making markets in bills, sterling certificates of deposit and certain short-dated public-sector securities;

- Providing short-term finance to the corporate sector and to the government via the discounting of bills;

- Underwriting the weekly Treasury bill tender;

- Acting as a buffer between the Bank of England and the commercial banks with regard to the:

    ○ adjustment of liquidity within the banking system, and

    ○ implementation of monetary policy.

3.4 The environment within which discount houses operate has been changing significantly in recent years, most notably in respect of the competition that the institutions face. The Bank of England has started to provide direct support to institutions other than the discount houses, while the development of the sterling inter-bank and sterling CD markets has provided effective alternative means for commercial banks to adjust their liquidity positions. The development of the commercial paper market (below), consequent upon the decision by the authorities in 1986 to allow such a market, has added to the competition faced by commercial bills in the provision of short-term corporate finance. Finally, the Bank of England allowed other banking institutions to apply for discount house (or equivalent) status. Despite these developments affecting the discount houses' environment, it should be emphasised that the discount market remains a *crucial* element within the Bank of England's monetary control framework. (The role of the discount market in the implementation of monetary policy is considered in more detail in Unit 7.)

Student Activity 3

1. What assets are purchased by the discount houses? *(Paragraph 3.1)*

2. What is the major source of funds for the discount houses? *(Paragraph 3.1)*

3. What is the role of the British merchant banks in the discount market?
   (Paragraph 3.2)

4. What are the roles of the Bank of England in the discount market?
   (Paragraph 3.2)

5. Which wing of the Bank of England is responsible for its operations in the discount market? *(Paragraph 9 of Unit 2)*

6. List the main functions of the discount market. *(Paragraph 3.3)*

The discount houses and the Bank of England's money market intervention

3.5 As noted above, the Bank of England is a very important participant in the activities of the discount market, alongside the discount houses themselves, the British merchant banks and the clearing banks. The Bank of England intervenes in the discount market to:

- Smooth the *flows of funds* between the government and the private sector;

- Influence the level and/or the structure of *short-term interest rates*.

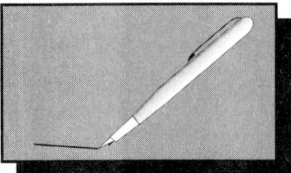

Smoothing flows of funds

3.6 The smoothing of flows of funds between the government and the private sector is necessary because on any particular day, due to variations in the patterns of government revenue and expenditure, there may be (and indeed is likely to be) an imbalance between the two. If, to take an example, there is a flow of revenue into the government's exchequer that is £1bn greater than the outflow on a particular day, the consequence of that imbalance is that the private sector has to find an additional £1bn to meet this commitment.

3.7 The immediate impact of this imbalance will be on the banking sector, however, which will find itself short of liquidity to the extent of £1bn. In the absence of any mechanism to alleviate this shortage, short-term interest rates would rise very substantially so that the banking system could find the £1bn to replenish its reserve base.

3.8 It may be, however, that the following day is characterised by a £1bn imbalance *the other way*, with government expenditures greater than revenues, so that the banking sector would find itself awash with cash. Plainly, the pressure on interest rates would be downward on that day, as the banking system struggled to find profitable outlets for this extra cash.

3.9 One objective of the Bank of England's intervention in the discount market is therefore to smooth the flows of funds between the government sector and the private sector in order to stabilise interest rates. In principle, the Bank of England achieves this smoothing of flows, and the consequent stabilising of interest rates, by supplying funds to the banking sector when a shortage is anticipated, and 'mopping up' excess funds when a surplus is anticipated.

3.10 In more detail, the process is as follows.

- The Bank of England, as banker to the government, will have details of the likely revenue inflows and expenditure outflows on any day, and will use this information to calculate a projected shortfall or surplus that would occur at the end of the day's clearing activities.

- This information is made available at stated times each day to the discount market.

- If there is a projected shortfall, the Bank of England will, in effect, invite the discount houses to sell some of their stock of bills to the Bank of England ('rediscount' the bills) which will have the effect of adding cash (liquidity) to the banking system, avoiding upward pressure on interest rates.

- If there is a projected surplus, the Bank of England will offer bills from its own stocks to the discount houses to buy, so that any excess cash in the system is used to purchase interest-bearing assets, thereby alleviating downward pressure on interest rates.

  However, in general the Bank of England prefers to keep the market short of liquidity, so as to help it (the Bank) control interest rates.

3.11 From the point of view of the *commercial banks* standing at one remove from the Bank of England relative to the discount houses, this intervention by the Bank of England underlines the importance of the discount houses in the

83

management of their liquidity positions. In the case of a projected shortfall, the commercial banks – particularly the clearing banks – will be suffering an outflow of funds at the clearing as cash is directed towards the government through the Bank of England. In order to restore their liquidity positions, they call in loans made to the discount houses. It is the discount houses that then experience a shortage of cash, which in their case is alleviated by the Bank of England standing ready to buy bills from the discount houses and providing them with cash. This intervention by the Bank of England therefore allows the commercial banks to operate on a lower cash ratio since it does, in effect, allow them to hold assets in the form of loans to the discount houses as an alternative to holding cash.

3.12   In the examples outlined above, the purpose of the Bank of England's intervention in the discount market was to smooth the flows of cash between the central government accounts and the private sector, and in doing so to avoid shortages or excesses of liquidity within the banking system that would give rise, respectively, to upward or downward pressure on interest rates. Note, however, that on occasions the purpose of Bank of England intervention in the discount market *will* be to create a surplus or a shortage of liquidity and hence to initiate a change in interest rates.

Changing short-term interest rates

3.13   Operations in the discount market is the way in which the Bank of England gives effect to the policy decisions to change the level of short-term interest rates. The key to understanding this is to recognise that the price at which the Bank of England purchases bills from the discount houses in the event of a shortage of liquidity, and the price at which it sells bills from its stocks in the event of a surplus of liquidity, are both *prices of the Bank of England's choosing*. When there is a shortage of liquidity in the market, the Bank of England may only be prepared to buy bills from the discount houses at a lower price, implying a higher interest rate, than currently prevails. Given the need by the discount houses for the liquidity in order to meet demands placed upon them for funds, they have little choice but to accept the lower prices being offered. In order to avoid having to sell bills to the Bank of England at these lower prices in future, the discount houses will bid more actively for funds from the clearing banks and other financial institutions, and hence the interest rate within the discount market will be driven up. In addition, the discount houses will only be prepared to purchase (that is, discount) bills at a lower price, thus reinforcing the rise in interest rates.

3.14   In order to enforce a rise in interest rates, the Bank of England may *deliberately engineer* a shortage of funds in the discount market. Recall that the discount houses, in return for having the Bank of England provide the lender of last resort facility, undertake to purchase the whole of the weekly Treasury bill issue. By making this issue larger than is required on financing grounds alone, the Bank of England can then ensure that the discount houses will need to sell bills to the Bank of England, which provides the opportunity for the Bank of England only to purchase them at a low price and hence to raise interest rates. An alternative ploy is to relieve a shortage one day, but to require repayment on a day when funds are likely to be plentiful. This can be achieved by specifying the maturity dates of the bills to be bought.

3.15   The Bank of England can, of course, also use the discount market to *lower* interest rates. If there is expected to be a surplus of liquidity in the discount market, such that without any Bank of England intervention in the market the interest rate will fall, the Bank will simply not offer to sell any bills to the discount market, or else will only offer to sell bills at a high price. The extra liquidity then remains in the market, causing downward pressure on the interest rate.

3.16   In practice, the Bank of England does not announce the price at which it will buy or sell bills from or to the discount houses. Instead, the discount houses make offers to the Bank of England of prices that they are seeking for bills to sell *to* the Bank of England or willing to pay to buy bills *from* the Bank. The Bank of England then accepts or rejects these offers, according to whether the interest rate implied in these offers is compatible with its unpublished target band. If the Bank accepts offers, then plainly it is content with the implied interest rate. However, if, for example, the discount houses receive refusals of offers of bills to sell to the Bank of England, signals will be sent to participants in the discount market about the Bank of England's intention with regard to short-term interest rates. The discount houses, having experienced the refusals, will need to reformulate their offers in order to be able to sell bills to the Bank of England, with those revised offers implying higher interest rates.

3.17   The Bank of England has established a maturity classification for bills, as follows:
   ● Band 1   1 to 14 days to maturity
   ● Band 2   15 to 33 days to maturity
   ● Band 3   34 to 63 days to maturity
   ● Band 4   64 to 91 days to maturity.

3.18   The majority of Bank of England intervention in the discount market in the form of buying or selling bills has in recent years been with regard to bills in Bands 1 and 2 (33 days or less to maturity) but often with particular emphasis on Band 1. The intervention has therefore been with the intention of influencing *very short-term* interest rates, with the rationale that the Bank of England seeks to leave the *general* structure of interest rates to be determined by free market forces whilst maintaining a high level of control over *short-term* rates. The Bank of England's control over liquidity is also enhanced by the use of bills close to maturity, since these are scheduled to give rise to an outflow of funds from the private sector when they mature, which, depending on the Bank of England's policy stance, may or may not be replaced by additional purchases of bills from the market.

3.19   In the 1990s, the Bank of England has usually signalled a change in bank base rates by 'posting' (creating) a minimum lending rate to the discount market, for one day. This method of changing interest rates has the advantage of being able to be announced at any time, even when the market is closed. The minimum lending rate (MLR) is the minimum rate for that day for all sterling assistance to the discount market.

3.20   Although the Bank of England will seek to use the discount market to influence short-term interest rates on a continuing basis, remember that it does this *in addition to* the function of providing liquidity to the system. The Bank of England always stands ready to provide liquidity to the banking system; what is variable is the *price* at which it will do so. This function of providing liquidity to the banking system is often referred to as the *lender of last resort* function, and refers to the provision of liquidity when necessary to the banking system *as a whole*, and does *not* refer to the bailing out of any individual bank which might, for one reason or another, have got into difficulties.

3.21   The environment within which discount houses have been operating, and thus the discount market itself, has been changing in recent years. The Bank of England has been instrumental in causing some of these changes, in particular by the use of REPO agreements whereby the Bank of England enters into agreements with banks and building societies to purchase relatively illiquid securities from them on the basis that they will be repurchased on a specified date in the future. These REPO agreements allow the banks and building societies to adjust their liquidity portfolios by means of direct deals with the Bank of England, and hence the discount market is bypassed and reduced in importance. The Bank of England has also, since 1986, provided direct borrowing facilities for certain institutions within the Stock Exchange, principally money brokers and gilt-edged market-makers, following upon the Stock Exchange deregulation. These developments, at the same time as bypassing the discount market, serve to provide the Bank of England with a *alternative* means of influencing the level of liquidity within the financial system. The introduction of open REPO facilities in the gilts market in January 1996 has increased the range of techniques open to the Bank of England in its market operations.

Student Activity 4

1. Why does the Bank of England act to smooth flows of funds between the government sector and the private sector?   *(Paragraphs 3.6–9)*

2. How does the Bank of England go about relieving a shortfall of funds in the discount market?   *(Paragraph 3.10)*

3. What is the importance for the commercial banks of the Bank of England's smoothing operations in the discount market?   *(Paragraph 3.11)*

4. How might the Bank of England use its discount market intervention to push up interest rates?   *(Paragraph 3.14)*

5. What approach does the Bank of England take in its setting of prices for bills purchased from the discount market?   *(Paragraph 3.16)*

6. Which intervention bands have been used most often by the Bank of England in recent years?   *(Paragraph 3.18)*

7. How are changes in base rate announced by the Bank of England?

    (Paragraph 3.19)

8. What is the 'lender of last resort' facility?   *(Paragraph 3.20)*

9. What is the relevance of REPO agreements to the position of the discount market?

    (Paragraph 3.21)

4   The other sterling money markets

4.1   Note first that transactions within the parallel markets are *unsecured*, meaning that the lender has to depend on the 'good name' of the borrower. In addition, there is no 'lender of last resort' facility within the secondary markets in the same way as that provided by the Bank of England to the discount market. Taken together, these differences mean that transactions within the secondary markets are somewhat *riskier* than those within the discount market, and this is reflected in higher interest rates within the secondary markets.

4.2   In the second place, although seven different parallel markets are identified, this is primarily for explanatory purposes and in order to recognise the *specialist role* that each market fulfils. Institutions are frequently active in a number of these markets simultaneously, however, with the result that funds flow very easily between them. The parallel markets are, therefore, in that respect strongly interlinked, and also strongly linked to the discount market via the CD market.

4.3   In the third place, although activities in the parallel markets first commenced during the 1950s, the markets are continuing to develop and evolve – most noticeably, in recent times, with the creation of the sterling commercial paper market in 1986 and also the medium-term note market. The development of the secondary markets reflects one of their most important characteristics: their ability to react quickly and flexibly to meet the requirements of participants. In the past, conventional banking channels have often failed to fulfil the requirements of the participants, due to the various official controls and restrictions that have been placed on banking activities. The evolution of the parallel markets has frequently, therefore, been a reflection of these controls and restrictions.

The sterling inter-bank market

4.4   This is the largest, and arguably the most important such market, concerned with the wholesale lending and borrowing of short-term funds between commercial banks. In this context, 'wholesale' would refer to a transaction of at least £0.5m, with an average transaction being perhaps of the order of £10m. 'Short-term' refers to a range of periods extending from overnight to five years, although the majority of transactions would be for less than three months. These inter-bank transactions invariably make use of the agency of a broker, known as a money broker.

4.5   Traditionally, i.e. before about 1960, a bank borrowing from another bank was frowned upon, since banks were supposed to be self-sufficient and, if they needed to borrow from another bank, this suggested imprudent policies. Borrowing and lending between banks is now firmly established as acceptable banking practice, and the inter-bank market has become an important means by which the commercial banks may adjust their liquidity positions. A bank that is faced with a shortage of liquidity, or has the possibility of immediate lending opportunities, is able to raise substantial volumes of funds at short notice by using the inter-bank market, and is able to do so at competitive interest rates. Similarly, a bank which has surplus funds is able to lend these out through the inter-bank market to other banks in order to obtain a competitive yield while at the same time retaining a certain amount of liquidity in those funds. For certain wholesale banks in particular which have only a limited *number* of depositors, the inter-bank market is crucial since it allows them to separate their decisions on lending opportunities from their deposit position.

4.6 This has become known as the trend towards *liability management*, meaning that much banking business has now become driven by *lending* opportunities, with banks subsequently arranging the funding of that lending through the use of the inter-bank market. It also means that banks do not need to match their deposits to their lending, in terms of size or in terms of maturity, to the same extent; a withdrawal of a large deposit from a particular bank can be covered by a loan on the inter-bank market. The inter-bank market therefore serves to raise the efficiency of the banking system as a whole, and to provide customers with both deposit and borrowing facilities that would not otherwise be available. Before the early 1960s, *asset management* prevailed: banks took deposits, and then allocated or managed the assets which these deposits were used to buy or create. With liability management, banks tend to identify good lending business and then bid for deposits on the inter-bank market to fund the lending.

4.7 The inter-bank market is also important in that it determines the *marginal cost of funds* to a commercial bank. If a bank wishes to obtain additional funds, then the cost of those funds will be determined by the rate ruling in the inter-bank market at the time, with the benchmark interest rate being the three-month London Inter-Bank Offered Rate (LIBOR). Much lending by commercial banks, particularly to the corporate sector, is at rates that are a set margin above LIBOR, and consequently this rate is of importance to borrowers with loans obtained on this basis. In addition, there are links between the *base rates* supposedly set by banks (but actually decided by the Chancellor of the Exchequer) and the inter-bank rates such as LIBOR, although the links are not straightforward.

4.8 Although the inter-bank market is recognised as the largest of the secondary money markets, the very nature of the market makes it difficult to establish its precise size. An estimate of its size can, however, be gained from the volume of sterling deposits held by UK banks that originated from *other* UK banks, which at the end of July 1996 stood at £116.6bn.

The sterling certificates of deposit market

4.9 Sterling certificates of deposit (£CDs) are negotiable bearer securities issued by banks and large building societies, usually with a minimum value of £50,000 and a maximum of £1.0m. Their initial term to maturity is normally between 28 days and five years, with a concentration towards the shorter end. CDs are attractive to their purchasers because no taxation on either interest or capital gains is deducted when the CD is sold or when it matures. This is unlike a conventional UK bank deposit from a personal customer and from whose interest a 20% tax is deducted, unless the customer is exempt from income tax. In addition, being bearer securities, for certain purchasers there may be benefits arising from the anonymity they confer. They are attractive to banks since they provide a facility for raising large sums of money for fixed periods of time at fixed interest rates. As such, they provide a very useful alternative to conventional deposits, since CDs cannot be 'withdrawn' in the same way as conventional deposits and hence the risk associated with portfolio management operations is reduced. £CDs issued by banks totalled £82.5bn (including other short-term paper) in July 1996. In addition, the comparable total for building societies was £9.2bn.

4.10 Margins on £CDs tend to be very competitive, and banks are able to attract substantial inflows in response to very slight increases in rates offered. Although the banks issuing the CDs form the *primary* market in these instruments, the success of the market is dependent on the liquidity in the *secondary* market., in which discount houses play an important role. In practice, the secondary market in £CDs is very liquid, with a wide range of institutions involved including banks, who frequently hold large volumes in their own asset portfolios as an important source of liquidity that also yields a market-related return. In addition to the interest return on holding CDs, holders also stand to make capital gains if they sell the CDs after a fall in market interest rates, although the risk of capital losses also exists in the event of having to sell CDs before their maturity after a *rise* in market interest rates.

Student Activity 5

1. What differences between primary money market and parallel sterling money market activities are likely to make transactions in the parallel markets slightly more risky than those in the primary market? *(Paragraph 4.1)*

2. In what sense has the evolution of the parallel sterling money markets reflected official controls and restrictions? *(Paragraph 4.3)*

3. Summarise the key characteristics of sterling inter-bank market transactions. *(Paragraph 4.4)*

4. What is the relevance of liability management in respect of activities in the inter-bank market? *(Paragraphs 4.5 and 4.6)*

5. What is LIBOR and what is its relevance for a commercial bank? *(Paragraph 4.7)*

6. List the attractions of sterling certificates of deposit to an issuing bank or building society. *(Paragraphs 4.9–10)*

7. What is the difference between the primary and the secondary market for sterling certificates of deposit? *(Paragraph 4.10)*

The sterling commercial paper market

4.11 The sterling commercial paper market is one of the newest of the secondary money markets, having commenced operations in May 1986. Prior to that time, the creation of commercial paper within the UK financial system was not permitted; however, the increasing use of eurocommercial paper, and the increasing use of commercial paper in other countries, especially the United States, had made the UK out of line with practice elsewhere. Following alterations to the provisions of the Banking Act 1979 (now the Banking Act 1987) to allow the creation of sterling commercial paper, this market has grown substantially and gained considerable importance to the financing of many corporate enterprises.

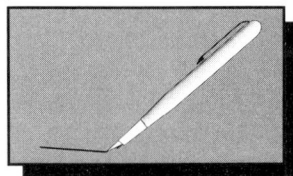

4.12   Sterling commercial paper (SCP) consists of a programme of short-term, marketable, unsecured promissory notes with a fixed maturity. The initial maturity is typically between seven days and three months (although longer maturities are permitted), and hence it is generally shorter-term than many instruments traded on the parallel money markets. SCP may be issued by any company, bank or building society, provided that it (or its guarantor, which may be a bank) has a listing on the Stock Exchange, has a net asset value of at least £25m, and the minimum denomination of such paper is £100,000. SCP is issued in bearer form, at a discount to its maturity value. A good credit rating is a prerequisite for the SCP to be sold readily.

4.13   Unlike commercial bills, SCP does *not* have to be issued as the counterpart to an identifiable commercial transaction. In this respect, it has a substantial advantage over commercial bills, since it can be used as a means of raising short-term finance for any purpose. Issuing SCP can also be a very *cheap* form of raising short-term finance; due to their high credit-rating, certain companies are better able to raise finance by issuing SCP than by borrowing from a bank. The lower costs of raising finance by an SCP programme may additionally be accompanied by a higher return for the *purchasers* of the paper, for the reason that it is an example of *disintermediation* – it bypasses the normal intermediation channels, with borrowers and lenders conducting business directly on a wholesale basis. The development of the SCP market, due to the disintermediation that it involves, is therefore of concern to the banks. At the same time, however, banks earn fee income from the management of SCP issues, and there are consequently some offsetting benefits.

4.14   As the majority of SCP is very short-term, figures for the market's outstanding debt tend to understate its importance. Nevertheless, some £7.3bn was outstanding at the end of April 1996. At one stage the discount houses made a secondary market in SCP but, when some companies became over-lent their SCP fell rapidly in price, the discount houses withdrew from the market.

Medium-term notes

4.15   In January 1990, the Bank of England lengthened the maturity of short-term paper which had been called SCP. The maximum maturity of SCP was to be one year, but paper issued to professionals, i.e. not private investors, could be issued for an original maturity of up to five years. If its maturity was greater than one year but no more than five years such securities were to be known as medium-term notes (MTNs). Both MTNs and commercial paper (with a maturity of not over one year) were permitted to be issued in foreign currency. The reasons for the different name are because the tax treatment of securities for over one year is different and to accord with practice in other markets.

4.16   The reason why the Bank of England is involved is that no prospectus is issued and that the transactions require to be exempted from the deposit-taking provisions of the Banking Act 1987. The denominations of the paper are large in order to limit the market to professional investors. At the end of April 1996, sterling MTNs outstanding totalled £17bn; of this total, £10bn had been issued by banks and building societies in the UK.

Student Activity 6

1. What is sterling commercial paper? *(Paragraph 4.12)*

2. What is the minimum permitted denomination of an issue of sterling commercial paper? *(Paragraph 4.12)*

3. What is the major advantage of sterling commercial paper over commercial bills from the point of view of the issuer? *(Paragraph 4.13)*

4. Why might borrowers prefer to raise funds via the issue of sterling commercial paper rather than via a bank loan? *(Paragraph 4.13)*

5. What threat might sterling commercial paper pose to the banks?

   (Paragraph 4.13)

6. Why is sterling commercial paper distinguished, as a form of short-term debt, from medium-term notes? *(Paragraph 4.16)*

The inter-company market

4.17   The inter-company market originated in 1969 and was a response to the problems faced at the time by companies wishing to raise finance from banks. The restrictions on bank lending caused companies to attempt to bypass the intermediation process (by borrowing from lenders other than banks), but the subsequent easing of bank lending restrictions and the development of additional means of raising finance by the issue of securities has meant that the attractions of this market have diminished.

4.18   The difficulties of bringing together two companies, one with funds to lend and the other needing to borrow funds, are considerable: the companies involved need to have compatible objectives with respect to maturity, size and interest rate on any loan, and the level of perceived risk must be deemed acceptable by the lender. The costs involved in overcoming these difficulties explain why the inter-company market is the smallest of the secondary money markets, and why brokers are active in the market to bring about deals.

The local authority market

4.18   The local authority market is the oldest parallel money markets, having commenced in 1955. The impetus for the creation of this market was the then restricted access for councils to borrowed funds from *central* government, leading the local authorities to seek to raise funds on their own account. Furthermore, the implicit guarantee of the Treasury for the debt issued by local authorities has ensured that such debt has had wide acceptance. The result was that the local authorities became important participants in both the bill and the bond markets during the 1960s and 1970s. In more recent years the tighter control over both the expenditure and the borrowing activities of local authorities has meant that its importance has diminished.

The finance house market

4.19   The finance house market is another example of declining importance within the parallel money markets. When finance houses were major providers of credit for both retail and commercial purposes, large volumes of funds were raised within this market. With the relative decline of this means of financing

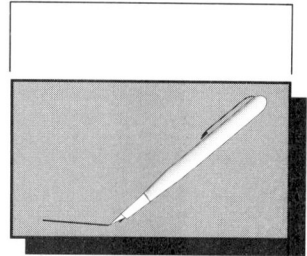

expenditure and the attainment of full banking status by a number of the larger finance houses, the market has declined. Nevertheless, significant sums of money are raised by the finance houses on this market, making use of issues of commercial bills in addition to direct borrowing from a range of institutions, including non-bank financial institutions such as pension funds and insurance companies as well as banks, non-financial organisations and individuals.

5 The primary (discount) market and the parallel money markets

Similarities

5.1 Some of the similarities are:

- Both the discount market and elements of the parallel markets *perform similar functions* in the adjustment of bank liquidity. Banks with shortages of liquidity are able to use the inter-bank market and the sterling certificates of deposit market as well as the discount market to cover any deficiency of liquidity, with the choice being influenced by the competing rates of interest involved. Similarly, banks with *surplus* liquidity will lend on the inter-bank market and buy CDs, in addition to lending to the discount market, in order to correct the position, again taking account of competing interest rates.

- The discount market is no longer the only avenue for *Bank of England intervention*. Since the mid-1980s the Bank of England has been prepared to provide liquidity to the banking system via REPO agreements and by direct assistance to certain institutions involved in the secondary markets.

- The *regulatory framework* for both the discount market and the secondary markets has become harmonised to some extent, with all markets supervised by the Bank of England's Wholesale Markets Supervision Division, and all participants expected to adhere to the London Code of Conduct (see Unit 9).

Differences

5.2 While recognising the similarities between the markets, it is also important to recognise the differences; differences which continue to make the distinction between the primary and parallel markets valid. For example:

- The discount market is still the *main* means by which the Bank of England seeks to *influence liquidity* within the banking system, and hence to *control short-term interest rates*.

- It is only to the discount market that the Bank of England provides the traditional *lender of last resort facility*.

- The *interest rates* that apply in the discount market are lower than those that apply for equivalent securities in the secondary market, because transactions within the discount market are *secured*, only *those institutions with a very high quality rating* operate within the discount market, and because of the *high quality* of financial instruments traded within that market.

- The discount market, in return for the lender of last resort facility provided by the Bank of England, is responsible for *underwriting the weekly Treasury bill issue*.

5.3   You must also remember that institutions will be operating in the discount market and perhaps several of the secondary sterling money markets simultaneously. While it is useful for expository purposes to examine the markets separately, the links between them must always be recognised. In addition, remember that these sterling money markets do not operate in isolation, and that, in particular, there are links with the *eurocurrency* markets, discussed later in this unit.

Student Activity 7

1.   What is the inter-company market?   *(Paragraph 4.17)*

2.   Why has the local authority market diminished in importance in recent years?
                                                                          (Paragraph 4 .18)

3.   In what ways do the finance houses utilise money market facilities?
                                                                          (Paragraph 4.19)

4.   State the similarities of the discount market and the secondary money markets.
                                                                          (Paragraph 5.1)

5.   Examine the key differences between the discount market and the secondary money market.   *(Paragraph 5.2)*

6   UK capital markets

6.1   Capital markets are concerned with two activities:

- Raising long-term finance for both private-sector companies and for public-sector organisations;

- Trading existing securities used by those organisations to raise long-term finance.

Primary market activity

6.2   The raising of long-term finance is termed *primary market activity.* This primary market activity is of crucial importance to both private-sector companies and public-sector organisations. Its importance to the former stems from the fact that it provides the funds for capital investment by industry and commerce, and therefore the means by which a company may develop and grow over time.

6.3   These long-term funds may be raised in the primary market in two different forms, by the issue of:

- *Equity shares*; and

- *Interest-bearing debt instruments.*

6.4   *Equity shares* may be issued in a number of different forms but the owners of those shares (the shareholders) are always the legal owners of the company. As such, the shareholders have the right at general meetings to determine the broad policies of the company and a claim on the profits of the company, with those profits being paid to shareholders in the form of dividends. As owners of the company, it is also the shareholders who have a claim on any residual value of that company in the event of it being liquidated.

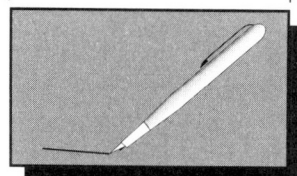

6.5   *Interest-bearing debt instruments* may also be issued in a variety of forms, with their distinguishing characteristic being that they are all forms of long-term borrowing. The majority of these instruments therefore normally commit the company to making regular interest payments, with the holders of these securities being creditors (or lenders – not shareholders/owners/investors) of the company concerned. Depending on the circumstances of the company, long-term borrowing by means of issuing interest-bearing debt instruments may give rise to certain advantages and greater flexibility relative to the issue of equity shares. In addition, it offers an alternative to the more conventional forms of borrowing from banks, which would be appropriate in situations where banks would not be prepared to lend in the amounts or for the period of time required by the company. (See generally, Unit 3.)

6.6   The issue of interest-bearing debt instruments in the UK capital market has been an important source of finance for the government to cover any budget deficit between income and expenditure. For the central government this has involved the issue of gilt-edged securities, with the sale of such debt *outside* the bank and building society sector constituting an important element of the control of the money supply. Local authorities were also traditionally significant issuers of debt on the UK capital market to finance any budget deficits they may have or to finance any large-scale projects.

Secondary market activity

6.7   The trading of *existing* securities issued by companies and government organisations in order to raise long-term finance is termed *secondary market activity*. The existence of a secondary market for these securities is of considerable importance, since it provides the holders with the means of liquidating their investments at very short notice. The significance of this is that the majority of equity shares have no date on which they will be redeemed (that is, they are irredeemable unless the issuing company decides otherwise), and much of the debt issued by both companies and government agencies has a long initial period to maturity. A small amount of government gilt-edged stock (consolidated loan stock, known as consols) has no maturity date, and it is common for much gilt-edged stock to have a maturity date 25 or more years into the future when issued. Given the irredeemable nature of the majority of equity shares and the long period to maturity of many debt instruments when issued, it would be very difficult to find buyers for such securities unless a secondary market for them existed, since few investors would be interested in buying a security that they could never sell or for which they would have to wait decades to mature. In this very real sense, therefore, the existence of a primary market for long-term finance is dependent on the existence of an active secondary market for the securities involved.

6.8   At the centre of the capital market in the UK is the *London Stock Exchange*, prior to May 1991 known as the International Stock Exchange. The majority of the activity on the London Stock Exchange involves the trading of existing securities (that is, secondary market activity), but this is to some extent a reflection of the need for a liquid secondary market for a primary market to exist, and you must remember that the London Stock Exchange is of major importance in the *raising* of long-term finance for both companies and government.

6.9 In addition to providing long-term finance for companies and government agencies within the UK, the London Stock Exchange engages in a substantial volume of trading in securities relating to *overseas* companies and official bodies, and in the trading of Eurobonds. This trading in overseas securities is a reflection of London's reputation as an international financial centre, but also a reflection of the increasing internationalisation of capital markets which, in London's case, has itself been stimulated by the deregulation within the market during the 1980s.

6.10 Although the London Stock Exchange is at the heart of the capital market in the UK, a significant proportion of the trade in capital-market securities takes place *outside* the London Stock Exchange. There is no *compulsion* for the trading of equity shares or interest-bearing debt instruments to take place within the ambit of the London Stock Exchange. In practice, substantial volumes of overseas securities and Eurobonds are traded outside, much of it by wholesale banks and securities houses based in London but with foreign ownership. Also, certain forms of specialist capital provision (such as venture capital) will not normally involve the trading of securities; the providers of venture capital will generally be investing in a business on a deliberately long-term basis in a way which does not give rise to any marketable securities for a significant period of time. These specialist providers of venture capital may be separate institutions (such as *3i*), or they may be subsidiaries or elements of other investing financial intermediaries able to take a long-term investment perspective, such as pension funds or investment trusts.

Student Activity 8

1. What are the two main activities of capital markets? *(Paragraph 6.1)*

2. What is primary market activity? *(Paragraph 6.2)*

3. What types of instruments are relevant for capital market activities? *(Paragraphs 6.2–5)*

4. What is secondary market activity? *(Paragraph 6.6)*

5. In broad terms, what type of activity dominates the operations of the London Stock Exchange? *(Paragraph 6.7)*

6. What types of capital market activity take place outside the London Stock Exchange? *(Paragraph 6.9)*

The London Stock Exchange

6.11 The London Stock Exchange currently comprises two separate markets: the *main market* (which accounts for the bulk of London Stock Exchange activity, in terms of both the number of securities listed for trading and in terms of turnover), and a 'junior' market, termed the *Alternative Investment Market* where the securities of some much smaller companies are traded.

6.12 We have noted that the money markets do not have a tangible, physical presence. The same is increasingly true of the UK capital markets. While the London Stock Exchange has a building in London with a large trading floor, only a very small proportion of trades are now executed on that trading floor,

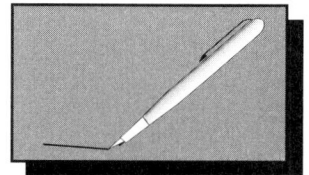

and the remaining space within the building, along with the London Stock Exchange staff, is devoted to the administration and supervision of the capital market. Like the money markets, the capital market essentially comprises a network of communications, making use of computer and telephone links particularly, with participants being geographically dispersed although concentrated in London.

Structure prior to October 1986

6.13 Prior to 27 October 1986 ('Big Bang'), the London Stock Exchange operated a *single-capacity* trading system. This system meant that the membership of the London Stock Exchange was split into two groups, *brokers* and *jobbers*, each with sharply distinct functions.

6.14 *Brokers* (stockbrokers) were those members of the London Stock Exchange whose principal task was to execute orders for clients, whether private individuals or institutions. Brokers were not permitted to deal with each other but were only permitted to buy securities from or sell securities to *jobbers*. Brokers charged a *commission* on all the deals they executed, with these commissions being subject to a *minimum scale* set by the London Stock Exchange, although many brokers supplemented their income by managing portfolios of securities, by selling investment advice and research findings, and other financial services.

6.15 *Jobbers* were those members of the London Stock Exchange who bought and sold securities on their own account (that is, as principals). Jobbers were permitted only to sell securities to and buy securities from the brokers: London Stock Exchange rules did not permit them to deal in securities directly with the general public.

6.16 The purpose of the sharp distinction between the roles of jobber and broker was to promote a competitive market in securities and to ensure that investors would not be subject to the conflicts of interest likely to surface under a dual capacity system (that is, one where a single firm both executes deals for investors and deals in securities on its own account). Under the single-capacity system, the broker had no reason for wanting to do anything but obtain the best deal for the client, since the securities that the client wished to trade could only be sold to or bought from a jobber. Furthermore, the system of minimum commissions guaranteed the broker a stable source of income and reduced the incentive to undertake deals that did not make use of a jobber. A system of *dual capacity* was, it was argued, likely to lead to conflicts of interest since it would be difficult to ensure that a client received the best prices and the best advice about which securities to buy and sell, if the broking firm was also holding quantities of securities on its own account.

6.17 The rules of the London Stock Exchange also extended to the *ownership* of member firms. Only in 1970 were London Stock Exchange firms able to form themselves into limited companies, and even then only 10% of the share capital of any firm could be held by an outsider. This limit of 10% was raised to 29.9% in 1982, but it nevertheless remained the case that, in comparison to stock exchanges in other parts of the world, the broking and jobbing firms in the UK were small-scale operations. The primary purpose of this restriction on ownership was to ensure a competitive market in the services provided;

in the case of *jobbing* firms, this was to increase the number of firms quoting prices on any particular security and therefore to minimise the spread between buying and selling prices.

Forces for change

6.18   The most important change was the rise of the institutional shareholder. Whereas in 1963 around 30% of the equity shares of UK companies were held by institutional shareholders (primarily insurance companies and pension funds), by 1990 it is estimated that some 70% was held by institutions. The corollary to this has of course been that the proportion of UK company equity shares held by private individuals has fallen very substantially. Although the privatisation policies of the government since 1979 have had the objective of increasing direct share-ownership by the general public, the effect of the privatisations has been only to increase the *number* of shareholders rather than to increase the proportion of equity shares held by the general public, which has continued its downward slide.

6.19   From the point of view of the jobbers within the London Stock Exchange, the important characteristic of institutional shareholders is that when they buy or sell securities they do so in very large deals, much larger than the deals by private investors. In consequence, the average size of transaction has been rising substantially; to match this, there needed to be an increase in the *capital base* of the jobbing firms, since in principle these jobbing firms needed to be able to take large blocks of securities on to their books, as well as to supply large blocks from their holdings. However, the restrictions on the ownership of London Stock Exchange firms meant that the matching increase in this capital base was not forthcoming. As a consequence, the ability of jobbing firms to quote prices for a wide range of securities fell, and jobbing firms began to specialise in a narrower range of securities and to merge with other jobbing firms. It became common for transactions to be set up between institutional shareholders by the *broker* concerned, making only nominal use of the jobber in order to comply with the London Stock Exchange regulations. The result, clearly, was a *decline* in the level of competition within the market.

6.20   From the point of view of institutional shareholders, the London Stock Exchange was starting to lose its attractions. The system of minimum commissions paid to brokers was based on a percentage of the value of a transaction, rather than a fixed sum, despite the fact that the work involved for the broker was essentially the same irrespective of the size of transaction. The system of minimum commissions also ensured that the broker had a source of income from which to subsidise the research and analysis of stocks typically undertaken by brokers, which was the main way for brokers to compete since competition on commissions was not permitted. This research and analysis was of considerable benefit to private investors, but of very limited value to the majority of institutional shareholders since they generally undertook their own investment research.

6.21   The net result was that the London Stock Exchange was proving to be *very expensive* for institutional shareholders and they, not surprisingly, started to look elsewhere. For larger companies that were quoted on other Stock Exchanges, institutions found it was cheaper to deal in securities on these exchanges, with the result that London was starting to lose business. Moreover, London was *failing to attract new business*, in the form of companies over-seas seeking quotations on the London Stock Exchange or else in the form of new types of security – the Eurobond market, for example, had virtually no contact with the London Stock Exchange. In this context, it is important to recognise the increasingly *international* nature of the capital markets; in an international market place, the London Stock Exchange was too expensive to be able to compete effectively.

6.22   Although the institutional shareholders were the major force for change within the structure of the London Stock Exchange, the member firms also wanted change. The London Stock Exchange regulations on the ownership of member firms were seen as particularly restrictive for the jobbing firms, since it prevented adequate access to capital and thus to an ability to compete with overseas firms. Meanwhile, the minimum-commissions system was seen as particularly harmful to the broking firms, as it resulted in an inability to compete on price, either within the UK market or on an international basis.

6.23   Finally, it is worth noting that the government, via the Office of Fair Trading (OFT), also wished to see change. The requirements relating to single capacity and to minimum commissions could be seen as anti-competitive, and the OFT initiated proceedings to test the legality of these agreements. These proceedings prompted the London Stock Exchange to make an arrangement with the OFT whereby it would end the single-capacity and minimum-commission arrangements in 1986 in return for the OFT dropping its proceedings. But note however, that the OFT's actions provided only the *immediate spur* for the reforms, and that other forces for change, particularly from institutional shareholders and from member firms, would most likely have brought about change within the system at around the same time, in the absence of the OFT action.

Student Activity 9

1. In the context of London Stock Exchange operations, what was single-capacity trading?   *(Paragraph 6.3)*

2. What was the primary purpose of single-capacity trading?   *(Paragraph 6.16)*

3. In relation to share ownership, what has happened to the importance of institutional investors during the past 20–30 years?   *(Paragraph 6.19)*

4. What have been the implications of the changing pattern of share ownership for jobbing (market-making) firms on the London Stock Exchange? *(Paragraph 6.20)*

5. What was the effect of the fixed-commissions system on institutional shareholders?
                                                                          (Paragraph 6.21)

6. What was the relevance of the Office of Fair Trading to the changes which took place in the London Stock Exchange's operations?   *(Paragraph 6.23)*

'Big Bang' reforms

6.24   'Big Bang' refers to the major changes in the operations of the London Stock Exchange that came into effect on 27 October 1986. These changes were essentially threefold:

- The system of minimum commissions on London Stock Exchange transactions was ended. After Big Bang, brokers were free to charge whatever commission rates they wished and were able to negotiate with their clients. This brought London into line with the practice in New York, where the exchange had abandoned fixed commissions in 1975.

- The 'single capacity' system was ended. The distinction between brokers and jobbers was abolished; brokers could now buy and sell securities on their own account, and jobbers could deal directly with clients. Hence, a 'dual-capacity' trading system was available for firms who wished to fulfil both functions. Although a number of firms *did* move into dual capacity trading, often through merger, note that it was mainly the *larger* firms that did so, and many of the smaller broking firms have continued to offer broking services only. This is particularly true of the broking firms that specialise in private client business, since the benefits of offering the jobbing facilities were much less apparent.

- The gilt-edged securities market was freed up to allow greater competition. The gilt-edged securities element of the capital market had been a very uncompetitive part of the capital market prior to Big Bang, with two jobbing firms accounting for some 75% of the jobbing activity. After Big Bang, some 27 institutions were granted licences by the Bank of England to operate as primary dealers in gilt-edged securities. These 27 institutions were termed gilt-edged market makers, since the dual capacity system was allowed in this part of the capital market also, with participants being able to deal in gilt-edged on their own account and to take orders direct from clients.

6.25 The level of competition in the gilt-edged market proved to be too great for all 27 participants to operate profitably, not least because the public sector borrowing requirement (PSBR) was starting to fall, eventually to become the public-sector debt-repayment (PSDR), with the implication that the value of gilt-edged securities in issue was rising only very slowly and subsequently *fell* when the PSDR started to apply. Consequently, the number of participants fell, although the return of large PSBRs after 1992 has given a major boost to the market.

6.26 Because of dual-capacity in the gilts market after Big Bang, the gilt-edged market makers needed to be able to adjust their positions in particular stocks by dealing with *other* gilt-edged market makers. However, no gilt-edged market maker would wish to indicate to other participants that it was short of, or had too much of, a particular stock. Hence, in order to provide anonymity in dealings between gilt-edged market makers, six *inter-dealer brokers* were established. By 1993 only three of these brokers were still active in the market.

6.27 Although these three changes – the ending of minimum commissions, the merging of the broking and jobbing functions, and changes in the gilts market – were the changes that occurred at Big Bang on 27 October 1986, another far-reaching change occurred at the beginning of March 1986. From that date, the restrictions on the ownership of London Stock Exchange firms were ended, meaning that member firms could be totally owned by another financial institution rather than a maximum ownership of 29.9%. With the other changes to the UK capital market in prospect in October 1986, this led to a flurry of merger activity involving London Stock Exchange firms. Much of that activity was centred around the intention of some financial institutions to become integrated securities houses, providing broking and market-making services for a wide range of securities under one roof, alongside comprehensive corporate finance and banking facilities. The widely held view was that this was necessary in the light of trends towards disintermediation and securitisation in the area of corporate financing, since only by becoming more heavily involved in the securities markets could these trends be offset. Further support for the view that it was necessary to become an integrated securities house was provided by the observation that, with both financial markets and industrial markets operating on a *global* basis, it was essential to provide corporate customers with a full range of banking and securities services in order to be able to attract their business.

6.28   Not all the institutions that have entered the securities trading business have been successful. The costs of entering the business have been high; the price of jobbing and broking firms reflected their attractiveness, while for those institutions setting up their operations from scratch, the costs of acquiring suitable buildings, fitting them out with appropriate communications and computing equipment and recruiting the appropriate personnel have been daunting. It is important to remember that the *profit* earned by any securities trading firm relies on individuals and institutions buying and selling securities – that is to say, it is dependent on *turnover*. For the first 12 months following Big Bang, turnover in the market as a whole was high, and hence the profitability of the majority of securities trading firms or subsidiaries was sufficient to keep them in operation. The Stock Market Crash of October 1987, however, caused turnover to drop substantially, and the inevitable consequence was a fall in profitability with a number of firms withdrawing or scaling down their operations within the UK capital market.

6.29   The impact of the Big Bang reforms of the London Stock Exchange on the *costs* of securities trading and on the services offered to those wishing to raise finance have been more clear-cut. For *institutional* investors, buying and selling blocks of securities of large value, the costs associated with such transactions have fallen substantially. As a consequence of not being bound by the scale of minimum commissions, institutions have been able to negotiate much lower commissions on their deals. Furthermore, the competition in respect of the more actively traded securities within the market has risen, leading to a general narrowing of spreads between bid and offer prices on such occasions. For *private client investors*, it is clear that costs have *not* fallen; these investors were, in effect, subsidised by the institutional investors under the minimum-commissions system and hence, with this subsidy removed, charges have correspondingly increased. For companies wishing to *raise funds* on the UK capital market, the conclusion is that there is now a wider range of instruments available through which to raise funds (and hence also a wider choice for investors to invest in), while the increased competition in the market has raised the quality of service provided.

Current changes

6.30   In 1996 media attention focused on a continuing debate, often acrimonious, as to whether deals should be quote-driven, as at present, or order-driven, with deals being matched by a computer program rather than by market makers. Currently, prices quoted by market makers are displayed on a computer screen, called SEAQ (Stock Exchange Automated Quotations) and the broker obtains, for his client, the best price quoted. However, many large deals are negotiated at finer prices than those available on SEAQ. The situation resembles that prevailing over fixed or negotiable commissions before Big Bang.

6.31 In mid 1996, a House of Commons Treasury Committee report was published, recommending a change to order-driven trading. The main advantage is 'transparency', meaning that investors will see who their real counterparties are and the size of the spread. Many brokers will welcome the use of a computer to match the deals, rather than waiting for their chosen market-maker to pick up the telephone. Naturally, market-makers are opposed to the change, although large deals will be routed via them because of the difficulty of matching such deals quickly. The change is likely to occur in the summer of 1997 when Crest (the new settlement system) is in full operation.

Crest
6.32 This is an electronic share settlement system which, during the period from July 1996 to April 1997, is gradually replacing the paper-driven system called Talisman. Deals under Crest will not use share certificates and will be settled on a five-day rolling settlement which, when any teething difficulties have been removed, will become a three-day rolling settlement. However, small investors may continue to use share certificates with a 10-day settlement period – and a slightly worse price because of the labour involved.

Student Activity 10

1. List the three main elements of 'Big Bang'. *(Paragraph 6.24)*

2. How did the environment for the gilt-edged securities market alter after 'Big Bang'? *(Paragraph 6.24)*

3. What is an 'inter-dealer broker'? *(Paragraphs 6.25–26)*

4. What regulatory change allowed the flurry of merger activity among London Stock Exchange firms and outside institutions during the mid-1980s?
   (Paragraph 6.27)

5. Why were banks particularly interested in becoming involved with stock market activities during the mid-1980s? *(Paragraph 6.27)*

6. What was the general effect of 'Big Bang' on the costs for institutional investors of trading on the stock market? *(Paragraph 6.29)*

6. Distinguish between order-driven and quote driven dealing. *(Paragraphs 6.30–31)*

7　The primary market for equities

7.1 One of the major activities of the London Stock Exchange is reviewing applications from companies for a quotation for their shares to be traded on the Exchange. The Exchange must ensure that companies seeking a quotation satisfy its requirements (the 'Yellow Book'), which involve providing the Exchange (and therefore the investing public) with a broad spread of information

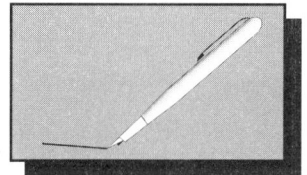

about the operations of the company. In order to maintain a quotation, a company is required to supply this information on a continuing basis, with quotations being suspended for those companies which do not comply. However, gaining a quotation does not imply a 'seal of approval' from the London Stock Exchange; rather, it means that sufficient information about the company has been provided for investors to form their own view as to the wisdom of investing in that company. It also enhances the liquidity of the shares.

7.2   When a company first raises capital funds via the London Stock Exchange, the event is referred to as a public flotation of that company. The flotation of a company is normally managed by a merchant bank, working in conjunction with a stockbroker, although when the company is relatively small the services of the merchant bank are invariably dispensed with.

7.3   A flotation may be achieved in one of several ways:

- Offer for sale;

- Tender;

- Intermediaries offer for sale;

- Placing.

Offer for sale

7.4   An offer for sale may be at a fixed price per share, so that investors have to decide whether, and how many shares they wish to purchase at that price. The difficulty with this approach lies in determining the correct price; too low a price will result in an over-subscription, which may be exacerbated by 'stagging' whereby investors will deliberately make applications for more shares than they intend to hold in the long term in the hope of being able to sell some, or all, of their allocation at an immediate profit. Any over-subscription also leads to difficulties in allocating the shares among the investors. Much of the difficulty in determining the appropriate price for a fixed-price offer is caused by movements in the stock market as a whole; what might be considered a 'fair' price relative to the market when the price is set may become very expensive if the market falls substantially, or very cheap if the market rises substantially, during the period in which the offer remains open.

7.5   An offer for sale may also be at a price to be set between two stated prices, e.g. for the public offer for Railtrack PLC it was 'expected to be between 340p and 380p'. The shares were to be paid for in two instalments, with the first being 190p on applying for the shares. The second, due before 3 June 1997, will be for the price (announced as 380p five days after the offer closed) less the first instalment, and appears on the interim certificates issued to successful investors. The detail of this procedure is appropriate for issues which are payable in instalments but if the purchase price is to be paid in full on application then an indication of the amounts required is given, e.g. '£1500 or £2000 etc'. Investors then receive shares almost to the value of their cheques, plus a refund of the difference.

Tenders

7.6   Tenders require investors to specify both the number of shares they wish to buy and the price they are willing to pay for them. Shares are then allocated in descending order of the bid price until all shares are allocated. It is, however, normal market practice to charge all those allotted shares a price that is equal to the price per share offered by the final bid accepted. This price is known as the 'striking price', and those investors bidding below the striking price do not receive an allocation of shares. The advantage of the tender method is that it ensures that the 'right' price is achieved (since all the shares are sold at the highest achievable price), but carries the disadvantages that, first, it may lead to a concentrated ownership of shares, and, second, that it tends to deter many investors since they are unsure about the price at which they will need to bid to secure an allocation.

Intermediaries offer for sale

7.7 In this method the shares are offered to a limited number of stockbrokers, to whom the public may apply to buy the shares. The company, or its bankers, then deal with a handful of brokers, rather than thousands of investors. It is cheaper than an offer for sale, but it does result in a larger register of shareholders, which can be expensive but which is an advantage to a company selling to the general public rather than selling to (say) wholesalers and distributors.

Placing

7.8 A flotation by means of a placing is particularly appropriate for relatively small companies. Under a placing, the merchant bank and/or stockbroker will arrange for the shares to be sold in blocks at agreed prices. These blocks will usually be large, and hence will normally be sold to investing institutions such as insurance companies, pension funds and unit trusts, but the London Stock Exchange will usually require that a block is sold to a dealer within the London Stock Exchange in order that there are shares available from which a market in that company's securities can be made.

7.9 The principal advantage of a placing over an offer is that it is substantially cheaper, but it carries the disadvantage that it necessarily leads to a concentration of shareholdings, since it involves the majority of shares ending up with a limited number of institutions. However, the register of shareholders is smaller and thus cheaper to maintain.

Alternative Investment Market (AIM)

7.10 This opened in July 1995, and replaced the Unlisted Securities Market (USM) at the end of 1996. The latter's companies have, in most cases, joined the main market, whose listing requirements were changed to bring them into line with the EU: The USM, in effect, became an anomaly.

7.11 The requirements for admittance to AIM are fairly simple: companies must be vetted by a 'nominated adviser', who is one of 50 stock exchange member firms approved for this purpose by the stock exchange authorities. No minimum number of shares need to be available for investors, so the market for some shares in AIM can be thin (illiquid).

7.12 Because shares quoted on AIM are not quoted on the London Stock Exchange, investors in some new issues on AIM may be eligible for tax relief, provided that the shares qualify under the rules of the Enterprise Investment Scheme. If so, then the investors receive 20% relief on the original investment to be set against income tax, plus a deferment of capital gains tax when they sell.

Ofex

7.13   This stands for 'off-exchange trading', and is a matched-bargain share trading facility for shares in unquoted companies. It is not the responsibility of the Stock Exchange, being run by a stockbroker (JP Jenkins) who 'matches' buying orders to selling orders. Hence, the speed of selling depends on the speed at which a buyer can be found. Unlike the main exchange and AIM, there is no market regulation except that the:

- Companies Act 1985 applies;
- SFA supervises;
- Companies must be approved by a stockbroker;
- Companies must publish a prospectus before joining the service.

Recent trends

7.14   The use of offers for sale declined in 1996, after the Stock Exchange withdrew its requirement that all flotations over £50m had to be in this form (partly at least). The sums raised in the primary market for new and existing companies – which includes debt instruments and equities – in recent years have been as follows:

	UK borrowers (£bn)	Overseas borrowers (£bn)
1991	20.5	4.0
1992	12.4	1.2
1993	26.7	9.3
1994	20.9	3.2
1995	11.0	2.1

Additional finance – rights issues

7.15   Rather different arrangements apply for any subsequent finance raised on the capital market. London Stock Exchange rules require that any additional issue of shares by a company must be first offered to existing shareholders. This system is known as a rights issue and involves inviting existing shareholders to subscribe to the new shares, usually at a price that represents a discount to the current market price. These 'rights' can be sold in the market and the purchasers incur the obligation to buy the shares attaching to the rights, e.g. two new ordinary shares per 'right'. When shareholders receive their rights – usually in a form known as 'allotment letters' – they face several choices, they can:

- Take up all their rights and buy all their shares. If they do not, then they will find that future dividends will be smaller, because the profits will have to be divided by a larger number of shares – dilution of the equity, as it is called. However if they take up all of their rights, they must find the cash with which to buy the new shares.

- Sell all their rights and bank the cash.

- Sell some of their rights and use the proceeds to take up only a part of the shares to which they are entitled. In this way, they lessen the impact of dilution and preserve their holdings of cash and other shares.

7.16   To ensure that the new money is raised, a rights issue is usually 'underwritten' by an investment bank, which will buy any shares not purchased with the aid of the rights which have been issued. The fees charged for this underwriting can be substantial and add to the expenses of the rights issue.

Vendor placing

7.17 The shareholders may, however, at a general meeting of the company, waive their rights to be offered the shares first, in which case the company may then sell the shares in blocks (usually) to investing institutions. This process is a vendor placing. A company may also raise additional capital by the issue of interest-bearing debt instruments, as an alternative to further issue of equity shares. Sometimes, the debt is issued together with warrants to subscribe for new shares on certain dates at determined prices. These warrants are, in effect, call options.

Open offer

7.18 Yet another way of raising further equity capital, often used by companies unwilling to pay for the charges for underwriting a rights issue, is to invite existing shareholders to subscribe for new shares in an open offer. This gives no rights to be sold in the market but the offer stays 'open' for several weeks.

Student Activity 11

1. What is a quotation on the London Stock Exchange? *(Paragraph 7.1)*

2. What is the significance of a quotation on the London Stock Exchange for a potential investor? *(Paragraph 7.1)*

3. What is a public flotation of a company? *(Paragraph 7.2)*

4. In which ways may a flotation be achieved? *(Paragraphs 7.3–9)*

5. What is a rights issue? *(Paragraph 7.15)*

6. What is the Alternative Investment Market? *(Paragraphs 7.10–11)*

7. What is Ofex? *(Paragraph 7.3)*

8 Securities indices

8.1 Stock exchange indices were introduced the USA over a century ago. They enable price and other calculations to be compared not only historically but also between securities – which in most cases mean ordinary shares.

FT Ordinary

8.2 The FT Ordinary Share index has 1 July 1935 for its base of 100 and is calculated hourly. It covers 30 leading shares and is an unweighted geometric average. 'Unweighted' means that no account is taken of the different totals of shares issued by each of the 30 companies and a geometric average is designed to avoid giving undue importance to excessive movements in one or two shares. For instance, take two shares A & B with prices of 2 & 2 on Day 1 and 2 & 7 on Day 2, and compare their arithmetic and geometric averages (AM and GM respectively).

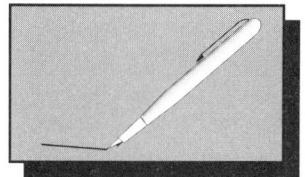

	AM	GM
Day 1	$\dfrac{2 + 2}{2} = 2$	$(2 \times 2) = 2$
Day 2	$\dfrac{2 + 7}{2} = 4.5$	$(2 \times 7) = (14) = 3.74$

8.3   The 'FT Ordinary' is used for long-term comparisons of share prices over periods of up to 60 years. It is the UK's equivalent of the Dow Jones index which has been in existence for over a century in the USA. However, with the development of computers, it has become easier to produce more comprehensive stock exchange indices, so the FT Ordinary Share index has declined in importance.

FTSE 100

8.4   Known as the 'Footsie', the correct title of this index is the Financial Times Stock Exchange Index of 100 Shares. It is compiled and published every minute and is a weighted arithmetic average of the stocks of the largest 100 companies: hence it also includes fixed interest securities where these have been issued. It is revised every three months to determine new entrants and leavers on the basis of market capitalisation (price times number of shares issued). Thus, market capitalisation determines entry/exit and, of course, the weighting accorded to each stock. 1984 is the base year (= 1000). The index is used to gauge short-term – daily, weekly, monthly – fluctuations in prices. There are no subdivisions into sectors. Some investment banks and managers calculate it on a real-time basis, rather than once every minute, and this is a very useful tool for trading in the derivative markets. In the USA, the Dow Jones is the Footsie's opposite number, indicating market sentiment.

FT-SE Actuaries Share Indices

8.5   These are a set of indices which now includes the 'Footsie' but most traders still regard this family as still separate. The largest of the set of indices is the FT-SE Actuaries All-Share Index, comprising 899 securities and calculated hourly as a weighted arithmetic average. There are many subdivisions, both by size and industry. The indices tend to be used for comparisons: between companies and their sectors, between companies and the 'All Share' and between sectors and the 'All Share'.

A pyramid of indices

8.6   FTSE 100 + FTSE Mid 250 = FTSE-A 350
which is split into higher yield and lower yield. In addition, there are four industry baskets:

- Building and construction;
- Pharmaceuticals;
- Water;
- Retail banks

+ FT-SE Small Cap(italisation) = FTSE-A All Share

In addition, there is a FT-SE-A Fledgling index.

8.7   In the 'All Share' there are eight industrial headings and 36 subdivisions. To avoid excessive detail, these are the headings, with the number of securities in each shown in brackets (as at mid-July 1996).

Mineral extraction	34
General industrials	276
Consumer goods	82
Services	253
Utilities	33
Non-financial	668
Financial	105
Investment trusts	126
FT-SE-A All Share	899

Index tracking

8.8 Index tracking has nothing to do with 'index-linking' (to inflation) but is a goal sought by fund managers, especially those managing some unit trusts and pension funds, to keep abreast of changes in the index – usually the Footsie. Hence, the prices of company shares about to go into the index tend to rise as demand increases in expectation – and vice versa. Replication can be achieved in two ways:

● Assembling a portfolio of the 100 companies, in similar proportions to their weightings. However, monitoring – and buying – 100 shares can be expensive;

● Building a smaller portfolio which behaves in a similar way to the Footsie.

Index-tracking is a new development in the financial services industry.

Student Activity 12

1. What is the purpose of a securities index? *(Paragraph 8.1)*

2. Compare and contrast the FT Ordinary, the 'Footsie' and the FT-SE Actuaries All Share indices. *(Paragraphs 8.2–5)*

3. Demonstrate the difference between a geometric average and an arithmetic average. *(Paragraph 8.2)*

4. Show how the FTSE 100 'nests' into the FT-SE-A All Share Index.
(Paragraph 8.6)

5. If you wished to compare share prices at 12 noon on a Monday with their level at the same on the previous Friday, which index should be used and why?
(Paragraph 8.4)

6. Explain what is meant by 'index-tracking'. How does it differ from 'index-linking'?
(Paragraph 8.8)

9 Efficiency of secondary securities markets

9.1 A distinction must be made between two types of 'efficiency':

● Operational efficiency, achieving a service at the lowest transaction cost, i.e. financial transactions.

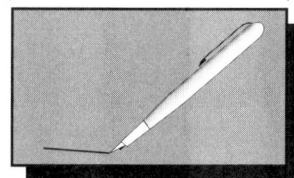

- Pricing efficiency, where prices reflect all the relevant information which affects the valuation of financial assets.

9.2   *Operational (internal) efficiency* is being achieved to some extent by the abolition of fixed commissions, which occurred in New York in 1975, Paris in 1985 and London in 1986 ('Big Bang'). However, the other element in transaction costs is the 'buy-sell' spread, plus any stamp duty.

9.3   *Pricing (external) efficiency* is at its maximum when all relevant information is translated and absorbed into the supply and demand of financial assets and hence their prices. Accordingly, it is argued, capital is being allocated as efficiently as possible, so that all the investor has to decide is the level of risk which is acceptable. 'You can't buck the market' is how a certain lady politician once stated this theory.

9.4   Over 40 years ago, Maurice Kendall, in the *Journal* of the Royal Statistical Society ('The Analysis of Economic Trends Series'; 'Part 1, Prices') could establish no predictable movements or patterns in equity prices, which seemed to change randomly. In the following years, the 'random walk hypothesis' developed, arguing that share prices behave in a haphazard way, and cannot be predicted or forecast. Certainly, it was argued, past performance was no guide to the future, so that 'chartists' who plotted share prices on squared paper and drew trend lines were wasting their time. From the random walk theory has developed the current academic orthodoxy – the efficient market hypothesis.

Efficient market hypothesis (EMH)

9.5   EMH states that the general availability of relevant information about companies, borrowers and other issuers of financial securities will lead to a correct valuation (pricing) of such securities, provided that:

- They are freely traded in markets;
- These markets are properly functioning (internally efficient).

Insider trading, by employees or stockbrokers with confidential information is contrary to EMH. Indeed, in many countries, including the UK, insider dealing is a criminal offence.

9.6   There are three forms or levels of EMH.

- Weak-form – the market currently reflects all relevant information implied in historic prices.
- Semi-strong-form – the market currently reflects all publicly available relevant information.
- Strong-form – the market currently reflects all publicly and privately available relevant information.

9.7   There is debate over EMH among academics, who support it, and market practitioners, who reject it. Three observations can be made here. First, some investment managers have better track records than others, and have 'outperformed' the market, at least for a time. If the EMH were true, this would not be possible. Second, just because information is available to all does not mean that all investors will incorporate it into their buying or selling decisions. Ignorance, loyalty and memory all play various roles when investment decisions are made. Third, some practitioners argue that, although the information is available, the institutions or organisations concerned take a long time to reach their decisions. Too often, the board or committee meets only weekly or fortnightly to take their decisions

Student Activity 13

1. Distinguish between the two types of secondary market efficiency.

    (Paragraph 9.1)

2. Explain what is meant by the random walk hypothesis.   *(Paragraph 9.4)*

3. Summarise the Efficient Market Hypothesis (EMH).   *(Paragraph 9.5)*

4. Describe the three forms of the EMH.   *(Paragraph 9.6)*

5. What criticisms can be made of the EMH?   *(Paragraph 9.7)*

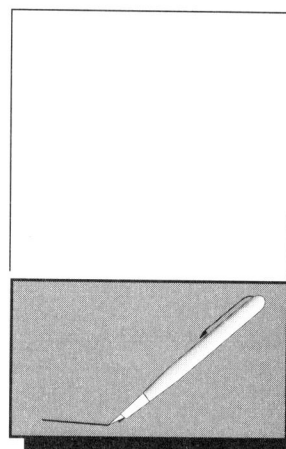

10   The fixed income (debt) market

Structure

10.1   As we noted earlier, the corporate debt market in London is dwarfed by the gilt market (government sterling bonds). Moreover, corporate bonds are regulated by the London Stock Exchange whereas the gilt-edged market is regulated by the Bank of England. This predominance of the gilt-edged market is likely to continue for the foreseeable future, in spite of the recent attempt to revitalise the corporate bond market by extending Personal Equity Plans (PEPs) to permit special PEPs for corporate bonds. Accordingly, we concentrate on the gilts market.

Primary market

10.2   Published towards the end of November each year, the government's budget includes forecasts of its Public Sector Borrowing Requirement (PSBR) for several years ahead. (The UK government's financial year currently runs from 1 April to 31 March, although this will change if the UK joins the single EMU currency). The PSBR, plus the amount of existing gilts maturing during the coming financial year give an indication of the total gilts which the authorities (the Treasury and its banker, the Bank of England) will have to issue in the primary market. However, a deduction must be made from this total to take into account the sales of National Savings products in the retail financial market: this is usually around £3 bn of 'new money'.

Auctions

10.3   Towards the end of March each year, the Chancellor issues a 'remit' to the Bank of England, outlining an auction calendar for gilts during the forthcoming financial year. There are usually 10 auctions, normally held on the last Wednesday of a month. However, this timetable is flexible, to avoid holding an auction too close to a budget day (by tradition a Tuesday) or Christmas and the New Year. Another example of this flexibility occurred in July 1996, when two gilts were auctioned – 8% Treasury Stock 2000 on the Tuesday and 8% Treasury Stock 2015 on the Thursday. Such events are called 'dual stock auctions'.

10.4   Auctions are the usual method of issuing conventional gilts, i.e. not index-linked, and are divided into two sections, non-competitive and competitive. All auctions are for conventional gilts.

10.5   *Non-competitive bids* are designed for smaller investors, and are priced at the average of the competitive bids. The minimum bid is £1,000 and the maximum is £500,000. When applying, investors make non-competitive bids at a stated price for their stock, e.g. £107 for the short-dated stock and £102 for the long-dated stock in the July 1996 auction. When the average price of the competitive bids is known, the differences are settled by cheque.

10.6   *Competitive bids* begin at £500,000 and successful applicants must pay their bid prices. Payment must be by CHAPS, and not by cheque.

Tap sales

10.7   These are a traditional way of selling gilts in line with market conditions and on a day-to-day basis. There is usually a 'short-tap' and a 'long-tap', i.e. a short-dated gilt and a long-dated gilt which are sold when the Bank thinks that such sales will not depress prices too much. The procedure is now formalised, with tap issues being announced at 10.15 am for bids at 10.45 am, giving investors a mere 30 minutes to decide. Tap issuance of conventional gilts is currently only 10% of total issuance. All index-linked gilts are issued through the tap at present

Secondary market

10.8   The participants include:

- The *holders* – banks, other financial institutions, companies and individuals in the UK and overseas.
- The *authorities*, i.e. the Treasury and the Bank of England.
- *GEMMs* – gilt-edged market makers. There are 20 of these, compared to 27 at 'Big Bang' (October 1986). Since 'Big Bang' their profits have fluctuated and provisional data at the end of 1995 showed a cumulative loss in the nine or so years from October 1986. The obligations of a GEMM are to make a two-way (buying and selling) market in all the gilts which they quote, and to deal at the prices quoted on the screen (some gilts are rarely traded, because the amounts outstanding are so small). Until January 1996, only GEMMs could participate in repos.
- *Stock exchange money brokers*, who enable GEMMs to borrow gilts from pension funds and insurance companies, in order to deliver the securities on the next day. The brokers receive a fee for arranging this borrowing, the GEMMs also paying the lending institutions for the use of the stock.
- *inter-dealer brokers*. Their role is to act as intermediaries between the GEMMs, so that the transactions between GEMMs are anonymous, i.e. the counterparties (the GEMMs) do not know each other's names. This anonymity is vital because the GEMMs are competing with each other for customers (the holders and potential holders) and do not wish to let their rivals know whether or not they have large holdings – or have 'gone short' – in particular stocks.

10.9 Unlike those in the equity market, transactions are settled the next working day. Moreover, they are relatively fewer in number but larger in amount. Annual turnover is around £1,500bn (£1.5 trillion) and is split fairly evenly between intra-market business and customer business. The number of transactions a year is about 700,000, with most deals being classed as 'customer business'.

New and recent developments

10.10 In Unit 2, we noted the repo market, which for gilts began in January 1996. Because a repo enables market participants to borrow cash against the security of gilt-edged stock, it can increase the money supply; likewise a reverse repo enables the parties to borrow stock against the deposit of cash and so cover a 'short' position in a gilt. This repo market now extends far beyond GEMMs, who alone could take part in repos until January 1996, and then only with stock exchange money brokers.

10.11 The objective of the new facility is to deepen the existing market, providing greater liquidity and to make it more attractive to overseas investors, who are much more familiar with the concept. Another motive is to provide an additional instrument for the discount market, in the run-up to the single currency. It would make the London sterling money market less dissimilar to Frankfurt.

10.12 Preparations are well under way for the introduction of stripped gilts, probably in the summer of 1997. New issues are now strippable, as soon as the facility has been introduced, and dividend payment days on such stocks are standardised at 7 June and 7 December each year. Each of these gilts will be 'stripped' into its component interest payments, plus the capital amount payable on maturity, as described in Unit 6 when discussing implicit forward interest rates. Thus, for a 10-year gilt, with interest paid every six months, there will be 20 interest strips (two for each of the 10 years) plus the capital repayment, making 21 securities in all. The new market will allow investors to buy and sell the capital repayment of a gilt and to receive no income and to buy and sell all or part of the income stream and to forgo the capital repayment.

Student Activity 14

1 If most gilts have their interest paid on 7 June and 7 December, will this not lead to a surplus of liquidity in the discount market on these days? How might the Bank of England react? *(Clue: Paragraph 3.9)*

2 How might those investors, who prefer to receive a stream of gilt dividends from month to month, react? *(Clue: a monthly income high interest deposit account)*

10.13 At present, the gilts market is quote-driven. It is not likely to come within the orbit of Crest, but over 50% of all gilts are held in accounts at the Central Gilts Office at the Bank of England, and not in paper form.

Student Activity 15

1. What are gilts and who trades in them? *(Paragraphs 10.1 and 10.8)*

2. Compare the primary gilts market in London with the primary equity market in London. *(Paragraphs 10.3–7 and 7.4–18)*

3. Compare the secondary gilts market in London with the secondary equity market in London. *(Paragraphs 10.8–9, and 6.30–32)*

4. What changes have occurred in the gilts market in the 1990s?
(Paragraphs 10.10–11)

5. What will happen in the summer of 1997? *(Paragraph 10.12)*

11 The eurocurrency markets

What are eurocurrencies?

11.1 The term *eurocurrency* relates to large-scale foreign-currency-denominated borrowing and lending activities. For example, eurodollar activity relates to large-scale deposits with or loans by banks situated outside the USA which are denominated in US dollars.

11.2 The prefix 'euro' tends to cause confusion in that it suggests that the market is confined to Europe or is connected in some way with the European Union's single currency. This is not the case, and although many eurocurrency transactions take place in Europe they can in fact take place in *any country* in the world. However, the name 'euro' for the EUs single currency will cause great confusion to students for many years to come, unless the markets change the name 'eurocurrency' to a more correct name such as 'external currency'. Originally, eurodollar transactions were all in Europe, so that the name was an accurate geographical description of the market's location. Today, there are important markets in Japan, Australia, SE Asia and the Caribbean.

11.3 The major eurocurrencies are the eurodollar, eurosterling, eurodeutschmark and euroyen. The eurodollar currently accounts for approximately 45% of all eurocurrency transactions.

The nature of eurocurrency transactions

11.4 Eurocurrency markets deal with the lending and borrowing of eurocurrencies in wholesale amounts. Transactions are normally *for a minimum US$1m equivalent*, and *unsecured*. Many eurocurrency transactions are short-term in nature and mature in one year or less. This short-term activity relates not only to *inter-bank deposits* but also to such instruments as *certificates of deposit*. In viewing the long term, the most popular instrument at present is the *Eurobond*.

Creation and growth of eurocurrency markets

11.5 The first euromarket originated in the early 1950s in eurodollars. Several eastern European banks wanted to disguise their ownership of dollar deposits and consequently placed them with correspondent banks mainly in Britain and France. With this sudden inflow of dollars, these banks began to offer dollar loans at attractive interest rates, lower than those being offered in the

USA. Coupled to this was the existence of direct monetary controls in the USA, which held down US deposit rates but which did not apply to dollars accepted from non-residents by American banks operating outside the USA. This precipitated an increase of overseas branches of US banks, particularly in London, in order to take a share of this new business. European banks also began to compete for this business. Thus, eurocurrency markets were born.

11.6 Other factors which have contributed to the successful expansion of the eurocurrency markets in the past include the:

- *Removal of currency exchange controls* by major Western countries; and

- *Large rises in oil prices* during the 1970s which resulted in a major recycling of funds between the oil-rich nations and those countries which had huge international payments problems.

11.7 Other influences which have continued to encourage the upsurge of the eurocurrency markets include:

- The ability of the markets to operate on very fine interest-rate margins. Compared to domestic markets, the eurocurrency markets have been able to offer *lower rates to borrowers* and *higher rates on deposits*. This has been one of the principal reasons for the eurocurrency markets' success. These rates have been achieved by *economies of scale* which have reduced unit administration costs.

- Formerly the *lack of specific reserve requirements* for either liquidity or capital which meant that banks operating in the eurocurrency markets did not have to hold huge amounts of relatively low-yield liquid assets nor have the capital backing which would be required for similar domestic operations. Some of the financial benefits of this were passed on to the customer which increased market activity. (In saying this, it must not be ignored that a higher return on funds will be expected by the ultimate lender due to the higher risk factor which is evident in eurocurrency transactions as opposed to normal domestic business.)

11.8 In the latter part of the 1980s the growth of the eurocurrency markets slowed, as steps were taken to *increase regulatory controls on international banking activities.* Of particular significance was the western world's major central banks' agreement to introduce common capital-adequacy requirements by the end of 1992. The third world debt problem also affected the markets' development.

11.9 However, even with eurocurrency and domestic markets competing on equal supervisory terms, the eurocurrency markets still have the benefits of *economies of scale* and other operational advantages which should still give them a competitive edge.

11.10 The predominant position which the US dollar enjoys as the main currency of world trade has led to international business maintaining dollar balances in order to meet their commitments. An advantage of this is that there is no need to switch into and out of dollars when payments are made and incomes received respectively, thus *negating the effects of any adverse exchange rate movements.* It also obviously *reduces administrative transaction costs.* This situation is naturally linked to the continued provision of funds to the eurodollar market and the raising of dollar loans against anticipated future dollar earnings.

11.11 A similar scenario is now being experienced with other major currencies such as the yen and the Deutschmark which are showing an increased presence on the international scene. This continuing trend can only add to the standing of the eurocurrency markets.

Student Activity 16

1. Define the term 'eurocurrency'. *(Paragraph 11.1)*

2. List the main eurocurrencies. *(Paragraph 11.3)*

3. What are the normal characteristics of eurocurrency market activity? *(Paragraph 11.4)*

4. What is the connection between oil prices and the growth of the eurocurrency markets? *(Paragraph 11.6)*

5. In what way have fine interest-rate margins stimulated the growth of the eurocurrency markets? *(Paragraph 11.7)*

6. Why have eurocurrency activities been able to operate on narrow margins? *(Paragraph 11.7)*

7. What has been the impact on eurocurrency market activities of increased regulation of banking activities throughout the western world as a whole? *(Paragraph 11.8)*

8. What is the advantage to a business operating internationally of holding US dollar balances? *(Paragraph 11.10)*

Recent developments

11.12 In addition to the factors already mentioned, the *Third World debt problem* has had a major influence on eurocurrency activity in recent years. During the 1970s less-developed countries borrowed huge sums in the eurocurrency markets. At the beginning of the 1980s, with real interest rates increasing with the strengthening of the US dollar, coupled with world recession and the collapse of primary commodity prices, many developing countries found that they could no longer service these loans and threatened to renege on their debts. This was a shock to the eurocurrency markets. Major banks have been forced to make massive provisions against possible losses on their eurocurrency lending to Third World countries as a consequence.

11.13 Some banks have negotiated the securitisation of Third World loans (effectively turning claims against individual borrowers into marketable securities), and have then attempted to sell their debt, often at a huge discount on international markets, so that they might recoup some of their funds. Needless to say, banks are loath to be involved in similar lending as a result of their experiences. In fact, lending to less-developed countries is now only normally contemplated if there are some safeguards built in, e.g. if the arrangement is IMF-backed.

11.14 This Third World debt problem has caused the eurocurrency markets to *change direction with their activities.* Transactions now tend to involve *corporate borrowers* and *developed countries*. The trend towards securitisation of debt has enabled eurocurrency market participants to deal in issues of securities without the on-lending risks of taking debt on their own balance sheets. This has obviously been attractive, given the problems encountered in lending to the Third World in the recent past. Despite this trend, there has been an *increase in the syndicated loans market* since 1987. Although this has mainly involved lending to corporate borrowers in OECD countries, there was an increase in such lending to less-developed countries more recently.

11.15 The continued growth of the eurocurrency markets is also due to the good economic growth experienced by many industrial nations particularly in the Far East, where adverse financial and economic conditions, which have had an effect elsewhere, have had little impact. This has led directly to a movement in eurocurrency activity towards the Far East with the importance of the markets in Japan and other Far Eastern centres increasingly coming to the fore. This has led to a fall in the importance of other centres (such as London), although the UK's share of activities still amounts to approximately 15% of the world's total and Western Europe as a whole has around 50% of all eurocurrency activities.

Student Activity 17

1. What major factors led to the Third World debt problem?   *(Paragraph 11.12)*

2. What is securitisation of debt?   *(Paragraph 11.13)*

3. What is the relevance of securitisation to the Third World debt problem?
                                                                    (Paragraph 11.14)

4. What has been the effect of the Third World debt problem on the pattern of eurocurrency lending?   *(Paragraph 11.14)*

5. Despite the problems caused by the Third World debt problem, the eurocurrency markets have continued to grow. Why?   *(Paragraph 11.15)*

Suppliers and users of eurocurrency funds

Suppliers

11.16 Suppliers can be classified into three categories:

- *Official institutions.* These were prominent providers of funds during the early 1960s and again, particularly, in the mid-1970s when oil monies were recycled through the markets. This category includes international monetary institutions, central banks and public sector bodies.

- *Commercial banks.* Commercial banks have proved to be an important gateway through which *new* funds have been able to flow into the markets, normally being on-lent by the banks on behalf of non-bank customers.

- *Private investors and non-bank private sector institutions.* This group includes wealthy individuals and multinational commercial and industrial companies.

11.17 We have already mentioned why funds have been drawn to the eurocurrency markets at the expense of domestic markets. But obviously some suppliers of

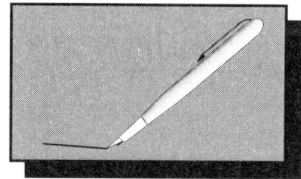

funds have additional reasons for using the markets. *Central banks* find it extremely convenient to maintain reserves in interest-bearing liquid assets denominated in internationally accepted currencies. *Commercial banks* have found that participation in the markets has helped in liability and asset-management operations. Added to this, the holding of eurocurrencies helps to minimise exposure to volatile exchange rate movements. This ability to aid the financial management of institutions will undoubtedly keep eurocurrency activity buoyant.

Users

11.18 Users again can be classified into three groups:

- *Official institutions.* Following the Third World debt problem, large loans now tend to be limited to central governments and other public bodies of the developed countries considered to be of high standing in the international financial markets.

- *Commercial banks.* These raise huge amounts on behalf of their customers in the markets.

- *Non-bank private sector institutions.* This is the main user group. Multinational companies are particularly evident in this area, raising funds through syndicated bank loans, Eurobonds and short-term paper.

11.19 We have already covered the advantages of using eurocurrency funds, e.g. fine interest rates, innovative debt instruments and flexibility of terms. However, as with suppliers of funds, users of funds have additional reasons for using the eurocurrency markets. *Central banks* have found them useful for the raising of funds without the unacceptable political ties and strict monetary conditions which often accompany borrowing from official sources. *Corporate borrowers* who are involved in international trade or overseas investment also find it convenient to be able to access huge amounts of internationally acceptable currencies. It also offers them an alternative source of funds when official restraints on borrowing in their home countries are in force.

11.20 Thus, you can see that the evolution of the eurocurrency markets will depend upon the progression of individual countries' financial systems and upon the growth of international trade. While the rapid rates of growth experienced 10 to 20 years ago are unlikely to be repeated, provided there is a need for these markets they will continue to play an important part on the international financial stage for the foreseeable future.

Student Activity 18

1. What is the particular advantage to a central bank of depositing reserves with the eurocurrency markets?   *(Paragraphs 11.16–17)*

2. Why are the eurocurrency markets popular with the commercial banks?
   (Paragraphs 11.16–18)

3. To what types of official institutions do the eurocurrency markets now tend to limit their lending?   *(Paragraph 11.18)*

4. Who are now the main borrowers in the eurocurrency markets?
   (Paragraph 11.18)

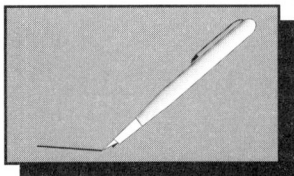

5. What are the advantages for central banks of raising funds through the eurocurrency markets? *(Paragraph 11.19)*

6. What are the advantages for corporate borrowers of raising funds through the eurocurrency markets? *(Paragraph 11.19)*

7. What broad factors are likely to affect the future prosperity of the eurocurrency markets? *(Paragraph 11.20)*

Eurocurrency interest rates

Influences on interest rates

11.21 Basically, interest rates on eurocurrency transactions are determined by the supply of and demand for eurocurrency funds. There are, however, four notable influences on those supply and demand conditions which have, over time, caused them to become major elements within the international financial system:

- Interest rates in the country from which the relevant currency originated.

- Previous lack of regulation.

- Higher levels of risk.

- Exchange controls.

11.22 The interest rates that apply within the country where the eurocurrency market is based will *not* be reflected in the rates applicable to a eurocurrency transaction. Rather, it is the *interest rates that apply in the country from which the relevant currency originated*. The reason for this is simply that, in order to obtain a foreign currency deposit, a bank must offer rates that are competitive with those quoted for deposits in that currency's country of origin. In addition, market forces and the possibility of arbitrage will guarantee comparability between rates. Hence, whatever factors are influencing the interest rates in the domestic market will also be influencing interest rates in the corresponding eurocurrency market for that currency. (These factors will be those which commonly determine the overall level of interest rates within an economy.)

11.23 The eurocurrency markets have until recently been largely *unregulated*. Liquidity and capital-adequacy ratios were not applied to eurocurrency activities and hence the banks involved could operate on narrower margins than applied to domestic business. Combined with the size of the transactions involved which enabled economies of scale to be generated, the result was that rates paid on eurocurrency deposits were higher and the rates charged on loans lower than on comparable domestic deposits and loans. This advantage has been eroded in recent years, however, by the trend towards the harmonisation of banking regulation throughout the world. The differentials between eurocurrency and comparable domestic interest rates have accordingly narrowed to some extent.

11.24 It is sometimes argued that the nature of the eurocurrency market activities means that the depositors of the funds are exposed to *higher levels of risk* than in comparable domestic markets. Although the increased regulation has reduced this extra risk, an element remains, which means that the higher rates paid on eurocurrency deposits are largely justified by the risk premium.

11.25 The existence of *exchange controls* in some form in a number of countries whose currencies are involved in the eurocurrency markets has meant that the differentials between domestic and eurocurrency rates have often been higher than would be justified by economic factors.

The links between foreign exchange rates and eurocurrency interest rates

11.26 Changes in eurocurrency interest rates are likely to have significant effects on the exchange rate of the currency involved. These effects may best be illustrated by following the consequences of a rise in, for example, eurosterling interest rates. Eurosterling deposits and loans are, you will recall, based *outside* the UK, and consequently represent foreign currency deposits and loans of banks in countries other than the UK. A rise in the level of eurosterling interest rates will lead, other things being equal, to a rise in the volume of eurosterling deposits. But the sterling will initially have to be obtained in order to make these eurosterling deposits, and consequently either bank balances denominated in other currencies or else assets denominated in other currencies will have to be sold and then switched into sterling using the foreign exchange markets in order to make the additional eurosterling deposits. The net result is that an increase in eurosterling interest rates will give rise to an increased demand for sterling on the spot exchange market, and hence to a *rise in the spot exchange rate.*

11.27 An appreciation of sterling on the spot foreign exchange market will not be the only effect, however; there will, other things being equal, be implications for the *forward* foreign exchange markets. The reason for this is that the relationship between spot and forward foreign exchange rates for a particular currency (that is, whether the forward exchange rate stands at a premium or a discount to the spot market) will depend on interest rates applicable to that currency relative to interest rates for other currencies. Again, the relationship can best be explained by means of an example. Suppose a bank based in the US undertakes to supply a customer with sterling in three months' time. In order to avoid the risk associated with this commitment to provide sterling in three months' time at a price agreed today, the bank will purchase the necessary sterling *now* on the spot market and then make a eurosterling deposit with three months to maturity. What the bank has in effect done is to convert a quantity of what would have been interest-bearing dollar assets into interest-bearing sterling assets (the eurosterling deposit). Now, if the interest rate on the eurosterling deposit is *higher* than could be achieved on the alternative dollar assets, plainly the bank is in an advantageous position – it is earning more on its assets – and hence it will be prepared to supply the sterling at a *lower* price (that is, at a discount) to the current spot price. The interest rate differential will therefore be reflected in the differential between spot and forward exchange rates (after taking account of the banks' administrative overheads). Alternatively, if the interest rate on the eurosterling deposit is *lower* than on the alternative dollar assets, the bank will charge a *premium* on the forward transaction in order to cover the interest rate differential. The existence of competition amongst the banks to supply currencies on a forward basis will ensure that any premiums or discounts are kept in line with interest-rate differentials.

11.28 With that principle in mind, you can see that if eurosterling interest rates were initially *below* those available for dollars, a rise in the eurosterling rates would *reduce the premium* on forward sterling sales. Similarly, if the eurosterling rates were initially *above* those available for dollars, a rise in the eurosterling rates would *increase the discount* on forward sterling sales. This analysis is, of course, on an 'other things being equal' basis; a change in eurocurrency rates may well be occasioned by changes in other economic variables which have an impact on exchange rates.

Student Activity 19

1. Broadly, what is the relationship between the rate of interest paid on euroyen deposits in London and interest rates paid on comparable yen deposits in Japan?
    (Paragraph 11.22)

2. For what reasons are rates of interest paid on eurocurrency deposits often higher than rates paid on comparable deposits in the country from where the currency in question originates?
    (Paragraphs 11.23–25)

3. What is likely to be the effect on the spot exchange rate for sterling of an increase in the eurosterling deposit rate?
    (Paragraph 11.26)

4. What is likely to be the effect on the forward exchange rate for sterling of an increase in the eurosterling deposit rate?
    (Paragraph 11.27)

12 Financial innovations as a stimulus

12.1 In the UK money markets, the first half of this century was extremely quiet. No new financial instruments were introduced after the treasury bill in the late 1870s until CDs were issued in the mid 1960s. However, the 1950s saw the launch of the parallel markets and the range of Eurocurrency markets. Since then, the pace of change has quickened, with SCP, MTNs and repos.

12.2 In the early 1970s, the Bretton Woods system of fixed exchange rates began to break up, and the resultant volatility was quietened by the introduction of financial derivatives.

12.3 Settlement is changing, in parallel with the growth of trading and the development of computers. Crest will be operative early in 1997, while the EU central banks are devising a new real-time clearing system called TARGET. Transactions will pass through central banks when they enter the system – real time – and not as a net figure after the close of business. The latter system is a relic of handwritten bookkeeping and is unlikely to survive the Millennium.

12.4 Crises do not affect the way in which markets operate as much as they can change policies and regulatory controls. 1931 caused the UK to change its monetary policy by leaving the gold standard and 1992 saw the UK rewriting its monetary policy after being forced out of the Exchange Rate Mechanism.

12.5 Technology is a prime mover of market methods, with computer-based trading taking over from face-to-face and telephone-based deals, especially in cash markets. However, 'open outcry' is still a feature in many derivative markets.

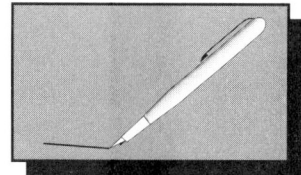

Student Activity 20

1. Assess the causes of change in cash financial markets.   *(Paragraphs 12.1–5)*

2. Construct a table along these lines, to show recent major changes in world financial markets. Use a separate sheet for each decade, in order to show as much detail as possible.

Decade	Event	Instrument	Market
1950s			
1960s			
1970s			
1980s			
1990s			

Appendix – classification of global financial markets

Internal (national) borrowers	*External (Eurocurrency international or offshore)*
Domestic market where domestic borrowers borrow in their national (domestic currencies	Where borrowers borrow in Eurocurrencies

Foreign market where foreign borrowers borrow in the national currency, e.g. Japan – Samurai; USA – Yankee; Netherlands – Rembrandt markets.

Example of borrowers and markets:

- UK company borrows sterling in London – domestic.
- UK company borrows guilders in Rotterdam – Rembrandt.
- UK company borrows US dollars in London – Eurocurrency.
- UK company borrows US dollars in New York – Yankee.

Note: some observers group the foreign and the external markets together.

Summary

After studying this unit you should be able to:

- **state the functions of financial markets;**

- **classify them and explain what is meant by the EMH;**

- **subdivide the UK wholesale sterling money markets into their various markets;**

- **describe the organisation of the London Stock Exchange and the problems which it has faced;**

- **distinguish between the equity and fixed-income (debt) markets;**

- **state the reasons for the growth of the eurocurrency markets**

- **examine the role of financial innovations on the markets and the financial instruments which are traded on them.**

Self-assessment questions

Short-answer questions

1. What types of transactions take place within the sterling money markets?

2. List the component parts of the sterling money markets.

3. Which institutions are the major players in the discount market?

4. What are the two broad reasons for Bank of England intervention in the discount market?

5. How does the Bank of England place upward pressure on short-term interest rates through its discount market intervention?

6. What is the Bank of England's objective in relation to the general structure of interest rates?

7. Why are transactions in the secondary sterling money market likely to be somewhat more risky than those within the primary money market?

8. What are the attractions of sterling certificates of deposit to an issuing bank?

9. What is the difference between primary and secondary capital market activities?

10. What types of securities are traded on the London Stock Exchange?

11. What must a company do in order to obtain a 'quotation' on the main market of the London Stock Exchange?

12. What is the difference between an offer for sale and a placing, in respect of shares traded on the London Stock Exchange?

13. What has been the importance of the structure of share ownership for the development of the London Stock Exchange in recent years?

14. Why was 'Big Bang' on the London Stock Exchange of such great importance to UK institutional investors?

15. What are eurocurrency bank deposits?

16. What has been the relevance of narrow operating margins to the growth of the eurocurrency markets?

17. What are the particular attractions of eurocurrency bank deposits to companies which operate internationally?

18 What has been the effect on the pattern of transactions in the eurocurrency markets of the Third World debt problem?

19. Why are interest rate margins on eurocurrency transactions often narrower than margins on comparable domestic transactions?

Multiple-choice questions

1. The London money markets
   (a) are concerned with the trading of currencies
   (b) are under the direct control of the Bank of England
   (c) exist via a network of communications linking participants
   (d) involve only the participation of banking institutions.
   (e) involve only the participation of money brokers.

2. An extremely important component of the London sterling money market structure is
   (a) the inter-bank market
   (b) the local authority market
   (c) the foreign exchange market
   (d) the Eurobond market.
   (e) the gilt-edged market.

3. An important function of the discount market is to
   (a) issue Treasury bills on behalf of the government
   (b) provide medium-term instalment credit to retail consumers
   (c) act as a buffer between the Bank of England and the commercial banks
   (d) make a market in long-dated gilt-edged securities.
   (e) link retail banks and building societies.

4. Bank of England intervention in the discount market
   (a) usually takes place in respect of bills within the band of maturity covering 64 to 91 days
   (b) involves inviting discount houses to buy or sell bills in specified bands at prices published in advance by the Bank
   (c) is solely concerned with manipulating short-term interest rates
   (d) involves inviting discount houses to make offers to buy or sell bills in specified bands, which the Bank is then free to accept or reject as it thinks fit.
   (e) occurs at 12 noon every day.

5. The sterling inter-bank market is of crucial significance to the clearing banks because

    (a) it sets base rates, relative to which all bank on-lending rates are fixed

    (b) it determines the marginal cost of funds to the banks

    (c) the prices of eligible bank bills are determined within this market

    (d) it is through this market that the Bank of England adjusts the amount of liquidity available to the banking system.

    (e) it is in this market where the Bank of England announces its Minimum Lending Rate to change banks' base rates.

6. The sterling commercial paper market

    (a) involves raising short-term funds which are effectively backed by outstanding debts arising from identifiable commercial transactions

    (b) involves the raising of funds with a minimum maturity of three months

    (c) poses a threat to the financial intermediation operations of banks by allowing certain companies to raise short-term funds at very fine rates

    (d) allows funds to be raised cheaply, as transactions are effectively underwritten by the Bank of England.

    (e) is declining, as a result of competition from the medium-term note market.

7. Capital market activity in the UK

    (a) relates to the raising of short-term funds by private and public sector organisations

    (b) involves the issue of both interest-bearing debt and equity claims on companies

    (c) does not involve transactions in Eurobonds

    (d) relates only to private sector debt instruments

    (e) relates to the raising of short-term and long-term debt.

8. A major difference between the money markets and the capital markets in the UK is that the money markets

    (a) operate via a communications network, whilst the capital markets involve face-to-face contact on the floor of the Stock Exchange

    (b) involve only private sector participation, whilst the capital markets involve both private and public sector participants

    (c) involve only UK-based organisations whilst the capital markets involve both UK-based and overseas-based organisations

    (d) relate to the raising of short-term finance, whilst the capital markets relate to long-term funding

    (e) the Bank of England operates only in the money markets.

9. A 'quotation' on the London Stock Exchange

    (a) means that the company concerned provides the London Stock Exchange regularly with required information about its operations

    (b) is the price set for the company's equity shares at any given time

    (c) is a seal of approval from the London Stock Exchange for the company's activities

    (d) means that the London Stock Exchange guarantees the resale value of the shares of the company concerned

    (e) means that current share prices appear on TV screens in peoples homes.

10. The former single-capacity trading system on the London Stock Exchange

    (a) was intended to control the income levels of the brokers and jobbers operating within the market

    (b) was vital to the ability of jobbers to meet large orders placed by institutional investors

    (c) was intended to promote a competitive market for securities and to protect investors from exploitation by London Stock Exchange firms

    (d) helped market participants to maintain their competitive position relative to firms based overseas

    (e) kept banks from providing facilities for buying and selling shares.

11. 'Big Bang' on the London Stock Exchange

    (a) involved major changes in the trading framework for gilt-edged securities

    (b) is the term used by the media to describe the London Stock Market collapse of October 1987

    (c) forced all London Stock Market firms to give up their single-capacity status and instead to become broker-dealers

    (d) was caused by amendments to the Banking Act 1979 which allowed non-financial companies to issue sterling commercial paper

    (e) resulted in the Banking Act 1987.

12. A major implication of the deregulation which occurred on the London Stock Exchange in March 1986 was that

    (a) it introduced single-capacity dealing as a means of protecting investors

    (b) for the first time Eurobonds could be traded on the London Stock Exchange

    (c) it allowed banking institutions to take full control of London Stock Exchange firms

    (d) foreign companies would in future be allowed to have their shares listed on the London Stock Exchange

    (e) it allowed UK banks to become members of continental stock exchanges.

13. Eurocurrency activity

    (a) never involves the borrowing and lending of sterling

    (b) always involves short-term borrowing and lending of foreign currencies

    (c) refers to foreign-currency-denominated borrowing and lending of wholesale funds

    (d) is related to the official transactions of the European Commission.

    (e) is involved in planning for the single currency.

14. Since the early 1980s, in relation to eurocurrency activities

    (a) the UK has become increasingly important

    (b) Europe as a whole has become increasingly important

    (c) Japan and Far Eastern offshore centres have become increasingly important

    (d) Japan and Far Eastern offshore centres have diminished in importance.

    (e) the former Soviet Union has become a leading player.

15. Transactions in the eurocurrency markets

    (a) are unsecured and rarely involve amounts of funds less than US$1m equivalent

    (b) are normally secured

    (c) always involve at least one participant based in a European country

    (d) never have an individual value in excess of US$1m.

    (e) are all controlled by the Bank for International Settlements.

16. Today the major users of eurocurrency funds are

    (a) UK local authorities

    (b) non-bank private sector institutions

    (c) central banks of developing countries

    (d) central banks of developed countries.

    (e) European central banks.

17. A major cause of the slowdown in the growth of the eurocurrency markets during the 1980s was

    (a) deregulation of banks operating in the USA

    (b) rapid fluctuations in the price of crude oil

    (c) the implementation of monetarist policies in many western nations

    (d) debt repayment problems faced by Third World countries.

    (e) a change in money market operating techniques by the Bank of England.

18. A reduction in the rate of interest paid on eurodollar deposits is likely to

    (a) cause the spot exchange rate for dollars to rise

    (b) cause an existing premium on forward purchases of dollars to rise

    (c) cause an existing discount on forward purchases of dollars to rise

    (d) leave the spot exchange rate for dollars unaffected unless other eurocurrency interest rates also alter.

    (e) leave all exchange rates unaltered, because Eurocurrencies are concerned with lending and borrowing and do not involve the foreign exchange market.

Unit 4

Derivative Instruments

Objectives

After studying this unit, you should be able to:

- **appreciate the significance of the financial derivatives markets;**

- **explain the role of derivative instruments;**

- **distinguish between futures and forward contracts;**

- **understand the role of the clearing house in a futures exchange;**

- **be aware of the importance of over-the-counter (OTC) derivatives markets;**

- **describe the basic features of options;**

- **understand the risk/reward relationships of call and put options;**

- **know what interest rate swaps are, and who uses them;**

- **describe the interest rate agreement market;**

- **examine the factors which affect the prices of:**
  - **futures**
  - **options;**

- **explain how arbitrage occurs between a derivatives market and the relevant cash market;**

- **construct very basic models for the pricing of:**
  - **futures**
  - **options.**

Note: If you have difficulty in understanding the complex nature of some of these instruments, you may wish to postpone further study of this unit until after Units 6 and 8, which cover interest rates, exchange rates and their 'cash markets'; these cash instruments form the bases from which many derivative instruments are derived.

1 What are derivatives?

1.1 Derivatives are contracts, with their own prices, involving rights and obligations relating to underlying purchases and sales of assets. In ordinary language, they are not the purchases and sales of, say, pigs and securities, but they are the buying and selling of rights and obligations to buy the pigs or securities.

1.2   These rights and obligations are related to – or, are derived from – the underlying transactions, so they have been given the general name of derivatives. However, they are separate from the underlying transactions. For instance, if a person agrees to buy pigs, he has to accept delivery of the animals and pay for them, but if he buys a right (but not the obligation) to buy pigs at a fixed price he can do one of several things:

●   Sell that right to another trader (for a profit);

●   Ignore it if he cannot sell it at a profit;

●   Exercise that right if the market price for pigs is higher than the fixed price under the right.

1.3   These rights and obligations are complex and can smooth out price changes in the underlying assets – on the cash market as it is often termed. However, speculators are very active in derivative markets and unwitting investors can make substantial losses. Barings, the UK's oldest merchant bank, had to cease business as a result of unauthorised derivatives trading by one of its dealers.

1.4   For there to be a derivatives market, the cash market needs to be liquid – easy to trade in without moving the price of an asset (although prices can change for other reasons) – and volatile. By volatile is meant 'changeable in price'. If the price is unmovable then there is no opportunity to make a short-term profit by trading in that asset. Moreover, if a market is illiquid then there will also not be much demand for that asset.

1.5   Strictly, forward contracts are not derivatives, because they involve the delivery or acceptance of the underlying asset (pigs or shares) at the end of the period and cannot be bought or sold. However, futures are derivatives, because once they have been agreed they can be bought and sold. So, we can identify (or list) some of the major types of derivatives, in order to become familiar with their names:

●   Futures;

●   Options;

●   Swaps;

●   Interest rate agreements.

2 Origins of derivatives

2.1   Although some historians have identified financial derivatives as being used over 350 years ago in the great Dutch tulip mania of 1634, the fact remains that they really began in Chicago in the early 1970s.

Why Chicago?

2.2   Nearly 150 years ago, the great plains of the American Mid-West were opened up to markets on the East Coast of the USA and in Europe by railways and steamships, and Chicago became the great trading centre for farm products, especially wheat and meat. Farmers were selling their produce and merchants were buying; both groups wanted stable prices – a forlorn hope, given the weather and the risk of disease. The least they could achieve was less volatility – less instability. Gradually, a futures market developed, trading in standard units of defined size and quality, so that the only variable was the price. The farmers and merchants were joined by hedgers – traders who would seek to iron out price differences and so reduce volatility.

2.3   As well as standard units, Chicago developed the idea of a clearing house, which vetted traders and positioned itself as a party to every deal. Farmers, merchants and hedgers thus dealt with the clearing house, rather than with each other, once they had agreed the deals. This 'interposition' of the clearing house virtually eliminated counterparty risk.

Why the 1970s?

2.4   Until then, there was little need for financial derivatives, because the volatility of exchange rates and interest rates had been limited by a number of factors.

2.5   With the exception of the First World War, exchange rates had been linked to the gold standard until the early 1930s, when many countries devalued their currencies. While this caused exchange rates to become more volatile, the world recession meant that the number of transactions fell. Moreover, the outbreak of the Second World War meant that countries wanted a return to exchange rate stability, using narrow bands within which exchange rates could fluctuate. This exchange-rate stability was known as the Bretton Woods regime and lasted until 1973.

2.6   Once the gold standard had broken down in the early 1930s, economists began to advocate the use of taxation and government spending as the instruments of economic policy. These became the orthodox policy variables, and not interest rates. Hence, while this policy remained unchallenged in the 1950s and 1960s, exchange rates were fairly stable, as were interest rates.

The breakdown of the Bretton Woods parities and the resurgence of monetary policy

2.7   In 1971, the US devalued the dollar against gold, from $35 an ounce to $38 an ounce, while the Bretton Woods 'bands' were widened from 1% either way to 2.25% each way. The world was experiencing a major boom, causing stresses and strains in the financial system. In 1973 the USA floated the dollar against gold, and many other countries also floated their currencies. The era of financial volatility had begun, and the world was booming. This scenario was very different to the 1930s, when the world was in deep recession.

2.8   There was thus a need for derivatives – futures and options – to reduce the instability (volatility) of exchange rates. Moreover, interest rates and exchange rates often move together, so that interest rates also became more volatile and new financial derivatives were devised – swaps, collars and caps.

2.9   At that time, economists began to place less importance on taxation and government spending and more importance on the quantity of money and its price – interest rates – as methods of achieving full employment and price stability. Thus, interest rates could now become more volatile as a result of policy decisions by central banks and politicians.

2.10 Other factors helped the development of financial derivatives at that time. Computers had become widely available to help with complex pricing calculations and mathematicians had devised a pricing model for option contracts. Until then, most derivatives had been futures contracts, because options were so complex. Moreover, computers and telexes made global trading possible – 24 hours a day, for five days each week.

2.11 Thus, there was a need for financial derivatives, the equipment – hardware and software – was there, and Chicago had a century of experience in commodity derivatives (largely futures). In May 1972, the Chicago Mercantile Exchange began trading in seven major currencies, in its International Monetary Market division.

Student Activity 1

1. Distinguish between a derivative and the underlying transaction in the cash market   *(Paragraphs 1.1–2).*

2. Explain why financial derivatives began in Chicago in the early 1970s.
                                                                (Paragraphs 2.2–11)

3. Why did they not begin in the currency upheavals of the 1930s depression?
                                                                (Paragraph 2.5)

4. Why do business people dislike uncertainty?

5. Why were exchange rates and interest rates fairly stable after the end of the Second World War?   *(Paragraph 2.5–6)*

6. Name some of the various types of financial derivatives.   *(Paragraph 1.5)*

7. Why should there be liquidity and volatility in the cash market before a derivative can be created?   *(Paragraph 1.4)*

3 Functions of derivatives

3.1 First, they give investors a *choice of location* where they can alter their portfolios of assets because, if there were no derivatives, the only market where these portfolios could be changed would be the cash market. Thus, investors can chose to alter their holdings of derivatives or underlying assets if new information makes them alter their opinions of the attraction of certain financial assets relatively to others. In other words, derivatives enable investors to change their risk exposure at lower cost.

3.2 The market in which investors will make these changes will be the cheaper or cheapest. And this cheaper market is hardly likely to be the cash market because dealings there involve settlement of the full transaction including delivery or receipt of the asset in question. The derivatives market is also likely to be cheaper for other reasons, such as:

● Liquidity;

● Transactions costs;

● Taxes (stamp duty especially);

● The gearing (leverage) which is possible with derivatives.

3.3   Thus, it is likely that the derivatives market will act as the 'price discovery' market, from which signals are sent to the other market – on this argument, the cash market. The derivatives market clarifies investors' opinions about spot prices, i.e. prices in the cash market, in the months ahead. It also enables investors to protect the values of their portfolios more cheaply.

3.4   The link between the cash market and the derivatives market is a process of buying and selling between the two, known as *arbitrage* – buying in one market or city and selling in another. If purchases are made in the cheaper market and sales are achieved in the higher market, then the purchases will tend to raise prices and the sales will tend to lower them, with the result that price differences will diminish.

3.5   Derivatives provide opportunities for three different kinds of investors:

● Hedgers;

● Arbitrageurs;

● Speculators.

3.6   *Hedgers* wish to avoid risks by eliminating as much as is possible the likelihood of price change. For this certainty, they are prepared to pay a cost. Obviously, if all traders were hedgers, then the chances of finding counterparties (people to trade with) would be linked to finding people who had opposite opinions as to the course of prices in the next year or so. Fortunately, derivative markets attract other types of traders, who seek profit rather than stability or certainty.

3.7   *Arbitrageurs* buy cheaply, sell dearly. Thus, if all the hedgers were selling, the arbitrageurs would become buyers, causing prices to move upwards from the lower levels resulting from the sales of the hedgers. The arbitrageurs would then try and sell in dearer markets, moving prices downwards. They seek a risk-less profit.

3.8   *Speculators* are attracted to risk, unlike hedgers and arbitrageurs. Speculators seek exposure and take up positions, i.e. over-bought or oversold, seeking not a small risk-less profit but the chance of a greater profit resulting from the greater risk to which they are exposed.

3.9   Speculators, in turn, can be grouped into various categories:

● *Scalpers*, who go short or long (run a position) for no more than a few minutes;

● *Day traders*, running a position during a single day, and not overnight in case the price changes substantially;

● *Position traders*, who hold excess instruments (or go short extensively) for longer periods, in the hope that they will profit from substantial price changes.

Student Activity 2

1. Describe the aims of the three types of investors in financial derivatives.
(Paragraphs 3.6–9)

2. What determines whether the cash or the derivatives market is the 'price discovery market'? *(Paragraph 3.2)*

3. What is meant by taking a 'position'? *(Paragraph 3.8)*

4. Why don't some investors wish to take 'positions'? *(Paragraphs 3.6–7)*

4 Derivatives markets

4.1 There are two types of markets in derivative instruments – exchange-based markets, such as LIFFE, and over-the-counter (OTC) markets.

Exchange-based markets and clearing houses

4.2 These were the first markets to be developed and are highly organised and regulated by their owners, who are usually the traders. It is the exchange which decides on the:

- Standard units – currency, size, maturity – to be traded, and the times when trading begins and ceases each day.

- Rules of the *clearing house*, through which all deals are routed, with the result that a deal between (say) X who sells to Y becomes a deal between X selling to the clearing house which in turn sells to Y. Conversely, Y pays the clearing house who pays X (irrespective of whether Y pays the clearing house or X delivers to the clearing house). The clearing house interposes itself between all counterparties, thereby shouldering the burden of default and lessening the risk. In effect, it standardises the counterparty, just as deals are for standard products; it also facilitates delivery.

- *Margining* requirements, which all members have to deposit with the clearing house, to ensure that default is unlikely. In addition, all investors must maintain margins with their brokers who are, of course, members of the exchange. The two types of margin are calculated slightly differently on the value of futures contracts traded on the exchange.

  Moreover, margins are calculated slightly differently in the USA to the way in which they are calculated in the UK, where they comprise (at LIFFE):

  Investor (maintained with broker).

  - initial margin

  - variation margin (lower than the initial margin) recalculated daily (marked to market).

  Broker (maintained with clearing house).

  - *variation margin* (often with sales/purchases netted) which is recalculated daily (marked to market).

4.3 *Marking to market* is a daily process by which all outstanding deals are revalued daily, because prices change so frequently. In other words, historic pricing/costing is not used because prices charge every minute, i.e. they are volatile. Marking to market is done by the clearing house for all the exchange's members and, again, by the members who act as brokers. The latter 'mark to market' all their transactions with their clients.

4.4 In London, most derivatives exchanges are members of the London Clearing House. They include:

- LIFFE – London International Financial Futures and Options Exchange;

- London Metal Exchange;

- London Commodity Exchange (formerly London FOX – Futures and Options Exchange). On 16 September 1996, this became the Commodity Products Division of LIFFE.

- The International Petroleum Exchange.

(Note: the London Clearing House is not the cheque and credit clearing system. It is currently owned by six large UK banks, but it is planned to transfer ownership to the traders and the participating exchanges.)

4.5 The two largest derivative exchanges in the world are the Chicago Mercantile Exchange and the Chicago Board of Trade. LIFFE is the world's third largest, closely followed by MATIF in Paris and DTB in Frankfurt.

4.6 Deals on exchanges are 'open outcry' (face-to-face) or electronic (Automated Pit Trading is the LIFFE name for it). LIFFE has both types of dealing – open outcry in the day and APT in the late afternoon – for most of its contracts.

Student Activity 3

1. What risk does the use of standard trading units on exchange-based markets eliminate? *(Paragraph 4.2)*

2. What risk is removed by the clearing house in a derivatives exchange? *(Paragraph 4.2)*

3. What is meant by 'margining'? *(Paragraph 4.2)*

4. What is meant by 'marking to market'? *(Paragraph 4.3)*

5. Name two commodity derivatives exchanges. *(Paragraph 4.4)*

6. Name four financial derivatives exchanges. *(Paragraph 4.5)*

OTC markets

4.7 The world's largest OTC market is a cash market – the foreign exchange market, based in the world's financial centres. There is no official membership, banks deal with each other by phone, fax and computer; regulation is undertaken by each country's regulator and co-ordinated by the Bank for International Settlements. Although a cash market, there are also large numbers of deals in derivatives in the foreign exchange market.

Bank of England Grey Book markets

4.8 This is the working name given to the OTC derivatives markets spawned in London by the banks in the foreign exchange market. The 'Grey Book' is the

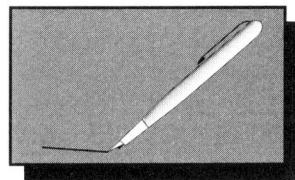

popular name for the Bank of England rules governing those professional investors in the wholesale money markets dealing with financial instruments not covered by the Financial Services Act 1986, whether by omission or by express exemption.

4.9 The Bank of England publishes the *London Code of Conduct*, detailing a code of best practice for a range of financial instruments. Some are cash – wholesale deposits, spot and forward foreign exchange – but others are derivatives, including:

- Options;
- Forward rate agreements (contracts for differences);
- Interest rate and currency swaps;
- Sale and repurchase agreements.

4.10 OTC markets are characterised by the existence of *quote vendors*, providing real-time price information on computer screens. Firms providing this service include:

- Reuters;
- Bloomberg News Service;
- Knight Ridder.

Quote vendors also link into the exchange markets, so providing a comprehensive price information service. They get their OTC prices from dealers in the markets.

4.11 As well as the Bank of England Grey Book Markets, London is host to two other OTC derivatives markets – in oil and base metals.

Advantages of OTC markets
4.12 These are that:

- Investors obtain a contract which is tailored exactly to their required quantity (amount) and maturity, unlike an exchange's standard contract.
- It is argued that the impact of deals on prices is more gentle than on an exchange where liquidity is said to be more 'concentrated'.
- The supervision by central banks and regulators lessens some of the risk arising from the absence of regulation by an exchange, especially when a highly-rated bank interposes itself as a counterparty in a currency or interest-rate swap.

Disadvantages of OTC markets
4.13 The important ones are that:

- There is no clearing house to eliminate counterparty risk;
- There is no daily margining.
- Documentation can be more complex than on an exchange.
- Prices can be less transparent than on an exchange, although quote vendors provide as much information as possible – at a price.

Student Activity 4

1. What is an OTC market? *(Paragraph 4.7)*

2. What are quote vendors? *(Paragraph 4.10)*

3. What is the Bank of England Grey book? *(Paragraph 4.8)*

4. What derivatives are traded in OTC markets? *(Paragraph 4.9)*

5. What are the advantages of OTC markets? *(Paragraph 4.12)*

6. What are the disadvantages of OTC markets? *(Paragraph 4.13)*

5 Forwards and futures

5.1 A forward contract is 'physical' in that the parties agree *now* on a price to be paid on a mutually acceptable date for the delivery of an agreed quantity on that date. An example from the foreign exchange market might be for A to agree on 31 July 1996 to sell to B £257,000 worth of DM on 31 January 1997 at a rate of (say) DM 2.3746. Both parties will build these amounts into their cash flows because they have every intention of honouring their contract. They have bought certainty – the exchange rate – because nobody knows what the spot rate will be. As will be seen from Unit 8, the forward rate is not a forecast of the spot rate for the end of January, but it is the spot rate on the day the contract was concluded which has been adjusted for the different interest rates obtaining on that day for the period until settlement.

5.2 *Forward* contracts have a number of distinctive features:

- The *amounts can be tailored to suit the parties' needs*, although periods in excess of one year may be hard to obtain – contracts are said to be 'personalised'.

- *There is no secondary market*: they are highly illiquid and the parties are 'stuck' with them.

- The only occasion when cash actually flows is *on delivery.*

- If one party cannot deliver from stock, then they must *buy the commodity* (or currency) on the spot market in order to honour the forward contract.

- There is a *risk of default*, because the contract is often agreed on an OTC market.

- Both parties expect the mutual obligations to be honoured.

5.3 In effect, although a forward contract 'looks to the future', it is not a derivative instrument because it resembles a cash contract with a very long delivery date. Nothing of any substance – no right or obligation – can be 'derived' from the underlying contract.

5.4 *Futures*, on the other hand, are very different from forwards, because they:

- Have standard terms, which are not negotiable between the parties.

- Can be sold and bought in their own right in a secondary market.

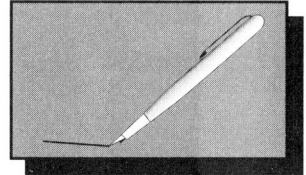

- Are not usually intended to be delivered – in the USA 98% of future contracts are sold or offset before delivery.

- Are usually offset, e.g. a purchase by a sale, or vice versa, before delivery.

- Come within the scope of the Financial Services Act 1986 if they are traded:

    ○ on a recognised investment exchange

    ○ for investment purposes on an OTC market;

- Involve cash flows from the outset, because of margining requirements.

- Have an element of gearing as result of the need to deposit this margin.

5.5   This gearing makes futures trading very attractive to investors, because most futures deals occur on exchange markets where margining is compulsory. This limits the amount of cash which has to be spent on the initial transaction. Also, marking to market keeps investors aware of price changes and the clearing house minimises counterparty risk. Another reason why futures tend to be traded on exchanges is that both parties are obligated to each other, with a symmetric risk/reward ratio.

Student Activity 5

1. Define a forward contract.   *(Paragraphs 5.1 to 5.3)*

2. Define a futures contract.   *(Paragraph 5.4)*

3. Compare and contrast forward and futures contracts under these headings:
   (a) Cash outlays;
   (b) Nature of contract;
   (c) Delivery;
   (d) Trading in a secondary market;
   (e) Liquidity;
   (f) Gearing.   *(Paragraph 5.4)*

4. What are the attractions of futures for investors?   *(Paragraph 5.5)*

5. Explain the phrase 'symmetric risk/reward ratio'.   *(Paragraph 5.5)*

6   Futures contracts

6.1   These are two-way contracts, obligating both parties – the buyer has a duty to pay the price and the seller has a duty to deliver the commodity or the asset. Most futures are traded on exchanges, and financial futures can be grouped under four headings:

- Stock index futures;

- Interest rate futures (short-term);

- Long-term interest rate (bond) futures;

- Currency futures.

Stock index futures

6.2 In the UK, LIFFE trades the FT-SE 100 index at £25 x index. This means that, if the index is 3,750 then one contract costs £93,750 (£25 x 3,750). At a 3% margin, the initial cash outlay is £2812.50. There is always a choice of three delivery months – the nearest three of March, June, September and December. In November, for example, investors can buy futures expiring in December, March and June (but not September). Delivery is the third Friday in the delivery month, e.g. 21 March 1997, and, because replicating the 100 companies securities in the exact proportion is well-nigh impossible, delivery is in cash. There is also a futures contract on the FT-SE Mid 250 index.

Interest rate futures (short-term)

6.3 LIFFE provides futures in the following three-month Eurocurrency interest rates – Eurodollars, Eurolira, Euro Swiss Francs, Euroyen – as well as ECUs. The final reference interest rate (on settlement day) is obtained from the British Bankers' Association. Settlement is by cash.

6.4 For sterling there is a three-month LIFFE future available for five quarters ahead, e.g. in August, for September, December, March, June and September. The contract size is £500,000; settlement is by cash and the price is quoted at 100 less the interest rate. For example, on 1 August 1996, when base rate was 5.75%, the September 96 price was 94.26. The September 1997 price was 93.12, implying a base rate of 6.88% for that month.

Long-term interest rate (bond) futures

6.5 The LIFFE long-gilt future is based on a £50,000 nominal value notional gilt with a 9% coupon. Delivery is physical, from a list of suitable gilts published by LIFFE. In addition, there are a number of futures in foreign government bonds. At expiry, the futures price of the bond will equal the cash price, so that futures prices tend to forecast interest rates.

Currency futures

6.7 Here the leading exchange is the IMM (part of the Chicago Mercantile Exchange) and the FT publishes the prices of its DM, yen, Swiss franc and sterling futures on the Currencies and Money page. In August 1996, delivery was for September, December and March.

6.8 Great competition for currency futures comes from the foreign exchange (= OTC) market, although LIFFE also trades futures in the four currencies named above, plus the DM against the US dollar.

Open interest and trading volume

6.9 There are two indicators of business traded in futures markets:

- *Open interest* is the number of contracts still open at any one time, i.e. not closed or offset by an opposite trade.

- *Trading volume* is the total of contracts traded over a period, e.g. a day, week or month.

Student Activity 6

1. Examine the reasons why futures are usually exchange-market traded derivatives.
   (Paragraph 5.5)

2. Identify the types of financial futures contracts.   *(Paragraph 6.1)*

3. Define the term 'open interest'.   *(Paragraph 6.9)*

4. How does it differ from 'trading volume'?   *(Paragraph 6.9)*

5. In the lists of LIFFE and IMM futures contracts, no mention was made of France, where MATIF dominates the French Franc and interest rate futures contracts. Why is this so? Is it chauvinism/nationalism? *(Clues: little time differences; liquid markets)*

7   Options

Differences between options and futures

7.1   We have mentioned above (paragraph 5.5) that futures had a symmetric risk/reward ratio. However, options do not, because they are equivalent to 'one-way bets'. Their risk/reward ratio is asymmetrical – which is very useful to investors seeking to hedge either a cash flow and/or an equity shareholding. In effect, the buyer of an option buys a right but not an obligation: it is up to the buyer what he does with the option – exercises it, sells it or lets it lapse.

7.2   The original seller of an option – the writer as he is known – is in a very different position. He is at the whim of the owner – if the owner exercises the option the writer must honour it. However, he does keep the price paid to him by the buyer.

7.3   On the expiry of a future, the contract has to be either honoured or offset by another future expiring on that day. Another difference in the USA between the two forms of derivatives is that margining occurs against futures but not against options. The reason is that cash passes immediately the option is written and sold to the buyer. However, LIFFE does require margining for options, although only initial margins.

7.4   To give an example of the risk which can be hedged against by an option: many investors might think that share prices would fall in the run-up to the next general election. So, they do not buy a future; they buy an option, possibly on the FT-SE 100. They buy a put option, which enables them to sell at a certain price (say) 3,750 if they so wish. Their cost is the price of one option; their reward is the sale at 3,750. The risk is asymmetric – people believe the index is more likely to fall than rise, but they cannot be certain.

7.5   For the buyers of such options, the most they can lose is their purchase price; for the sellers, the most they can gain is that same purchase price (their sales price). It is very lopsided (asymmetric).

American and European options

7.6   It is very easy to remember the difference between these two types of options:

- American options can be exercised at any time during the life of the option: American = A = Any time.

- European options can be exercised only at the end of their life, i.e. on expiry: European = E = End/Expiry.

Call options

7.7 These enable the buyer of the option the right (not the duty) to buy the asset at a stated price, known as the exercise price, i.e. call the asset from the market. The exercise price is also known as the strike price. The price paid for this option – a price which varies considerably during its life – is the option price (or premium, as it is sometimes called).

Put options

7.8 These enable the buyer of the option the right (not the duty) to sell the asset at the exercise price, i.e. put the asset into the market. It, too, has a change-able option price (premium).

'Trading of volatility'

7.9 This phrase is sometimes used to describe the role of options in derivative markets. Options enable price changes to be used by hedgers, arbitrageurs and speculators. Hedgers seek protection and minimal risk, arbitrageurs seek small profits and slightly more risk while speculators seek greater profit and face greater risk. Options enable 'volatility to be traded'.

Financial instruments on which options are traded

7.10 Options are available on many cash and derivative financial instruments – on equity share prices, equity indices, cash markets, swaps and even futures, to name but a few.

Equity options

7.11 Once known as 'traded options', the market in these moved from the London Stock Exchange to LIFFE in 1990. These are available for some 70 shares, with new ones being added occasionally, as with Railtrack in May 1996.

7.12 The exercise prices are determined by LIFFE; units are of 1,000 shares and the options are American-style. Prices are published in the London Equities section of the World Stock Markets page of the *Financial Times*. For instance, on 1 August 1996, LIFFE had exercise prices of 330 and 360 for options on Lloyds-TSB Group plc ordinary shares. On 2 August (a Friday) the share price (spot market price) rose to 354p (a new high for the share) and so, on Monday 5 August, LIFFE introduced a higher exercise price of 390.

7.13 The range of exercise prices is also determined by LIFFE, and varies according to the price of the underlying share, e.g. a share trading at 500p is likely to have equity options available at 50p intervals – 500 and 550 – whereas a share priced at about 100p is likely to have options with 10p intervals.

7.14 Each of the 70-odd shares is allocated to one of three-monthly cycles – January, April etc; February, May etc or March, June etc. Delivery is physical, i.e. the actual shares.

Equity indices

7.15 LIFFE has two options on the FT-SE 100 index – one American and one European style. Both are virtually identical. Each point is valued at £10 (£25 is the value of each point of the future).

7.16 Other LIFFE options are:

- Short sterling;
- 3-month Eurodollars;
- 3-month Euromark;
- Long gilt;
- German government bond;
- US Treasury bond;
- Italian government bond.

Student Activity 7

1. Distinguish between American and European options. *(Paragraph 7.6)*

2. Distinguish between 'put' and 'call' options. *(Paragraphs 7.6–8)*

3. What is the meaning of the statement 'Options enable volatility to be traded'? *(Paragraph 7.9)*

4. Why are options riskier than futures? *(Paragraphs 7.1–5)*

8 Interest rate swaps

8.1 Swaps are private agreements between two parties to exchange cash flows on a notional principal for some future period according to some prearranged formula. In effect, these are portfolios of forward contracts for any length of time from two to 15 years. Interest-rate swaps began in 1981. The simplest form of swap – and the most common – is a 'plain vanilla' swap of a fixed rate of interest for a floating rate on the same notional principal for a given period and in the same currency. The payments from one party to the other are net, not gross.

8.2 The reason why this swap is profitable to both parties is that one has a greater comparative advantage than the other in one of the markets – fixed or floating rates of interest on securities. A company either seeking new money will go to that market – with fixed or floating rates of interest – in which it has the greatest comparative advantage. However, this may not be the type of finance it needs – for instance, it may require fixed-rate finance but it can borrow relatively more cheaply on a floating rate of interest.

8.3 It is not just the case of borrowing at a fixed rate of interest and swapping with a floating rate but rather that the global financial market has imperfections so that some borrowers can get better deals in some markets than can their competitors. So borrowers search out the best deals and, if the loan product is not to their liking, they will also seek out an interest rate swap – a bit of 'financial customising'.

8.4 Interest rate swaps enable financial intermediaries to change the cash flows of their assets and liabilities, converting from fixed to floating and vice versa. This enables them to market their loans in the most attractive form desired by their customers, e.g. fixed rate mortgages and yet preserve their profitability by swapping their liabilities' cash flows from floating to fixed.

8.5 The basic format of the transaction is:

- A borrows at his best rate
- B borrows at his best rate
- A & B swap the interest rates, using the notional principal, but still paying their original lenders.

8.6 Consider this arithmetical example:

Dogger Bank – needs fixed rate funds for 10 years.
Cucumber plc – needs floating rate funds for 10 years.

We can demonstrate their borrowing choices in this table

UK domestic market	Eurosterling market	Quality spread
Dogger Bank 8.5% fixed	Cucumber 9.0% fixed	50 bps
Cucumber plc LIBOR + 80 bps	Dogger LIBOR + 20 bps	60 bps

So Dogger:

- Borrows £1m at LIBOR + 20 bps, in the Eurosterling market where it has the greater comparative advantage; and
- Swaps into (say) 8.7% fixed.

Cucumber:

- Borrows £1m at 9.0% fixed, in the Eurosterling market where it has the lesser comparative disadvantage;
- Swaps at LIBOR + 45 bps.

8.7 Dogger Bank:

Pays	LIBOR + 20 bps	(original loan)	(1)
+	8.7% fixed (swap)		(2)
=	8.7% + LIBOR + 20 bps	(total payments)	(1) + (2)

Receives	LIBOR + 45 bps (swap)		(3)
=	8.7% – 25 bps (fixed)	(net payments)	((1) + (2)) – (3)
=	8.45% (fixed)		

8.8 Cucumber plc:

Pays	9.0% fixed	(original loan)	(1)
+	LIBOR + 45 bps (swap)		(2)
=	9.0% + LIBOR + 45 bps	(total payments)	(1) + (2)
Receives	8.7%	(swap)	(3)
=	0.3% + LIBOR + 45 bps		((1) + (2)) – (3)
=	LIBOR + 30 bps + 45 bps		
=	LIBOR + 75 bps	(which is cheaper than LIBOR + 80 bps)	

So both have profited.

8.9 A number of reasons have been given for the rapid growth of this market to several $trillons in about 15 years – credit arbitrage, with some markets preferring certain types of debt instruments and becoming segmented; prudential regulations requiring matching of domestic liabilities in domestic markets, different tax regimes; greater volatility in interest rates, in so far as changes are more frequent.

Primary market

8.10 This is an OTC market comprising the world's leading retail and investment banks, and is regulated by their regulators and the Bank for International Settlements, helped by the International Swap Dealers Association (ISDA). Many banks have moved from being mere intermediaries to becoming principals: in effect, they add their names to deals in this OTC market, in a somewhat similar way in which the clearing house eliminates counterparty risk on a derivatives exchange. The leading banks have their own master agreements, often drafted in consultation with the ISDA, and bringing uniform practice into operation.

Secondary market

8.11 This is a growing OTC market and offers such contracts as:

- Swap reversals, with identical details for the remaining period of the original swap but with a different price and counterparty. The problem is that the 'reversing' party now has two counterparties and thus greater default risk.

- Swap sales or swap assignments ensure that the new counterparty takes over the seller's liability to the old counterparty, who has to agree to the substitution.

- Buy-backs (close-out sales or cancellations) are where the swap is sold back to the original counterparty.

Student Activity 8

1. Describe an interest rate swap. *(Paragraphs 8.2 and 8.6)*

2. What makes such a swap attractive to both parties? *(Paragraph 8.3)*

3. When does money change hands in an interest-rate swap? *(Paragraph 8.2)*

4. Outline the primary market for these derivatives. *(Paragraph 8.1)*

5. How can parties to such a swap get out of their obligations by trading in the secondary market? *(Paragraph 8.11)*

9 Interest rate agreements

9.1 These are made between two parties when one, in return for an immediate premium, agrees to recompense the other if a designated interest rate (the reference rate) exceeds or falls below a stated level (the strike rate). There are three generic types:

- Cap, where the reference rate must not exceed the strike rate.

- Ceiling, when the reference rate must not drop below the strike rate.

● Collar, which comprises a cap and a ceiling. The party requiring to be compensated buys a cap and sells a ceiling.

9.2 Settlement is made, if necessary, once every six months during the agreement and payments relate to a notional stated principal. It is possible to buy options in caps and ceilings.

9.3 Forward rate agreements (FRAs) are interest rate agreements which begin not now but at some time in the future. Pricing is based on rates in the futures market (there often is one) or from the yield curve for cash deposits. Using the yield curve involves comparing the 3-month rate with the 6-month rate to get the 3-month forward rate for months 4, 5 and 6 (expressed as 3 × 6 FRA) as described in Unit 6.

Student Activity 9

1. Examine how a building society might wish to use interest rate swaps.
   (Paragraph 9.1)

2. Describe how people borrowing on mortgages would wish to purchase an interest rate cap.
   (Paragraph 9.1)

3. How do banks help to make the interest-rate swap market (which is an OTC market) more like an exchange market.
   (Paragraph 8.10)

4. When are there cash flows (and which way) in an interest rate agreement?
   (Paragraphs 9.1–2)

5. Explain what a FRA is.
   (Paragraph 9.3)

10 Pricing of futures

10.1 To give 'supply and demand' as the answer to a question seeking the factors determining the price of a futures contract is, unfortunately, far too elementary. Such an answer needs to examine the underlying costs and incomes resulting from trading in derivatives and these are different as between futures and options. Moreover, with futures prices, these converge to the cash price as the delivery date approaches, with the futures contract eventually merging into a cash contract for spot delivery.

10.2 The costs involved in trading are the:
   ● Cost of the underlying asset;
   ● Cost of borrowing the purchase price of the underlying asset.

10.3 The rewards/incomes involved in trading are the:
   ● Proceeds of the sale of the underlying asset;
   ● Cash yield (dividends, interest) received by the owner of the asset during the futures contract.

10.4 The next stage of the process is to use what are called 'arbitrage arguments', examining the arbitrage profits (losses) arising from given prices. The equilib-

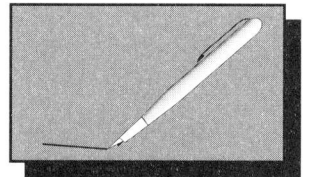

rium price is where there is zero profit/loss possible from risk-free arbitrage (buying or selling between the cash and futures markets). The arbitrage strategies are simple.

Either (argument 1):

● Buy the futures contract now;

● Sell the asset now on the cash market;

● Invest the sale proceeds until the futures contract matures;

or (argument 2):

● Sell the futures contract now;

● Buy the asset now on the cash market;

● Borrow the money to finance this cash purchase.

10.5 One way of presenting a simple (ignoring spreads and back-office costs) formula is:

Futures price = Price of asset (cash) + Price of asset (cash) (% cost of finance – less % yield from asset)

If the asset costs £100 and finance is at 6% and the asset yield is 7%, then:

$$Price = 100 + 100(0.06 - 0.07)$$
$$= 100 + 100(-0.01)$$
$$= 100 - 1$$
$$= 99$$

10.6 This formula involves percentages, and can be restated as the 'cost of carry' model which is:

Futures price = Spot price + Carry costs – Carry return

Using the data in the previous example gives (in £):

$$= 100 + 6 - 7$$
$$= 99$$

10.7 We mentioned that this is a simple model, ignoring such factors as:

● The cash flows from dividends and interest payments which are reinvested at varying dates and at unknown rates of interest.

● Transactions costs, including margining.

● Price restrictions imposed by exchanges and markets on selling short.

● The futures contract may give a choice of delivery instruments (as with the LIFFE long gilts future) or a choice of delivery dates.

● There may be a spread of interest rates, so that the arbitrage argument for selling the futures contract involves a higher cost of carry than the carry return yielded by selling the asset now and buying the futures.

● The taxation treatment of futures transactions may be different from cash transactions.

Student Activity 10

1. What are the underlying factors which determine the price of a futures contract?
   (Paragraphs 10.2–3)

2. Explain the two 'arbitrage arguments' used to determine the equilibrium price.
   (Paragraph 10.4)

3. State the pricing formula in its two forms:　　　*(Paragraphs 10.5–6)*
   (a) In percentage terms
   (b) In monetary terms.

4. What is meant by:　　　*(Paragraphs 10.6–7)*
   (a) cost of carry;
   (b) carry return.

5. In what ways do the actual prices of futures differ from those calculated by a model?　　　*(Paragraph 10.7)*

11　The pricing of options

11.1　This is more complex than the pricing of futures but it does involve 'arbitrage arguments'. However, there are some complicated mathematical models described in more advanced textbooks, and these will be mentioned in the next section.

11.2　The price of an option involves two elements – an intrinsic value which can be nil or higher, and time value (sometimes called a time premium). The intrinsic value can never be negative, i.e. less than nil. Here we use equity options, once known as traded options.

In the money/out of the money

11.3　These two terms describe the relationship between the current (spot or market) price of the asset and the exercise price. If the market price is higher than the exercise price then the option is 'in the money'. If the market price is lower than the exercise price then the option is 'out of the money'. If both prices are equal, then the option is 'at the money'.

Intrinsic value

11.4　For a *call option* this is the current price of the asset (the underlying price) less the strike (or exercise) price. Thus, on 6 August 1996, for a call option at 160 for August on Hanson (share price of 156) the intrinsic value was 156 less 160 = NIL (not –4). Another example on the same day was a 240 February 97 call on Railtrack (share price 226). 226 less 240 gives NIL. (Remember c = call option, start with current underlying price).

11.5　For a *put option*, this is the strike (exercise price) less the underlying price. Again, there are no negative values, so the lowest value is always nil. On 6 August 1996 a 160 February 97 put on Hanson (underlying price 156 still) had an intrinsic value of 160 less 156 = 4. For Railtrack's 240 Feb 97 put, the intrinsic value was 240 less 226 = 14.

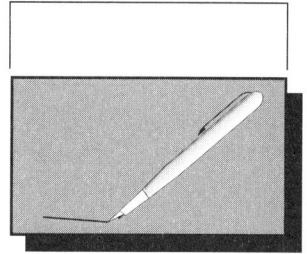

Time value

11.6   This is often called a premium because it is the extra amount over and above the intrinsic value which a buyer is prepared to pay in order to enjoy the prospect of the underlying price changing and so increasing the option's intrinsic value. By definition, the time value is obtained by deducting the intrinsic value from the option price.

Option price less intrinsic value = time value (premium)

11.7   It should now be obvious why the intrinsic value is never negative. If it were then we should be deducting a negative value from the option price, which is the same as adding a positive value to it.

11.8   To go back to our two examples from 6 August 1996. In the table below, prices are from the FT, while the intrinsic values were calculated earlier in this section.

Hanson

August Call	160	February Put	160
Price of option	1	Price of option	16.5
Intrinsic value	NIL	Intrinsic value	4
Time value	1	Time value	12.5

Railtrack

February Call	240	February Put	240
Price of option	7	Price of option	35
Intrinsic value	NIL	Intrinsic value	14
Time value	7	Time value	21

11.9   The August 160 call on Hanson had only a few days to run, so its time value was only 1. The market has taken a bearish view on this share for some time. With the February 240 call on Railtrack, investors still knew little about this new company, believing the share price would remain low, so the value was 'all in the time' because the contract still had six months to expiry.

11.10 The two put options are both February 97 but there was little support for Hanson, with a low intrinsic value. For Railtrack, sentiment was more uncertain, with more support for being able to sell profitably at 240, i.e. hoping that the underlying price would fall well below 240. Thus, speculators could sell at 240 and buy at 226 (that day's price) or even lower.

11.11 For put options, speculators want the underlying price to fall; for call options they want it to rise.

Put-call parity relationship

11.12 There is a relationship between put and call options on the same underlying instrument, provided that the options have similar exercise (strike) prices and similar maturities. The following formula assumes that European options are used (PV = present value).

Put option price less call option price = PV of exercise price plus PV of cash distribution less price of underlying asset

Factors affecting an options price

11.13 These can be summarised as follows:

- When price of underlying asset changes:
  - call option changes price in same direction because the intrinsic value increases when the share price rises;
  - put option changes price in opposite direction (because owner's profit diminishes the higher the price he has to pay for it).

- When strike (exercise) price changes:
  - call option price changes in opposite direction because for call options the total from which an unchanged share price is deducted has risen, so intrinsic value rises.

- Time to expiry:
  - the longer to maturity the greater the time value in the price.

- When price volatility (measured by standard deviation and not by beta – and thus not systematic risk) increases:
  - the option price rises because there is more likelihood of the underlying price moving to investors' benefit.

- When short-term interest rates increase:
  - call option prices will rise, because call option holders have sold the asset short, and have invested the sales proceeds;
  - put option prices will fall, because assets are financed with borrowed money.

- Expected cash receipts for asset-holders increase:
  - call option prices will fall, because these cash distributions make it more attractive to hold the asset than the option;
  - put option prices will rise because the distributions increase the value derived from holding the asset.

Student Activity 11

1. Separate the price of an option into its two component elements.

   (Paragraph 11.2)

2. Explain what is meant by the 'Put-Call Parity Relationship'. *(Paragraph 11.12)*

3. Give an aide memoire for calculating the intrinsic value of a call option.

   (Paragraph 11.4)

4. Construct a table showing how the six factors affect the prices of
   (a) call options;
   (b) put options. *(Paragraph 11.13)*

12 Option pricing models

12.1 Although the discussion in the preceding section seems almost as elementary as the section on the pricing of futures, a theoretical model for options pricing is much more complex because of the inherent price instability of the

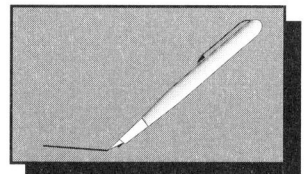

underlying asset. Such price volatility is, along with liquidity, one of the two underlying requirements for a derivatives market.

12.2 The first options pricing model was devised in 1973 by Black and Scholes, who were mathematicians working on European call option prices. Their assumptions include:

- No transaction costs or taxes.
- Interest rate has no spread, is risk-less and constant.
- Security pays no dividends.
- Trading is continuous and markets are always open.
- Security prices follow a random walk.

12.3 An alternative model is the binomial option pricing model, using a hedged portfolio comprising:

- A long position in the asset; protected by
- A short call position in it.

This portfolio is protected, i.e. it is risk-free, so that the price of the option is equal to the risk-free interest rate on the value of the portfolio.

Measures of option risk

12.4 Option risk measures bear the names of letters of the Greek alphabet and two are given below. However, there are several more.

12.5 Delta is the change in the option price resulting from a given change in the price of the underlying asset. In ordinary language, delta measures speed. Gamma measures the change in delta resulting from changes in the price of the underlying asset, i.e. the volatility of delta. In ordinary language, gamma measures acceleration or deceleration.

Student Activity 12

1. Name two option pricing models.   (Paragraphs 12.2–3)

2. State the assumptions of the more famous model.   (Paragraph 12.2)

3. Explain what are meant, in relation to options, by:
    (a) delta;
    (b) gamma.   (Paragraph 12.5)

Summary

Having studied this unit, you should be able to:

- **appreciate the significance of the financial derivatives markets;**

- **explain the role of derivative instruments;**

- **distinguish between futures and forward contracts;**

- **understand the role of the clearing house in a futures exchange;**

- **be aware of the importance of over-the-counter (OTC) derivatives markets;**

- **describe the basic features of options;**

- **understand the risk/reward relationships of call and put options;**

- **know what interest rate swaps are, and who uses them;**

- **describe the interest rate agreement market;**

- **examine the factors which affect the prices of:**
  - **futures**
  - **options;**

- **explain how arbitrage occurs between a derivatives market and the relevant cash market;**

- **construct very basic models for the pricing of:**
  - **futures**
  - **options.**

Self-assessment questions

Multiple choice questions

1. Scalpers are speculators who:
   (a) run a position for no longer than a few minutes
   (b) run a position until the next day
   (c) buy in one market and sell in another
   (d) seek maximum profit at minimum risk
   (e) seek maximum profit from long-term price changes.

2. The 'Grey Book' markets are:
   (a) commodity markets outside LIFFE
   (b) OTC derivatives markets in London connected to the foreign exchange market
   (c) OTC derivatives markets in London not covered by the Financial Services Act 1986
   (d) supervised by the Securities and Future Authority
   (e) supervised by the London Clearing House.

3. In London, margins are imposed by:

   (a) LIFFE

   (b) London Clearing House

   (c) Bank of England

   (d) Securities and Investments Board

   (e) Securities and Futures Authority.

4. Which of these products have/has a symmetric risk/reward ratio?

   (a) derivatives traded on a secondary market

   (b) all products traded on a derivatives exchange

   (c) futures and options

   (d) options

   (e) futures.

5. The London Clearing House is:

   (a) owned by the Bank of England and leading UK banks

   (b) a member of APACS

   (c) owned by all the UK retail banks

   (d) becoming part of the European System of Central Banks in January 1999

   (e) planning to be owned by the participating derivative exchanges.

Short-answer questions

1. What are the economic functions of derivative markets. Need they attract speculators?

2. Distinguish between the two main types of derivative markets, with special reference to supervision in the light of the collapse of Barings in 1995.

3. Show how the use of financial derivatives can indirectly help a person in the UK who has:

   (a) a floating rate mortgage

   (b) a defined contributions pension

   (c) an endowment policy for £40,000 with profits

   (d) an elderly relative in Canada, and who they support by making regular remittances.

4. Distinguish between the primary and secondary markets on:

   (a) gilt-edged

   (b) interest rate swaps.

5. Distinguish between an interest rate agreement and an interest rate swap.

Unit 5

Regulation of Financial Institutions and Financial Markets

Objectives

After studying this unit, you should be able to:

- know the purpose of governmental regulation of financial markets;

- indicate the different ways in which governments regulate markets;

- list the regulatory reforms of the 1980s;

- describe self-regulatory organisations, particularly in the UK;

- know, in outline, the implementation of regulation in the world's major economies;

- comment on the role of the Bank of England in supervising the banking system;

- analyse the commercial banks' and building societies, needs for liquidity, capital adequacy and profitability, and the structure of their balance sheets in relation to these concepts;

- comment on the regulatory environment resulting from the Financial Services Act 1986;

- describe the roles of the Building Societies Commission and the Department of Trade and Industry respectively, in the regulation of building societies and insurance companies;

- discuss the influence of international institutions (Bank for International Settlements and the EU) on the framework for supervising and regulating the financial system;

- know the major requirements of the main EU Banking Directives on capital adequacy and solvency ratios;

- understand the causes of reform, including financial crises, financial innovation and globalisation.

1 The need for regulation and the way it is implemented

1.1 Financial markets are so complex and so important in the economy that regulations are required to:

- Promote the stability of financial institutions;

- Promote competition and fairness in financial markets;

- Ensure that issuers of securities do not conceal relevant information;
- Regulate foreign participation in a market;
- Control the level of activity in an economy.

Promoting the stability of financial institutions

1.2   This is probably the most important reason because the failure of financial intermediaries can cause insolvencies and unemployment. The need for stability applies not only to deposit-taking financial intermediaries but also to investing ones. The failure of motor insurance companies in the 1970s and the collapse of some of the Maxwell companies' pension funds in the early 1990s show the distress which can be caused. This type of control is often called 'prudential regulation' to distinguish it from the implementation of economic policy and to emphasise its aim of preventing reckless or imprudent business practices.

Promoting competition and fairness in financial markets

1.3   Here five areas can be identified:

- Preventing insider dealing, e.g. employees and managers dealing in their companies, or client companies, securities before market sensitive news is published.

- Disclosing charges made by insurance companies, unit trusts and investment trusts.

- The complexity of insurance contracts and the promissory element in them – the insured person is relying on the company paying out should a claim be made.

- The need for a 'level playing field' in international markets, especially banking, where the Bank for International Settlements (BIS) has published a uniform code for capital adequacy. In addition, the BIS monitors the eurocurrency markets and the OTC markets in derivatives. Without a level playing field, countries with less stringent regulations could gain a competitive advantage over the rest.

- The existence of minimum commissions, as on the London Stock Exchange before 'Big Bang'.

Ensuring that issuers of securities do not conceal relevant information

1.4   There is an asymmetry of information in such markets because the users of funds almost invariably have a greater knowledge of their affairs than have their potential lenders and investors. If the latter are professionals, then they will ascertain as much as possible by research, taking references or going to credit rating agencies (as with commercial paper). However, if the potential lenders and investors are private individuals, there is a far greater chance of their being enticed into dealing with such companies without making the necessary enquiries. Moreover, they may not be able to make such enquiries, so the market regulator will often require such information, e.g. contracts between a company and its directors, to be published before a company's security can be issued.

Regulating foreign participation in a market

1.5   For example, in Brazil a foreign bank is limited to a set number of branches and if it wants to open a new branch it must close an old one. In the UK, non-EU insurance companies are treated somewhat differently to UK insurance companies. This is not just chauvinism, but the result of the need to protect a country's citizens if they have to institute legal proceedings against a party domiciled overseas and thus subject to different laws.

Controlling the level of activity in an economy

1.6 Most countries control the activities of financial intermediaries as part of their economic and monetary policy. This is usually regarded as separate from prudential regulation and investor protection but, at time of economic crises, such measures can affect financial markets quite dramatically. Examples can be a sudden rise in interest rates or the imposition of minimum down payments on HP sales or personal loans to buy 'consumer durables'. The downturn in the housing and mortgage markets in the UK in the early 1990s can be attributed to the policy measure taken to reduce inflation – raising interest rates.

Ways of implementation

1.7 Regulation by a government department is one way. Examples are insurance company regulation in the UK and the regulation of most financial institutions in Japan, where the Ministry of Finance (MoF) implements its regulations through seven bureaux. The Bank of Japan, although it is the central bank, is subordinate to the MoF.

1.8 Regulation by the central bank or a commission is another. In the UK, the examples are the Bank of England and the Building Societies Commission. In the USA, the Federal Reserve is the equivalent of the Bank of England, but it is much more independent. In Germany, the central bank is the Bundesbank, and it too is more independent than the Bank of England, but prudential regulation in Germany is the responsibility of a separate body.

1.9 Self-regulation, typified by the three SROs (self regulatory organisations) in the UK and by the National Association of Securities Dealers (NASD) in the USA, is a third way.

Student Activity 1

1. Outline the reasons why financial institutions and markets are regulated.
   (Paragraph 1.1)

2. How does such regulation ensure fair competition? *(Paragraph 1.3)*

3. Why is fair competition needed? *(Paragraph 1.3)*

4. What is meant by the 'asymmetry of information'? *(Paragraph 1.4)*

5. What forms does financial regulation take? *(Paragraphs 1.7–9)*

2 Prudential regulation by the Bank of England

2.1 The Bank of England is just *one component* of the regulatory and supervisory system within the UK financial system, having particular responsibility for

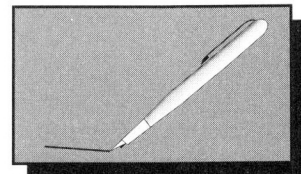

the supervision of banking activities and the operations of certain financial markets. The other components of financial regulation and supervision in the UK, and the way in which these fit together with the Bank of England's responsibilities, are discussed later in this unit.

The Banking Act 1987

2.2   While the activities of the Bank of England in supervising the domestic banking system may appear to relate to individual banks within the system, the overall thrust of the supervisory efforts is directed towards maintaining the integrity of the sector, since only in such circumstances can the general public's confidence in its stability be maintained.

2.3   Traditionally, the supervision of commercial banks by the Bank of England was on an informal basis, with the Bank seeking to ensure, on a case-by-case basis, that individual banks were not over-exposed to risk in their lending portfolios, that they had an appropriate level of liquidity, and so on. Since the enactment of the 1979 Banking Act, however, the supervision of the domestic banking system by the Bank of England has had a formal legal basis, with these legal aspects being extended by the 1987 Banking Act (which repealed almost all the 1979 Act).

2.4   The Banking Act of 1987 was intended to make the supervision of banks within the UK more rigorous following the failure of the Johnson Matthey Bank in 1984, and to introduce a unified system of regulation for banking institutions. As a consequence, under this Act there is just one category of authorised banking institutions, with all banks required to operate within the same statutory supervisory requirements. The 1987 Act made two significant changes to the supervisory framework, it increased the:

- Volume and frequency of the data concerning a bank's activities to be channelled to the Bank of England, thereby allowing a closer monitoring to be made; and

- Powers – including discretionary powers – of the Bank of England for the supervision of banking activities.

2.5   Under the 1987 Banking Act, a bank must satisfy certain minimum criteria before it can receive authorisation. These criteria require, in particular, that:

- The bank's directors, controllers and managers are 'fit and proper' persons to hold such positions;

- The bank is effectively directed by at least two individuals;

- For banks incorporated within the UK, there must be as many non-executive directors as the Bank of England considers appropriate;

- The business be conducted prudently, with regard to liquidity, capital adequacy, foreign currency exposure, provisions for bad and doubtful debts, accounting and other records, and internal management controls;

- The institution has a minimum value of net assets when authorisation is granted (set at ECU 5m since the beginning of 1993).

2.6   In respect of the 'fit and proper' test and the criteria relating to the prudent conduct, the Bank of England has substantial discretionary powers. In addition, though, within the provisions of the 1987 Act the Bank of England:

- Retains the discretion to set prudential standards on a case-by-case basis; and

- Has the power to object to proposed takeovers and mergers involving UK banking institutions.

2.7 Also, under the Act:

- The provision of false or misleading information to the Bank of England was made a criminal offence;

- The auditors of a bank are expected to pay close attention to the Bank of England's supervisory information requirements as a further check on the provision of adequate information to the Bank of England; and

- Banks are required to give notice to the Bank of England when their exposure to individual borrowers is expected to exceed 25% of their capital, and to report exposures of 10–25% to the Bank of England.

2.8 In order to buttress the ability of the Bank of England to fulfil its supervisory responsibilities, the 1987 Act established a Board of Banking Supervision, which advises the Governor of the Bank of England on matters relating to the:

- Supervision of authorised institutions;

- Development and evolution of supervisory practice;

- Administration of banking supervisory legislation; and the

- Structure and staffing of the Banking Supervision Division of the Bank of England.

2.9 The Board comprises the Governor, Deputy Governor and the executive director of the Bank of England responsible for banking supervision, together with six other members from *outside* the Bank of England, selected by the Chancellor of the Exchequer and the Governor of the Bank on the basis of their relevant skills and experience.

2.10 The Governor of the Bank of England has the right to ignore the advice of this Board of Banking Supervision but must inform the Chancellor of the Exchequer when he does so. It is clear, therefore, that the Bank of England retains ultimate responsibility for banking supervision within the UK, a fact which has led to a certain amount of criticism. Critics argue the need for a completely *independent* statutory body to be responsible for supervision, on the basis that the ties and the long-standing relationships that the Bank of England has with a variety of City institutions prevent it from being totally objective in the exercise of its supervisory responsibilities.

Student Activity 2

1. What was the broad intention of the Banking Act 1987?   *(Paragraph 2.4)*

2. List the minimum criteria which a bank must satisfy in order to gain authorisation from the Bank of England.   *(Paragraph 2.5)*

3. What requirements does the Banking Act 1987 place upon authorised banks in relation to their exposure to individual borrowers?   *(Paragraph 2.7)*

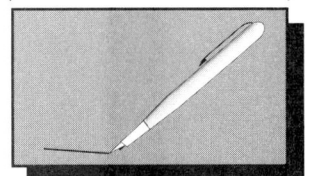

4. What is the function of the Board of Banking Supervision?   *(Paragraph 2.8)*

5. Why do some people argue in favour of the establishment of a completely independent statutory body to be responsible for banking supervision?

(Paragraph 2.10)

The supervision of bank liquidity

2.11   An important component of the supervision of banking institutions by the Bank of England is with regard to their *liquidity positions*. In broad terms, the objective here is to ensure that all banks will be able to meet their obligations when they fall due. The major obligations relate to the repayment of deposits, both sight deposits and time deposits, but banks will generally also have outstanding commitments on the lending side of their business in the form of unutilised overdraft facilities and commitments to lend to particular customers at a specific date in the future. Given that the maturity transformation of funds by banks will result in the average maturity of their deposits being significantly shorter than the average maturity of their advances (constituting the major element of a bank's assets), the problem of ensuring that a bank is able to meet its obligations when they fall due is a significant one.

2.12   In principle, a bank is able to ensure that it can meet its obligations by means of one or more of the following methods. The bank may:

●   Hold cash or other liquid assets, recognising that the value of many liquid assets will be variable due to fluctuations in market prices.

●   Attempt to match the maturity characteristics of its assets with the maturity characteristics of its deposit base, so that (after allowing for defaults on loans) there is an appropriate cash flow from maturing assets.

●   Seek to maintain a diversified deposit base and an appropriately high standing in the money markets such that it is able to attract deposits as and when required, without having to pay excessive interest rates.

2.13   Although there has been some discussion about the possibility of introducing a standardised requirement for all banks to hold a similar stock of liquid assets as a 'safety net', the basic principle of liquidity control remains one of self-regulation. The Bank of England sets the broad guidelines for evaluating the quality of assets and for classifying liabilities, and then leaves the institutions to select that combination of assets and liabilities they consider appropriate to their commercial objectives. Furthermore, the Bank of England does not specify which, or what combination, of the three approaches to ensuring adequate liquidity identified above should be utilised.

2.14   Although this regime may give the impression of a relatively lax attitude towards the supervision of bank liquidity, it must be remembered that the continual flow of confidential information that a bank provides to the Bank of England regarding the nature of its assets and liabilities, together with the regular meetings that senior managers are required to hold with Bank of England supervisors, ensures that the Bank is kept informed of the liquidity position of any bank. Should the Bank of England consider that the policies being followed by a bank are not giving rise to an adequate level of liquidity, it will issue a warning, and failure by the bank concerned to act on such a warning is likely to lead to the suspension of authorisation. In general terms, it is the intention of the liquidity controls to provide encouragement for banking institutions to follow prudent policies with regard to their overall liquidity positions, and to ensure that the internal management systems of the banks are capable of monitoring their liquidity positions and dealing with unanticipated liquidity problems.

Student Activity 3

1. In relation to liquidity controls, what are a bank's major obligations?

   (Paragraph 2.11)

2. What is the overall objective of liquidity controls? *(Paragraph 2.11)*

3. List the ways in which a bank may meet its liquidity commitments.

   (Paragraph 2.12)

4. To what extent does the Bank of England dictate the liquidity management policy to be pursued by individual banks? *(Paragraph 2.13)*

5. How does the Bank of England maintain the effectiveness of its supervision of bank's liquidity? *(Paragraph 2.14)*

The supervision of capital adequacy

2.15 The capital that a bank has is an important consideration since it is a measure of the bank's ability to absorb losses which can arise from bad debts or trading losses (as with Barings). It is also a source of finance for investment in technology and acquisitions of other financial institutions. An adequate level of capital in relation to a bank's lending is therefore, along with an adequate level of liquidity, an essential requirement for the maintenance of a sound banking system and the maintenance of confidence in that system.

2.16 The Bank of England has had a legal duty to regulate the capital adequacy of banking institutions since the enactment of the Banking Act of 1979, and this duty was strengthened by the Banking Act of 1987. Despite that legal duty to regulate the banks' capital adequacy, during the 1980s there was no common minimum level of capital adequacy applied to banks in the UK, and the requirement imposed on any bank was the result of the Bank of England's assessment of that bank's position and capabilities.

2.17 Different assets in a bank's portfolio carry different levels of risk, and given that the characteristics of a portfolio will vary widely from one bank to another, it is inappropriate to require a bank to hold capital equal to a particular proportion of its assets. A necessary first step, therefore, was for the Bank of England to assess the risk attached to the various items in a bank's portfolio and then to weight that portfolio according to its riskiness. The outcome was that the greater the level of risk in a bank's portfolio, the greater the amount of capital required in order to maintain a given degree of capital adequacy. There was a clear recognition, therefore, that a particular level of protection for depositors would have to take account of the risk associated with the bank's lending activities.

2.18 The Bank of England, in addition to setting down the parameters for assessing risk in the asset portfolio, also set down a clear definition of what could be regarded as the 'capital' of a bank for the purposes of specifying capital adequacy

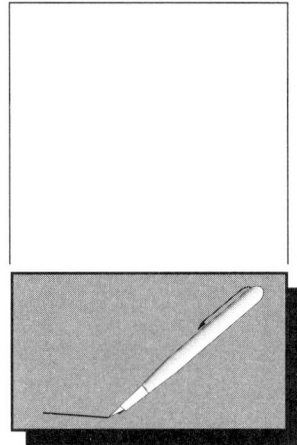

ratios. The Bank retained the flexibility, however, to specify the ratio of capital to the risk-weighted assets that any individual bank would be required to hold, with this ratio taking account of the Bank of England's assessment of the bank's managerial capacity with regard to its risk position, its profitability and its overall prospects. The Bank of England therefore set a *minimum* ratio (termed the 'trigger' ratio) below which it would be likely to intervene, with the expectation that in normal circumstances the bank would maintain a 'target' ratio which included a margin over the value of the trigger ratio.

The Basle Accord

2.19   Moves at an international level to harmonise the capital adequacy ratios of banks in different countries have led to some change in the nature of the capital adequacy regime facing banks in the UK, towards a more rigorously defined framework. The Committee on Banking Regulations and Supervisory Practices of the Bank for International Settlements (BIS) put forward a framework in July 1988 for the harmonisation of standards of capital adequacy, with the objective of strengthening the world's banking system and placing it in a better position to withstand any future problems in world financial markets. In addition, the requirements are intended to provide a more equal basis for competition between banks in different countries and to remove the incentive for a bank to relocate activities in another country in order to take advantage of its relatively lax regulatory requirements. Because the BIS is located in Basle, the requirements are known as the Basle Accord.

2.20   The majority of western banks undertook to implement the BIS proposals by the end of 1992. Although in strict terms they only relate to banks that are internationally active, the Bank of England is applying them as a common standard to all authorised banks in the UK. Furthermore, the Bank of England announced that it would make use of the discretionary powers allowed under the proposals for individual central banks to set capital adequacy requirements *above* the minimum level specified, and that it would continue to set 'trigger' and 'target' ratios. These latter ratios are confidential and very important in day-to-day supervision.

2.21   On the *risk* side of the capital adequacy proposals, and along the lines of the system for weighting the risk characteristics of different assets used by the Bank of England, the BIS proposals specify risk weightings for the various categories of assets. These include:

- Cash: 0%
- Call money at the discount houses: 10%
- Fixed interest securities issued by OECD central governments: 20%
- Mortgage loans to owner-occupiers: 50%
- Commercial loans: 100%.

2.22   In addition, account is also taken of off-balance-sheet risks, i.e. risk-carrying activities with which a bank might be involved which do not need to appear on the bank's balance sheet, such as forward currency exchange contracts, underwriting commitments and guarantees. Such items are included in the calculations by means of 'credit conversion factors' that are designed to provide a measure of their value weighted for credit risk.

2.23 On the *capital* side of the proposals of the BIS, capital is split into two types:

- Tier 1 capital (core capital), which comprises shareholders' equity and disclosed reserves; and

- Tier 2 capital (supplementary capital) which consists of revaluation reserves, general provisions, hidden reserves, subordinated debt and certain other approved capital instruments.

2.24 The requirement of the BIS proposals is that banks should have capital equal in value to *at least 8% of total risk-weighted assets*, and that within this ratio at least half of the capital should be Tier 1 capital.

Prudential controls on foreign currency exposure

2.25 A further important aspect of the Bank of England's supervisory responsibilities relates to the control of banks' exposures to foreign currency risks. As movements in currency exchange rates may have adverse effects on a bank's net worth, if its assets and liabilities are not balanced in terms of their currencies of denomination, the Bank seeks to measure, monitor and discuss with banks their foreign currency exposures. It also sets out guidelines for the maximum desirable exposures in individual currencies and for total net positions in all currencies. These controls relating to foreign currency risk are separate from, and additional to, the monitoring of each bank's overall risk position in respect of large exposures to individual borrowers or types of assets.

Student Activity 4

1. Why is an adequate level of capital vital for a bank's financial stability?
   (Paragraph 2.15)

2. Why is the evaluation of the risk associated with assets of importance to the determination of a bank's desired capital base? *(Paragraph 2.17)*

3. In relation to the Bank of England's supervision of capital adequacy, what are a bank's trigger and target ratios? *(Paragraph 2.18)*

4. What is the relevance of the BIS requirements for the way in which the Bank of England supervises UK banks' capital adequacy? *(Paragraphs 2.19–24)*

5. What is the Bank of England's role in respect of foreign currency exposure of banks? *(Paragraph 2.25)*

BCCI/Barings and banking supervision in the 1990s

2.26 In July 1991 the Bank of England moved to close down the UK operations of the Bank of Credit and Commerce International (BCCI), a major international bank incorporated in Luxembourg. At the same time, or shortly afterwards, in a co-ordinated operation, banking supervisors in a number of other countries took similar action in respect of BCCI operations falling within their jurisdiction. The reason for this extraordinary action was the discovery of overwhelming evidence of gross banking irregularities and strong suspicion that massive fraudulent transactions had been perpetrated by BCCI employees.

2.27 Whilst the closure of BCCI had extremely serious implications for many of its

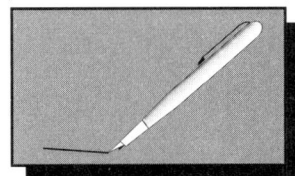

depositors and borrowers, the immediate impact on banking markets as a whole was muted. The major effect of the BCCI affair came some time later through its influence on the way in which international banks are supervised.

2.28 Following the closure of BCCI there was widespread criticism of the failure of banking supervisors to act sooner to protect the interests of depositors. The Bank of England was a particular target for criticism because of the importance of UK-based operations for BCCI. Consequently, amid allegations that the Bank had been made aware of improper activities at BCCI several years before its closure, the UK Government appointed Lord Justice Bingham to undertake an official independent enquiry into the supervision of BCCI.

2.29 The Bingham Report was published in October 1992, and whilst it was not unduly critical of the Bank of England's actions or of the basic system of banking supervision used in the UK, it nevertheless questioned the emphasis and rigour of the Bank's supervisory activities, and put forward suggestions and recommendations for improving the supervisory regime. The outcome of the enquiry was a reinforcement of changes which the Bank had already begun to make in respect of its approach to banking supervision.

2.30 In February 1995, it became apparent that Barings, the UK's oldest merchant bank, was unable to continue in business. The reason was that most of its capital and reserves had been transferred to a subsidiary in Singapore to finance losses incurred by a derivatives trader. No other banks would help and the Chancellor of the Exchequer refused to sanction taxpayers' money being used to support a failed merchant or investment bank. Thus, Barings ceased trading momentarily and was bought shortly afterwards by a Dutch bank (ING Bank) for a nominal sum. It now operates as Barings ING Bank.

2.31 Naturally, there was an outcry and the Board of Banking Supervision was asked to enquire into the bank's collapse. For the purposes of this enquiry, the Bank of England members of the Board did not take part. A Bank of England manager who had exceeded his discretion in 'authorising' the transfers of funds from Barings in London to Singapore, so that well over 25% of the bank's capital was committed to this one operation, later resigned. However, the episode and the report highlight two problem areas, the:

● Relations between the Bank of England and the Singapore Monetary Authority, its counterpart in that offshore banking centre;

● Fact that a central bank is more used to supervising lending, deposit-taking and foreign exchange trading than the buying and selling of securities and derivatives. Better co-operation is required between the Bank, the SIB and the Securities and Futures Authority (SFA) which supervises the securities markets in the UK.

2.32 In the immediate post-Baring days, it is difficult to discern the stance taken by the Bank of England. However, there are two examples of its views.

● In mid-1996, in its annual report on the Banking Act, the Bank expressed concerns over the growth of price-cutting in mortgage finance, particularly by cash discounts given to borrowers. Within weeks, this practice became less common.

- In July 1996, a report in a Sunday newspaper gave details of a letter sent to all banks by the Bank's executive director in charge of banking supervision, commenting adversely on:

  ○ failure to provide and take up detailed references on employees;

  ○ mixing the duties of dealers and back-office staff – a separation which has become almost mandatory since Lugano in 1974 (see paragraph 9.5) and which had been ignored by Barings in the Singapore dealing room where Nick Leeson had worked;

  ○ failure to undertake routine checks in back offices, such as checking suspense accounts regularly;

  ○ allowing dealers to act as both proprietary dealers (for the bank) and client dealers (for customers).

  Note that a number of these concerns relate to trading rather than lending.

2.33   In July 1996, two documents were published in the aftermath of the Baring collapse. One was a paper prepared by Arthur Andersen, the chartered accountants, on its review of the Bank's supervision and surveillance procedures, and the second was the Bank's Review of Supervision. Basically, more human and financial resources were to be devoted to supervision, a more systematic model of a risk assessment was to be developed and quality assurance was to be given a higher profile. Former bankers, nicknamed 'grey panthers', were to be recruited.

Student Activity 5

1.   Why was BCCI closed down by the Bank of England in July 1991?

(Paragraph 2.26)

2.   Why was the Bank of England criticised following the closure of BCCI?

(Paragraph 2.28)

3.   The Bingham enquiry was set up in order to examine the quality of banking supervision in the light of BCCI. What was the broad tenor of the Bingham Report?   *(Paragraph 2.29)*

4.   Why did Barings collapse in 1995?   *(Paragraph 2.30)*

5.   What problems were brought to light by the inquiry into the collapse?

(Paragraph 2.31)

3   Banking regulation within the EU

3.1   The EU's internal markets initiative set the end of 1992 as the target date for the completion of a Single European Market. This Single Market means that there should be now completely free movement of goods, services, labour and capital between EU member states. Since services are included in the Single Market initiative, the relevance of EU legislation to banking activities within the UK has been given a major boost.

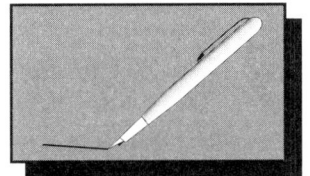

3.2   In January 1993 the Second Banking Co-ordination Directive came into force. This legislation has crucial implications for the future of banking activities within the EU. Its two major elements are that:

● It has introduced a *Single European Banking Licence* which will ensure that EU-incorporated banks which are authorised within their own country's regulations (e.g. UK banks authorised by the Bank of England under the terms of the Banking Act 1987) are automatically recognised as banks in any part of the EU by virtue of their home country recognition.

● *Home country supervisors* are now responsible for the supervision of all operations within the EU of banks incorporated in the home country. However, the local monetary authorities retain exclusive responsibility for measures imposed upon banks in respect of monetary policy. In addition, for the time being host countries have primary responsibility for the supervision of liquidity and position risk. (Position risk relates to risks which banks run if their assets and liabilities are not matched, particularly in respect of currency and interest rates. For instance, if a UK bank had large amounts of French franc deposits which had been used to fund sterling lending, that bank would be at risk if the French franc strengthened against the pound, assuming no action had been taken beforehand to hedge this risk.)

3.3   Thus, a bank which is authorised within the UK by the Bank of England is now able to set up branches in any other EU member state and is allowed to provide a wide range of cross-border banking services without the need for separate authorisation by the authorities of the host country.

3.4   Clearly, it is necessary for banking authorities in the various EU countries to *harmonise* their banking authorisation regulations if there is to be mutual recognition of each other's banks. Thus, the Second Banking Co-ordination Directive sets out:

● Minimum levels of capital (set at ECU5m) required before authorisation can be granted;

● Supervisory control of major shareholders and banks' participation in the non-banking sector;

● Accounting and internal control mechanisms.

3.5   In addition to the Second Banking Co-ordination Directive, there are several other directives relevant to banks wishing to offer a range of financial services. Examples are the:

● *Capital Liberalisation Directive*, which aims to make illegal the imposition of exchange controls on movements of capital within the EU;

● *Admissions Directive* on the requirements to be fulfilled before a company can have its shares listed on any EU Stock Exchange;

● *UCITS Directive* (Undertaking for Collective Investment in Transferable Securities) which relates to investments such as unit trusts.

3.6   There has been a flood of EU legislation over the past few years. Even banks wishing to concentrate on their traditional domestic markets will find that the impact of free competition and harmonisation of banking regulations within the EU cannot be ignored. Many institutions have already found that the EU legislation has had an effect on operating procedures and internal management structures.

3.7   Some banks have adopted an aggressive strategy to try to take advantage of the harmonisation of EU supervision and regulation. A number of major UK financial institutions have formed alliances with institutions based in other EU countries to take advantage of new business opportunities as they arise.

Student Activity 6

1. What was the ultimate objective of the EU's 1992 initiative?   *(Paragraph 3.1)*

2. What are the two major elements of the Second Banking Co-ordination Directive?
    (Paragraph 3.2)

3. Why is it important that minimum regulatory standards applying to banks should be harmonised within the EU?   *(Paragraph 3.4)*

4. List some of the aspects of harmonisation of regulations to which the Second Banking Co-ordination Directive refers.   *(Paragraph 3.4)*

5. In addition to the Second Banking Co-ordination Directive, what other directives are likely to be of importance to the future activities of UK banks?
    (Paragraph 3.5)

6. Even when a UK bank wishes to restrict its activities to the UK, it is still likely to be affected by the 1992 initiative. Why?   *(Paragraph 3.6)*

4   Supervision and regulation of building societies

The main functions of the Building Societies Commission

4.1   The Building Societies Commission is responsible for:

- *Supervision and regulation* of all building societies in accordance with the Building Societies Act 1986. Such societies are exempt from the provisions of the Banking Act 1987, unless they apply to convert to PLC status. Such conversion requires the approval of the Commission and the Bank of England.

- *Representing* the building societies and acting as their spokesman, e.g. to appropriate government departments on matters relevant to the operations of building societies.

- Safeguarding the *financial stability* of building societies.

- Promoting the *protection of shareholders'* funds and *depositors'* funds in building societies.

- Promoting the *principal purpose* of building societies, which is to raise funds from members to enable them to grant mortgage loans for residential property to members.

- Ensuring that societies exercise *prudently* the powers granted to them under the Building Societies Act 1986.

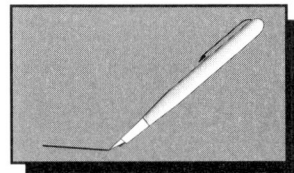

The powers of the Building Societies Commission

4.2 The Commission has considerable powers to restrict the activities of individual building societies and to interfere with their operations. The Commission:

- Is responsible for the *authorisation* of building societies and has the power to revoke such authorisation if a society fails to meet the criteria for prudent management set down in the Building Societies Act 1986. These criteria relate to:

  ○ the maintenance of adequate reserves, adequate liquid assets and adequate capital resources;

  ○ provision of effective accounting, records and internal controls; and the use of suitable arrangements for assessment of the adequacy of securities for advances.

- May *issue a directive* requiring a society to submit an appropriate restructuring plan where the society has breached the limits for wholesale funding, deposit liabilities, commercial assets or liquid assets. The society must then either submit a restructuring plan or, alternatively, seek the approval of its members to convert to plc status. If the society fails to comply with a restructuring plan or if it fails to apply for plc status, the Commission may apply for a court order to wind up the society.

- Can issue a *prohibition order* if it decides that a particular activity of a society is beyond its powers under the 1986 Act.

- May direct that any *advertising* which it considers to be misleading or unsuitable be withdrawn.

4.3 Finally, it should be remembered that the Single European Market in services is bound to affect the building societies. So far the effect of EU legislation has been minimal, but the Second Banking Co-ordination Directive, which in future may be joined by a Mortgage Credit Directive, could have far-reaching implications, although it is too early to make any firm predictions.

Student Activity 7

1. Which institution is responsible for the regulation of building societies which convert to plc status? *(Paragraph 4.1)*

2. What are the main functions of the Building Societies Commission? *(Paragraph 4.2)*

3. When considering the authorisation of a building society, what criteria are taken into account under the Building Societies Act 1986? *(Paragraph 4.2)*

4. List the ways in which the Building Societies Commission may restrict the activities of building societies. *(Paragraph 4.2)*

5 Other deposit-taking institutions

5.1 Within the UK financial system, there are two other deposit-taking financial institutions:

- Finance houses; and
- The National Savings Bank.

Finance houses

5.2 The primary function of finance houses is to provide medium-term instalment credit to both individuals and businesses. With regard to individuals, this finance is principally for the purchase of consumer durables, while for businesses it is primarily for machinery and other capital equipment. Factoring of book debts is provided, along with leasing of small items such as photocopiers and cars.

5.3 The provision of instalment credit to businesses is a comparatively recent development, stemming from the inability of the finance houses to expand in the personal sector because of former restrictions on consumer credit and from increased competition from credit cards and personal loans from banks and building societies.

5.4 The major source of funds for the finance houses is the wholesale money markets, particularly via commercial bills and CDs. In addition, finance houses take in substantial short-term deposits from the banking sector. In contrast to the retail banks and the building societies in particular, therefore, the intermediation activity of finance houses does *not* involve the *aggregation* of savings; typically, finance houses will take in large blocks of funds and lend in very much smaller quantities.

5.5 Several of the larger finance houses chose to take on the status of banking institutions under the Banking Act 1979 and are consequently included in the 'other British banks' category. As a consequence, many of these have expanded outside the traditional finance house activities. A much larger number of finance houses (many of them relatively small individually) chose not to do so and are classified as the *non-banking sector finance house* group.

The National Savings Bank

5.6 The National Savings Bank is part of the Department for National Savings, and as such provides deposit facilities and other simple banking services through post offices in the UK. It offers three types of account:

- *Investment accounts* which pay interest gross (but liable to tax), at a reasonably competitive rate in line with the inter-bank 12-month LIBID rate on funds that are subject to one month's notice of withdrawal. A recent change is to allow, after the first 30 days, immediate withdrawals, subject to the loss of 30 days' interest.

- *Ordinary accounts*, where access to funds does not require notice and is relatively easy through post offices. The rate of interest is lower than on investment accounts, with the first £70 of interest being tax-free.

- *Treasurer's accounts*, with a minimum balance of £10,000 for societies, clubs, etc. Launched in the late summer of 1996, this is the bank's third product in 135 years.

At the end of 1995 the total funds in investment accounts was approximately £9.9bn, and approximately £1.4bn in ordinary accounts.

5.7 The funds in the National Savings Bank are invested exclusively in British government securities, and hence investments in the National Savings Bank are, in effect, default-free.

5.8   The Bank is outside the scope of the Banking Act 1987. In reality, it is not a financial intermediary because it is part of the final user (the government). However, it is a financial institution.

Student Activity 8

1.   What is the primary function of the finance houses?   *(Paragraph 5.2)*

2.   What is the major source of funds for the finance houses?   *(Paragraph 5.4)*

3.   What facilities are offered by the National Savings Bank?   *(Paragraph 5.6)*

4.   What happens to the funds which are deposited with the National Savings Bank?
                                                                                          (Paragraph 5.7)

5.   Why is the National Savings Bank not regulated in the same way as retail banks or building societies?   *(Paragraph 5.8)*

6   Non-deposit-taking financial intermediaries

6.1   The final group of financial intermediaries whose regulation is to be examined are those intermediaries that do not take in deposits, represented by pension funds, insurance companies, unit trusts and investment trusts. Since they do not take in deposits, they acquire funds in a number of different ways, for example by means of selling insurance policies and pension contracts. They were described in Unit 2.

Pension funds

6.2   The pension funds considered here are the funds that arise out of occupational schemes operated by employers, rather than the state pensions system. A significant proportion of the working population are members of an occupational pension scheme, whereby the employer and (usually) the employee make regular payments into a scheme which will provide the employee with a pension when he or she retires. The objective of the pension fund managers is therefore to collect the regular contributions and to build up a fund in order to be able to pay the pensions at some point in the future, taking account of uncertainties such as inflation and mortality rates. A key element in minimising the cost to the employer of the pension scheme is the return on the funds invested, and hence considerable attention is paid to the investment performance of the fund managers.

6.3   After the death of Robert Maxwell in 1991, it was found that a number of pension funds in companies in his group had lost some of their assets. Litigation and criminal proceedings resulted and the government appointed the Goode Committee to report on how to prevent a re-occurrence of this problem. As a result, the Pensions Act 1995 was enacted: it is enabling legislation to facilitate the implementation of more detailed rules to control pension funds. Previously, they had been controlled largely through the law relating to trustees, i.e. principles of equity, as amended by statute. Although fund managers were supervised by IMRO, the trustees themselves did not come under the Financial Services Act: the fund managers advised on the investments, but these were owned by the trustees.

Pension fund regulation

6.4   Under the Pensions Act 1995, the new regime of supervision is beginning to take shape. Two essential features are a:

- Minimum Funding Requirement, comparable to that for insurance companies; and

- Statement of Investment Principles.

An Office of the Pensions Regulatory Authority (Opra) has been created to be the regulator for the funds.

Insurance companies

6.5   Insurance consists of two broad types of activity:

- General insurance; and

- Long-term insurance.

General insurance

6.6   General insurance involves covering risks such as fire, theft, accident and damage from weather. Claims that arise on such policies are generally met from incoming premiums, but in addition a *fund* is accumulated from which to meet unusually large losses. The time lag that generally occurs between the receipt of a premium by the insurance company and the payment of any claim on that policy also ensures that a 'pool' of funds is available for investment. As a consequence, companies involved in general insurance have large funds invested in various assets, especially government securities and equities, and as such are significant participants within the financial system, quite apart from their insurance activities.

6.7   Long-term insurance involves covering the risk of the death of an individual. In practice, the majority of long-term insurance policies carry comparatively little insurance cover for death, and are used much more as *long-term savings vehicles*. It is in this context, in particular, that the long-term insurance companies build up substantial funds and are, in effect, aggregating the relatively small savings of individuals to enable indirect investment in equities, gilts, property and so on to take place, to provide the individual policyholder with specialist investment expertise, and to allow the individual to benefit from certain tax advantages.

Regulation

6.8   The major legislation affecting UK insurance companies is the Insurance Companies Act 1982, which consolidated existing UK legislation and incorporated EU directives on insurance business.

6.9   The *objects* of this legislation are to protect:

- Policyholders from the insolvency of an insurance company;

- Individuals from being sold insurance which is unsuitable for their needs.

6.10   The implementation of the Act's provisions is the responsibility of the Department of Trade and Industry (DTI), which has powers to grant or revoke authorisation of insurance companies, to stipulate solvency margins for insurance companies, to monitor insurance companies and to intervene in their operation if necessary.

6.11   Under the Act, there are three classifications of ownership of insurance companies:

- UK companies, supervised by the DTI;

- EU companies, supervised by the government of the EU country where their head office is located;

- External companies, based in non-EU countries. These are supervised by the DTI if they operate in the UK. They must appoint a UK agent, whose executives and underwriters must be 'fit and proper' persons under the Act.

6.12   It is a criminal offence to undertake insurance business in the UK without prior authorisation of the DTI; authority will be granted only if the applicant is deemed to be fit and proper to undertake such business.

6.13   The DTI maintains regular surveillance of insurance businesses through the various returns which the companies must submit. If the DTI is not satisfied that the business is properly conducted it may revoke authorisation. Alternatively, some less severe sanction may be adopted, such as a directive forbidding the issue of new policies or ordering a restructuring of the assets of the insurance company. Since the Act, new companies may not be composite companies (see Unit 2), they must be either general or long-term insurance companies.

6.14   Insurance has been regulated, in one way or another, for a considerable time. As well as the reasons for regulation listed in section 1, in a modern society, some activities must be insured – motoring is the most common example. All motorists must have at least third-party insurance cover for accidents. Other examples include nuclear power stations, dangerous animals and solicitors (professional indemnity cover).

Solvency margins

6.15   As with some banking regulations, figures are now expressed in ECUs to calculate the solvency margins which insurance companies must maintain under the Act. There are two ways of calculating these margins, which are adjusted downwards by the percentage of claims which have been reinsured with other insurers:

- Premium basis

    18% of the first ECU 10m of premiums

    + 16% of the remaining premiums (expressed in ECUs).

- Claims basis

    26% of the first ECU 7m of claims

    + 23% of the remaining claims.

6.16   There are also three levels for the *minimum guarantee fund*: ECU 200,000; ECU 300,000; ECU 400,000.

Student Activity 9

1. What is an occupational pension scheme?   *(Paragraph 6.2)*

2. What sort of risks does general insurance relate to?   (Paragraph 6.5)

3. What are the three classes of ownership insurance companies? *(Paragraph 6.10)*

4. What are the key elements of the regulation and supervision of insurance companies in the UK?   *(Paragraph 6.9)*

5. How are solvency margins calculated for insurance companies? *(Paragraph 6.14)*

Unit trusts

6.17   Unit trusts are collective investment vehicles designed to allow, in particular, relatively small-scale investors indirect access to equity markets and to benefit from specialist investment management. An individual invests in a unit trust by purchasing a number of 'units', which gives rise to a transfer of funds to be managed by the unit trust and which provides the investor with the right to a portion of the income or capital gains achieved by the trust.

6.18   Unit trusts are required to operate under a *trust deed* which specifies the objectives of the fund and how it is to be managed. All unit trusts involve two separate companies, the

●   *Management company*, which is responsible for matters such as the investment strategy of the trust, the calculation of the buying and selling prices of the units, and for the administration of the selling and repurchasing of units.

●   *Trustee company*, which is responsible for holding the trust's assets, receiving and distributing to unit-holders the income from the underlying investments, and ensuring that the conditions of the trust deed are met. Trustee companies are substantial financial institutions in their own right and are frequently clearing banks.

6.19   The volume of funds under management by a unit trust are variable and will be dependent on the level of sales and repurchases of units. Unit trusts are therefore termed 'open-ended' funds, and there is no secondary market in the units; units have to be bought from and sold back to the management company. The costs of administering the trust, as well as brokerage charges, fees to the trustee company and the profit to the management company, are met by an annual charge on the assets under management (typically 1.5% per annum) and by the difference between the price at which the investor buys units (the offer price) and sells units back to the management company (the bid price).

6.20   The regulation of unit trusts was brought to the attention of the media in September 1996, when sales were suspended in three of Morgan Grenfell's unit trusts, because of investments made, apparently without authority, in obscure European companies. The problem is the first major one to occur in the unit trust sector.

Investment trusts

6.21   Despite their title, investment trusts are legally not trusts at all, but *companies*.

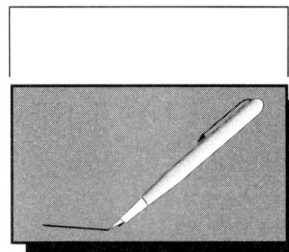

The purpose of these companies is to use shareholders' funds to make investments, particularly in other companies. Accordingly, investment trusts obtain their funds for investment initially from an issue of shares and subsequently from borrowing, from retained income and from realised capital gains.

6.22 As with any company, an investment trust is under the control of its board of directors who usually determines the broad investment strategy of the company and then appoints fund managers to deal with the day-to-day investment management.

6.23 As with unit trusts, the investment objectives vary widely; some investment trusts are large and 'general', having investments spread widely, while others are smaller and specialise in particular sectors or geographical areas. The trend in recent years has been towards launching specialist investment trusts to take advantage of particular circumstances, with some launches being specifically directed at institutional investors. As a consequence, the industry has regained some of its buoyancy, but the continued threat of takeover (which is possible, given that they are companies like any other) and subsequent disinvestment remains a significant consideration.

7 Supervision and regulation of investment business

7.1 The Gower Report (1984) concluded that the supervision and regulation of investment business was excessively complex, inequitable and inefficient. As a result of the Gower Report, the Financial Services Act 1986 (FSA) was enacted in order to lay down a comprehensive framework for the regulation of investment business and for investor protection. It established the Securities and Investments Board (SIB) to oversee the regulation of investment businesses via self-regulatory organisations (SROs) and recognised professional bodies (RPBs).

The Financial Services Act 1986

Allocation of responsibilities
7.2 The FSA made the DTI responsible for the regulation of investment business in the UK. In turn the Secretary of State for Trade and Industry delegated operational powers to the SIB. In June 1992, the DTI's responsibilities in respect of the FSA were transferred to the Treasury, in order to consolidate a wide range of financial regulations under one ministry.

7.3 It must be emphasised that the SIB system does not cover all activities which might be included under the heading of investment business. Its scope of responsibility includes:

- Securities markets (other than gilts which are the responsibility of the Bank of England);
- Futures and options;
- Unit trust management;
- Insurance broking;
- Fund management;

- Investment advice;
- Corporate finance.

7.4 The FSA explicitly makes the Bank of England responsible for the regulation of the gilts market, the bullion markets, the wholesale money markets, and the foreign exchange market. Also, the DTI maintains considerable power in respect of the operations of insurance companies and unit trusts, despite responsibility for their marketing activities resting ultimately with the Treasury. Note that the FSA does not cover the selling of mortgages or the operation of *bureaux de change.*

SIB/SRO structure

7.5 An initial function of the SIB was to formulate a rule book embodying codes of conduct and regulations for institutions and individuals involved in investment business. Once this rule book had been approved by the Director General of Fair Trading (because all regulations tend to reduce competition and may lead to restrictive practices) and the Secretary of State at the DTI, formal powers were transferred to the SIB (in April 1987), which then set about the job of delegating specific responsibilities to a number of SROs. Between them, the SROs cover the bulk of activities as prescribed by the FSA. In order to obtain their own delegated powers, each SRO had to produce its own rule book, which had to be approved by both the SIB and the Director General of Fair Trading. The rule books are intended to give investors equivalent protection to that implicit in the SIB's own rule book.

7.6 Initially, there were five SROs, but this was subsequently reduced to three by merger:

- Securities and Investment Authority;
- Personal Investment Authority;
- Investment Management Regulatory Organisation.

7.7 *The Securities and Futures Authority (SFA).* This was formed in 1991 from the merger of The Securities Association (TSA) and the Association of Futures Brokers and Dealers (AFBD). The overlap in the responsibilities of these two SROs made their amalgamation a logical development. TSA supervised the activities of the members of the London Stock Exchange, whilst the AFBD supervised the trade and broking in financial and commodities futures and options. The SFA has now assumed these responsibilities for the securities and derivative markets.

7.8 *The Personal Investment Authority (PIA).* This is responsible for supervising the marketing and management of unit trusts and life assurance businesses and of the independent financial advisers who deal with the general public in respect of investments such as unit trusts and life assurance. It also covers the activities of licensed dealers and those providing investment management services for retail clients. The PIA resulted from the merger of two of the original five SROs, LAUTRO and FIMBRA, creating a single self-regulatory body for those individuals and institutions involved directly in the provision of investment services to the general public.

7.9   *The Investment Management Regulatory Organisation (IMRO).* This is responsible for the activities of independent investment managers and advisers, especially those managing institutional funds, collective investment schemes and in-house pension funds.

7.10   A major criticism of the formal basis of the SIB/SRO structure was that it was excessively legalistic and detailed in its requirements, and hence potentially damaging to investors' interests, by restricting choice and increasing costs. As a result of this criticism, the SIB simplified its operating procedures and requirements. Since 1990 investment firms have been expected to operate in line with 10 broad principles laid down by the SIB and in 1991 a series of 'core rules' were published by the SIB which now from the basis for the production of simplified rule books by the individual SROs. Less than half of these core rules apply to dealings between professional investors.

7.11   Within the SIB structure, there are also:
   ● *Recognised Professional Bodies* (RPBs), e.g. the Law Societies; the Chartered Accountants. Where an individual undertakes investment business as a minor element of his or her professional activities (and not all do), then so long as certification is obtained from one of the RPBs, there is no need for full authorisation from the SIB or an SRO. A professional body will only be granted RPB status if its standards and codes of practice are compatible with those of the SIB.
   ● *Recognised Investment Exchanges*, e.g. the London Stock Exchange, LIFFE, and *Recognised Clearing Houses*, e.g. TALISMAN (LSE). They are responsible for the regulation of specific financial markets and transactions, and via recognition from SIB they escape direct supervision of their activities.

Student Activity 10

1.   What did the Gower Report conclude about the supervision and regulation of investment business?   *(Paragraph 7.1)*

2.   Which government departments have had responsibility for the implementation of the Financial Services Act 1986?   *(Paragraph 7.2)*

3.   For which areas of investment business regulation is the SIB responsible?   *(Paragraph 7.3)*

4.   For which areas of financial supervision was the Bank of England made responsible by the Financial Services Act?   *(Paragraph 7.4)*

5.   What is the relevance of rule books within the SIB regulatory framework?   *(Paragraph 7.5)*

6.   List the three SROs together with their areas of responsibility.   *(Paragraphs 7.6–9)*

7.   What action did the SIB take in order to counter the criticism that its regulatory framework restricted choice and increased costs for investors?   *(Paragraph 7.10)*

8.   What is the Personal Investment Authority?   *(Paragraph 7.8)*

9.   What are Recognised Professional Bodies and Recognised Investment Exchanges?   *(Paragraph 7.11)*

Authorisation of investment businesses

7.12   Under the FSA, a person (or firm) is deemed to be carrying on an investment business if he or she buys or sells investments (unless acting in purely a personal capacity), arranges for others to buy or sell investments, manages investments on the behalf of others, advises others on their investments, or operates a collective investment scheme. Unless exempt under the Act, it is a criminal offence for any person to operate an investment business within the UK without prior authorisation.

7.13   Individuals and institutions may obtain authorisation in one of five ways:

- Directly from SIB, although its fees are set so as to discourage this.

- Through membership of an SRO. Currently the scope of responsibility of each SRO is limited, hence an individual or institution offering a wide range of investment services may require membership of more than one SRO.

- Certification by an RPB, where the investment business is only a minor part of a person's activities.

- From the DTI in respect of endowment and unit-linked insurance policies.

- From the relevant regulatory body of another EU state, where the level of investor protection given is comparable to that in force in the UK, and where the business does not have a permanent place of residence within the UK.

7.14   In order to obtain authorisation from SIB or an SRO, the firm must meet criteria which establish that it is 'fit and proper' to run an investment business. These criteria relate to:

- Capital adequacy;

- Previous business record;

- Compliance arrangements in respect of supervision;

- The good character of the firm's owners, directors and employees.

The firm must also produce a business plan which sets the approved limits of the investment business which may be undertaken.

7.15   To maintain authorised status, an investment firm must comply with the conduct of business rules laid down by its regulator. These rules relate to:

- Advertising;

- Disclosure of commissions;

- Making unsolicited calls;

- Fair treatment of clients;

- Provision of customer agreements;

- Maintenance of records to be produced if complaints are made.

Sanctions against investment firms and individuals

7.16   An investment firm believed to be in violation of the conduct of business rules may be investigated by the relevant SRO. The SRO may take action to protect the firm's clients. It may issue private or public warnings, limit the scope of the firm's activities, or suspend or withdraw authorisation. For instance, the SFA forbade Nick Leeson to trade in London.

7.17   SIB may investigate any authorised firm, and any other business suspected of undertaking investment activities without authorisation. It may seize documents and require people to give evidence. Its powers override those of the SROs, and in addition to the sanctions available to the SROs, SIB may also apply to court for a winding-up order and may undertake criminal prosecutions. The SIB may, and does, fine firms and individuals for infringement of the rules.

Compensation fund

7.18   The FSA established a compensation fund to provide compensation to investors with authorised firms which go into liquidation or which are involved with fraudulent operations. The fund gives 100% cover for the first £30,000 of individual investments, and 90% cover for the next £20,000, i.e. a total of £48,000.

7.19   The fund is financed by a levy on the SROs, which recoup their contribution via levies on their individual members. The initial burden of compensation falls upon the SRO which authorised the firm in respect of which claims are made. If claims exceed a preset sum, the other SROs must also contribute. There has been some criticism of the fund, both in terms of the cover given, and on account of the levies not reflecting the inherent riskiness of the different authorised firms.

The cost of regulation

7.20   As suggested above, there has been some criticism of the costs associated with the regulation process within the SIB/SRO framework. In particular, costs arise in respect of:

- Gaining authorisation;
- Annual membership fees;
- Compliance arrangements;
- Auditing of accounts;
- Production of financial statements;
- Contribution to the compensation fund.

7.21   Whilst some cost is unavoidable, the question arises as to whether the investor is getting value for money as, ultimately, it is the investor who pays for the regulation via lower returns and higher fees. If the quality of protection, and hence the stability of the markets is improved, then all parties involved may benefit substantially. However, if the associated costs are seen as being excessive, firms may be forced out of business and activities may be pushed to more lightly regulated markets overseas.

Student Activity 11

1. In what circumstances is an individual deemed to be undertaking an investment business?   *(Paragraph 7.12)*

2. In what ways may individuals and institutions obtain authorisation within the provisions of the Financial Services Act 1986?   *(Paragraph 7.13)*

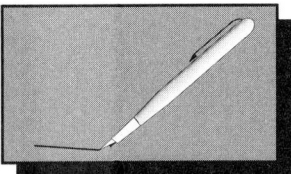

3. What factors are covered by the criteria for authorisation within the provisions of the FSA? *(Paragraph 7.14)*

4. What do the conduct of business rules relate to? *(Paragraph 7.15)*

5. What sanctions may be applied to an investment business found to be in violation of the conduct of business rules? *(Paragraphs 7.16–17)*

6. What compensation is available to investors in authorised firms which go into liquidation? *(Paragraph 7.18)*

7. How is the investors' compensation scheme financed? *(Paragraph 7.19)*

8. In what ways do costs arise in respect of investor protection, and what problems do they cause for investors and investment firms? *(Paragraph 7.21)*

8 Regulation overseas

USA

8.1 Here the regulatory structure is largely the result of crises, especially the Great Depression of the 1930s and the earlier stock market crash of October 1929. The two statutory pillars are the Securities Act 1933 and the Securities Exchange Act 1934:. Both require great detail in companies' new issues, while the 1934 Act created the Securities and Exchange Commission (a federal agency) to enforce the two Acts.

8.2 The Banking Act 1933 created the Federal Deposit Insurance Corporation for bank deposits and separated commercial banking from investment banking operations. However, since the 1980s, there has been some relaxation in this rigid distinction.

8.3 Self-regulatory roles are played by the New York and American stock exchanges, together with the National Association of Securities Dealers (NASD).

8.4 The USA is a federal state, but markets are supervised by the federal government in Washington; monetary policy is the responsibility of the Federal Reserve System. However, some banks are 'chartered' by the 50 states which comprise the union. Nationwide commercial banking is about to start; until now, banks have been restricted to one state.

Japan

8.5 Japan, like the UK, is a unitary state and highly centralised. Securities markets are supervised by the Ministry of Finance (MoF) through the Securities Bureau, which is one of seven specialised bureaux under the MoF. National commercial banks are permitted, unlike the USA. The Bank of Japan is the central bank and is subject to control by the MoF.

Germany

8.6 Germany, like the USA is a federal state, and the individual states (known as Länder) are responsible for the eight stock exchanges. However, the central bank (Bundesbank) supervises the bond market, which tends to be dominated by government bank and mortgage bonds. Companies, on the other hand, raise capital from banks or on the Eurobond market.

8.7   Like the USA, Germany has a very independent central bank, although its discretion in exchange rates is minimal. However, it has virtual independence in setting interest rates, unlike the Bank of England.

9   Causes of regulatory change

9.1   Three major causes of change can be identified:

- Crises;

- Innovation;

- Globalisation.

Of these, perhaps crises have been the most important.

Crises

9.2   The Great Depression of 1929–1934 resulted in the US legislation of 1933 and 1934 and, also, in the creation of the *Bank for International Settlements* (BIS) in 1930. The BIS was created by most of the world's central banks as a sort of 'central bank for central banks' to monitor the German World War 1 debt repayments which had caused so many problems in the 1920s. Located in Basle, Switzerland, it survived World War 2 when its shareholding central banks were on opposing sides and then took on a new lease of life administering European Iron and Steel Community loans. The BIS has subsequently:

- Become the monitor of the Euro-markets.

- Drafted the Basle Concordat on Capital Adequacy, which forms the 'level playing field' for global banking.

- Spawned the European Central Bank. This began as the Committee of Governors of the EC central banks, with a secretariat provided by the BIS. This Committee became the European Monetary Institute, and then moved to Frankfurt.

- Begun to monitor the OTC markets in financial derivatives.

9.3   In the UK, the failure of a number of insurance companies in the 1960s and 1970s prompted the Insurance Companies Act 1982. In the 1970s, the failure of Norton Warburg, an investment firm, resulted in the appointment of the Gower Committee to consider the problem of the financial regulation. This, in turn, led to the 1986 Financial Services Act. The death of Robert Maxwell and the fate of pensioners in some of the companies which he had bought caused a public outcry: the result was the Goode Report and the Pensions Act 1995.

9.4   In banking, cause and effect can be listed in a similar fashion. The 'secondary banking crisis' of 1973–74 recorded gaps in regulation between the Bank of England and the DTI, resulting in the Banking Act 1979. However, the Act was also prompted by the need to have a statutory regulatory framework to harmonise with that on most of mainland Europe. In 1984, the failure of Johnson Matthey Bankers (a full bank under the 1979 Act and not a mere 'licensed deposit-taker) led to the Banking Act 1987. As we have seen, the BCCI and Barings crises led to administrative changes rather than new primary legislation.

9.5 Lugano is a word which triggers a knee-jerk reaction in many bankers. It is a town in Switzerland where Lloyds Bank Europe (as it then was) had established a small branch to buy 'suitcase money' coming across the border from Italy. Collusion occurred between the management and the only foreign exchange dealer, who blatantly exceeded his limits. When the deception was discovered, both lost their jobs, and the losses cost Lloyds Bank the equivalent of four years' profits from South America. As a result, there developed the practice of separating dealers (traders) in the 'front office' or dealing room from the clerks and supervisors in the 'back office'.

Innovation

9.6 In 1980, UK banks began to move into the mortgage market, designing new products to increase their share of what is perceived to be a low-risk area of lending. Building societies responded by seeking powers to challenge the banks on current accounts – powers which they received in the Building Societies Act 1986. Meanwhile, they had been granted access to the sterling wholesale money markets in 1983.

9.7 The two great market developments in the second half of this century have been the growth of the eurocurrency markets, followed by the growth of financial derivatives. The response of the financial regulators was, as we have seen, the assumption of a regulatory role by the Bank for International Settlements.

Globalisation

9.8 To some extent, this dovetails into 'innovation' and has resulted in a need for regulators to consult with their opposite numbers in other countries. In many markets there is now 24-hour trading five days a week, so that no single government or central bank can regulate all the deals occurring within its territory, because so many of them involve an overseas counterparty. However, in the UK, increasing competition from overseas caused the government to insist on the abolition of fixed commissions on the London Stock Exchange.

Student Activity 12

1. Compare and contrast financial regulation in the USA with that in Japan.
   (Paragraphs 8.1–5)

2. Compare and contrast financial regulation in the UK with that in Germany.
   (Paragraphs 8.6–7, plus rest of unit)

3. Compare and contrast financial regulation in Germany with either that of Japan or the USA.
   (Paragraphs 8.1–7)

4. Assess the role of crises in the development of financial regulation in this century.
   (Paragraphs 9.2–5)

5. To what extent is globalisation an underlying cause of changes in financial regulation rather than one aspect of innovation?
   (Paragraph 9.8)

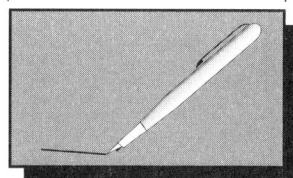

Summary

After having studied this unit, you should be able to:

- **know the purpose of governmental regulation of financial markets;**

- **indicate the different ways in which governments regulate markets;**

- **list the regulatory reforms of the 1980s;**

- **describe self-regulatory organisations, particularly in the UK;**

- **know, in outline, the implementation of regulation in the world's major economies;**

- **comment on the role of the Bank of England in supervising the banking system;**

- **analyse the commercial banks' and building societies, needs for liquidity, capital adequacy and profitability, and the structure of their balance sheets in relation to these concepts;**

- **comment on the regulatory environment resulting from the Financial Services Act 1986;**

- **describe the roles of the Building Societies Commission and the Department of Trade and Industry respectively, in the regulation of building societies and insurance companies;**

- **discuss the influence of international institutions (Bank for International Settlements and the EU) on the framework for supervising and regulating the financial system;**

- **know the major requirements of the main EU Banking Directives on capital adequacy and solvency ratios;**

- **understand the causes of reform, including financial crises, financial innovation and globalisation.**

Self-assessment questions

Short-answer questions

1. What are the basic criteria which must be satisfied by a bank in order to obtain authorisation from the Bank of England?

2. In what ways may a bank seek to ensure its ability to cover its obligations when they fall due?

3. In what way did the acceptance of the BIS proposals affect the Bank of England's approach to the supervision of capital adequacy?

4. In what way did the closure of BCCI influence the development of international banking supervision?

5. What is the SIB?

6. Does the Financial Services Act framework cover all investment businesses?

7. In what ways may the Building Societies Commission restrict the activities of individual building societies?

8. What is the role of the Department of Trade and Industry in the regulation of insurance companies?

Multiple-choice questions

1. As a result of the Banking Act 1987

   (a) a bank's auditors must now be deemed to be 'fit and proper' by the Bank of England

   (b) it is now a criminal offence for a bank to lend funds equal to more than 25% of its capital base to a single borrower

   (c) the Bank of England is required to set uniform reserve ratios for all banking institutions in respect of their liquidity and capital adequacy

   (d) it is now a criminal offence for a bank to provide false or misleading information to the Bank of England.

2. In relation to the supervision of banks' liquidity

   (a) the Bank of England sets minimum required ratios of liquid assets to deposit liabilities for all banks

   (b) the Bank of England sets broad guidelines for evaluating the quality of assets and for classifying liabilities, but leaves reserve ratios to the discretion of the banks themselves

   (c) the overriding principle of self-regulation means that the Bank of England does not interfere with individual banks' liquidity policies

   (d) all banks are required to hold minimum amounts of high quality liquid assets on the approval of the Bank of England.

3. Under the provisions of the Banking Act 1987, an authorised banking institution must

   (a) inform the Bank of England when any single borrower accounts for more than 25% of its total loans

    (b) return an annual report on its liquidity position to the Board of Banking Supervision

    (c) have owners, controllers and managers who are deemed to be fit and proper persons by the Bank of England

    (d) hold liquid assets equal to at least 8% of its risk-weighted asset base.

4.   Under the BIS capital adequacy requirements, all banks are required to

    (a) hold designated types of capital equal to at least 8% of a risk-weighted asset base

    (b) hold risk-weighted assets which are equal in value to at least 8% of total asset holdings

    (c) hold designated types of capital equal to at least 8% of a risk-weighted liabilities base

    (d) make quarterly returns to the BIS demonstrating the adequacy of their capital holdings.

5.   The Second Banking Co-ordination Directive

    (a) is the only piece of EU legislation to be of direct relevance to UK banking institutions

    (b) specifies minimum capital adequacy requirements for all the western world's banking institutions

    (c) lays down regulations on the maximum amount of capital which an EU bank may hold

    (d) sets out guidelines for the harmonisation of bank supervision within the EU.

Unit 6

The Analysis of Interest Rates

Objectives

After studying this unit, you should be able to:

- **explain what interest rates are;**

- **distinguish between nominal and real rates of interest;**

- **examine the two theories concerning the determination of interest rates;**

- **understand why there are so many rates of interest;**

- **outline the effects of interest rate changes;**

- **calculate the yield to maturity of a bond;**

- **classify the various types of bonds;**

- **identify and draw yield curves, and explain the significance of their shapes and slopes;**

- **understand what spot rates and implied forward rates are;**

- **describe the most important UK interest rates.**

---

1 Introduction

1.1 Every unit of this workbook has mentioned interest rates, to explain either how they influence certain financial flows in the economy or how they influence the profitability of particular groups of financial institutions. This repeated reference to interest rates underlines their crucial role within the financial system. The primary purpose of this unit is to examine the process by which interest rates are determined, although section 10 and Appendix A of the next unit consider the impact of interest rate changes.

1.2 Reference is frequently made in the media to 'the rate of interest', as if there were one single interest rate throughout the economy. Even the most casual observation reveals, however, that there are a multitude of interest rates ranging, for example, from a figure of 2.5% pa quoted on a number of government-issued gilt-edged securities, through to interest rates exceeding 30% pa quoted on credit cards issued by several high street stores. Hence, an additional purpose of this unit is to consider the *range* of interest rates that exists within the economy and to examine the determinants of the pattern of interest rates that apply at any one time.

Definitions

1.3   It is important to appreciate that an interest rate is a *price*, and that the price relates to *present* claims on resources relative to *future* claims on resources. An interest rate is therefore the price that a *borrower pays* in order to be able to consume resources now rather than at a point in time in the future. Correspondingly, it is therefore the price that a *lender receives* to forgo current consumption in order to take advantage of consumption of resources at some point in the future. Like all prices in free markets, interest rates are established by the interaction of supply and demand; in this context, it is the supply and demand of future claims on resources. We may therefore adopt as our definition of an interest rate that it is a

> price established by the interaction of the supply of, and the demand for, future claims on resources.

That price will usually be expressed as a proportion of the sum borrowed or lent over a given time period – hence, an interest rate of 10% pa states that the price of that loan will be 10% of the value of the loan for each year that the loan remains outstanding.

1.4   Note here the importance of time in our concept of interest rates. Thus, most interest rates are calculated on an annual basis – 'per annum' is usually understood. In wholesale money market dealings in sterling, Belgian francs, Irish pounds and Kuwaiti dinar, the year has 365 days; in all other currencies there are 360 days to a year. Some UK retail banks, however, charge interest on a monthly basis, partly because (they say) their customers are paid monthly and prefer it.

1.5   'Interest on interest', or compounding, can have substantial effect on the value of debt where the interest is not paid by the borrower. Such compounding is usually calculate, every six months but, for the banks which charge interest monthly, it occurs monthly. To give two arithmetical examples: 1% per calendar month (pcm) becomes 12.7% pa; 10% a year, if unpaid, increases the total debt to 21% after two years and to 33% in three years. Compound interest can be a boon to savers, but a curse to borrowers.

Real and nominal interest rates

1.6   An important distinction is made between *real* and *nominal* interest rates. A *nominal* interest rate is what is normally observed and quoted and represents the actual money paid by the borrower to the lender, expressed as a percentage of the sum borrowed over a stated period of time. A *real* rate of interest, on the other hand, is a nominal rate that is adjusted to take account of the impact of inflation on the real value of the loan.

1.7   A bank might, for example, pay an interest rate of 10% pa on deposits. The 10% is the *nominal* interest rate and represents the nominal price that the investor receives in return for delaying his consumption of resources for a year. However, that investor will only be able to purchase an additional 10% of goods and services with his funds at the end of the year if the price level of those goods and services *remains constant* over that year. If the price level is *not* constant and rises by, say, 6% over that year, then while the nominal interest rate is 10% the *real* interest rate is only 4%, since the investor can only purchase an additional 4% of goods and services when the loan matures, due to their increase in price. Thus, the real interest rate will always be less than the nominal interest rate when inflation occurs (when the purchasing power of money is falling). If, with a nominal interest rate on deposits of 10% pa, the inflation rate were to be, say, 12% pa, then the real interest rate would be minus 2% – that is, it would be negative, since the nominal interest payments would be insufficient to maintain the purchasing power of the capital as a result of the inflation of 12% pa.

Measuring the real interest rate

1.8   One of the major problems surrounding the concept of the real interest rate lies in its *measurement*. For a period of time *in the past*, calculation of the real interest rate involves deflating the nominal interest paid by an appropriate price index. There is no 'perfect' price index and, in principle, each individual within an economy is likely to have had their own price index based on the unique combination of goods and services that they purchased. Hence, any real interest rate calculated for a previous period is necessarily an approximation to some degree, although the choice of an appropriate price index will usually bring this approximation to within acceptable limits.

1.9   For a period of time into the *future*, the calculation of the real interest rate to be paid by the borrower (and received by the lender) is considerably more problematic. In addition, although the calculation of the real interest rate that applied for a *previous* period may be of some use, the calculation of the real interest rate that will apply in the *future* is of much greater use, since it is with regard to future interest rates that decisions will be made on the allocation of funds for investment purposes.

1.10   The calculation of the future real rate of interest involves deflating the future nominal rate of interest by the future rate of inflation. The difficulty surrounding the future rate of inflation is not only that it involves the problem of choosing an appropriate price index, as explained in the previous paragraph but, also, given that future rates of inflation are not known with certainty, it can only be an *expected* rate of inflation. By extension, therefore, any future real interest rate can only be an *expected* real interest rate. Given that future rates of inflation, especially for anything but a short period into the future, are extremely difficult to forecast accurately, the actual real interest rate paid and received will often vary substantially from what was expected.

1.11   A particular real interest rate can be achieved on a loan extending into the future, with both the borrower and lender protected from unanticipated changes in the rate of inflation, through the use of *indexation*. The principle of indexation is that, in order to protect the capital value of the loan, that capital value would be linked to an appropriate price index, thus having the effect of ensuring that the real purchasing power of the capital at the end of the period of the loan would be the same as it was at the start. In order to protect the value of interest payments, these would be paid as a proportion of the index-linked capital sum, which would have the effect of guaranteeing the agreed real rate of return on the loan. The overall effect, therefore, is to make the real rate of return on the loan totally independent of the rate of inflation. Despite the attractions of such an agreement, index-linked loans are comparatively uncommon in the UK. The only major borrower in this form is the government through the issue of index-linked savings certificates and gilts, as was seen in Unit 2. In the USA, such loans are even rarer, and index linked Treasury bonds are to be introduced in early 1997.

1.12 The main alternative to index-linking loans is for funds to be lent at market-related (i.e. not fixed) rates of interest. The basis for this arrangement is that market rates of interest tend to move in line with the rate of inflation and, consequently, if there is an unexpectedly high rate of inflation during the life of the loan, this will be compensated for by an increase in the rate of interest payable on the loan.

1.13 While historical experience tends to show that market rates of interest do indeed move in line with inflation, two points should be noted:

- The movement of interest rates often tends to occur some time *after* the rise in inflation, with the result that loans maturing within that time lag are not protected.

- The adjustment is invariably much less than total. In other words, while the movement in interest rates is usually in the right *direction*, it has frequently not been of a sufficient *amount* to protect fully the value of the loan from the effects of inflation, since the market interest rate has often been less than the rate of inflation.

1.14 The reason for the incomplete adjustment of market interest rates to inflation rates is simply that, as we shall see later in this unit, there are other influences on market interest rates in addition to the level of inflation. While use of market-related interest rates therefore represents an imperfect means of protecting a loan from inflation, its widespread use would indicate that it offers sufficient protection for many borrowers and lenders, and it should be remembered that it avoids the complexities associated with the use of a price index.

Positive and negative interest rates

1.15 We can see that if the rate of inflation over the period of a loan is greater than the nominal interest rate paid, the *real* rate of interest on that loan will be negative as it was on many occasions in the 1980s. It is equally possible for *expected* real interest rates to be negative. In these circumstances, lenders expect the inflation rate to be greater than the nominal interest rate and thus expect a negative real return, but they may choose to accept this if it constitutes the best use of their funds at that time.

1.16 *Nominal* interest rates, however, should always be positive (subject to the exceptions in paragraph 1.22) for the following reasons.

Hoarding becomes attractive

1.17 The self-evident reason that nominal interest rates will never be less than zero is that no rational individual is going to lend out £100 now to get back £95 in a year's time: the lender would clearly do better simply by putting the £100 under the mattress or in a safe so that they would still have £100 at the end of the year.

1.18 There are three additional and closely related reasons for nominal interest rates being positive (rather than just zero), however:

- Compensation for risk

- Compensation for loss of liquidity; and
- Compensation for delayed consumption.

Compensation for risk

1.19 Any loan involves some risk of default of either interest or principal. In some instances, such as the purchase of government securities, the risk is negligible, but in other instances it will plainly be considerable. For a financial intermediary making a number of loans at the same time, the risk of default on any one loan will be reflected in the interest rate being higher, for all loans made, than it would have been in the absence of any risk.

Compensation for loss of liquidity

1.20 Lending a sum of money will generally involve a loss of liquidity, since only a minority of loans are subject to repayment on demand. For most lenders, therefore, there is a loss of the immediate purchasing power associated with holding money. Consequently, the lender will require compensation for this loss of liquidity, which will be reflected in the interest rate paid on the loan, with higher interest rates (other things being equal) being paid on less liquid loans.

Compensation for delayed consumption

1.21 Lending funds involves forgoing consumption in the current period in favour of consumption in a future period. Given that individuals prefer consumption now to consumption in the future (while recognising that the *rate* of time preference will vary between individuals), it is inevitable that compensation will be required by lenders for their delayed consumption. Once again, this compensation will be reflected in the interest rate. For individuals who have a very strong preference for consumption now rather than at a point in the future, the interest rate will need to be correspondingly high to persuade them to forgo current consumption. Note, however, that some individuals will not so much be forgoing current consumption as taking the opportunity to accumulate sufficient funds (in the form of financial claims) with which to make a larger purchase in the future than they can at present.

Negative interest rates

1.22 There are, however, occasions when the nominal rate of interest becomes negative, although banks and building societies describe the negative nominal rate of interest as a 'maintenance charge'. For instance, the Swiss banking laws have provided secrecy for many depositors, who are quite willing to pay a fee for such a service, guaranteeing the safety of their funds denominated in a strong currency and free from prying eyes of regulators and (perhaps) Interpol. Another example occurs in the UK where some building societies, eager to see adequate balances maintained in small accounts, have on occasion levied a quarterly fee should the balance fall below the stipulated balance.

Student Activity 1

1. State the general definition of an interest rate. *(Paragraph 1.3)*

2. What is a nominal rate of interest? *(Paragraphs 1.6–7)*

3. What is a real rate of interest? *(Paragraphs 1.6–7)*

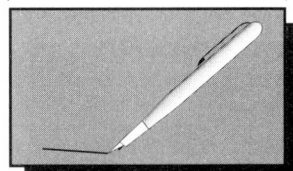

4. Why can a past real rate of interest only be measured approximately?

(Paragraph 1.8)

5. Why can a future real rate of interest only be an expected rate when the nominal rate paid on an asset is fixed? *(Paragraphs 1.9–10)*

6. How does indexation make the real rate of return on a loan independent of the rate of inflation? *(Paragraph 1.11)*

7. List the reasons for nominal rates of interest being positive. *(Paragraphs 1.17–21)*

2 Theories of interest rates

2.1   Fisher's classical theory is the older of the two major interest rate theories and has a number of assumptions:

●   The market/economy consists only of individuals who are saving/consuming out of current income (not using up past savings) and firms investing in asset-based projects. There are no financial intermediaries – such as banks and pension funds – no government and no overseas transactions.

●   There is no risk of borrowers defaulting.

●   Inflation is assumed to be zero, so the real rate of interest and the nominal rate are the same.

●   There is no investment in cash, only in firms' debt (bonds).

2.2   Savings are the results of people's choices between consuming now or in the future; such choices are influenced by their time preferences, especially their marginal rate of time preference. Savings are also influenced by people's incomes (the higher they are the more people will save – given similar time preferences).

2.3   Using Marshall's scissors diagram, we get the familiar diagram of this.

Figure 6.1

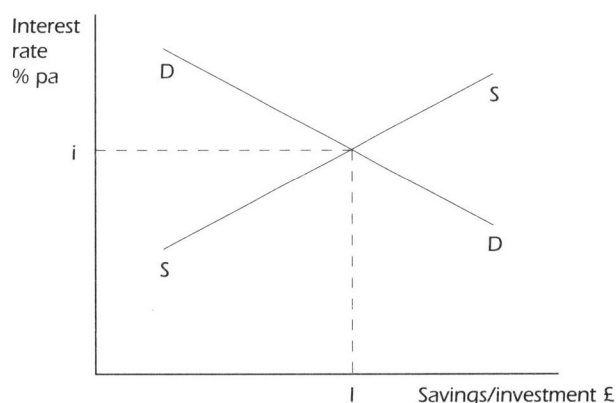

Equilibrium is at a rate of i% pa, where S = I and where supply and demand are equal. Shifts in the supply and demand curves produce changes in price (interest rate) and the 'quantity' (the equilibrium level of savings and investment).

Fisher's law

2.4   This starts from a different point from paragraphs 1.8 and 1.9 above. It states that the nominal rate of interest (which can be observed in transactions) comprises two unobservable elements:

● The real rate of interest (y below);

● A premium to compensate for the loss of purchasing power of savings caused by inflation (p below).

Expressed algebraically, the nominal rate of interest (i) equals (y + p). The law is found more in American textbooks than in UK ones, because the UK has been plagued by inflation to a greater extent than the USA. Hence, our problem in the UK has been to ascertain the real rate of interest rather than the nominal rate, i.e. ours is a practical problem, which Americans view in a more theoretical way. In the UK, i = y + p is often expressed as y = i – p. However, years of negative real rates of interest have probably convinced many UK investors that there is no premium above inflation, so that they rewrite the formula:

y = i – inflation.

The Loanable Funds Theory

2.5   This is an extension of Fisher's Theory to include banks and the government, with similar scissors-shaped diagrams. It includes bank deposits, but not notes and coin. Because the only investment is in assets (by governments, firms or by banks), it has been called a real theory. There is no investment in cash.

Keynes' Liquidity Preference Theory

2.6   This approaches interest rates from a different angle – from the supply of money and people's demand for it. At any one point in time, the supply of money is fixed – by the central bank – so the supply curve becomes a vertical line, as in the diagram below in Fig. 6.2.

2.7   The demand for money has, as you may recall from earlier studies, three elements; of which the third is by far the most important:

● *Transactions demand* – for spending on goods and services. This is determined by the frequency with which people receive their incomes – monthly, weekly (or daily in a hyperinflation!) and by the level of their incomes. Interest rates play little part in these decisions.

● *Precautionary demand* - for emergencies (rainy day money). Again, interest rates play only a minor role in determining this demand.

● *Speculative demand.* Keynes includes investors in his theory; such investors switch in and out of money or bonds according to the level of interest rates. The demand curve for money is, like most demand curves, downward sloping, because there is a negative relationship between the rate of interest (on bonds) and the demand for money (in those days when Keynes devised his theory, current accounts paid no interest).

2.8   Keynes assumed, in his theory, that wealth could be held in only two forms – money and/or bonds. There was no default risk on bonds, which can have maturities of up to 30 years, and the rate of inflation was zero, so that real and nominal rates of interest were equal. The supply of money was fixed.

2.9 The diagram for the price of money is shown in Fig. 6.2.

Figure 6.2 The price of money

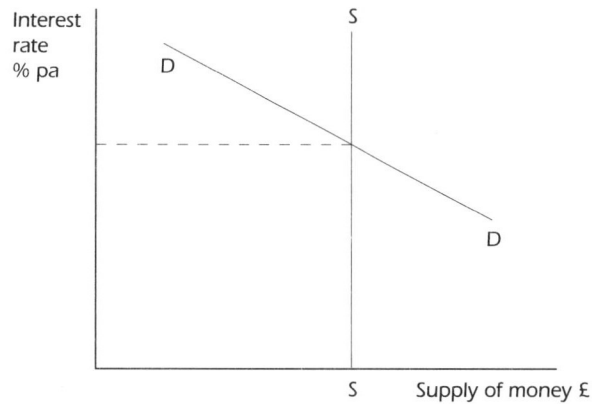

2.10 We can now examine changes in demand:

- Investors expect interest rates to rise (bond prices to fall), so they sell bonds and move into money. Their selling causes bond prices to fall, so their expectations are fulfilled. The demand curve has shifted to the right (the demand for money has increased).

Figure 6.3

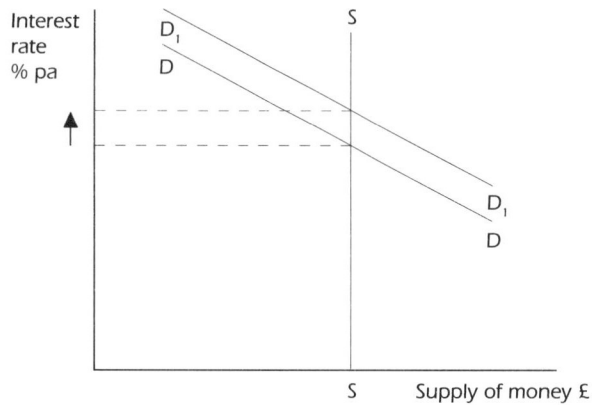

- Investors expect prices to rise, so more money is needed to maintain the purchasing power (in goods and services) of the balances held for spending saving. Again, the demand curve has shifted to the right.

So far, the analysis is along the lines of that studied on the Foundation Course.

2.11 Changes in supply, however, are slightly different because they result in at least two differing and opposing effects – a liquidity effect and an income effect. Furthermore there is also an inflationary expectations effect.

Liquidity effect

2.12 Here the money supply curve (still vertical) shifts to the right and the rate of interest falls, because there is more money than was there before. Hence, borrowers need not pay so much for their loans. Investors are faced with

Figure 6.4

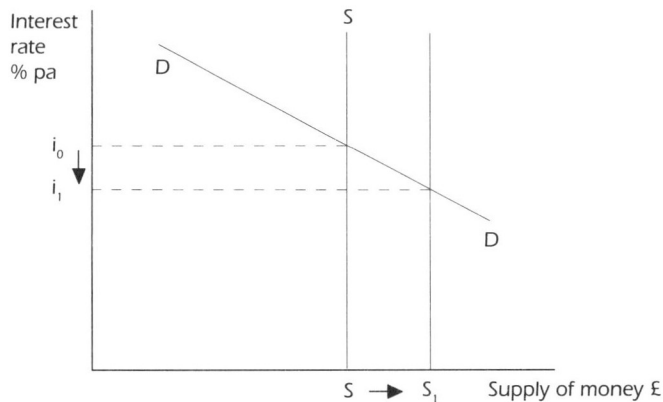

more money than they had, so they move from money into bonds, forcing up bond prices (which are the reciprocal of interest rates); hence interest rates fall. The diagram is shown in Fig. 6.4

Income effect

2.13 Here the increase in the money supply is examined with regard to its effect on the overall economy, which has not been shown on the diagrams in this section until now. These merely refer to money – its quantity and price. However, ion many cases, more money in the economy will increase demand for goods and services, partly because people do not wish to hold so much money – they would rather spend it. This spending will result in more output or more imports – in real terms (volume) or in prices or a combination of both. If an economy is working at less than full capacity, then real output is likely to increase, rather than inflation, unless there are bottlenecks in some industries or services which hamper the growth of output. This is shown in the Fig. 6.5, which should be read in conjunction with Fig. 6.4.

Figure 6.5

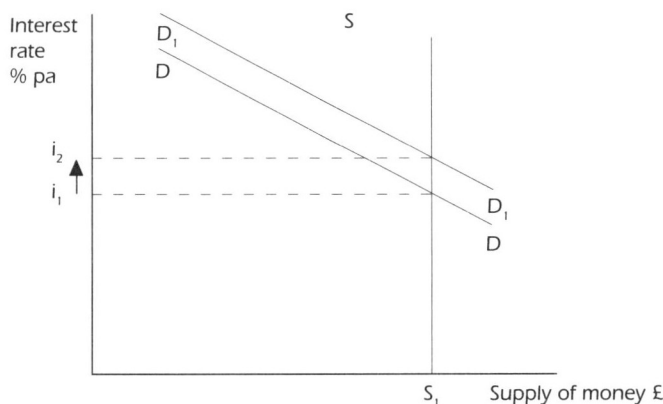

S_1 is the new money supply – notice that it is to the right of S in Fig. 6.4 and D_1 is the new demand curve, but it is not possible to deduce whether i_2 is above or below i_0, its original level. The extent of the increase in the interest rate depends mainly on the spare capacity in the economy at the time if the original increase in the money supply. The less the slack in the economy, the greater will be the rise in the interest rate.

Price expectations effect

2.14 If the economy is working at or very close to full capacity at the time of an increase in money supply, then people and firms will observe that output rises more in price than in volume. In other words, they will see an increase in inflation, and act accordingly. They will expect prices to rise and so the purchasing power of their money balances , i.e. their demand curve for money shifts to the right. Similarly, the investors realise that the purchasing power of their money balances will fall, so, to maintain it, they increase their demand for money. The diagram is very similar to Fig. 6.5 in the previous paragraph.

2.15 Because the liquidity preference theory views interest rates as the price of money, it is often regarded as a 'monetary theory' of interest rate determination. This can be confusing to new students, because Keynes and his supporters have little in common with the monetarist theories of Milton Friedman and his associates.

Student Activity 2

1. What are the assumptions of Fisher's theory?   *(Paragraph 2.1)*

2. What is Fisher's Law?   *(Paragraph 2.4)*

3. Explain why his theory is often called a real theory of interest rate determination.
                                                                              (Paragraph 2.5)

4. What are the assumptions of Keynes' theory?   *(Paragraph 2.8)*

5. What are, according to Keynes, the three elements in the demand for money?
                                                                              (Paragraph 2.7)

6. Examine the two effects, in his theory, of an increase in the supply of money.
                                                                          (Paragraphs 2.11–14)

7. Explain why Keynes's theory is regarded as a 'monetary theory' of interest rate determination.   *(Paragraph 2.15)*

3   Explaining the overall level of interest rates

3.1 As we have just seen, two major theories have been advanced to explain the overall level of interest rates in an economy: the Classical theory (otherwise known as the loanable funds theory and based on Fisher's theory) and the Keynesian theory. These two theories take radically different approaches to the explanation of the overall level of interest rates but they can in practice be reconciled quite easily by making use of the differing time horizons to which they are intended to apply. Thus, while they are in a sense alternatives, it is more useful to regard them as being two halves of a more complete explanation than either theory could provide on its own. Note also that both these theories seek only to explain the *overall* level of interest rates and do not seek to explain the distribution of interest rates that may apply at any particular point in time. Explanations of the distribution of interest rates at a point in time are considered in section 7 of this unit.

3.2 Quite simply, the *Classical theory* focuses upon what might be termed the real economic variables, and argues that the level of *real* interest rates is determined by the level of saving (which provides a flow of loanable funds) and the level of investment in capital equipment and so on (which provides a demand for loanable funds). The more that people wish to save, the lower will be the level of interest rates, as the supply of loanable funds rises relatively to demand. Conversely, the more that people wish to invest, the greater will be the demand for borrowed funds and, other things being equal, the higher will be the rate of interest.

3.3   The Classical theory dismisses the relevance of money, arguing that its use is merely to determine the absolute price level and does not influence the real amounts of saving and investment. By contrast, the *Keynesian theory* emphasises the supply of and demand for money, arguing that it is the interaction of these two variables which determines the rate of interest. Basically, the more money (or liquidity) that people wish to hold, other things being equal, the higher will be its price (the rate of interest); the greater the supply of money, the lower the price, and so on.

The reconciliation of the Classical and Keynesian theories

3.4   The two theories can in practice be reconciled by making reference to the *time period* over which they are intended to apply. The Keynesian approach is essentially concerned with the causes of *short-term* changes in interest rates. Thus, while (for example) an increase in the money supply would exert downward pressure on the interest rate without spilling over into increased prices in the rest of the economy, in the longer term any increases in the money supply *would* cause increased prices, which should in turn raise the demand for money in order to meet the costs of transactions at these higher prices, and hence would bring about a return to the original level of interest rates.

3.5   The Classical theory, on the other hand, is primarily concerned with *longer-term* changes in interest rates. While the Classical theory maintains that an increase in the money supply will only have an impact on the price level in the longer term, it accepts that due to imperfections within the economic system this will not occur over shorter time periods. In the short term, an increase in the money supply, the Classical theorists accept, will probably increase the supply of loanable funds and hence bring about a fall in interest rates. In the longer term, as the effects of the increased money supply feed through into the general price level, the interest rate will return to its previous level since all the additional liquidity will have been absorbed into increased prices.

3.6   Thus, we are left with the position that while the Keynesian theory seeks primarily to explain short-term changes in interest rates, it is not inconsistent with the explanation for the longer-term changes in interest rates proposed by the Classical theory. Equally, while the Classical theory is primarily concerned with explaining longer-term changes, it is not, in turn, inconsistent with the explanation of short-term changes in interest rates put forward by the Keynesian theory.

Summary of causes of changes in the overall level of interest rates

3.7   Having examined the Classical and Keynesian theories of the determination of interest rates, we turn next to the use of these theories in summarising the major causes of changes in interest rates within the real world. For this purpose we must look separately at the factors giving rise to changes in *nominal* interest rates on the one hand and *real* interest rates on the other.

Nominal rates

3.8 The causes of *increases* in nominal interest rates are as follows.

● *A reduction in the money supply*, or the introduction by the authorities of policies to reduce the rate of growth of the money supply, would generally result in higher nominal rates of interest. The techniques for controlling the money supply that are considered in Unit 7 may all be utilised, and in this respect the attainment of a higher level of interest rates might constitute a deliberate target in order to curb the demand for borrowed funds within the economy.

● *Increased actual or expected rates of inflation* are likely to give rise to increases in interest rates, as lenders within the economy, in the absence of index-linking, seek to protect the real purchasing power of their financial assets.

● *Increases in the level of economic activity* will cause increases in nominal interest rates, since with an increasing number of transactions to be financed by a constant stock of money a shortage of liquidity will become apparent at the original level of interest rates.

● *Increases in interest rates in overseas financial markets* are likely to cause an increase in interest rates in the domestic economy. The increasingly international nature of financial markets means that higher interest rates overseas will cause a relocation of funds towards those overseas markets to benefit from the higher rates. To limit the loss of deposits, domestic financial intermediaries are likely to increase their rates, or else the government, in order to avoid a large outflow of funds and an associated drop in the exchange rate, may initiate an increase in interest rates. (This is expanded in the final paragraphs of section 9 of this unit.)

3.9 These sources of upward pressure on interest rates will, when operating in reverse, cause decreases in nominal interest rates. In addition, note that all these factors will operate to increase nominal interest rates on an 'other things being equal' basis. It should be recognised, however, that other things will frequently *not* be equal, and certain factors will be operating in opposite directions. For example, while an increase in the expected rate of inflation may be acting to raise nominal interest rates, increases in the money supply (which may itself be the cause of the raised expectations of inflation) may be operating to keep nominal interest rates low.

Real interest rates

3.10 Factors which are likely to cause a rise in *real* interest rates include:

● *Factors causing increases in nominal interest rates which are not accompanied by equal increases in inflation* will, by definition, give rise to increases in real interest rates. Thus, any factor which operates *solely* to increase nominal interest rates will have this effect, an example of which would be an increase in the demand for money, under the Keynesian theory, with the money supply constant. Alternatively, any factor which operates *solely* to reduce the inflation rate while leaving nominal interest rates unchanged would raise the real interest rate. The majority of influences on the inflation rate will, in practice, also cause changes in nominal interest rates (indeed, many of the counter-inflation policies deliberately make use of higher nominal interest rates). However the operation of a prices and incomes policy by the government, if successful and unaccompanied by any monetary or fiscal policy instruments, would reduce inflation whilst leaving nominal interest rates unchanged. By extension, of course, any factor which causes a proportionately greater reduction in inflation than in nominal interest rates would also raise the real interest rate.

● *Increases in the desired level of investment or reductions in the desired level of saving* would, in terms of the Classical theory, increase the real interest rate. Given the emphasis of the Classical theory, this will be a longer-term influence with increases in the desired level of investment originating perhaps from technological developments.

● *Monetary policy*, designed to reduce the rate of growth of the money supply, may require increases in the *real* interest rate. The monetary authorities may need to raise nominal interest rates substantially above either the current or the expected inflation rate in order to bring down the rate of growth of the money supply to target rates.

● *The fiscal policy* of the government may have implications for real interest rates. If the government is running a large budget deficit, the financing of this deficit in a non-inflationary manner may give rise to a high level of real interest rates due to the increased demand within the economy for borrowed funds.

● *A high level of uncertainty* will generate higher real interest rates through an increase in the perceived risk associated with lending in financial markets. The increased level of uncertainty could have a number of causes, both short-term and long-term, which would include social and political changes either within the country itself or in major overseas countries, given the international nature of financial markets.

All these five factors will operate in reverse to bring about a fall in real interest rates. In addition, we have again assumed that they operate on an 'other things being equal' basis, whereas in practice they would tend to operate together either to offset or to reinforce the direction of change of real interest rates.

Student Activity 3

1. What is the 'Classical theory' of the level of interest rates?

    (Paragraphs 3.2–3)

2. What is the 'Keynesian theory' of the level of interest rates?   *(Paragraph 3.3)*

3. In what sense are the Classical theory and the Keynesian theory of interest rates complementary?   *(Paragraphs 3.4–6)*

4. Summarise the factors which may cause nominal rates of interest to rise.

    (Paragraphs 3.8–9)

5. Examine the factors which may cause real rates of interest to rise.

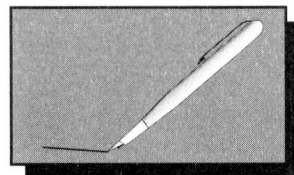

    (Paragraph 3.10)

4 Types of bonds

4.1   Strictly, *fixed-interest rate securities* can be classified into two groups:

- *Discounted securities*, such as UK treasury bills and CDs, which are issued at a price below their redemption value, so that the increase in their market value is, in effect, the rate of interest. However, in arithmetical terms, we are looking at rate of discount, which is not the same as a rate of interest.

- *Coupon securities*, such as, for example, Treasury 8% 2009, which pays £8 in two half-yearly instalments every year for every £100 of stock. At a price of 99.25% (£99.25) this would yield 8.06% (£8/99.25 × 100).

4.2   One very large borrower in most countries' fixed-interest securities markets is the government of that country. In the USA, it is the Federal Treasury – the world's largest borrower. In the UK, it is the UK Treasury. However, there the similarity ends because in the USA there is a very wide range of borrowers in the bond market whereas in the UK there is, for most purposes, only the UK government.

4.3   In the USA there are 50 state governments, with their bond issues, and a host of municipal borrowers. In the UK there are no state governments, while local authorities have been rigorously controlled for years and there are few of their issues which remain. For instance, at the end of June 1996, the *Financial Times* quoted the prices and yields of 71 of the most frequently traded gilts, but under 'other fixed interest' it published data for only 14 securities. However, fixed-interest securities issued by UK companies feature in the companies section, along with all the equities, e.g. Fiscal Properties 7.5% Loan 2020 is quoted immediately after its ordinary shares. Accordingly, the US market is the better one from which to quote examples of bonds.

4.4   *Floating rate securities* are found mainly in the Eurocurrency markets and have been mentioned in the section on interest rate swaps in Unit 4. In the domestic markets, they are less common, particularly in the UK gilt market. Thus, there are only two floating rate gilts whose prices are quoted in the *FT*.

4.5   Floating rate securities are popular with lenders/borrowers wishing to match their cashflows. Companies may prefer them to having to issue repeated short-term fixed rate bonds. If inflation is high when the debt is issued, then the floating rate will capture the fall in interest rates when inflation falls: hence a 'floater' can be cheaper than a 'straight' as a fixed rate security is often known. Finally, issuing a floater can enable a borrower to enter into an interest rate swap.

4.6   However, most borrowers prefer the certainty of fixed rate borrowing for their cashflows and profit forecasting and also tend to borrow when interest rates are low and markets are buoyant.

Risk premium

4.7   This is the yield on a non-governmental borrower's debt compared to that on a 'on-the-run' US Treasury stock of a similar maturity ('on-the-run' means 'tap' gilt in the UK). The latter is termed a 'base interest rate', which is confusing to UK readers, who are almost certain to confuse it with 'base rate', which is decided by the Chancellor of the Exchequer. In Europe, we talk of such an interest rate as a benchmark rate. The yields on government bonds are invariably lower than on other bonds; hence the premia. Risk premia arise for a number of reasons:

- Type of issuer;
- Perceived credit-worthiness of issuer;
- Term to maturity;
- Terms of the issue;
- Tax treatment of interest;\
- Anticipated liquidity of the market in an issue.

Type of issuer

4.8   This can be a company (domestic or foreign), a foreign government, or an international organisation, such as the World Bank. In the USA, the bond market is divided into a number of sectors, one of which comprises corporations (companies). This, in turn, is subdivided into four:

- Utilities (gas, water, electricity);
- Transportations;
- Industrials;
- Banks and finance companies.

Perceived credit-worthiness of issuer

4.9   In the USA, there are five commercial rating companies. Two of these are also widely used in the UK – Standard & Poor's and Moody's – which also uses IBCA for banks and building societies. Other US agencies are Duff and Phelps, McCarthy's and Fitch.

Term to maturity

4.10   The greater the time before the security matures, the greater is its price volatility. The difference between the yields in any two maturity sectors of the same type of security is known as the maturity spread. In the UK, the converse of this is known as the pull to maturity which makes short-dated stocks more stable than long-dated stocks.

Terms of the issue

4.11   For example, the inclusion of options to convert into another stock. If the option is a put or conversion option, then the spread against a comparable issue without such an option will be less than if the option were a call. The reason is that the call favours the borrower whereas the put favours the lender.

Tax treatment of interest

4.12   In the UK, interest from gilts is subject to income tax, but in most cases there is no liability to capital gains tax.

Anticipated liquidity of the market

4.13   The greater the expected liquidity in an issue, then the smaller the spread against a Treasury stock.

1. Give two examples, from the UK, of discounted securities. *(Paragraph 4.1)*

2. Calculate the interest yield on 8% Treasury Stock 2009, at a price of 101.
   (Paragraph 4.1)

3. In which section of the *FT* are found the prices of UK company loan stocks?
   (Paragraph 4.3)

4. What are the advantages of floating rate debt to company borrowers?
   (Paragraph 4.5)

5. Explain why there is a 'spread' between company loan stocks and gilts of the same maturity. *(Paragraphs 4.7–13)*

6. Who measures the creditworthiness of a corporate borrower? *(Paragraph 4.9)*

5   Calculating yields

Interest yield

5.1   This yield has several other names – flat, current, or running yield. It also has two subdivisions – whether it is gross or net of income tax. And, when net of income tax, there are several rates of tax to consider – 20%, 24% or 40% for 1996/97. Apart from that, it is relatively simple to calculate:

$$\text{Gross interest yield} = \frac{\text{Coupon of the stock}}{\text{Price of the stock when bought}} \times 100\%$$

Thus, on 22 July 1996, 7% Treasury 2001 stood at 98.5, so that an investor who bought at that price would calculate his gross running yield as:

$$\frac{7}{98.5} \times 100$$

$$= 0.071066 \times 100$$

$$= 7.11\% \text{ (to two decimal places)}$$

5.2   This stock is a FOTRA gilt (free of tax to residents abroad) but it is likely that the investor is a UK resident and subject to income tax at one of the three rates quoted above. The investor therefore has to deduct tax at the appropriate rate to obtain a *net interest yield*. For simplicity's sake, it is easier to multiply by the percentage not taken in tax. For example:

Tax rate	multiply by	and divide by 100
20%	80%	

$$7.11 \times \frac{80}{100} = 5.69\%$$

24%	multiply by 76%	
40%	multiply by 60%	

5.3   The calculations are simple ratios, and do not have to take into account the length of time to maturity. In other words, the same calculation is done whether the stock matures in 1998 or 2028.

Redemption yield

5.4 Although they appear daily in the financial press, redemption yields are very difficult to calculate without the aid of a computer. The reason is that they contain two components, both of which are discounted to today's value and then added. One is the stream of income to be received and the other is the capital gain or loss on redemption. The formula is:

$$P = \frac{C_1}{(1 + i)} + \frac{C_2}{(1 + i)^2} + \frac{C_3}{(1 + i)^3} \ldots\ldots\ldots + \frac{C_n}{(1 + i)^n} + \frac{R}{(1 + i)^n}$$

Where:

P is the price paid

C is the coupon (say 7%)

R is the redemption value

n is the number of years to maturity

i is the unknown (the yield)

$\dfrac{C_1}{(1 + i)}$ is the present value of the first dividend to be received, and

$\dfrac{C_2}{(1 + i)^2}$ is the present value of the next dividend, duly discounted

and so on ...

Solving this equation is a complex process involving algorithms and using iteration – in ordinary language, trial and error.

5.5 Although there is an answer to such an equation, its accuracy does depend on the assumption – which many people may make instinctively – that interest rates remain unchanged. In other words, when the interest received is reinvested then that reinvested money receives a constant rate of interest. When phrased like that, the response is obvious – interest rates change.

Performance yield

5.6 This type of yield is not used so frequently, but it resembles the redemption yield except that it is looking forward only to a date of sale rather than the maturity of the security. Once the stock is sold, the value P is certain (not an unknown) and so the performance yield can be calculated exactly. However, when looking to a prospective sale, the future price can be only an estimate based on forecasts of the yields and on possible dates.

Student Activity 5

1. Using the example above, calculate the net running yields at 24% and 40% income tax rates. *(Paragraph 5.2)*

2. Explain the three types of yield on fixed-interest securities.

3. State their formulae.

4. Calculate the net interest yield on Exchequer 13% 2013–17 when its price is 133³/₄. *(Paragraph 5.2)*

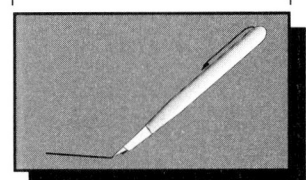

5. Explain why its price is 133³/₄ when it will be redeemed at only 100 (i.e. much less). *(Clue: look at the coupon and present day yields)*

6. The Treasury can repay this at any time in the years 2013 to 2017. If base rate in those years is 5%, when is the stock likely to be repaid? If base rate in those years is 15%, when is the stock likely to be repaid?

   (Clue: how much interest is saved after repayment?)

7. Explain why performance yields are not published on a regular basis in the financial press. *(Paragraph 5.6)*

6   The term structure of interest rates

Introduction

6.1   This unit has concentrated so far on explaining the *overall level* of interest rates – either nominal or real – that will apply within an economy at a point in time. In this section, we turn to considering the *distribution* of interest rates at a point in time, specifically the *term structure* of interest rates. The term structure of interest rates may be defined as

> the spread of interest rates that are paid on the same type of assets with different terms to maturity.

6.2   This concept of the term structure of interest rates is only of relevance in the case of those assets which have a fixed term to maturity and pay a fixed interest at specified periods. The major group of such assets in the UK is gilt-edged securities issued by the government, although other groups, such as sterling certificates of deposit, also satisfy the requirements and the general principles involved can be applied to financial assets more widely.

6.3   Examination of the list of 'British funds' (gilts) in the *Financial Times* will reveal that there are a number of different gilts with the same coupon rate (for example, 10%) but with differing periods to maturity. The list also reveals that the *yield* on these gilt-edged securities – which differ only in terms of their period to maturity – normally varies quite markedly. It is this *spread* of interest rates paid on the same type of assets (in this case gilts) with different terms to maturity that theories of the term structure of interest rates seek to explain.

The yield curve

6.4   The term structure of interest rates on a particular type of asset may be represented diagrammatically in the *yield curve*. Strictly speaking, the yield on an asset includes not only the interest income from that asset but also any capital appreciation (due to the current price being less than the sum paid on maturity) or capital depreciation (due to the current price being greater than the sum paid on maturity). In the list of gilts in the *Financial Times*, the return that includes any capital appreciation or depreciation is termed the *redemption yield*, while the return that only takes account of the interest income is termed the *interest yield* (as described in section 5 of this unit).

6.5   For the vast majority of gilts, the redemption and interest yields are very similar; only for short-dated gilts where the coupon rate is substantially different from the current market interest rate will the difference be noticeable. For our purposes, however, the difference between the two is of little importance, and hence the terms 'yield' and 'interest rate' will be used interchangeably. The 'normal' yield curve (note: for nominal and not real interest rates) is represented in Fig. 6.6.

Figure 6.6 Normal yield curve

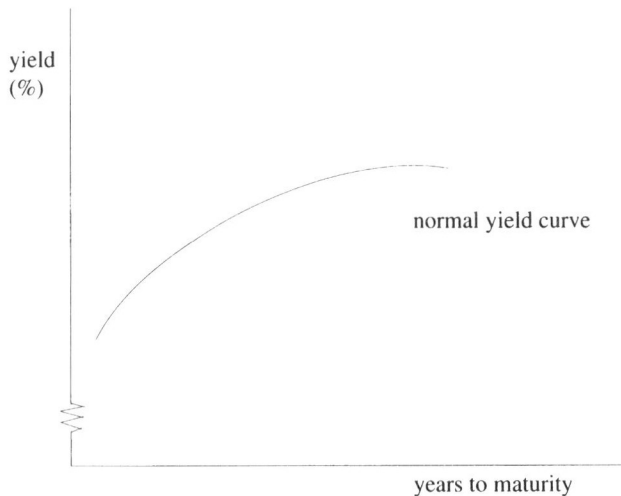

6.6　The curve depicted in Fig. 6.6 is referred to as the 'normal' yield curve because it is constructed on the assumption that within the market there is no specific expectation of interest rate movements in either direction. It is furthermore assumed that there exists some element of uncertainty within the financial environment. Given those two assumptions, the characteristic upward slope of the normal yield curve is attributable to *liquidity preference* and to *risk*.

6.7　With regard to *liquidity preference*, note first that any lending involves a loss of immediate purchasing power. When lending for a short period of time, this loss of immediate purchasing power may be relatively slight and so the lender may not require much compensation. When lending for longer periods of time, however, the lender would generally require a higher level of compensation. This compensation is, of course, reflected in the interest rate and so is one explanation why, under 'normal' conditions, interest rates on long-dated loans will be higher than on short-dated loans. It is important to appreciate that this principle applies just as strongly to marketable securities as to non-marketable loans, the reason being that while with marketable securities the lender can sell the security, there is a risk of capital loss associated with a premature sale, and the possibility of premature sale increases with the maturity of the security.

6.8　The overall *risks* associated with lending increase over time, because other risks increase. These are the risks of:

- *Default*, of either interest or principal, which will generally increase with the length of the loan;

- *Real capital loss due to inflation*, which increases with the length of the loan;

- *Capital loss on marketable securities* which, if they have to be sold prior to maturity, increases with the length of the loan;

- *Changes in the lender's circumstances* which, making a particular loan within a portfolio inappropriate to new circumstances, will increase with the length of the loan.

6.9 For all these four reasons, lenders will seek compensation, in the form of higher interest rates, for loans of long maturity compared with loans of short maturity. When taken in conjunction with the liquidity preference principle, it is clear to see why the normal yield curve slopes upward. The strength of the attitude towards liquidity preference and towards risk will determine the slope of the curve, with the observed tendency for the curve to rise gently over longer maturities reflecting the fact that it becomes difficult to evaluate the compensation required for the increased risk or for the loss of liquidity associated with, say, an extra year to maturity when a loan already has several years to maturity.

The influence of interest rate expectations on the yield curve

6.10 Having considered the determinants of the shape of the 'normal' yield curve when there are no specific expectations of changes in interest rates, the next issue to address is: what will be the impact on the shape of the yield curve if there *are* specific expectations of changes in interest rates?

Expectations of a fall in interest rates

6.11 When there is a general expectation of a fall in interest rates, the effect is for long-term rates to be depressed relative to short-term rates. The reason for this is that lenders prefer to make longer-term loans now at the higher rate; they want to avoid lending short-term now because they will only be able to re-lend the funds at low interest rates after those short-term loans have matured. Hence, there will be an increased supply of long-term funds to the market and a reduced supply of short-term funds, which will serve to lower long-term rates and raise short-term rates. These effects will be *reinforced* by the preferences of borrowers; expecting a fall in interest rates, borrowers will wish to borrow short-term in order to be able to rollover their loans at the new, lower rates when those short-term loans mature. Equally, they will seek to avoid borrowing long-term until the fall in interest rates materialises. Hence, there will be an *increased demand* for short-term loans which, in conjunction with the reduced supply from lenders, will serve to increase short-term interest rates; there will also be a reduced demand for long-term loans which, in conjunction with the increased supply from lenders, will serve to lower long-term interest rates. The impact on the yield curve is to make it flatter, as shown in Fig. 6.7.

6.12 If the expectations of falls in interest rates are particularly strong, then it may be the case that the influence of these outweighs the influences of risk and of liquidity preference that give rise to the upward-sloping 'normal' yield curve. In such circumstances, the yield curve will become *downward*-sloping, with interest rates on securities with long maturities being *lower* than those with short maturities.

6.13 Downward-sloping yield curves were observed in the UK gilts market and in several other UK securities markets in a number of periods between the early 1980s and autumn 1992. As we have just discussed, for downward-sloping yield curves to be observed, the expectations of lower interest rates have to be

**Figure 6.7 Effect on yield curve of expectations of
an interest rate fall**

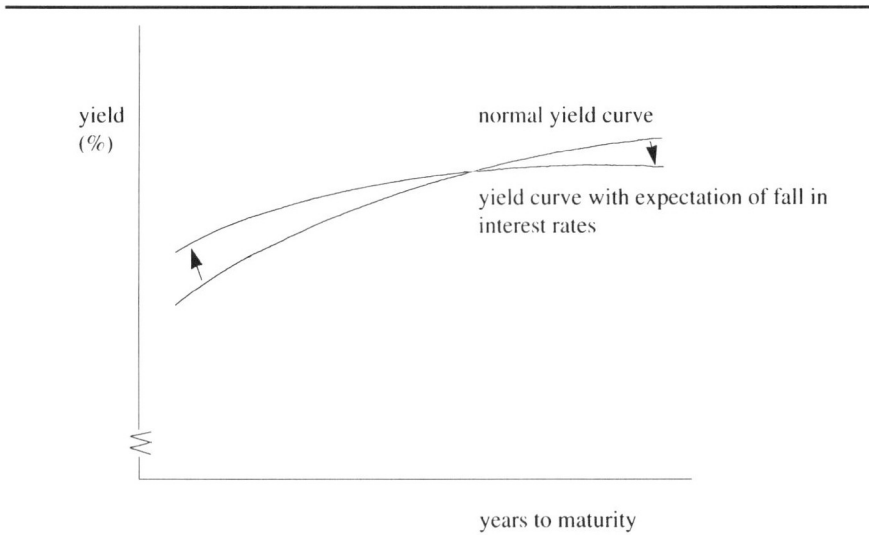

sufficient to swamp the normal risk– and liquidity-preference influences. Within the UK markets, this in turn was a reflection of the very high nominal interest rates observed periodically, when combined with the expectation that inflation-reducing policies would prove successful, thus leading to reductions in interest rates in due course. Frequently, these expectations were for falls in interest rates in the *medium* term, with the result that the yield curve was upward-sloping over the span of shorter maturities and only became downward-sloping over the longer maturities (Curve 1 in Fig. 6.8. Only on those occasions when interest rates were particularly high and were seen as a short-term expedient, expected to last only a short period of time, was the yield curve downward-sloping throughout (Curve 2 in Fig. 6.8).

Figure 6.8 Downward-sloping yield curve

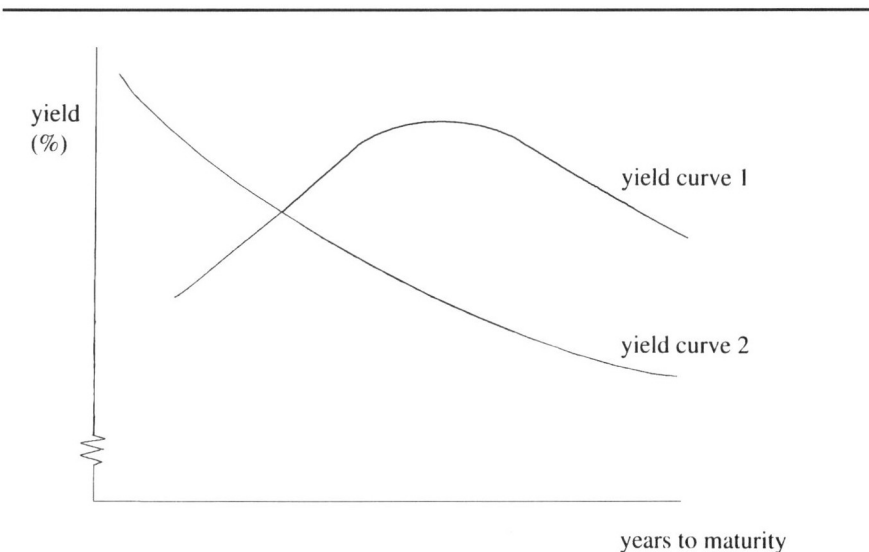

Expectations of a rise in interest rates

6.14   When a rise in interest rates is generally expected, the impact will be for long-term rates to be increased relative to short-term rates. The reasons for this are largely the reverse of the reasons for a rise in short-term rates relative to long-term rates when a fall in interest rates is expected. If there are generalised expectations of a rise in interest rates, borrowers will seek to borrow long-term in order to lock in at the current low rates, and will seek to avoid borrowing short-term since this may involve rolling-over loans at higher interest rates. Hence, there will be an increased demand for long-term loans and a reduced demand for short-term loans. Lenders, on the other hand, will be unwilling to lend long-term if rates are expected to rise, and will instead seek to lend only short-term in order to profit from the high rates when they materialise. The combination of a reduced demand from borrowers and an increased supply from lenders of short-term loans means that short-term rates will fall, while the increased demand from borrowers and reduced supply from lenders of long-term loans means that long-term rates will increase. The effect will be for the yield curve to become more steeply upward-sloping than the 'normal' yield curve, as is shown in Fig. 6.9.

6.15 In practice, the yield curves that are observed will frequently *not* be smooth curves; they invariably display humps or dips. We have already considered why the yield curve might initially be upward-sloping and subsequently downward-sloping when there are expectations of falls in the interest rate in the medium term, but the patterns are often considerably more complicated than this. The reason is that the precise shape of any yield curve will be influenced by the particular format of the expectations about interest rate changes. We have only taken a general form here, in terms of a rise or fall in interest rates; in practice, they may, for example, be expected to fall in nine months' time followed by a rise in two years' time, and this would be reflected in the shape of the yield curve.

**Figure 6.9 Effect on yield curve of expectations of
interest rate increases**

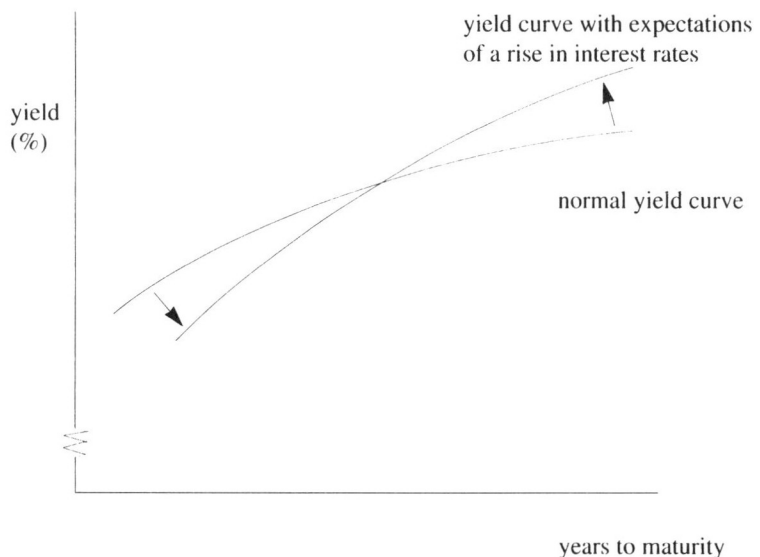

Student Activity 6

1. Define the 'term structure of interest rates'. *(Paragraphs 6.1–2)*

2. To what type of assets is the 'term structure analysis' relevant?
   (Paragraphs 6.2–3)

3. What is a yield curve? *(Paragraphs 6.4–6)*

4. Why does the 'normal' yield curve slope upward from left to right?
   (Paragraphs 6.6–9)

5. In what way do expectations of a fall in interest rates affect the shape of the yield curve? *(Paragraphs 6.11–13)*

6. In what way do expectations of a rise in interest rates affect the shape of the yield curve?

7. Which one of the four diagrams in this section could be said to have applied in the first half of 1996? *(Clue: were interest rates expected to rise or fall?)*

More advanced theory

6.15 Two main theories seek to explain the shapes of yield curves.

- Expectations, which is subdivided into:
  - ○ pure expectations, i.e. only expectations
  - ○ liquidity – biased expectations, in that other factors are important
  - ○ preferred habitat – biased expectations, in that factors are important.
- Market segmentation, which disallows large-scale arbitrage between the various segments of the market.

Pure expectations

6.16 If we assume a flat yield curve, but with investors/borrowers now expecting rates to rise (prices to fall), then lenders would invest at the short end of the market, profiting when prices had fallen by enjoying higher yields. This would push up prices (force down the curve) at this end. Borrowers would, of course, want to borrow for much longer periods, forcing up the yield at that end. These actions will tilt the curve in an anticlockwise direction from its horizontal position.

6.17 The theory fails to consider the risks involved, so that the investors in the previous paragraph and the borrowers are taking on risks – nobody knows future prices (price risk) or future rates of interest (reinvestment risk).

Liquidity

6.18 Investors are willing to pay a premium for not being liquid, i.e. buying long-dated stocks, and this urge to be compensated for illiquidity will be more important than the expectations which may result in a downward sloping curve. This premium has an upward bias on the curve, so that it usually has a positive slope (upwards from left to right).

Preferred habitat

6.19 This variant of the expectations theory argues that investors prefer to match their assets with known liabilities – because they are risk-averse. Hence, they

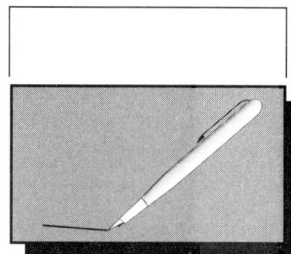

often 'lock-in' to a fixed rate. Also, life assurance companies, and pension funds, as we saw in Unit 2, try to match the maturities of their assets and liabilities.

6.20   In order to be encouraged to shift out of their 'preferred habitats', such investors will require to receive a substantial premium on the yield (which can be negative in some cases). This premium will, therefore, cause the yield curve to have a positive or negative slope, or even be horizontal.

Market segmentation

6.21   A lay person might describe this theory as 'a highly structured and inflexible version of the preferred habitat theory'. It assumes that neither investors nor borrowers are able or willing to move along the yield curve to take advantage of arbitrage opportunities.

6.22   The reason for this highly inflexible compartmentalisation (segmentation) of the market is that regulators and/or the investing institutions' own rules require them to keep certain strict percentages of their assets in each of the market sectors , e.g. less than six months; six months to two years, etc.

6.23   Under this theory, the yield curve is constructed from the yield curves of the various segments of the fixed-interest securities market. Some economists regard this theory as unsustainable because it presupposes that there is absolute risk aversion, whereas evidence shows that investors are willing to take risks and arbitrage along the yield curve. In other words, its critics regard it as a structured version of the preferred habitat development of the expectations theory.

Student Activity 7

1.   Outline the two main theories of the shape of yield curves.   *(Paragraph 6.15)*

2.   Describe the variants of the expectations theory.   *(Paragraphs 6.16–20)*

3.   Distinguish between the preferred habitat version of the expectations theory and the market segmentation theory.   *(Paragraphs 6.19–23)*

4.   Examine the effects on the credibility of these theories if the new European Central Bank were to introduce complex and rigid assets ratios so as to match the known liabilities of commercial banks.   *(Paragraph 6.22)*

5   What might be the 'preferred habitats' of an investor aged 30 who has:

   (a) borrowed £65,000 on a 25-year mortgage
   (b) borrowed £8,000 over five years to finance his MBA studies
   (c) no liabilities such as these, but who has an invalid child who needs constant attention. The court has awarded the child £500,000 in compensation.
                                                                                    (Paragraph 6.19)

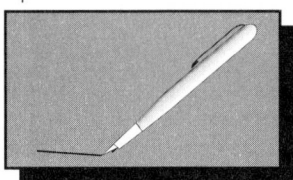

7 Using a yield curve to price a bond

Spot rates

7.1 In section 4 of this unit we discussed, under the heading of risk premia, the factors causing the spread between company loan stocks and gilts of a similar maturity. This technique can be used to calculate yield curves and then to price a fixed-interest stock.

7.2 In paragraph 5.4 the formula for calculating redemption yields was explained. We now separate the interest payments (strip is the technical word) from the capital sum and view the cash flow of (say) 6% stock due in 2001 as:

£6 due on (say) 1/10/96 as £6 due then but discounted to today's (23/7/96) value

£6 due on 1/4/97 and discounted to today's value

£6 due on 1/10/97 and discounted

and so on until

£6 due on 1/10/01 and discounted

+ £100 due on 1/10/01 and discounted

(In fact, this stripping will begin in the London gilts markets in the summer of 1997, as was mentioned in Unit 3.)

7.3 Using lay people's language, we are discounting these stripped interest payments to ascertain their value today (rather than £6 in (say) two years' time). In the USA, these discount rates are called 'spot rates' and can be plotted on a graph to show a 'spot rate curve'.

7.4 By a process known in American as 'bootstrapping' (lifting oneself by one's boots in English), it is possible to construct from actual Treasury bill and bond yields a 'theoretical spot yield curve' for a coupon security discounted in this way.

Forward rates

7.5 These are used in such decisions as: 'Faced with a choice of investing in a six month Treasury bill now, or a three-month Treasury bill now and then another in three months' time, at what interest rate do I need to borrow in three months' time to be indifferent to both alternatives?'

7.6 The forward rate is the yield on the three-month Treasury bill in three months' time. It can be calculated from the spot rate for a six-month Treasury bill, less the spot rate for a three-month bill. Such rates are called 'implied' or 'implicit forward rates'.

7.7 In the same way, implied forward rates for (say) a two-year security in three years' time, can be calculated from the spot yield curves for three and five years for that security (2 = 5 less 3). (Care: avoid confusion with spot and forward exchange rates). Such implied forward rates are most important for decisions on:

- Investing – go for the whole term, or a series of shorter investments?
- Borrowing – borrow long-term, or borrow short-term and renew on expiry?

Student Activity 8

1. Explain what is meant by 'stripping'. *(Paragraph 7.2)*

2. What is a theoretical spot rate curve? *(Paragraph 7.4)*

3. What is an implied forward rate? What is it implied from? *(Paragraph 7.7)*

4. Why are implied forward rates important to managers in company treasuries?
   (Paragraph 7.5)

8 Differentials between interest rates on different types of assets

8.1 There is a danger in regarding loans as being somehow uniform, varying only in terms of maturity. In practice, every loan – whether or not it involves the issuance of a security – is unique since it represents a composite of characteristics that are particular to that loan (asset), and the interest rate on that loan is only one characteristic. It is the combination of these various characteristics that influences the demand for and supply of that asset, and hence determines the price – which here means the interest rate. The extent to which the various characteristics underlying each asset are demanded or supplied determines the pattern, and any changes in the pattern, of interest rates across different assets within the economy.

8.2 This section seeks to draw together some of the characteristics involved in loans that have already been identified, at the same time as identifying others that have not been considered so far. Given that every loan involves a *combination* of characteristics, remember that these will vary in importance; and indeed some will not figure at all in particular loans. It is the particular combinations that do, indeed, generate the spread of interest rates applying at any one time.

Characteristics of borrowing and lending transactions

Term to maturity

8.3 As we discussed in the context of the term structure of interest rates, the longer the term to maturity of a loan the higher will be the interest rate, if fixed for the duration of the loan, which is sought by the lender as compensation for the loss of liquidity. This, of course, assumes that any expectations of future interest rate reductions do not outweigh the underlying risk and liquidity preference factors. Moreover, the longer this period of a loan, the greater is the chance that the other characteristics – such as government policy – may change.

Risk

8.4 The default risk associated with the payment of either interest or principal on a loan was identified above in paragraph 1.19. The higher the perceived risk involved in lending to a particular borrower, the larger will be any risk premium charged by the lender, in the form of a higher interest rate. With large financial intermediaries this may be formalised by means of charging a borrower a certain margin, over a reference interest rate such as LIBOR, according to the perceived risk.

Expectations of changes in interest rates

8.5   As we also saw in the discussion of the term structure of interest rates above, an expectation of a rise in interest rates would induce lenders to seek higher interest rates for any long-term loan. Equally, an expectation of lower interest rates would induce lenders to accept lower interest rates than would otherwise be the case. However, expectations of interest rate movements will not be identical across all borrowers and lenders. Hence, at any one time the interest rate that a borrower and a lender are prepared to pay and accept for a transaction may well be different from that for another transaction elsewhere in the economy. To avoid becoming locked in to interest rates which bear little relation to market interest rates after the loan has commenced, both borrowers and lenders may be inclined to agree loans on a floating interest rate basis at times of high interest rate volatility.

Size of the loan

8.6   Because of the existence of economies of scale on both the borrowing and the lending sides, a large-scale loan may attract preferential interest rates. From the point of view of a financial intermediary, a large deposit would attract lower administration costs (per £1 deposited) and hence the financial intermediary would be prepared to offer a higher interest rate to attract such deposits. Similarly, large-scale loans may justify a lower interest rate charged by the financial intermediary because lower administration costs are associated with servicing that loan. However, both large-scale deposits and large-scale loans may involve an increase in *portfolio risk* for the financial intermediary – the withdrawal of a large-scale deposit may pose problems and a large-scale loan may involve an undesirable concentration of risk due to inadequate diversification. Both these aspects of increased portfolio risk may serve to offset – in some cases, more than offset – the benefits of enhanced economies of scale.

Interest rates elsewhere

8.7   The high level of international interdependence of financial markets means that most domestic interest rates will be influenced by changes in interest rates in other financial markets, particularly in the USA (see paragraph 10.6).

Expectations of inflation

8.8   These will cause lenders to seek, and borrowers to be prepared to pay, higher interest rates than if price stability were anticipated. As with expectations of interest-rate changes, however, expectations of inflation will vary across the participants in borrowing and lending transactions. The borrower and lender in one transaction in which both parties have relatively low expectations of inflation would result in a lower interest rate on that transaction than one in which the parties have higher expectations of inflation. In this way, another cause of a *spread* of interest rates is established.

Tax considerations

8.9   The taxation regime applicable to particular assets and the taxation position of the borrower and of the lender is likely to affect the interest rate applicable to one asset compared with others. By way of example: examination of the list of gilts in the *Financial Times* will often reveal short-dated gilts with a redemption yield somewhat higher than fixed rate National Savings Certificates (NSCs), due to the different tax treatment of capital gains and interest income from a gilt-edged security and the complete exemption of NSCs from these two taxes.

Marketability of an asset

8.10   Where a loan transaction results in the issue of a security, the marketability of that security will influence the interest rate, with higher marketability being associated with lower interest rates.

Business strategy of the financial intermediary

8.11   A particular financial intermediary may decide to follow a strategy of maximising its short-term profits, in which case you would expect to see low rates for depositors and high rates for borrowers, whereas another may be following a strategy for short-term growth by squeezing its margins and offering relatively high rates for depositors and low rates to borrowers. The effect, along with other alternative strategies, is for financial intermediaries to be offering a spread of lending and borrowing rates at any one point in time.

Fixity of the interest rate

8.12   The degree to which the interest rate on a loan is fixed (both the range within which it is fixed and the time period over which it is fixed), together with the terms for negotiating 'rolling over' the loan, will influence the rate that the lender is willing to accept. Facilities for indexation of a loan may reduce the *real* interest rate that a lender is willing to accept.

Type of loan

8.13   Term loans offered by a financial intermediary where interest is paid on the sum of money lent regardless of whether the money is used by the borrower or not, will generally attract a lower interest rate than an overdraft facility where interest is paid only on the funds used by the borrower.

Government intervention

8.14   This is likely to influence the spread of interest rates at a point in time in a number of ways. The various methods of financial regulation established by the government will influence the cost structures, and hence the interest rates paid and required by financial intermediaries, to different extents. The policies pursued by government to control monetary conditions may also influence the structure of interest rates, through the use of open-market operations, restrictions on hire-purchase agreements, interest rate ceilings and officially administered rates. As we saw in the discussion of the influences on the money supply of the form of financing the PSBR or PSDR in Unit 14, the form chosen may well have an impact on the interest rate structure according to the type of security traded and the institutions or individuals involved.

Market imperfections

8.15   Finally, it is important to recognise that sizeable participants in a financial market, other than the government, may distort the interest rate structure. Legal constraints on the participation of certain groups of institutions in particular markets may also give rise to a distorted pattern of interest rates.

The interest rate cartel operated by the building societies until the early 1980s, buttressed by restrictions on the ability of banks to enter the housing finance market, resulted in mortgage rates being out of line with rates elsewhere for long periods of time.

8.16 Taken together, these 13 factors provide ample explanation for a spread of interest rates being observed within the economy at any one point in time. They do not, however, cover variations between interest rates in domestic and Eurocurrency markets.

Student Activity 9

1. Why might each type of loan be thought of as being unique?

    (Paragraphs 8.1–2)

2. In what way might the size of a loan affect the rate of interest charged?

    (Paragraph 8.6)

3. What is the relevance of expectations of inflation to the pattern of interest rates established? *(Paragraph 8.5)*

4. What is the importance of a financial intermediary's business strategy to the pattern of interest rates established? *(Paragraph 8.11)*

5. How may market imperfections affect the pattern of interest rates established?

    (Paragraph 8.15)

9 Key UK interest rates

Money market rates

9.1 The London sterling money market interest rates are crucial for the financial system of the UK. The reason for this is that they determine the cost of acquiring funds for many financial institutions and the *marginal* cost of funds for many more. As a consequence, they influence the interest rates applied to every loan transaction within the economy. A number of the money market interest rates in the London sterling markets on 2 October 1996 are reproduced in Table 6.1.

9.2 As regards the *level* of interest rates, since the maximum maturity of the transactions to which these interest rates apply is one year, the Keynesian (liquidity preference) theory of the determination of interest rates is relevant. However, it is important to remember the influence of the *Bank of England* on these rates. The Bank seeks to influence interest rates by intervention in the discount market (the 'primary' money market). In recent years the emphasis has been on the manipulation of very short-term rates (by means of dealing in bills in Bands 1 and 2 – bills of up to 33 days' maturity), and hence for these rates the influence of the Bank of England is an important additional factor. However, given the portfolio adjustment that occurs if interest rates of any particular maturity are affected, in practice the influence of the Bank of England will spread outwards from these two bands to other maturities. If the Bank engineers a rise in very short-term rates, for example, then rates for slightly longer-dated assets will become more attractive to borrowers and less

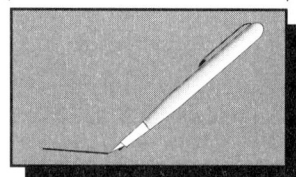

Table 6.1 London money market interest rates, 2 October 1996 (% pa)

	Overnight	7 days' notice	One month	Three months	Six months	One year
Interbank Sterling	$7^{1}/_{4}$–$5^{1}/_{2}$	$5^{7}/_{8}$–$5^{5}/_{8}$	$5^{15}/_{16}$–$5^{13}/_{16}$	$5^{15}/_{16}$–$5^{13}/_{16}$	$6^{1}/_{16}$–$5^{15}/_{16}$	$6^{5}/_{16}$–$6^{3}/_{16}$
Sterling CDs	—	—	$5^{27}/_{32}$–$5^{25}/_{32}$	$5^{27}/_{32}$–$5^{25}/_{32}$	$5^{15}/_{16}$–$5^{7}/_{8}$	$6^{1}/_{8}$–$6^{1}/_{16}$
Treasury bills (buy)	—	—	$5^{11}/_{16}$–$5^{9}/_{16}$	$5^{11}/_{16}$–$5^{9}/_{16}$	—	—
Bank bills (buy)	—	—	$5^{23}/_{32}$–$5^{21}/_{32}$	$5^{23}/_{32}$–$5^{21}/_{32}$	$5^{13}/_{16}$–$5^{3}/_{4}$	—
Local authority deposits	$5^{13}/_{16}$–$5^{11}/_{16}$	$5^{13}/_{16}$–$5^{11}/_{16}$	$5^{13}/_{16}$–$5^{3}/_{4}$	$5^{7}/_{8}$–$5^{13}/_{16}$	6–$5^{7}/_{8}$	$6^{1}/_{8}$–$6^{1}/_{16}$
Discount market deposits	$6^{3}/_{4}$–$5^{3}/_{4}$	$5^{7}/_{8}$–$5^{3}/_{4}$	—	—	—	—

Source: Financial Times, 3 October 1996

attractive to lenders, thereby giving upward pressure to those slightly longer-term rates.

9.3 The *term structure* of the interest rates in this table may be explained by the theory of the term structure of interest rates which, in turn, makes use of risk, liquidity preference and interest-rate expectation characteristics. The data in the table demonstrate that the yield curve for the securities identified there was generally upward-sloping throughout, hence implying that there were no expectations of future falls in interest rates to offset the normal upward-sloping tendency associated with risk and liquidity preference.

9.4 Finally, the *spread* of interest rates in the table will be determined by the *particular set* of characteristics of each asset. The instruments with the lowest rates (Treasury bills, bank bills) are those associated with the primary market; those with the higher rates are associated with the secondary markets and reflect the higher risk and, in some instances, reduced marketability.

9.5 A short supply of day-to-day credit on the London money market on 2 October 1996 was responsible for the high overnight inter-bank offered rate of $7^{1}/_{4}\%$ on that day, and for some distortion to the pattern of overnight interest rates. The spread between the inter-bank offered bid rates is usually much finer, but shortages or surpluses on any particular day will cause the spread to be wider.

Bank base rates

9.6 Bank base rates are another important set of interest rates; whereas money market interest rates attract little attention from the media, changes in bank base rates are very widely reported because they are usually initiated by the Chancellor of the Exchequer. Partly as a consequence of their prominence within the media, they have become an indicator of the health of the economy, with any changes in them also attaining political importance. Such political importance derives partly from the politician who decides to change them but also because of their effect on the economy.

9.7 It is important to bear in mind that bank base rates are indeed *base* rates. They are the *starting point* from which a bank determines its lending rates and, to some extent, its deposit rates also. Lending rates are calculated as a percentage above the bank's base rate, with a loan regarded as being low-risk charged at a rate a percentage point or two above base rate and loans of higher risk several percentage points above base rate.

9.8 A proportion of term loans provided by banks are at rates linked to money market rates, and so bypass the base rate calculation altogether. This is not to say, however, that the principles involved in the calculation of base rates are overlooked; the money market rates will generally represent the interest cost to a bank of acquiring *additional* funds, and the margin over money market rates will reflect the perceived risk and the administration costs. Lending at rates linked to money market rates does, of course, have the advantage of reducing the interest rate risk associated with lending.

9.9 Finally, although bank base rates are the starting point for determining the lending rates charged by banks, many other lending rates are linked to bank base rates and acquire an increased importance as a result. Since base rates are an important competitive tool, differences of any size between the base rates of competing banks would lead to large switches of loans and deposits between them. Consequently, bank base rates tend to be very similar, if not identical, at least for the larger banks. Furthermore, any *changes* in bank base rates will all tend to be announced at the same time for the same reasons.

Student Activity 10

1. Why are the London sterling money market rates of such crucial importance for the operation of the UK financial system? *(Paragraph 9.1)*

2. Which theory is relevant to the explanation of the level of sterling money market interest rates? *(Paragraph 9.2)*

3. What factors affect the level of bank base rates? *(Paragraph 9.6)*

4. What is the advantage to a bank of making loans at rates linked to market rates? *(Paragraph 9.8)*

The relationship between sterling money market rates and commercial bank lending rates

9.10 We have noted that both sterling money market interest rates and bank base rates represent very important sets of interest rates within the financial system. In this section we look more carefully at the relationship between sterling money market rates and bank base rates, emphasising particularly the link between sterling money market rates and the lending rates charged by commercial banks.

9.11 The commercial banks are important participants in the sterling money markets, both in lending funds and in borrowing funds. In this respect, the markets are crucial to the adjustment of the banks' liquidity positions since it is virtually impossible for a bank to increase its funds at short notice through increasing its retail deposits when profitable lending opportunities arise – and

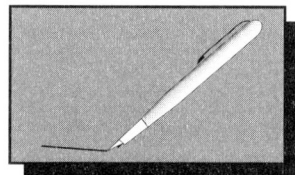

equally, it is virtually impossible to *reduce*, at short notice, its funds obtained through retail deposits when it has excess funds due to a shortage of lending opportunities. Retail deposits generally take a long time to respond to any changes in interest rates, but furthermore, any changes in rates will have to be applied to *all* the funds to which those rates apply – a bank cannot just pay a higher rate on the *additional* deposits that it attracts to a particular type of account.

9.12 The *marginal* cost of raising additional funds from retail sources is therefore very high and sufficient to encourage greater use by the banks of the whole-sale money markets for liquidity adjustment purposes where the markets are relatively sensitive to small changes in rates, and where transactions are negotiated individually and quickly. The short-term inter-bank interest rates therefore provide a good indicator of the marginal cost of funds to a bank, and it is the three-month LIBOR (London Inter-Bank Offered Rate) and three-month LIBID (London Inter-Bank Bid Rate) that have become the benchmark interest rates in this respect. (Three-month rates are used due to their stability relative to shorter-term rates, and due to the widespread use of three-month maturity in many money market instruments and transactions.)

9.13 The impact of changes in short-term inter-bank interest rates on the rates charged by commercial banks on their lending will depend upon the basis on which the loan has been agreed. There are three alternative bases relevant here, at a fixed margin above:

- An inter-bank rate (for example, LIBOR);
- The bank's base rate; and at a
- Fixed rate.

At a fixed margin above an inter-bank rate

9.14 The relationship between the inter-bank rate and the rate charged on a commercial bank loan is straightforward here, since if a loan has been made at, say, 3% above three-month LIBOR, a rise in LIBOR will give rise to an immediate rise in the rate charged by the bank.

At a fixed margin above the bank's base rate

9.15 The relationship is somewhat more complicated here, since it depends on the link between a bank's base rate and the inter-bank rates. Base rates tend to follow the general trend in short-term inter-bank rates over the longer term, due to the fact (considered above) that the short-term inter-bank rates represent the marginal cost of funds to a bank. For some banks, where a significant proportion of their lending is funded from these wholesale sources, these short-term inter-bank rates come close to representing the *average* cost of funds in addition to the marginal cost. However, over the short term, inter-bank rates will tend to diverge from bank base rates due to the cost and perhaps the loss of customer goodwill associated with frequent changes in base rates. Accordingly, banks will tend to adjust their base rates when the change in inter-bank rates is expected to be long-lasting, when it is a relatively large change, and when the proportion of a bank's funding at these inter-bank rates is relatively high. The result is that adjustment tends to take place with a lag, and in relatively large steps when it does occur, but in certain cases a very narrow profit margin on lending activities may cause a bank to change its base rates quickly.

9.16 Banks will not wish to let the divergence – in either direction – between base rates and inter-bank rates become too large, since this will encourage *arbitrage* at the bank's expense. Arbitrage involves, for example, borrowing from the banks when base rates are low in order to on-lend in the wholesale markets. In this instance, it is the divergence between very *short-term* wholesale rates and base rates that is important, since arbitrageurs will generally only wish to lend short-term in case base rates rise when they will find themselves locked into an arbitrage transaction at rates that lose them money. If money lent on the wholesale markets can be regained quickly in order to end the borrowing from the banks, the risk is naturally reduced.

At fixed rates

9.17 Some lending – particularly to the personal sector – is undertaken by banks on a fixed-rate basis. Clearly, changes in inter-bank rates will have no impact on existing fixed rate loans, but as they mature and new loans are negotiated, the new fixed rates are likely to reflect the altered cost of funds to the bank.

The relationship between mortgage rates and short-term interest rates

9.18 Given that mortgage repayments constitute a substantial element of the total outgoings of many households, changes in mortgage rates have become an important and politically sensitive issue. The UK housing finance system is dominated by *variable rate mortgages* (which are by no means universal in other countries), which means that while the mortgage loan may be for an initial maturity of 25 years, this is of little importance in determining the interest rate charged. Typically, the provider of the housing finance has to obtain funds on a very short-term basis, and hence the rate charged will necessarily reflect the cost of these funds. If the cost of funds rises, the need to maintain profitability will ensure that the rate charged to borrowers increases, and if it falls, competitive pressures will ensure that this change is also reflected.

9.19 Short-term money market rates will clearly be important in the determination of mortgage rates where mortgage providers obtain their funds from the money markets. An increasing proportion of mortgage funds have been obtained from the money markets in recent years. Where a mortgage provider does obtain a significant proportion of funds from the wholesale markets, any change in short-term money market interest rates will be reflected that much more fully and quickly in changes in the mortgage rate. Even where a mortgage provider obtains all the funds from retail sources, however, changes in short-term rates will still have an impact. Changes in money market rates now filter through to change rates in the rest of the financial system relatively quickly as borrowers and lenders of all types adjust their portfolio positions to reflect the changed structure of interest rates, and hence lead to changes in the rates that have to be paid to attract retail deposits. Nevertheless, there is likely to be a time-lag involved here and the movement may not be of the same amount. A consequence of this is that different mortgage providers may be charging different mortgage rates at any one point in time, because the composition of their sources of funds gives rise to a varying cost of funds, rather than because of any differences in competitive strategy. These relative cost positions will, of course, vary over time with changing money market and retail rates.

9.20 Although short-term interest rates will therefore have an impact on mortgage rates, other factors, especially in the longer term, will exert their influence also. The overall profile of the demand for and supply of long-term mortgage funds will be a significant factor in the establishment of rates, alongside the shorter-term influences from the money market. In this regard, those factors which affect the overall level of interest rates discussed in section 3 are relevant. In addition, there may be particular considerations that apply to the demand for and supply of mortgage funds, such as the extent to which housing is seen as a tax-efficient and profitable investment, and demographic changes in the population. Such considerations and other market imperfections (see section 8) may lead to a differential between rates on mortgage funds and those elsewhere.

9.21 As with commercial bank lending, mortgage providers will seek to avoid very frequent changes in rates due to the administrative cost and lost goodwill associated with such changes. Some mortgage providers now only change the repayments due from borrowers once a year (although the rates charged on the loan may be changed more frequently). Overall, mortgage rates do not adjust particularly quickly to changes in short-term rates. Fixed-rate mortgages, at least over a limited number of years, are becoming more familiar within the UK system.

The relationship between domestic and international interest rates

9.22 Section 3 above noted that one of the influences on the overall level of interest rates in an economy would be the interest rates that applied in other financial centres in the world. This influence will be greater the more open is the financial system of the economy and it is notable that the UK represents one of the most open financial systems. Given that openness, the links between interest rates in the UK and interest rates elsewhere in the world are likely to be very complex. Nevertheless, three broad influences linking interest rates in one country with those elsewhere in the world may be identified:

- The economic environment;

- Expectations of movements in exchange rates;

- Actual and expected inflation rates relative to other countries.

The economic environment

9.23 A robust economy that is experiencing, and is expected to continue to experience, a high growth rate normally generates considerable confidence. In the current context, that high level of confidence will be reflected in a low rate of expected defaults on loans. With that low risk premium incorporated into the interest rates, you would expect such economies, other things being equal, to have low interest rates relative to other economies. (Conversely, of course, countries where investments are perceived to carry greater risk – due to doubts about economic prospects or about political or social stability – would see higher interest rates than elsewhere.)

Expectations of movements in exchange rates

9.24 Expectations that the value of a currency is going to depreciate relative to other currencies will lead investors to require a premium to compensate for any loss in international purchasing power resulting from such a depreciation.

This premium will naturally make interest rates higher in that country than elsewhere. Conversely, in circumstances where there are general expectations of an appreciation of a currency, interest rates on assets denominated in that currency will tend to be lower than elsewhere. When an expectation of an appreciation or a depreciation of a currency develops, unless there is a sufficient differential in interest rates, funds are likely to be moved between currencies in order to take account of the better return to be gained from holding assets in that currency (in the case of an expected appreciation) or in another currency in the case of an expected depreciation.

Actual and expected inflation rates relative to other countries

9.25 A country with a high rate of inflation relative to those in other countries will carry a higher (nominal) interest rate since investors will require a premium in terms of interest rates to compensate for the loss in purchasing power that the high rate of inflation involves. A higher expected rate of inflation would have corresponding implications for the term structure of interest rates relative to other countries.

9.26 These three broad influences on a country's interest rates relative to those elsewhere may also be the source of pressure for *changes* in interest rates. As was implied in paragraph 9.24, expectations involving a depreciation of the exchange rate may induce the government to raise interest rates in order to prevent this, but they may also induce financial intermediaries to raise their deposit rates in order to avoid the outflow of funds that would otherwise occur.

Student Activity 11

1. Why do banks use money markets to adjust their liquidity positions rather than retail deposit markets? *(Paragraph 9.11)*

2. Examine the ways in which an increase in money market rates may affect banks' on-lending rates. *(Paragraphs 9.12–17)*

3. Other than money market interest rates, what factors are likely to affect the rate of interest charged on mortgage loans? *(Paragraph 9.20)*

4. In what way is the general condition of a country's economy likely to affect the level of its interest rates relative to those existing in other countries? *(Paragraph 9.23)*

5. What is the relevance of expected exchange rate movements for the determination of domestic interest rates? *(Paragraph 9.24)*

10 Recent trends in UK interest rates

10.1 While real interest rates on the majority of retail, and frequently wholesale, financial assets were *negative* during the 1970s, since the early 1980s the position has changed significantly. Since 1981 real interest rates have been positive for the majority of both retail and wholesale financial assets and in several years, furthermore, have been historically *high*. The UK has not been unique in this respect; most industrialised countries have experienced similar trends.

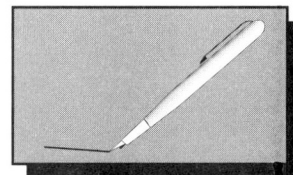

10.2   It is useful to identify some of the causes of this trend in real interest rates. Note that the emphasis here is on explaining the trend rather than the more detailed changes and levels that have applied at particular points in time.

Inflation

10.3   Given that real interest rates are nominal rates adjusted for inflation, the inflation rate is an important influence on real interest rates. With nominal interest rates remaining at high levels, the fall in average inflation rates experienced during the 1980s saw real interest rates rise. In addition, it appears that nominal rates adjusted more quickly to the increase in inflation during the early 1980s, perhaps due to learning from experience in the 1970s. It has also been suggested that expectations of inflation were very slow to fall, with the result that nominal interest rates lagged well behind the fall in inflation. More recently nominal interest rates have fallen substantially, but so too has the rate of inflation, thereby having only a limited impact on real interest rates.

Monetary policy

10.4   The government has a major influence over nominal interest rates through monetary policy, and it is notable that the UK government has made extensive use of monetary policy in order to control inflation. Tight monetary controls have periodically pushed up interest rates which, in so far as the controls led to a fall in inflation, thereby pushed up real interest rates.

Sterling exchange rate

10.5   During the latter half of the 1980s, the government became more acutely aware of the implications of depreciation in the value of sterling on the international exchanges, particularly for the inflation rate in the UK. As a result, monetary policy increasingly took into account the sterling exchange rate, with high interest rates being used to sustain the value of sterling when depreciation looked likely. Since Autumn 1992, policy has been more relaxed in this context, with the result that interest rates have been set to reflect the strengths and weaknesses of the domestic economy, with special emphasis on the outlook for underlying inflation two years ahead.

Economic policy in the USA

10.6   The US dollar dominates the international financial system, with the consequence that the economic policies followed by the US government impinge upon all other countries in the system. During much of the 1980s, large fiscal expansion in the USA was accompanied by a relatively tight monetary policy, leading to high nominal interest rates. Since inflation rates were relatively low in the USA, this implied high real rates. The ease of movement of funds between the UK and the USA meant that the rates offered to attract deposits within the UK had to be high to offset the competition from the US.

Problems within the international financial system

10.7   A major influence here was the Third World debt crisis which pushed up the risk premium and therefore the interest rate charged by financial institutions on international lending. The relatively severe world recessions of the early 1980s and early 1990s also served to increase the default risk associated with much commercial lending, leading once again to upward pressure on interest rates.

Increasing financial sophistication

10.8   It has been suggested that the lenders of funds within the private sector are now much more sensitive to the real interest rate as a consequence of their experience of the 1970s. Funds are no longer deposited at low or zero nominal interest rates to the extent that they were, and a greater readiness to search out and shift money to assets with higher interest rates has put upward pressure on rates.

Competition between financial institutions

10.9   The growth of competition between financial institutions (a notable example being that between banks and building societies) has also put upward and downward pressure on rates. At least until the recession at the beginning of the 1990s, the high level of demand for credit – especially within the housing market – allowed higher rates to be paid. Afterwards, a reaction set in, and competition in the mid 1990s caused interest rates to fall as a number of banks and building societies competed for market share in a stagnant market.

Long-term trend in interest rates

10.10 It has been argued that the *normal* pattern for interest rates is for real rates to be positive. On this basis, the negative interest rates seen in the 1970s were the deviation from the norm that requires explanation, and the situation since the early 1980s should be seen as being the normal situation. The experience of the 1970s can be explained by a combination of rapid monetary growth and a slow adjustment of expectations of inflation to reality. However, real interest rates were, on a historical basis, 'above trend' in the 1980s and early 1990s; these can, though, be attributed to the combination of the other seven influences identified here. It can be said that the high real rates of interest hurt over-borrowed companies and individuals during these periods.

Student Activity 12

1. Examine the main factors which are believed to have influenced the level of interest rates in the UK in recent years.

2. How dependent is the UK on world interest rates?   *(Paragraph 10.6)*

3. Are real interest rates in the UK ever likely to become negative again?
                                                                                        (Paragraph 10.10)

4. Compare and contrast the effect of competition between bank and building societies in the late 1980s and in the mid 1990s.   *(Paragraph 10.9)*

5. When the large building societies have converted to banks by the end of 1997, what is likely to happen to interest rates?   *(Paragraph 10.9)*

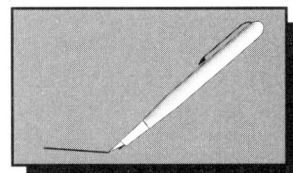

Summary

Now that you have completed this unit you should be able to:

- **explain what interest rates are;**

- **distinguish between nominal and real rates of interest;**

- **examine the two theories concerning the determination of interest rates;**

- **understand why there are so many rates of interest;**

- **outline the effects of interest rate changes;**

- **calculate the yield to maturity of a bond;**

- **classify the various types of bonds;**

- **identify and draw yield curves, and explain the significance of their shapes and slopes;**

- **understand what spot rates and implied forward rates are;**

- **describe the most important UK interest rates.**

Self-assessment questions

Short-answer questions

1. Real rates of interest can only be measured approximately even when nominal rates are absolutely fixed. Why?

2. What is the relevance of money to the Classical theory of interest rates?

3. What is shown by a term structure of interest rates?

4. Why are there so many different rates of interest in a modern economy?

5. List the major characteristics of a borrowing and lending transaction relevant to the determination of its interest rate.

6. What factors will tend to speed up the response of base rates to an increase in sterling money market rates?

7. List the three broad influences which tend to link one country's interest rates to those of other countries.

8. What is likely to be the effect on the current account of the UK balance of payments of an increase in UK interest rates?

Multiple-choice questions

1. Indexation:
   (a) guarantees to the lender a minimum nominal return on funds lent
   (b) means that the borrower is uncertain of the nominal amount of interest to be paid until the time it is due for payment

    (c) removes all risk for the lender associated with lending

    (d) provides the borrower with a ceiling to the amount of interest which will have to be paid on a loan in nominal terms.

2. Which of the following is most likely to cause nominal rates of interest to rise?

    (a) reduced levels of inflation and expected inflation

    (b) a slump in the domestic economy

    (c) a fall in the level of real interest rates required by lenders

    (d) a tightening of official monetary controls.

3. The real rate of interest:

    (a) will rise if the rate of inflation falls more quickly than the level of nominal interest rates

    (b) will fall if the rate of inflation rises more slowly than the level of nominal interest rates

    (c) depends entirely upon the position of the government's monetary policy

    (d) will tend to fall over time as the desired level of capital investment in the economy rises, other things being equal.

4. If there are general expectations that interest rates are to fall, yield curves for gilt-edged securities:

    (a) will always slope downward from left to right

    (b) will slope downward from left to right as long as the expectation effect outweighs the underlying risk and liquidity preference effects

    (c) will only slope downward from left to right when there is felt to be no risk attached to lending

    (d) will always slope upward from left to right because of the underlying risk and liquidity preference effects.

5. Bank base rates:

    (a) will always rise when sterling money market rates rise

    (b) are the rates which banks charge on their loans (other than those linked directly to market rates)

    (c) form the starting point only for the calculation of interest rates charged to some borrowers

    (d) tend to differ quite significantly between banks due to the high degree of competition which now exists.

6. Higher real rates of interest will tend to:

    (a) reduce the 'endowment' effect which retail banks experience

    (b) cause bank turnover to increase as it is much easier for them to attract deposits

    (c) cause banks to narrow their profit margins in order to remain competitive

    (d) have adverse effects on banks' profitability due to ensuing reduced demands for loans and increased provisions for bad debts.

Unit 7

Monetary Policy

Objectives

After studying this unit, you should be able to:

- state the objectives of monetary policy and relate monetary policy to the other types of economic policy;

- appreciate the need for immediate targets, with stable relationships between them and the goals of economic policy, as a means of monetary control;

- describe in detail the instruments of monetary policy in the UK;

- analyse the effects of monetary policy on the banking and financial system and the rest of the economy;

- assess the effectiveness of the UK's monetary policy since 1980;

- identify the goals and targets of monetary policy in the world's three major economies.

1 Monetary policy in context

1.1 An emphasis on monetary policy is appropriate for two reasons:

- Since the beginning of the 1980s the UK government – along with governments in many other industrialised nations – has attached considerable importance to monetary policy within the overall framework of its macroeconomic policy.

- It is relevant to this course, given its title of 'The Monetary and Financial System'.

1.2 Remember, however, that monetary policy constitutes only one possible element of a macroeconomic policy package. The emphasis placed upon monetary policy in recent years, and the control of the money supply in particular, is not the historical norm. Prior to the 1980s macroeconomic policy packages comprised a balance of alternative policies, and there are indications that many governments are returning to this view.

Economic policy objectives

1.3 Although it may seem obvious, it is nevertheless a point worth making, that the purpose of economic policy is to attain *objectives*. By extension, only if those objectives are clearly identified can the *design*, *implementation* and *evaluation* of economic policy be conducted. Conventionally, the four objectives of economic policy are usually held to be:

- *A high and stable level of employment.* This does, of course, have its equivalent in a low and stable level of *unemployment*. It does not, however, imply zero unemployment: a certain level of unemployment is appropriate for the efficient operation of a changing economy, since, for example, it will take people a period of time to switch between jobs, or to retrain for a new job, and so on.

- *A low and stable rate of inflation,* which is considered a necessary objective of economic policy, in order to try to avoid the costs associated with inflation. In particular, many economists (but by no means all) argue that low inflation is a necessary prerequisite for achieving sustainable economic growth.

- *A high rate of economic growth,* since economic growth provides for the increases over time in the living standards of the population. This rate of economic growth should be at least comparable to those of competing nations.

- *A satisfactory balance of payments,* which is usually taken to mean an equilibrium, or a modest surplus, over the longer term. A long-term equilibrium on the balance of payments implies that a country is able to pay its way in international terms and to purchase imports, while a surplus would imply that its stock of overseas assets is, in addition, increasing.

1.4   While these four factors constitute the major objectives of economic policy, other objectives should not be overlooked. A *satisfactory distribution of income and wealth* is put forward as a fifth objective. This distribution of income and wealth can be held to refer to either *individuals,* i.e. there should be neither very rich nor very poor individuals, or *regions,* i.e. there should not be particularly rich and particularly poor regions in the country.

Conflicts between economic policy objectives

1.5   A serious problem surrounding the attainment of the four major economic policy objectives identified above is the existence of *conflicts* between those objectives. In other words, the attainment of any one objective is often at the expense of the attainment of one or more of the other objectives.

1.6   The major conflicts are between full employment and economic growth, and between low inflation and balance of payments equilibrium. In more detail: policies to raise the level of employment (and hence reduce unemployment) will generally involve raising the overall level of demand for goods and services within the economy (the level of 'aggregate demand'). This will encourage producers to produce more and perhaps to invest in new production facilities, and will generally lead to an improved rate of economic growth. But policies which raise the level of aggregate demand will tend to *raise prices* (and hence be inconsistent with the low inflation objective), and in addition a high level of aggregate demand will frequently spill over into a raised level of *imported* products (a particular problem for the UK) with the consequence that the *balance of payments worsens.*

1.7   The inconsistency between two pairs of objectives can, of course, be seen between inflation and the balance of payments: a policy to achieve a low rate of inflation may often be consistent with a balance of payments equilibrium since it may involve a low demand for imported goods. However, it may involve a low demand for goods and services generally, and hence be *inconsistent* with low unemployment and high economic growth objectives.

1.8 In practice, much of the debate about how economic policy should be operated is ultimately concerned with how a *package* of policies may be put together which will allow the attainment of all four objectives at once – or, at least, the attainment of two or three while maintaining the remaining one or two within 'acceptable' ranges. Invariably, however, the government is left with the need to make choices and to trade off one policy objective against another, in order to identify an appropriate balance between the objectives. Into this problem enters the additional consideration of the *timescale* involved. For example, most economists would agree that an increase in employment and economic growth can be achieved by means of pursuing expansionary policy. Monetarists, however, would maintain that this increase in employment and economic growth would be only *temporary*, and that the expansionary policies would lead to an increase in inflation in the longer term, concurrent with falls in employment and economic growth. Monetarists see low inflation as a prerequisite for longer-term economic growth and employment and therefore advocate policies to reduce inflation – which would generally involve *contractionary* policies *reducing* employment and growth in the short term. In this context, therefore, the importance is that not only does the government have to decide on the trade-off between different objectives, it has also to decide over what *time period* it wishes to pursue those objectives.

1.9 In the 1980s, governments of many industrialised countries allocated priorities to these targets, with inflation first and economic growth second. Conflict can occur in international relations when governments of important countries have differing priorities in economic policy.

Student Activity 1

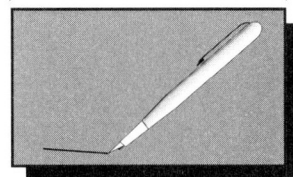

1. What are the four objectives normally listed in respect of a government's economic policy? *(Paragraph 1.2)*

2. Give some examples of the ways in which economic policy objectives may conflict. *(Paragraph 1.5)*

3. Why is it generally accepted that governments require a 'package' of economic policies? *(Paragraph 1.7)*

4. Why is it important for a government to be clear over the time period for which a policy objective is to be pursued? *(Paragraph 1.7)*

2 Forms of economic policy

2.1 Bearing in mind our concentration on macroeconomic policy, the five major forms of economic policy are:

- Monetary policy;
- Fiscal policy;

- Exchange rate policy;
- Prices and incomes policy; and
- National debt management policy.

This section will look briefly at what each of these forms of economic policy involves. In doing so, remember that any one policy will form part of a policy *package*, and that the way in which that policy is employed will be dependent upon the other components of that package.

Monetary policy

2.2   The purpose of monetary policy is to control some measure (or measures) of the money supply and/or the level and structure of interest rates. The importance attached to monetary policy within a government's policy package will depend not only upon its view of the operation of the economy (monetarist/ Keynesian) but also upon the decision it has reached regarding the priority given to different objectives. For example, if the attainment of low inflation is seen as being the major objective and the government is of a monetarist persuasion, considerable importance will be attached to monetary policy. If, on the other hand, inflation is the major objective but the government is of a Keynesian persuasion, different policies such as prices and incomes policies or interest rate policies are likely to be emphasised, with monetary policy being allocated a supporting role.

Fiscal policy

2.3   Fiscal policy is concerned with decisions regarding the level and structure of government expenditure and taxation. Given the importance of the levels of government expenditure and taxation in determining the size of the Public Sector Borrowing Requirement (PSBR) or the Public Sector Debt Repayment (PSDR), fiscal policy therefore also involves decisions regarding the size of the PSBR/PSDR.

2.4   As with monetary policy, the importance of fiscal policy within an economic policy package is dependent upon the prioritisation of objectives and of the view taken of the operation of the economy. Fiscal policy has traditionally been regarded as having its impact through its influence on the level of aggregate demand within the economy.

- An *expansionary* fiscal policy would involve increasing government expenditure relative to taxation in order to boost the level of spending within the economy and thereby bringing more people into employment and enhancing economic growth.

- Alternatively, a *contractionary* fiscal policy would involve raising taxation relative to government expenditure, with the purpose of reducing aggregate demand and lowering inflation and the demand for imports – though with the side-effects of lowering employment and growth.

Exchange rate policy

2.5   Exchange rate policy involves the targeting of a particular value of the exchange rate. While the exchange rate relative to any one currency may carry particular weight (for example US$, DM), the value of the currency relative to the country's major trading partners in general is more likely to be the objective. A major purpose of exchange rate policy is to influence the flows within the balance of payments, and may be used by some countries in conjunction with other measures such as exchange controls, import tariffs and quotas. However, the latter three practices are restricted or forbidden under a number of trade agreements (such as the EU and the World Trade Organisation), so their use is generally confined to smaller countries which are not yet members.

Prices and income policies

2.6   A prices and incomes policy is intended to influence the rate of inflation by means of either statutory or voluntary restrictions upon increases in wages, dividends and/or prices. The range of prices and incomes over which such a policy may prevail, and the degree of statutory control involved, is subject to considerable variation. Within the UK, prices and incomes policies have been avoided by the government since 1979, although extensive use was made of them, in various formats, during the 1960s and 1970s.

National Debt management policy

2.7   *National debt management policy* is concerned with the manipulation of the outstanding stock of government debt instruments held by the domestic private sector with the objective of influencing the level and structure of interest rates and/or the availability of reserve assets to the banking system. Given that fiscal policy, through its relation to the PSBR/PSDR, involves decisions regarding the issue of new government securities and monetary policy has as one of its concerns the level of interest rates, it is inevitable that national debt management policy is closely related to both fiscal policy and monetary policy.

2.8   From this brief discussion of the different forms of economic policy, it should be clear why a *package* of economic policies will be required. Any one particular policy may have a beneficial impact upon one – or perhaps more than one – of the economic policy objectives. However, it may also often have a *detrimental* impact on one or more of the other objectives, and hence *additional* economic policies may be required in order to offset those detrimental impacts. By juggling the form and severity of the different economic policies – and taking into account the expected future trends within the economy – a package of policies may be put together to achieve the objectives identified.

2.9   By way of illustration, consider an example where the economy has high unemployment, moderate inflation and an approximate equilibrium on the balance of payments. In order to cure the high unemployment, an expansionary fiscal policy may be advocated. Such a policy may, however, initiate a rise in inflation and an increased volume of imports giving rise to a balance of payments deficit. Accordingly, a prices and incomes policy may be instituted in order to prevent inflation rising, along with an exchange rate policy to maintain a low exchange rate to deter imports and maintain the competitiveness of exports.

2.10   It is important to appreciate that, in the context of the formation of a package of economic policy measures, the government *has* to make a decision about the position of most components of such a package. While the decision regarding a prices and incomes policy is (at least initially) an either/or decision, this does not apply, for example, to fiscal policy; the government is forced to take decisions about expenditure and taxation, and hence a stance on fiscal policy is automatic. Similar considerations apply to monetary policy and to exchange rate policy; even a decision to 'do nothing' to interest rates and the exchange rate is a conscious decision with corresponding policy implications.

Student Activity 2

1. What determines the importance of monetary policy in the government's economic policy package? *(Paragraph 2.2)*

2. What does fiscal policy involve? *(Paragraph 2.3)*

3. What are prices and incomes policies? *(Paragraph 2.6)*

4. In what ways is debt management policy closely related to monetary and fiscal policies? *(Paragraph 2.7)*

3   Objectives, targets and instruments

3.1   We have, so far, been assuming that a particular economic policy – say, monetary policy – will have a direct impact upon one of the objectives of economic policy, such as inflation. This is not, in practice, the case; in reality, there will be a *chain* that links policies to objectives, with policies having their impact through instruments and intermediate targets.

- *Economic policies* are the group of five policies, such as monetary policy and fiscal policy, identified in paragraph 2.1. Each of the policies has, working from grassroots level upwards, a number of instruments, intermediate targets and policy objectives.

- *Instruments* are those variables over which the authorities have some control, and through which they hope to influence the intermediate targets.

- *Intermediate targets* are, in turn, those variables through which the authorities attempt to achieve their objectives.

- *Objectives* are the ultimate goals of economic policy.

The relationship between policies, instruments, intermediate targets and objectives may perhaps best be illustrated by means of some examples.

3.2   Taking *monetary policy*: one of the associated *instruments* is open-market operations which involves official sales and purchases of government debt. Open-market operations may be regarded as an instrument since they constitute a variable over which the authorities have some control. They have no particular purpose of their own, however; rather, they may be used to facilitate the attainment of one or more *intermediate targets*, which in this case would constitute the level of short-term interest rates and the rate of growth of a measure of the money supply. Those intermediate targets, rather than constituting ends in themselves, are the variables through which the authorities attempt to achieve the *objective*, which in this case could be the rate of inflation.

3.3   As another example, but with *fiscal policy* as the economic policy, the *instrument* might be income tax rates, the *intermediate targets* the level of disposable income (since a rise in tax rates reduces disposable income) and the level of aggregate demand (since a lowering of disposable income will lower aggregate demand), with the ultimate *objective* of attaining a satisfactory balance of payments through a lowering of imports. Alternatively, with fiscal policy remaining as the economic policy, the *instrument* might be government expenditure plans; the *intermediate targets* the *actual* level of government expenditure and the level of aggregate demand, and the *ultimate objective* the level of employment.

3.4 The particular policy–instrument–intermediate target–objective chain will depend upon the way in which policy is perceived to work in practice. Consequently, a range of intermediate targets would be consistent with a particular instrument of economic policy according to the perception of the operation of economic policy taken.

3.5 In conclusion, we stress that the chain of causation is instrument ➜ intermediate target ➜ objective. It is also vital that the relationship between the intermediate target and the objective is stable and predictable. In the case of monetary aggregates, such as M0 and M4, this is not the case (see section 7). The ratio between money supply and output does vary over time.

4 Problems in the implementation of economic policy

4.1 Even when a chain linking economic policy to instrument, intermediate targets and ultimate objective has been identified, there will frequently be additional complications in the implementation of that economic policy. Some of the major ones are discussed below.

4.2 It may be the case that the *intermediate target may not be effectively controlled by the instrument chosen*. For example, one of the problems associated with ceilings on bank lending when used as an instrument of monetary policy is that the money markets could bypass this restriction by means of various forms of lending (so-called disintermediation) so that the purchasing power within the economy would not be curtailed.

4.3 The *intermediate target variables may be difficult to define*. For example, open-market operations may be the instrument used to control the rate of growth of the money supply but there are many different measures of the money supply which do not grow at identical rates, and the choice of measure is problematic.

4.4 The *relationship between an instrument and a target variable may be subject to change over time*. For example, the reaction of the private sector to wage demands may well differ from one period of prices and incomes policy to another. Experience of a prices and incomes policy may cause people to ignore calls for 'voluntary restraint' or to seek out more quickly alternative means of receiving increases in wages. As we noted in paragraph 3.5, there is no long-term stable relationship between the monetary aggregates and output.

4.5　The *wrong instrument to achieve a particular variable may be chosen*. The instrument that is appropriate at one time may well *not* be the instrument appropriate at another. For example, if an increase in investment expenditures is the intermediate target, a cut in interest rates will not boost investment if there is a large surplus of productive capacity at that time. Instead, an increase in the level of aggregate demand would first be required.

4.6　The *links between an intermediate target and the final objective may not be known with precision*. Of particular note has been the long-running debate regarding the relative importance of aggregate demand on the one hand and the money supply on the other in the determination of the rate of inflation. Clearly, the operation of economic policy will inevitably be a hit-and-miss affair unless such links are reasonably well established.

4.7　*Timing considerations may be important*. Changing the value of an instrument will not have an *immediate* impact on the policy objective, even if the links in the policy chain are well established. For example, the decision to raise government expenditure takes some time to put into effect, since money cannot be spent immediately (hospitals, for example, take time to design and build); when it does rise, it will take some time to have its full impact on aggregate demand; and when it does have its full impact on aggregate demand there will be a lag before employers recruit the labour, and hence lower the unemployment rate, to cope with that raised aggregate demand.

4.8　A *government has to anticipate the way the economy is heading*, for which purpose forecasting is crucial. However, remember that the collection of statistics about the state of the economy occurs only after a time lag, and hence policy-makers also have to estimate where the economy *currently is*. In addition, they have to forecast where unemployment will be, on present policies, at some point in the future in order to implement policies *now* to move that level of unemployment towards its target level. If the estimate of the time lags is wrong (and there is evidence that many time lags are *variable*), such policies may end up doing more harm than good by moving the economy *further away* from the intended position.

4.9　It is for this reason that managing economic policy has been compared to driving a car which only has a rear window and where the accelerator and brake pedals only operate with a variable time lag; it is like a car with only a rear window because you only know with accuracy where the economy *has been*, not where it is and still less where it is going, and like a car where the brake and accelerator pedals only operate with a variable lag since any expansionary or contractionary policies only operate with a variable lag. If driving such a car would prove difficult, then insofar as the comparison is valid, so too is the management of economic policy!

4.10　These problems of implementation – particularly that associated with time lags – has led some economists to put forward the view that the government should not attempt discretionary economic policies, since there is a very real danger that more harm than good will be done. Instead, they advocate that economic policy should be guided by policy 'rules', with the intention of creating a stable background against which free market forces can operate.

5 The interrelationship of monetary and fiscal policy

5.1 So far we have assumed that the various instruments of economic policy will be independent of each other, whereas in practice this will not always be so. The major area where one set of instruments will be dependent upon another lies in the link between monetary and fiscal policy. Consider the following example.

5.2 Suppose that the government wishes to lower the level of unemployment and that it seeks to do this by raising government expenditure and/or lowering taxation. Such a policy is clearly an act of fiscal policy, intended to have its effect by altering the level of aggregate demand. *But* raising government expenditure and/or lowering taxation will *also* either raise the PSBR or lower the PSDR which will have *monetary* implications. It *may* be that these monetary implications fit what the government had planned for monetary policy anyway, but it is more likely that they will not. The essential point, however, is that monetary and fiscal policy are not independent, and policy-makers will have to ensure that the stance they take with regard to the one is consistent with that taken for the other.

5.3 The key figure connecting monetary policy with fiscal policy is the PSBR. Its size, and the way in which it is financed, is a channel between the two policies.

Student Activity 3

1. Define policy instruments, intermediate targets and objectives. *(Paragraph 3.1)*

2. Give an example from either monetary policy or fiscal policy of a chain of instrument, target and objective. *(Paragraphs 3.2–3)*

3. List the main types of problems which governments may face in the implementation of their economic policies. *(Paragraphs 4.2–9)*

4. Why do some economists argue that governments should not tinker with the operation of the economy, but rather should set policy 'rules'? *(Paragraph 4.10)*

5. Give an example of how monetary and fiscal policy may be interrelated. *(Paragraph 5.2)*

6 The basics of monetary policy

6.1 The money supply within the economy is the outcome of a wide array of different forces. These forces can, in broad terms, be split into two: the 'free market' forces and the influence of the government. The 'free market' forces would generate a specific quantity of money on their own account, taking into consideration factors such as the prudential reserve ratios operated by banks, the propensity of the general public to hold cash relative to bank money, the demand from the private sector for loans and so on. The actions of the authorities (that is, the Treasury and the Bank of England) with regard to monetary controls are, in effect, *in addition to* these free market forces, the primary reason for such intervention being that the money supply and/or the

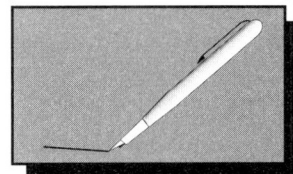

level and structure of interest rates implied by that is not consistent with the economic policy objectives.

6.2   Thus, monetary policy is concerned with the attempts of the authorities to influence some measure (or measures) of the money supply or the level and/ or structure of interest rates. At any one point in time the authorities are only able to control *either* the money supply *or* the rate of interest; what they are unable to do is to control both simultaneously. The reason for this is straightforward. The interest rate is the *price* of money and seeking to control the interest rate therefore implies seeking to control the price of money. The money supply is plainly the quantity of money, and therefore control of both the interest rate and the money supply implies controlling both price and quantity simultaneously.

6.3   In terms of a supply and demand diagram illustrating the money market (Fig. 7.1), the authorities are, to some extent at least, able to control the supply curve; if they choose to fix the quantity of money (say at M^*) then they have to accept whatever interest rate then results from the interaction of that supply with the private sector demand – in this case i^*. From the alternative viewpoint, if the authorities decide to fix the interest rate at i^*, then they have to adjust the money supply in order to maintain that (in the figure that is M^*) but if the demand for money should increase (and the curve shift to the right) the authorities will have to *expand* the money supply in order to retain the interest rate of i^*.

6.4   The *caveat* to the authorities' inability to control the interest rate and the money supply simultaneously is that they may be able to do so in the short term through the use of very restrictive monetary controls. For example, the authorities might institute very tight controls, including specific requirements on banks and building societies to limit the extent of credit creation, and thus fix the money supply within narrow limits. *On top of* those controls limits could be

Figure 7.1

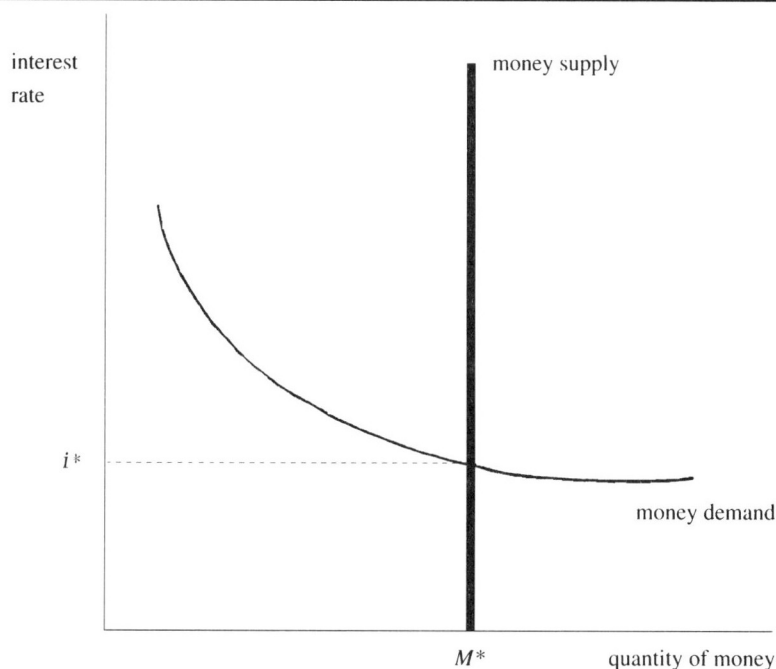

imposed (by means of directives) on interest rates that could be charged on loans by banks and building societies. If that interest rate was below the market clearing rate, then the interest rate would not adjust so as to equate the supply and demand for loans, so that these institutions would have to initiate some other rationing procedure – which might, in practice, be solved for them as a result of further directives from the authorities stipulating the preference to be given to particular categories of borrowers. Clearly, the authorities will have achieved control of both the interest rate and the money supply.

6.5   Note that the authorities will have achieved control of both variables by means of *suspending* the operation of free market adjustments. In particular, the interest rate would not be allowed to adjust in response to forces within the financial system. Within any market that is controlled in this way, there will be suppliers (in this context, the potential lenders of funds) and those with a demand for the product or service (in this context, potential borrowers) whose needs are not being satisfied, and this will lead to transactions taking place *outside* the regulated market.

6.6   What is likely to happen here is that there will be a process of *disintermediation* as prospective borrowers find lenders of funds outside the controlled institutions. The borrowers involved in this disintermediation process will in all likelihood be prepared to pay higher interest rates than those determined by the authorities, and lenders will also be likely to receive more than those the banks and building societies would be permitted to pay, so that there is a strong incentive for such disintermediation activity to take place. The rise of the inter-company markets in the late 1970s is a classic example of disintermediation resulting from the 'corset' (see paragraph 8.14).

6.7   The result is that the volume of borrowing and lending within the economy will continue to rise, which then calls into question the appropriateness of the measure of the money supply being controlled – with an increasing proportion of borrowing and lending activity taking place *outside* that measure, will it not become inappropriate, for policy purposes, to continue to seek to control that measure? Equally, with the interest rates being paid and received on this disintermediation activity being *higher* than the officially determined rate and increasing volumes being involved, will not that officially determined rate become increasingly meaningless? Thus, while the authorities are able to control both the interest rate and the money supply simultaneously by means of very restrictive controls in the short term, the bypassing of such controls means that this will be impossible in the longer term.

7   The intermediate targets of monetary policy

7.1   The two intermediate targets of monetary policy are usually regarded as the:

- Rate of growth of the money supply; and
- Level and/or structure of interest rates.

Rate of growth of the money supply

7.2   This intermediate target was widely employed during the 1980s in the UK because of its perceived link with the rate of inflation. The immediate problem raised by its use is, however, the issue of the measure of the money supply to be utilised, along with the fear that targeting any particular measure, even if the targets are achieved, is likely to lead to distortions with the effect that other measures of the money supply, and their associated impact on the real economy, grow at different rates than they would otherwise.

Figure 7.2   Ratio of M0 to GDP

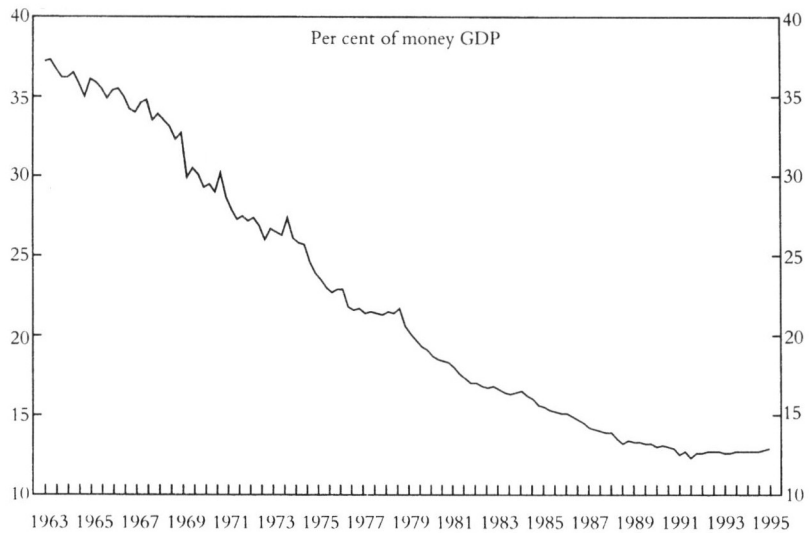

Per cent of money GDP

1963 1965 1967 1969 1971 1973 1975 1977 1979 1981 1983 1985 1987 1989 1991 1993 1995

Figure 7.3   Ratio of M4 to GDP

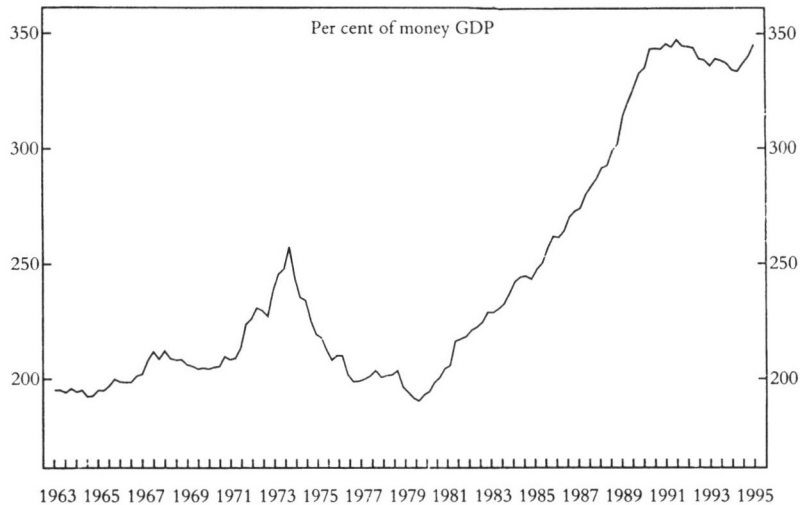

Per cent of money GDP

1963 1965 1967 1969 1971 1973 1975 1977 1979 1981 1983 1985 1987 1989 1991 1993 1995

7.3   Figs. 7.2 and 7.3, taken from the 'Red Book', a Government Budget publication, show how GDP and M0 and M4 have varied, in their ratios to each other, over the last 30 years. M0 grew less rapidly than GDP, at a stable rate until recently, largely as a result of the growth of 'the banking habit'. The market for banks is saturated at present, and this could be the prime reason for the new stability in the ratio. Other suggested causes are low interest rates and the rise of the 'informal economy' with its preference for cash.

7.4   M4's ratio shows great swings, largely as a result of changes in bank and building society lending policies. In turn, these depend on the stance of monetary policy, e.g. tight in the early 1990s, resulting in a stabilising of the ratio.

Level and/or structure of interest rates

7.5 Although less widely employed than the money supply during most of the 1980s, interest rates have in the past been important intermediate targets. In 1989, the Chancellor used to repeat 'interest rates will stay as high as is required for as long as is required to bring down the rate of inflation'. The essential rationale for employing interest rates as a target is that those elements of expenditure that are subject to the influence of interest rates – investment expenditure and credit-based consumer expenditure in particular, as noted above – will be altered as a consequence of changes in interest rates initiated by the authorities. In addition, however, there may be important supplementary rationales:

- Since international currency flows are influenced by interest rates, they will have an impact on the balance of payments.

- Interest rates may be used as a means of attaining other intermediate targets, most notably the rate of growth of the money supply. By raising interest rates the authorities may be able to reduce the demand for bank and building society credit and hence reduce the rate of growth of the money supply.

Additional intermediate targets

7.6 While control of the money supply and of interest rates are the two major intermediate targets of monetary policy, there may from time to time be additional intermediate targets. These will include:

- Exchange rates;
- Credit creation by banks and building societies;
- Nominal domestic expenditure (or nominal national income).

Exchange rates

7.7 Exchange rates may constitute an intermediate target, since by affecting the relative prices of imports and exports, trade flows will be influenced. Altered trade flows will obviously have an impact on the attainment of the balance of payments objective, but they will also impact upon the level of domestic output and hence employment, and upon the rate of inflation.

Credit creation by banks and building societies.

7.8 Credit creation by banks and building societies may be an intermediate target for the straightforward reason that it constitutes an important element of any growth in the money supply, and may in this respect be one of a chain of intermediate targets. Such credit creation may also constitute an intermediate target of monetary policy, however, because of a perceived link between credit provided by banks and building societies on the one hand and private sector expenditures on the other, thereby enabling the authorities to influence such expenditures and hence the overall level of aggregate demand.

Nominal domestic expenditure (or nominal national income)

7.9 The primary rationale for having the nominal level of domestic expenditure as an intermediate target is that this variable would be expected to be a determinant of the rate of inflation, and the levels of output and employment. Monetary policy would then be designed so as to achieve a particular growth rate of nominal domestic expenditure, taking into account the prevailing rate of inflation. The advantage of using this variable as an intermediate target is its close relationship to the ultimate objectives of inflation and employment, but there is the corresponding disadvantage in that the link between the instruments of monetary policy and this intermediate target are rather weak.

Choice of intermediate target

7.10 The main influence on the choice of intermediate target will be the perception on the part of the policy-makers of the economic determinants of the ultimate objectives (that is, broadly how the economy works) and hence on the reliability of the relationships between the ultimate objectives and the intermediate targets used to attain them. If the policy-makers are of a monetarist persuasion, you would expect to see an emphasis on the money supply (in view of the importance placed on money being the major determinant of inflation, particularly in the longer term), but also paying attention to the growth of nominal domestic expenditure because of difficulties with the appropriate measurement of the money supply. Policy-makers of a more Keynesian/demand management persuasion might be expected to pay more attention to the level and structure of interest rates, with correspondingly less attention to the money supply.

7.11 Particularly in the use of the money supply as an intermediate target, there has been much debate as to whether the target should be generally announced. This would take the form of a figure – or a range – for the growth of one or more measures of the money supply.

7.12 The major argument *in favour* of such announcements is that, if the private sector believes that the government is intent on achieving that intermediate target, the *expectations* by that sector of variables such as inflation will be reduced. If expectations are reduced, then wage settlements in particular are likely to be pushed downward, bringing about a lowering of inflation. Thus, inflation will have been lowered quickly and relatively painlessly through the lowering of expectations.

7.13 There are disadvantages however.

- The non-achievement of the intermediate target may lead to an element of political embarrassment and give rise to a suspicion and disbelief about *future* announcements, so that their beneficial impact on the lowering of expectations is reduced.

- The announcement of intermediate targets may lock the authorities into a particular path for economic policy and reduce their flexibility to respond to developments – though it has to be recognised that this is also seen as an *advantage* since it reduces the ability of the authorities to initiate *destabilising* economic policy.

- It has been argued that as soon as any particular variable is targeted publicly it starts to react in an unpredictable fashion because the private sector makes use of alternative channels to avoid the restrictions implied by the targeting of the one variable.

Student Activity 4

1. Except in the short term, the authorities are able to control either the growth of the money supply or interest rates, but not both, Why? *(Paragraph 6.3)*

2. What is the relevance of disintermediation to the authorities' attempts to control both the money supply and interest rates? *(Paragraphs 6.6–7)*

3. Why might the rate of interest be used as an intermediate target of monetary policy? *(Paragraph 7.5)*

4. In addition to the growth of the money supply and the level/structure of interest rates, what other variables might be set as intermediate targets of monetary policy? *(Paragraph 7.6)*

5. What is likely to determine the choice of intermediate target variable for monetary policy? *(Paragraph 7.10)*

6. List the advantages and disadvantages of announcing publicly the intermediate target variable for economic policy. *(Paragraphs 7.12–13)*

8 Monetary control methods

8.1 The purpose of monetary policy, as we have seen, is to control some measure (or measures) of the money supply and/or the level and structure of interest rates in order to attain a particular policy objective. Recall, however, from section 6 that the authorities are not able to control both the money supply and interest rates simultaneously. Furthermore, unless the authorities are prepared to use directives to control interest rates, interest rates are controlled by means of controlling the money supply. The authorities therefore have the choice of controlling the money supply as an end in itself, because of the link with inflation, or manipulating the money supply in order to influence interest rates and hence aggregate demand, output and employment. In any event, it is clear that monetary policy is crucially dependent upon controlling the money supply.

The targets of monetary control

8.2 The components of the money supply that will be the targets of monetary policy will be dependent upon the particular measure of the money supply that is selected. Nevertheless, there are essentially two elements to any widely accepted measure of the money supply:

- Notes and coin;
- Bank and building society deposits.

8.3 Although notes and coin constitute only a small element of the money supply in the UK, it is a very important element because it forms a vital part of the reserve base that is the prerequisite for the credit creation process by banks and building societies. Control of the cash base of the financial system may therefore be a desirable target of the authorities since it constitutes a means of controlling the broader money supply measures. The quantity of notes and coin within the financial system may be controlled within quite fine limits by the authorities; however, their willingness to do so will be

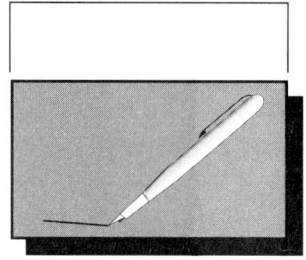

countered by the possibility of a loss of confidence in the stability of the financial system if any decline in the availability of cash is too sharp. In practice, the total of notes and coin is loosely controlled, being largely demand determined by the growth of output (nominal GDP).

8.4   For the most part, however, monetary control is targeted towards bank and building society deposits as these constitute a much greater proportion of most measures of the money supply. The control here can take one of two forms:

●   It can be directed towards limiting the *supply* side – by limiting the ability of banks and building societies to supply credit; *or*

●   It can be directed towards the *demand* side – by limiting the willingness of the non-bank, non-building society private sector to borrow funds.

8.5   The *instruments* used to limit either the demand or supply of credit are considered below, but note that they are likely to influence the holdings of other liquid assets in addition to bank and building society deposits.

Monetary control instruments

8.6   It is useful to place the instruments through which monetary control is achieved into three groups:

●   Instruments of market intervention;

●   Instruments of portfolio constraint;

●   Longer-term control mechanisms.

Instruments of market intervention

8.7   As the title suggests, the instruments of market intervention are designed to achieve the intermediate targets of monetary policy by means of the authorities intervening in the operation of the money markets. Within the UK financial system, this involves the setting of the *discount rate* (intervention rate) and the use of *open-market operations*.

8.8   The discount rate is the rate at which the Bank of England is prepared to lend money to the discount houses in cases where there is a shortage of liquidity within the financial system. The Bank of England is able to engineer a shortage of liquidity in order to force the discount houses to borrow from the Bank of England at this discount (intervention) rate, which then has a knock-on effect throughout the whole structure of interest rates within the economy since it is representative of the marginal cost of funds to the banking system as a whole.

8.9   Open-market operations involve the Bank of England in buying and selling securities within the market to alter either the level and/or the structure of interest rates or the volume of liquidity. In this respect, it is open market operations that can be used to engineer a liquidity shortage within the discount market. Most of the open-market operations undertaken by the Bank of England are within the discount market, with their greatest impact therefore on short-term interest rates, but by buying and selling long-dated gilts an impact upon longer-term interest rates can be achieved.

8.10   One of the advantages of changes in the discount rate and the use of open-market operations over other methods of monetary control is that they impinge upon financial institutions in general rather than on banking institutions in particular. While the initial impact may well be felt by the discount houses, the effects will quickly filter through to affect all institutions through the changed interest rates prevailing in the markets.

Instruments of portfolio constraint

8.11 Instruments of portfolio constraint refer to those controls that may be imposed by the authorities on the portfolio structure of financial institutions, with the purpose of influencing either the volume and/or the type of lending and hence credit creation. In contrast to the market intervention instruments discussed above, the problem is that these instruments of portfolio constraint have had a narrow and therefore distorting impact. Although in principle they could be applied to a wide range of financial institutions, in the UK they have been applied only to banking institutions. The result of this is that they have, in effect, been discriminated against but also note that disintermediation has tended to occur as those institutions not subject to the controls take over unfulfilled opportunities. As a consequence, less use has been made of these instruments in recent years. Nevertheless, the instruments are potentially available for use, with the major components being:

- Reserve requirements;
- Special deposits;
- Supplementary special deposits;
- 'Moral suasion'; and
- Direct controls.

8.12 *Reserve requirements.* Banks and building societies need to hold a base of reserve assets for prudential purposes. If and when a bank or building society falls to its minimum desired reserve asset ratio it will have to turn away any incoming demands for loans or else seek to acquire additional reserve assets from which to expand its lending. The result in either case will generally be a rise in interest rates which will serve to reduce the demand for loans. The purpose of any imposed reserve requirements is, in effect, to duplicate this process; if the authorities impose a reserve requirement in excess of the desired reserve ratio (or else reduce the availability of reserve assets) the consequence will be that the institutions involved will have to curtail their lending and/or acquire additional reserve assets, serving to raise interest rates and reducing the demand for loans. This, in turn, will curb the rate of growth of the money supply.

8.13 *Special deposits.* Special deposits are deposits that the Bank of England may require certain banking institutions to deposit with it. These deposits, equal to a specified proportion of certain elements of their deposit liabilities, are then 'frozen' at the Bank of England and may not be used as part of the reserve asset base for lending purposes. While they are particularly discriminatory as regards the institutions to which they apply, they do have a very rapid impact upon the ability of these institutions to create credit and are useful for drawing off any excess reserve assets within the system. At present, they are not used.

8.14 *Supplementary special deposits.* Supplementary special deposits are additional deposits that banking institutions had to make at the Bank of England if and when a category of their deposit liabilities exceeded an upper limit set by the Bank of England. This mechanism, referred to as the 'corset', was operated on a periodic basis by the Bank of England between 1973 and 1980 and was phrased in terms of a *growth rate* for certain interest-bearing eligible liabilities. Institutions which exceeded the specified growth rate of these liabilities were required to make supplementary special deposits with the Bank of England on a scale dependent upon the extent of the overshoot. The penalty involved was not only that, like ordinary special deposits, they could not be used as part of the reserve asset base then required but also that (unlike ordinary special deposits) they attracted no interest payment.

8.15 The *advantages* of this mechanism are that it can be adjusted quickly in the light of developments and the requirements of monetary policy and that it allows very direct control over a major element of the money supply. The corresponding *disadvantage* is that it constitutes a distortion of the banking mechanism and hence is once again liable to lead to disintermediation.

8.16 *'Moral suasion'.* This refers to the range of informal requests and pressure that the Bank of England may exert over banking institutions. The extent to which this is a real power of the Bank relative to direct controls (see 'Direct controls') is open to question, since much of the pressure that the Bank would exert would involve the institutions taking actions that were not in their commercial interest. However, the position and potential power of the Bank of England probably provides it with some power with regard to 'moral suasion' which may perhaps be utilised most effectively in the context of establishing lending priorities rather than absolute levels.

8.17 *Direct controls.* Direct controls involve the Bank of England in issuing directives in order to attain particular intermediate targets. Thus, for example, the Bank of England might impose controls on interest rates payable upon deposits, impose limits on the volume of credit creation or direct banks to prioritise lending according to type of customer. Although these direct controls have the benefits of speed of implementation and precision, they are discriminatory towards the institutions involved and are likely to lead to disintermediation as both potential borrowers and potential lenders seek to pursue their best interests. Their use, therefore, is perhaps best reserved for short-term requirements, not least since their effectiveness will decline the longer they are applied.

Reasons for the decline of portfolio constraints

8.18 Since 1980, there have been few portfolio constraints in use for monetary policy purposes. The reasons have been summarised from time to time in ministerial speeches and are as follows:

- Prior to 1980, banks and building societies operated in separate markets in the personal sector and did not compete on product range. That has now changed, so that *constraints on banks must be replicated not only on building societies but also on the remaining centralised mortgage lenders (see Unit 10).* Although some of the largest societies, including those about to become banks, maintain accounts and relations with the Bank of England, this is not the case with the majority of building societies. At present, joint portfolio constraints would have to be imposed by the Building Societies Commission and the Bank of England, working in tandem – and there is no administrative machinery for this.

- *Disintermediation*, largely by companies, is a 'knee-jerk' reaction to portfolio constraints and this became conspicuous in the late 1970s. 'Interest rates reach those parts of the economy which portfolio constraints don't reach' is one description of why credit is controlled by price rather than quantity.

- Throughout the 1950s, 1960s and 1970s, when portfolio constraints were used by both major political parties when in government, the UK maintained a system of *exchange control*. This restriction on the movement of funds to and from abroad prevented borrowers from seeking finance from overseas when UK monetary policy was restrictive. Moreover, most European countries had similar restrictions preventing their banks and investors from moving funds outside their countries. These exchange controls had the effect of supporting the portfolio constraints but they now no longer exist, with the result that UK borrowers can ask banks overseas for loans in sterling.

- Portfolio constraints are regarded as *inimical to competition* because they place ceilings – of one kind or another – on the growth of banks and other deposit-taking intermediaries.

Longer-term control mechanisms

8.19   The approaches available to the authorities to control the longer-term growth of the money supply will, to a large extent, have been considered in your previous studies, but it will be useful to summarise the main considerations here.

8.20   A major influence on the longer-term growth of the money supply is the size of the public sector borrowing requirement (PSBR). A *reduction in the size of the PSBR* through altering levels of taxation and/or government expenditure will have a direct influence by reducing the demand for borrowed funds within the economy and will therefore serve to lower interest rates.

8.21   The *financing method* of any PSBR is also important because any financing through the sale of short-term government debt instruments will alter the availability of potential reserve assets to the banking system. In addition, the larger the proportion of any PSBR that is financed by sales of gilt-edged securities and National Savings instruments to the non-bank, non-building society private sector, the smaller the impact upon the money supply.

8.22   A policy of *funding* the national debt in order to reduce the availability of liquid assets to the banking system may also assist in the control of the money supply in the longer term. The use of the surplus funds arising from the existence of a PSDR will also have an impact on the money supply, since a PSDR results in a withdrawal of funds from the non-bank non-building society private sector, unless those funds are used to repay debt held by that sector. In addition, of course, the greater the PSDR the greater the scope for reducing money supply growth. On the *demand* side, it is possible that the use of taxation penalties or other disincentives to borrowing may serve to slow down any increase in the demand for credit and hence to slow the growth of the money supply.

The effectiveness of monetary controls

8.23 We have concentrated on what monetary controls can achieve in principle. The practice is often far removed from the principle, however, and in countries where there have been strenuous attempts to use monetary policy (emphasising the control of money supply growth rather than the maintenance of interest rates) the success in attaining the money supply growth targets has been generally modest.

8.24 The reason for the limited ability to reach money supply growth targets is essentially twofold.

- The instruments of monetary control have proved to be inadequate to achieve the desired precision of control over money supply growth.

- There exists only a limited understanding of how the participants within the financial system will react to changes in the values of the instruments and targets used to implement monetary policy.

Taken together it is clear that monetary policy will remain a difficult policy to use for the attainment of the ultimate policy objectives.

Student Activity 5

1. Why might it be thought desirable for the authorities to control the cash base of the financial system? *(Paragraph 8.3)*

2. Why, for the most part, are monetary controls targeted towards bank and building society deposits? *(Paragraph 8.4)*

3. What is the nature of the impact of instruments of market intervention in respect of monetary control? *(Paragraphs 8.7–10)*

4. List the instruments of portfolio constraint in respect of monetary control. *(Paragraph 8.11)*

5. Why do instruments of portfolio constraint tend to distort the operation of the financial system? *(Paragraph 8.18)*

6. List the ways in which the authorities might seek to influence money supply growth in the longer term. *(Paragraph 8.20–22)*

9 The operation of monetary controls in the UK

9.1 The operation of monetary controls in the UK has seen considerable change over time, partly as a consequence of the increased importance attached to monetary policy in recent years but also as a consequence of developments within the financial system. Up to 1980 the emphasis was upon the use of portfolio constraints for the purposes of monetary control in the form of special deposits, supplementary special deposits and various direct controls on both lending and interest rates. As we have seen, the problem with such portfolio constraints is that they tend to be distortionary and lead to disintermediation, but in addition, in the case of the UK, they appear to have been of limited efficacy.

9.2   The introduction of new monetary control provisions in August 1981 resulted in a switch of emphasis towards market intervention, combined with measures to ensure longer-term control of the money supply. The key element of this market intervention has been the manipulation of interest rates, achieved through the use of open-market operations and the Bank of England's discount (intervention) rate, one result of which has been the prevalence of high *real* interest rates in the UK as the inflation rate has fallen and the authorities have sought to attain only modest growth in the money supply. This policy has been described as a 'one club' policy by critics using the analogy of a golfer playing with only one golf club in their bag instead of the usual 14 (the package of instruments). Longer-term policies to restrain the growth of the money supply have centred around the PSBR, with the stated objective of the government being to attain a balanced budget (that is, a zero PSBR) on average over the longer term. The reduced need for borrowing from banks given by a lower PSBR will, it is intended, lead to a lower rate of credit creation and lower interest rates.

9.3   Use has also been made of *funding policy* to try to limit the supply of liquid assets available within the financial system. A strategy of over-funding of the PSBR during the early to mid-1980s meant that sales of gilt-edged securities and National Savings instruments to the non-bank non-building society private sector often exceeded the PSBR, with the result that there was a *negative* impact on the money supply arising from public sector financing. During the years 1987/88 to 1990/91 a PSDR existed, and the strategy was to fund fully such surpluses by means of debt repurchases from the non-bank non-building society private sector in order to neutralise the contractionary impact on the money supply that a PSDR would otherwise have.

9.4   Comparisons of the actual growth of the money supply over various periods since 1980 relative to the target rates demonstrate that the authorities in the UK have achieved only limited success in meeting them, with the early years of the 1980s (when the rate of growth of the money supply was seen as being a major target for economic policy) showing persistent overshoots. It may be argued, of course, that the growth of the money supply itself is of little importance and it is the ultimate objectives of economic policy that are of primary concern. As section 11 demonstrates, however, the success of the UK in meeting the policy objectives has, at best, been mixed.

Developments in the framework of economic policy

9.5   We have already noted that economic policy prior to the late 1970s in the UK was dominated by the 'demand management' framework. Successive governments therefore paid attention to managing the level of aggregate demand with the intention of 'fine tuning' the economy to keep the level of employment, the balance of payments and the rate of inflation on their appropriate paths. This management of the level of aggregate demand was achieved primarily by the use of fiscal policy, with monetary policy given the supporting role of stabilising the interest rate. In consequence the money supply was permitted to accommodate the money demand.

9.6   The need to borrow substantial sums of money from the International Monetary Fund in 1976 (occasioned by the marked international payments problems experienced at the time) led – under additional pressure from the

IMF – to a reappraisal of the framework within which economic policy was to operate in the UK. The significant shift that resulted was towards greater attention being paid to the role of monetary policy and to the targeting of the growth rate of the money supply in particular, in order to curb inflation. This shift of emphasis towards the control of the money supply and towards the lowering of inflation as a policy objective was strengthened by the change of government in 1979. The commitment of the incoming Conservative government towards monetarism installed monetary policy as the major element of economic policy; but a parallel commitment of that government to the free operation of market forces also gave rise to a number of other changes in the framework of economic policy.

9.7   The overriding policy objective of the post-1979 government was the control of inflation, which stood in contrast to the full-employment objective of all postwar governments. However, note that one of the underlying precepts of the monetarist philosophy is that the economy is inherently self-regulating and that any intervention by the government in the form of active macroeconomic policies would be likely merely to create distortions and to move the economy *away* from its optimal employment position and economic growth path. Furthermore, the attainment of a low rate of inflation was necessary for the free market forces to operate satisfactorily to bring about full employment in the longer term. Thus, the adoption of monetarist policies may be seen as consistent with the objective of full employment, but only on a longer time scale than that associated with demand management policies.

The Medium-Term Financial Strategy (MTFS)

9.8   The Medium-Term Financial Strategy (MTFS) is the title given to the broad approach to the implementation of its economic policy by the successive Conservative governments since 1979. It is important to avoid equating the MTFS too closely with monetarism and with the aim of controlling inflation. Although one of the main aims of the MTFS is indeed to reduce inflation by means of tight monetary control, the strategy also includes the aims of reducing the burden of taxation on the working population in order to boost incentives and thereby raise the rate of economic growth, and of reducing the proportion of national resources that are absorbed by the public sector.

9.9   The MTFS has the purpose of mapping out in broad terms how the government intends to achieve its longer-term objectives of low inflation, sustainable economic growth and low unemployment consistent with broad equilibrium of the balance of payments. Targets and projections are subsequently added to those broad aims of the MTFS. The targets and projections are formulated for four years ahead on a rolling basis, with the figures being updated each year, and relate to the size of the PSBR/PSDR, of government expenditure and taxation, and to the growth of the money supply. For all these components, the intention was for the targets to be progressively reduced over time, with the purpose of informing the private sector exactly what the government's intentions were regarding the management of the economy, in the hope of influencing favourable expectations, and therefore behaviour, in critical areas such as the setting of wages. The practice has not gone entirely as planned and the targeted reductions in money supply growth were not consistent from one year to the next, with the consequence that the potential benefits from reducing inflation expectations were less than hoped.

9.10   Although the strict adherence to the MTFS has been reduced, compared with the early 1980s, the framework of economic policy remains the MTFS and a section on it has appeared in each Budget 'Red Book' so far. Although no specific targets (they are now termed 'monitoring ranges') are set for growth rates of measures of the money supply, targets for government expenditure and taxation are still set in terms of achieving a balanced budget as an average over the longer term. The absence of specific targets for growth rates of measures of the money supply has not, however, been projected – nor indeed interpreted by the financial markets – as an indication that their rapid growth would be of limited importance. It is clear that the authorities are still mindful of the importance of rapid money supply growth, with the consequence that financial markets pay attention to such figures, but the importance attached to them is reduced compared with earlier years.

9.11   The abandonment of specific targets for money supply growth may be seen as a reflection of a shift towards a less rigid application of the MTFS in recent years. Indeed, even before this time, the authorities had been placing increasing emphasis upon the need for policy instruments to be set in the light of a range of indicators of monetary conditions, and not simply on the basis of the growth rates of precisely defined monetary aggregates. In this context, the authorities looked increasingly towards movements in sterling exchange rates during the second half of the 1980s. The ultimate step in this regard was the placing of sterling into the European Union's (then European Community's) Exchange Rate Mechanism (ERM) in October 1990. This action undoubtedly constrained the extent to which monetary policy instruments could be directed towards controlling the growth of the domestic money supply, and hence modified further the practical operation of the MTFS.

Economic policy since September 1992

9.12   The most fundamental turning point for government economic policy in the UK in recent years came with the withdrawal of sterling from the EU's ERM in September 1992. This event followed an apparent widespread loss of confidence in the authorities' ability to maintain the exchange value of sterling within its parity bands relative to other ERM currencies. The withdrawal from the ERM led to a substantial reduction in the exchange rate of sterling, and allowed the authorities to sanction significant reductions in interest rates (on the grounds that the recessionary forces prevalent in the UK economy were sufficient to counteract any ensuing inflationary pressures). In February 1994 base rates were reduced to $5^{1}/_{4}$% (their lowest level since 1977). The lower rates of interest, the reduced exchange value for sterling and subdued inflation rates during 1993 undoubtedly contributed to an improvement in business conditions in the UK, with unemployment falling marginally as output began to rise.

9.13   Base rate was subsequently increased in three $^{1}/_{2}$% steps, to $6^{3}/_{4}$%, but by early July 1996 it had fallen to $5^{3}/_{4}$%. This was in a series of cuts of 25 basis points and, like most base rate changes since 1990, they were announced by the introduction of a Minimum Lending Rate (to the discount market) at that new level for the day.

9.14   Despite the extreme change of policy introduced in September 1992 (summarised in Appendix B to this unit), the overall approach to implementing policy continues to be couched in terms of the MTFS, although this is now regarded more simply as providing a framework for achieving sustainable economic growth based on permanently low inflation. However, an important development of the strategy was the introduction of the *inflation target*. This target effectively commits the government to directing its economic policy instruments to the maintenance of the underlying rate of inflation within the range of 1% to 4% p.a.. In order to support this policy, the Bank of England now provides a quarterly report on the progress being made towards the achievement of the inflation target, and the Treasury is being more open on policy matters via the publication of the minutes of meetings between the Chancellor and the Governor some six weeks later. The idea here is that debate on policy will be better informed, and the government will find it more difficult to take actions which are not consistent with its stated policy objectives.

9.15   Choosing to target the rate of inflation directly means that the government has bypassed all the conventional targets of monetary policy. Thus, the monitoring ranges announced for M0 (0–4% p.a.) and M4 (3–9% p.a.), along with monitoring the exchange rate for sterling and changes in asset prices, are effectively early warning devices to indicate when policy may be running off course. Such variables will be taken into account in the setting of monetary controls (interest rates).

9.16   The new approach to policy still recognises the importance of fiscal policy. In particular, considerable concern has been expressed in respect of the need to reduce the huge PSBR, which was approximately £46bn during 1993/94 and will still be over £25bn in 1996/97. Measures introduced in recent Budgets have been aimed at raising additional revenue and holding back the growth of government expenditure. Nevertheless, it is anticipated that large PSBRs will remain for many years to come, despite the natural improvement which is likely to follow recovery in the economy. In particular, receipts form VAT have failed to meet their budgeted totals.

Student Activity 6

1. What have been the main instruments of control used by the UK monetary authorities since the early 1980s?   *(Paragraph 9.2)*

2. What has been the success of the UK authorities in meeting their money supply growth targets since the early 1980s?   *(Paragraph 9.4)*

3. In what fundamental way did the economic policy objectives of the Conservative government which came to power in 1979 differ from those of other postwar governments in the UK?   *(Paragraph 9.7)*

4. What is the Medium-Term Financial Strategy?   *(Paragraphs 9.8–11)*

5. In what ways has the UK government's approach to economic policy altered since the mid-1980s?   *(Paragraph 9.10)*

6. What changes in economic policy were precipitated by the withdrawal of sterling from the ERM in September 1992?   *(Paragraphs 9.14–15)*

10 Effects of monetary policy on deposit-taking financial intermediaries

Interest rates

10.1 Changes in base rate will immediately affect the returns from all lending products priced at a margin over base rate. This applies mainly to banks, and certainly not to building societies. Also, the change in money market interest rates associated with the base rate change will affect the returns on liquid assets – with capital values changing in the reverse direction – and also on the cost of wholesale funds used to finance the assets side of the balance sheets.

10.2 Not all lending products are priced at a margin over base rate and, moreover, the use of base rate in the pricing of products has been declining for some time. A far greater percentage of bank products are priced by managed rates, changes in which are decided by looking at the cost of funds, competitors' reactions and market strategies. Thus, a succession of $1/4\%$ cuts in base rate is likely to result in interest rates falling on most products, but the extent of these falls cannot be predicted with arithmetic certainty.

10.3 Banks and, indeed, all financial intermediaries with large portfolios of short-term fixed interest securities will be significantly affected by changes in capital values. In particular, a rise in base rate may be unexpected, so that the market will reduce the prices of such assets to the full extent of the increase. On the other hand, a cut in base rate may have been expected, so that the rise in the value of such assets is more muted.

10.4 Some retail banks still have perhaps 10% of their deposits in non-interest bearing form, giving them a ratchet or 'endowment' element in their profits when interest rates rise because the cost of such non-interest bearing deposits does not rise. However, the reverse is true when interest rates fall, because the costs of operating such accounts are unaffected.

Exchange rate volatility

10.5 Although banks are tightly controlled by their regulatory authorities in their ability to run over-bought or oversized positions in foreign currency assets, changes in exchange rates will result in concomitant losses or profits. In particular, banks are well advised not to run such 'open positions' at weekends, when the chances of a revaluation or devaluation of a fixed-rate currency are most likely.

10.6 A second effect of changes in exchange rates occurs when a bank's overseas profits, denominated in foreign currency, are exchanged into its domestic currency for the purposes of preparing the annual accounts. Its operations in a foreign currency may not be any more or less profitable than in the previous year but, if the exchange rate of that foreign currency has risen, then the equivalent in the domestic currency will rise too.

Portfolio constraints

10.7 These can inhibit the ability of financial intermediaries to grow, especially to increase market shares. Originally, in the 1950s and 1960s, they operated largely on the assets of banks and building societies. However, in the late

1970s a device, termed the 'corset', severely limited the ability of the banks to increase their interest-bearing deposits. Thus, by operating on the liabilities side of balance sheets, restrictions were individually imposed on the growth of bank assets in general. The result was large-scale disintermediation by business customers.

Effect on customers and the quality of loan books

10.8 The effects on the economy as a whole are outlined in Appendix A but the indirect effect on deposit-taking financial intermediaries is to change the quality of their loans and advances. A rise in interest rates will lead to more borrowers defaulting and an increase in the lenders' provisions for bad debts. However, a fall in interest rates may not necessarily result in an increase in the quality of lending if borrowers are, as they were in the mid-1990s, unwilling to increase their borrowing. Too many remembered the high mortgage rates of five years earlier, the rise of unemployment at that time, the repossessions and, finally, substantial falls in house prices leading to negative equity.

Effects on profits

10.9 These are difficult to quantify because, while a rise in interest rates could lead to wider profit margins for lenders, these beneficial effects could be outweighed by an increase in the total of bad debts written off against trading profits. Indeed, as the volatility of interest rates has increased during the second half of this century, so has the volatility of bank profits.

Student Activity 7

1. How are banks affected by changes in:

   (a) interest rates   *(Paragraphs 10.1–4)*
   (b) exchange rates?   *(Paragraphs 10.5–6)*

2. Why are portfolio constraints no longer used to implement monetary policy in the UK?   *(Paragraphs 8.18–10.7)*

3. How are the banks' customers affected by monetary policy in the UK?
                                                                 (Paragraph 10.8)

4. How are homeowners buying their houses with mortgages affected by monetary policy in the UK?   *(Paragraph 10.8)*

5. Would they be affected in the same way if they had fixed-rate mortgages?
                                                                 (Paragraph 10.8)

11 The success of economic policy

11.1 The success of the government's economic policy in recent years can only really be assessed in the light of the objectives of economic policy which, you will recall, consisted of a:

- High and stable level of employment;
- Low and stable rate of inflation,
- High rate of economic growth; and
- Satisfactory balance of payments.

However, in the autumn of 1992, inflation was given a specific target and was accorded greater priority than the other goals. This section reviews the success achieved in attaining these four objectives from a starting point of 1980.

A high and stable level of employment

11.2   This objective is usually evaluated in terms of *unemployment* rather than employment. The evidence demonstrates that the objective of achieving a low and stable unemployment rate has not been achieved, since unemployment rose from 5.8% in 1980 (an historically high figure) to 11.1% in 1986, before falling back to 5.8% in 1990. Unemployment rose again, and stood at 10.3% in 1993; after which it has fallen steadily to 7.7% in May 1996. These figures do, furthermore, relate to the official unemployment statistics. There have been a number of changes in the basis of collection which have served, overall, to depress the figures. This record is not, however, markedly worse than that of many other industrialised nations, although the unemployment rate in the UK rose faster and fell more slowly than in most countries. Nevertheless, the unemployment rate in 1996 remains well above that of 1980, although it has to be recognised that the attainment of low unemployment was always regarded as a longer-term objective which would be facilitated by reductions in the rate of inflation. The government also points to the fact that a large number of new jobs have been created – that is to say, the growth in *employment* that has been achieved – as a better indicator of its success in achieving this particular objective of economic policy.

A low and stable rate of inflation

11.3   This has been the government's major economic policy objective, but even here fortunes have been mixed. During 1983–88 inflation was on average lower than it had been at any time since the 1960s, and remained significantly lower than the rates experienced during the 1970s and at the beginning of the 1980s. Between 1988–91, the rate of inflation once again gave cause for concern, and in the autumn of 1990 reached almost 11%. More recently the rate has fallen substantially. In June 1993 it reached a 30-year low of 1.2% although it touched 3.9% in September 1995. By May 1996 it had fallen to 2.2%. However, note that throughout much of the past decade the UK's inflation rate has generally remained higher than the rates experienced by most of the UK's major trading partners. Therefore, it is not possible to conclude without qualification that the major objective of economic policy has been achieved in recent years.

A high rate of economic growth

11.4   The success of the government's economic policy in achieving a high rate of economic growth since 1980 is more difficult to evaluate, due to the substantial variation in experience. Over the decade 1980–89, economic growth at an annual average rate of 2.3% was slightly higher than that achieved during the 1970–79 period and *lower* than that achieved in the period 1960–69 (2.9%) and 1950–59 (2.6%). However, the evidence reveals that between 1983 and 1988, economic growth was significantly higher than the average of preceding years and comparable, if not exceeding, that achieved by many of the UK's major trading partners. The experiences of 1980–82 and 1990–92 may then be attributed to the world recessions at the time although, in terms of economic growth, the recessions in the UK were markedly more severe than in the many other countries, and this requires some explanation.

More recently the rate of growth has improved somewhat, especially since the relaxation of economic policy following 'Black Wednesday' in September 1992.

A satisfactory balance of payments

11.5 Here we consider the broad trends only, using concepts found in most textbooks. However, the UK has recently divided the current account into the:

- Trade in goods and services; and

- Investment income.

11.6 The *current account* of the balance of payments, reflecting the value of goods and services imported relative to the value of those exported, has displayed very marked fluctuations since the early 1980s. In the first half of the 1980s large oil surpluses contributed to a series of large current account surpluses, but in the second half of the 1980s there was a succession of very large deficits on the current account of the balance of payments, culminating in a deficit of almost £23bn in 1989. Closer examination of the figures reveals that there was a steady worsening of the non-oil component of the current account of the balance of payments over the decade, giving rise to concerns about the ability of the UK to pay its way in international terms. More recently the position has improved, although the deficit was about £11bn in 1993, but only £2bn in 1994 and £6.7bn in 1995.

11.7 The former division of the current account into its *visible* and *invisible* components reveals some additional worrying trends. Traditionally, the invisible component of the balance of payments has generated strong surpluses which have to a large extent offset any deficits on the visible component. In recent years, however, the surplus on the invisibles account has declined and when combined with the massive deficit on the visible component, has contributed to the huge current account deficit mentioned earlier.

11.8 On the *capital account* of the balance of payments, the flows involved have been volatile since the early 1980s. This is partly attributable to the high real rates of interest that applied at times, leading to large inflows of short-term investment funds (the so-called 'hot money') which has in turn contributed to the instability of exchange rates.

11.9 Overall, it is clear that while the government has achieved some success in attaining its economic policy objectives, there remain areas where its success has been very limited. It is also clear that the *conflicts* between economic policy objectives identified earlier remain, and that the government is experiencing considerable difficulty in reconciling the objectives of high economic growth and low unemployment on the one hand with low inflation and a stable balance of payments on the other.

Student Activity 8

1. What has been the success in recent years of UK economic policy measured in terms of achieving a low level of unemployment? *(Paragraph 11.2)*

2. What has been the UK's record in inflation since the early 1980s?

(Paragraph 11.3)

3. Has the UK succeeded in achieving its objective in respect of economic growth in recent years?

(Paragraph 11.4)

4. How has the UK's current account on the balance of payments fared in recent years?

(Paragraph 11.6)

12 Monetary policy in the three major world economies

12.1 Most of the world's major economies pursue similar economic policy objectives, with stable prices having a somewhat greater priority than economic growth. However, not all of these countries are at the same stage of the economic cycle at any particular time, so that conflicts can occur if one country is contracting aggregate monetary demand at a time when others are seeking to expand it. Moreover, although the political leaders exchange views at their regular G7 summits (held between the USA, Japan, Germany, France, UK, Italy and Canada) they are answerable only to their electorates at different times and in different ways. A third point is that their central banks have varying degrees of independence, ranging from great discretion in interest rates for the US and German central banks to minimal discretion for Japan and the UK.

USA

12.2 In the USA, goals of economic policy are similar to those of the UK, except that greater priority may be given to interest rate stability, possibly in view of the importance of bond markets in the American financial system. In mid-summer 1996, the US economy is some six months or more ahead of the UK economy, with non-farm payroll (employment) data making investors fear that the Federal Reserve will raise its discount rate to 'cool the economy'. The fact that there are to be elections in November 1996 is, in the American scene, irrelevant because both the President and the members of Congress have no power over interest rates. This is far removed from the UK, where decisions on base rate are taken by an elected politician (the Chancellor of the Exchequer).

12.3 The Federal Reserve uses the full range of traditional methods in implementing monetary policy, but it does use one which is not found in the UK. This is to operate on the reserve assets of commercial banks, i.e. the balances which they keep with the 12 regional reserve banks. If a bank has more reserves in its account than it is required to keep then it can increase its lending – with the inevitable result that these reserves will gradually fall to the minimum level. Alternatively, that bank can lend its excess reserves to banks which are below their minima, or it can buy government securities. In its open market operations, the Federal Reserve will be seeking to contain the growth of the money supply, stabilise interest rates and adjust the level of the banks' total reserves.

12.4 Another instrument of monetary policy used in the USA is one which has only just begun to be used in the UK – the repurchase agreement (or 'repo') and the reverse repo. Under these, the central bank provides reserves for a stated period – usually when the banks are likely to be flush with funds – so that a shortage can be perpetuated. They are likely to be used in the EMU (paragraph 12.100.

Germany

12.5 Again, the goals of monetary policy are similar, except that there is a greater consensus over the overwhelming priority of low inflation. This arises from two brief periods of hyperinflation this century: the first in 1922–23, the second in 1947–48. It was no coincidence that both occurred shortly after the end of each of the two world wars. As we noted earlier, the central bank has great independence in setting interest rates but little discretion over exchange rates. This asymmetrical distribution of discretion can cause problems, because exchange rates and interest rates are closely connected (see Unit 8). The head of the central bank resigned shortly after the reunification of East and West Germany in 1990, largely because he disagreed with the government's decision for the exchange rates between the two currencies.

12.6 German monetary policy is consequently very cautious and there is great reluctance to reduce interest rates in case the reduction causes a rise in retail prices. In midsummer 1996, Germany had four million people unemployed and some observers believed that, eventually, a cut in interest rates was inevitable. It came in late summer.

12.7 Germany, like the USA, does not have a target for inflation but it does have a target for the growth of broad money: M3, as the Germans term it. The target is for a calendar year, being announced in December, but it is by no means an absolute level; quite often it is breached rather than observed.

12.8 Instruments of monetary policy are largely three interest rates and ample use of 'repos'. The interest rates are the repo rate, usually posted for one month, the Lombard rate for loans from the central bank, and the discount rate for special advances.

Japan

12.9 The Japanese economy is in a structural recession, and interest rates are extremely low, with the result that observers do not even talk about 'when interest rates might rise' but rather 'if interest rates rise'. Further cuts are out of the question and increases may not be on the agenda because they could trigger a rise in the exchange rate and so depress exports.

EMU

12.10 Under EMU (Economic and Monetary Union) the EU is likely to introduce a single currency (the euro) on 1 January 1999, with it replacing many individual currencies in the first half of 2002. At present, it seems likely that the new European Central Bank will implement its monetary policy by means of interest rates and repos. It will be 'independent of instruction' and its goals are likely to be to achieve 'monetary stability'. This is not a term commonly used in the UK but it means stability of:

- Prices;
- Interest rates;
- Exchange rates.

Appendix A:
The transmission mechanism of monetary policy

This is the way (or ways) in which the changes in monetary policy – at present changes in interest rates – affect the firms and individuals in the economy.

The monetary channel

Changes in short-term interest rates affect longer-term rates as switching occurs between shorter- and longer-term securities. This affects asset valuations and the composition of the various assets in the portfolios of institutions, firms and individuals.

Changes in nominal interest rates affect consumption by individuals whose interest payments, mainly on mortgages, will change. If interest rates rise, so will interest payments on variable-interest-rate mortgages (still traditional in the UK). Unless earnings rise faster, this will reduce personal consumption.

The effects on businesses are on the cost of:

- Holding stocks and work-in progress, when financed by borrowed money or, if financed by cash, the interest forgone on such cash;

- Capital investment – gross domestic fixed capital formation.

Real interest rates change fairly quickly (real = nominal rates less the RPI), because wages and prices are 'sticky'. As a result, wages and prices will be slow to follow a rise in interest rates, so that the RPI will not react immediately. Hence, if (nominal) interest rates rise following a rise in base rate, then real interest rates will rise at first then fall slowly as the RPI gradually reflects the eventual rise in prices. If base rate is reduced, short-term interest rates will also fall but, with prices being sticky, there is a sharper fall in real interest rates. This will moderate when prices readjust to lower interest rates by rising more slowly than before.

These changes in real interest rates in turn affect:

- Spending, because saving becomes more attractive if real interest rates rise and less attractive if they fall. This spending will be for both consumption and capital investment. So, if real rates rise, spending falls, and *vice versa*.

- The totality of wealth, because prices of assets usually move inversely to changes in interest rates. This also affects expenditure, particularly through the so-called 'feel good' factor.

- Exchange rates and hence the prospects for imports and exports. If real interest rates rise, the exchange rate will tend to rise so that exports become dearer in foreign currency and imports are cheaper in domestic currency. The trade balance will deteriorate and the gross domestic product (which includes net exports of goods and services) will be adversely affected.

These various ways in which changes in interest rates affect the real economy are often called the monetary channel.

251

The credit channel

However, there is an additional route through which these changes occur – the credit channel. Banks have a unique source of information about their customers – the current accounts which their customers maintain with them – and it can be quite expensive for other lenders to purchase this information, e.g. from credit reference agencies. Hence, other types of loans may be imperfect substitutes for bank loans, so that bank lending decisions affect the expenditure of those firms which cannot borrow from the capital market more than they affect the spending of other firms which can borrow from it.

If banks widen their lending margins after a base rate fall, or lower them after a base rate increase, then the effect of the base rate change is lessened. On the other hand, if they increase their lending rates more than the basis point rise in base rate then this will increase the effect on expenditure. The other option – lowering their lending rates by more than the fall in base rate – is, in practice, inconceivable.

Several problems can arise when:

- Changes in nominal interest rates have a much earlier effect on the real economy, which is likely to occur when there is a sharp or unexpected rise in base rate, triggering 'knee-jerk' reactions from households and firms.

- The 'feel-good' factor, brainwashed by steady employment and years of rising house prices, is inoperative. For the first half of the 1990s, house prices fell and then went on to a plateau, from which they may be starting to rise; while large corporates are still reducing their work forces. It is therefore no wonder that the general public finds it difficult to adjust to the new economic policy. It could be argued that this adjustment could continue for a decade rather than two years.

- Banks are reluctant to lend, irrespective of changes in interest rates, and potential borrowers are reluctant to borrow. It could be argued that this situation still prevailed in 1995.

(Reprinted, with slight amendments, from *The New Financial Review*, February 1995.)

Appendix B:
The government's monetary framework

Focus on explicit inflation target

Achieving low inflation is a key feature of the government's economic policy to deliver prosperity and secure jobs. In order to achieve this the Government set out an explicit inflation target in October 1992. The Chancellor reaffirmed this target in July 1995 and also extended it:

> the Government's current aim is to keep underlying inflation (measured by RPI excluding mortgage interest payments) within the range 1–4%, and to get down to the lower half of the range – that is $2^1/_2$% or less – by the end of the present Parliament. ... Beyond this Parliament, the aim will be to continue underlying inflation of $2^1/_2$% or less. Monetary policy will be set consistently to achieve this target. This should ensure that inflation will remain in the range 1–4%.

Transparent process

The framework has become increasingly transparent over the last three years. The Bank of England publishes a completely independent inflation report every quarter. Minutes of the monthly monetary meetings are released around two weeks after the following meeting. The Treasury publishes a monthly report covering all the available data on the same day as the meeting. Interest rate changes are always accompanied by a press notice, explaining the reason for the move.

Forward looking, based on a broad assessment of all the data

Since monetary policy influences inflation with a lag, interest rate decisions are based on an assessment of the prospects for underlying inflation over the next two years. This assessment is based on a wide range of information, including:

- Monetary and other financial indicators (including narrow and broad money, movements in the exchange rate and asset prices, and expectations about future inflation);

- Indicators of activity (including measures of spare capacity, retail sales growth and labour shortages) and the overall stance of fiscal policy;

- Indicators of costs, in particular, wage costs and material input prices (including commodity prices).

As the minutes make clear:

- Monetary policy decisions are not based on any one indicator, but on an overall assessment of all the relevant information.

- While medium-term monitoring ranges have been set for narrow and broad money, the information from these variables is interpreted alongside all the other data.

- While inflation forecasts are one useful way of summarising much of this information, decisions are not just based on a single point forecast but an assessment of the risks and uncertainties surrounding the outlook for inflation.

Response to shocks

Ever since the inflation target was first introduced, the government has explicitly acknowledged that events outside its control, such as sharp movement in commodity prices, might temporarily take inflation away from its target. The government cannot predict how large these shocks might be, or whether they will be favourable or unfavourable, but the government believes that, by setting interest rates consistently at the level judged to be necessary to achieve the inflation target of $2^1/_2$% or less, it should ensure that inflation will remain in the range 1–4 per cent.

Furthermore, as the framework is forward looking, monetary policy responds to changes in demand pressures which alter the outlook for inflation. Thus, concern last year that the economy was growing at an unsuitably fast rate was one of the factors behind the increases in interest rates.

HM Treasury 3 November 1995

Student Activity 9

1. How is US monetary policy likely to affect the UK in the near future?
   (Paragraph 12.2)

2. What is meant by making monetary policy 'transparent'? *(Appendix B)*

3. Why is UK monetary policy said to be 'forward-looking'? *(Appendix B)*

4. How are external shocks likely to affect the UK's monetary policy? *(Appendix B)*

5. Why is German monetary policy so cautious? *(Paragraphs 12.5–6)*

6. What are the two channels for the transmission of monetary policy to the real economy? *(Appendix A)*

Summary

Now that you have studied this unit you should be able to:

- **state the objectives of monetary policy and relate monetary policy to the other types of economic policy;**

- **appreciate the need for intermediate targets, with stable relationships between them and the goals of economic policy, as a means of monetary control;**

- **describe in detail the instruments of monetary policy in the UK;**

- **analyse the effects of monetary policy on the banking and financial system, and the rest of the economy;**

- **assess the effectiveness of the UK's monetary policy since 1980;**

- **identify the goals and targets of monetary policy in the world's three major economies;**

Self-assessment questions

Short-answer questions

1. List the objectives normally specified for government economic policy.

2. Why is it often argued that governments require a package of economic policies in order to achieve their policy objectives?

3. What factors are likely to affect the importance attached to monetary policy by a government?

4. The occurrence of disintermediation means that the authorities are unable to control both the money supply and interest rates simultaneously. Why?

5. List the possible intermediate targets of monetary policy.

6. Cash is only a minor element of the money supply in the modern economy. Why, therefore, might control of the cash base be seen as a desirable target for monetary policy?

7. To what extent has the UK government achieved its major economic policy objectives since the early 1980s?

Multiple-choice questions

1. An intermediate target of economic policy is
   (a) a variable over which the authorities have some control and through which they hope to influence a policy instrument
   (b) the ultimate objective of the policy
   (c) a variable through which the authorities attempt to achieve a policy objective
   (d) a concept which is only relevant in respect of monetary variables.

2. Fiscal policy
   (a) may have important implications for the rate of growth of the money supply through its impact on the PSBR/PSDR
   (b) relates to the setting of money supply growth targets
   (c) is particularly useful for the authorities as changes in fiscal variables have an immediate impact on the economy
   (d) has not been used in the UK since the present government turned to monetarism at the end of the 1970s.

3. Demand management
   (a) is just a different term for fiscal policy
   (b) is normally directed towards managing the demand for money, and the growth of the money supply
   (c) involves the manipulation of aggregate demand within the economy with a view to influencing the levels of output and employment
   (d) will always affect the level of output and employment in the economy, as its instruments are never directed towards balance of payments variables.

4. Within the context of monetary control, instruments of portfolio constraint

   (a) have a generalised effect on all borrowing and lending activities within financial markets

   (b) include the use of the Bank of England's intervention rate

   (c) tend to distort the financial system the longer the term for which they are applied, and hence lead to disintermediation

   (d) involve the setting of targets for the size of the PSBR/PSDR.

5. Since the early 1980s the UK monetary authorities have

   (a) placed emphasis on the use of portfolio constraints in order to control the money supply

   (b) used instruments of market intervention backed by prudent public financing in order to control the money supply

   (c) relied solely on reducing the PSBR in order to control the money supply

   (d) attempted to control money supply growth by a mixture of reserve asset requirements, special deposits and intervention on the foreign exchange market.

6. In recent years the UK government's economic policy has

   (a) adhered strictly to the original framework of the MTFS

   (b) concentrated less heavily on money supply growth, and now takes into account a range of variables affecting monetary conditions

   (c) relied heavily on the setting of targets for the growth of broad measures of the money supply

   (d) been explicitly directed towards the reduction of unemployment using standard demand management techniques.

Unit 8

The Analysis of Exchange Rates

Objectives

After studying this unit you should be able to:

- **define foreign exchange rates and cross rates;**

- **explain what is meant by currency baskets, especially the ECU;**

- **describe the structure of the foreign exchange market;**

- **discuss the fundamental determinants of exchange rates;**

- **explain how a forward exchange rate is determined using the concept of covered interest parity;**

- **describe the structure of a country's balance of payments and its terms of trade;**

- **analyse how changes in the terms of trade affect a country's balance of trade and balance of payments;**

- **appreciate how changes in a country's balance of payments affect its currency's exchange rate;**

- **identify the different types of exchange rate systems, especially the European Monetary System;**

- **assess the arguments for and against a country joining the single currency of the EU;**

- **identify the types of foreign exchange risk, and the various financial derivatives which have been devised to manage such risk.**

---

1   Exchange rates

1.1   Exchange rates are prices of one country's money, in terms of other countries' money, e.g. £1 = DM 2.25 or £1 = USD 1.54. Expressed in that way, it seems so simple but, in reality, there are problems arising from the:

- Way in which prices are expressed;

- Factors which cause the changes in demand and supply which in turn cause the price changes.

1.2   In general business, we quote prices as money per unit of the item being traded, e.g. apples are 10p each or lunches are £6. We may express the price as 'Apples – 10 for £1' but we never say 'Lunches are 1 for £6'. However, this reversal of the price statement occurs in foreign exchange where in the UK we say 'the DM is 2.25' (meaning we get 2.25 units of German currency for one major unit of our currency) and never 'the DM is 0.4444 against the £'. And yet 'DM1 = £0.4444' is the same arithmetically as sterling '£1 = DM2.25'.

1.3   To revert to our greengrocer shouting his price of 'apples are ten for £1', when he lowers his price it becomes 'eleven apples for a £1' and, when lower still, 'a dozen apples for £1'. When the price rises, he charges '9 apples for £1'. In other words, under this way of pricing, you buy on the higher number, e.g. at 12 to £1 and sell at a lower number, e.g. 9 for £1. This rule applies to all foreign exchange transactions in this country – 'buy high, sell low' – and it is taught to all trainee clerks in foreign exchange sections.

1.4   To complicate matters further, some countries do not follow this practice, so that foreign exchange rates would be quoted in the same way as all other prices, e.g. DM are 44.4 pence each, so we buy (if we can) at 44.2p and sell (if we can) at 44.7p. This is the same as buying at $1/44.2 \times 100$ (= 2.262) and selling at $1/44.7 \times 100$ (= 2.237).

Cross rates

1.5   Foreign exchange dealers are paid to make profits and so they are continually testing rates in different cities to see if they can make a profit 'on the cross'. A cross rate is the exchange rate of one foreign currency against another foreign currency instead of against our own currency. The most common cross rate is US dollars against Canadian dollars (there is no mention of pounds here). If traders can sell US dollars for sterling in London and then use that sterling to buy Canadian dollars in London or New York or Zurich or Paris or Frankfurt, then they might be able to make a small profit. If there is no profit then they will not deal.

1.6   Using the *Financial Times* and the rates of 29 July 1996, the arithmetic becomes:

$$£1 = \text{US\$ } 1.5580$$
$$£1 = \text{Can\$ } 2.1382$$

so $\text{US\$ } 1.5580 = \text{Can\$ } 2.1382$

$$\text{US\$}1 = \text{Can\$ } \frac{2.1382}{1.5580} \text{ (dividing both sides by 1.5580)}$$

$$= \text{Can\$ } 1.3724$$

We then look at the table for US dollar rates, where:

$$\text{US\$}1 = \text{Can\$ } 1.3725$$

(Source: *Financial Times*: 30 July 1996)

1.7   That may seem close enough to most people but, on deals of one million dollars and over, that difference is worth $100. So, why is there a slight difference? Why haven't the arbitrageurs eliminated it?

1.8   One reason is that this is 'riskless arbitrage', taking no account of counterparty risks (which are probably minimal because the parties are invariably banks of undoubted integrity) but also the risk that the exchange rate could move against the arbitrageurs whilst they were completing the transaction. For one moment, the arbitrageurs owned sterling as a vehicle to get from US dollars to Canadian dollars.

1.9 The second reason is probably more important – cost. Deals cost money in the shape of back office labour, computer time, telex/telephones. There comes a point where the profit does not cover the cost, and the arbitrageur might be better employed in (say) trading the DM against the Austrian schilling in (say) Paris or Milan.

Student Activity 1

1. Explain, in everyday words what exchange rates are. *(Paragraph 1.1)*

2. Using the phrase 'they are cheap, they are two a penny' describe how exchange rates are expressed. *(Paragraph 1.2)*

3. What are meant by 'cross rates'? *(Paragraph 1.5)*

4. What is meant by exchange rate arbitrage? *(Paragraph 1.5)*

5. List some of the costs involved in foreign exchange deals. *(Paragraph 1.9)*

2 Currency baskets

2.1 Currency baskets are combinations of foreign currencies, devised as artificial currencies which do not fluctuate in value as much as individual currencies. Two major baskets have been created since currencies became more volatile in the early 1970s – the Special Drawing Right (SDR) and the European Currency Unit (ECU).

Origins

2.2 You will recall that one of the functions of money is to act as a unit of account and that one of the characteristics needed by an asset used as money is that it must be stable in its value (purchasing power). One very popular asset for use as money has been gold, which had its heyday in the 19th century, when the gold standard ensured that foreign exchange rates linked to gold did not fluctuate significantly. The reason for this stability was that gold could be exported to sell currencies rising in value and buy currencies falling in value.

2.3 However, there were problems with gold: its supply is limited and was dependent on discovery of new fields, leading to 'gold rushes'; second, some countries have more gold fields than others. In the great depression of the 1930s, many countries left the gold standard and even the USA devalued the dollar against gold in 1933, from $20.67 an ounce to $35 an ounce.

2.4 After the great depression came the Second World War when the allies decided at Bretton Woods in 1944 to revert to stable exchange rates, linking their currencies to the US dollar, and thus indirectly to gold. These Bretton Woods 'parities' worked well until the strains of a worldwide boom in the 1970s put too much pressure on them, and they were widened from one per cent either side of parity to 2.25%.

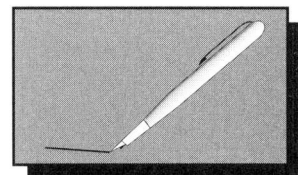

Special drawing rights

2.5   In the mid-1960s, agreement was reached on a new form of international money, nicknamed 'paper gold' and called the Special Drawing Right (SDR), with an exchange rate of 1 to 1 with the US dollar. However, in the early 1970s, the US dollar itself devalued against gold and in 1973 most leading countries began to float against each other. This caused the SDR to float exactly in line with the US dollar, so the link was broken and the SDR was occasionally devalued against the US dollar.

2.6   From 1974 to 1980, the SDR was calculated as a weighted average of the world's most important currencies – defined as the currencies of all countries with more than 1% of the world's total trade in goods and services for the years 1968–1972. This gave a basket of 16 currencies which proved to be unwieldy.

2.7   Since January 1981, the SDR has been a basket of five leading currencies – US dollar, DM, yen, sterling, and the French franc – with their weights changed every five years. The International Monetary Fund publishes exchange rates for the SDR one day in arrears, as will be seen from the data on the 'Currencies and Money' page of the *Financial Times*.

2.8   As well as being a unit of account, the SDR is a form of money because allocations of SDRs were made to member nations of the International Monetary Fund in the late 1960s. In this role, it functions as an international 'reserve asset', i.e. as a liquid store of value.

European Currency Unit

2.9   This originated in the early 1970s, as the European unit of account, as a bookkeeping mechanism for the budget of the European Communities (as they then were) . At the same time, the EEC tried to keep its currencies linked together rather than through the US dollar, by means of an arrangement nicknamed the 'snake in the tunnel' with the snake referring to the exchange rates and the tunnel being the upper and lower limits beyond which the member currencies could not float. In 1979, this European Monetary System was, to use a marketing concept, re-launched with the creation of the European Exchange Rate Mechanism (ERM). (The ERM is covered in section 10 of this unit, but here we are concerned with the currency basket, the ECU, which was created as part of the European Monetary System.)

2.10   On joining the EU, all member nations swap 20% of their official holdings of gold and US dollars into ECUs. Thus, ECUs exist but they are created by exchange of existing money rather than by what is a gift (as was the issue of SDRs some 30 years ago). The ECU is calculated as a weighted basket of the currencies of the first 12 members of the EU, being revised in 1984 and, for the final time, in 1989. The EU now has 15 member states and is likely to grow still further, so that recalculating the ECU every time a new country joined would be a laborious and costly exercise.

2.11   The currency with the greatest weight in the ECU is the DM which, incidentally, has its weight related to the old West Germany. Had reunification occurred before the final re-weighting then the DM's weight would have been even larger.

Interest rates

2.12   As you will see from the 'Currencies and Money' page of the *Financial Times*, interest rates are quoted by banks for both SDR and ECU denominated accounts These are calculated by weighting the relevant interest rates for the member currencies by their weights in the SDR or ECU, as the case may be.

Comparisons of the two baskets

2.13   The SDR has been heavily weighted by the US dollar and so lenders and borrowers have often avoided it, particularly as oil – the most important commodity in world trade – is priced in dollars. The ECU has become more popular as a device for limiting currency fluctuations but, at the time of writing, there is uncertainty among traders as to the details of how it will link into the euro, the new single currency of the EU.

Student Activity 2

1. Describe, in general terms, how the two most important currency baskets are calculated.   *(Paragraphs 2.7 and 2.10)*

2. Which section of the *Financial Times* provides detailed information on exchange rates, including currency baskets?   *(Paragraphs 2.7 and 2.12)*

3. Are there interest rates for currency baskets?   *(Paragraph 2.12)*

4. When a country joins the European Union, what must it do with 20% of its holdings of gold and US dollars?   *(Paragraph 2.10)*

5. What is so special about gold and US dollars?   *(Paragraphs 2.2–4)*

3   Foreign exchange markets

3.1   Within a country's domestic economy, inter-party transactions can normally be settled by the transfer of domestic currency from one party to the other by cash, cheque or other funds-transfer mechanism. However, once trade between different countries or currency areas is instigated the situation becomes more complex. The parties to the trade need to decide in which currency the transactions will be denominated – seller's, buyer's or that of another country. For example, oil exports from Saudi Arabia to Japan could be invoiced in Saudi riyals or Japanese yen. In fact, trading practice in the oil industry means that most oil shipments are invoiced in US dollars so that would be the most likely currency of the transaction. Whatever method is chosen, one party (or possibly both) will be faced with the prospect of paying or receiving payment in a currency other than its own. *Currencies will have to be traded*, and to meet this need a network of foreign currency exchange markets has evolved, interlinked today by a sophisticated communications network. There is no central market place as such; groups of dealers around the world communicate with each other by telephone, telex, facsimile and computers, trying to match the supply of and demand for various currencies, according to the needs of governments, commerce, industry and individuals. It is, in effect, a global OTC market.

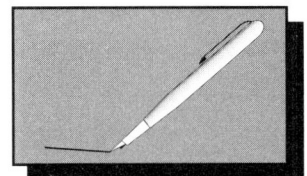

3.2 The main centres for foreign exchange (forex) dealing are at present London (daily turnover in April 1995 was US$464bn), New York ($244bn) and Tokyo ($161bn).

Who are the players?

3.3 The actual market participants can be either dealers or principals or both. A *dealer* buys or sells currencies for third parties, selling at a margin above the market rate and buying at a margin below. The difference between his buying and selling rate is called the 'turn', in addition to which the dealer may well charge a fee or commission for his services. The commercial banks are the main dealers, acting for the whole spectrum of their customers from holiday-makers to multinational investors.

3.4 A *principal* buys and sells currencies on his own account, speculating on favourable exchange-rate movements to enable him to profit from his dealing. He is prepared to hold currency for short periods in the hope that its ex-change rate will improve so that he can sell at a profit. Many dealers will also act as principals in the market to try to enhance their profitability. Indeed, most of the banks acting as dealers have now designated their forex opera-tions as profit centres, so the dealers have an incentive to act as principals if they are sure they can read the market trends correctly.

3.5 Often, a country's official monetary authorities will enter the forex market, usually in order to reduce undesired short-term fluctuations in exchange rates. By buying or selling currencies they can raise or lower currency ex-change rates, funding transactions from official reserves or loans from international institutions. Currency swap arrangements with overseas mon-etary authorities are sometimes utilised in order to support these operations.

Student Activity 3

1. Why are foreign exchange markets required? *(Paragraph 3.1)*

2. What form do foreign exchange markets take? *(Paragraph 3.1)*

3. In 1995 where were the world's three main foreign exchange markets located? *(Paragraph 3.2)*

4. What is the role of a dealer in the foreign exchange market? *(Paragraph 3.3)*

5. What is the role of a principal in the foreign exchange market? *(Paragraph 3.4)*

6. Why do national monetary authorities become involved with foreign exchange activities? *(Paragraph 3.5)*

The 'commodity'

3.6 This market is where bank deposits in various currencies are bought and sold: it must be distinguished from the market in bank notes of different countries, which is separate. The size of the bank deposits is large, because this is a wholesale market – one million for most currencies.

3.7 It is a global financial market, operating around the clock for five days a week. The week really begins (about 10.30pm on Sunday London time) when

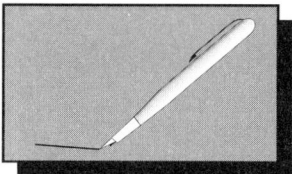

the foreign exchange dealing rooms open in Tokyo (Monday morning there), although the market is already open in New Zealand. Soon afterwards they are joined by dealers in Sydney, Hong Kong and Singapore. By 6.30am in London, the markets are opening in Frankfurt and Paris, but the Far East markets are about to close. Normally, the continent is one hour ahead of London, except for one month in the autumn, when the continental countries have reverted to mean time one month earlier than the UK. (Soon, they will keep the same period of summer time as the UK.) At 2.00pm London time, New York opens, to be followed in the early evening by California, to be followed in the late evening by Tokyo ... The market is highly automated and deals are executed by pressing the appropriate buy or sell button on the keyboard.

Delivery (settlement\the back office)

3.8   'Spot' deals are for delivery (settlement) in (at the most) two working days' time, i.e. a spot deal concluded on a Thursday will be settled on the next Monday; a Tuesday deal will be settled on the next Thursday. The other detail needed is which bank account to pay and which bank account will receive the proceeds. Spot deals can also be for tomorrow or even, early in the morning London time, for today. If one of the currencies is sterling, then the cutoff for 'same day' deals is the closing time for CHAPS, provided the other centre (in the Western Hemisphere) is still open.

3.9   Suppose Lloyds Bank buys yen from and sells DM to Citibank New York. Citibank will specify to which bank account in Frankfurt it will require the DM to be paid. It could be its account with Deutsche Bank, or it might be its own branch there. Lloyds Bank must then instruct a bank in Frankfurt to transfer the DM from its account with that bank to Citibank's account with Deutsche Bank. Similarly, Lloyds Bank will inform Citibank of the bank in Tokyo which is to receive the yen.

3.10   For the past 20 years, following a fraud in Lugano, it has been the practice to separate dealers (traders in US-speak), who buy and sell, from the clerks and bookkeepers who keep the records and make the payments. This practice has extended into other financial markets, e.g. where Nick Leeson dealt. However, there he had access to the records (but did not make the payments) ...

Student Activity 4

1. Why was it essential for the fate of Barings to be decided before about 10.30pm in London that Sunday?   *(Paragraph 3.7)*

2. If it is 7am in London, what time is it in Tokyo?   *(Paragraph 3.7)*

3. Is it possible to sell US dollars against sterling, value the same day, in London at 1.30pm?   *(Paragraph 3.8)*

4. Is it possible to buy US dollars against DM, value the same day in London at 1.30pm?   *(Paragraph 3.8)*

5. Why must dealers be separated from the back office?   *(Paragraph 3.10)*

4   Types of foreign exchange transactions

4.1   *Spot* currency transactions are those for which settlement must be completed within two business days. *Forward* transactions take place when an exchange rate has been booked at which currency will be delivered on a fixed future date or on a day between two future dates. In the first instance, a *fixed forward currency contract* is arranged between buyer and seller, and in the second, an *option forward currency contract* is written, the 'option' being *when* to deliver between the agreed dates not *whether* to deliver. Delivery of agreed currencies *must* be made by the final date of the contract.

4.2   Forward contracts are useful to importers or exporters who are carrying out transactions denominated in a (to them) foreign currency. At the time of quoting for or agreeing their trading deal, they can crystallise the domestic currency value of the expected future foreign currency invoice, and hence ensure that the profitability of the deal is not eroded by adverse future movements in foreign exchange rates. This is known as 'hedging' exchange rate risk, and forward currency contracts are one of several hedging tools used by international traders.

How are rates for forward transactions determined?

4.3   When quoting forward currency rates dealers will add a discount or deduct a premium from the spot rate to reflect the differential between interest rates prevailing for the two currencies concerned. If, for example, interest rates on sterling funds are higher than those on US dollar funds, then the forward dollar will be quoted at a premium against sterling to compensate for the loss by the writer of the forward contract (usually a bank) of interest earned on dollars compared with sterling for the contract period involved. This interest rate differential is used to calculate *forward* exchange premiums and discounts from the spot rate and which dealers quote to clients according to the length of the contract required. Forward exchange rates are not forecasts of the spot rate on future dates, they are today's spot rate adjusted for interest rate differentials.

Practical examples

4.4   An example may be from the data of 20 September 1995, reported in the FT of the next day. We use Japan, because their interest rates are so low:

	USA	Japan
Three months' money market rates	5.75% p.a.	0.5% p.a.
Exchange rate spot	JEY 102.915	
three months' forward	JEY 101.575	

If we express the forward rate as a percentage of the spot rate we do this calculation:

$$\frac{101.575}{102.915} \times 100$$

$$= 0.98698 \times 100$$

$$= 98.698$$

This can be rewritten:

$$(98.698 - 100)$$

$$= -1.302\% \text{ for three months}$$

Multiply by four to give an annual rate:

= –5.208%

= –5.21%

And the difference between the two interest rates is:

5.75% – 0.5%

= 5.25% which is very close to 5.21%.

Forward exchange rates are not forecasts of future spot rates

4.5 Forward exchange rates are spot exchange rates adjusted for the difference in interest rates prevailing in the two currencies concerned.

4.6 If investors (say a multinational, or George Soros) see interest rates rise in one country then they may wish to buy that currency in order to benefit from the higher rate of interest. However, there is one unknown – how much will that foreign currency be worth when they come to sell? The forward exchange market gives them the chance to sell that currency now for settlement in (say) six months' time, so that they know now what profit on the whole transaction will be. Thus, the investors buy the spot currency, with the result that the spot rate rises, but they sell the forward currency, so that the forward rate falls.

4.7 The rules are: *Buy spot, sell forward*
Sell spot, buy forward.

Student Activity 5

1. What are 'spot' foreign exchange transactions'? *(Paragraph 4.1)*

2. What is a fixed forward exchange contract? *(Paragraph 4.1)*

3. What is an option forward exchange contract? *(Paragraph 4.1)*

4. What use are forward exchange contracts to importers and exporters?
(Paragraph 4.2)

5. What determines the premium or discount on forward exchange rates? *(Paragraph 4.3)*

6. Using data from a recent FT, check the three month forward premium/discount between two currencies. *(Paragraph 4.4)*

7. Explain how you can construct a forward rate for two currencies provided that:
   (a) there is a spot rate;
   (b) there are interest rates quoted for the forward periods, e.g. three months fixed deposit in both currencies. *(Paragraph 4.4)*

5 The balance of payments and the terms of trade

Basic concepts

5.1 The balance of payments accounts are effectively a systematic record of all transactions between domestic residents of a country, such as the UK, and residents of foreign nations, over a given time period. All transactions are

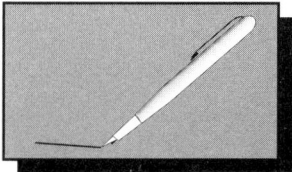

recorded in sterling, *credit items* having a positive sign and *debit items* a negative sign. Credit items include exports of goods and services and earnings of interest from overseas and investment from overseas. Debit items include imports of goods and services, dividend payments made to overseas residents and domestic investment made overseas.

Structure of the balance of payments accounts

5.2   The accounts can be split into three parts, the:

- Current account;
- Capital account;
- Balancing item.

Current account

5.3   The current account is now subdivided into four sections:

- Visibles;
- Services;
- Investment income;
- Transfers.

5.4   *Visibles* include the export and import of tangible items, e.g. basic raw materials, manufactured goods, fuels, and so on. The balance of imports and exports in visible trade is called the balance of trade in goods.

5.5   *Services* include:

- Earnings from and payments for private sector services (such as financial services, tourism, transport);
- Government sector services, e.g. running overseas embassies.

5.6   *Investment income* includes:

- Interest, profits and dividends arising from international financial activities.

5.7   *Transfers* includes:

- Private-sector current transfers (such as gifts overseas, private pensions and remittances of private pensions); and
- Government sector current transfer payments, e.g. official overseas aid, payments relating to the EU budget, and retirement and war pensions paid to overseas residents who have emigrated from the UK.

5.8   The aggregation of the visible and invisible balances yields the *current account balance*. This is considered the most important component of the accounts because of its implications for other major macroeconomic variables such as output and employment.

Capital account

5.9   The main components of the capital account (also termed 'transactions in external assets and liabilities) are:

- Overseas investment in the UK – divided into direct investment (investment in physical assets) and portfolio investment (involving financial instruments).

- UK private-sector investment overseas (divided as above).

- Foreign currency and sterling borrowing/lending by UK banks.

- Deposits with and borrowing from banks overseas by the UK non-bank private sector and public sector.

- Changes in official reserves.

- Transactions in other external assets and liabilities, e.g. borrowing from or repaying of funds to the IMF.

Balancing item

5.10 The balancing item is included to deal with errors and omissions in the accounts. If more currency flows into the country (in net terms) than is recorded in real transactions the balancing item will be positive.

Student Activity 6

1. What are the balance of payments accounts? *(Paragraph 5.1)*

2. Give some examples of credit items in the current account of the balance of payments. *(Paragraphs 5.3–7)*

3. Give some examples of debit items in the transactions in external assets and liabilities? *(Paragraph 5.9)*

4. What is the difference between the balance of trade in goods and the current account balance? *(Paragraphs 5.5–7)*

5. What type of items are included in the capital account of the balance of payments? *(Paragraph 5.9)*

6. What is the balancing item in the balance of payments? *(Paragraph 5.10)*

Official financing

5.11 Should the sum of the current account, the private sector elements of the capital account and the balancing item be negative, there is said to be a balance of payments deficit, in which case *official financing* (changes in official reserves) has to be positive. The reverse case applies if the sum is positive and a balance of payments surplus occurs. Possession of official reserves is vital to finance balance of payments deficits (and hence for the authorities to be able to influence currency exchange rates). Reserves are made up of the following assets:

- *Convertible currencies* – normally the major component of reserves.

- *Gold* – used as a 'second line of defence' rather than on a day-to-day basis.

- *Special Drawing Rights (SDRs)* – a reserve asset created by the IMF and available to member countries (see paragraphs 2.5–8).

- *Reserve positions at the IMF* – effectively overdraft facilities in foreign currencies.

5.12 The sum of these items provides a *narrow* definition of a country's international liquidity. Recently, however, more attention has been focused on a broader definition which includes borrowing facilities made available to sovereign states from the IMF, commercial banks and central banks of other countries. The

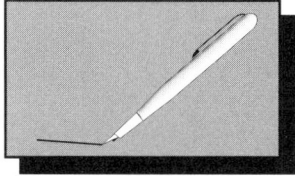

broader definition is a better guide to the liquidity available to a 'creditworthy' country but is far more difficult to calculate than the narrow definition.

Accounting equality and economic equilibrium

5.13   The balance of payments accounts are compiled using *double entry bookkeeping*, and hence always balance in accounting terms. Effectively, every international transaction must be financed by international payments. If the sum of the current account, private sector capital account and the balancing item is –£x, this will be balanced by +£x of official financing, making the accounts sum to zero.

5.14   *Economic equilibrium* occurs only when official financing is zero. When a balance of payments deficit or surplus occurs, there is economic disequilibrium. If disequilibrium persists in the long run a fundamental disequilibrium is said to exist and has important implications for the level of official reserves and overseas official borrowing. In recent years the focus has been on the current account because it represents a country's ability to pay its way internationally. Hence the balance of payments may be regarded as being in equilibrium only when there is a zero balance on the current account.

5.15   Ignoring the balancing item, if the current account is in deficit this must be balanced by a surplus of equal size on the private sector capital account, otherwise official financing has to be used and reserves are run down or overseas debt is increased.

5.16   If exchange rates are clean floating rates, the balance of payments will always be in equilibrium as by definition there is no official intervention in the currency markets. Problems may exist, however, if a large capital account surplus is balanced by a large current account deficit due to the latter's implications for the export of goods and services and hence domestic employment.

Student Activity 7

1.   Under what circumstances will official financing be positive?   *(Paragraph 5.13)*

2.   List the main components of the official reserves.   *(Paragraph 5.12)*

3.   What is the difference between the narrow definition and the broad definition of international liquidity?   *(Paragraph 5.13)*

4.   Why must balance of payments accounts always balance?   *(Paragraph 5.14)*

5.   In what circumstances does economic equilibrium occur on the balance of payments?   *(Paragraph 5.15)*

6.   In what sense does a clean floating exchange rate imply a permanent equilibrium position for the balance of payments?   *(Paragraph 5.16)*

Terms of trade

5.17   The terms of (visible) trade for any particular country relative to the rest of the world are defined as:

$$\frac{\text{Index of export prices}}{\text{Index of import prices}} \times 100$$

5.18   Initially both price indices are set at 100 and therefore the terms of trade are also 100. Now, if export prices rise while import prices remain constant, the terms of trade rise above 100 and are said to have improved. This means that for every unit of goods exported the country will obtain a larger quantity of imports. The converse is true for a deterioration in the terms of trade.

5.19   Care must be taken when interpreting a change in the terms of trade. An improvement in the terms of trade will be beneficial if the price of a country's exports has increased due to increased demand. This will have a favourable effect on the balance of trade. If the price of exports has risen due to rising domestic production costs then the improvement in the terms of trade will be beneficial only if the demand for that country's exports is price inelastic (that is, demand falls by a proportionately smaller amount than prices rise). If the converse case is true (demand is price elastic), then the balance of trade is likely to deteriorate.

5.20   If the terms of trade deteriorate due to rising import prices, whether this is beneficial to the balance of trade and hence to the economy as a whole, again depends on the elasticity of demand for imports. If the imported goods are seen as necessities (that is, low price elasticity of demand) the balance of trade will deteriorate.

5.21   Due to the importance of the terms of trade and their implications for a country's economy, a government may want to influence their value. The government will have a limited influence on the terms of trade because the relative prices of imports and exports are at the mercy of world supply and demand. Despite this, there are a number of ways in which the government can influence the terms of trade, first, by influencing the exchange rate; secondly, by trying to reduce domestic price inflation through tight monetary or fiscal policy and so causing the terms of trade to deteriorate. If we assume an elastic demand for the country's exports, this will then improve the balance of trade. It is unlikely that the government would use the reverse of the above policy to improve the terms of trade. Instead, it would try to encourage the production of high-quality goods thereby stimulating higher demand and pushing the prices of the goods upwards.

Student Activity 8

1. Define the terms of trade.   (Paragraph 5.17)

2. What happens to the terms of trade if export prices rise, other things being equal?   (Paragraph 5.19)

3. In what circumstances will an improvement in the terms of trade be good for the balance of trade?   (Paragraph 5.19)

4. Why is the influence of a government on the terms of trade likely to be limited?   (Paragraph 5.21)

5. What actions might be taken by a government to influence the terms of trade?   (Paragraph 5.21)

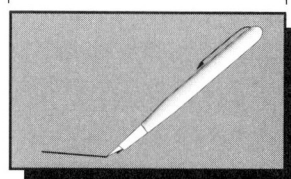

6 The economic significance of the balance of payments

The current account

Deficits

6.1 As we mentioned earlier, a current account deficit means that a country is not paying its way internationally, and therefore is either increasing its foreign debt, or running down its reserves, or both. It is possible that the deficit is financed by a surplus on the capital account.

6.2 The extent to which a deficit is regarded as being unfavourable depends, first, on its size and, second, on its persistence. The underlying economic and financial strength of the country is also important. Hence, a short-term deficit may not be looked on as being too harmful, as long as it is easily financed by running down reserves. It may even lead to an increased standard of living.

6.3 If it is believed that a current account deficit will persist into the future, the implications become more serious. The longer a deficit has to be financed the more the (finite) official reserves will be run down or the more the foreign borrowing will have to increase. The larger the deficit, the worse this situation will become.

6.4 Clearly, the larger the size of debt that is amassed the progressively more onerous the servicing requirements will be. This may lead to a loss of confidence in the debtor nation and therefore, to prevent investment funds flowing out of the country, interest rates may have to be raised. This is clearly at odds with trying to correct the current account deficit through a low exchange rate.

6.5 The international debt problem of the early 1980s came about due to less-developed countries borrowing heavily to finance current account deficits. Unfortunately, the advent of high real interest rates and the strengthening of currencies led to unmanageable debt repayments. Only major rescheduling exercises and the provision of extra funds prevented a global financial crisis.

Surpluses

6.6 A persistent surplus is seen as a favourable situation for a country to be in, as it can use the surplus either to build up overseas investments, to increase official reserves or to repay overseas debt (or a combination of all three).

6.7 A country may come under political pressure to reduce its surplus, if it is excessively large, due to it being matched by a current account deficit in at least one other country. A more attractive solution to curing a country's deficit on the current account is for the surplus country to increase its imports rather than for the deficit country to depress demand for goods and services in its economy or to introduce tariffs. The surplus country may also benefit from a higher standard of living without increasing its international indebtedness.

The capital account

6.8 Due to the rather varied nature of the components of the capital account, great care must be taken when interpreting capital flows. Even if a country has a balanced capital account it may be relying on short-run capital inflows which are extremely volatile and likely to flow out of the country in response to a small change in relative interest rates.

Deficits

6.9 A deficit means there is a net outflow of funds. The implications here are far less disturbing than for a current account deficit. For instance, the deficit may be due to heavy investment in capital goods by that country in a foreign country, and may therefore lead to inflows of profit in the current account in future years. In addition, capital account outflows are likely to hold down the domestic currency's exchange rate, and hence help to improve the competitiveness of exports.

6.10 Capital outflows may be detrimental if output is raised and jobs created abroad at the expense of the domestic economy. It may also have detrimental effects on the demand for exports produced by the domestic economy.

Surpluses

6.11 If the capital account surplus involves long-term capital investment from foreigners in domestic industry this will encourage the production of more goods domestically, perhaps increasing visible exports and decreasing imports. On the other hand, the capital may be withdrawn in the future and also generate interest, profits and dividends which flow abroad, worsening the invisibles balance on the current account.

6.12 Problems may also occur if capital inflows consisting of 'hot money' (that is, short-term investments that flow in due to relatively high domestic interest rates) takes up a considerable part of the capital account. Large flows of hot money tend to destabilise the domestic currency's exchange rate and may contribute towards a current account deficit by raising outflows of interest payments.

Student Activity 9

1. What factors will influence the extent to which a current account deficit on the balance of payments is seen as unfavourable? *(Paragraph 6.2)*

2. Why might a current account deficit eventually lead to a loss of confidence in the country? *(Paragraph 6.4)*

3. Why might a persistent current account surplus be seen as a good thing by a country? *(Paragraph 6.6)*

4. Give some reasons for a country seeking to reduce its current account surplus. *(Paragraph 6.7)*

5. In what sense may a deficit on the capital account of the balance of payments be detrimental for the economy? *(Paragraph 6.10)*

6. How might a surplus on the capital account be a good thing for the current account? *(Paragraph 6.9)*

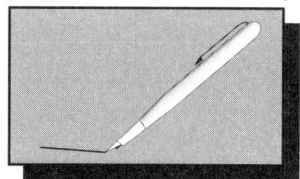

7 Correcting a balance of payments imbalance

The basic payments problem

7.1   Above we discussed how certain imbalances within components of the balance of payments may cause problems for a country's economy. Sometimes, however, these problems may be self-correcting over time; for example, a current account deficit reduces demand for domestic goods and therefore puts downward pressure on domestic inflation, increasing competitiveness of exports and therefore improving the current account position.

7.2   However, these natural mechanisms may be too slow, necessitating government intervention to deal with such imbalances. Care must be taken with timing when implementing these policies, and the government will also have to make sure such policies do not conflict with other economic objectives.

A current account imbalance

Deficits

7.3   The following policies may help to reduce a current account deficit:

- Reduce the sterling exchange rate.
- Demand management policies.
- Direct controls.
- Exchange controls.
- Quality improvement.

7.4   *Reducing the sterling exchange rate* reduces the foreign currency price of exports and raises the sterling price of imports. This will be successful as long as 'the sum of the price elasticity of demand for imports plus that for exports is greater than one' (the Marshall-Lerner condition). Hence the above policy is most successful when the demand for exports and imports is highly price elastic. The result is that eventually total receipts from exports rise and total payments for imports fall by a greater percentage. This policy is sometimes known as the 'elasticities approach'.

7.5   One short-run problem this policy has to contend with is the 'J-curve effect'. In the short run, before demand for exports has had time to increase, revenue from exports will decrease due to a fall in price, while expenditure on imports will increase – worsening the current account. As demand for exports increases and for imports decreases over time the current account will start to improve. The bottom of the 'J' shows the deficit worsening at first and then improving.

7.6   *Demand management policies* aim to improve the current account by reducing the volume of imports bought. The authorities may tighten monetary policy (but note the problems of higher interest rates), reduce government spending or increase taxation. This approach to policy may also free spare capacity to service export markets.

The above policies are the only two *seriously viable policy options*. The policies mentioned below are theoretically possible but run into problems in practice:

7.7 *Direct controls* include tariffs (taxes on imports) and quotas (quantity restrictions on imports). Both these may result in retaliation from other countries.

7.8 *Exchange controls* limit the use of foreign currency by UK residents.

7.9 *Quality improvement of* exports enhances their competitive position, and hence the current account of the balance of payments will also be enhanced.

Surpluses

7.10 A current account surplus may also be undesirable (see paragraph 6.7) and therefore governments may want to eradicate such a surplus. This is done by using the reverse of the policies just outlined:

- *Raising the sterling exchange rate* may be done by buying sterling and selling foreign currency. Alternatively, the government may try to attract foreign currency capital inflows. Again, this policy will only be successful if the Marshall-Lerner criterion holds (see 7.4).

- *Raising domestic demand* by expansionary monetary and/or fiscal policy, hence drawing in more imports. Both of these policies also fuel inflation, decreasing the competitiveness of exports. These policies are successful as long as the demand for imports/exports is elastic.

- *Abolition of import controls*; alternatively *export controls* may be introduced.

- The government may *encourage foreign holidays for its residents*, or encourage students to study overseas and so on.

Capital account imbalance

Deficits

7.11 Inflows of capital funds or the stemming of outflows of such funds are aided by the implementation of the following policies:

- *The raising of domestic interest rates* through tight monetary policy. This makes domestic financial instruments more attractive to overseas investors.

- *Stabilising the exchange rate* in order to discourage speculative outflows.

- *Government incentives* for foreign investment in the domestic economy, via grants, subsidies or tax free allowances.

- Reduction of government capital expenditure outflows.

7.12 The above policies do have their drawbacks. The magnitude and timing of such policies may be hard to judge. Also, if too much capital is attracted this will put the current account under extreme pressure due to an appreciating exchange rate.

Surpluses

7.13 The policies to deal with a capital account surplus are basically the *reverse* of those outlined above. These policies will be pursued if a large capital account surplus is sustained at the expense of a current account deficit.

Student Activity 10

1. Give an example of how a balance of payments problem may be self-correcting.
   (Paragraph 7.1)

2. What condition is required for a reduction in a country's exchange rate to have a positive effect on the current account of its balance of payments? *(Paragraph 7.4)*

3. What is the 'J-curve effect'? *(Paragraph 7.5)*

4. How might demand management policies be used to influence a country's current account on the balance of payments? *(Paragraph 7.6)*

5. List the policies which might be implemented to reduce a surplus on the current account of the balance of payments. *(Paragraph 7.10)*

6. State the policies which might be implemented to reduce a deficit on the capital account of the balance of payments. *(Paragraph 7.11)*

8 Determinants of exchange rate movements

Long-term trends in exchange rates

8.1 In the longer term, the relative economic performances of different countries determine the broad structure of exchange rates. The major contributory factors are usually referred to as the 'economic fundamentals', and are:

- Relative inflation rates;
- Relative interest rats (interest rate parity)
- The position of the balance of payments.

Relative inflation rates

8.2 One theory linking exchange rates and differing inflation rates between countries is the *purchasing power parity* (PPP) theory, which claims that the equilibrium exchange rate between currencies will be the rate at which the domestic purchasing powers of these currencies is equalised. For example, if a basket of goods costs £1 in the UK and DM3 in Germany, then the equilibrium exchange rate would be £1 = DM3. If this is not the case, people will in theory import goods from the 'cheaper' country, which will experience a trade surplus tending to force up the value of that country's currency.

8.3 This theory might work if all goods and services were traded internationally and international capital flows were zero or equal between the two countries concerned. As this is rarely the case, the PPP theory is too simplistic for the real world and, in any case, ignores transport and other trading costs. The PPP theory does help to explain, however, why the exchange rate of a country with high inflation will tend to fall relative to a country with a lower rate of inflation. The high-inflation country's export prices will rise but its imports will be relatively cheaper. In time, balance of payments problems will arise and official policy actions may be needed to correct the imbalance.

Relative interest rates

8.4 The level of *real* domestic interest rates (that is, nominal rates adjusted for the effects of expected domestic inflation) compared with those abroad is usually thought to have a strong influence on international capital flows, particularly in the short term. High interest rates attract capital funds from overseas and also add to investor confidence, since they suggest that the government has strong policies to control domestic inflation. Capital inflows from abroad create an increased demand for the domestic currency, thus pushing its exchange rate higher, all other things being equal. As the government's monetary policy determines inflation rates to a large extent, it can be seen that it has a strong knock-on influence on the level of exchange rates and the state of the balance of payments capital account, if the government is prepared to accept the *domestic* implications of holding interest rates persistently high by international standards.

The position of the balance of payments

8.5   The balance of payments accounts reflect the actual flow of currencies related to international trade and capital movement, and the longer-term trends in these accounts influence exchange rate patterns. The current account shows the ability of a country to finance current overseas expenditure with current overseas earnings. A persistent *current account surplus* will tend to put *upward pressure* on the domestic currency's exchange rate – current account deficits will have the opposite effect. However, *capital account flows* can counteract the effects of current account deficits or surpluses, but to the extent that balance of payments accounts are out of balance overall there will be an effect on long-term exchange-rate trends.

Other influences

8.6   In addition to the above three key economic variables, the following factors can have some influence on exchange rates:

- *Changes* in consumers' tastes, real income levels and productive capacities.
- *Expectations* concerning future economic conditions or government policies.
- Actual or expected changes in the *political and social environment*.
- Effects of *government policies* on the economy and investor confidence, inflation, investment, import controls and so on.

Short-term movements in exchange rates

8.7   In addition to the long-term effects of the above variables, they can also cause short-term changes in exchange rates. For example, a sharp reduction in interest rates could trigger off an outflow of short-term international capital. This outflow, added to the domestic effects of lower interest rates (such as cheaper credit taken to purchase imports) can only serve to undermine the domestic currency's exchange rate.

8.8   More important, however, in the short term is the effect of *official currency market intervention* by the monetary authorities both at home and abroad. Large-scale purchases or sales of currencies by a central bank, *if unanticipated by the market*, can have a substantial effect on the exchange rates. Changes in *government economic policies* on trade or investment, if not previously anticipated and discounted by the market, are also likely to alter exchange rates if they are thought to be of serious intent.

8.9   There are many other short-term factors influencing the forex markets, including industrial unrest (particularly in vital sectors of the economy), forthcoming general elections, the health of influential leaders and bad weather.

Student Activity 11

1. What is the purchasing power parity theory, and what is its relevance for exchange rate determination? *(Paragraphs 8.2–3)*

2. What is the relevance of the level of real domestic interest rates for the determination of a country's exchange rates? *(Paragraph 8.4)*

3. Why is the occurrence of a current account deficit or surplus on the balance of payments regarded as being important for the determination of exchange rates? *(Paragraph 8.5)*

4. What is the relevance of official exchange market intervention for exchange rate determination? *(Paragraph 8.8)*

5. List the types of factors which are likely to influence exchange rates in the short run. *(Paragraphs 8.7–9)*

8.10 Governments can raise interest rates in order to attract short-term investment. Because some invested funds flow in from abroad, if all other conditions remain unchanged the extra demand for sterling for this inward investment will strengthen the exchange rate. Conversely, if interest rates fall, foreign investors will tend to seek better returns elsewhere and will sell the sterling proceeds of their realised UK investments to purchase foreign currency to invest elsewhere. In this case the pressure on the sterling exchange rate will be downward.

8.11 We are assuming, of course, in the above scenarios that interest rates are the only factor influencing spot exchange rates. Obviously other factors affect the forex market's view of a currency's worth: inflation, balance of payments position, political stability and many more. If these factors are volatile, then increases in interest rates will have less influence on the exchange rate. On the other hand, a stable country with low interest rates and an apparently appreciating currency may well continue to attract foreign investment funds, particularly if investment opportunities elsewhere are unattractive for political or other reasons. It has been known, for example, for Switzerland to impose negative interest rates on foreign holders of Swiss francs to prevent large inflows of foreign investment forcing up the Swiss franc exchange rate.

Spot and forward exchange rates

8.12 As we have seen above, it is difficult to quantify a *direct* relationship between interest rates and *spot* exchange rates because of the many other factors affecting the equation. However, it is possible to show a direct relationship between interest rates and forward exchange rates, or at least the margin between spot and forward rates. The basic rules for calculating forward rates relate directly to the interest rate differential between the two countries involved. A currency with a higher interest rate will be quoted at a *discount* on the forward exchange market (that is, cheaper than spot). A currency with a lower interest rate will be quoted at a *premium* (more expensive than spot). The premiums and discounts quoted are calculated directly on an annualised basis by using the differences between the eurocurrency interest rates of the two currencies involved. This means that an investor will not gain by buying foreign currency for investment abroad and booking a forward exchange rate for repatriation of his funds on completion of the investment.

Conclusion

8.13   If all other factors remain unchanged, interest rates throughout the world would tend to converge as funds move from low-interest currencies to higher-interest ones, directly affecting exchange rates accordingly. In the real world many other factors come into play and distort the neat mathematical connection.

Student Activity 12

1. Other things being equal, what is likely to be the effect on a country's spot exchange rate of an increase in domestic interest rates?   *(Paragraph 8.10)*

2. Why might a change in the level of domestic spot interest rates have no effect on the country's currency exchange rate?   *(Paragraph 8.11)*

3. What determines the discount or premium on a forward exchange transaction relative to a corresponding spot transaction?   *(Paragraph 8.12)*

4. Why will an investor not gain simply by buying foreign currency for investment abroad, and then booking a forward exchange rate for repatriation of the funds on completion of the investment?   *(Paragraph 8.12)*

9   Different types of exchange rate regime

Clean floating exchange rates

9.1   If exchange rates are left purely to market determination, with no direct or deliberate intervention from the monetary authorities, then there is said to be a *clean floating* exchange rate regime in force. Exchange rates will be determined solely by the interaction of supply of and demand for currencies on the open market.

9.2   As far as the UK is concerned, credits to the balance of payments accounts represent a supply of foreign currencies (that is, a demand for sterling) from foreigners buying UK exports, investing or making other payments in the UK. Debits to the accounts represent a demand for foreign currencies (that is, a supply of sterling) from UK residents wishing to purchase imports, to invest or make other payments overseas. The interaction of this supply and demand, and supplies of and demands for foreign currencies, will determine sterling's exchange rate against other currencies. Hence, any factor which increases (or decreases) the supply of sterling relative to demand is likely to push the value of sterling downward (or upward) in terms of other currencies.

9.3   The *advantages of clean floating* may be summarised as follows:

- In theory it provides an automatic mechanism for dealing with balance of payments problems. A current account deficit will lead to foreign currency borrowing to cover current expenditure. Foreign holders of sterling assets will seek higher interest rates to compensate them for holding weak assets or will sell them. This will depress the exchange value of sterling as supply exceeds demand. If the price elasticities of demand for traded goods are high enough the current account balance should improve.

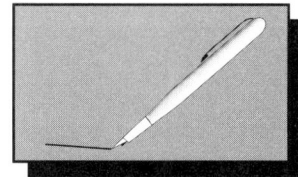

- Official international currency reserves are not required as government exchange market intervention does not take place.

- Market forces determine the exchange rate, thus relieving the government of making economically and politically difficult decisions.

- The government's economic policy may therefore be directed towards domestic problems, e.g. unemployment, inflation and slow economic growth.

9.4   The *disadvantages of clean floating* may be summarised as follows:

- With no official intervention to stabilise short-term exchange rate fluctuations, markets may become unstable, caused perhaps by pure currency speculation.

- If price elasticities of demand for internationally traded goods are low, then an ongoing balance of payments problem may result in persistent pressure on exchange rates.

- A continuing depreciating exchange rate, leading to higher prices for imported raw materials and consumer goods, may generate inflationary pressures within the domestic economy. These pressures may well offset the competitive advantage to exporters given by the depreciating exchange rate.

Managed floating exchange rates

9.5   The above disadvantages of clean floating tend to undermine its attractiveness in practice, particularly in view of the economic instability and financial uncertainty which could arise. However, the *principle* of allowing exchange rates to move broadly in line with market forces, producing a gradual adjustment of exchange rates to reflect underlying real economic factors, is sound enough. A compromise would appear to be a system in which market forces are permitted to determine the longer-term trend in exchange rates with the authorities taking discretionary action to control short-term fluctuations. This system has been used by the UK for most of the period since 1972–3 (except for the 23 months in the ERM).

9.6   Within such a system, normally referred to as a *managed floating* regime, the authorities intervene by *buying and selling currencies* on the forex markets, using the official reserves or official borrowing from overseas. For example, they can sell domestic currency (increase supply) to depress the domestic currency's exchange rate, or buy it (increase demand) to give the exchange rate an upward push. Alternatively, the authorities may *adjust short-term domestic interest rates* to alter net inflows of short-term capital funds from abroad, and increase or reduce demand for domestic currency relative to its supply. One problem with this regime is in deciding when and by how much to intervene; and there are limits to which the authorities are able to intervene.

9.7   It should be recognised that, irrespective of the degree of official intervention to smooth exchange rate fluctuations, there is no guarantee that balance of payments problems will be automatically solved. In fact, experience has shown that substantial deficits and surpluses may persist, as it takes time for trade flows to adjust, and speculative capital flows may cause further problems. However, it is generally agreed that managed floating rates have helped the world economy to adjust to various disturbances, such as the massive oil price rises of the 1970s.

Student Activity 13

1. What is meant by a clean floating exchange rate regime?   *(Paragraph 9.1)*

2. What determines exchange rates in a clean floating regime?   *(Paragraph 9.2)*

3. List the key *advantages* of clean floating exchange rates.   *(Paragraph 9.3)*

4. List the main *disadvantages* of clean floating exchange rates.   *(Paragraph 9.4)*

5. What is a managed floating exchange rate regime?   *(Paragraph 9.5)*

6. What instruments do the authorities use in order to operate a managed floating exchange rate regime?   *(Paragraph 9.6)*

Fixed exchange rates

9.8   A fixed exchange rate system is one where the authorities attempt to hold the exchange rate of their currency at a fixed rate, or within a narrow margin of a predetermined value, against other currencies. Extensive exchange market intervention is usually needed by all parties, but there will often be some facility for the adjustment of fixed currency parities if economic pressures demand it. The difference between this system and managed floating is that there is an *overriding commitment to the stability of exchange rates within agreed, narrowly defined margins.* Adjustments to currency parities are not expected to be commonplace, and will usually be countenanced only after extensive negotiations between the countries involved in order to accommodate *fundamental* shifts in their relative economic performances.

9.9   A past example of a fixed exchange rate system, the Bretton Woods adjustable peg system, operated between 1945 and 1972 with each of the world's major western currencies being pegged to within a plus/minus 1% margin of a fixed US dollar par value. Central banks were obliged to intervene on a day-to-day basis to hold their currencies within the accepted range. Devaluation or revaluation of the currency was allowed only when a country experienced serious balance of payments difficulties, and then only with the permission of the International Monetary Fund if a change in parities of more than 10% was needed. The Bretton Woods system collapsed because the USA ran huge balance of payments deficits in the late 1960s but refused to devalue the US dollar against gold (suspending the gold convertibility of the US dollar instead), and nations with large balance of payments surpluses (particularly Japan and West Germany) refused to revalue. (The system of fixed exchange rates known as the Exchange Rate Mechanism (ERM) of the European Monetary System in the EU will be examined in section 11).

9.10   Obviously, there are many advantages for countries which are able to achieve stable exchange rates. Business confidence is much higher when international traders and investors can easily assess the value of foreign currency transactions without resorting to (sometimes) expensive currency hedging tools. Of course, domestic inflation in one country may make devaluation of its currency essential if it is to maintain international competitiveness. Therefore, fixed rate systems incorporate 'safety valves' which enable such actions to be taken, albeit after appropriate negotiations with other members of the system.

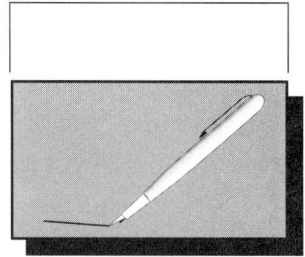

9.11 However, fixed exchange rate systems suffer from certain disadvantages:

- Authorities must hold sufficient reserves for foreign exchange market intervention purposes to fend off speculative pressures.

- Governments must define exactly how far they are prepared to intervene to protect their exchange rate against market pressures, before they resort to domestic deflationary policies.

- The authorities face the difficult problem of deciding when and by how much fixed exchange rates should be altered if intervention policies do not succeed.

- Sudden alterations in fixed parities under fixed rate schemes cause periodic destabilisation in financial markets and are also slow to take effect, as trade takes time to adjust to the new exchange rate structure. In the short term, therefore, the underlying problems may well persist.

- Unless the economic performances of the parties to a fixed exchange-rate mechanism converge (particularly with respect to inflation rates), then fixed parities will continuously come under pressure. If they can converge, however, the benefits can be substantial;

- If the parties have differing economic objectives, e.g. growth is espoused by one party, and price stability by the other – then the system will be difficult if not impossible to maintain.

Student Activity 14

1. In modern usage, what is meant by a 'fixed exchange rate regime'? *(Paragraph 9.8)*

2. Under what circumstances is it thought to be appropriate for the authorities to alter 'fixed' exchange rates? *(Paragraph 9.8)*

3. What is the major *advantage* of a fixed exchange rate system? *(Paragraph 9.10)*

4. What are the main *disadvantages* of a fixed exchange rate system? *(Paragraph 9.11)*

5. What basic economic condition is required for a system of fixed exchange rates to be successful? *(Paragraph 9.11)*

10 Portfolio balance and monetary theories – and others

10.1 These are two theories seeking to explain movements in exchange rates and the working of adjustment policies to improve the current account of a country's balance of payments.

Portfolio balance theory

10.2 The portfolio balance theory focuses on international flows of investment, which now dominate foreign exchange markets. International investors will, it is argued, spread their portfolios of investments in such a way as to maximise their returns. A rise in interest rates in one financial centre (relatively to interest rates in other centres) would lead to funds moving there, and purchasing its currency. The spot exchange rate would rise, and interest rates ease until they reached a level where there was no advantage for investors to continue the process. In other words, their portfolios would be in balance.

10.3   The theory can be extended to include forward premia and discounts, when it becomes one of 'interest rate parity'. Not only do investors watch current interest rates and exchange rates but they also have expectations of future changes which will cause them to alter their portfolios or, at least, hedge their positions. This theory focuses on forward rates, futures and options.

Monetary approach

10.4   The monetary approach to the balance of payments emphasises the links between the money supply and the current account of the balance of payments. There are two variants: one for currencies with a fixed rate of exchange and the other for currencies with a floating exchange rate.

Fixed exchange rate

10.5   Here the central bank has a duty to buy and sell its currency in order to keep the exchange within the permitted limits. If the central bank sterilises inflows of its own currency purchased from foreign investors selling their holdings of it as they withdraw their investments (or receive payments for their exports to that country), then the outflow of payments will soon be halted. This sterilising involves the central bank not increasing the cash reserves maintained with it by the commercial banks. Domestic prices would cease to rise as credit became tighter, and interest rates would tend to rise to equate the demand and supply of credit. Foreign investors would cease to leave the country and might even return. The problem, it is argued, is that central banks prefer to increase credit by buying bonds in open market operations. The reason for these open market purchases could be that the country was pursuing a policy of stable interest rates. Another reason could be that the central bank was automatically investing the sterling bank deposits which it had purchased in the foreign exchange market in order to support the exchange rate.

Floating exchange rate

10.6   Here a current account deficit causes the exchange rate to fall and also the money supply to fall. The latter's fall results from the fact that the excess outflows of sterling are bought by foreigners or UK banks, the money balances of whom do not count for measuring money supply.

Absorptions approach

10.7   In paragraph 7.4 we encountered 'the price elasticities' approach, where a devaluation of a currency could improve a country's current account if the price elasticities of demand for exports and imports were greater than one. However, for the extra exports to be produced, the price elasticities of supply must be greater than one.

10.8   Another way of rephrasing that last sentence is that there must be sufficient spare capacity in the economy – and stocks of goods – for the extra production both for export and in substitution for imports, This brings attention to the whole economy rather than just demand and supply curves.

10.9   The absorptions approach argues that net exports need to be increased and that net exports equal GDP minus domestic expenditure. To increase net exports, therefore, either GDP must be increased more than domestic expenditure or domestic expenditure must be reduced. Either the devaluation must reduce domestic expenditure or it must be accompanied by restrictive demand management policies to achieve such a reduction.

10.10 Supporters of this approach do not deny that price elasticities are important but argue that more attention needs to be given to the effects of devaluation on output and incomes and on the income-related changes in consumption, savings and investment. Two areas of concern, they maintain, are the hoarding caused by the increase in income resulting from the extra output and an increase in imports also caused by the increase in income.

Student Activity 15

1. Outline the portfolio balance theory. *(Paragraph 10.2)*

2. Summarise the interest rate parity theory. *(Paragraph 10.3)*

3. What is the monetary approach to the balance of payments? *(Paragraph 10.4)*

4. Distinguish between its operation with:
   (a) fixed-exchange rate regimes
   (b) floating-exchange rate regimes. *(Paragraphs 10.5–6)*

5. Explain the elasticities approach. *(Paragraph 7.4)*

6. Describe the absorption approach. *(Paragraph 10.9)*

11   The European Monetary System (EMS)

Background

11.1   For many years there has been much debate on the view that the EU (formerly the EC) should move towards full economic and monetary union (EMU). At the extreme, EMU may imply the introduction of a single EU currency, with monetary controls being implemented by a European Central Bank, and with substantial power over economic policy being vested with EU institutions. However, as might be expected, there have often been major reservations expressed about such objectives, and in particular a number of EU governments have resisted strongly any proposal which would undermine their sovereign powers in respect of economic policy.

11.2   In 1970 the Werner Report put forward the first comprehensive plan for a movement towards EMU. This plan was accepted in principle, but due to adverse economic conditions during the first half of the 1970s, and with a general lack of practical support from several EC member states, the plan only had a limited impact on exchange rate arrangements within the EU.

11.3   An important step forward was taken at the Bremen Summit of EC Heads of Government in July 1978, when proposals for the formulation of the European Monetary System (EMS) were accepted. The objectives of the EMS are far more limited than those of full EMU, and relate primarily to the stabilisation of EU currency exchange rates, and mutual financial support for member states. In the 1980s, it was summarised as a 'zone of monetary stability' (exchange rates, interest rates and prices). In the 1990s, this has become rephrased to be a 'zone of increasing monetary stability'. Nevertheless, the successful operation of the EMS is generally seen as being an important first step on the road towards EMU, and the requirements for its operation are likely to force the necessary economic convergence between EU member states.

The European Monetary System (EMS)

11.4 The European Monetary System was set up in March 1979 and, although not obligatory, all the then member states of the EU joined. Greece, Spain, Portugal, Austria, Finland and Sweden followed when they became members of the EU, making 15 members of the EMS at present. Note the following:

The Exchange Rate Mechanism (ERM)

11.5 This mechanism operates on the basis of two criteria:

- A 'parity grid' arrangement sets upper and lower intervention rates for each pair of currencies. Initially, the grid allowed a maximum of $+/- 2^{1}/_{4}\%$ relative movement (with $+/- 6\%$ for a small number of currencies). However, following extreme turbulence on the currency exchanges, in July 1993 the band was widened to $+/- 15\%$ for most currencies (officially a temporary expedient). Once any two currencies reach their relative value limits the central bank of the country with the weak currency is required to sell the other country's currency on the currency exchanges, whilst the central bank of the country with the strong currency is required to buy the weaker currency. These purchases and sales, with supporting currency swaps among central banks if required, continue until pressure is taken off the currencies' values and they are pushed away from their parity limits.

- *The European Currency Unit Divergence Indicator* provides early warning of exchange rate pressures. The ECU is used as the basis for calculating a central rate for each member's currency. Each currency is allocated divergence limits against its ECU central rate. In the event of a currency's value moving beyond 75% of the maximum deviation permitted, it is expected that the relevant government will take some form of remedial action. For a country with a weak currency this may involve the raising of domestic interest rates or perhaps a tightening of fiscal policy. For a strong currency country, some form of expansionary policy might be expected. Thus, the ECU indicator relates to the broad position of a currency relative to all other EU currencies taken as a group.

11.6 The values of individual currencies may be realigned within the parity grid and in terms of the ECU central rate if the fundamental economic relationships underlying the exchange rates alter.

11.7 Whilst all EU states are members of the EMS, at June 1996 Greece had still not joined the ERM, and the memberships of the UK and Italy were still suspended following the EU currency crisis of September 1992.

The European Currency Unit (ECU)

11.8 The ECU is a 'basket' of EU currencies, and may be regarded as a form of international money, performing all the functions which are normally associated with money assets. Thus, for example, the ECU is used as a means of payment between EU central banks; it is used as the unit of account for both the intervention and credit element of the EMS; and it may be used for its medium of exchange, store of value, unit of account and standard of deferred payment properties in private sector financial transactions.

11.9 Note, however, that since its introduction, in March 1979, the ECU has developed along two distinct routes. The official ECU, as explained above, is a key element in the operation of the EMS. This is quite separate from the private ECU which is created by private institutions out of the ECU's component currencies, and may be bought and sold on the foreign exchange market. Both individuals and companies may hold ECU assets (such as bank deposits and marketable securities) and incur ECU liabilities (such as bank loans and securitised debts).

11.10 The major advantage in using the ECU is that its international purchasing power value is likely to be more stable than the corresponding values of the individual component currencies.

11.11 The value of the ECU is calculated as a weighted average of all 12 currencies. The weights reflect each member's relative economic size in terms of gross national product and the importance of its trade within the EU, and the access which each member has to short-term financing from the EMCF. The weights were reviewed every five years, but since the ratification of the Maastricht Treaty the weights are to remain fixed at their current values, which were determined in June 1989, when there were 12 members of the EU.

The European Monetary Co-operation Fund/Exchange Rate Stabilisation Fund

11.12 The European Monetary Co-operation Fund (EMCF) provides financial support to EMS members with international payment problems. It issues ECUs to EU central banks in exchange for deposits of 20% of their gold and dollar reserves. These swaps are renewed every three months; gold and dollar reserves do not actually change hands so central banks continue to manage and earn interest on their dollar deposits. The 'official' ECUs created by these swaps can only be used for transactions between EMS central banks and certain other monetary institutions, e.g. for settling debts incurred in operating the ERM. All EMS members currently participate in the EMCF swap arrangements, although non-members of the ERM are not obliged to.

The Very Short-term Financing Facility (VSTFF)

11.13 Under this scheme central banks which are members of the ERM open to each other short-term credit facilities in their own currencies in unlimited amounts to finance intervention when currencies threaten to breach ERM margins. The facilities are short-term in nature, but repayment may be deferred if the borrower's international payments position deems this necessary.

Student Activity 16

1. Why has the plan for Economic and Monetary Union often generated opposition from individual EU states? *(Paragraph 11.1)*

2. What were the main objectives of the European Monetary System? *(Paragraph 11.3)*

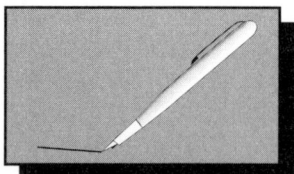

3. Describe the ERM. *(Paragraph 11.5)*

4. What is the ECU? *(Paragraph 11.8)*

5. What are the uses of the ECU in the private sector? *(Paragraph 11.9)*

6. What is the function of the European Monetary Co-operation Fund?
   (Paragraph 11.12)

7. What are 'Very Short-term Financing Facilities' within the context of the EMS?
   (Paragraph 11.13)

The objectives of the EMS

11.14 The long-term aim of the EMS is now to promote full EMU, but in the medium term it is intended to create *a zone of monetary stability* within the EU, providing a sound base for trade and payment between members.

11.15 To achieve these objectives, as with any fixed exchange rate regime, it is essential that the economic performances of all members should be broadly similar. The successful operation of the EMS will therefore require a high level of economic policy co-ordination between EU governments to this end. Their policies will have to provide:

- Similarly low levels of inflation in each country;

- A narrowing of interest rate differentials between members;

- Tight limits on balance of payments imbalances.

11.16 If these are not achieved, then intervention will only limit exchange rate fluctuations in the short term and eventually exchange rate adjustments will have to be made, thus undermining the objectives of the system.

Operation of the EMS and recent developments

11.17 Between its establishment in March 1979 and September 1992, the EMS appears to have operated reasonably successfully, although it was necessary to realign currency exchange values on a number of occasions. Despite these realignments, the exchange rates of ERM participants' currencies were more stable than those of the other main Western currencies, and to the extent that this helps to support business confidence this is clearly a positive outcome. However, it must also be recognised that some critics of the ERM have argued that its operation has tended to undermine economic growth within the participating countries. Indeed, it must never be forgotten that in order to achieve exchange rate stability in the longer term, it is necessary that the economic performances of the countries involved should be broadly similar. In consequence, the successful operation of the EMS requires the subordination of domestic policies within individual countries to this purpose. In July 1993, as a result of speculative sales of French francs, the narrow bands were widened to 15% either side and the ERM became a shadow of its former self. However, by the mid-1990s, most member currencies were well within these much wider bands.

11.18 It is the implied loss of sovereignty over economic policy decisions which has often been used by the British government to justify sterling being kept out of the ERM. Indeed, when sterling was put into the mechanism, in October 1990, there was much controversy over the parity chosen, and the fears that because of sterling's importance in international trade and investment, it might generate instability within the ERM (especially relative to the DM), thereby requiring excessive exchange market intervention, proved to be well-founded. As events turned out, excessive speculation against sterling caused it to be withdrawn from the ERM in September 1992.

11.19 Despite the possible difficulties which might arise with the UK's full member-ship of the EMS, it is important to recognise that there are several substantial benefits which should accrue. In particular, as the EU now accounts for over a half of all the UK's overseas trade, a more stable relationship between ster-ling and other EU currencies should help both exporters and importers in their business planning and pricing decisions.

11.20 Also, if UK producers were no longer able to rely upon a depreciating value for sterling in order to maintain their international competitiveness, they would be under greater pressure to hold down wage and price rises, in the face of generally modest inflation rates within the rest of the EU. (Failure to hold down UK inflation rates relative to other ERM members could have dire consequences for UK output and jobs, assuming that devaluation of sterling was not seen as an acceptable option). Finally, the political advantage of full membership of the EMS cannot be ignored, especially in the light of the Maastricht Treaty, which sees full participation of all EU members in the EMS as a vital part of the first stage for achieving EMU.

11.21 The ratification of the Maastricht Treaty in July 1993 did little to quell the debate on the future shape of EU monetary arrangements. The Treaty envis-ages that by as early as 1997 (a date put back to 1999) there could be the irrevocable fixing of exchange rates within the EU, as the precursor to the introduction of a single EU currency. This move would be subject to a quali-fied majority of EU states being in favour (meaning that no one member state could veto the move) and at least seven member states meeting the economic convergence criteria. However, not only has the UK Government reserved the right to decide nearer the time whether or not the UK would proceed to join a single currency arrangement, but also the EU currency crisis of July 1993 raised doubts as to whether a single EU currency is viable. Since the crisis (caused by intense speculation against the French franc), most EU currencies within the ERM have operated within fluctuation bands of +/− 15%, which could hardly be regarded as a rigid framework for currency stability. The dangers in attempting to force convergence through the implementation of an inflexible exchange rate regime between EU currencies have been clearly demonstrated since the summer of 1993.

11.22 An important aspect of the Maastricht Treaty is the proposal that a European Central Bank (ECB) will be established, and will take up its full powers when a single EU currency is introduced in 1999 (within the conditions stated above). At present, it functions as the European Monetary Institute, based in Frankfurt and planning for the single currency. It is intended that the ECB will be politically independent, and will have as its main objective the mainte-nance of price stability within the EU.

11.23 Each member state's own central bank will be maintained as part of the European System of Central Banks, and will be expected to support the ECB in the implementation of agreed policy. Each individual central bank will also be required to be politically independent of its own country's government. The responsibilities of the ECB will include the conduct of EU monetary policy and control, foreign exchange market operations, the holding and management of member states' foreign exchange reserves, and the promotion of the smooth operation of EU payments systems. These developments are now regarded as virtual certainties and are outlined in the next section.

Student Activity 17

1. What is the long-term aim of the EMS? *(Paragraph 11.14)*

2. What is the medium-term aim of the EMS? *(Paragraph 11.14)*

3. What economic conditions are required for the EMS to achieve its desired objectives? *(Paragraph 11.15)*

4. How successful has been the operation of the EMS, at least until the summer of 1993?

5. Why did the ratification of the Maastricht Treaty not signal the end of the controversy over the EU's movement towards EMU? *(Paragraph 11.21)*

6. What is the role of the proposed European Central Bank? *(Paragraphs 11.22–3)*

12 The Single European Currency

12.1 This is scheduled to be introduced on 1 January 1999, after which new public debt, as and when issued, will be denominated in euro, and all open market operations in the money markets will be in euro, not national currencies. There will be a change over period for notes, coins and retail banking operations in the first half of 2002. By 1 July 2002, those EU member states which have joined the single currency area will have, as their legal tender, the euro. At present it is not known which states, especially the UK, will be joining. Decisions are expected to be taken in 1998, once statistics for 1997 have become available.

12.2 Arguments for and against a single currency are complex and divisive, and electoral majorities for and against it could be small. Because a single currency means a single form of money and a single monetary policy, the decision is political as well as economic and commercial. It also affects taxation and public expenditure, because changes in government borrowing affect the money supply and monetary policy.

Arguments in favour

12.3 The following is a summary of the arguments in favour.

- There will be a substantial saving in costs – no foreign exchange costs, no separate currency accounts for businesses exporting to and importing from other participating countries.

- At present UK interest rates are higher than those in the EU – especially German interest rates. If the UK joins, then our interest rates will fall.

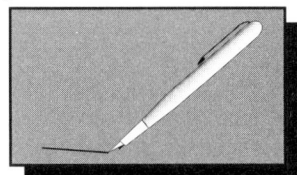

- A fall in interest rates helps consumers, firms and also reduces the budget deficit.

- The cost of converting machines etc is offset by the increased orders for computers and vending machines.

- Economic growth will be higher because lower interest rates mean more purchases of new plant and machinery.

- The goal of monetary policy will be low or zero inflation – stable prices, stable interest rates and stable exchange rates with non-EU currencies such as the US dollar and yen. The monetary stability will require fiscal policy to be more flexible.

Arguments against

12.4   Arguments against include:

- The UK loses control of monetary and fiscal policy. (But many argue that it already has lost it before joining a single currency and that independence of action is illusory.)

- There would be huge budget transfers from richer to poorer EU regions. Supporters counter this argument by stating that private capital flows can perform this role.

- Europe is not 'an optimal currency area' because:
  - all its regions are not subject to common real economic change with common effects; in particular, labour productivity varies greatly;
  - labour is not mobile between its regions (this latter point is countered by arguments that capital is mobile).

  Canada and the USA have all the characteristics needed for a single currency, except the desire for one. Canada has zero inflation and a floating exchange rate with its major trading partner.

- The costs of conversion far exceed the benefits, especially when much of the machinery will be imported.

- The UK will lose the possibility of devaluing to overcome the external demand shocks which are likely to lead to unemployment. Supporters argue that devaluation is not a remedy because inflation is an inherent result and price rises eliminate the temporary benefits brought by devaluation.

Student Activity 18

1. Outline the likely programme for the introduction of a single currency.

    (Paragraph 12.1)

2. Summarise the arguments in favour.   *(Paragraph 12.3)*

3. State the arguments against.   *(Paragraph 12.4)*

4. If there is a referendum on the UK joining the single currency, are you likely to vote for, against or abstain? Give your reasons.   *(Paragraphs 12.3–4)*

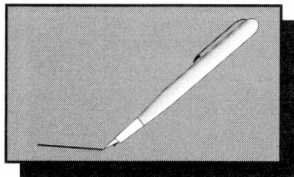

13   Foreign exchange risks

13.1   Foreign exchange risks can be conveniently classified under three main headings:

- Transaction risk;
- Translation risk;
- Economic risk.

Transaction risk

13.2   Transaction exposure arises from normal trading activities when goods and services are invoiced in a foreign currency. Exporters will gain if the foreign currency appreciates in value between the time of invoicing and the time of settlement of the obligation, whereas importers will lose in such a situation. The converse applies if the foreign currency depreciates in value between invoice date and settlement.

13.3   Since exchange rates are volatile and often unpredictable, it is difficult for a business to anticipate the effect on its earnings of changes in foreign exchange rates.

Translation risk

13.4   Translation exposure arises when there is a mismatch between the currencies of denomination of the assets and liabilities of a company. For example, a major UK-based company whose balance sheet and accounts are reported in sterling may have the following asset and liability mix:

Assets		*Liabilities*	
Sterling	75%	Sterling	50%
US$	25%	US$	50%

13.5   If the US dollar appreciates in value relative to sterling, then the company's balance sheet must be affected detrimentally because the sterling equivalent of the US dollar-denominated liabilities will rise in absolute terms more than the sterling equivalent of the US dollar-denominated assets. The converse will apply if the US dollar depreciates against sterling, and in this situation there will be a translation gain.

13.6   These changes will show (be translated) in the balance sheet. Any net increase in assets will be balanced by an increase in the reported reserves and hence reported net worth of the business. Any net reduction in assets will be reflected in a reduced net worth.

13.7   Since lenders, creditors and shareholders study balance sheets and net worth when analysing the performance of a company, changes in net worth could affect attitudes and influence the ability of the company to raise money on favourable terms. In addition, translation losses or gains may influence shareholder attitudes in a takeover bid.

13.8   Sometimes a company can take a financing decision which results in the creation of both transaction and translation exposures. For instance, a company may have a sterling overdraft and decide to borrow US dollars, convert them to sterling and pay off the sterling borrowing. The rationale behind this action may well be that interest rates on US dollar borrowing are much lower than those for sterling borrowing. Assuming the company does not have any income or assets denominated in US dollars, then it has incurred a translation exposure because of the US dollar liability, and a transaction exposure because of the need to provide US dollars to meet the interest payments on the US dollar loan. If the dollar appreciates in value after the loan has been made, the real cost of the interest payments will rise because more sterling will be required to obtain the dollars to cover the interest payments. Likewise, there will be a translation loss shown in the accounts because the sterling equivalent of the dollar loan will have increased.

Economic risk

13.9   Economic risk relates to the effects on the overall international competitiveness of a company resulting from exchange rate movements.

13.10 A company need not be trading internationally to be affected by economic exposure. For example, suppose a British coal mine sells its coal only within the UK and only has one competitor, an Australian mine, for the sale of its coal in the UK (in practice the position is far more complex). Any fall in the value of the Australian dollar against sterling will provide the Australian coal with a competitive advantage against British coal because the Australian coal will become cheaper in terms of sterling.

13.11 Exposure to economic risk is difficult to quantify and it is not reported in the published accounts. Nevertheless, in the long run, failure to monitor and control economic exposure can result in a serious decline in international competitiveness.

Student Activity 19

1. Explain what is meant by the term 'transaction risk' in relation to exchange rate movements.   *(Paragraph 13.2)*

2. What is the importance of 'translation risk' to a company? *(Paragraphs 13.4–8)*

3. Explain what is meant by the term 'economic risk' in relation to exchange rate movements.   *(Paragraphs 13.9–11)*

14   The hedging of exchange rate risk

Forward exchange contracts

14.1   A forward exchange contract is a contract between a customer and a bank whereby the parties agree a rate of exchange for the sale or purchase of a fixed amount of foreign currency at a fixed future date or between two set future dates. Banks are willing to enter into forward exchange contracts for most currencies for up to one year in advance of the agreed maturity date. For major currencies such as the yen, the US dollar or the Deutschmark, banks may agree forward contracts for up to five year periods. In effect, the forward contract fixes a rate of exchange today for a deal which it is agreed will take place at a set future date or within a set agreed period in the future.

14.2 Remember that a forward exchange contract imposes an obligation on the customer to put into effect the transaction to which the contract relates. Hence, if the relevant foreign exchange rates have moved in favour of the customer at the time the contract matures, the customer must still deal with the bank at the agreed forward rate of exchange.

14.3 If the customer does not honour his obligation to deliver or take delivery of the foreign currency as specified in the forward contract, the bank will close out the contract. This involves the bank in honouring the customer's obligations by buying the currency at the spot rate and then selling back at the agreed forward rate if the contract was for the bank to sell currency. Alternatively, a close-out will involve the bank in selling the currency at the spot rate and then buying it back at the agreed forward rate if the forward contract was for the bank to buy. The resultant profit or loss on the close-out is then passed on to the customer.

14.4 Forward exchange contracts are appropriate when the company is relatively certain of the amount and timing of future receipts or payments denominated in foreign currency and when the company expects exchange rates to move against it. If there is a little uncertainty over the timing of the receipt or payment, then the trader can purchase a foreign exchange option. This gives him the choice of (say) a month in which to deliver the currency or sterling. If not, then the contract is 'closed out'.

Currency options

14.5 A currency option operates in a similar manner to an interest-rate option (described in Unit 4). Thus, the holder has the right, but not the obligation, to buy or sell (depending on the type of option chosen) a set amount of foreign currency at a set future date or, if the option is an American option, at any time up to a set expiry date. The holder must pay a premium to acquire the option. It is completely different from a foreign exchange option.

14.6 Options are useful when the timing and amounts of payments or receipts denominated in foreign currency are uncertain, because the holder is under no obligation to complete the underlying foreign exchange transaction.

14.7 Options are also applicable when the company expects the rate of exchange to move in its favour, but feels it necessary to have cover in case rates move the other way. If the rate does move in favour of the company it can abandon the option and deal at the spot rate. However, if rates move against the company it can exercise the option and thus protect itself from these adverse foreign exchange movements.

14.8 Options are particularly applicable when a company makes a bid for a large contract with payment denominated in foreign currency. The company may wish to fix the sterling equivalent of the completion proceeds right from the start, but if a forward exchange contract is arranged there is a danger of a potential loss on a close-out if the contract is not subsequently awarded. However, if an option is used, there is no obligation on the holder to exercise it. Hence, if the contract is not awarded, the holder can abandon the option or, depending on which way rates of exchange have moved, the holder may be able to sell the option back to the bank for its intrinsic value.

Currency futures

14.9 Currency futures operate on exactly the same principles as interest rate futures. A company which has future monetary payments or receipts which are denominated in foreign currency may buy or sell a relevant futures contract at the outset, expecting that the resultant gain or loss on closing-out the futures contract may offset the loss or gain on settlement of the currency transaction.

Currency swaps

14.10 A currency swap arises when two parties agree to exchange equivalent borrowed sums of two different currencies, together with the associated interest commitments on those sums.

14.11 For example, let us suppose that a German company needs to borrow £1m to acquire a UK outlet, and a UK company needs to borrow DM3m to take over a German business. Let us suppose that the current rate of exchange is DM3 = £1. The German company could borrow DM3m and the UK company could borrow £1m. The companies could then swap their respective borrowed principals and the respective servicing commitments. Thus, the UK company would acquire the necessary Deutschmarks whilst the German company would obtain the required sterling. However, each company has benefited because the companies will probably be able to obtain better borrowing terms in their own markets. Hence the UK company has obtained the lower rates which only the German company can obtain in its own market, and vice versa.

14.12 The effect of the swap is that each company has hedged its translation exposure by borrowing in the currency in which the newly purchased asset is denominated but the foreign currency borrowing has been acquired on more favourable terms than would have applied had each borrowed the foreign currency directly.

14.13 In practice, the swap is usually arranged through an intermediary bank which guarantees the obligations of both parties. This is particularly important because each party is legally responsible for servicing its original borrowing and this commitment still remains even if the counterparty fails to honour its obligations under the swap.

Currency borrowing for exporters and currency deposits for importers

14.14 A UK company expecting to receive a foreign currency payment at a future date may borrow that amount of foreign currency immediately and convert it into sterling at the current spot rate, thus fixing the exchange rate on the transaction. When the foreign currency payment arrives it will be used to pay off the foreign currency loan. Some adjustment to the amount borrowed will be required in order to take account of the interest to be paid on the loan, and, of course, the company takes the risk that the foreign currency payment will not materialise, and hence that it will be left holding a foreign currency debt requiring servicing.

14.15 A similar device may be used by a company expecting to make a foreign currency payment at a future date. In this case a UK company would purchase foreign currency at the current spot rate, and would then deposit the funds into an interest-bearing account in readiness to make the future foreign currency payment. The risk here is that the expected future transaction will not occur, and that the foreign currency funds will not be required, thus leaving the company holding foreign currency funds that have to be converted to sterling at the ruling spot rate.

Concluding remarks

14.16 There is a wide variety of techniques which can be used to manage interest rate and foreign exchange rate exposure. The UK's re-entry into the Exchange Rate Mechanism of the European Monetary System and then entering the single currency area would involve the management of foreign exchange exposure becoming less important for companies which confine their activities to the EU. This would be particularly the case if the permissible fluctuation band is narrow and if the frequency of realignments involving sterling is kept low. However, interest rate risk management could assume even greater importance for such companies because interest rates would have an even more important role in maintaining currency stability within the EMS.

Student Activity 20

1. What is a forward exchange contract? *(Paragraph 14.1)*

2. In what sense does a forward exchange contract impose an obligation on the parties to the contract? *(Paragraph 14.2)*

3. In what circumstances is the use of forward exchange contracts appropriate? *(Paragraph 14.4)*

4. What is a currency option? *(Paragraph 14.5)*

5. In what circumstances is the use of currency options appropriate? *(Paragraphs 14.6–8)*

6. What is a currency swap? *(Paragraphs 14.10–11)*

7. In what respect does a currency swap allow a company to manage its risks? *(Paragraphs 14.11–12)*

8. How might exporters use currency borrowing and importers currency deposits in order to manage risk? *(Paragraphs 14.14–15)*

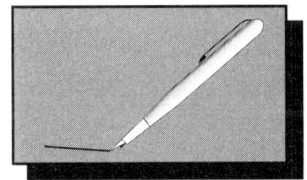

Summary

After studying this unit you should be able to:

- **define foreign exchange rates and cross rates;**

- **explain what is meant by currency baskets, especially the ECU;**

- **describe the structure of the foreign exchange market;**

- **discuss the fundamental determinants of exchange rates;**

- **explain how a forward exchange rate is determined using the concept of covered interest parity;**

- **describe the structure of a country's balance of payments and its terms of trade;**

- **analyse how changes in the terms of trade affect a country's balance of trade and balance of payments;**

- **appreciate how changes in a country's balance of payments affect its currency's exchange rate;**

- **identify the different types of exchange rate systems, especially the European Monetary System;**

- **assess the arguments for and against a country joining the single currency of the EU;**

- **identify the types of foreign exchange risk, and the various financial derivatives which have been devised to manage such risk.**

Self-assessment questions

Short-answer questions

1. As at 1995, where were the world's three major foreign exchange markets based?

2. What is the difference between a 'spot' currency transaction and a 'forward' currency transaction?

3. What is an option forward currency contract?

4. What is the purchasing power parity theory, and what is its relevance for the pattern of exchange rates?

5. What is likely to be the effect on a country's exchange rate if it experiences persistent and substantial balance of payments current account deficits?

6. What is the basic principle of a managed floating exchange rate regime?

7. What basic economic conditions are required for a fixed exchange rate regime to be successful in the longer term?

8. What is the membership of the EMS?

9. What is the ECU?

10. What are the uses of the ECU in the private sector?

11. What is the Very Short-term Financing Facility of the EMS?

12. What economic conditions must be met for the successful operation of the EMS?

13. Other things being equal, an increase in the UK interest rate on sterling funds is likely to cause the spot rate for sterling funds to rise relative to the US dollar, causing a premium to increase or discount to decrease, on forward sales of sterling for dollars. Why?

14. What risk does a borrower run if he borrows at fixed rates of interest?

15. List the three types of exchange rate risk which might be faced by a company.

16. What is a forward rate agreement?

17. What are the major limitations of forward rate agreements?

18. What is the maximum loss which a company can make when it buys an interest rate option?

19. What is a forward exchange contract?

20. What is the difference between a European currency option and an American currency option?

21. Why do companies engage in currency swaps?

Multiple-choice questions

1. Foreign exchange markets
   (a) are located physically in all the western world's major financial centres
   (b) exist through a sophisticated network of communications
   (c) engage in foreign currency denominated borrowing and lending activities
   (d) have not been subject to official intervention for many years in the UK
   (e) are regulated by the Bank for International Settlements.

2. A principal on the foreign exchange market makes a profit by
   (a) buying and selling currencies for third parties
   (b) managing a bank's foreign exchange dealing room
   (c) administering the official government body responsible for dealing in foreign exchange
   (d) buying and selling currencies on his own account
   (e) using agents to act for him around the world.

3. The major long-term determinant of exchange rate movements is normally thought to be:
   (a) central bank intervention in the foreign exchange markets

(b) political developments in major western nations

(c) industrial unrest in major western nations

(d) variations in the economic fundamentals

(e) changes in the oil price.

4. For much of the period since the early 1970s, the exchange rate for sterling has been:

(a) pegged to the US dollar

(b) determined by agreement with other EU countries within the EMS

(c) determined within a clean floating exchange rate regime

(d) determined within a managed floating exchange rate regime

(e) aligned to the SDR.

5. In a clean floating exchange rate regime

(a) a current account surplus must be balanced by a deficit on official financing

(b) a balance of payments deficit must be balanced by a surplus on official financing

(c) a current account surplus must be balanced by a deficit on the combined capital account balance and balancing item

(d) a current account surplus cannot occur

(e) a country's net receipts from services should affect a deficit on trade in goods.

6. As at June 1994, the Exchange Rate Mechanism of the EMS had the active involvement of

(a) all members of the EU

(b) all members of the EMS

(c) all members of the EMS except for UK, Greece and Italy

(d) all members of the EU except Spain and Portugal

(e) all members of the EU plus Switzerland.

7. The Exchange Rate Mechanism of the EMS involves

(a) each member-country committing itself to keeping the value of its currency within a specified margin of an agreed amount of every other member currency

(b) the fixing of exchange rates of all EU member states relative to each other

(c) regular realignments of currency values in order to avoid the purchasing power parity theory taking effect

(d) an agreement to introduce a single currency into the EU once the Single European Market is complete

(e) members of the EMS depositing their currencies with each other.

8. If a country raises its domestic rates of interest relative to those ruling in other major countries, the country's currency exchange rate will

(a) probably depreciate

(b) always appreciate, given time

    (c) probably appreciate, other things being equal

    (d) be largely unaffected in the short term

    (e) moved downwards and then upwards (the J curve effect).

9. The medium-term objective of the EMS is to

    (a) bring about a single European currency

    (b) create a zone of monetary stability within the EU

    (c) cause EU interest rates to fall to the level of those experienced in Japan

    (d) bring about political union within the EU

    (e) bring new members into the EU.

10. If an investor buys spot foreign currency to invest abroad at higher interest rates than those available in the domestic economy

    (a) he will definitely make a profit as long as he arranges a forward contract to return his money to sterling when his investment matures

    (b) the higher overseas interest rates will benefit him when he brings the money back home, even using spot rates

    (c) he will make a loss on the deal even if he arranges a forward contract to repatriate the funds

    (d) he will not gain by booking a forward exchange contract for repatriation of his funds on completion of the investment

    (e) he needs to sell the domestic currency forward to protect his investment abroad.

11. A UK-based company purchases all its raw material from within the UK and all its sales are within the UK. The competitors for the market of that company are a mixture of UK-based and overseas-based companies. The UK company is therefore exposed to

    (a) transaction risk

    (b) economic risk

    (c) default risk

    (d) translation risk

    (e) default risk and translation risk.

12. A company has bid for a contract in an overseas country, and if the bid is successful a large payment, denominated in foreign currency, will be received. The company needs to protect the value of the potential foreign currency receipt in terms of home currency, but realises that if the contract is not awarded there will be no foreign currency. Which of the following would be the most appropriate hedging instrument?

    (a) a forward exchange contract

    (b) a currency future

    (c) a currency option

    (d) a currency swap

    (e) a currency deposit.

13. Which of the following constitutes a right but not an obligation on the part of the holder?

    (a) a forward exchange contract

    (b) a forward rate agreement

    (c) a currency option

    (d) a financial futures contract

    (e) a currency swap.

14. A major advantage of a forward rate agreement for a borrower is that

    (a) it allows the borrower to fix the total amount of interest which is to be paid on an outstanding loan for a fixed period of time

    (b) it allows the borrower to convert a fixed interest rate commitment to a floating rate and hence take advantage of falling market rates

    (c) it gives the borrower a right to fix interest payments over a set period of time, but not an obligation

    (d) it may be taken out for any principal sum.

15. A currency swap arises when two parties

    (a) trade two different currencies with the same value

    (b) exchange equivalent borrowed sums of two different currencies, together with the associated interest commitments

    (c) exchange interest rate commitments on two separate borrowed sums

    (d) exchange currencies raised during trading operations in order to avoid domestic exchange controls

    (e) barter the currencies to avoid the foreign exchange market.

Unit 9

Corporate Sector Finances & Portfolio Theory

Objectives

After studying this unit, you should be able to:

- discuss the broad trends in corporate sector financing in the UK and identify the various financing alternatives available to companies;

- appreciate the importance of credit ratings and the role of rating companies with special reference to commercial paper;

- distinguish between medium-term notes, note issuance facilities, Euronotes and syndicated loans;

- understand the key provisions of a corporate bond issue;

- assess the risks involved with investing in corporate bonds;

- describe the Eurobond market and the different types of bond structures issued, together with the role of Euroclear and CEDEL;

- distinguish between preference shares, corporate debt and ordinary shares;

- examine the fundamental principles of portfolio theory;

- calculate the historic single-period investment return for a security or a portfolio of financial assets;

- calculate the expected return and the variability of expected return on a portfolio;

- assess the components of a portfolio's total risk: systematic risk and unsystematic risk;

- explain what is meant by the beta of a stock;

- demonstrate how diversification through risk management eliminates unsystematic risk;

- distinguish between the different ways of hedging against interest rate risk.

1   Background issues

1.1   One of the most important functions of the financial system is to meet the financing requirements of the corporate sector, i.e. all private sector companies which are not classified as banks or other financial institutions. Companies are major borrowers from the banking sector, as well as being important customers for other banking services. They are also the source of equity and debt securities, the issue and trading of which dominate capital market activities; and a significant proportion of the turnover of the money markets relates to short-term corporate financing. Therefore, the financing operations of the corporate sector have crucial implications for the prosperity and development of financial institutions and markets.

1.2   In the UK, the corporate sector fluctuates from being a net provider of funds, i.e. running a surplus, for the rest of the economy to being a net recipient, i.e. running a deficit. The peak deficit was £21.5bn in 1990 but since then it returned to surplus in 1993 and 1994, before reverting to a deficit in 1995 and the first quarter of 1996. In other words, there is a pronounced cyclical pattern, unlike the personal sector which is usually in surplus (see Unit 10, paragraph 1.2), and the public sector, which is usually in deficit.

UK corporate sector aggregate balance sheet

1.3   The aggregate balance sheets for 1991 and 1995 are shown in Table 9.1. The key aspects are summarised below

Financial assets

1.4   These consist of:

- Notes and coin – a small fraction of the total, largely held by retail outlets for day-to-day transactions.

- Public sector debt instruments – secure, interest-bearing investments.

- Bank deposits – an important item, showing steady growth in recent years; the main liquid asset held.

- Building society deposits – much less important than bank deposits, and likely to fall as societies become banks.

- Claims on other businesses – these are the dominant items, and include trade credit outstanding, holdings of UK and overseas company securities, and direct and other investment overseas. Note that the value of marketable securities depends upon market forces, and that movements in exchange rates may influence the sterling value of foreign currency denominated assets.

Financial liabilities

1.5   These consist of:

- Public sector lending – this largely relates to purchases of commercial bills by the Bank of England.

- Bank lending – a major item of corporate sector debt which grew steadily until 1990, but which contracted somewhat during the recession of the early 1990s and has now stabilised.

- Other financial institution lending – demonstrates a similar pattern to bank lending, but is of much less significance.

- Trade credit – an important source of finance.

- Securities issues – by far the largest item, effectively representing the nominal value of equities and marketable debt issued by corporates. The total value outstanding is influenced by new issues and redemptions. In

Table 9.1 UK corporate sector, aggregate balance sheet (end-year figures), £bn

	1991	1995
Financial assets		
Notes and coin	1.6	1.9
Public sector debt instruments	5.7	3.1
Bank deposits – sterling	63.8	80.5
– foreign currency	12.5	14.2
Building society deposits	5.5	4.0
Credit extended by retailers	2.5	2.5
Trade credit extended to purchasers	84.3	83.8
Company securities – UK	38.6	50.3
– overseas	1.2	2.7
Direct and other investment overseas	167.0	181.1
Miscellaneous and adjustments	28.6	40.7
Total financial assets	356.3	466.8
Financial liabilities		
Public sector lending	7.8	6.4
Bank lending – sterling	130.9	124.9
– foreign currency	33.5	30.2
Other financial institution lending	7.6	8.3
Trade credit received from suppliers	95.0	100.1
Finance leasing	14.4	14.2
UK company securities	603.6	959.8
Overseas direct and other investment in the UK	92.6	112.2
Miscellaneous and adjustments	67.3	105.5
Total financial liabilities	1052.7	1461.6
Net financial assets	−696.4	−638.9

Sources: Financial Statistics, Table 9.1I National Income and Expenditure, Central Statistical Office

turn, stock market conditions influence the attraction of this source of finance.

- Overseas direct and other investment – this has grown significantly in recent years, reflecting the relative attractions of investment in the UK.

1.6 In recent years, the UK corporate sector has had substantial net financial liabilities. However, the special position of equity claims on companies must be recognised, as must the fact that in a capitalist economic system individuals ultimately own a large proportion of all national wealth, either directly or indirectly (via claims on financial institutions). Also, the corporate sector holds substantial amounts of tangible assets, such as buildings, plant and equipment, stocks and work-in-progress.

UK corporate sector sources and uses of funds

1.7 Examination of a balance sheet shows the relative importance of various assets and liabilities held at a specific point in time. However, in order to understand how companies are financed and the uses to which they put their net inflows of funds, we must consider the sector's sources and uses of funds data. Table 9.2 shows the UK corporate sector's sources and uses of funds during 1991 and 1995.

Sources of funds

1.8 These may be divided into internal and external sources, i.e. external to each company. *Internal funds* basically relate to the net income generated by a company which has been retained rather than distributed to shareholders. The importance of internal funds grew significantly between 1991 and 1995, as the amount of funds raised externally fell markedly. *External funds* relate to borrowing from banks and other financial institutions, issuing of securities (both equity and debt), and flows of other investment funds. It was the reduction in bank borrowing during the early 1990s which bore the brunt of the corporate sector's financial adjustments.

1.9 During 1991 and 1992 there were unprecedented net repayments of bank loans by the sector, whilst fairly substantial share and other capital issues occurred. This development was quite understandable in the light of the uncertain economic environment, and following the pressures placed upon banks themselves to take extra care to avoid unnecessary risk. Also note that overseas sources have made important contributions to the external funds used by UK companies, via purchases of securities, direct investment and overseas bank loans. It was only during the later stages of the UK recession in 1992, and at a time when many major overseas economies were themselves slipping into recession, that the inflows of funds from overseas began to diminish. In 1995, the situation changed, with companies using bank borrowing to invest in UK company securities by takeover bids.

Use of funds

\1.10 The table demonstrates the surge in corporate takeovers in 1995, as mentioned in the previous paragraph. Some of the new finance was also used to finance increases in the book value of stocks of raw materials and finished goods, which had been reduced four years earlier. Another use for the funds raised was the purchase of more financial (i.e. not liquid) assets. In fact, liquid assets were reduced, which is not surprising in view of the low level of interest rates.

Student Activity 1

1. In general terms, why is the corporate sector of major importance to the operations of the financial system?   *(Paragraph 1.1)*

2. What has been the overall financial position of the corporate sector in recent years?   *(Paragraph 1.2)*

3. What are the most important groups of financial assets on the corporate sector's balance sheet?   *(Paragraph 1.4)*

4. What is the importance of bank lending to the corporate sector, and in what way did its position alter during the early 1990s?   *(Paragraph 1.5)*

5. What are the most important groups of financial liabilities on the corporate sector's balance sheet?   *(Paragraph 1.7)*

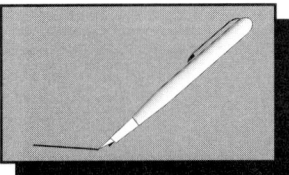

Table 9.2 UK corporate sector, sources and uses of funds, £bn

	1991	1995
Sources of funds		
Internal funds	34.9	54.6
External funds:		
Bank borrowing	−1.4	14.0
Other loans	5.1	2.5
Ordinary share issues	12.8	11.4
Debentures and preference share issues	4.5	11.7
Other capital issues	5.4	8.2
Overseas investment	10.0	5.2
Import credit, etc.	1.1	1.1
Total identified sources	72.4	108.7
Uses of funds		
Liquid assets:		
Bank deposits, notes and coin	3.4	5.6
Other liquid assets	2.1	−1.3
Other financial assets	1.7	9.2
Gross domestic fixed capital formation	49.9	51.6
Increase in book value of stocks	−3.1	8.3
Investment in UK company securities	8.2	22.5
Investment overseas	4.9	5.8
Other uses of funds	1.3	1.4
Total identified uses	68.4	103.1
Balancing item	4.0	5.6

Source: Financial Statistics, Central Statistical Office

6. What is meant by internal financing for a company? *(Paragraph 1.8)*

7. What is meant by external financing for a company? *(Paragraph 1.8)*

8. In what ways did the sources of funding used by companies alter between the late 1980s and the early 1990s? *(Paragraph 1.9)*

9. In what ways did the uses of funds for companies alter between the late 1980s and the early 1990s? *(Paragraph 1.10)*

2   Overdraft facilities

2.1   The overdraft facility is provided by banks and allows corporate customers to overdraw their current accounts up to an agreed maximum amount. Interest is charged on the overdrawn balance at close of business each day. The facility usually lasts for one year, and then can be renewed by mutual agreement.

2.2   The *benefits* of the overdraft from the point of view of corporate borrowers are that:

●   The facility is flexible and is ideal for financing day-to-day working capital needs. The facility is not tied to any specific transactions. In this respect, it is different from an acceptance credit.

- The documentation is simple and can be quickly arranged.

- Interest is charged on the daily debit balance and thus interest costs are minimised.

- If the facility is secured, a lower rate of interest may be available because of the lower risk for the lender.

2.3   The *drawbacks* of overdraft facilities from the borrower's point of view are that:

- Overdraft facilities are, in theory, repayable on demand. However, it is unlikely that a bank would exercise this right unless the position of the borrower had deteriorated dramatically. Nevertheless, remember that in difficult times companies would be safer with committed facilities, such as loans, which cannot be called in unless there is a breach of one of the covenants in the loan agreement.

- Overdrafts are sometimes linked to base rate whereas other facilities for major corporate borrowers could be linked to LIBOR. Generally speaking, base rate will be higher than LIBOR.

- Because interest rates are linked to base rate or LIBOR, the borrower is exposed to interest rate fluctuations, although base rate does not experience such volatile movements as other interest rate benchmarks, such as LIBOR.

2.4   There is also a drawback for lenders, when companies use cheques for large amounts on their current accounts – whether in debit or credit – these cause substantial swings in the operational balances of the banks involved. The need to keep these balances at the target levels agreed with the Bank of England can cause extra work for the treasury dealers who manage the banks' liquid assets. Hence, banks tend to increase the margin over LIBOR at which the overdraft is priced.

3   Committed LIBOR-linked loan facilities

3.1   These are known as committed facilities because a bank allows its customer to take out various LIBOR-linked loans of various maturities (usually one to three months), subject to a maximum total amount outstanding at any one time. The minimum total facility is usually £250,000 and the minimum individual loan is usually £100,000. There is no maximum.

3.2   The *benefits* of a LIBOR-linked loan facility for the corporate borrower are that:

- The documentation is standardised and simple.

- There are many banks which offer these facilities, hence the margins over LIBOR are kept relatively low because of competitive pressures amongst the providers of such finance.

- The facility is committed, hence the borrower knows that the funds will be available if needed (except in the comparatively rare case where the bank has insisted on a demand clause whereby the facility may be withdrawn without notice after a demand is made and not immediately met).

- As with overdrafts, there is no need for the loans to be tied to specific transactions.

3.3   The *drawbacks* from the corporate borrower's point of view are that:

- A non-utilisation fee is payable on undrawn facilities, thus making these loans more appropriate where the borrower has a fairly certain financing requirement. In addition, the bank may well charge a commitment fee for setting up the facility.

- The borrowing is linked to three month sterling LIBOR which is more volatile than base rate. Hence, there is a greater interest-rate exposure than would apply with an overdraft linked to base rate.

Uncommitted LIBOR-linked loan facilities

3.4   Note that major companies whose shares are included in the *FTSE-100* Index can *enter the money market directly* for the purposes of raising immediate short-term funds. There are no commitment fees or non-utilisation fees to pay since the facility is uncommitted. The minimum amount via this direct borrowing facility is usually £1m. The margin over LIBOR is narrower than for the committed LIBOR-linked loans raised in the normal way, because the company deals directly with a bank which wishes to make a deposit for the period and amount which matches the borrower's requirements.

4   Acceptance credits

4.1   A company may raise short-term finance by drawing a *bill of exchange* on a bank. The bank accepts the bill of exchange in return for a fee. By accepting the bill, the bank is effectively *guaranteeing payment* to the holder at maturity. Once a bill has been accepted by a bank, the company should easily be able to find a third party who will discount the bill (that is, purchase the bill for an amount below its face value at maturity). The difference between the face value of the bill and the amount paid by the discounter represents the effective rate of interest; the lower the difference (or discount), the lower the effective rate of interest. The finest rates of discount apply to eligible bills, which are bills rediscountable at the Bank of England.

4.2   When a commercial bill has been accepted by a bank, it becomes a commercial bank bill and if that bank is an eligible bank, then the bill becomes an eligible bank bill. (Eligible banks are banks which meet the minimum criteria of the Bank of England for the quality of their acceptance business, market standing and, for foreign banks, the treatment of UK banks in the relevant overseas market.)

4.3   The bill itself must be related to an *underlying trade transaction*, and there must be a brief mention of this transaction on the bill itself. The original term of the bill must not exceed 187 days and the bill must be payable in the UK.

4.4   The *benefits* of acceptance credit finance for corporate customers are that the:

- Company can arrange a total facility (usual minimum amount £500,000) and within this total individual bills of not less than £50,000 each can be drawn. In exchange for a commitment fee, these facilities can be guaranteed, so that individual bills can be drawn without negotiations once the overall facility amount has been agreed.

- Discount rate is a fine rate, known as eligible bill rate, which is usually below LIBOR.
- Discount (that is, the effective rate of interest) is fixed at the outset, hence the cost of borrowing is not affected by subsequent interest rate changes.
- Facility is flexible since bills can be drawn for varying amounts and varying maturities up to 187 days.
- Facility is self-liquidating, provided the underlying trade transaction is completed and the buyer pays.
- Company is not tied to the accepting bank and can discount the bill with another organisation if that organisation offers a better discount rate.

4.5 The *drawbacks* to acceptance credit finance are that the:

- Facility is only available if there is an underlying trade transaction.
- Discounter of the bill may subsequently sell the bill (rediscount it) to another party. Thus, the drawer's name and the underlying transaction (which must be specified on the bill) could become public knowledge, with obvious implications for the drawer's commercial position.

Student Activity 2

1. Describe an overdraft facility to a continental business person. *(Paragraph 2.1)*

2 List the benefits and drawbacks of an overdraft facility for a corporate borrower.
   (Paragraphs 2.2–3)

3 What is a LIBOR-linked loan facility? *(Paragraph 3.1)*

4. What are the benefits of a LIBOR-linked loan facility for a corporate borrower?
    (Paragraph 3.2)

5. List the drawbacks of a LIBOR-linked loan facility for a corporate borrower.
    (Paragraph 3.3)

6. What types of companies may raise funds directly from the money markets?
    (Paragraph 3.4)

7. What are the advantages of raising money directly from the money markets for a corporate borrower? *(Paragraph 3.4)*

8. What is an acceptance credit? *(Paragraphs 4.1–3)*

9. What are the benefits of using acceptance credits for a corporate borrower?
    (Paragraph 4.4)

10. What are the drawbacks to acceptance credit finance for a corporate borrower?
    (Paragraph 4.5)

5   Commercial paper and medium-term notes

5.1   Commercial paper relates to marketable, unsecured promissory notes issued by companies and purchased directly by investors. The notes are issued at below their face value but are redeemed at par by the issuing company. This form of corporate borrowing bypasses the normal financial intermediary (since investor and borrower deal direct) and hence the process provides a good example of disintermediation.

5.2   The three main commercial paper markets are US dollar commercial paper (USCP), Euro-commercial paper (ECP) and Sterling Commercial Paper (SCP). If the paper is issued for periods between one and five years, it is known as medium-term notes (MTNs).

5.3   Commercial paper is usually issued under a *programme* managed by a bank or syndicate of banks, while MTNs are often issued as part of a *Note Issuance Facility* arranged and managed by a syndicate of banks.

5.4   The *benefits* of commercial paper finance for companies wishing to raise finance are that:

- It does not have to be tied to an underlying trading transaction, thus giving greater flexibility.

- Because of the disintermediation process, whereby the traditional bank deposit/lending function is omitted, it is possible for borrowers to obtain lower rates whilst investors receive higher rates.

- The facility is flexible, since the notes can be issued with original maturities of between seven days and five years. Notes with an original maturity of between one year and five years are called medium-term notes to distinguish them from the commercial paper with an original maturity of below one year.

5.5   The major *disadvantages* of commercial paper are that:

- The minimum denominations are relatively high (£100,000 for an individual note for SCP, as opposed to £50,000 for individual bills with acceptance credits).

- It is necessary to make fairly regular issues of commercial paper to establish a high market profile and to maintain investor interest.

- The documentation requirements may be demanding.

- There is a minimum net asset requirement (of £25m in the case of SCP) which precludes many companies from using this facility.

- In the case of USCP and ECP, it is necessary for the borrower to obtain a rating from one of the commercial rating organisations such as Moodys or Standard & Poor. These ratings are costly to obtain and so set an initial cost for entry into the market. However, if the rating is high enough the company may be able to issue commercial paper at lower effective interest rates.

- There is no guarantee that investors will always take up any issue of commercial paper and thus it may be necessary to arrange stand-by funding, perhaps from a bank, in order to cover the risk of an issue being under subscribed. Naturally, the bank will charge a commitment fee for the stand-by facility.

(For further details of CP and MTNs, see Unit 3.)

6 Bank loans and their documentation

6.1 In today's competitive market, banks are willing to structure bank loans on a made-to-measure basis to meet the specific needs of corporate customers. Consequently, it is difficult to generalise. However, we can summarise the key characteristics of a *loan facility letter* to enable you to appreciate the vast range of lending packages available from banks.

6.2 The *term to maturity* can be anything from one to 10 years, but it is not uncommon for loans to be made with repayments scheduled over 30 years.

6.3 *Early repayment* of fixed term loans is possible but the bank may levy a cancellation fee.

6.4 *Interest can be fixed or variable.* Variable rates can be linked to LIBOR or to base rate. There can be an arrangement whereby fixed interest rates will only apply for part of the loan period and then rates will be subject to renegotiation for the remainder of the loan.

6.5 The majority of long-term loans are *secured* against specific assets of the borrower, or alternatively there may be a floating charge covering all the assets. In fact, the usual charge includes a comprehensive combination of fixed and floating charges.

6.6 There will usually be covenants in the loan agreement by which the company agrees to *maintain minimum financial ratios* such as gearing (ratio of debt to equity).

6.7 The majority of banks charge *commitment fees* for arranging the facility and there may well be specific charges to cover the cost to the bank of tying up its capital in the loan (the capital adequacy requirements of central banks now impose a cost on commercial banks for lending, see Unit 5).

6.8 Where the amount required by a single customer is too great for one single bank (because the bank does not wish to become too exposed to one borrower or to one market sector), *syndicated loans* may be offered. Here, one bank acts as lead bank and undertakes negotiations with the borrower on behalf of a syndicate of banks. Syndicated loans enable banks to obtain business which would not otherwise be available and to spread the risk among themselves and to earn fees for selling participations. They enable the borrower to obtain a loan with lower transaction costs than would have applied if the funds had been raised through a number of separate loans from different banks for smaller amounts.

6.9 At times when confidence in the economic system is high, syndicated loans are not as popular as other facilities such as commercial paper which involve disintermediation. However, when confidence ebbs, corporates prefer the safety of a loan. This was illustrated by the surge of syndicated loans which occurred just after the October 1987 world stock market crash. Another example is Ferranti, an engineering company which ran into difficulties in about 1990. Its commercial paper and notes were down-rated by rating agencies and it had to resort to bank finance.

7 Lease financing

7.1 Large companies, such as airlines, often finance their asset purchases by lease finance from a bank. The bank acquires the assets, obtaining any tax reliefs and allows the company to operate the asset in the company's livery. Railway rolling stock is another example.

7.2 Leasing is available from most banks but a new development in the UK has been the formation of three companies to own railway rolling stock for leasing to the operating companies. One of these leasing companies has received a takeover bid from a leading bus company, which proposes to finance part of its bid by selling securitised lease receivable assets of the leasing company. This is the first example of securitisation being applied to lease receivables: previously, it has been applied to mortgages, credit card and HP receivables.

Student Activity 3

1. Define commercial paper. *(Paragraph 5.1)*

2. What are the three main types of commercial paper? *(Paragraph 5.2)*

3. What are the benefits for a company of raising finance through an issue of commercial paper? *(Paragraph 5.4)*

4. What are the main disadvantages for a company of raising finance through an issue of commercial paper? *(Paragraph 5.5)*

5. List the key characteristics of bank loans. *(Paragraphs 6.2–7)*

6. What is a syndicated bank loan? *(Paragraph 6.8)*

7. Under what conditions are syndicated loans likely to prove popular with corporate borrowers? *(Paragraph 6.9)*

8 Sterling debentures

8.1 Sterling debentures (sometimes called sterling bonds) are transferable registered secured loan stocks by which a company can raise funds. The stocks are issued by way of an offer for sale to the general public or by a private placing with the clients of a merchant bank or other major financial institution. The debentures of public listed companies are quoted on the London Stock Exchange.

8.2 The sterling debenture is only suitable for raising large amounts of funds, with a typical issue being in the range of £30–100m. The original maturity period must exceed five years. (The medium-term note market has superseded the sterling debenture market for issues of less than five years' original maturity.)

8.3 The launch of corporate bond PEPs is likely to provide a stimulus for managers of unit trusts and investment trusts to purchase more sterling debentures than has been their practice. However, such bonds carry an interest-rate risk

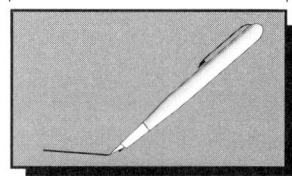

and no possibility of substantial capital gain. If secured, their credit risk is less than that of equity shares.

8.4   The *benefits* of sterling debentures to the corporate borrower are that the:

●   Rate of interest is fixed for the period of the loan.

●   The cost of servicing is fixed for the whole loan period.

●   Company may be able to repurchase the loan stock in the market, subject to certain legal formalities, and this will prove beneficial if interest rates in general have fallen and refinancing at lower cost is available.

8.5   'Junk bonds' are a derisory term for poor quality debt issued by companies in the USA and usually standing in line for repayment after more senior debt issues. They are not found in the UK, although there have been suggestions that attractively priced bonds of this type could be issued by companies seeking to bid for government 'Private Finance Initiative' construction and operating projects.

9   Eurobonds

9.1   Eurobonds are foreign-currency-denominated securities which may be issued in a third country by way of an offer for sale to the general public or by a private placing with investors. Public issues are normally made through a syndicate of banks which underwrites the bonds and distributes them to investors. Public issues are usually listed on one of the major stock exchanges whereas private placements are rarely announced publicly and are rarely listed on any stock exchange. Clearly, the private placements will tend to result in a narrow ownership with fewer opportunities for the holder to sell the bond prior to maturity.

9.2   Eurobonds are only suitable for raising large amounts of funds with a typical acceptable minimum issue being in the region of US$75m or its equivalent. In addition, the issuer must have a high credit rating and, preferably, be an internationally known name.

9.3   Eurobonds are unsecured and this helps the issuer to maintain creditworthiness with other providers of finance, as it is unnecessary to commit assets as security for Eurobonds. Such assets may therefore be used to support other types of financing. (For further details of Euro-currency markets, see Unit 3.)

Types of Eurobonds

9.4   The most popular type of Eurobond is a fixed-rate bond with 'bullet' repayment, i.e. the whole of the principal debt is repaid on maturity.

9.5   Floating rate bonds are linked to LIBOR; because they can be used to match assets they are popular with banks and with borrowing governments.

9.6   Equity warrant bonds give holders the right to buy some of the issuing company's equity.

The markets

9.7   Most Eurobonds are listed on the London or Luxembourg stock exchanges, but both the primary and secondary markets are OTC based. The bonds are bearer in form, so that ownership passes by delivery. Settlement is made by one of two specialised organisations – EUROCLEAR and CEDEL, based in Brussels and Luxembourg respectively. They run accounts for their clients (the investing financial institutions), and keep the securities in their vaults.

Student Activity 4

1. How can a company finance the purchase of a large asset by leasing it?
    (Paragraph 7.1)

2. How can a leasing company raise finance from the leases it owns? *(Paragraph 7.2)*

3. What are sterling debentures?   *(Paragraph 8.1)*

4. For what type of fund-raising are sterling debentures appropriate?*(Paragraph 8.2)*

5. What are the benefits for a corporate borrower of using sterling debentures to raise funds?   *(Paragraph 8.4)*

6. What are Eurobonds?   *(Paragraph 9.1)*

7. For what type of fund-raising are Eurobonds appropriate?   *(Paragraphs 9.2–3)*

8. Describe some of the different types of Eurobonds.   *(Paragraphs 9.4–6)*

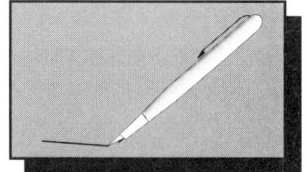

10   Equity finance

10.1   Equity finance is a method of raising long-term funds by issuing shares, the most common of which are *ordinary shares*. An ordinary shareholder is a part-owner of the company and his return comes by way of dividends and capital gains on the shares. Ordinary shareholders have a claim to the residual profits of the company after all other claims have been met; they have the right to vote at general meetings, and can vote to elect or dismiss the directors.

10.2   In the event of liquidation, the ordinary shareholders are entitled to participate in the surplus, if any, which is left after all outside creditors have been paid in full and after the claims of any prior equity holders, such as preference shareholders, have been met.

10.3   The *benefits* of ordinary shares as a means of finance from the company's perspective are:

- Dividends can be paid only from available profits (from the current year or from profits retained from past years) and, even if profits are available, dividends need not be paid. The directors recommend the rate of dividend, subject to available profits, and whilst ordinary shareholders can vote to reduce the dividend, they cannot vote to increase it. This contrasts with interest due on a loan which is a commercial debt and must be paid irrespective of profits.

- Equity capital is not generally redeemable, except with the consent of the courts or the shareholders, so long-term capital is committed to the company which does not have to be serviced if trading conditions are unfavourable.

10.4 However, the *disadvantages* of ordinary shares are:

- Dividends are not tax-deductible expenses, whereas interest *is* tax-deductible.

- If a new issue of ordinary shares is made, the decision-making power of the original shareholders can be diluted as the new shareholders become part-owners. In the UK most new issues are by way of rights issues, which means that the original shareholders are given the opportunity to buy the shares on favourable terms. However, it is almost inevitable that some of the new shares will subsequently find their way on to the open market.

10.5 *Preference shares* are another form of equity. The holder can only receive a dividend if there are available profits, but the amount of the dividend is a fixed monetary amount per share. In liquidation, the preference shareholder ranks behind all outside creditors although he ranks before the ordinary shareholder.

The importance of capital structure

10.6 All companies wish to raise their funds (or capital) at the minimum possible cost. The greater the ratio of loan capital to equity, the greater the gearing ratio. To some extent, highly-geared companies should find their cost of capital is less than that of lower-geared companies since the cost of debt finance, being tax-deductible, is generally lower than that for equity. However, once gearing is raised beyond a certain level, companies are perceived as being more risky because of the commitment to service the debt. Hence, providers of debt and equity finance may expect a higher return from a relatively highly-geared company to compensate for the greater risk.

10.7 It is, therefore, a highly complex matter to decide on the optimal capital structure for any company. The balance has to be struck between using relatively cheap loan funds and avoiding the financial instability which may flow from an excessively high gearing ratio.

Student Activity 5

1. What are the rights of ordinary shareholders? *(Paragraph 10.1)*

2. What is the position of ordinary shareholders if the company in which they hold shares goes into liquidation? *(Paragraph 10.2)*

3. From the point of view of a company, what are the benefits of ordinary shares as a means of raising funds? *(Paragraph 10.3)*

4. From the point of view of a company, what are the disadvantages of ordinary shares as a means of raising funds? *(Paragraph 10.4)*

5. What are preference shares? *(Paragraph 10.5)*

6. Why is it important for a company to obtain the 'right' balance of debt and equity in relation to its capital structure? *(Paragraph 10.6)*

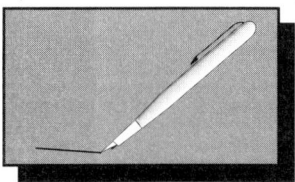

11 Elementary portfolio theory

11.1   The return from any investment is, in simple terms:

Final value less original value plus cash received as a percentage of the original value.

Algebraically it is:

$$R = \frac{(V_1 - V_0) + \text{Cash}}{V_0}$$

where V_1 = final value

V_0 = original value

11.2   This equation is too simple for the real world but it shows the principles clearly. The real world has to take account of dealing costs, shares (and gilts) going ex-dividend before cash is received as a dividend, and the fact that dividends are not usually paid at the end of the period under review. They are paid during these periods and need to be reinvested in an interest-bearing account or, if sufficiently large, in the actual security.

11.3   Elementary theory states that, in constructing a portfolio of financial assets, investors seeks to maximise their expected return from the portfolio, at a level of risk which they are willing to accept. We discussed financial assets in Unit 2 but risk has been an ongoing topic in a number of units. We can identify a number of risks – fire, accident, death – but, for this purpose, we can measure risk as:

the extent to which the actual outcome (value) differs from the expected outcome (value).

11.4   The calculations are:

1.   Square all the differences between actual and expected returns (this eliminates positive and negative values, so that shortfalls are treated in the same way as excesses).

2.   Weight these squared numbers by the value of the original investments.

3.   Add the weighted amounts together (known as the variance).

4.   Take the square root (to arrive at the standard deviation).

Expected return

11.5   This is calculated in a similar fashion, but the weights are the investor's subjective probabilities of the outcome occurring, and not the original cost. The exercise is also simplified by treating the portfolio as a single entity, whereas in real life the investor would have detailed opinions on the individual assets in the portfolio. Moreover, as we show later in paragraph 11.8, a portfolio will comprise assets with risks which offset each other, so that the portfolio does have a 'life of its own'.

11.6   In the table below, there are five possible outcomes (or scenarios), which the investor reckons have different chances of occurring.

Outcome	Return	Subjective probability
A	50%	0.1
B	30%	0.2
C	10%	0.4
D	−10%	0.2
E	−30%	0.1
Total		1.0

Notice that the probabilities are symmetric and that they sum to one.

The sum of the weighted returns is:

$$0.1(50) + 0.2(30) + 0.4(10) + 0.2(-10) + 0.1(-30)$$
$$= 5 + 6 + 4 - 2 - 3$$
$$= 10\%$$

Diversification and risk

11.7 If you have one or two shares, perhaps as a result of profit-sharing schemes, you may have been annoyed to find, on occasion, that all share prices move in one direction. Sometimes this occurs as a result of a similar change in New York but it can be disconcerting to see perhaps no direct relevance between the overall change in share prices and the attraction of any particular share or shares which you own. The overall change is an example of *systematic risk*, affecting all or nearly all securities in a portfolio.

11.8 *Unsystematic risk* is unique to that particular security – perhaps a change of chief executive, a new product, a fire, a strike. It is possible to offset these unsystematic risks by constructing a large portfolio of (say) 50 securities (we ignore the costs of managing them and dealing in them) such that 'pluses' on some securities balance the 'shortfalls' on others. For instance, an investor may hold shares into two exporters and two importers, in companies in the consumer goods and capital goods industries and so on. Eventually, unsystematic risk can be eliminated or, at least, compensated against, by diversification.

11.9 *Systematic risk* is defined, not very positively, as risk which cannot be eliminated by diversification. It results from the economic cycle and political events. The two types of risk and their relationship to portfolio size can be shown on a diagram (Fig. 9.1).

The risk return of individual securities

11.10 Using the systematic/unsystematic divide, we can divide the return of a security into two elements:

● Systematic return, which is linked to market return;

● Unsystematic return which is nothing to do with market return.

(Remember that risk is the square and deviation of the returns.)

Beta

11.11 This is the link between the systematic return for a particular security and the market return, expressed as beta times the market return. Beta is different for every security and, moreover, it is likely to change over time. The reasons for a change include changes in the economy, new product ranges, growth or decline of the firm, etc. Beta is calculated by using a technique called regression analysis.

11.12 For simplicity, analysts often talk of just beta for a share, leaving the market return implied. Thus, a share with a beta of 3 will tend to react to changes in market returns to a greater extent than a share with a beta of 2.

Student Activity 6

1. Calculate the return on a share bought for £4.20, sold for £5.10 and on which you received a dividend (net) of 18p on the day you sold it. Ignore dealing costs and tax.   *(Paragraph 11.1)*

2. Why is this calculation too simple for the real world?   *(Paragraph 11.2)*

3. Why are the differences between actual and expected returns squared before they are weighted?   *(Paragraph 11.3)*

4. If a share has a beta of 2.5 and the all-share index has fallen by 10%, then by how much is that share's price likely to have fallen?   *(Paragraph 11.11–12)*

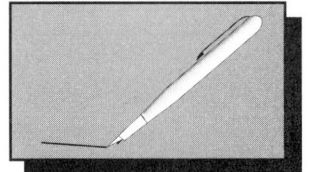

12   The nature of interest rate risk

Interest rate risk and borrowers

12.1   A company may borrow at *fixed or floating rates* of interest, although fixed-rate borrowing facilities may not always be available for smaller companies. In addition, a company, if it is a major borrower, may borrow at fixed rates and arrange to switch into floating rates by an interest rate swap, or the company could use a swap to achieve the opposite result if it borrows at floating rates and swaps into fixed. Whatever means of borrowing are used, it is normal for borrowers to be committed to a fixed or to a floating rate of interest for a period of time.

Figure 9.1

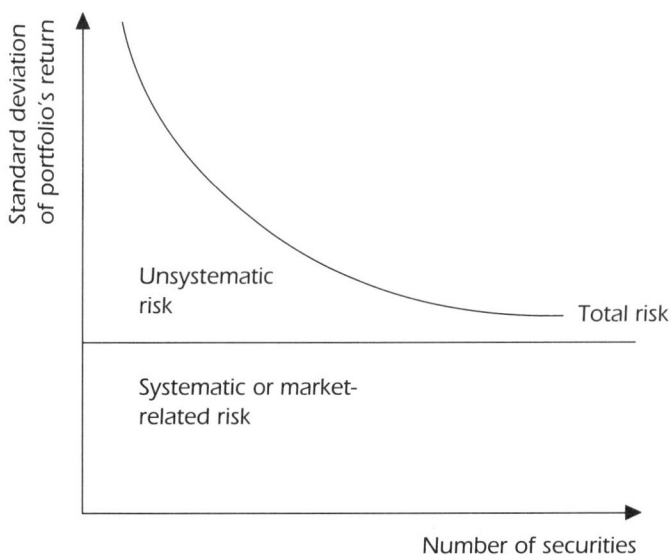

12.2   The factors which influence the choice between fixed rate and floating rate borrowing are:

- Expectations of future interest rate movements during the period of the loan.

- The current level of fixed interest rates which are on offer.

- The margin over LIBOR or base rate which is available.

12.3   The *risks* which a borrower faces with *floating rate borrowing* are:

- The benchmark to which the interest rate is tied, e.g. LIBOR, may rise. This can lead to cash flow problems because the servicing cost of the debt rises.

- If competitors have borrowed at fixed rates, they will be unaffected by any rise in base rate or other benchmarks. Hence the floating rate borrower will be at a competitive disadvantage if interest rates in general rise.

12.4   For *fixed rate borrowers* there is still a risk. Cash flows and servicing costs are not affected by changes in the general level of interest rates during the period of the fixed rate agreement, but if market rates in general fall during the loan period, the borrower will be paying an uncompetitive rate of interest. In these circumstances, competitors who have borrowed at floating rates will gain a competitive advantage.

Interest rate risk and lenders

12.5   Financial intermediaries such as banks face the opposite risks to those of borrowers when they lend money. When funds are lent at floating rates the lender loses out if rates in general fall. When loans are made at fixed rates of interest the lender loses if rates in general rise.

12.6   Clearly, such losses can be mitigated if the financial intermediary raises funds (that is, deposits) which match the lending in maturities and type of interest (fixed or floating).

Student Activity 7

1.   What factors influence the choice between fixed and floating rate borrowing?
(Paragraph 12.2)

2.   What risks are faced by a borrower taking on floating rate debt? *(Paragraph 12.3)*

3.   What risks are faced by a borrower taking on fixed rate debt? *(Paragraph 12.4)*

4.   In what sense do lenders face opposite risks to borrowers in respect of interest rate movements?
(Paragraph 12.5)

Hedging of interest rate risk

12.7   There are many techniques by which interest rate exposures can be hedged and most of these mechanisms turn what was in effect floating-rate borrowing into fixed-rate borrowing. Remember that although fixed-rate borrowing can still result in a competitive disadvantage if interest rates in general fall, at least the cost of servicing the borrowing and the resultant cash flow implications are known for the period for which the rates are fixed.

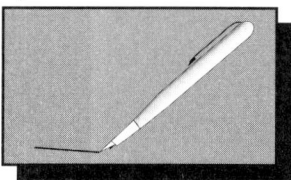

12.8   The main techniques for hedging interest rate risk are:

- Forward rate agreements;

- Interest rate options;

- Interest rate swaps; and

- Financial futures.

Forward rate agreements (FRAs)

12.9   FRAs involve the fixing of an interest rate for a specific period of time in advance and independently of the principal sum borrowed. Thus, a borrower with a floating rate loan outstanding may wish to hedge against a possible increase in the market rate of interest beyond a certain level. If the market rate rises above this level, the bank entering into the FRA (which is not necessarily the bank from which the loan was obtained) will cover the excess interest payments. If the market rate falls below the agreed level, the borrower will pay the difference between the actual rate and the agreed rate to the bank.

12.10   *Major limitations* of FRAs are that they are normally only available when the principal sum on which they are based is £100,000 or more, and FRAs to cover borrowings in excess of a year are rarely available.

Interest rate options

12.11   An interest rate option is the *right*, but not the obligation, to borrow or to deposit a specified sum at a set rate of interest (the striking rate), for an agreed period of time which commences on a known future date. The company will pay a premium to the bank for this right.

12.12   In the case of an option to borrow, the borrower will decide on the expiry date of the option whether to exercise his right to borrow at the striking rate. If interest rates in general are below the striking rate at the expiry of the option the borrower will allow the option to lapse and will borrow at current market rates. If interest rates are above the striking rate the option will be exercised.

12.13   Thus, for a premium, the company can fix the maximum borrowing costs of a known future commitment, but if interest rates subsequently fall, the company can abandon the option and can take advantage of the favourable interest rate movements.

12.14   One further benefit of the option is that if the borrowing is not in fact required, the option can be sold back to the bank if interest rates in general have risen at expiry date. Such an option is said to have an intrinsic value, since the right to borrow at below current market rates must be worth something.

12.15   Interest rate options can be tailor-made by banks to meet the specific perceived borrowing (or depositing) requirements of a corporate customer.

Interest rate swaps

12.16   Interest rate swaps occur when two borrowers raise funds independently for the same principal sum and for the same borrowing period, but one company borrows at a fixed rate and the other at a floating rate of interest, or one borrows at a rate linked to LIBOR whilst the other borrows at a rate linked to base rate. The two companies then swap their associated debt servicing commitments.

12.17 From the point of view of hedging interest rate risk, interest-rate swaps are useful for smaller companies which may not be able to borrow at fixed interest rates. The smaller company borrows at floating rates and the larger company borrows at fixed rates. The resulting interest rate payments are swapped, and in addition the smaller company pays a fee to the larger company. As a result, the smaller company has obtained fixed-rate financing which would not normally be available to it, whilst the larger company has obtained floating-rate borrowing at a lower-than-normal rate when taking into account the fee.

12.18 In practice, such swaps are often arranged through an intermediary bank so that the obligations of both counterparties are guaranteed by the bank and the standard bank documentation can be used to simplify and clarify the legal position. Naturally, banks charge a fee for undertaking this role.

12.19 The main role of the interest rate swap in interest rate exposure management for smaller companies is to enable them to hedge interest rate exposure by borrowing at fixed rates which would not otherwise be possible.

Financial futures

12.20 A financial future is an agreement to buy or sell a standard quantity of a specific financial instrument at a future date and at an agreed price. The futures contracts which hedge interest rates have prices which are set by supply and demand, but the main factor which influences supply and demand is the level of interest rates in general. If interest rates rise, the prices of the relevant futures contracts fall.

12.21 If a company wants to hedge a perceived future borrowing requirement against a rise in interest rates it can sell futures contracts. If interest rates do rise by the time the underlying borrowing is taken up, the interest cost of that borrowing will be greater than would have been the case if the interest rate had been fixed at the same time as the futures contract was sold. However, the company can cancel out its obligations under the futures contract by buying back the same number of contracts at the lower price. Hence, the gain on the sale and subsequent repurchase of the futures contracts will offset the extra interest costs on the underlying borrowing.

12.22 If interest rates were to fall by the time the borrowing was due to be taken up, then the lower cost of borrowing would be offset by the loss on the futures contracts (the price of the futures contract would have risen by the time the company had to cancel its obligations by repurchasing futures contracts).

12.23 It is not always possible to buy a number of interest rate financial futures contracts to match exactly the potential extra interest rate costs if rates rise, because financial futures contracts are for standard amounts and periods. These standard periods on offer from the futures contracts may not exactly match the borrowing requirements of the company.

Interest rate caps, floors and collars

12.24 A cap may be purchased from a bank in order to protect the holder of an existing floating rate loan from the interest rate moving upwards beyond the level specified by the cap contract. The borrower is still able to benefit if interest rates fall, but may claim any excess interest charge over the cap level from the seller of the cap.

12.25 A floor has the same characteristics as a cap, except that it protects an investor or depositor against a floating rate of interest falling below the specified floor level. The seller of the floor will pay the purchaser any interest losses below the floor rate. The purchaser is still able to benefit from increases in interest rates.

12.26 A collar is effectively a combination of a cap and a floor, and may be purchased by a company wishing to protect itself against the interest rate on outstanding debt going beyond a capped level, but prepared to forgo the gain from the interest rate falling below a lower specified level in exchange for a lower premium on the cap.

Student Activity 8

1. What is a forward rate agreement? *(Paragraph 12.9)*

2. What are the major limitations of forward rate agreements? *(Paragraph 12.10)*

3. What is an interest rate option? *(Paragraph 12.11)*

4. Under what circumstances will the buyer of an interest rate option allow it to lapse? *(Paragraph 12.12)*

5. In what sense does an option have a market value? *(Paragraph 12.14)*

6. Give an example of the operation of an interest rate swap. *(Paragraph 12.16)*

7. What is the main role of interest rate swaps? *(Paragraph 12.17)*

8. What is a financial future? *(Paragraph 12.20)*

9. Describe caps, floors and collars. *(Paragraphs 12.24–26)*

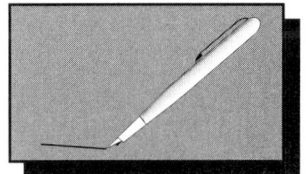

Summary

Now that you have studied this unit, you should be able to:

- discuss the broad trends in corporate sector financing in the UK and identify the various financing alternatives available to companies;

- appreciate the importance of credit ratings and the role of rating companies with special reference to commercial paper;

- distinguish between medium-term notes, note issuance facilities, Euronotes and syndicated loans;

- understand the key provisions of a corporate bond issue;

- assess the risks involved with investing in corporate bonds;

- describe the Eurobond market and the different types of bond structures issued, together with the role of Euroclear and CEDEL;

- distinguish between preference shares, corporate debt and ordinary shares;

- examine the fundamental principles of portfolio theory;

- calculate the historic single-period investment return for a security or a portfolio of financial assets;

- calculate the expected return and the variability of expected return on a portfolio;

- assess the components of a portfolio's total risk: systematic risk and unsystematic risk;

- explain what is meant by the beta of a stock;

- demonstrate how diversification through risk management eliminates unsystematic risk;

- distinguish between the different ways of hedging against interest rate risk.

Self-assessment questions

Short-answer questions

1. A creditworthy company, the shares of which are listed on the London Stock Exchange, wishes to borrow for capital expenditure purposes. Why is an acceptance credit facility unlikely to be available for this purpose?

2. Why will a lender normally accept a lower rate of interest for secured as opposed to unsecured lending?

3. What are the benefits of overdraft facilities for corporate borrowers?

4. What are the possible disadvantages of sterling commercial paper from the point of view of corporate borrowers?

5. How do preference shares differ from ordinary shares?

6. Why is a highly geared company considered to be more risky than a low-geared company, other things being equal?

Multiple-choice questions

1. During the early 1990s, for the UK corporate sector:
   (a) holdings of notes and coin far outweighed deposits with building societies
   (b) sterling bank deposits were greater than sterling bank loans outstanding
   (c) sterling bank loans outstanding exceeded the value of trade credit outstanding
   (d) debt owed to the public sector was a major item amongst financial liabilities
   (e) more trade credit was granted than received.

2. Bank borrowing for the UK corporate sector:
   (a) has never been a major source of funding
   (b) is the main internal source of funding
   (c) rose substantially during the early 1990s, due to the difficulties experienced in raising equity funds
   (d) saw an unprecedented reduction during the early 1990s
   (e) is now largely in foreign currencies rather than sterling.

3. Which one of the following can be considered as a disadvantage of an overdraft facility as opposed to a loan, from the point of view of a corporate borrower; the overdraft is:
   (a) less flexible than a loan
   (b) calculated on the closing debit balance each day
   (c) repayable on demand
   (d) only available for the borrowing of sums in excess of £1m
   (e) not usually available in a foreign currency?

321

4. Which of the following borrowing facilities must be linked to an underlying trade transaction:

    (a) an overdraft

    (b) a loan

    (c) sterling commercial paper

    (d) an acceptance credit

    (e) a medium-term note?

5. What is the original maturity of medium term notes:

    (a) 187 days

    (b) 187 days to one year

    (c) one to five years

    (d) 187 days to three years

    (e) over five years?

6. In order to be eligible to issue sterling commercial paper, a company must have net assets of at least:

    (a) £10m

    (b) £15m

    (c) £20m

    (d) £25m.

7. An important motive for a company raising finance through an issue of ordinary shares, as opposed to through long-term debt instruments, is that:

    (a) this reduces the gearing ratio and hence improves the financial stability of the company

    (b) equity finance is much cheaper than debt finance

    (c) this protects the existing owners' control of the business

    (d) the dividends which are paid on equity shares are tax-deductible for the company, whilst interest payments on debt are not.

Unit 10

Personal Sector Finances and the Housing Market

Objectives

After studying this unit, you should be able to:

- analyse the structure of the personal sector balance sheet;

- name the sources and uses of funds for the personal sector;

- appreciate the financial risks faced by the personal sector;

- understand the broad nature of the UK housing market and how house prices are determined;

- identify the main types of mortgage loan and the associated types of interest payments and repayments of principal;

- describe the operation of housing finance in the UK and how it differs from housing finance in North America and the rest of the European Union.

1 The structure of personal sector finances

The personal sector within the UK economy

1.1 The UK personal sector is defined as comprising all individuals resident in the UK, as well as unincorporated businesses (such as sole traders and partnerships), and non-profit-making institutions (such as registered charities and trade unions).

1.2 With the exception of a short period at the end of the 1980s, the personal sector has been a major net provider of funds to the other sectors of the economy in recent years. In 1988, in the 'mortgage' boom, a record financial deficit was generated by the personal sector with the amount spent on consumption and investment in real capital assets exceeding personal disposable income by £14.5bn. A large part of this net borrowing (which financed the extra spending on house purchase) was from building societies and retail banks, in the form of mortgage loans. By 1990, the sector had returned to an overall financial surplus, which grew rapidly to reach a record £31.3bn in 1992; in 1995 the surplus was £22.6bn. The impact of the recession on consumer confidence, and the downturn in the housing market were crucial factors underlying this return to a surplus.

1.3 Personal sector financial requirements are of crucial importance to the operation of the UK financial system. A large proportion of the activities of the retail banks, and almost all of the activities of the building societies, are directed towards satisfying the demands of personal sector customers, who also dominate the work of pension funds and many insurance companies, unit trusts and investment trust companies.

UK personal sector aggregate balance sheet

1.4 The aggregate balance sheets for 1991 and 1995 are shown in Table 10.1. You must take care in respect of the interpretation of the data on personal sector finances, as most of the information available has to be collected indirectly, from financial institutions, and some figures quoted are estimates or residuals. Nevertheless, the broad patterns of personal sector financing are clear, and the key aspects of the balance sheets are summarised below.

Financial assets

1.5 These consist of:

- *Notes and coin* – total holdings have grown steadily, but their relative importance has diminished, as you would expect given the evolution of payments methods and increased financial sophistication.

- *UK government securities and National Savings* – holdings reflect the demands of UK public sector finances, and have risen slightly.

- *Bank and building society deposits* – these are extremely important for the personal sector, accounting for 21% of total financial assets at the end of 1995.

- *Trade credit* – relates to credit granted to suppliers by unincorporated businesses.

- *Company securities* – direct holdings are significant (over 12% of total financial assets at the end of 1995), but of much greater importance are indirect holdings via investments in life assurance, pension funds and unit trusts.

- *Life assurance and pension funds* – now comprising over half of the personal sector's financial assets. As we have seen, these financial intermediaries invest in gilts and property as well as in equities, but around a half of all personal sector financial assets are in the form of company securities, both directly and indirectly.

Financial liabilities

1.6 These consist of:

- *Bank lending* – for purposes other than the purchase of residential property, once accounted for around 20% of the sector's total outstanding financial liabilities but this figure is now about 16%. Moreover, the rate of growth of new bank lending fell markedly during the early 1990s. Total outstanding debt actually fell in 1992 and 1993, partly as a result of the writing-off of bad debts.

- *Loans for the purchase of residential property* – by far the largest category of debt (around 70% of the total), continued to grow throughout the recent recession, although at a much reduced rate. The dominant providers of these funds have been the building societies, with banks making a significant contribution and gradually increasing their share.

- *Trade credit and credit extended by retailers* – have maintained their importance in recent years, although overall growth has been relatively slow.

**Table 10.1 UK personal sector, aggregate balance sheet
(end-year figures), £bn**

	1991	1995
Financial Assets		
Notes and coin	14.1	18.4
UK government securities	10.4	21.3
National Savings	37.7	54.4
Other public sector debt	0.7	0.6
Bank deposits – sterling	159.5	194.3
– foreign currency	3.0	3.6
Building society deposits	177.4	208.2
Domestic trade credit 46.7	48.0	
Unit trust units	20.0	54.1
Company securities – UK	141.0	224.4
– overseas	12.7	18.2
Life assurance and pension funds	611.0	995.3
Miscellaneous and adjustments	40.9	43.7
Total financial assets	1280.0	1898.8
Financial liabilities		
Bank lending – sterling	85.6	86.0
– foreign currency	1.6	0.6
Credit extended by retailers	2.5	2.6
Domestic trade credit 32.5	34.0	
Loans for house purchase – building societies	197.2	223.8
– other	122.5	166.9
Overseas investment in the UK	7.8	8.7
Miscellaneous and adjustments	21.1	21.5
Total financial liabilities	473.3	551.3
Net financial assets	806.7	1347.4

Source: Financial Statistics, Central Statistical Office, Table 9.1J

1.7   Total personal sector financial liabilities have grown far more slowly than the sector's financial assets in recent years, so that a healthy balance of net financial assets has been maintained. The personal sector also holds substantial amounts of tangible assets, the most important element of which is residential property. The importance of financial institutions for personal sector finances is clearly shown by the balance sheet. Banks and building societies have a crucial role on *both* sides of the balance sheet, although non-bank financial intermediaries dominate the assets side, with life assurance companies, pension funds and unit trusts being especially important. The liabilities side is dominated by banks and building societies.

Table 10.2 UK personal sector, sources and uses of funds, £bn

	1991	1995
Sources of funds		
Saving	40.9	50.5
Borrowing:		
Bank borrowing	2.0	6.8
Credit extended by retailers	0.1	−0.1
Loans for house purchase:		
Public sector	−0.9	−0.3
Banks	4.8	7.8
Building societies	20.9	9.2
Other	1.1	−1.5
Other loans and mortgages	1.3	2.0
Other sources of funds and adjustments	1.4	0.4
Total identified sources	71.6	74.8
Uses of funds		
Liquid assets:		
Notes and coin	0.4	1.2
National Savings	2.2	3.2
Deposits with banks	6.2	13.2
Deposits with building societies	17.3	14.2
Other	−0.2	0.5
UK government securities	1.4	2.1
Other public sector debt	0.2	0.4
Company securities	−4.0	−16.8
Life assurance and pension funds	29.2	29.8
Investment in fixed assets and stocks	25.3	29.9
Other uses of funds	2.6	2.3
Total identified uses	80.6	79.2
Balancing item	−9.0	−4.4

Source: Financial Statistics, Central Statistical Office, Table 10.7B

UK personal sector sources and uses of funds

1.8   The personal sector balance sheet shows the relative importance of various assets and liabilities held at a specific point in time. However, in order to understand the nature of personal sector financing, in terms of the generation and disposition of its funds, we must consider the sector's sources and uses of funds data. Table 10.2 shows the UK personal sector's sources and uses of funds during 1991 and 1995.

Sources of funds

1.9 These may be divided into saving and borrowing. The ratio of saving to personal disposable income has risen substantially since the mortgage boom of the late 1980s. The ratio stood at the historically low level of 5.6% in 1988; by 1995 it was 11.0%. In 1988, 25% of the sector's sources of funds came from saving; in 1995 the corresponding figure was over 67%. The savings ratio averages around 10% but rises in times of inflation – in 1980, when the second oil crises occurred, it was over 14%.

1.10 During the early 1990s there was a massive reduction in the flows of borrowed funds, with bank lending for purposes other than the purchase of residential property largely collapsing. The weak state of the UK economy, lack of consumer confidence, high unemployment and the debt overhang from the 1980s are thought to be the main factors underlying this trend.

Uses of funds

1.11 Total amounts of funds utilised by the personal sector have remained relatively stable in recent years, compared to the late 1980s.

1.12 Purchases of public sector debt have largely reflected the public sector's borrowing requirement, which remains higher than forecast. Purchases of company securities have remained negative, i.e. net sales, partly due to sales of deceased's people's holdings to pay Inheritance Tax. However, the two main uses of personal sector funds have continued to be investments in life assurance policies and pension funds, and purchases of fixed assets and stocks (the most important element of which has been purchases of residential property). The weakness of the economy, and especially fears of unemployment, have been major factors in containing the flows of funds into fixed assets and stocks in recent years.

1.13 Holdings of liquid assets have continued to rise, but at a reduced rate. Financial pressures on members of the personal sector and falling interest rates on liquid assets are probably responsible for this trend. One outcome has been a rise in holdings of notes and coins, which comprise most of M0, the narrow monetary aggregate. As a result, the growth of M0 has kept pace with the growth of output, reversing a 30-year trend when people switched from notes and coin to bank accounts.

Student Activity 1

Before reading the next section of the text, answer the following questions and then check your answers against the paragraph(s) indicated.

1. Define the UK personal sector. *(Paragraph 1.1)*

2. What has been the overall financial position of the personal sector in recent years? *(Paragraph 1.2)*

3. What types of financial institutions are heavily dependent upon the financial needs of the personal sector? *(Paragraph 1.3)*

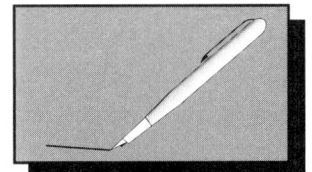

4. List the main groups of financial assets held by the personal sector in order of their importance in the sector's balance sheet. *(Paragraph 1.5)*

5. What is the criterion for the original order of the items on the assets side of the balance sheet? (Clue – think of a drink.) *(Paragraph 1.5)*

6 What is the largest group of financial liabilities held by the personal sector? *(Paragraph 1.6)*

7. To what extent are banks important to the personal sector's balance sheet? *(Table 10.1)*

8. In broad terms, how have the sources of funds for the personal sector altered in recent years? *(Paragraphs 1.9–10)*

9. In what ways have the uses of personal sector funds altered in recent years? *(Paragraphs 1.12–13)*

10. What have been the most important uses for personal sector funds in recent years? *(Paragraph 1.12)*

2 Financial risks faced by the personal sector

2.1 In managing their financial positions, members of the personal sector face a range of risks. The existence of these risks is likely to have an important influence on the structuring of the personal sector's balance sheet and upon its selection of sources and uses of funds. The major risks which should be recognised are discussed below.

Default

2.2 The most obvious default risk for the personal sector relates to the granting of trade credit by unincorporated businesses to buyers of their products. The only protection is for creditors to screen carefully the creditworthiness of potential debtors before credit is granted. Also, traders may consider withdrawing credit facilities altogether, and offering discounts for cash in order to maintain the level of business.

2.3 The bulk of personal sector financial asset holdings represent claims on financial institutions. An institution may fail, due to inept management or fraud, and depositors/investors may lose all of their deposits/investments. However, in the UK this occurrence is rare due to the existence of officially-sponsored depositor/investor protection schemes, as outlined in earlier units. The liquidation value of failed institutions is also available to compensate depositors/investors such as those who had substantial deposits in BCCI.

2.4 Direct ownership of company securities is inherently risky, especially when they relate to smaller, unlisted companies. Investors are wise to hold diversified portfolios of securities and to seek professional advice.

2.5 Government securities issued by major Western countries are effectively default-free, but capital losses may still be incurred if premature realisation is required at a time when market rates of interest are higher than those ruling when the securities were purchased. The only truly capital-safe investments are National Savings and other UK government instruments.

Inflation

2.6   The main problem is in predicting the future rate of inflation. If the actual rate of inflation turns out to be significantly different from the rate expected, either the borrower or the lender will experience unanticipated gains or losses. Unexpectedly high inflation will effectively transfer wealth to the borrower holding a fixed interest debt. Linking interest payments to market rates of interest or to a suitable price index may help to alleviate this problem, although uncertainty in relation to actual cash payments is then introduced into the transaction.

2.7   Purchasing company equity shares or residential property may serve as a hedge against inflation, but experience has shown that this may only be true in the longer term. Short-term price fluctuations may make such investments particularly risky.

2.8   Personal sector financial behaviour may be affected in a general sense because inflation may alter the balance between saving and consumption. Whilst some people may seek to spend their funds before their value is eroded by inflation, the evidence suggests that the opposite reaction occurs. The uncertainty created by inflation causes saving to rise to protect financial security, and try to preserve the real value of wealth holdings.

Changes in financial requirements

2.9   Unanticipated change in personal circumstances may cause serious problems for both borrowers and lenders. For example, someone with a large mortgage loan may be unable to cope with the servicing commitments if income is reduced due to illness, loss of employment, the break-up of a relationship or marriage, and so on. Sensible financial planning is always important – if possible there should be flexibility to adjust commitments in response to changes in circumstances, without fundamentally disrupting living standards. Unfortunately, these risks are very difficult to avoid within a market economy.

2.10   For a lender, the choice is often between relatively low-risk liquid assets, which pay only modest returns, or higher return, illiquid risky assets. Once a portfolio has been selected, unanticipated changes in circumstances may result in the forced sale of securities, with associated risk of capital loss, or the premature withdrawal of deposits, which may incur interest penalties. This possibility provides a good reason for investors to hold diversified portfolios of assets, as far as their personal circumstances will allow.

Interest rate movements

2.11   The interest rate risks faced by members of the personal sector are basically the same as those faced by companies (see Unit 9, section 12**)**. Thus, variable rates of interest lead to uncertainty in respect of future cash flows, whilst fixed rates mean that benefits of favourable interest rate movements may be forgone. The market value of fixed interest securities is also likely to be affected by movements in market rates of interest, and the market value of company shares may alter depending upon the perceived impact of interest rates on company profitability and cash flows. However, mortgage interest payments in some households may be a far higher percentage of income than occurs in most companies.

2.12 Other than not holding interest-bearing claims and not borrowing funds, there is little that members of the personal sector can do to avoid interest rate risk entirely. The holding of diversified portfolios of assets helps to spread risk and borrowers should ensure that they are able to cope with the cash flow implications if interest rates were to rise to the maximum level which appears realistically possible.

2.13 In the UK, base rate changes will affect mortgage rates in a way different to that seen in the Europe, as discussed at 10.9.

Government economic policy changes
2.14 Sudden changes in government economic policies may have adverse effects on personal sector finances. Monetary policy, affecting interest rates, inflation, bankruptcies and unemployment will impact as implied above. Constraints on money supply growth may limit the ability of financial institutions to lend. The policy overall is likely to influence the broad economic environment, and affect consumer confidence and attitudes to investment and borrowing.

2.15 Fiscal policy changes may lead to alterations in the tax regime in respect of interest earnings, or payments, or capital gains. The balance of portfolios may need to be altered if the tax privileges granted to pension schemes, PEPs, National Savings and mortgage interest payments were to be changed or removed. The public sector's expenditure plans and overall budgetary position will not only influence broad economic developments but also will affect the availability of and returns on public sector debt instruments. Business and consumer confidence is also likely to be affected if excessively large public sector borrowing is forecast.

2.16 Changes in almost any aspect of economic policy may have potentially serious effects on personal sector finances. Both direct and indirect impacts on decision-making should be recognised.

Student Activity 2

1. Outline the types of default risk faced by members of the personal sector.
(Paragraphs 2.1 and 2.2)

2. What actions might members of the personal sector take in order to reduce the default risk which they face? *(Paragraphs 2.2–5)*

3. Why is the occurrence of inflation a problem for someone lending money?
(Paragraph 2.6)

4. How might the balance of personal sector saving and consumption be affected by the occurrence of inflation? *(Paragraph 2.8)*

5. Give some examples of the problems which might be caused for both borrowers and lenders as a result of changes in their personal circumstances.
(Paragraphs 2.9 and 2.10)

6. In what ways might both borrowers and lenders be adversely affected by interest rate movements? *(Paragraph 2.11)*

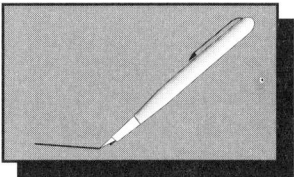

7. How might individual borrowers and lenders attempt to limit the adverse impact of movements in interest rates? *(Paragraph 2.12)*

8. In what general ways might changes in government monetary policy adversely affect personal sector finances? *(Paragraph 2.13)*

9. In what general ways might changes in government fiscal policy influence personal sector financial decisions? *(Paragraph 2.14)*

10. If base rates had risen to 20% after Black Wednesday (in September 1992) and stayed high for some months, analyse the likely affects on personal borrowers.

3 The UK housing market and house prices

3.1 For many people, the ownership of residential property is their single most important investment, and the purchase of such property is probably the largest single expenditure that most people will ever make in their personal capacity. However, as most people entering the housing market for the first time or trading up to more expensive property need to borrow funds for this purpose, the provision of housing finance is an extremely important aspect of personal sector finances.

3.2 To obtain a clear understanding of the nature of UK housing finance, the structure of the UK housing market, the way in which the government supports the housing market, and the broad factors affecting the determination of house prices must be understood. (Note that in the following sections, the terms 'residential property' and 'houses' are used interchangeably, although the former is the more accurate description.)

UK housing market

3.3 As is shown in Table 10.3, owner-occupation dominates housing tenures in the UK, currently, around two-thirds of all housing tenures are in owner-occupation. This is one of the highest proportions amongst Western nations, and its popularity has grown steadily this century.

3.4 A large proportion of purchases of residential property is financed, at least in part, by mortgage loans. In other words, houses are bought and sold, rather than inherited; the average length of a mortgage was eight years, now about 10 years. For the UK personal sector in aggregate, such loans dominate total financial liabilities. In 1980, mortgage loans accounted for 57% of financial liabilities; by 1995 this proportion was near to 71%.

The housing market and the economy

3.5 The nature of the UK housing market and its associated financing has important implications for the implementation of government economic policy and the operation of the economy. Changes in interest rates may have significant effects on the spending power of people with outstanding variable rate mortgage loans. As such people often have high propensities to consume, the impact on the economy as a whole may be substantial. Also, changes in the real value of residential property may affect personal sector expenditure decisions. When the real value is rising, owners may feel better off and hence may

Table 10.3 UK housing tenure, 1985 to 1994 (end year figures)

Year	Owner-occupied		Public sector rented *		Private sector rented		Housing association rented		Total dwellings
	m	%	m	%	m	%	m	%	m
1985	13.5	60.55	6.0	26.8	2.3	10.2	0.6	2.5	22.4
1986	13.9	61.5	5.9	26.1	1.3	9.8	0.6	2.5	22.6
1987	14.3	62.6	5.8	25.3	2.2	9.5	0.6	2.6	22.8
1988	14.8	64.0	5.6	24.2	2.2	9.1	0.6	2.7	23.1
1989	15.2	65.2	5.4	23.0	2.1	9.0	0.7	2.8	23.3
1990	15.5	65.8	5.2	22.1	2.1	9.1	0.7	3.0	23.5
1991	15.6	66.0	5.1	21.4	2.1	9.4	0.7	3.1	23.7
1992	15.8	66.2	5.0	20.8	2.2	9.6	0.8	3.4	23.9
1993	16.0	66.5	4.9	20.2	2.3	9.6	0.9	3.7	24.1
1994	16.2	66.8	4.8	19.6	2.3	9.6	1.0	3.9	24.2

* From local authorities or new town corporations.

Source: Housing and Construction Statistics, Department of the Environment, Table 9.3

spend a higher proportion of their disposable income, thus underpinning economic growth and supporting business confidence. This, in turn, may encourage people to enter the housing market for the first time or to trade up to more expensive property, which may push up house prices further. A virtuous cycle may be created. This pattern occurred in the UK in the late 1980s, fed by competing mortgage lenders. Unfortunately, if underlying economic conditions alter, the accumulated mortgage debt may cause serious problems.

The determination of house prices

3.6   House prices are determined in the free market by the forces of supply and demand. The key characteristics of the housing market which you must bear in mind are:

●   Residential property is extremely durable;

●   The vast majority of the population is housed at any point in time;

●   The total stock of houses can only be increased at a very slow rate;

●   The bulk of house purchases/sales relate to second-hand houses;

●   First-time buyers have considerable discretion over the timing of entry into the market.

3.7   The net supply of houses for sale on the market is the sum of:

●   New houses made available;

●   Houses vacated as a result of the owner's death, emigration or move to rented accommodation;

●   Houses transferred from rental status, but not involving sitting tenants.

3.8   The net supply is reduced to the extent that properties are demolished for slum clearance or redevelopment purposes. Houses placed on the market by owner-occupiers wishing to move have no net effect on supply, as they create an equal demand (albeit possibly for a different type of property).

3.9 The net supply is likely to be influenced by the general state of the economy, and expected trends in earnings, unemployment, inflation, and interest rates. This is especially so in respect of the activities of property developers. When economic conditions are good, more houses are likely to come on to the market. The only qualification relates to people with financial difficulties who may have to withdraw from owner-occupation as economic conditions deteriorate.

3.10 The sources of net demand for houses are potential first-time buyers and separated partners. This demand is influenced by the general economic conditions as noted above, and in the longer-term by demographic factors and social conventions. The availability of alternative types of tenure is also important.

3.11 The interaction of supply and demand determines prices, but demand is able to adjust much more quickly than supply. Therefore, if economic conditions are favourable, expectations in respect of employment and earnings are good, and interest rates are felt to be relatively low, the boost to demand is likely to place upwards pressure on prices, at least in the short term. The speed of adjustment of supply will determine the extent and persistence of the price rise. Ultimately, the impact on building costs and land prices, and expectations of property developers will be the key factors. Supply may never catch up with demand, and prices may continue to drift upwards until there is a change in conditions sufficient to reduce the level of demand. In this case, excess supply may arise in the market. As property developers do not wish to hold stocks of vacant houses, and as some owner occupiers feel obliged to sell their houses due to pressing financial problems, there may well be downward pressure on house prices.

UK house prices

3.12 Trends in UK house prices in recent years are easy to explain. During the late 1980s the UK economy was growing steadily, unemployment was falling, income taxes had been reduced, and there was a high level of competition between mortgage lenders. Thus, despite relatively high rates of interest, house prices were pushed up significantly. The word 'gazumping' was coined, describing instances where sellers broke their undertakings to sell when another buyer offered a higher price. The apparent investment value of houses merely reinforced demand.

3.13 At the beginning of the 1990s, consumer confidence was dented by rising unemployment, and interest rates remained high. The boom of the late 1980s had left many people with unmanageable debts and the levels of arrears on mortgage loans and possessions began to rise. Lenders repossessed properties and then sold them cheaply to regain most of their loses quickly. The housing market stagnated, undermining confidence still further, and unprecedented reductions in housing prices (in nominal terms) became widespread.

3.14 The appearance of negative equity – where the value of a property falls below the outstanding associated mortgage debt – for some borrowers also made matters worse. Thus, if the property is sold, the owner must raise additional funds to discharge the debt. Technically, mortgage lenders find themselves with unintended unsecured loans. The risks involved for borrowers and lenders are fairly obvious, and the negative equity overhang is one factor still holding back recovery in the housing market. Uncertainty on economic conditions is the other major factor.

3.15 In the mid 1990s house prices have failed to rise, in spite of forecasts that they would.

Government support for the housing market

Owner occupation

3.16 The main source of support given to owner-occupation is the tax relief on mortgage interest payments. Tax relief may be claimed on the interest payments associated with the first £30,000 of a mortgage loan for a single property occupied by the borrowers. The relief is given at 15% of the payment, and not at basic rate (24% for 1996–97). This relief is normally available through MIRAS (mortgage interest relief at source), whereby the borrower pays interest net of tax relief, and the lender collects the amount of the tax relief from the Inland Revenue.

3.17 Tax relief on mortgage loans has often been criticised as being a public sector subsidy to people who are often amongst the better-off in society. It may also have led to inflated house prices and made it harder for first-time buyers to enter the market. The government has gradually limited the amount of relief available in recent years, but it seems unlikely that it will be abolished in the near future due to the state of the housing market and government's desire for electoral popularity.

3.18 The impact of abolition would depend upon what the government did with the savings to the Exchequer (approximately £4.3bn in 1993/4). Housing benefits for the poor could be improved or the income tax burden for low earners could be reduced. However, whilst the positive impacts on the economy might encourage demand for housing in general, the relative cost of borrowing to finance owner-occupation would rise. Therefore, it is likely that house prices would be lower than they otherwise would be, and builders and landowners would lose out. Competition in the mortgage loan market would probably intensify, and this could put downward pressure on deposit rates offered by mortgage lenders. The rented housing sector might be given a boost, as owner-occupation became less attractive in terms of both finance and investment value.

Private rented homes

3.19 In the early 1990s, private rented homes became more popular, halting a decline in popularity which began with the imposition of rent controls in World War One. The Housing Act 1988 created a new form of tenancy, an assured shorthold tenancy (AST), which tries to balance the rights of landlord and tenant. An AST gives the tenant six months' security at first (unless a longer period is stated) and, after that, the landlord has to give the tenant two months' notice. ASTs began in January 1989, before which date most tenants had much better protection under regulated tenancies. However, it is not usually possible to convert regulated tenancies into ASTs.

Social housing

3.20 Once known disparagingly as 'council houses', this type of accommodation has undergone great changes since 1980. First, many council house tenants have been able to buy their homes from the local council, at a generous discount, as a result of the government's 'Right To Buy' legislation.

3.21 Second, the government has encouraged the formation of mutual housing societies, known as housing associations. There are over 2200 of these (about the same as the number of building societies 100 years ago) and, as shown in Table 10.3, they are the landlords for about one million householders. In 1964, the Housing Corporation was established to supervise all the housing associations registered with it. The Corporation receives grants and loans from the government, using these to give further grants and loans to housing associations. In addition, the Corporation 'markets' the housing association movement to banks and building societies, which lend the associations the rest of the finance they require. The total of such lending is over £9bn, making the housing associations an important group of borrowers in the wholesale markets.

3.22 The housing associations provide most of their homes on a rental or shared ownership basis. Nevertheless, as Table 10.3 shows, local authorities and new towns still own a great deal of the UK's housing stock.

Student Activity 3

Before reading the next section of the text, answer the following questions and then check your answers against the paragraph(s) indicated.

1. What proportion of housing tenures are accounted for by owner-occupation?
   (Paragraphs 3.1–2)

2. What is the importance of mortgage loans amongst personal sector financial liabilities? *(Paragraphs 3.1–2)*

3. In general terms, how might changes in the state of the housing market affect economic activity? *(Paragraph 3.5)*

4. List the key characteristics of the housing market. *(Paragraph 3.6)*

5. What factors determine the net supply of houses for sale on the market?
   (Paragraphs 3.7–9)

6. What are likely to be the most important factors determining the level of house prices? *(Paragraphs 3.8–10)*

7. Describe and explain the recent trends in the UK house prices. *(Paragraphs 3.12–15)*

8. Outline the nature of the support which is given to the housing market by the government. *(Paragraph 3.16)*

9. Why has government support for the housing market been criticised?
   (Paragraphs 3.17–18)

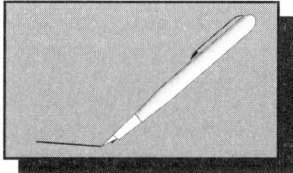

4 Nature and regulation of housing finance

4.1 The key concept is the mortgage, which is a charge over property, given by the owner of the property (the borrower/mortgagor) to a lender in order to secure the loan. If the borrower defaults, the lender may apply for possession of the property, which can then be sold to discharge the debt. The lender taking possession has a duty to obtain the market price for the property.

4.2 The Consumer Credit Act 1974 is the legal basis for the Advertisements and Quotations Regulations which mortgage lenders must adhere to. The aim here is that potential borrowers are made fully aware of the commitments that they are intending to take on.

4.3 The Building Societies Act 1986 and the Banking Act 1987 provide the regulatory frameworks within which the main mortgage lenders must operate. This legislation is intended to ensure that operations undertaken by building societies and banks meet minimum standards of good practice, that their customers are protected from fraud and incompetence, and that the integrity of the financial system is maintained (see Unit 5). However, the Financial Services Act 1986 does not apply to mortgage lending. This is regarded by many as a serious gap in the consumer protection legislation which is likely to be remedied soon.

5 Types of mortgage loans

5.1 All types commit the borrower to make regular payments to the lender, usually for a period of 20–25 years:

Annuity (repayment) mortgage
5.2 This involves the repayment of the loan plus interest by equal instalments (assuming that the mortgage interest rate does not alter) over the life of the loan. During the early years of the loan, a large proportion of each instalment is consumed by the interest element, and only a small amount of the principal is repaid.

Endowment mortgage
5.3 This links the loan to an endowment assurance plan. The borrower pays only interest to the lender during the term of the loan, but at the same time pays a regular premium to an insurance company. The proceeds from the matured policy should be sufficient to pay off the loan and leave a residual for the borrower. Until the mid 1980s, this form (or at least the 'low-cost' version) was dominant, at least in part because tax relief was at one time available on premiums. Whilst these loans are attractive when the stock market performs well and house prices rise steadily, the repayment arrangements are relatively inflexible. There has also been criticism of lenders being too eager to push this type of loan in order to earn the substantial commissions generated on the sale of the endowment policies.

5.4 Endowment mortgages are of three types, distinguished by differences in the endowment policy which repays the mortgage. Consequently the borrower pays interest on the whole mortgage for the whole period, unlike a repayment mortgage, where the debt reduces over the whole period, with the last year's payments comprising almost wholly repayments of principal.

With profits endowment policy

5.5 Each year, the value of the policy rises in line with reversionary bonuses which are added to the capital sum assured and never deducted. In addition, at the end of the term of the policy, a variable bonus (the terminal bonus) is also added. However, this terminal bonus, e.g. '29% of the sum assured and attaching bonuses [the reversionary bonuses of former years]' really is variable and, in the above example, could be reduced to (say) 25% or 30%, according to investment conditions. Recently, the reversionary bonuses have fallen and companies have had to announce cuts in their reversionary bonuses for forthcoming years, with the result that the proceeds of endowment policies may not be sufficient to repay a mortgage, especially if its term was around 12 or 15 years rather than the traditional 25 years. Accordingly, borrowers faced with a possible gap are being advised to take out savings plans with a building society (the 'up-front' charges of an extra life policy would make it an unattractive way of topping up the repayment, as would the fact that the borrowers would face higher premiums because they are older than when they took out the mortgage).

Unit-linked policy

5.6 This type of policy has no attaching reversionary bonuses, but its value fluctuates much in the same way as the price of a unit trust fluctuates. Neither is there a terminal bonus.

Low-cost endowment mortgage

5.7 Here, the life cover provided by the policy is below the debt, with the difference being covered by a mortgage protection policy (a sort of extended term life policy). The advantage for the borrowers is that they do not have to pay such large premiums but, of course, they cannot take all the profits when the policy matures. Instead, most of the profits go to repay the loan, and what remains (if anything) is paid to the borrower.

PEP mortgage

5.8 This is another form of interest only mortgage, with the proceeds of the PEPs being used to repay the borrowing at the end of the term. Term assurance is also required for the whole debt for the whole term.

5.9 PEP mortgages have a number of advantages:

- If the PEPs rise in value, then the monthly payments may be able to be reduced;

- The Government may increase the maximum amount payable each year to a PEP.

5.10 There are some disadvantages:

- The Government may reduce the limits on PEPs or alter their tax exemption.

- The values of the PEPs may fall – when it will be necessary to increase the monthly repayment, provided that they do not breach the maximum allowed.

Pension mortgage

5.11   This involves the borrower paying only interest to the lender during the term of the loan, whilst contributing to a pension scheme. On retirement part of the lump-sum pension payment is used to discharge the loan. The borrower gains from the tax relief on the pension contributions. For legal reasons they are more risky than endowment mortgages for lenders.

Interest-only mortgage

5.12   This involves a commitment only to pay interest for the term of the loan. The borrower must make separate arrangements for the ultimate repayment of the debt, e.g. a savings plan may be set up.

Flexible mortgage

5.13   This is a new product, giving the borrower (the mortgagor) the choice of varying the capital repayment programme while continuing to pay the interest. It has been developed by lenders as a device to increase their share of a stagnant mortgage market. Should the market begin to grow in line with possible increases in house prices, such products may be withdrawn for new borrowers. They have the disadvantage of increasing the volatility of a lender's cash flow.

Bridging loans

5.14   These are a special type of interest-only short-term 'mortgage', enabling a seller of a house with a mortgage on it to buy a second property before completion of his sale. A 'closed bridge' is where contracts have been exchanged for the sale of the first house, repayment comes from the sale proceeds which should be received four weeks after exchange. An 'open bridge' is riskier and rarer, covering the possible sale of an existing house before contracts are exchanged and the purchase of another house: repayment could come from the sale of either property if the loan were outstanding for too long.

5.15   Bridging loans are not true mortgages because the income(s) of the borrower(s) are usually insufficient to service the mortgages on two properties, particularly if the borrower is 'trading up' or increasing his or increasing his gearing. Hence, bridges are sanctioned for short periods, in order to keep the lending under review.

6   Types of interest payments

6.1   In the UK the vast majority of mortgage loans are associated with variable rates of interest, although some lenders are willing to fix rates for a period of, say, 2 or 3 years, and a very few have recently fixed rates for the whole term of some loans. The advantages and disadvantages of fixed and variable rates for the borrower were discussed in paras 2.11–13. For the lender, an important advantage of variable rates is that short-term funds may be raised to finance long-term mortgage loans without exposure to risk from short-term rates rising, as occurred in the USA. Short-term funds are normally cheaper than long-term funds, and hence the borrower is also likely to benefit.

6.2   Variable rate loans may dampen the impact of interest rate movements (monetary policy) on the housing market and house prices, as potential borrowers will tend to view extreme levels of interest rates as being only temporary aberrations from normal levels, and will expect their interest commitments to adjust appropriately in the future. However, memories of repossessions, negative equity, falling house prices and two base rate rises announced on 'Black Wednesday' will be slow to fade.

Student Activity 4

1. What is a mortgage? *(Paragraph 4.1)*

2. What is the relevance of the Building Societies Act 1986 and the Banking Act 1987 for the provision of housing finance in the UK? *(Paragraph 4.3)*

3. What major Act does not apply to mortgage finance? *(Paragraph 4.3)*

4 List and describe the main types of mortgage loan. *(Paragraphs 5.1–12)*

5. What is the dominant form of interest arrangement associated with mortgage loans in the UK? *(Paragraph 6.1)*

6. What are the advantages and disadvantages of fixed and variable rate mortgage loans for borrowers? *(Paragraph 6.1)*

7. What are the advantages and disadvantages of fixed and variable rate mortgage loans for lenders? *(Paragraph 6.1)*

8. In what way might variable rate mortgage loans interfere with the implementation of monetary policy? *(Paragraph 6.2)*

7 Structure of UK housing finance

Table 10.4 Providers of housing finance in the UK, £bn outstanding, 1985 to 1995 (end year figures)

Year	Building societies	Banks	Insurance companies and pension funds	Public sector	Other financial institutions	Total
1985	97.2	21.1	2.7	5.4	1.0	127.4
1986	116.6	25.9	3.2	5.0	3.5	154.2
1987	131.6	35.9	4.0	4.6	7.5	183.6
1988	155.3	45.3	4.5	4.4	14.2	223.7
1989	152.3	79.2	4.5	4.3	17.4	257.9
1990	176.7	85.7	3.2	3.9	24.0	293.4
1991	197.6	90.4	2.9	3.0	26.2	319.7
1992	209.9	96.4	2.8	2.5	25.1	336.8
1993	217.7	108.5	2.1	2.2	22.7	253.2
1994	231.8	115.9	1.4	1.8	25.3	376.2
1995	223.8	139.9	1.2	1.5	24.2	390.7

Source: Financial Statistics, Central Statistical Office, Table 91J

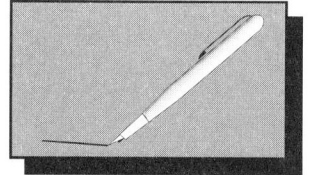

7.1   You can see from Table 10.4 that the dominant providers of housing finance in the UK are the building societies. At the end of 1995 they accounted for 57% of the UK housing finance market. At the beginning of the 1980s the building societies were very much more important in the market (80% of the total), and the second largest provider of housing finance was then the public sector. The retail banks were then only minor players. However, following deregulation of the financial sector, the banks rapidly became a major force in the market. By 1988, before the conversion of Abbey National Building Society to bank status, the banks' share of outstanding loans had reached 20%. By the end of 1992 the banks' share was 28% and by the end of 1995 nearly 36%. In August 1996, the Abbey National took over the National and Provincial Building Society, and five further societies plan to convert into banks or be taken over by a bank.

7.2   Specialist mortgage lenders funded entirely from wholesale sources first appeared in the market in the mid-1980s. By 1990 they accounted for around 10% of new advances, although more recently they have been badly affected by the downturn in the housing market, and have reduced their exposure to the market. Some building societies, seeking to expand in a depressed market, have bought the 'mortgage books' of some of these lenders, who have then withdrawn from providing mortgages.

7.3   In line with government policy, the public sector (mainly local authorities) is in the process of withdrawing from the mortgage loan market. Insurance companies and pension funds are also relatively minor players, having reduced their exposure to the market somewhat in recent years.

8   Competition in the UK housing finance market

8.1   Since the beginning of the 1980s, there has been a significant increase in the level of competition in the market for housing finance in the UK. Major factors influencing this trend were the:

- Removal of unofficial barriers to competition, such as the abandonment in 1983 of the interest rate fixing cartel by the building societies;

- Easing of monetary controls on retail banks;

- Enactment of the Building Societies Act 1986, allowing building societies to engage in a wider range of financial activities;

- Advances in technology; and

- Increased financial sophistication within the personal sector.

8.2   The main outcomes of increased competition have been:

- The end to mortgage queues, which were common before 1980, when building society head offices gave monthly mortgage allocations to their branches;

- Interest rates now reach market clearing levels (in 1990 they reached a new peak);

- Some upwards pressure on both mortgage interest rates and retail deposit rates initially due to excess demand for mortgage loans;

- Pressure for mortgage lenders to improve their efficiency and reduce their costs;

- Increasing innovation and product differentiation;

- Some backwards integration by mortgage lenders attempting to improve access to potential customers, (for example, via the purchase of estate agency chains); and

- Increased marketing and advertising.

8.3 Competition for market share was probably also responsible for an increasing proportion of the purchase price of property being covered by mortgage loans, and loans growing relative to borrowers' earnings. Together with squeezed profit margins, these developments increased the riskiness of mortgage lending in the late 1980s. The outcome has been clear to see during the early 1990s, with record levels of mortgage arrears and possessions. More recently, the weakness of the market has curtailed the excesses of free market competition.

9   Over-funding of the housing market

9.1 This is sometimes referred to as equity withdrawal, and relates to leakages of funds from the housing market. Basically there is controversy associated with this occurrence as mortgage loans, which have a privileged tax position, are used for purposes other than the purchase or improvement of residential property. Effectively, the consumer credit market is distorted as a state subsidy is inadvertently paid on one type of interest charges but not on others.

9.2 Leakages may occur when borrowed funds are used:
- to purchase a house owned by someone who has died – the beneficiaries of the estate may spend the proceeds as they wish, but the borrower, in this case, has genuinely used the funds for a house purchase;

- by an existing owner-occupier moving house, but where not all of the net proceeds from the sale of the initial property are reinvested in the newly-acquired property;

- for purposes other than the purchase or improvement of residential property, but where residential property is used as security (often as a second mortgage) – this is a genuine withdrawal of equity.

9.3 In the early 1990s, it seemed that unless the authorities either abolished tax relief on mortgage interest payments or introduced restrictive controls on the use of mortgage funds, there would appear to be little that can be done to stop this distortion of the consumer credit market. However, MIRAS is now only 15%, and positive equity has fallen because of the same factors which have created negative equity.

Student Activity 5

1. Describe the pattern of the provision of housing finance in the UK during the early 1990s. *(Table 10.4)*

2. In what ways has the pattern of housing finance provision altered since the early 1980s? *(Paragraphs 7.1–2)*

3. Where do the specialist mortgage lenders raise their funds for on-lending? *(Paragraph 7.2)*

4. What factors might explain the increased level of competition occurring in the market for housing finance since the beginning of the 1980s? *(Paragraph 8.1)*

5. In what way has the increased competition in the housing finance market altered the characteristics of that market? *(Paragraph 8.2)*

6. What factors contributed to the increased riskiness of mortgage lending in the late 1980s? *(Paragraph 8.3)*

7. What is meant by equity withdrawal from the housing market? *(Paragraph 9.1)*

8. Why is equity withdrawal less of a problem in the mid 1990s than it has been. *(Paragraph 9.3)*

9. Forty years ago, second mortgages were far less common than they were at the end of the 1980s. Assess the role that second mortgages might be playing in the 2030s. (Clue: consider inflation.)

10 Housing finance in the USA and Europe

Housing finance in the USA

10.1 In the USA, finance for owner occupiers began along the same lines as it did in the UK, except that the building societies are termed savings and loan associations (S&Ls or 'thrifts') in the USA. Also, the US legal system, based on common law, is similar to the English, although the statutes in the USA are different. Both thrifts and building societies indulge in maturity transformation – 'borrowing short' and 'lending long'.

10.2 There the similarity ends, however, because S&Ls have developed in a very different way to British building societies, many of which are becoming (technically at least) banks. The differences encompass:

● the way in which they perform the function of moving funds across the nation;

● interest rate structures.

10.3 In the UK, the movement of funds across the nation is achieved by very large building societies with virtually national coverage of large towns, and by permitting the larger societies to raise finance in the wholesale money markets, by means of PIBs, CDs, syndicated loans and Eurobond issues.

10.4 In the USA, this is achieved by thrifts selling parts of their mortgage books to outside investors. Thrifts are not permitted to have national branch networks. This US market is called the mortgage pass-through market.

10.5   The traditional mortgage in the UK has a floating rate of interest, so that lenders match their lending and deposit-taking rates. In the USA, the typical mortgage has a fixed or 'hard-to change' rate of interest, although thrifts have to pay short-term market rates of interest. However, US thrifts have an awesome problem – their interest rates can be mismatched, with lending rates below their deposit-seeking rates. This mismatch resulted in a severe financial crisis for most of them in the 1980s, after worldwide interest rates rose sharply to curb inflation. Finally, many of them had to be rescued, at enormous cost to the US taxpayer.

10.6   In effect, under the US system, high interest rates threaten the lenders (the thrifts); in the UK, high interest rates threaten the borrowers. The latter face repossession and negative equity, which are virtually unknown in the USA.

Asset securitisation

10.7   This technique, of which the US mortgage pass-through market is an excellent example, can be found in other countries. In the UK, for reasons mentioned above, there is no need for it, but it can be used by banks and other lenders to 'free up' HP or credit card debts and to increase cash flow.

10.8   Mortgage debts, however, are much larger than HP or credit card balances and so potential investors in collateralised mortgages, as they are also termed, prefer to see the debts insured or guaranteed by a reputable name.

Housing finance in continental Europe

10.9   In mainland Europe, there is a thriving mortgage market, but the lenders – specialised mortgage credit institutions, usually – do not engage in maturity transformation. Instead, they match the maturities of their mortgages by seeking finance in the long-term bond markets and not the money markets. This has the considerable advantage to borrowers that their rates of interest do not suffer from the volatility of short-term money market rates caused by the monetary policy operations of central banks. The stability also engenders a certain reluctance to buy and sell houses as frequently as the British do – 'trading up' is probably little known on the continent.

10.10   In France and Germany there are specialised mortgage lenders, with securities quoted on the stock exchange – the Credit Foncier and the Hypothekenbanken respectively. However, Germany does have financial institutions akin to the UK's building societies – the Bausparkassen. But, the resemblance is only superficial, because Germans do not have 'accounts' with the Kassen – instead, they have a 'savings contract' with one of them for a number of years, after which the contract becomes a 'mortgage contract' with that Kasse. Although operating in the retail financial market, the Kassen have long-term relationships with their members, who eventually receive a first mortgage of about 60% of the value of their houses, topping up the balance from their savings or from a second mortgage. There is no sign of the Kassen entering retail banking.

Transferable mortgages

10.11   These can be found in Canada and Denmark, and enable sellers of houses to sell them along with the mortgages on them; the buyers can buy both.

Student Activity 6

1. How does US housing finance differ from that of the UK? *(Paragraphs 10.1–7)*

2. Why does it seem unlikely that the UK will have a large market in securitised mortgages? *(Paragraph 10.8)*

3. Why didn't the UK have a mortgage finance crisis comparable to that in the USA in the 1980s? *(Paragraphs 10.5 and 10.6)*

4. What are the major differences between the UK's mortgage market and that commonly found in continental European countries? *(Paragraphs 10.9 and 10.10)*

5. How do Bausparkassen differ from the building societies? *(Paragraph 10.10)*

6. Give examples (and reasons) where the UK might benefit by adopting features found in the housing finance systems of other countries. *(Paragraphs 10.3 and 10.4)*

7. Assess the speed at which the UK may move towards the continental system of fixed-interest-rate mortgages. (Clue: look at EU monetary policy convergence.)

8. What problems with a transferable mortgage might face:

   (a) the lender

   (b) the buyer?

   (Consider: creditworthiness and size of debt.)

9. 'The continental *mortgagor* enjoys low interest-rate *volatility*, unlike the UK *mortgagor* and the US *mortgagee*.'

   (a) Explain the words in italics

   (b) Comment on the facts underlying the statement

   (c) Which of the three systems is the best, and why?

Summary

Now that you have completed this unit you should be able to:

- **describe the structure of the personal sector balance sheet;**

- **appreciate the sources and uses of funds for the personal sector;**

- **understand the financial risks faced by the personal sector;**

- **appreciate the broad nature of the UK housing market and the determination of house prices;**

- **appreciate the main types of mortgage loan and the associated types of interest payments;**

- **understand the nature of housing finance in the UK, in the EU and in North America.**

Self-assessment questions

Short-answer questions

1. What is the importance of company securities to personal sector financial asset holdings?

2. Which groups of financial institutions dominate the assets side of the personal sector balance sheet?

3. In what way did the sources of funds for the personal sector alter between 1988 and 1995?

4. List the main types of financial risk which members of the personal sector face.

5. What are the component parts of the net supply of houses for sale on the market?

6. What have been the main factors influencing the trend towards increased competition in the market for housing finance since the beginning of the 1980s?

Multiple-choice questions

1. Between 1988 and 1995 the UK personal sector:
   (a) moved from a position of record financial deficit to one of record financial surplus
   (b) persistently generated financial deficits
   (c) persistently generated financial surpluses
   (d) moved from a position of small financial deficit to one of record financial deficit
   (e) moved from a position of small financial surplus to one of record financial surplus.

2. Loans to the personal sector for the purchase of residential property:
   (a) are of minor significance to the activities of the retail banks
   (b) account for around 80% of all personal sector financial assets
   (c) are by far the largest category of debt on the personal sector's balance sheet
   (d) increased dramatically during the early 1990s
   (e) account for around 50% of all personal sector financial assets.

3. In relation to the UK housing market:
   (a) renting property from the public sector has largely disappeared due to the government's policy on home ownership
   (b) almost one half of all tenures are in the form of owner-occupation
   (c) the main form of support for owner-occupation provided by the government is via tax relief on mortgage loan interest payments
   (d) the recession of the early 1990s led to a substantial reduction in the level of home ownership

   (e) the most significant change since 1988 has been a substantial rise in privately rented housing.

4. Annuity mortgage loans:

   (a) involve proportionately larger amounts of the principal sum borrowed being repaid as the debt approaches maturity

   (b) have often been criticised on the grounds that they involve the payment of large commissions to lenders on the sale of the associated endowment (insurance) policy

   (c) involve only the commitment to pay interest for the term of the loan

   (d) have been the dominant form of housing finance in the UK in recent years

   (e) assist elderly people eke out their savings.

5. In respect of the provision of housing finance in the UK:

   (a) banks account for around two-thirds of the outstanding mortgage debt

   (b) insurance companies and pension funds withdrew completely from the market during the 1980s

   (c) specialist mortgage lenders (using wholesale funding sources) grew far more rapidly than any other group of providers of finance during the second half of the 1980s, but have since diminished somewhat in importance

   (d) the building societies accounted for less than a half of outstanding mortgage debt during the early 1990s

   (e) housing associations are the fastest growing source of housing finance.

6. A major outcome of the increase in competition in the housing finance market since the early 1980s has been:

   (a) a reduced need for lenders to differentiate their mortgage products

   (b) the elimination of mortgage queues

   (c) interest rates for borrowers being lower than they otherwise would have been

   (d) interest rates paid by mortgage lenders for their funds being lower than they otherwise would have been

   (e) the entry of foreign banks into the mortgage market.

Unit 11

Examination Questions

1. (a) What attributes must an asset possess in order to be considered liquid?
   [6]

   (b) To what extent do the following assets possess the attributes referred to in (a) necessary for them to be considered liquid?
   (i) Treasury bills;
   (ii) gilt-edged stock;
   (iii) bank notes;
   (iv) building society term shares;
   (v) certificates of deposit issued by a commercial bank;
   (vi) sterling commercial paper. [12]

   (c) Classify the assets set out in (b) according to whether they are included in the measures of money stock in the UK [7]

2. (a) Explain the basic role of financial intermediaries. [10]

   (b) Classify the main types of financial intermediary in the UK according to whether their liabilities are included in official measures of the money supply. [15]

3. 'Recent developments have led to a convergence between the activities of the clearing banks and the building societies, to the point where they are now identical as financial institutions.' Discuss.

4. (a) What are the basic benefits arising from financial intermediation? [12]

   (b) What do you understand by the term 'disintermediation'? [5]

   (c) Outline the clearing banks' response to challenges from the building societies in the area of financial intermediation. [8]

5. Discuss the effects of each of the following on a clearing bank's balance sheet and interest rates:
   (a) regulations concerning capital adequacy; [7]
   (b) the need for liquidity; [11]
   (c) an increased demand for advances. [7]

6. Discuss the role of the following in the UK financial system:
   (a) Treasury bills; [8]
   (b) Gilt-edged securities (gilts); [8]
   (c) Eligible commercial bills. [9]

7. Why and how does a bank raise funds in the following markets?
   (a) the retail market; [5]

(b) the wholesale market; [10]

(c) the capital market. [10]

8. (a) Explain why 'liquidity' and 'capital' are important to commercial banks. [10]

(b) Outline the basic principles of the Bank of England's current prudential controls relating to banks' liquidity and capital adequacy. [15]

9. 'The nature of the functions performed by the Bank of England are such that it would be both impractical and undesirable for them to be carried out by private commercial enterprises.' Discuss.

10. (a) Discuss the role of the parallel sterling money markets in London. [15]

(b) Is it still valid to distinguish the parallel markets from the discount market? [10]

11. Discuss the significance of the following in the UK financial system:

(a) the inter-bank market; [9]

(b) commercial (eligible) bank bills; [8]

(c) the London Stock Exchange, including reference to the changes introduced by 'Big Bang'. [8]

12. (a) What is meant by bank lending in 'eurocurrencies'? [7]

(b) Consider the impact of the following on the eurocurrency bank lending market:

(i) the debt problem of the developing countries;

(ii) securitisation;

(iii) liberalisation in the domestic markets. [18]

13. (a) Discuss the factors which determine the level of eurocurrency interest rates. [13]

(b) Why are changes in Eurodollar rates of importance to the foreign exchange market? [12]

14. (a) Discuss the factors which affect the level and pattern of money market interest rates in the UK. [13]

(b) To what extent do changes in money market rates lead to changes in commercial banks' base rates? [12]

15. (a) What is meant by the term 'yield curve'? [7]

(b) Examine:

(i) the factors which, in normal conditions, produce higher rates for long-term than for short-term maturities;

(ii) the relationship between short-term inter-bank rates and commercial bank lending rates. [18]

16. In seeking to achieve the ultimate objectives of monetary policy, the authorities can set intermediate targets.

(a) Discuss the intermediate targets that might be selected. [17]

(b) List the techniques that could be used to achieve these targets. [8]

17. (a) A country is experiencing a rate of inflation approaching 10% p.a.. Examine the likely effects on:

    (i) the functions of money; [10]

    (ii) interest rates. [5]

    (b) If a country's inflation rate is higher than that of its major trading partners, what will be the likely consequences for:

    (i) the exchange rate; [5]

    (ii) the balance of payments? [5]

18. (a) Outline the different techniques available to monetary authorities for controlling the money supply. [15]

    (b) Discuss the techniques for controlling the money supply which have been used in the UK since the early 1980s. [10]

19. (a) How can a government rectify:

    (i) a deficit on the current account of the balance of payments; and [12]

    (ii) a deficit on the capital account of the balance of payments? [8]

    (b) What is the purpose of a country's foreign exchange reserves? [5]

20. In the absence of official intervention in the foreign exchange market, what factors are likely to influence changes in a country's exchange rate? [25]

21. (a) Outline the main objectives of the European Monetary System (EMS). [5]

    (b) What economic conditions are essential for the objectives of the EMS to be achieved? [8]

    (c) Discuss the case for and against full UK entry into the EMS again. [12]

22. (a) Distinguish between a country's 'balance of trade' and its 'terms of trade'. [12]

    (b) To what extent can a government influence its balance of trade and its terms of trade? [13]

23. (a) Within the context of corporate finance, what is meant by the terms 'internal funding' and 'external funding'? [7]

    (b) Outline the main types of external funding available to a large company. [18]

24. (a) Outline the broad types of exposure to foreign currency exchange rate risk which a company may face. [12]

    (b) Explain how a company may use interest rate swaps as a means of managing interest rate risk. [13]

25. (a) What risks are faced by a company which borrows substantial amounts of long-term funds:

    (i) at a market-related rate of interest;

    (ii) at a fixed rate of interest? [12]

    (b) Explain how a company may use interest rate swaps as a means of managing interest rate risk. [13]

26. (a) In relation to the housing market, what do you understand by the term 'negative equity'? [5]

(b) What problems might the existence of negative equity entail for:

(i) an owner-occupier;

(ii) a provider of housing finance? [10]

(c) Discuss the main factors likely to influence the average price of new houses. [10]

27. Discuss the significance of the following for the UK personal sector's finances:

(a) building societies; [9]

(b) life assurance companies and pension funds; [8]

(c) company securities. [8]

28. (a) What are the main types of financial risks faced by a personal sector investor? [12]

(b) Describe the actions which might be taken by a personal sector investor in order to minimise the risks identified in (a). [13]

Appendix 1

Answers to Self-Assessment Questions

Unit 1

Short-answer questions

1. Gilts, equities, foreign exchange and money markets; the latter two markets will affect the first two, where much of my pension fund's assets will be invested.

2. Financial assets are the broader group, being assets which are expressed in money – dollars or euros. Money is any financial asset which performs the functions of a medium of exchange, liquid store of value, unit of account and standard of deferred payments.

3. The Chancellor of the Exchequer might raise base rate to reduce the rate of inflation; the exchange rate might fall as exports become expensive to overseas purchasers; prices of financial assets may fall. If other EU countries' inflation rates are unchanged, then the UK will be ineligible to join the single currency.

4. By calculating today's value (present value) of all the cash flows which the owner will receive from the financial asset.

5. Risk can be defined as the chance of returns from an asset being lower than expected – which can occur with property and farming. It is possible to philosophise that life itself is risky, which is why we take out life assurance policies.

Multiple-choice questions

1. (e)
2. (b)
3. (c)
4. (a)
5. (b)
6. (b)

Unit 2

Short-answer questions

1. A branch network; this could be superseded by more telephone banking and, next century, by having sites on the internet.

2. The fixed costs of the banks are much lower – both total fixed costs and average fixed costs.

3. Cash, cheques, bank giro credits, standing orders, direct debits, debit cards, CHAPS.

4. No.

5. They comprise about 70% of total assets and liabilities.

6. Opening their branches for longer each day, introducing more ATMs and telephone banking facilities, paying interest on current accounts, introducing more savings accounts and interest rate tiers.

7. Bidding for term deposits and making term loans, i.e. not usually sight deposits and loans.

8. Balancing the maturity, currency and type of interest rate (fixed or floating) of specific assets with comparable liabilities, e.g. if two-year loans in currency Z at fixed interest rates are (say) 4% of total assets, then 4% of total liabilities will be two-year loans in currency Z at fixed interest rates.

9. To act as a 'cushion' between the Bank of England and the rest of the banking system and, if necessary, to buy any unsold Treasury bills at the weekly tender organised by the Bank of England.

10. Because the Bank of England is prepared to lend them the funds they require but at a rate of interest of its choosing.

11. Sharp rises in interest rates have led to losses on their holdings of financial assets, so newcomers have been reluctant to become discount houses. Existing houses have diversified into other financial assets, such as SCP and leasing. Moreover, the Bank of England has instituted a system of repos directly with the banks which supply most of the houses' borrowed funds.

Multiple-choice questions

1. (c)

2. (a)

3. (c)

4. (c)

5. (a)

6. (c)

7. (c)

8. (c)

9. (b)

10. (c)

11. (b)

12. (d)

13. (a)

14. (d)

Unit 3

Short-answer questions

1. Borrowing and lending of short-term wholesale funds.

2. Discount market, together with the following parallel markets: inter-bank, CD, CP, MTN, intercompany, finance house and local authority.

3. Bank of England, the discount houses and the 100 or so commercial banks – both retail and wholesale – which lend very short-term money to the houses.

4. To keep short-term interest rates (a) stable and (b) at a level consistent with the government's monetary policy (which is largely interest-rate policy).

5. By keeping the houses short of funds.

6. To keep short-term interest rates in line with the government's monetary policy and to keep longer term interest rates low, so as to enable the government to borrow as cheaply as possible.

7. All transactions are unsecured and also because the Bank of England does not supply day-to-day liquidity to the parallel money markets.

8. The banks receive funds which are not repayable until the CDs mature; yet the purchases of the CDs can obtain cash immediately by selling in the secondary market.

9. Primary markets raise new money. Secondary markets enable owners of financial assets to sell them – they are markets in existing securities.

10. Gilt-edged securities issued by the Treasury, bonds issued by companies and shares issued by companies.

11. Undergo stringent vetting of its recent trading record and accounts by the exchange authorities.

12. An offer for sale involves inviting members of the public to buy the new shares. A placing is where a merchant bank or stockbroker buys all the shares for sale to its clients. Members of the public have to buy in the secondary market, using a stockbroker.

13. Share ownership has become concentrated among the pension funds and insurance companies, who have pressed for narrower dealing spreads and faster settlement.

14. It gave the institutions much lower dealing costs, especially in connection with overseas securities which are also traded on overseas stock exchanges.

15. Eurocurrency bank deposits are denominated in a foreign currency which is not the currency of the country of the bank where the money is deposited, e.g. US dollars deposited in a bank in Zurich.

16. Narrow interest-rate margins have attracted more depositors and borrowers to the eurocurrency markets.

17. Eurocurrency bank deposits are attractive to international companies because the interest rates are attractive and the companies do not have to

switch their holdings of foreign currencies on the foreign exchange market before and after making a deposit.

18. Borrowers are now corporates and governments in the developed world rather than governments of developing countries.

19. Because the deposits are very large, so that the average total costs of overheads are small for the banks and because central bank liquidity requirements are not so stringent.

Multiple-choice questions

1. (c)

2. (a)

3. (c)

4. (d)

5. (b)

6. (c)

7. (b)

8. (d)

9. (a)

10. (c)

11. (a)

12. (c)

13. (c)

14. (c)

15. (a)

16. (b)

17. (d)

18. (a)

Unit 4

Short-answer questions

1. Derivative markets give investors a choice of location as to the market in which they can change their portfolios They also act as 'price discovery' markets in which they form their opinions of the future course of prices. They need not attract speculators but, if they do, then the presence of speculators will increase the liquidity of the markets.

2. Derivative markets are exchange-based or OTC markets. Derivative exchanges are strictly controlled by the exchanges themselves, whereas OTC markets rely on self-regulation by the ISDA and prudential regulation of their members by the relevant authorities in the countries concerned.

The Baring collapse occurred because of poor internal controls within a participant in an exchange-based market and not in the market itself.

3. (a) The borrower can seek a fixed-rate mortgage from a lender who has purchased caps and collars so as to offer stable interest rates for some years ahead.

    (b) This is also called a 'money purchase' pension and its final value depends totally on the performance of the fund managers, who need to hedge the value of the assets in the pension fund. Index options could be used to achieve this.

    (c) Again, derivatives should be used by the fund manager to hedge the values of the assets in the life fund.

    (d) Unfortunately, unless the remittances are very large, the person in the UK is unlikely to be able to purchase the currency forward from his bank or buy a currency option on Canadian dollars.

4. (a) The primary market in gilt-edged securities comprises investing intermediaries whereas that in interest-rate swaps is likely to involve corporate borrowers and deposit-taking financial intermediaries (such as banks and building societies). The gilts market is exchange-based, whereas the interest-rate swap market is an OTC market.

    (b) The secondary markets in both financial instruments have similar participants as do the respective primary markets, except that the Bank of England is a much less active player in the secondary market for gilts.

5. An interest-rate agreement involves one party compensating the other if the reference rate is different from the strike rate, in return for an immediate payment.

    There are very few cash flows in the agreement. With an interest-rate swap there is a constant flow of cash between the parties, who also have additional borrowing which is being protected by the swap.

Multiple-choice questions

1. (a)
2. (b)
3. (a)
4. (e)
5. (e)

Unit 5

Short-answer questions

1. Under the Banking Act 1987 a bank must satisfy certain minimum criteria before it can receive authorisation. These criteria require that:

    (a) The bank's directors, controllers and managers are 'fit and proper' persons to hold such positions;

(b) The bank is effectively directed by at least two individuals;

(c) For banks incorporated in the UK, there must be as many non-executive directors as the Bank of England considers to be appropriate;

(d) The business is conducted prudently, with regard to liquidity, capital adequacy, foreign currency exposure, provisions for bad and doubtful debts, accounting and other records and internal management controls;

(e) The institution has net assets of not less than ECU 5m when authorisation is granted.

2. There are basically three ways in which a bank may ensure that it has sufficient liquidity to meet its obligations when they fall due:

(a) Cash and other liquid assets may be held;

(b) Assets may be matched with liabilities in respect of their maturity, so as to ensure an appropriate cash flow from maturing assets;

(c) The bank may seek to maintain a diversified deposit base and an appropriately high standing in the markets, so that it is able to attract deposits without undue cost, as and when required.

3. The BIS proposals specify risk weightings for assets held by banks, as well as the items which may be included in core capital and supplementary capital. It is required that all banks involved in international business must hold capital equal to at least 8% of their risk-weighted assets; and of this capital, at least one-half must be in the form of core capital. These proposals led to a tightening-up of the Bank of England's approach to capital-adequacy supervision, in the sense that formerly it declined to specify minimum standards which would be applied to all banks. Instead, the Bank had taken each bank on its own merits, and set trigger and target capital ratios on a case-by-case basis. The Bank still applies these ratios where they are greater than the minimum BIS requirement.

4. The closure of BCCI was followed by serious criticism of the role of banking regulators. It was argued that the standards of banking supervision in a number of countries, including the UK, had proven to be inadequate, and that as a consequence large number of depositors had suffered needlessly. Therefore, in response to this criticism a number of enquiries were set up, including one in the UK which led to the Bingham Report. Whilst this Report was not unduly critical of the Bank of England or of the basic system of banking supervision in the UK, it did make a range of recommendations for strengthening the supervisory framework and for enhancing the rigour with which regulatory requirements should be implemented. All the recommendations were accepted by the UK authorities, and most were acted upon quickly. A similar tightening of supervision was also recommended by bodies such as the EU Commission and the BIS.

5. The SIB is the Securities and Investment Board, which is at the heart of the regulatory mechanism for UK investment businesses, as established by the Financial Services Act 1986. The SIB has delegated powers from the Treasury in respect of the supervision of investment businesses, and in turn is able to delegate operational responsibility for day-to-day supervision to self-regulatory organisations each responsible for a particular sector of the investment industry.

6. No. Whilst the bulk of investment business activities are taken within the SIB structure, certain activities still remain the responsibility of other regulatory bodies. For example, the Bank of England is responsible for the regulation of the gilt-edged securities market, and the Department of Trade and Industry still has important powers in respect of the operations of insurance companies and unit trusts.

7. The Building Societies Commission has considerable powers in respect of the activities of building societies. In the first instance, societies must meet the Commission's criteria for prudent management if they are to obtain and then maintain authorisation. In addition, the Commission may issue directions to societies on financial restructuring if specified financing and lending ratios are violated; it may issue prohibition orders forbidding the provision of particular services by individual societies; and it may direct that advertising be amended or withdrawn if it considers it to be misleading.

8. The Department of Trade and Industry operates under the requirements of the Insurance Companies Act 1982 and has overall responsibility for the authorisation and supervision of insurance companies operating in the UK. The DTI has the power to grant or revoke authorisation for all types of insurance business; to stipulate solvency margins; to monitor the activities of insurance companies; and to intervene in their operation if necessary.

Multiple choice questions

1. (a)

2. (d)

3. (c)

4. (a)

5. (d)

Unit 6

Short-answer questions

1 This is because in order to calculate a real rate of interest from a fixed nominal rate it is necessary to deduct the concurrent rate of inflation. Even for a past time-period, inflation is measured using price indices which relate to particular samples of goods and services, and hence only provide an approximation of the rate of inflation for any individual. Therefore, it is only possible to obtain an approximate measure of the real rate of interest. For future real rates of interest the situation is even more problematic as it is only possible to work in terms of expectations, which means that there is additional uncertainty introduced into the calculation.

2 Money is irrelevant to the Classical theory, in the sense that it is held to determine only the absolute level of prices and does not affect the amounts of real saving or real investment (that is, the amounts of loanable funds supplied and demanded). An increase in the money supply will merely

raise the nominal amounts of saving and investment by the same proportion.

3   A term structure of interest rates shows the spread of interest rates that are paid on the same type of assets with different terms to maturity.

4   There are so many different rates of interest because there are so many different types of borrowing and lending transaction. Each transaction comprises a set of characteristics, such as the risk attached, term to maturity, tax implications, size of loan/deposit and so on. It is these characteristics which will determine the supply of and demand for the type of transaction and hence its price (that is, the rate of interest charged). Different sets of characteristics may lead to different prices for different transactions.

5   Risk;

Term to maturity;

Expectations of changes in interest rates;

Size of loan/deposit;

Interest rates elsewhere;

Expectations of inflation;

Tax considerations;

Marketability of the asset (where securities are involved);

Business strategy of financial intermediary;

Fixity of the interest rate;

Type of loan/deposit;

Government intervention;

Market imperfections.

6   Bank base rates will respond more quickly the narrower the bank's initial profit margin, the greater the increase in money market rates, the greater the expectation that the higher money market rates are to persist, and the greater the proportion of funds raised from the money markets.

7   The economic environment in the countries concerned;

Expectations of movements in exchange rates;

Actual and expected rates of inflation in the countries concerned.

8   Assuming that the increase in interest rates is a real increase relative to rates in other countries, it is likely that the exchange rate for sterling will be strengthened as 'hot' funds are attracted to the UK, and hence the UK's trading position will become less competitive. If elasticities of demand for traded goods and services are sufficiently high, the value of exports will fall as the value of imports rises, and the current account position will deteriorate. The main qualification to this result is that higher interest rates may dampen down domestic demand in the UK, and hence import flows may be held back.

Multiple-choice questions

1. (b)

2. (d)

3. (a)

4. (b)

5. (c)

6. (d)

Unit 7

Short-answer questions

1. It is generally agreed that all governments would like to attain the following objectives, a:

   (a) High and stable level of employment;

   (b) Low and stable rate of inflation;

   (c) High rate of economic growth;

   (d) Satisfactory balance of payments position.

   Individual governments may seek to achieve additional objectives depending upon their political stance: for example, in respect of income and wealth distribution.

2. A major problem in implementing economic policy is that the objectives may often conflict. Thus, for example, a policy designed to reduce unemployment by way of raising domestic demand may also cause the balance of payments to deteriorate (by sucking in imports) and may push up inflation (if bottlenecks occur in domestic production). Consequently, the authorities are likely to require a set of policies aimed at achieving a set of policy objectives. It is most unlikely that just one policy (say, of raising demand or reducing monetary growth) will cause all policy objectives to be achieved, especially in the shorter term. Different policies may, therefore, be aimed at achieving different specific objectives.

3. The importance attached to monetary policy within the government's policy package will depend upon the views it holds as to how the economy operates (and hence, as to the impact of the money supply on economic activity), and upon the priorities which the government has in respect of its policy objectives. For example, a high priority for the defeat of inflation from a government committed to monetarist principles will cause monetary policy to be applied to the single most important element of the policy package.

4. If the authorities attempt to control the supply of money, the free market demand will determine the price (the rate of interest). Conversely, an attempt to peg interest rates must mean that private-sector demand for money is accommodated, irrespective of its level. If the authorities attempt to control both the money supply and interest rates, this can only be done by overriding the free market mechanism; for example, by dictating to banks how much they may lend and at what rates. However, because individual potential borrowers are frustrated by these controls they are likely to seek out funds from channels not involving the controlled institutions. If the latter are limited in their lending, they have only limited

requirements for funds, and hence the rates they are willing to pay for deposits are likely to be less than potential lenders would hope for. Thus, the potential exists for disintermediation to occur. Borrowers and lenders may come together directly and funds may be exchanged at rates different from those ruling in the controlled sector. This also raises questions about the extent to which the authorities are actually controlling a meaningful money supply variable.

5. The rate of growth of the money supply;

    The level and/or structure of interest rates;

    Exchange rates;

    Credit creation by banks and building societies;

    Nominal domestic expenditure (or nominal national income).

6. Whilst cash is only a relatively small part of the money supply, it is a vital element of the reserve base for credit creation. Hence, if the authorities are able to limit the growth of the cash base they may be able to exert pressure on the growth of the money supply overall.

7. The major policy objective specified by the government has been the control of inflation. The results of policy in this respect have been somewhat mixed. Certainly the rate of inflation fell to relatively low levels during the middle years of the 1980s, but by 1990 the rate had crept back up towards the level which the government inherited in 1979. However, more recently the rate of inflation has been held at a relatively low level. Furthermore, until recently, the UK's rate of inflation has tended to remain above that experienced by the majority of its major trading partners.

Multiple-choice questions

1. (c)

2. (a)

3. (c)

4. (c)

5. (b)

6. (b)

Unit 8

Short-answer questions

1. London

    New York

    Tokyo.

2. A spot currency transaction takes place at the current quoted market exchange rate, and settlement must take place within two business days of the transaction. By contrast, a forward transaction relates to an agreement to exchange currencies before a future date (or between set future dates) at a premium or discount to the spot exchange rate.

3. An option forward contract gives the purchaser the option over when to deliver the currency (which is the subject of the contract) between the two set future dates. The option does not relate to whether the currency is delivered. The currency must be delivered at some point between the set dates at the agreed premium or discount to the spot rate.

4. The purchasing power parity theory states that the equilibrium exchange rate between any pair of currencies will only be achieved when the domestic purchasing power of each currency is equal. Where this is not the case, it will be worthwhile for traders to import goods and services from the country with the relatively cheap products into the country with relatively expensive products. The deterioration in the latter country's balance of payments is likely to push the exchange rate downwards; whilst the other country will experience an appreciating exchange rate. This adjustment will continue until purchasing powers are brought into line and adjustments in trade flows cease. The main relevance of the purchasing power parity theory is that it explains why countries with inflation rates persistently greater than their major trading partners' tend to experience steadily depreciating exchange rates. As the purchasing power of a given amount of domestic currency diminishes more quickly than in other countries, the exchange rate will tend to adjust under pressure from balance of payments flows.

5. The exchange rate of the country's currency is likely to drift downward over time relative to the currencies of countries experiencing balance of payments surpluses. Not only must a current deficit be financed period by period, with the obvious demands for foreign currencies from domestic residents, but also overseas suppliers of funds will begin to question the country's ability to service its debt, which is likely to grow (as reserves are finite). However, it should be recognised that, at least in the shorter term, capital inflows for investment purposes may be able to swamp the effect of the current deficit, and the exchange rate may be supported at its existing level or even pushed upwards.

6. A managed floating exchange rate regime attempts to combine the gradual adjustments in exchange rates which may occur in a clean floating system in response to changes in the underlying economic relationships, with the stability of rates which may be achieved when the authorities are committed to intervene in the foreign exchange markets to limit undesired fluctuations in rates. In the long term it is expected that market forces will determine the broad trend of exchange rates; however, the authorities are willing to intervene on a day-to-day basis to iron out short-term fluctuations which may undermine international business confidence.

7. As fixed exchange rates are held within their set margins by official intervention in the foreign exchange markets, the fixed rate system can only operate successfully if the required intervention is kept within manageable limits. This will only occur when the economic performances of the countries concerned converge over time. An especially important factor is the relative rate of inflation. If the countries concerned have markedly different rates of inflation, their relative international competitiveness will alter (with fixed exchange rates), balance of payments problems will probably arise and pressure will build up on the structure of exchange rates. As there are limits to any country's reserves and international

borrowing power, it is likely that sooner or later the countries with growing balance of payments deficits will be forced to devalue their currencies, thus violating the spirit of stability embedded in a fixed rate system.

8. All EU members are also members of the EMS, although some states do not participate in all aspects of EMS operations.

9. The ECU is the European Currency Unit. Currently, this is a monetary unit used mainly by EU institutions, which has a value calculated by reference to fixed quantities of all EU members' currencies. The whole 'currency basket' is valued daily against all major currencies.

10. The ECU is used in the private sector as a unit of account, recognising that its exchange value tends to be more stable than those of the individual component currencies. In particular, the ECU is used to denominate bank deposits, invoices, travellers' cheques, eurobonds and various types of loans and capital funding.

11. The Very Short-Term Financing Facility of the EMS is a scheme whereby the central banks of ERM members make available unlimited short-term borrowing facilities in their own currencies to other member states when their currency values threaten to breach the ERM margins. Repayment of these borrowed funds may be deferred if the borrower faces serious international repayment problems.

12. The successful operation of the EMS implies that members' exchange rates are stabilised and realignments of parity values are avoided. In order to bring this about, member states' economic performances must be broadly similar, and to this end it is likely that there will have to be general agreement on economic policy objectives and the means of achieving these objectives. In particular, policies will have to be aimed at bringing EMS members' inflation rates broadly into line at a relatively low level; interest rate differentials will have to be narrowed in order to avoid excessive international short term capital movements, and balance of payments imbalances will have to be kept to a minimum.

13. An increase in interest rates on sterling funds, other things being equal, is likely to increase the demand for sterling from investors wishing to take advantage of the more attractive returns. This will have the immediate effect of pushing up the spot rate for sterling on the exchange market against other major currencies, including the US dollar. In respect of rates for forward transactions, the premium or discount relative to the spot rate will depend upon the differential between interest rates on comparable funds denominated in the two currencies concerned. Thus, for a future sale of sterling for US dollars, any premium required (because interest rates on dollar funds are lower than those paid on sterling) will be raised, as the forgone interest earnings of the bank willing to sell the dollars will be increased; alternatively, if dollar interest rates are above comparable sterling interest rates, the increase in the latter will make the discount available fall (as the interest benefit to the bank selling the dollars at the future date will be reduced).

14. The main risk is that market rates of interest will fall, and hence that the fixed rate will prove to be high relative to the rate at which funds might have been raised. If competing companies have raised funds at floating

rates, the borrower with fixed rate debt has a competitive disadvantage when market rates fall.

15. Transaction risk;

   Translation risk;

   Economic risk.

16. A forward rate agreement is effectively a contract between a bank and a borrower (not necessarily from the bank in question), whereby the bank agrees to fix the rate of interest on an outstanding loan for a fixed period of time. Thus, a company may have a floating rate loan outstanding and may be fearful that market rates are about to rise. To protect itself it may negotiate a forward rate agreement which pegs the interest paid on the loan to a specified amount. If market rates rise above this value, the bank entering into the agreement will cover the excess interest cost; if market rates are below the agreed rate, the borrower will pay the difference to the bank entering into the agreement. The effect is that the borrower converts a floating rate debt into a fixed-rate debt for a set period of time.

17. The major limitations of forward rate agreements are that they are normally only available when the principal sum on which they are based is more than £100,000 and when the period of cover required is less than one year.

18. When an option to borrow at a specified rate of interest is taken out, the buyer has to make a premium payment to the seller. If, when the time comes around for the borrower to take up its funds, market rates of interest are below the rate specified by the option, it makes little sense to borrow by the exercise of the option (it is cheaper to go straight to the open market), and hence the option is allowed to lapse. Therefore, the maximum loss to the buyer of the option is the premium payment, which could have been avoided had it been known in advance that market rates were going to be so attractive at the time of borrowing.

19. A forward exchange contract is a contract between a bank and one of its customers, whereby the parties agree a rate of exchange for the sale or purchase of a fixed amount of foreign currency at a fixed future date or between two set future dates.

20. A European option relates to a right to buy or sell a set amount of foreign currency at a set future date. An American option may be exercised at any time up to a set expiry date.

21. Companies may engage in currency swaps to exploit imperfection in markets, whereby each can borrow in particular markets at different rates to those at which the other can borrow. Thus, a UK firm may wish to borrow French francs but may be charged a higher rate of interest than a French company wishing to borrow francs. Similarly, a French company may require sterling funds but may be charged more than a UK company for such funds. It may, therefore, make sense for the UK company to raise sterling funds and the French company to raise francs, and for the two companies to swap the funds and the associated servicing commitments. Companies are also able to manipulate the balance of their assets and liabilities in terms of their currencies of denomination by using swaps, thus hedging translation exposure.

Multiple-choice questions

1. (b)

2. (d)

3. (d)

4. (d)

5. (c)

6. (c)

7. (a)

8. (c)

9. (b)

10. (d)

11. (b)

12. (c)

13. (c)

14. (a)

15. (b)

Unit 9

Short-answer questions

1. Quite simply, acceptance credit facilities are available only if there is an underlying trade transaction to which the associated bills of exchange may be attached. Thus, raising money for general capital expenditure is not possible by this means. In addition, capital expenditure implies a long-term commitment of funds which should ideally be financed by long-term sources of funds. Acceptance credits are short-term financing instruments.

2. With secured lending the lender obtains a legal claim to realisable assets owned by the borrower. In the event of the borrower being unable or unwilling to service the debt, the lender may activate the security and force the borrower to meet his commitments by realising the assets in question. Where lending is unsecured, the lender has to depend upon the good name of the borrower and, in the event of default on the debt, cannot fall back upon a legal claim to property owned by the borrower. Therefore, secured loans normally attract a lower rate of interest than unsecured loans as the lender is less exposed to the risk of losses on the transaction.

3. Overdraft facilities are easy to arrange with simple documentation. Interest is charged on a daily basis on the closing debit balance. The funds are not tied to specific transactions, and hence overdrafts provide a useful source of working capital.

4. The main disadvantages of sterling commercial paper are the relatively

high minimum denominations (£100,000), the associated documentation requirements and the minimum net asset requirements (£25m) which may exclude many companies from the market. In addition, it is necessary to make fairly regular issues of commercial paper in order to establish a high market profile and maintain investor interest.

5. Preference shares give their owners preferential treatment over ordinary shareholders in their company's dividend payments and in the case of the liquidation of the company. Thus, in any given year, if dividends are to be paid preferential shareholders will be paid before any distributions are made to ordinary shareholders. However, the dividends on preference shares tend to be a fixed amount (when paid), whereas dividends on ordinary shares tend to vary with the company's profitability. If the company goes into liquidation, the proceeds from the sale of its assets are used, firstly, to meet the claims of creditors and only then to make payments to shareholders. Before ordinary shareholders can receive any payment the preferential shareholders must have been paid their due amount. Finally, whilst ordinary shareholders have voting rights at general meetings of the company, it is only in extreme circumstances (such as when liquidation is proposed) that such rights are extended to preferential shareholders.

6. Gearing measures the ratio of long-term loan capital to equity capital held by a company: the higher the gearing ratio the greater the amount of interest-bearing debt of a company relative to its share capital. Thus, the greater the gearing ratio, the greater the commitment for the company to make regular interest payments. Consequently, the stability of the company depends upon its being able to generate sufficient profits (before interest and tax) to meet these interest payments, and hence the company is in a more risky situation than if it had depended more heavily on equity finance (where dividends can be waived in times of low profitability).

Multiple-choice questions

1. (c)

2. (d)

3. (c)

4. (d)

5. (c)

6. (d)

7. (a)

Unit 10

Short-answer questions

1. Company securities are of great importance in the personal sector balance sheet. Around a half of all personal sector financial assets are in the form of company securities, although their value may fluctuate according

to market forces. Direct holdings of company securities are significant (around 10% of total financial assets at the end of 1992), but of much greater importance are indirect holdings via investments in life assurance, pension funds and unit trusts.

2. Non-bank financial intermediaries dominate the assets side of the personal sector balance sheet. Life assurance companies, pension funds and unit trusts are especially important.

3. Between 1988 and 1992 there was a substantial increase in the rate of saving in the personal sector. In 1988 the ratio of saving to personal disposable income stood at the historically low level of 5.6%; by 1992 it had risen to 11.6%. In 1988, 25% of the sector's sources of funds came from saving; in 1992 the figure was 74%. During the period in question there was a huge reduction in the flows of borrowed funds, with bank lending for purposes other than purchase of residential property largely collapsing.

4. The main types of financial risk faced by the personal sector relate to:
    ● Default
    ● Inflation
    ● Changes in personal financial circumstances
    ● Interest rate movements
    ● Changes in government economic policy.

5. The net supply of houses for sale on the market is the sum of:
    ● New houses made available;
    ● Houses vacated as a result of the owner's death, emigration or move to rented accommodation;
    ● Houses transferred from rental status, but not involving sitting tenants.

    The net supply is reduced to the extent that properties are demolished for slum clearance or redevelopment purposes. Houses placed on the market by owner-occupiers wishing to move have no net effect on supply, as they create an equal demand (albeit possibly for a different type of property).

6. The main factors influencing the trend towards increased competition in the housing finance market have included the removal of unofficial barriers to competition (such as the abandonment of the interest rate fixing cartel operated by the building societies); the easing of monetary controls on retail banks; the Building Societies Act 1986 (allowing building societies to engage in a wider range of financial activities); technological advances; and increased financial sophistication within the personal sector.

Multiple-choice questions

1. (a)

2. (c)

3. (c)

4. (a)

5. (c)

6. (b)

Appendix 2

Answers to Examination Questions

Question 1

(a)   An asset is said to be liquid if it can be realised quickly and cheaply and without capital loss or interest loss. The liquidity of an asset is a matter of degree, depending on how well it fulfils the criteria set out above. Cash is, by definition, the most liquid of assets and it acts as a benchmark against which other assets are judged.

Assets which are easily saleable may not necessarily be liquid. For instance, stocks and shares in major companies quoted on the London Stock Exchange are easily saleable, but their price fluctuates throughout the trading day in accordance with market conditions.

Assets which are close to maturity and which have a guaranteed price are liquid, for instance a gilt which is due to mature in one week's time. The original time between first issue and maturity date is irrelevant in this context. What matters is how long there is between the present time and the maturity date.

(b)   (i) *Treasury bills* The bills have original terms of 63, 91 or 182 days and will be redeemed at par on maturity. Being negotiable, the bills can be sold at any time prior to maturity at a price determined by market conditions. Clearly the price cannot be too far below face value because of the imminent redemption date. The bills are government guaranteed.

(ii) *Gilt-edged stock* Gilts are government guaranteed with original maturities of five years or more. Some gilts are undated. There is an active secondary market in gilts so that holders can quickly sell them for cash. Clearly, longer-dated and undated gilts are not liquid assets. Short-dated gilts become more and more liquid as redemption approaches.

(iii) *Bank notes* By definition, bank notes are the most liquid of assets since they represent immediate purchasing power. The attractiveness of their liquidity is undermined by the fact that notes do not pay interest, and hence there is no protection against the detrimental effect of inflation on this form of money as a store of value.

(iv) *Building society term shares* These are deposits with building societies which are committed for a fixed term. The deposits cannot be withdrawn on demand and there is no secondary market. These assets cannot be considered liquid on basic criteria, but as maturity approaches the shares may begin to be considered liquid, provided there is no interest penalty for early redemption. Nowadays, some societies allow premature withdrawals against an interest penalty. Although such a penalty would not involve a capital loss, such shares could not be considered as liquid.

(v) *Certificates of deposit issued by commercial banks* These instruments are issued with original maturities of between three months and five years. The certificates are negotiable and can be easily sold on the secondary market for the current market price. Certificates can be denominated in sterling or foreign currency. The liquidity of certificates of deposit can be considered to be similar to that of short-dated gilts (see above).

(vi) *Sterling commercial paper* These assets should be secure, being issued by quoted companies with minimum net assets of £25m. Thus the considerations are similar to those for Treasury bills, with liquidity increasing as maturity approaches. However, market prices on the secondary market could be affected by credit considerations at times of stock market uncertainty. This factor would not apply to Treasury bills. Hence, a Treasury bill for the same amount would always be more liquid than sterling commercial paper.

(c)   (i)   Bank notes: these are included in all monetary measures, including M0.

(ii) Gilts, Treasury bills and sterling commercial paper: these are not included in any of the measures of the money supply.

(iii) Building society term shares: included in M2, M4 and M3H.

(iv) Sterling certificates of deposit are included in M4 and M3H; foreign currency certificates of deposit are included in M3H.

Question 2

(a)   The most fundamental role of financial intermediaries is to channel funds between those who wish to lend (those with budget surpluses) and those who wish to borrow (those with budget deficits). It is important to appreciate, though, that financial intermediaries do *not* just act as 'agents' or 'middlemen', and that they are responsible for *transforming* the funds that pass through their hands, creating new financial assets in the process. An individual might, for example, deposit funds with a building society on the basis of seven days' notice of withdrawal; this deposit is an asset of the depositor but a liability of the building society. All or part of those funds may be on-lent to an ultimate borrower; in the case of a building society it might be for a period of 25 years. That loan is an asset of the building society but a liability of the borrower. Thus, the process of financial intermediation has led to a *maturity transformation of funds*. The ultimate lender holds a claim on the financial intermediary which is more liquid than the claim that the financial intermediary holds on the ultimate borrower; that is, the financial intermediary's liabilities are more liquid than its assets.

The ability of the financial intermediary to undertake the maturity transformation of funds is dependent upon the 'law of large numbers'. The financial intermediary uses its experience to show that on any one day the net withdrawal of funds will only amount to a relatively small proportion of total deposits. As a consequence, so long as adequate liquid reserves are maintained, the financial intermediary will be able to remain solvent whilst utilising a large proportion of its funds to purchase fairly illiquid assets. In addition, the law of large numbers allows the financial intermediary to spread the risk of on-lending between a large number of ultimate lenders. Defaults on interest payments and repayments of principal by ultimate borrowers are not attributable to any individual lender.

A financial intermediary also acts to aggregate the small savings of individuals into sums which are large enough to be of use to ultimate borrowers. On the borrowing side of a financial intermediary's business there are economies of scale in the collection and the interpretation of financial information in relation to investment opportunities. The ultimate lender effectively obtains a stake in a diversified portfolio managed by professionals. The borrower also gains through the easier access to funds, probably at a lower rate of interest than would otherwise be the case.

(b)   *Banking institutions'* liabilities are included in all currently used measures of the money supply, although for M0 only Bank of England Banking Department liabilities are relevant. Also, in respect of M2, it is only those deposits which constitute retail transactions balances which are included. Both sight and time sterling deposits are relevant for M2, M3H and M4. Bank sterling certificates of deposit are included only in the broad measures M3H and M4, whilst foreign currency deposits and certificates of deposit appear only in the M3H measure.

Building society sterling retail deposits and shares are included in M2. All forms of building society sterling deposits and shares and sterling certificates of deposit are included in M3H and M4, whilst foreign currency deposits and certificates of deposit appear only in the M3H measure.

The liabilities of *other non-bank financial intermediaries* (the most important of which are the long-term investment institutions; i.e. the insurance companies, pension funds, unit trusts, and investment trust companies) are not included in any of the currently used measures of the money supply. The deposits of finance houses and credit unions also do not feature in the money supply data.

Question 3

The activities of building societies prior to the early 1980s were largely restricted to attracting savings deposits from their members and other depositors on the one hand, and on-lending funds, in the form of mortgage loans for the purchase of residential property, on the other. The major reason for this very limited role of the building societies within the UK financial system was the restrictive legislative framework within which they were compelled to operate. A crucial aspect of this was their mutual status, and the traditional view that they were to be operated for the benefit of their members on a non-profit-making basis. In other words, the ethos of the building societies was not primarily directed towards commercial objectives, as was the norm for other major financial institutions.

The financial environment for the building societies began to alter significantly during the early 1980s when they began to find that they were being challenged, especially by the clearing banks, in areas of activity in which they had been the dominant force for many years. However, the event that brought about the major changes in the range of activities that building societies were permitted to undertake was undoubtedly the enactment of the

Building Societies Act 1986. This Act formally recognised that the building societies constituted a major element within the UK financial system, and attempted to provide them with a regulatory framework which would allow them to develop the provision of financial services for their customers, without losing their basic identity as savings and mortgage loan institutions. Indeed, if societies wish to undertake activities falling outside the provisions of the Act (as subsequently altered by amendments to Schedule 8 of the Act), they now have the option (with the permission of their members) of renouncing their mutual status and becoming public limited companies. Any building societies taking this option then operate within the same regulatory framework as the clearing banks.

It can therefore be seen that the natural evolution of the UK financial system, along with the changed legislative framework, has led to a marked convergence of the activities of banks and building societies in recent years. This convergence of activities has, however, been almost wholly in respect of *retail* personal-sector business (with the exception of the raising of wholesale funds where the building societies are subject to a 50% ceiling on such funds within their liabilities portfolio). As implied above, the clearing banks are now major providers of mortgage loans, although the building societies still dominate this activity; both banks and building societies offer a wide range of savings facilities; and building societies may now make unsecured loans (although the amounts which may be lent to individual customers and the amounts which may be lent in total are strictly limited); and they may provide a wide array of money transmission services, including full cheque book account facilities. Indeed, several large building societies are now members of the clearing system (formerly societies had no option but to operate through the clearing banks in this respect), and in many ways they are leading the banks in the provision of interest-bearing cheque accounts and cheque support cards with a larger guarantee value than is provided by some banks. On a broader level, societies now have the powers to take equity stakes in both life and general insurance companies; to undertake fund management; to establish and manage Personal Equity Plans and unit trusts through associated bodies; to take equity stakes in stockbroking firms; and to offer a wider range of banking and related services than was formerly the case. Therefore, as time passes it is likely that many societies will move even further into the areas of activity which have traditionally been associated with the clearing banks and other financial institutions.

It would, nevertheless, be quite wrong to suggest that the substantial convergence in the activities of the building societies and the clearing banks has led to them becoming identical financial institutions. There are still several quite fundamental differences to be found between the institutions, particularly in respect of wholesale/corporate activities and international transactions. Thus, whilst the building societies have only limited access to the wholesale money markets, banks have no specific restrictions applied to such operations; and neither are they limited in their ability to undertake transactions with the corporate sector or with overseas residents. Consequently, a large proportion of the clearing banks' overseas lending is to the corporate sector, whilst building society lending is almost wholly directed towards the personal sector. Also, the banks offer a much wider range of banking and related financial services to their much more diverse customer base. This is especially so if the clearing banks are defined to include their subsidiary and associated companies which operate within their group structures.

It should also be recognised that in respect of most activities the clearing banks and the building societies are regulated by separate bodies. The banks fall within the control of the Bank of England, operating under the provisions of the Banking Act 1987, whilst the building societies are regulated by the Building Societies Commission, which was established within the framework of the Building Societies Act 1986. It is only in respect of certain investment activities that both the clearing banks and the building societies fall within the same body of controls, as specified by the Financial Services Act 1986. As a result of these arrangements the specific regulations on liquidity, capital adequacy and so on tend to differ between the two groups of institutions, although in respect of activities which are similar within each sector it would appear probable that some form of harmonisation of controls will evolve over time.

The clearing banks and the building societies also differ in their legal status. Technically, all building societies are mutual institutions, whose objectives are not directed towards the maximisation of profits. The clearing banks are commercial companies with the need to meet their shareholders' requirements for dividends and capital growth. However, market pressures have been tending to push the building societies towards a greater recognition of operating efficiency, and many now place a great emphasis upon their ability to generate profits. In fact, as mentioned above, societies may now elect to alter their status to that of public limited companies. Once conversion has taken place, the institution will no longer be governed by the Building Societies Act, but must instead apply for authorisation from the Bank of England and become, in effect, a clearing bank. Several leading societies have shown interest in pursuing this line of development, arguing that the Building Societies Act 1986 still inhibits their ability to offer the range and quality of services demanded by their customers. In 1997, four large societies are expected to become banks.

Question 4

(a) The term *financial intermediation* refers to the activity of channelling funds between those who wish to lend (those people and institutions with budget surpluses) and those who wish to borrow (those with budget deficits). Most people think of financial intermediaries as including banks, building societies and the like, but it is important to understand that whenever an individual or institution undertakes, as a business venture, the channelling of funds between borrowers and lenders, then the process of financial intermediation takes place. This process forms an extremely important aspect of the modern financial system, and hence it may be concluded that it generates significant benefits for all parties involved and for society as a whole.

The major benefits generated by the financial intermediation process may be thought of within the context of its *key characteristics*:

(i) *Maturity transformation of funds.* It is often the case that the assets of a financial intermediary are less liquid than its liabilities. For example, the average maturity of deposits with a bank may be seven days, whilst the average maturity of its loans and investments may be one year. The bank is able to perform this maturity transformation by utilising the 'law of large numbers'; that is, because it has a large number of depositors it is able to estimate fairly accurately the maximum likely net withdrawal of funds on any given day, and hence it needs to cover only a small percentage of its total deposits with immediately liquid assets. Consequently, a large proportion of its funds may be used for long-term lending. The ultimate borrower benefits from having access to funds which are likely to be available for longer than would have been the case had they been obtained directly from the ultimate lenders, and the latter benefit from holding claims against the financial intermediary which are likely to be more liquid than had the funds been lent directly to an ultimate borrower.

(ii) *Risk spreading.* As the financial intermediary normally lends to a large number of individuals and/or institutions, any defaults on debt may be regarded as losses from the intermediary's overall portfolio of assets. The losses are not attributable to any individual ultimate lender, but are shared between all lenders supplying funds to the financial intermediary. However, such losses are normally absorbed within the operating margin of the intermediary, and so are rarely recognised by the ultimate lenders. Thus, there is a reduced risk for the ultimate lender, whilst the ultimate borrower will probably be able to raise funds at a lower cost than would have been the case had direct borrowing been necessary (with the consequently higher risk for the lender).

(iii) *Reduction of transactions costs and aggregation of savings.* As financial intermediaries usually operate on a large scale, they are able to take advantage of economies of scale in the accumulation and interpretation of financial information, to spread the fixed overheads often associated with financial transactions, and to employ specialist personnel capable of assessing the creditworthiness of potential borrowers and the earnings potential of available investments. Also, they are able to advertise their presence and so reduce search costs for both prospective borrowers and lenders. Indeed, as many lenders often have only relatively small amounts of funds available, financial intermediaries are able to bundle small deposits into amounts sufficient to meet the needs of ultimate borrowers.

The existence of financial intermediaries is also likely to generate *benefits for society as a whole*, through encouraging the lending of funds for innovative but risky projects which might otherwise not be able to elicit the necessary financial support. Thus, the economic growth of the nation may be enhanced.

(b)   *Disintermediation* refers to the situation where ultimate lenders and ultimate borrowers come together directly, and thus bypass the established channels of financial intermediation. There are two major sets of circumstances which cause disintermediation activity to occur:

(i) Where artificial *restrictions* are placed upon the free market mechanism (such as the application of monetary controls on bank lending), it is quite possible that prospective borrowers will be unable to raise the funds they require from financial intermediaries. These borrowers may be willing to pay higher rates of interest than are currently being charged by the intermediaries, and it might be possible for an ultimate lender to earn a higher rate by lending funds directly rather than by lending through a financial intermediary. This rate of interest must, of course, be sufficient to persuade the lender to forgo the benefits normally offered by the deposit of funds with a financial intermediary. The sterling intercompany money market was formed on this basis in 1969.

(ii) Where the ultimate borrower possesses a very *high credit rating*, it may simply be cheaper for that borrower to raise funds directly from ultimate lenders, perhaps via the issue of marketable securities. The evolution of the sterling commercial paper market provides a good example of this form of disintermediation.

(c)   The traditional role of building societies is the provision of long-term loans for the purchase of residential and other real property. A relatively small proportion of their assets has been held in the form of government and local authority securities, and hence they have also acted as financial intermediaries in this context. However, since the major provisions of the Building Societies Act 1986 came into force at the beginning of 1987, the building societies have had available the powers to extend significantly their financial intermediation activities, as well as the range of other financial services which they may offer. Of particular relevance is the ability of societies to make unsecured loans to customers, although initially the amount which could be lent to an individual customer was limited to £5,000 (this has since been raised to £10,000). In addition, the societies may now also establish and manage pension schemes, and through subsidiaries of associated companies establish and manage PEPs and unit trusts and engage in life and general insurance business. They may also offer investment services (agency broking, portfolio management and the provision of investment advice), trusteeship, executorship, land services (including estate agency and property development) and general banking services. When taken with their existing range of savings and current account facilities, it is clear that the building societies are now capable of providing a high level of competition to the banks over a broad front of activities, and especially in the personal savings and loans markets.

The banks' response to these developments has taken several forms and understandably has focused upon the maintenance of the personal customer base. In particular, the banks have broadened the range of savings facilities available and have improved the flexibility of access to funds, whilst offering more competitive interest rates. Interest-bearing current accounts are becoming increasingly common and various automatic overdraft facilities and free banking services have been introduced. Banks have also attempted to attack the building societies in their own traditional area of mortgage lending. Not only have they allocated large amounts of funds to this purpose, but they have also introduced various innovations, including fixed rate mortgage loans for fixed periods. In addition, the banks have become somewhat more aggressive in their marketing and advertising strategies, trying to acquire a more up-to-date and accessible image. There is now much more explicit recognition of customer needs, through longer opening hours (especially Saturday morning opening) and the provision of ATMs. Indeed, the banks have once again been seen to take the initiative in the implementation of computer technology.

Three retail banks have decided to buy building societies. In 1995, Lloyds bought the Cheltenham & Gloucester; in 1996 the Abbey National (itself only a bank since 1989) bought the National & Provincial and in 1997 the Bank of Ireland plans to buy the Bristol & West. Also, it can be argued that the merger of Lloyds Bank with TSB Bank at the end of 1995 was a response to competition in a stagnant personal finance market from the four societies planning to become banks in 1997.

Question 5

(a)   The capital of a bank is basically the difference between the value of its assets and the value of its liabilities. The capital base effectively comprises the bank's paid-up share capital and accumulated capital reserves, together with certain special forms of loan stock. Capital is vital for the protection of a bank's depositors from losses on assets (i.e. defaults on loans and capital losses on investments), and hence for the maintenance of confidence in the bank. The adequacy of a given capital base will depend upon the quality of assets held by the bank. The more risky are the assets held, the less adequate a given amount of capital will be in respect of protecting depositors. Conversely, the more risky are assets, the greater will be the amount of capital required in order to maintain a given level of protection.

The regulations as currently applied flow from internationally-agreed principles put forward by the Committee on Banking Regulations and Supervisory Practices of the Bank for International Settlements (BIS) in July 1988. These specify risk weightings for assets, ranging from a zero weight for cash through to a 100% weight for commercial loans, and define the balance sheet items which are acceptable as capital. The regulations require that all banks which undertake international activities must hold capital with a value *at least* equal to 8% of risk-weighted assets. Of this capital requirement, at least a half must be in the form of Tier 1 (or core) capital, which comprises shareholders' equity and disclosed reserves; the remaining capital is known as Tier 2 (or supplementary) capital, and includes revaluation reserves, general provisions, hidden reserves and subordinated debt. In the UK, these minimum requirements are applied to all banks, and the Bank of England has reserved the right to apply higher ratios to individual banks, depending upon the quality of their management and the nature of their operations.

Clearly, the above-specified capital adequacy requirements have important implications for the structure and growth of banks' balance sheets. The total of risk-weighted assets can only grow so long as there is sufficient capital to allow this to occur, although the book value of assets may be raised by switching to lower risk assets, hence reducing the risk weighting per unit of assets. If the bank does not wish to restructure its assets portfolio, and is already operating on the minimum capital ratio allowed, it can only expand its assets base by raising additional capital – either by raising more share or loan capital in the market or by ploughing back profits and thus increasing capital reserves.

The raising of capital funds involves a commitment to pay dividends or interest, and hence the bank's costs will be raised, thus putting pressure on profit margins. Indeed, if the bank decided instead to reduce the riskiness of the assets held, this would probably have a similar effect, as less risky assets also tend to be those which are less profitable. Therefore, in order to raise the level of capital adequacy, or to maintain the level in the face of balance sheet growth, it is probable that a bank will be forced to widen its interest rate margin if it is to maintain its profitability.

Thus, in order to generate extra profits, interest rates charged to borrowers are likely to be higher, and rates paid to depositors are likely to be lower than they would have been had the bank not been obliged to adhere rigidly to the capital adequacy requirements. The bank is also likely to take special care when considering making marginal loans to all but the most creditworthy of borrowers, as expected profitability will be vital for the internal generation of capital funds.

(b)   All banks need liquidity, in order to be able to meet demands from depositors for withdrawals of funds, inter-institution indebtedness, unforeseen borrowing requests from customers, and so on. The Bank of England requires that banks should manage prudently their liquidity positions, and the broad objective of current regulations is that banks should be able to meet their obligations when they fall due. The Bank of England does not specify formal liquid assets ratios, rather it lists the major types of obligations which banks must take into account (including sight deposits, time deposits, commitments to lend at a specific date, and unutilised overdraft facilities, where the timing of commitments is uncertain), and then specifies the various means by which these obligations may be covered. An important aspect of this liquidity cover is the holding of cash and other liquid assets, which has obvious implications for a bank's balance sheet structure. The types of liquid assets which are held, in addition to cash, include operational balances with the Bank of England, Treasury Bills, eligible bank bills, secured money with discount houses, inter-bank deposits and certificates of deposit. In addition, careful management of asset portfolios, such that maturities are matched, at least to some extent, with those of liabilities, is important to the maintenance of a satisfactory liquidity position. Finally, by maintaining a diversified deposit base and a good reputation within the financial markets, a bank will be able to raise additional funds relatively easily without undue cost, and hence will be able to supplement its liquidity if required. The Bank of England takes each bank on its own merits, and has to be satisfied that its total liquidity cover is adequate in the light of its particular operations and the management expertise which it has available. However, within this constraint, each bank is left to determine its own combination of approaches to liquidity management.

In relation to the effect on bank's interest rates, it must be remembered that liquid assets tend to pay lower returns than many other forms of assets, and hence the need for liquidity is likely to cause interest rates charged on loans to be somewhat higher than they would be in the absence of liquid asset holdings. Also, by limiting the extent of mismatch between asset and liability maturities, a bank is likely to forgo some of the benefits of maturity transformation of funds (i.e. borrowing short-term at relatively low rates of interest, and lending long-term, at relatively high rates), and hence may widen its interest rate margins so as to make good some of this loss. Indeed, in simply maintaining the quality of operations, and hence a good market standing, costs are likely to be incurred which will be reflected in the interest rates charged on loans and paid on deposits.

(c)   If a bank wishes to meet an increased demand for advances it may do this by running down holdings of other assets. Thus, it may have excess liquid reserves which may be turned into loans, although this may involve the need to sell short-term instruments with the associated risk of capital loss if funds are required immediately. Alternatively credit creation may take place on the basis of existing reserve assets, and this will inflate both sides of the balance sheet (a deposit will be created on the liabilities side to match the loan created on the assets side), at least until funds are withdrawn or transferred to other financial institutions.

In many cases, an increase in the demand for advances will necessitate the raising of additional funds by a bank. In the short-term, these are likely to come from money market sources, and especially via inter-bank deposits and issues of certificates of deposit. Clearly, this form of adjustment would cause both sides of the bank's balance sheet to grow. However, it must be emphasised that balance sheet growth would only be feasible if the bank held sufficient capital to support its larger portfolio of risk-weighted assets. Also, liquidity constraints would have to be borne in mind, and it might be necessary for the bank to hold some of its additional funds in liquid asset form. An increased demand for advances persisting into the longer term is likely to cause the bank to consider its strategy in the market for retail funds, and it may make positive efforts to increase inflows of funds from this source.

If the increased demand for advances was sufficiently large, it is probable that the consequently higher demand for funds from banks would push upwards wholesale money market rates, (and perhaps retail deposit rates in the slightly longer term). In turn, this higher cost of funds will put pressure on banks to raise their on-lending rates to borrowers. Thus, the overall effect is likely to be a general upwards movement in interest rates.

Question 6

(a)   *Treasury bills* are short-term marketable debt instruments issued by the Bank of England on behalf of the government. These bills are the main source of short-term financing for government sector budget deficits, and normally have original maturities of 91 days, although 63 day and 182 day bills are sometimes issued. The difference between the issue price of the bills and their (higher) maturity value is known as the discount on the bills, and this effectively measures the rate of interest paid on the funds borrowed. Technically, this source of funding is guaranteed for the government by the commitment from the discount houses to underwrite the weekly Treasury bill tender. Thus, if the competitive bids placed for a Treasury bill issue should fall short of the total amount on offer, the discount houses stand ready to purchase the unsold bills from the Bank of England.

In practice, most Treasury bills are held as risk free liquid assets by the discount houses, other UK banks and building societies, although some bills are also held by overseas central monetary institutions as sterling reserve assets.

In addition to acting as a government sector financing instrument, Treasury bills also play an important role in the Bank of England's money market operations. For example, if the authorities believe that there is an excessive amount of liquidity within the money markets, the Bank may seek to mop up the surplus funds via an issue of Treasury bills. The discount houses' underwriting commitment will ensure that the bills are always taken up by the private sector, and hence that the desired amount of funds is withdrawn from the markets. The consequent squeezing of banks' liquidity bases is also likely to place upwards pressure on short-term interest rates within the financial system. Conversely, when the authorities detect a shortage of liquidity in the money markets, they may seek to make good this shortage by repurchasing Treasury bills from the discount houses. In this case it is normal for the Bank of England to invite the discount houses to make offers for the sale of bills. If the prices (rates of discount) offered by the discount houses are compatible with the Bank's unpublished band for officially desired short-term interest rates, the offers will be accepted by the Bank, and funds will be pumped into the markets in exchange for the bills. Rejection of offers will naturally lead to upwards pressure on short-term interest rates. Therefore, by manipulating its sales and repurchases of Treasury bills, the Bank of England is able to influence both the liquidity of the financial system and the level of short-term interest rates. However, it should be noted that, in recent years, whilst Treasury bills have often been used for this purpose, the Bank has tended to concentrate its intervention operations on eligible commercial (bank) bills.

(b) *Gilt-edged securities* are long-term marketable debt instruments issued by the Bank of England, via a network of primary dealers, on behalf of the government. Gilts provide by far the most important source of borrowed funds for the government sector, and have original maturities normally in the range of 5 to 25 years; although several issues of undated gilts are currently in circulation. Gilts guarantee a fixed annual coupon (interest) payment, and may be issued at prices different to their maturity value. There have also been several issues of index-linked gilts, which have nominal maturity values related to a price index, and which guarantee a fixed real interest payment on the index-linked capital value. The attractive default-free characteristics of gilts have, for many years, ensured their position as a major element in the asset portfolios of UK investment institutions, such as insurance companies and pension funds. They are also popular investments with individuals and with the overseas sector.

The importance of gilts for the financing of Public Sector Borrowing Requirements (PSBRs) cannot be overemphasised. For not only are gilts the main instrument of financing, but also purchases by the non-bank non-building society private sector have a neutral impact on money supply growth, and hence effectively support the implementation of monetary policy. If the government was unable to sell sufficient gilts to this particular sector of the economy, it would be forced to borrow from banks or building societies, or from the Bank of England, which would have an immediate impact on money supply growth.

During the period 1987 to 1991 the UK government ran budget surpluses. Wherever possible, the Bank of England undertook 'full funding' of these surpluses by making repurchases of gilts from the non-bank non-building society private sector. In effect, these repurchases allowed the authorities to recycle the surplus funds back to the private sector, thus avoiding any net impact on the money supply or the liquidity base of the banking sector.

(c) A *commercial bill* is a bill of exchange which is issued as the counterpart to a commercial transaction. The vendor of goods may be willing to allow the purchaser a period of credit before making payment. Thus, the vendor may issue a bill of exchange which will be accepted by the purchaser of the goods, who effectively promises to pay the amount due on a specified future date. The vendor of the goods could then simply hold this bill until its maturity date, at which time (it is hoped) the purchaser will make the appropriate payment. However, the vendor might wish to obtain funds before the date of maturity of the bill. In which case the bill may be discounted, i.e. the bill may be sold to a third party, for an amount below the maturity value of the debt. (The difference between the maturity value and the discounted value reflects the implicit interest payment on the funds locked away in the debt.) The discounting process will be made easier and the rate of discount reduced, if the bill is accepted (underwritten) by a reputable bank. Effectively, for a fee, the bank will guarantee the payment of the amount outstanding on the bill at the maturity date.

Upon acceptance by a bank, the commercial bill becomes a commercial bank bill. If the bank happens to be classified as an eligible bank, the bill becomes an *eligible commercial (bank) bill*. As eligibility status is only endowed upon banks which meet minimum criteria laid down by the Bank of England (in respect of the quality of their acceptance business, their market standing, and, for foreign banks, the treatment of UK banks in the relevant overseas market), eligible bills command very fine rates of discount. This position is further enhanced by the fact that eligible bills are rediscountable at the Bank of England.

Whilst eligible bank bills serve a useful function in respect of the short-term financing of trade and commerce, it may be argued that their greatest importance relates to the operation of official monetary controls. It is primarily through dealings in such bills that the Bank of England smooths cash flows between the public and private sectors of the economy, and through which it may seek to influence short-term interest rates. Thus, for example, if there is a shortage of liquidity on the money markets (perhaps resulting from tax payments being in excess of government expenditures), the Bank of England will announce its estimate of the extent of the shortage, and invite the discount houses to make offers to it for the sale of bills. If the rates of discount offered to the Bank are compatible with its undisclosed band for desired short-term interest rates, the offers will be accepted, the bills will be purchased by the Bank, and the liquidity shortage will be relieved. The rates at which offers are accepted or rejected provides a signal to the markets as to the level of short-term rates desired by the authorities. By accepting or rejecting offers as appropriate, the Bank is able to put pressure on interest rates to bring them into line with its policy objectives. As the bills held by the Bank mature, funds are drawn out of the private sector, and this provides a useful channel (along with sales of Treasury bills) for mopping up excess liquidity in the markets. The bills involved in these transactions are largely eligible bank bills, and in recent years bills falling within maturity bands 1 and 2 (up to 33 days to maturity) have dominated.

Question 7

(a)   Retail banks raise funds in the *retail market* in order to finance their lending activities. As these funds are normally raised from a large number of personal and small business customers, the banks are also likely to attempt to develop the business relationships formed as a basis for marketing other banking products and services. The opportunity to cross-sell insurance and investment products, plastic card-based credit and payments services, financial advice, and so on, is seen as being of great importance to the prosperity of retail banks in the increasingly competitive business environment.

In order to attract retail funds, the banks offer a range of current and savings accounts for customers. Current accounts are characterised by their associated money transmission services, with the traditional cheque book, direct debit and standing order facilities increasingly being supplemented by various forms of plastic card-based electronic payments mechanisms. Many current accounts now also pay interest on credit balances, which provides a further attraction for depositors. Indeed, in recent years, the distinction between current and savings accounts has become increasingly blurred. At the same time, the variety of terms, conditions and interest returns on savings accounts has been extended significantly in an attempt to meet the needs of the widest possible range of retail savers.

The retail banks have been helped in their task of raising retail funds by being able to utilise their extensive branch networks. The convenient location of branches in major centres of population and business activity and their increasingly extended opening hours have been an important competitive factor in being able to tap the retail market. The spread of ATMs, and the introduction of telephone banking facilities, are of increasing importance.

(b)   Banks may use the *wholesale market* to raise funds for lending. For retail banks, such funding may be seen as supplementing their retail market sources; for wholesale banks undertaking no retail operations, the wholesale market is their sole source of funding for lending. The nature of wholesale funds means that they are used extensively by all types of banks in respect of liquidity management operations. Wholesale term deposits, ranging in maturity from overnight upwards, may be raised quickly at competitive market rates, thus allowing banks to maintain a prudent balance of maturities within their assets and liabilities portfolios. The raising of foreign currency denominated funds on the eurocurrency markets also allows banks to manage their foreign currency exposure, and hence minimise the risk which might otherwise arise from unexpected movements in currency exchange rates.

A major source of wholesale funds is the parallel sterling money markets. In particular, fixed term borrowing on the inter-bank market and the issue of sterling certificates of deposit (£CDs) on the primary CD market are of great significance to UK banks. Inter-bank borrowing may also take place on the eurocurrency markets where foreign currency funds are required, and various forms of foreign currency denominated marketable instruments may be issued on the relevant eurocurrency market.

Banks may also raise funds by selling part of their holdings of marketable securities. For example, holdings of £CDs, issued by other financial institutions, may be sold on the secondary CDs markets, or eurocurrency instruments may be sold on the relevant secondary eurocurrency market. Alternatively, holdings of commercial or Treasury bills may be sold on the discount market, and the discount houses may be willing to make secured loans to clearing banks wishing to raise short-term funds.

(c)   The capital of a bank may be defined as the value of its net assets (i.e. total assets less total liabilities). The capital base effectively comprises the bank's paid up share capital, its accumulated capital reserves, and, under certain circumstances, issues of hybrid debt/equity instruments such as subordinated loan stock. A bank may raise funds in the *capital market* as a means of contributing to its capital base, which is vital for the protection of its depositors, and hence for the maintenance of general confidence in its operations, and for the underpinning of its long-term stability and growth. If the bank suffers from defaults on advances or incurs losses on investments, these will reduce the value of net operating profits. However, large provisions for bad debt may be greater than the concurrent gross operating profits of the bank, and hence the excess loss will have to be absorbed by the bank's capital base. In other words it is the bank's shareholders who incur the loss (through reduced capital reserves, as well as lower dividends), rather than the bank's depositors.

The adequacy of any given capital base depends not only upon the absolute volume of assets to be covered, but also is affected by the quality of the bank's assets. Thus, the more risky are the assets, the greater must be the cushion of capital funds, other things being equal, in order to maintain a given level of capital adequacy. It should be recognised that official requirements in respect of capital adequacy are laid down by the Bank of England, in compliance with the Basle Agreement on capital standards and relevant EU Directives. Basically, in order to maintain authorisation to operate in the UK, a bank must hold capital equal in value to at least 8% of its risk-weighted assets, (with the weights attaching to each category of assets being specified by the authorities). At least a half of this minimum capital requirement must be in the form of Tier 1 (core) capital, which comprises ordinary paid-up share capital plus disclosed reserves. The remaining capital, termed Tier 2 (supplementary) capital, may comprise undisclosed reserves, asset revaluation reserves, general provisions and hybrid debt/equity instruments (including subordinated loan stock).

A bank may add to its capital base, and hence, other things being equal, raise its capital adequacy, by issuing equity shares on the capital market. If the bank is making a public issue of shares for the first time in the UK it may float the shares on the London Stock Exchange. Alternatively, a rights issue of shares may be made to existing shareholders. In addition to ordinary shares, a bank may issue other types of equity, such as preference shares or convertible preference shares, but for official regulatory purposes the precise nature of the equity will be of importance. As stated above, only ordinary paid-up share capital is included in Tier 1; preference share capital is included in Tier 2. The capital market may also be used for the issue of hybrid debt/equity instruments including loan stock, which will bolster Tier 2 capital so long as it meets the specified official requirements.

Question 8

(a)   The liquidity of a commercial bank relates to its ability to meet its obligations as they fall due. An important factor in this respect is the broad structure of its assets portfolio, although the liquidity position of the bank involves its general ability to raise new funds and its expected future cash flows from maturing assets.

Banks require adequate liquidity, relative to their commitments, in order to maintain the confidence of their customers (particularly their depositors) and their shareholders. The specific reasons for banks requiring liquidity include: the need to be able to cover withdrawals of funds by customers; to meet interbank indebtedness, which may arise on a day-to-day basis following the payments clearing process; to be able to meet any unforeseen borrowing requests from customers; and to be able to cope with interruptions to their normal cash inflows. In addition to these commercial factors, there are also official requirements laid down by the Bank of England in respect of banks' liquidity positions.

The capital of a commercial bank may be defined as the value of its net assets (that is, total assets less total liabilities). The capital base normally comprises the bank's share capital, various forms of accumulated capital reserves and certain types of subordinated loan stock.

The capital base of a bank is vital for the protection of its creditors (its depositors) and hence for the maintenance of general confidence in its operations and the underpinning of its long-term stability and growth. If the bank suffers from defaults on advances or incurs losses on investments these will reduce the value of operating profits. However, large provisions for bad debts (for example, those which have arisen for many banks as a result of corporate failures, and especially those relating to property loans in the early 1990s) may be greater than the concurrent operating profits of the bank, and so these excess losses will have to be absorbed by the bank's capital base. In other words, it is the bank's shareholders who incur the loss (through reduced capital reserves, as well as through lower dividends) rather than the bank's depositors.

The adequacy of any given capital base depends not only upon the absolute volume of liabilities to be covered, but is also affected by the quality of the bank's assets. Thus, the more risky the assets, the greater must be the cushion of capital funds, other things being equal, to maintain a given level of capital adequacy. It should also be recognised that official requirements for capital adequacy are laid down by the Bank of England, within the provisions of the Banking Act 1987, and so capital adequacy is necessary for a bank to obtain and keep its authorisation to operate.

(b) The Bank of England's current prudential controls on banks' liquidity have the broad objective that institutions should be able to meet their obligations when they fall due. In this context, banks' major obligations are their sight deposits, time deposits, commitments to lend at a specific date and unutilised overdraft facilities. Institutions are expected to be able to cover demands for funds made in respect of these obligations by one or more of three means: by holding cash or other liquid assets; by careful asset-management designed to provide an appropriate cash flow from maturing assets; or by the maintenance of a diversified deposit base which allows funds to be raised quickly and without undue cost.

The basic principle of liquidity controls is one of *self-regulation* by institutions, so that, having established the broad guidelines for the evaluation of the quality of assets and for the classification of liabilities, the Bank of England leaves it to the individual institution to select the combination of assets and liabilities which it believes to be optimal, given its own commercial objectives. In order to ensure adequate liquidity, the management of an institution may choose any combination of the above-mentioned approaches. However, as all banks are required to make regular accounting returns to the Bank of England and senior managers of all banks are required to meet with Bank supervisors on a regular basis, the Bank is able to monitor closely the adequacy of liquidity management. If it is felt that an institution is not pursuing appropriately prudent liquidity management policies it will undoubtedly be warned by the Bank. Failure to act on such a warning risks the suspension of its authorisation, and hence its ability to continue in business.

Since the enactment of the Banking Act 1979 the Bank of England has had a legal duty to regulate the capital adequacy of banking institutions and this duty was strengthened by the 1987 Act. However, it was only towards the end of the 1980s that the Bank first stipulated a common minimum level of capital adequacy which must be met by all authorised banking institutions. Before that time there was no general minimum requirement, and each bank was dealt with separately on its own merits.

Throughout the 1980s the Bank's approach to measuring capital adequacy was to evaluate the various risks attached to a bank's assets portfolio, and then to *weight the portfolio according to its riskiness*. The more risky the assets held, the greater the weight given to the assets, and hence the larger the amount of capital required in order to maintain a given degree of capital adequacy. The Bank also provided a clear definition of the items which could be included within the capital base for regulatory purposes. Consequently, the control regime laid down strict parameters for the treatment of particular assets and capital items, but it left the Bank of England with the flexibility to set *specific ratios of capital to risk-weighted assets for individual banks*, reflecting its assessment of each bank's capacity to manage its risk position, profitability and general prospects.

To a large extent the Bank of England has maintained its established approach to the supervision of capital adequacy into the 1990s. However, the UK's acceptance of the proposals on the *harmonisation of capital adequacy standards*, put forward by the Committee on Banking Regulations and Supervisory Practices of the Bank for International Settlements (BIS) in July 1988, has led to the introduction of a more *rigorously defined framework* and the publication of *minimum required capital ratios* for all banking institutions. Indeed, most of the western world's major central banks agreed to implement the BIS capital adequacy convergence proposals by the end of 1992. Strictly, these proposals relate only to banks which are internationally active, but the Bank of England is applying them as a common standard to all authorised banks in the UK.

Question 9

The Bank of England performs three broad functions:

(a) provision of banking services;

(b) implementation of monetary controls;

(c) application of regulatory controls.

The Bank of England provides a range of conventional banking services to its customers, but it should be noted that the customer base is significantly different from that of the typical commercial bank. In particular, the Bank of England:

(a) holds the accounts of the central government and other public authorities, and has responsibility for ensuring that budget deficit financing requirements are satisfied, and for organising national debt management activities;

(b) holds accounts for overseas central banks and monetary institutions, and may provide assistance with international borrowing and lending activities, administer payments arising from official exchange market intervention, and so on;

(c) acts as banker to the commercial banks and largest building societies, holding deposits which may be used to cover inter-institution transactions resulting from payments-clearing operations.

The Bank of England does have a number of private non-bank, non-building society customers, but these constitute a fairly insignificant part of the total banking activity undertaken. And the view generally taken is that these accounts are not provided for commercial reasons but rather to help the Bank appreciate the type of problems which might be faced by the commercial banks for which it has supervisory responsibility.

The implementation of monetary controls represents an extremely important element of the Bank of England's functions since it is the means by which the government's monetary policy objectives are achieved. Clearly, when those objectives are monetarist in nature, the efficiency of the Bank of England in achieving strict control of the money supply is crucial to the success of the government's policy. However, even for a more pragmatic use of monetary policy, perhaps in support of other elements of the economic policy package, the Bank's role is still of great importance. The Bank may attempt to influence the money supply and/or interest rates through the use of market means (such as open-market operations and the manipulation of the rate of interest which it effectively charges on funds lent to the banking sector), or it may use non-market methods (perhaps involving the setting of minimum liquid reserve requirements or interest rate ceilings on deposits or qualitative lending guidelines, etc.). It should also be recognised that the Bank of England is likely to participate in the formulation of the details of monetary policy, providing the government with the relevant banking and monetary data as well as with its expert advice on the progress of monetary policy.

The third broad function of the Bank of England is to supervise the operations of the banking sector. In addition to providing a safeguard for the banks' depositors against imprudent on-lending activities, the Bank of England's overall objective is to maintain confidence in the financial system.

In addition to the three major functions identified above, the Bank of England also has responsibility for:

(a) issuing bank notes within England and Wales;

(b) intervention in the foreign exchange markets, to smooth or to peg exchange rates;

(c) liaison with overseas central banks and monetary institutions, in relation to international banking and finance matters.

Whilst some of the less important roles of the Bank of England might be performed effectively by a variety of private sector institutions, it is likely to be impractical for the majority of the functions to be dealt with in this way. The legal powers which would be required by a private institution to control or even to influence the activities of other private sector institutions, whether for monetary or regulatory purposes, would in many respects turn that institution into a central bank in all but name. Also, there is the problem that the majority of private financial institutions operate to make profits, and this could cause serious conflicts of interest to arise. For example, an operation which might be deemed necessary in the national interest might be extremely unattractive commercially, and perhaps would not be undertaken unless appropriate remuneration was received from the government. In fact, the whole notion of endowing extensive legal powers on a commercial enterprise would appear to be totally impractical and of dubious merit. Indeed, as many of the activities of the central bank may be both economically and politically sensitive (domestically and/or internationally), clear policy guidelines would have to be enforced by the central government. It would be most undesirable that the commercial considerations of a private-sector enterprise be allowed to impinge on the execution of important public duties. Furthermore, all this assumes that private institutions would be willing and able to take on such activities. The prospect of continual government interference in the carrying out of specific tasks would probably dissuade many institutions from becoming involved at all. Insufficient resources would also limit the number of institutions capable of carrying out many of the Bank of England's functions.

None the less, it might be possible for some of the Bank of England's functions to be carried out by private institutions. For example, provision of banking services for overseas monetary institutions and governments might be feasible, although only the largest of the commercial banks would probably wish to engage in this activity. Bank note issue and printing might also be undertaken by a private body, but there would have to be controls in order to protect the general public from exploitation. However, it is most improbable that the monetary policy and banking regulatory functions could be performed effectively by bodies other than the Bank of England. The government requires a direct link to the private financial sector which is both independent of commercial profit-making pressures and which puts the nation's interests before its own. In reality, an established and respected central bank such as the Bank of England is often able to execute its duties without explicit use of its legal powers (which are held very much in the background), relying instead on the voluntary co-operation of the institutions under its control.

Question 10

(a)   The parallel sterling money markets in London are one component of the London money markets. All money-market activity relates to short-term, wholesale borrowing and lending transactions. In sterling markets, the minimum transaction is normally in the region of £50,000 to £100,000, with the term to maturity of loans or debt instruments rarely being in excess of one year, and often being for periods of three months or less. Transactions in the parallel markets are unsecured, and consequently the lender has to depend upon the good name of the borrower. As a result, there tends to be a somewhat greater risk attached to lending in the parallel markets than in the (secured) discount market.

The parallel markets have been continually evolving since their commencement in the mid-1950s, and significant developments have taken place since the early 1980s. One of the important characteristics of the markets has been their ability to react quickly to the requirements of actual and potential participants and to provide facilities which have often been denied to them in more conventional banking channels. In this context, official controls and restrictions placed on normal bank lending have been an important catalyst to the growth of the markets. It should also be recognised that whilst it is usual to talk of a number of separate parallel markets, in practice many institutions are active in several markets simultaneously and hence funds tend to flow quite freely between different market segments. Identifying the separate markets is, however, useful since they fulfil individual specialist roles.

The *inter-bank market* is probably the most important of the parallel sterling money markets, due to its large size and its position within the financial system. This market serves to smooth the fluctuations in banks' cash flows, providing banks with a convenient means of adjusting their day-to-day liquidity positions. Thus, banks with surplus short-term funds are often willing to lend them to other banking institutions through the inter-bank market. Interest rates tend to be marginally greater than those earned on funds placed on the discount (primary) market, in recognition of the additional risks involved. The market also acts as an indicator of general trends in interest rates, in particular through the three-month London Inter-Bank Offered Rate (LIBOR). This rate is used as a measure of the cost of marginal funds to an individual bank, and hence changes in its value have important implications for the setting of rates on bank lending. LIBOR has a strong influence on movements in bank base rates, and so ultimately on the trend in mortgage and other longer-term rates.

The major role of the *sterling certificates of deposit market* is to provide the banking sector with an important alternative source of wholesale funds. Sterling CDs are negotiable bearer securities issued by banks in amounts ranging from £50,000 up to £1m, and are normally for terms ranging from twenty eight days to five years. Sterling CDs provide a useful way for the issuing bank to raise large sums of money for fixed periods at fixed rates of interest, thus reducing risk in portfolio management operations. Margins are very competitive and flows of funds tend to be sensitive to small changes in interest rates paid. Technically, the banks issuing the sterling CDs form the primary market in these instruments, whilst institutions which deal in issues, irrespective of whether or not they are the issuing banks, form the secondary market. The efficient operation of this secondary market is vital to the maintenance of the sterling CDs' liquidity, and hence their attractiveness to borrowers.

The *finance house market* relates to the wholesale fund-raising activities of the UK finance houses. This market has become progressively less important since a number of the larger finance houses gained full bank status in the late 1970s and began to raise funds on the inter-bank market as a consequence. Nevertheless, the market is still very active, with regular issues of commercial bills by the finance houses. The non-bank finance houses also raise wholesale funds directly from banking institutions, as well as from insurance companies, pension funds, non-financial companies and individuals.

The *local authority market* relates to the raising of funds by local authorities in both bill and bond markets and through wholesale bank loans. The attractiveness of the instruments issued by local authorities has been significantly enhanced by their implicit support from the Treasury. In more recent years the market has diminished in importance as a result of the government's attempts to hold back local authority expenditure and as it has sought to exert a greater direct influence over their borrowing activities.

The *sterling commercial paper (SCP) market* is the newest of the parallel sterling markets. SCP relates to short-term, marketable, unsecured promissory notes with a fixed maturity, typically between seven days and three months, that are issued in bearer form at a discount to their maturity value. SCP may be issued by companies (including banks) in the UK which have a net asset value of £25m or more, and where either they or their guarantors have a listing on the Stock Exchange. The major role fulfilled by the SCP market is that of allowing companies to raise short-term funds through the issue of marketable instruments which are *not* the counterpart to specific commercial transactions; unlike commercial bills, they may be issued for general business financing purposes. Some companies, owing to their financial standing, are able to borrow more cheaply through the issue of SCP than by taking out bank loans, and yet the purchasers of the paper may obtain higher returns than they would through making bank deposits. The development of the SCP market represents a further form of disintermediation and is becoming increasingly popular with larger companies in the UK, with a corresponding growth in the size of the market.

Finally, the *intercompany market*, which is the smallest of the parallel markets. This market allows lending by companies with surpluses directly to other companies who wish to borrow, making use of the agency of a broker. The market originated in 1969 in response to the difficulties faced by fundamentally creditworthy companies in raising finance through normal banking channels. With the relaxation of bank lending restrictions, the relative attractiveness of this disintermediation activity has diminished somewhat, and consequently the market now only operates on a modest scale.

(b)   It is widely agreed that it *is* still valid to distinguish between the parallel sterling money markets and the discount market, despite the fact that there are similarities between the two types of market.

A major reason for distinguishing between them is that the discount market still plays a vital role in official money market intervention operations. On a day-to-day basis the Bank of England seeks to smooth flows of funds between private sector and government accounts held at the Bank, and may also harness these cash flows as a means of influencing short-term interest rates. The Bank does this by inviting the discount houses to sell bills to it when there is a shortage of funds on the market, or to buy bills from it if the Bank wishes to mop up excess liquidity. Today the discount houses are expected to make offers to the Bank for the purchase or sale of bills and, depending upon the Bank's response, pressure may be exerted on short-term interest rates, and ultimately on the whole structure of interest rates in the economy. In addition to this form of intervention, the Bank also stands willing to act as a *lender of last resort* to the discount market, a privilege which is not extended to the parallel markets which have to depend upon being able to adjust their liquidity positions through transactions within the financial system, and do not have direct access in this context to the Bank of England.

It is also valid to distinguish between the two types of market because the transactions within the discount market are *secured* while those within the parallel markets are *unsecured*. Taking into account the fact that only the major clearing banks, certain merchant banks, the Bank of England's Banking Department and the discount houses themselves are permitted access to the discount market, it is to be expected that the rates at which funds are borrowed and lent in this market are the finest available and are often significantly less than those rates generated by comparable transactions within the parallel markets.

While recognising the important sources of difference between the two types of market, the similarities also need to be recognised. In particular, the banks which have access to the discount market will consider competing opportunities for the adjustment of their liquidity positions. These banks will look for the best deal for depositing surplus funds on either the discount market or the inter-bank market, and the purchase of sterling CDs provides a further use for such short-term funds. Similarly, to cover short-term deficiencies in liquidity, the discount market, the inter-bank market and the issue of sterling CDs provide competing sources of funding. Also, the Bank of England periodically provides liquidity directly to institutions operating in the secondary markets via the use of REPO agreements. In addition, the regulatory framework within which both types of market now operate has been harmonised somewhat; all markets are exempt from the provisions of the Financial Services Act 1986, but are supervised by the Bank of England's Wholesale Markets Supervision Division and are expected to adhere to the London Code of Conduct.

Question 11

(a) *The inter-bank market*
The activities of the sterling inter-bank market involve the borrowing and lending of short-term wholesale funds between banks, often via the agency of a broker. It is the largest of the parallel sterling money markets. The funds are borrowed and lent on an unsecured basis, and hence transactions in this market are slightly more risky than those which take place with the discount market where the transactions are both secured and have the lender-of-last-resort facility of the Bank of England available for support.

The importance of the inter-bank market has progressively increased since the mid-1970s, primarily because it provides the banks with a means of adjusting their liquidity positions relatively quickly and efficiently. On a day-to-day basis, banks are able to place surplus funds on the inter-bank market and thus earn a reasonably good return whilst maintaining some degree of liquidity for those funds. Conversely, banks experiencing pressure on their liquidity or seeing immediate on-lending opportunities may raise substantial amounts of funds within the market at competitive rates. The use of the market has tended to develop alongside the trend towards liability management whereby, rather than adjusting their assets to accommodate their liabilities, banks seek to adjust their liabilities position to reflect their assets.

The inter-bank market is also responsible for establishing the inter-bank rates which determine the marginal cost of funds to the commercial banks. Movements in inter-bank rates are therefore carefully monitored by the banking community, with the key rate in this respect being the three-month London Inter-Bank Offered Rate (LIBOR) which is taken as a crucial indicator of market trends. Substantial amounts of commercial bank lending, especially to the corporate sector, are now charged at a percentage over LIBOR, and hence changes in this rate have an immediate impact on the financing position of borrowers with such loans outstanding. In addition, changes in inter-bank rates will also have implications for the setting of bank base rates, although the final decisions are taken by the Chancellor of the Exchequer.

(b)   *Commercial (eligible) bank bills*
A commercial bill is a bill of exchange which is issued as the counterpart to a commercial transaction. It is upon acceptance by a bank that the commercial bill becomes a *commercial bank bill*. If the accepting bank happens to be classified by the Bank of England as an eligible bank, the bill then becomes an *eligible bank bill*. Eligibility status is awarded to banks meeting certain minimum criteria laid down by the Bank of England, which ensures that they command very fine rates of discount. This is in turn enhanced by the fact that eligible bills are rediscountable at the Bank of England.

The origin of eligible bank bills is plainly in the short-term financing of trade and commerce. However, it may be argued that their greatest importance relates to the operation of official monetary controls, since it is primarily through dealing in such bills that the Bank of England smooths cash flows between the government sector and the private sector of the economy, and through which it seeks to influence short-term interest rates. Thus, for example, if there is a shortage of liquidity on the money markets, the Bank of England will announce its estimate of the extent of the shortage, and invite the discount houses to make offers to it for the sale of bills. If the rates of discount offered to the Bank are compatible with its undisclosed band for desired short-term interest rates, the offers will be accepted, the bills purchased by the Bank and the cash shortage will be relieved. The rates at which offers are accepted or rejected provides a signal to the markets as to the level of short-term rates desired by the authorities. By accepting or rejecting offers as appropriate, the Bank is able to put pressure on interest rates to bring them into line with its policy objectives. As the bills held by the Bank mature, funds are drawn out of the private sector, and this provides a useful channel (along with sales of Treasury bills) for mopping up excess liquidity in the market. The bills involved in these transactions are largely eligible bank bills, and in recent years activity has been dominated by bills falling within maturity bands 1 and 2 (up to 33 days to maturity).

(c)   *The Stock Exchange*
The London Stock Exchange is the major constituent of the UK capital market. Activities within the London Stock Exchange relate to the issue of long-term securities (primary market activity) for both private sector companies and public sector organisations, and to the trading of existing securities (secondary market activity).

The primary market is of obvious importance for raising funds to support capital investment in industry and commerce. Funds may be raised through the issue of various forms of equity shares which constitute claims upon the profits of the companies issuing them. Companies may also raise capital funds through the issue of interest-bearing debt instruments such as debentures. Purchasers of these instruments normally have a claim to regular interest payments and are creditors of the issuing company. This mechanism for raising funds provides an important alternative to taking out bank loans. In the government sector, the issue of gilt-edged securities has traditionally been an extremely important aspect of budget deficit financing. The ability to issue large quantities of such debt to the non-bank, non-building society private sector is of great importance for monetary control purposes.

The secondary market is also of crucial importance, as it provides holders of both equities and interest-bearing securities with the opportunity to liquidate their investments at very short notice. Indeed, whilst a large proportion of the interest-bearing debt is dated, and hence would mature automatically at some point, some debt instruments, such as consols, have no fixed maturity date, and the bulk of equities are irredeemable (unless the issuing company deems otherwise). Thus, without the facilities offered by the London Stock Exchange, it would be considerably more difficult for private companies and the public sector to raise long-term funds, as the borrower would be required to take on a high degree of illiquidity together with the associated risks.

It should also be recognised that the London Stock Exchange is not only of importance for financing domestic businesses and the UK government sector. It also provides an active market for trading securities issued by foreign companies and overseas governments and official institutions. In addition, the London Stock Exchange has become increasingly involved with trade in Eurobonds.

During the mid-1980s there was significant deregulation of London Stock Exchange activities. Since March 1986 it has been possible for non-members of the London Stock Exchange to purchase a 100% stake in London Stock Exchange member firms. This has resulted in a large proportion of former broking and jobbing firms either being taken over by, or going into partnership with, other financial institutions, including many major banking organisations. This takeover and merger activity has also led to a significant increase in the capital backing for London Stock Exchange firms, which was thought to be vital if such firms were to become serious contenders in the securities business on an international level. In October 1986 further substantial changes in activities occurred within the framework of what became known as 'Big Bang'. These changes included the abolition of fixed minimum commissions on London Stock Exchange transactions, thus introducing a competitive pricing basis for trading in the secondary market. The distinction between brokers (who acted as agents for non-London Stock Exchange members, and who were not allowed to act as principals by holding securities on their own account) and jobbers (who acted as market-makers and were only allowed to deal with other London Stock Exchange members) was also abolished. There is now a single category of member, namely the broker/dealer, who may act as both a broker and a market maker. In other words, if London Stock Exchange members so wish, they may take on dual capacity dealing. In addition, the gilt-edged securities market was opened up to a larger number of primary dealers.

A significantly freer competitive environment within the primary and secondary markets was the major intention of these developments, with the London Stock Exchange offering an improved service to both investors and those wishing to raise finance. As things have turned out, there has been a great deal of restructuring within the capital market, and commissions paid by the larger institutional investors would appear to have been reduced significantly. The same cannot be said for small investors, the services for whom were formerly subsidised by the fixed commissions framework. There is now also a greater choice of instruments available through a wider variety of institutions for those organisations wishing to raise funds and for those investors seeking longer term investment opportunities.

Question 12

(a)   Bank lending in eurocurrencies refers to wholesale bank lending that is denominated in foreign currencies. Thus, for example, a bank located in Sydney that makes a wholesale loan denominated in yen would be making a euroyen loan; a bank located in Paris that makes a wholesale loan denominated in Deutschmarks would be making a euro-Deutschmark loan, and so on. The term 'wholesale' in this context relates to transactions that normally involve the equivalent of at least US$1m. The 'euro' prefix is given purely because the eurocurrency markets originated in Europe; it should be appreciated that eurocurrency loans can be made by banks located in any country (provided that the local banking regulations permit) and may be made in any (convertible) currency.

(b)   (i) Many less-developed countries (LDCs) borrowed vast sums of money during the 1970s and 1980s through eurocurrency bank loans. However, the easy access to these loans was probably an important factor in causing many LDCs to avoid dealing with their underlying balance of payments problems, which ultimately precipitated severe financing difficulties during the early and mid-1980s. In simplified terms, the non-oil producing LDCs attempted to borrow their way out of their international payments problems following the large oil price rise of 1978–9. In comparison with the oil price rise of 1973–4, however, the tightening of monetary and fiscal policies by many western nations in response to the oil price rise and consequent inflationary pressures led to rising real interest rates and depressed demands for basic raw commodities. In addition, during the first half of the 1980s the US dollar strengthened markedly, and with a large portion of LDC debt being denominated in dollar terms, the real cost of servicing the debt became severe. The overall result was that by 1982 the major LDCs were threatening to default on their international loans.

The impact of these developments has been that many banks are now very reluctant to provide new loans to heavily indebted LDCs, with additional funds frequently being made available only as part of an IMF-backed rescheduling exercise. Many banks have made very large provisions for the writing-off of their LDC debt, in addition to attempting to reduce their exposure to the worst risks amongst the LDCs. The attempts to reduce this exposure have involved attempts to 'securitise' the LDC debt held by specific banks, in order to recoup part (albeit only a small part) of the funds they originally lent by selling the securitised debt on international markets at a (usually) heavy discount. In total, the developments have had the result of markedly undermining the growth of the eurocurrency bank lending market.

(ii)   *Securitisation.* Securitisation refers to the process whereby borrowers issue marketable securities as an alternative to raising funds by means of bank loans. The popularity of this method of borrowing by the corporate sector has increased recently, with the result that the growth of bank lending has tended to fall, including the growth in the eurocurrency markets. An important factor stimulating the growth of this activity has been the deregulation of financial markets, since this has allowed companies greater freedom to issue securities, but the major driving force behind the trend towards securitisation has been the cost of borrowing for those companies with high credit ratings. Many large companies are now able to borrow *more cheaply* by issuing securities directly to the ultimate lenders than by borrowing from banks. The reason for the lower cost associated with issuing securities is that companies frequently have credit ratings equal to those of commercial banks, itself partly a consequence of the downgrading of many banks as a result of their Third World debt problems. Although there are administrative costs associated with issuing securities, these may be lower than the charges (excluding interest) that are effectively levied on loans by banks. The result is that the corporate borrower may be able to raise funds at a lower total cost than if the funds had been raised through bank loans, whilst at the same time the ultimate lender may be able to earn a higher return on funds than would be available through making deposits with banks.

Whilst securitisation has undermined the growth of eurocurrency bank lending, it should be emphasised that it has not necessarily harmed the eurocurrency markets in general. The reason for this is that many companies (and indeed official institutions) raise long-term funds through the issue of Eurobonds, while shorter-term requirements are met by Euronotes and euro-commercial paper issues. However, even here the banks do not lose out entirely, since they often provide underwriting facilities for Euronotes issues and acting as agents for (but not underwriting) euro-commercial paper issues.

(iii) *Liberalisation in the domestic markets.* A reduction in the rate of growth of eurocurrency bank lending has also come about as a consequence of the removal of official restrictions and the easing of regulatory requirements for activities in *domestic* financial markets. An initial stimulus to the growth of the Euromarkets was the freedom which they offered relative to the comparable domestic markets. The need to comply with fewer regulatory requirements than in domestic markets allowed participants in the Euromarkets to operate on very fine margins, thus being able to pay higher rates to suppliers of funds than could be obtained in domestic markets, whilst often charging borrowers lower rates than available for domestic funds. Therefore, as domestic financial markets have been liberalised, the relative cost advantages of the Euromarkets have diminished, thus tending to reduce their popularity. This trend has been supported by the wider array of business financing opportunities now available within domestic markets for both banks and their corporate customers. Many new forms of financial instruments and modes of operation have been introduced in recent years, within the evolving regulatory framework, and it is now possible for a high proportion of the constantly changing corporate financing needs to be met without difficulty by the domestic markets, whilst avoiding the financial risks which have always been attendant upon eurocurrency market activities (but which, in the past, were outweighed by the cost advantages of the market). Since the late 1970s important aspects of the liberalisation of the domestic markets have included the removal or reduction of foreign currency exchange controls (particularly on capital account items); the removal of direct monetary controls which tended to constrain banks' purely domestic operations (as in the UK before 1981); the easing of banking regulations on the allowable scope of domestic activities (for example, the removal of certain restrictions on interstate banking in the USA); the removal of restrictions on the issue of certain forms of securities by domestic companies (for example, the issue of sterling commercial paper by UK companies); and the general deregulation of domestic capital markets, allowing many banks to become much more directly involved with activities in areas of the financial markets that were previously prohibited to them.

Question 13

(a)   The level of interest rates paid on eurocurrency deposits and charged on eurocurrency loans is broadly determined by the forces of supply and demand for eurocurrency funds. However, given the special nature of the eurocurrency markets it is possible to identify a number of specific key factors which affect the level of interest rates in these markets:

(i) The rate of interest paid on a eurocurrency deposit or charged on a eurocurrency loan will reflect the level of *interest rates ruling in the country from which the relevant currency originates* (rather than the rates ruling in the country where the eurocurrency market is based). The reason for this is that, for activities to take place, banking institutions must obtain foreign currency funds and these will only be forthcoming if the rates of interest offered on deposits are at least as good as those available in the country where the currency originates. Therefore, the factors which affect the level of interest rates within any particular domestic market will also influence the level of rates to be found in the corresponding overseas eurocurrency market. Thus important factors include the current and expected rates of domestic *inflation*; the official *monetary policy* position of the domestic authorities; the general *economic environment* including the international payments position and prospects for future economic growth; the *confidence* of investors in future economic and financial prospects; and the *risk premium* required by investors in the light of the inherent political and economic stability of the country.

(ii) Until fairly recently, eurocurrency market activity was largely *unregulated*. Intermediaries were not required to hold low-yield liquid assets or to maintain specific capital backing relative to their risk-weighted assets, and hence they were able to operate on very *fine margins*. The large scale of transactions has also tended to hold down unit administration costs. Thus, for any given maturity of funds, the rates paid on eurocurrency deposits have tended to be somewhat *higher* than those rates paid on comparable domestic deposits; whilst the rates charged to borrowers have often been *lower* than rates charged for comparable domestic loans. However, since the mid-1980s the comparative advantage of the eurocurrency markets has been eroded by the movement towards the *harmonisation of regulation* within international banking markets. This has come about both through the strengthening of domestic supervisory requirements and through the pressures exerted by the Basle Committee agreement which required all banks to achieve minimum capital-adequacy standards. In consequence, the differentials between eurocurrency and comparable domestic interest rates have tended to narrow somewhat in recent years.

(iii) Notwithstanding the moves outlined above, which have tended to reduce the risk faced by providers of funds to the eurocurrency markets, the nature of activities in the markets generally involves *higher levels of risk* than those experienced in comparable domestic markets. Thus, the higher rates paid on deposits may be largely justified in terms of the risk premium required by depositors.

(iv) A very small number of western countries still maintain some form of *exchange controls* on movements of capital funds. Where this occurs, the differential between interest rates in eurocurrency markets and the rates in comparable domestic markets may be greater than can be explained purely on the basis of economic factors.

(b)   As the level of eurodollar rates shows the nominal return which may be earned on dollar deposits held with banks outside the USA, it would seem reasonable to suggest that, other things being equal, an increase in such rates will tend to raise the volume of eurodollar deposits. However, in order to make dollar deposits, investors must obtain the necessary dollars. Consequently, and irrespective of the precise portfolio adjustments undertaken, a *higher* level of *eurodollar interest rates* is likely to lead to an *increase* in the *US dollar spot exchange rate* as investors raise their demand for dollars. A lower level of eurodollar interest rates is likely to have the opposite effect, as investors liquidate their eurodollar deposits and switch to investments denominated in currencies which now offer relatively more attractive returns.

Changes in eurodollar rates, other things being equal, will also have implications for forward transactions on the foreign-currency exchange markets. This is because the *premiums and discounts on forward exchange rates* reflect the *differences between interest rates* on assets denominated in the currencies involved. The relationship can best be explained by a simple example. A UK-based bank may agree to sell dollars to a customer in three months' time. The bank will immediately purchase an appropriate amount of dollars on the spot market and will then use these dollars to make a eurodollar deposit with a three months' maturity. Thus, the bank effectively converts a quantity of funds which would otherwise have been held as interest-bearing *sterling* assets into an equal value of interest-bearing *dollar* assets. If the *rate of interest* which can be earned on the *eurodollars* is *less* than that which can be earned on *comparable sterling assets* on the domestic market, the bank will charge a *premium* on the forward transaction in order to cover the interest-rate differential, which amounts to a cost imposed on the bank. (This premium is in addition to charges which the bank will make for the various administrative expenses incurred.) Consequently, the higher the rate of interest which the bank is able to earn on the eurodollar deposit, the smaller the premium which it will charge the customer. The existence of competitive financial markets will ensure that the premium is reduced and that benefits from the higher eurodollar rate are passed on to the customer. Alternatively, if the *rate of interest* paid on the *eurodollar* deposit is initially *higher* than that which could be earned on domestic *sterling deposits*, the bank will offer a *discount* on the forward sale of dollars for sterling relative to the ruling spot rate. In this case, an increase in the eurodollar rate will cause the discount to be raised, as the bank benefits from the increased interest-rate differential in favour of eurodollars. A fall in the eurodollar rate would lead to a reduction in the discount or an increase in the premium on forward dollar sales to the bank's customer, depending upon the magnitude of the reduction of the eurodollar rate and the value of the initial interest-rate differential.

Question 14

(a)   Money market activity involves the borrowing and lending of wholesale funds for relatively short periods of time (usually for less than one year and often for periods ranging from overnight up to three months). The short-term nature of the market implies that the Keynesian theory of liquidity preference is appropriate in providing an explanation for the determination of the general level of interest rates within the market. However, whilst the supply of and the demand for liquidity undoubtedly influence the overall level of interest rates, there are many important considerations underlying this relationship. A particularly important factor relates to the position of the Bank of England, which, for many years, has been closely involved with the operations of the primary (discount) money market. This is an important channel for monetary controls and the adjustment of liquidity within the financial system. Furthermore, as all the London money markets (including the parallel sterling markets and the eurocurrency markets) are to some extent interconnected, the Bank's influence may percolate quickly throughout the whole market system.

The Bank's declared policy on interest rates since August 1981 (when MLR was formally suspended), has been to keep very short-term rates within an unpublished band, whilst allowing market forces to play a leading role in the determination of longer-term rates. The Bank stands ready to smooth cash flows between the government's accounts and private-sector accounts at the Bank, and hence it is always willing to provide/mop up cash whenever there is a shortage/surplus in the market. The discount houses make offers to sell/buy paper (of late, especially commercial bills) to/from the Bank. The intervention rates at which sales/purchases of paper occur effectively determine very short-term money market rates, and clearly this has a crucial influence on all short rates. The greater the need to relieve cash shortages, the greater the influence of the Bank. When the Chancellor of the Exchequer changes base rate, the Bank of England often publishes a Minimum Lending Rate for that day. It signals to the commercial banks that they must change their base rates by the appropriate number of basis points. The next day the Bank reverts to its usual mode of operations – inviting offers from the houses etc.

Looking towards longer-term rates within the money markets, the standard term-structure analysis applies; thus, when there are no general expectations of interest rate movements, the longer the term to maturity the higher the rate will be. This reflects the liquidity preference of lenders and the increased risks over time, so that the yield curve slopes upward. However, once expectations of future changes in rates are recognised the situation is not so simple. An expected rise in rates will tend to increase the demand for long-term fixed-rate funds but will reduce the supply, thus tending to make the yield curve steeper; and expected falls in rates will increase supply relative to demand at longer maturities and may even lead to a negatively-sloped yield curve. Government policies, exchange rate movements, general economic/inflation conditions and so on, will frame the expectations.

Interest rate differentials between different money market instruments (for example, Treasury bills, local authority deposits, sterling CDs) with the same maturity will be influenced by the set of characteristics which each instrument embodies – factors such as inherent risks, specific demand and supply conditions, ease of marketability, liquidity and so on will be important.

(b)   The importance of money markets for commercial banks' liquidity positions cannot be overemphasised, for it must be remembered that it is virtually impossible for a bank to adjust its short-term liquidity position through its retail funds flows. Thus, for all practical purposes, the marginal cost of funds for commercial banks is broadly reflected by money market rates, and in particular by the three-month sterling LIBOR. Therefore, bank base rates will tend to be strongly influenced by money market rates over time, but they only follow the broad trends, not the temporary fluctuations.

The setting of banks' base rates will be affected by longer-term considerations, including expectations of future movements in money market rates, and hence the factors listed above. Also retail banks must consider customer loyalty, as ordinary retail customers may be inconvenienced by continually changing interest rates, and indeed their finances may not be able to cope with such changes. In addition, the number of retail customers is now so large that the mechanics of altering retail deposit and base rates involve substantial costs for banks, despite the advances of computer technology. Thus, their interest rates tend to be 'sticky' relative to the more volatile money market rates.

Clearly, as all interest rates are interlinked, changes in money market rates will always have some influence on bank interest rates in the broadest sense, and consideration by banks of their longer-term profitability in respect of the raising and on-lending of funds will affect the nature of that influence. Also, the decision as to whether or not to alter interest rates following a change in market rates will be influenced by the proportion of total funds raised at market rates, the proportion of funds on-lent at market-related rates, and the size of the initial overall interest rate margin.

Question 15

(a) A yield curve shows the relationship between yields on a particular type of asset with different terms to maturity. Yield curves can only exist for instruments which carry fixed interest rates and have fixed maturity dates: for example, gilt-edged securities, certificates of deposit, and Eurobonds.

Figure 1 Normal yield curve

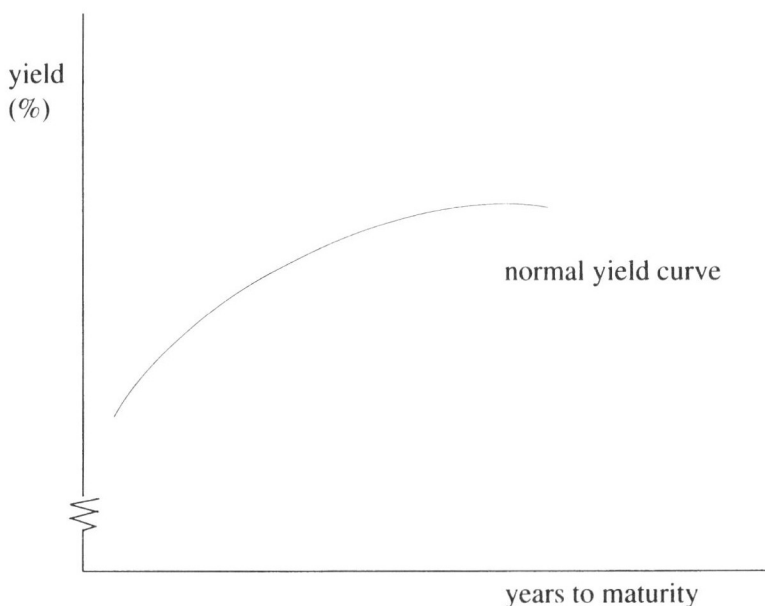

Figure 1 illustrates a 'normal' yield curve, which shows that the longer the term to maturity of the asset, the greater the yield generated. The curve levels off at higher maturities, since beyond a certain time into the future it becomes almost impossible to differentiate between different degrees of risk and liquidity preference, which are the basic factors responsible for the upward slope.

If there are general expectations that interest rates are going to rise in the future, this will tend to make the yield curve steeper as investors hold back on longer-term commitments to lend until rates have risen. Conversely, expectations of future reductions in interest rates will tend to cause the yield curve to become flatter as lenders increase long-term lending as a means of taking advantage of currently high rates of interest, whilst borrowers hold back their requirements in readiness for future lower rates of interest.

(b)   (i) The two basic factors which cause yield curves to slope upward from left to right are *risk* and *liquidity preference*.

The longer the term to maturity of an asset, the greater the risk which must be accepted by the holder of the asset. For example, whilst a borrower might appear to be highly creditworthy at the time a loan is made, the longer the period for which the funds are to be lent the greater the risk that conditions may alter, and hence the greater the risk of default. Therefore, the lender will seek a higher return in order to compensate for this higher risk. Similarly, the further one looks into the future, the harder it becomes to predict accurately the rate of *inflation*, and hence the degree of erosion of real capital value which might be expected in a nominal amount of funds lent or invested. Again, the lender will seek a higher return to cover this greater risk of *capital loss*. Indeed, concern over the risk of capital loss may be extended to the possibility of adverse movements in interest rates making the premature sale of marketable instruments unattractive, and hence perhaps causing difficulties if the lender's personal situation necessitates a reappraisal of his financial portfolio.

Lenders usually require compensation for the loss of access to *immediate purchasing power* which is entailed when funds are used to make fixed-term loans. The longer the term to maturity, the greater the amount of compensation that will be required by the lender. The liquidity issue is still relevant even when marketable debt is purchased, as the risk of capital loss from premature sale of the debt means that liquidity is lost in the strict sense.

The existence of risk and liquidity preference explains why longer-term rates of interest are higher than shorter-term rates, when there are no specific expectations of interest movements; that is, in what are sometimes referred to as 'normal' circumstances. However, when expectations of interest rate movements do exist, additional forces are exerted on the shape of the yield curve. Specifically, if there are general expectations of an increase, this will tend to push up long-term rates relative to short-term rates. This occurs because lenders, wishing to avoid being locked into relatively low yield assets, will increasingly prefer to lend short-term hoping that when the loans mature they will be able to reinvest the funds at the expected higher rate. Thus, there is an increase in the supply of short-term funds and a corresponding reduction in the supply of long-term funds. Conversely, borrowers will wish to borrow long-term today at the currently relatively low rate of interest. They would be foolish to borrow short-term only to have to reborrow the funds at higher rates of interest at some time in the future. Thus, there will tend to be an increase in the demand for long-term funds and a reduction in the demand for short-term funds. Therefore, considering the behaviour of both lenders and borrowers, the effect of an expected increase in interest rates is to create an excess demand for long-term funds and an excess supply of short-term funds at the initial term structure of interest rates. This will tend to result in market forces pushing down short-term rates and pushing up long-term rates, thus making the yield curve steeper.

(b)   (ii) *Short-term inter-bank interest rates* provide a good measure of the *marginal cost of funds* to individual banks attempting to adjust their liquidity positions. The importance of the inter-bank market cannot be overemphasised, for it must be remembered that it is virtually impossible for a bank to adjust its short-term liquidity position through its retail funds flow. By contrast, the inter-bank market is sensitive to relatively small changes in rates, terms for individual transactions are negotiated separately, and the sophisticated communications networks ensure that financing needs can be met quickly and efficiently.

The effect of changes in short-term inter-bank interest rates on commercial bank lending rates depends very much upon the *types of lending activity* involved and upon the *nature of the changes* in inter-bank rates. Thus, in relation to on-lending at a *fixed margin above inter-bank rate*, the relationship is direct. For example, a wholesale loan may be made to a corporate customer at a fixed percentage over the three-month LIBOR, and consequently an increase in inter-bank rates will cause an immediate increase in the rate charged to the corporate customer. However, where lending rates are *linked to base rates* the relationship is somewhat more complex. Although decisions on base rates are taken by the Chancellor of the Exchequer, the individual banks still determine the margins above base rate and, of course, al the managed interest rates which are free from any direct link to base rate.

Lending rates tend to follow the general trend in short-term inter-bank rates, but are not adjusted to reflect every short-term fluctuation in such rates. The reason for this is that the cost of inter-bank funds is only one factor in the determination of lending rates. The direct effect on a bank's operating margin of having to pay a higher rate for inter-bank funds would have to be weighed against the cost of adjusting lending rates, both in terms of the administration expenses and the effect on customer loyalty. Banks will be more willing to raise lending rates the greater the increase in inter-bank rates; the more permanent the increase in inter-bank rates is expected to be; the larger the proportion of total funds that the bank raises at inter-bank rates; the finer the bank's pre-existing operating margin; and the greater the response from competing financial intermediaries.

Finally, it should be recognised that some on-lending by commercial banks takes place at *fixed rates*. However, changes in inter-bank rates are still likely to influence the average of such rates, as term loans mature and are renegotiated and as new loans are made at rates reflecting the new (and future expected) cost of funds to the bank.

Question 16

(a)   Intermediate targets are those variables through which the authorities intend to achieve their economic policy objectives. In turn, the intermediate targets are themselves influenced by the authorities' policy instruments (that is, those policy variables over which they have reasonably close control). In addition, some intermediate targets may be manipulated to affect other target variables, which will then, it is hoped, influence the ultimate policy objectives.

The intermediate targets of monetary policy include the following:

(i) The level and/or structure of interest rates. The fundamental idea is that by altering interest rates the authorities may be able to influence interest-sensitive expenditure relating to both business investment and consumer spending. Changes in interest rates may also have implications for international currency flows, and hence for the balance of payments. In addition, it is important to recognise that changes in interest rates may be used as a means of influencing other intermediate target variables, and hence may be part of a chain of intermediate targets. For example, an increase in the level of interest rates may be effected by the authorities in the hope of damping down the demand for bank and building society credit, and thereby reducing the rate of growth of the money supply.

(ii) The rate of growth of the money supply. This became a more important intermediate target of monetary policy, during the 1980s in particular, as a consequence of the increased popularity of monetarism. Monetarists would argue that the rate of growth of the money supply must be controlled if the price level is to be stabilised. Unfortunately, a major problem in utilising this target variable is in determining which measure of the money supply to use. This caused particular difficulties in the UK in the 1980s.

(iii) Bank and building society credit creation. It is sometimes argued that members of the non-bank, non-building society private sector obtain credit primarily to finance expenditure on goods, services and real assets. Hence, there is likely to be a predictable relationship between the extension of bank and building society credit and the total level of private sector expenditures.

(iv) Exchange rates. The exchange rate of a country's currency may be a target variable, to affect the relative prices of exports and imports, and hence influence the current account of the balance of payments, domestic output and employment and the rate of inflation.

(v) Nominal domestic expenditure (or national income). It is quite acceptable to consider the level of domestic expenditure as a target for policy, as ultimately the manipulation of this variable may be expected to have an influence upon the rate of inflation and/or the levels of output and employment.

In addition, some economists would suggest that the Public Sector Borrowing Requirement (PSBR) may also be regarded as an intermediate target of monetary policy. The size of the PSBR may have important implications for both the rate of growth of the money supply and the level of interest rates.

(b) The *techniques* which may be used by the authorities in order to achieve their monetary policy targets include the following:

(i) *The central bank's discount rate* may be changed, as a means of affecting the marginal cost of funds for the financial system, and hence interest rates in general.

(ii) *Open market operations* may be undertaken in either the discount market or the gilt-edged securities market, with the intention of affecting the structure of financial assets held by the private sector and/or the level and structure of interest rates.

(iii) *The authorities may intervene in the foreign exchange market* by purchasing and selling currencies in order to influence the domestic currency's exchange rate, and possibly international currency flows.

(iv) *Direct controls* may be imposed on lending by financial institutions. These could be in the form of lending ceilings or qualitative guidelines.

(v) *Special deposits*, or the imposition of *restrictive reserve requirements* by the authorities, may influence the reserve bases of financial institutions.

(vi) *Moral suasion* may be applied to financial institutions in an attempt to persuade them to restrain their lending activities.

(vii) The authorities may set *maximum target growth rates for interest-bearing deposits* with financial institutions, as a means of limiting their willingness to bid for funds for on-lending. Penalties may be enforced against institutions violating the target rates. *Interest rate ceilings* may be imposed with a similar aim in mind.

(viii) Strictly speaking, the PSBR and PSDR are fiscal variables but they may be manipulated with the intention of influencing interest rates and credit and money supply growth. The precise *means of financing* a PSBR/PSDR is particularly important in this respect.

Question 17

(a)   (i) *Medium of exchange.* With annual inflation at around 10% there is *unlikely to be any significant effect* on the use of money as a medium of exchange. Experience has shown that inflation rates have to rise considerably above this value before people stop using money in the transactions process. The convenience of money is so great and the loss in purchasing power so small that reverting to the use of commodity monies or barter is out of the question.

Store of value. The impact of inflation on the store-of-value function of money depends very much upon the particular definition of money being considered. Thus, where money bears *no interest* (as in the case of cash and ordinary current account deposits) any amount of inflation erodes its *real purchasing power*, and hence it is likely that people will switch to holdings of other assets as *hedges against inflation*. However, a large proportion of the money stock as defined by the broader measures of money does pay interest, and this offers at least some *compensation* for the effects of inflation. If the real rate of interest on money is positive (which implies a nominal rate greater than 10% within the context of the question), then it is unlikely that people will move into non-money assets to any great extent (given the convenience factor associated with holding wealth in money form); although expectations of persistent inflation at even higher rates may cause a somewhat more substantial shift to other types of assets with better inflation-hedging qualities.

Unit of account The performance of money as a *measure of value* would be increasingly *undermined* the longer inflation persisted. Comparisons of money values over time would become increasingly difficult. With inflation at 10% the interpretation of company accounts could be distorted, especially if costs and revenues were compared at different points in time. To assess the true financial performance of a company it might be necessary to use inflation-adjusted accounting methods.

Standard for deferred payment The existence of inflation will undoubtedly undermine the *credit function* of money. Unless funds are lent on an index-linked basis, both lender and borrower will face *uncertainty* as to the real rate of interest to be received or paid. If funds are lent at a fixed rate of interest and inflation turns out to be higher than expected, the borrower will gain at the expense of the lender. Quite simply, the real value of the amount owed will diminish over time, and unless real interest rates are positive, the lender will not even receive sufficient compensation to make good the loss in purchasing power of the funds lent, let alone receive a return for the risk and loss of liquidity incurred.

(a)   (ii) If the rate of inflation rises towards 10%, it is likely that *nominal rates of interest* will also *increase*. There are basically two reasons for this: firstly, the lender will seek to *protect the purchasing power* of his outstanding loans and hence will push for higher nominal rates of interest. If he has in mind a desired real rate of interest, then nominal rates will have to be held above the concurrent rate of inflation. Indeed, financial institutions may feel obliged to raise the rates offered on savings deposits to dissuade savers from shifting their funds into other forms of assets which offer hedges against inflation.

Secondly, a rising rate of inflation will probably cause the authorities to tighten their *monetary policy* and so engineer an increase in nominal interest rates. Higher rates of interest are seen as a means of damping down the demand for credit and therefore money supply growth; and higher borrowing costs associated with outstanding debt will reduce the ability of borrowers to purchase goods and services, thus helping to reduce *inflationary pressures*. In addition, higher rates of interest will tend to support the *exchange value* of the domestic currency (by providing compensation to overseas investors for the effects of domestic inflation), and so help to hold down import prices whilst putting pressure on domestic producers to contain their costs.

(b)   (i) If a country's inflation rate is higher than the rates experienced by its major trading partners then, other things being equal, its exports will become *increasingly uncompetitive* in overseas markets, whilst *imports* become *increasingly attractive* in the domestic market. Assuming that the *price elasticities of demand* for traded goods and services are sufficiently high (technically, if the Marshall-Lerner condition holds; that is, that the sum of the elasticities is greater than one), then the country will find its current account deteriorating. In the short term, it may be able to draw upon its accumulated currency and gold reserves to cover any deficit or it may borrow from overseas, possibly pushing up interest rates in the process. However, as both reserves and international borrowing power are limited for any particular country, it is likely that in the longer term international *confidence* in the country's ability to pay its way will be undermined, and the domestic currency's *exchange rate* will begin to *depreciate*. The exchange rate movement may be seen as a necessary adjustment for the effects of above-average inflation on the country's international competitiveness. This natural adjustment mechanism is explained by the *purchasing power parity theory*, which states that, in the long run, movements in exchange rates are determined by the inflation differential between the relevant countries. Equilibrium exchange rates will only be achieved when the domestic purchasing powers of equivalent amounts of the relevant currencies are equal. However, in the short run capital flows may counteract the effects of inflation differentials on exchange rates.

(b)   (ii) As stated above, the *current account* of the balance of payments is likely to *deteriorate* (unless price elasticities are low, which is unlikely for most traded items). Any subsequent depreciation in the exchange value of the domestic currency may limit the impact of above-average inflation; and if the exchange rate falls sufficiently the country may be able to regain its former trading competitiveness. The effect on the *capital account* is likely to depend critically upon what happens to *domestic rates of interest*. Without any increase in interest rates there is likely to be an outflow of capital funds as investors seek higher real returns and as financial uncertainty undermines confidence. However, if the authorities cause interest rates to rise, perhaps to protect the exchange rate, investors may be willing to maintain their initial position. Somewhat ironically, this occurrence will make it harder for domestic producers to maintain their position in international markets, and hence confidence may still be damaged in the longer term; although higher domestic rates of interest may help to reduce the domestic rate of inflation and hence aid competitiveness in this way.

Question 18

(a) The instruments of monetary control may be divided into three broad groups:

(i) instruments of market intervention;

(ii) instruments of portfolio constraint;

(iii) longer-term control mechanisms.

The instruments of market intervention comprise the Bank of England's *open-market operations* and the setting of its *discount rate* (currently referred to as the intervention rate). This latter rate is effectively the price charged by the Bank for funds supplied to the markets in the event of a general shortage of liquidity. In recent years it has normally represented the rate of discount which the discount houses have been 'forced' to accept from the Bank in respect of their bill sales to the Bank. Clearly, the influence of the discount rate on the financial system is pervasive, as it measures the marginal cost of funds to the system as a whole. Changes in the discount rate give important signals in respect of the likely future trend of interest rates in general, but especially the trend in short-term rates.

Open-market operations occur when the Bank intervenes in the markets for securities, either buying or selling, depending upon its objectives in relation to the level and structure of interest rates and/or the volume of liquidity in the financial system. The Bank trades extensively in the discount market and so its greatest influence is exerted upon short-term interest rates, but it may also buy or sell long-term gilt-edged securities, thus having a more direct effect on long-term rates.

The instruments of market intervention are likely to have a fairly generalised effect on financial conditions. Thus, if interest rates are pushed upward, this may dampen the demand for mortgage loans from building societies and hire-purchase credit from finance houses as well as the demand for bank loans.

Although the instruments of portfolio constraint could be applied broadly, in practice they have been normally applied to specific groups of financial institutions, and hence they tend to operate in a discriminatory manner. This is clearly inequitable, and the controls may generate conditions which undermine their own effectiveness in the longer term. In other words, disintermediation may occur as non-controlled institutions attempt to take up any business driven away from the controlled parts of the financial system. The major portfolio constraints are reserve requirements, special deposits and supplementary special deposits, moral suasion and direct controls. Currently, they are in abeyance.

In order to create deposits, banks and building societies must hold a *reserve asset base*, usually in the form of cash or other liquid assets. When the institution reaches its desired minimum reserve ratio, assuming that there are unsatisfied demands for loans, it either has to turn away potential borrowers or it has to attract more deposits and/or purchase reserve assets. In either event, it is likely that interest rates will be pushed upward, which will restrain the demand for loans. Thus, if the authorities are able to influence the total supply or price of reserve assets, perhaps by the use of open-market operations or a call for special deposits, or if they are able to dictate a change in the required reserve ratio, they should be able to exert pressure on the level of deposit creation and hence the rate of growth of the money supply.

Special deposits (here termed SDs) are funds which must be deposited by (banking) institutions with the Bank of England. The Bank has the right to call for SDs in amounts related to individual institutions' eligible liabilities. These SDs do not count as part of institutions' reserve bases, and hence calls have an immediate affect on their ability to create credit. SDs have a similar ultimate effect to open-market operations, although they tend to act quicker and are useful for mopping up excess reserves within the banking system without having an undue destabilising effect. After a call has been made, banks are able to adjust their reserve positions steadily over time. *Supplementary special deposits* referred to the 'penalty' which had to be paid by institutions in violation of a fixed maximum target growth rate for a certain category of their deposit liabilities. When this system operated in the UK it was referred to as the 'corset' mechanism and focused attention directly upon a major element of the money supply. SDs were paid on a scale related to the degree of target overshoot; they could not be used by banks as part of the reserve base; and they attracted no interest payment from the Bank of England (unlike ordinary SDs).

Moral suasion occurs when the Bank applies informal pressures on financial institutions to act in a manner which is conducive 'to the national interest', although this might not be in the best commercial interest of the institutions. The Bank may make suggestions about lending priorities and may ask institutions to limit the amount of credit granted to certain categories of customers.

Direct controls limit the freedom of financial institutions to pursue their commercial objectives. The Bank of England might, for example, issue directives limiting the volume of credit creation for some or all borrowers; it may specify qualitative lending guidelines; or it may set ceilings on interest rates (thus limiting the ability of institutions to bid for new deposits).

Finally, there are a number of policies which may be applied with a view to influencing the rate of growth of the money supply in the *longer term*. In particular, the authorities may seek to reduce the level of the *Public Sector Borrowing Requirement* or increase the size of a *Public Sector Debt Repayment*. If a PSBR is to be reduced this not only has a direct effect on the demand for borrowed funds within the economy but also, and particularly to the extent that the PSBR would have been covered by sales of short-term government debt instruments, the supply of potential bank reserve assets is limited. In addition, for any given size of PSBR, the greater the proportion which is covered by the issue of gilt-edged securities and National Savings instruments to the non-bank, non-building society private sector, the smaller the monetary implications of the deficit financing. Indeed, as existing debt matures, the authorities may pursue a *funding policy* which is aimed at reducing the stock of liquid assets in the economy suitable for reserve asset purposes. In the case of a PSDR, funds are withdrawn from the private sector and the money supply will be reduced, unless the authorities use these funds to retire debt held by the non-bank, non-building society private sector. Clearly, the greater the PSDR the greater the opportunity for reducing money supply growth.

(b)   Since the new monetary controls provisions were introduced by the authorities in August 1981 the emphasis has been placed upon the use of market intervention and the implementation of policies directed towards the longer-term control of the money supply. Portfolio constraints have been largely abandoned, and since 1990 interest rates have frequently been changed by announcing a Minimum Lending Rate for the discount market for one day.

The emphasis of monetary controls since the early 1980s has been focused upon the manipulation of *short-term interest rates*. This has been achieved through the use of open-market operations, changes in the Bank's intervention (discount) rates and, on occasions, somewhat more direct pressures by the Bank. In addition, the government has pursued a policy of holding down the *PSBR* within its Medium Term Financial Strategy framework. Clearly, such policies have important implications for taxation and public expenditure decisions. It is hoped that reduced public-sector dependence on bank finance will take the pressure off interest rates at all levels and will encourage corporate borrowers to raise funds in the capital markets rather than through bank loans.

Finally, the authorities have also attempted to facilitate their monetary objectives through the careful implementation of *funding policy*. In fact, during part of the 1980s extensive *over-funding* of the PSBR took place, which means that sales of gilt-edged securities and National Savings instruments to the non-bank, non-building society private sector often exceeded the concurrent PSBR, thus having a negative impact on the growth of M4.

Question 19

(a)   (i) The following measures could be implemented with the objective of reducing a current account deficit:

(i) The authorities could seek to *reduce the exchange rate for the domestic currency.* This action would be aimed at reducing the foreign currency price of domestic exports, whilst raising the domestic currency price of foreign imports, other things being equal. Whilst it is probable that the domestic demand for imported goods and services would be depressed, total expenditure on imports would only fall if the *price elasticity of demand* for these imports was greater than one (i.e. the proportionate reduction in the quantity demanded must be greater than the proportionate increase in the domestic currency price of the goods and services). Similarly, whilst the volume of exports would probably increase, overseas earnings would only rise if the price elasticity of demand for exports was greater than one. Clearly, for there to be an overall improvement in the balance of traded goods and services, it is not necessary that both these elasticity conditions should be met. Strictly, if the sum of the two elasticities is greater than one, the balance of trade will improve (this is known as the Marshall-Lerner condition).

The required adjustment in exchange rates may be brought about by the authorities allowing market pressure to depress the value of the domestic currency (which would probably occur at some point due to the existence of a current account deficit). Alternatively, the downwards pressure could be intensified by official exchange market intervention involving sales of the domestic currency, or by a loosening of monetary controls with the aim of pushing interest rates downwards and hence undermining the attractiveness of domestic deposits for foreign investors. However, a possible side effect of this type of policy action is that domestic money supply growth may be stimulated, and hence the level of demand within the economy may be raised, thus counteracting at least some of the effect of the policy on the level of imports. In addition, it should also be noted that irrespective of the means by which the exchange value of the domestic currency is reduced, there may be a J-curve effect to contend with. That is, as it takes time for trading patterns to adjust, in the short-term it is likely that the deficit will be made worse. It is only as the demand for the now cheaper export goods and services begins to rise that export earnings will recover; and it is only as the demand for the now more expensive imports falls that total expenditure on such items will fall back. The final outcome will depend upon the relevant price elasticities of demand, as mentioned above.

(ii) *Demand management policies* may be directed towards reducing the volume of imports. Specifically, the authorities could tighten monetary policy (although higher interest rates could place upwards pressure on the domestic currency's exchange rate, through the attraction of foreign currency funds), reduce the level of government spending or raise taxes. The ensuing reduction in aggregate demand would not only depress the demand for imports, but also would possibly lead to the creation of spare capacity in the domestic economy, thus providing industry with the ability (and the motivation) to service export markets more effectively.

(iii) *Direct controls* could be introduced as a means of making imports less attractive to domestic consumers, or simply limiting the volume of such imports. For example, the authorities might apply tariffs to specific imports in order to raise their price within the domestic market, and hence improve the relative competitiveness of domestically produced goods. So long as the price elasticity of demand for the imports is greater than zero, demand would fall, and, other things being equal, total payments made to foreign exporters would be reduced. The problem with this measure is that it may lead to retaliation by overseas countries, which may adversely affect domestic exports. So too may the application of quotas (physical limits) on imports, and any subsequent price increases for the imports would offset the benefit for the current account payment flows.

(iv) *Exchange controls* could be applied in order to limit the use of foreign currency by domestic residents. This measure would effectively require the authorities to give their explicit permission before domestic residents could spend foreign currency, and hence their ability to purchase goods and services from overseas would be severely restricted.

It should be recognised that both exchange controls and direct controls would raise serious issues for many industrialised countries, in respect of their international commitments to support free trade and capital movements.

(v) *Overseas investment by domestic residents might be encouraged* as a means of improving the net inflow of interest, profits and dividends in the longer term. However, the feasibility of this policy, in the face of current account deficits, would depend upon the availability of foreign currency reserves, and a willingness to see those reserves run down.

(vi) Any policy designed to *improve the quality* of domestically-produced goods and services and their associated *marketing* on an international level, would help to improve the current account position, although probably only in the longer term.

(vii) The government might seek to *reduce its net payments* to official institutions and organisations overseas, and its expenditure on military and diplomatic commitments overseas. However, the feasibility of such actions is likely to be severely restricted by political factors.

(a)   (ii) The following measures could be implemented with the objective of reducing a capital account deficit:

(i) The authorities may use monetary policy as a means of *raising domestic interest rates,* and hence making domestic interest-bearing assets more attractive to international investors. This policy may also help to depress inflationary pressures, and hence give increased confidence to investors in respect of the holding of assets denominated in the domestic currency.

(ii) An official commitment to the maintenance of a *stable currency exchange rate* will reduce the perceived risk of losses, in international purchasing power terms, from the holding of assets denominated in the domestic currency.

(iii) The broad stance of the *government's economic policy* will be important to foreigners' expectations of the possible future development of the domestic economy. Policies may be used to promote stable economic growth, and hence to raise the rate of return on direct investment. They may also be formulated in a manner designed to generate confidence in international financial markets.

(iv) *Direct controls* may be introduced in the form of limits on the amounts of foreign currency which may be withdrawn from the country for overseas capital investment purposes. Alternatively, direct limits may be imposed on the amounts of overseas investment which may be undertaken by domestic residents. Unfortunately, such policies may lead to retaliation by other countries, which may see a direct threat to their own capital account position.

(v) The government may offer *incentives for investment* in the form of grants, subsidies or tax free allowances, which may be directed either towards the potential foreign investor in the domestic economy, or towards the domestic investor on the brink of investing abroad. Indeed, the authorities may use the threat of taxation as a weapon to dissuade domestic residents from investing abroad.

(vi) The government may *reduce its own capital expenditure overseas*, perhaps by drawing back from political and military commitments. It may also encourage foreign governments to undertake capital expenditure within the domestic economy. However, the nature of such expenditure could generate serious political problems.

(vii) In relation to the *official financing* elements of the capital account, the authorities might seek to lengthen the repayment period on any outstanding official overseas debt. They may also negotiate with international monetary authorities and overseas central banks to raise official overseas borrowing, and may borrow from private capital markets via bond issues.

(b) The possession of official foreign currency reserves allows the authorities to support the exchange value of the domestic currency. If a country operates a managed floating exchange rate regime, official reserves may be used to purchase the domestic currency as a means of preventing an undesired depreciation in its value. Where the authorities are committed to pegging the value of the domestic currency to some other currency or group of currencies (as is the case for currencies within the EU's Exchange Rate Mechanism), the possession of official reserves is vital for day-to-day foreign exchange market intervention, in order to iron out fluctuations in the balance of supplies of and demands for currencies which might threaten the stability of the domestic currency's value.

For countries with weak current account positions, and especially for developing countries with poor credit ratings, holdings of foreign exchange reserves provide overseas companies with confidence that they will be paid for imports into such countries. An adequate level of reserves, measured in terms of the cover they provide for imports, is therefore likely to enhance the prospects of international trade taking place.

Question 20

The exchange rate of a currency is its *price* relative to other currencies, with the exchange rate for any particular currency being dependent upon the supplies of and the demands for that currency on the foreign exchange markets.

The following factors have important effects on international trade and capital flows, and hence are likely to influence exchange rates:

(a) *Relative inflation rates.* A country with relatively high inflation will tend to lose competitiveness against its trading partners. Assuming that the price elasticities of demand for traded goods are sufficiently high then, other things being equal, the value of exports/imports will fall/rise, and downward pressure will be put on the exchange rate. The purchasing power parity theory may be relevant here.

(b) *Relative interest rates.* Changes in interest rate differentials between nations may cause a reallocation in international investment portfolios. However, raw nominal interest rates have to be taken with the expected inflation rates and exchange rate changes to form a meaningful calculation of relative real yields.

In addition, transaction costs and official impediments to flows may limit such influences.

(c)   *Expectations of economic conditions.* Foreign exchange markets may anticipate the likely effects on the balance of payments position of actual or expected events, and hence currencies may strengthen or weaken before the events have noticeable effects on the balance of payments; for example, expected changes in oil prices have implications for the future trading position of oil exporters; or expected interest rate or productivity changes may imply future capital movements.

(d)   *Non-economic factors.* Actual or expected changes in the political/social environment may have implications for a country's future trading/economic position, and hence foreign currency flows. Political unrest can badly undermine confidence.

(e)   *Government economic policies.* Even without direct intervention on the foreign exchange market, a government can have a significant influence of the exchange rate, not only through the general stance of its monetary and fiscal policies (affecting business confidence, and so on), but also by the specific effects of the policies on the demand for imports, supply of export goods, general inflation rate, and so on. Import controls, investment incentives and government expenditure overseas might also be included, as might policies to improve the quality and marketing of exported products.

Question 21

(a)   There are three main objectives for the EMS:

(i) It was intended that in the *medium term* the EMS would lead to the creation of a *zone of exchange rate stability* within the EU. In other words, it was desired that exchange rate fluctuations between the currencies of the EU members should be kept to a minimum in the interests of providing a sound base for trade and payments between EU members.

(ii) In the *longer term*, the successful operation of the EMS is now seen as an important step on the road to full *economic and monetary union* within the EU. Indeed, the Maastricht Treaty lays down specific criteria in relation to full participation in the EMS as part of the transition process to EMU. Clearly, the progressive reduction in exchange rate fluctuations is critical if a truly integrated European economy is to be achieved.

(iii) The technical requirements of the EMS should promote *convergence* of EU states' *economic performances*, by encouraging the less successful economies to adopt policies of the type used by the more successful member states.

(b)   In order to achieve a stable set of exchange rates between eucurrencies it is necessary that the *economic performances* of EU member states should be broadly similar. If this does not occur, then it is likely that the countries with relatively strong economies would tend to have persistent surpluses on their trade with the countries whose economies are relatively weak. The resulting international payments imbalances would then tend to destabilise exchange rates, as market adjustments brought the supplies of and the demands for the various EU currencies into equilibrium. In consequence, the successful operation of the EMS is likely to require a high level of *economic policy co-ordination* between EU governments, with a view to bringing about a convergence in individual members' economic performances. In particular, policies will be aimed at:

(i) bringing *inflation rates* in member states to similar low levels;

(ii) reducing differentials between the levels of *interest rates* ruling in comparable markets in the respective countries;

(iii) limiting the extent of *balance of payments* imbalances.

If these economic conditions are not met, then it is unlikely that exchange rate stability will be maintained in the medium term. Whilst central bank intervention on the foreign currency exchange markets may be able to limit exchange rate fluctuations in the shorter term, such intervention is not normally successful over longer periods in the face of persistent market pressures.

(c) Assuming that relatively narrow exchange rate fluctuation bands were to be used, it is argued that the UK's participation in the ERM would generate several substantial benefits for the UK economy:

(i) As the EU now accounts for over a half of all the UK's overseas trade, a more stable relationship between sterling and other EU currencies would help both exporters and importers in their business planning and pricing decisions. For example, an exporter would be able to set prices in another EU currency, and would be fairly confident of the sterling revenue to be generated at a future date. Similarly, the sterling cost of imports could be estimated more accurately, thus avoiding unforeseen cost increases which would arise from a weakening in sterling's value. For both exporters and importers there would be less pressure to operate on wide profit margins (in order to cover exchange rate risks or hedging costs), and hence there should be a greater chance of gaining business.

(ii) By stabilising the value of sterling relative to a strong currency such as the deutschmark, the control of domestic inflation may be assisted. Thus, pressure would be placed on domestic producers to hold down their production costs or face being priced out of overseas markets. Inflation rates in the domestic economy which were above the average of EU trading partners would necessarily translate into increasingly uncompetitive export prices. In addition, import prices would be held down relative to what they otherwise would have been had sterling been allowed to depreciate. In effect membership of the ERM should provide an anchor for UK monetary policy. However, it must be emphasised that these anti-inflation benefits would only accrue so long as other EU countries maintained low rates of inflation.

(iii) The influence of the UK in EU decision-making at a time of great economic and political change in Europe can only be enhanced by the UK's full commitment to the EMS. Without this, it is argued, the UK will become isolated politically, and might find that important economic opportunities are missed. The publication of the Delors Report in 1989, and the subsequent Maastricht Summit in December 1991, merely served to highlight the political discomfort of the UK government in respect of its European credentials.

Full membership of the EMS is not, of course, without its problems:

(i) The need to co-ordinate economic policies within the EU, if the EMS is to operate successfully, implies that domestic policies within individual EU countries may have to be subordinated to this purpose. This suggested loss of sovereignty over economic policy decisions has often been used as an argument by the UK government for keeping sterling out of the ERM. It is feared that the effective loss of economic independence would deny the authorities the power to respond to events which might be unique to the domestic economy.

(ii) When sterling was placed within the ERM, the question arose as to the appropriateness of the exchange rate on entry. There would appear to be little agreement on an appropriate rate, and yet this is a critical factor in determining not only the UK's competitive position but also the chances of stability being maintained within the ERM.

(iii) If the UK failed to achieve an economic performance on a par with the other major EU states, the relatively fixed exchange rate structure could prove to be damaging to both UK output and job prospects. (The essential economic conditions which would have to be satisfied are outlined above in part (b)).

(iv) It is sometimes argued that the importance of the UK in world trade and finance makes sterling an inherently unstable currency; or, perhaps more strictly, makes its exchange rate vulnerable to changes in certain economic and financial conditions. Thus, possible friction could be generated between sterling and other EU currencies, which may be affected differently by external events. In this context, the position of the deutschmark is of particular significance, given its growing importance in world financial affairs. Indeed, some commentators have argued that attempting to bring together two such important currencies within the ERM may undermine its basic stability. Also, to the extent that sterling did not settle down easily within the ERM, the authorities would be required to undertake excessive amounts of exchange market intervention, which could have adverse effects on the wellbeing of the domestic economy.

Note: The last section of this question has been overtaken by events. The UK's re-entry into the EMS, i.e. the ERM, would now be seen as a prelude to membership of the single currency area, with the Bank of England becoming a member of the ESCB. As such, the decision must be taken on much broader grounds.

Question 22

(a)   The *balance of visible trade* measures the difference between the value of visible exports and the value of visible imports. Visible imports and exports involve trade in:

(i)   food, beverages and tobacco;

(ii) basic raw materials;

(iii) fuel;

(iv) manufactured goods.

The *terms of trade* can be defined as:

$$\frac{\text{index of export prices}}{\text{index of import prices}} \times 100$$

At a particular base-date, both indices are given a value of 100, and so the starting point of the terms of trade is also 100. If there is a subsequent rise in the average price of imports with the average price of exports remaining constant , the terms of trade will fall below 100; conventionally this is described as a 'deterioration' in the terms of trade. A fall in the index of export prices relative to import prices would have the same effect. If the opposite adjustments occur, there is said to be an 'improvement' in the terms of trade. Therefore, in effect, movements in the terms of trade show changes in the real purchasing power (in terms of imports) of a given quantity of exports. If the terms of trade improve, for every unit of goods exported the country will obtain a larger quantity of imports; the converse is true for a deterioration in the terms of trade. Another name for 'terms of trade' is 'barter terms of trade'.

(b)   The government is able to influence the *balance of trade* to the extent that it is able to affect overseas trade flows. The major approaches which may be taken include the following:

(i) *Alteration of currency exchange rates*. For example, by reducing the exchange value of the domestic currency, other things being equal, the overseas price of exports will be reduced whilst the domestic price of imports will rise. As long as the price elasticity of demand for exports is greater than one, the additional demand for exports will be sufficiently great to cause the value of exports to rise; similarly, as long as the price elasticity of demand for imports is greater than one, the reduction in the demand for imports will be large enough to cause the value of imports to fall. Clearly, as long as the elasticities of demand for traded goods taken in aggregate are high enough, the balance of trade will move in favour of the country reducing the value of its currency. In addition, there should be sufficient spare capacity in the economy to enable the output to export markets to be increased. An increase in the value of the currency will have the opposite effect on the balance of trade.

(ii) *Domestic demand management*. If the authorities are able to depress domestic demand, perhaps through an increase in taxation, government spending cuts or a tightening of monetary policy, the flow of imports is likely to be reduced and spare capacity created within the domestic economy for the production of additional goods for export. Indeed, depressed home markets are likely to act as a stimulus to domestic businesses to seek out overseas markets for their products. In addition, reduced demand within the domestic economy is likely to ease inflationary pressures and so help domestic producers to maintain their competitive position in overseas markets. Expansionary economic policies would have the opposite effect on the economy and hence on the balance of trade.

(iii) *Direct controls*. Notwithstanding international free trade agreements, the authorities may introduce import controls, export incentives or exchange controls. To the extent that imports are held back or exports are raised, the balance of trade may be improved. However, it is important to recognise that such direct controls may simply lead to retaliation by overseas governments and so domestic exports may also be adversely affected, making the overall effect questionable.

Clearly, the authorities have a wide range of means through which they may seek to influence the balance of trade, and potentially the effects may be great.

The government's influence over the *terms of trade* is likely to be much more limited than its influence over the balance of trade. The reason for this is that in order to affect the terms of trade the authorities must alter the relative prices of export and import goods, and these are very much at the mercy of *world market prices*. Thus, whilst the government may be able to alter the terms of trade by an adjustment in the domestic currency's exchange rate, a subsequent change in market conditions which alters the prices of traded goods may wipe out the effect on the terms of trade. Nevertheless, by implementing policies which affect the level of domestic prices relative to prices overseas, the government will have some influence on the terms of trade.

As we mentioned above, alterations in the *domestic currency's exchange rate* will affect the terms of trade, for given sets of domestic prices. Alternatively, the authorities may introduce policies to hold down the rate of *domestic price inflation*, with a view to keeping price-rises below those experienced by overseas countries. This approach, which might involve a tightening of monetary or fiscal policies, would tend to cause the terms of trade to deteriorate. It seems unlikely that a government would attempt to cause domestic inflation as a means of improving the terms of trade. A far more sensible approach would be to encourage domestic industries to produce high-quality output and undertake aggressive marketing in overseas markets. Thus, if overseas demand for domestic exports can be stimulated, the prices of these goods may be pushed upwards (and hence the terms of trade improved) as a by-product of a favourable shift in trading patterns.

Question 23

(a)   Internal funding occurs when a company raises funds from internal sources such as from the sale of assets or from the retention of profits. If a company can reduce its dividends or boost profits then it will be raising funds internally.

Such funds do not have to be repaid or serviced in any way. However, internally generated funds can involve a cost, in that reduced dividends may result in shareholder dissatisfaction and a reduction in assets may result in reduced productive capacity.

Externally raised funds are funds raised by borrowing or by the issue of new shares for cash. Borrowings have to be serviced to meet both interest obligations and agreed capital repayments. New shares do not involve any servicing costs but the new shareholders may expect greater dividends. If new shares come into the hands of new shareholders, as opposed to being taken up by the existing shareholders as in a rights issue, then there will be some dilution of control in the company.

(b)   The main means by which companies can raise external finance are as follows:

(i) *Overdraft facilities.* There is a maximum borrowing limit marked on the current account, and the balance can fluctuate at will up to the maximum permitted overdraft limit. Overdrafts are repayable on demand. Interest is usually at floating rates and is charged on the closing daily debit balance.

(ii) *LIBOR-linked loans.* Within an agreed total limit the company may withdraw blocks of funds of maturities normally of between one and three months. The minimum facility is usually £250,000 and the minimum individual loan is usually £100,000. The total facility is usually committed by the bank, since the bank guarantees to keep the total facility available for a certain minimum period. A commitment fee is payable if the facility is committed, and banks usually charge a non-utilisation fee on any part of the facility which is not drawn.

LIBOR is usually more volatile than base rate, so interest costs are likely to be less predictable than for a base rate linked facility such as an overdraft.

(iii) *Acceptance credits*. A company draws a bill of exchange which is accepted by a bank. If the bill fulfils the following criteria, it becomes an eligible bill which can be discounted at the Bank of England:

(1) the bank must be deemed 'eligible' according to the Bank of England criteria;

(2) the bill must have a maximum original term of 187 days;

(3) the bill must be issued in connection with some underlying trade transaction, brief details of which must be noted on the bill itself.

Because eligible bills can be rediscounted at the Bank of England, the holder can discount the bill at a fine rate which can be below LIBOR.

The minimum total facility is usually £500,000 and the minimum amount for an individual bill is usually £50,000.

(iv) *Commercial paper*. This consists of unsecured promissory notes issued by companies to investors at a discount to face value. The minimum amount is very large (for example, £100,000 for a single promissory note with sterling commercial paper, as opposed to the £50,000 minimum for a single bill under an acceptance credit).

Sterling commercial paper is more flexible than acceptance credits because there is no need to link the issue to an underlying trade transaction. However, SCP requires a higher effective rate of interest than does an acceptance credit because of the lower security of SCP.

Sterling commercial paper has an original maturity of between seven days and five years, but the one to five year maturities are called Medium Term Notes.

Other commercial paper markets are the US commercial paper market and the EuroCommercial paper markets.

(v) *Bank loans*. Given the competition between banks, there is a tremendous variety of loans available to suit the needs of company borrowers. Terms to maturity can be from one to ten years, but in suitable cases 30-year maturities can be arranged. Interest can be fixed or floating, and floating rates can be LIBOR-linked or linked to base rate.

Security will normally be required for longer term loans and there may be covenants in the loan documentation which bind the company to maintaining certain minimum financial ratios.

(vi) *Sterling debentures*. These are registered transferable loan stocks which usually pay a fixed rate of interest and are redeemable at par on the set maturity date. The stocks are listed on the London Stock Exchange. The minimum original maturity period is now five years, since stocks with an original maturity of under five years must now be issued as Medium Term Notes on the sterling commercial paper market.

Large amounts of funds can be raised, with the typical range being £30–100m.

(vii) *Eurobonds.* Eurobonds are foreign currency denominated bearer securities which may be issued by way of an offer for sale to the general public or via a private placing with investors. Public issues are normally made by a syndicate of banks which underwrite the bonds and place them with investors. Such bonds are normally listed on one or more of the main stock exchanges. Private placements are rarely listed on a stock exchange.

Eurobonds are only applicable where large amounts of funds are required, with a typical issue being in excess of US$75m or its equivalent. Issuers must be major corporate bodies with an international reputation and a first-class credit rating. Companies which have issued a Eurobond find that this gives them added credibility with other providers of finance, thus ensuring that if additional funds are ever required, they can be raised at the finest rates.

(viii) *Leasing.* Assets such as aircraft, ships and machinery with the aid of lease finance from a bank or group of banks. Even the largest companies occasionally use this source of external finance, whereas the factoring of book debts is only used by smaller companies.

(ix) *Equity shares.* New issues of equity capital provide long-term funds without the need to service the repayment of capital or to make interest payments. There are two main classes of equity capital: ordinary shares and preference shares.

Ordinary shareholders are legally the owners of the company, with the power to appoint directors by a majority vote at meetings. Dividends can only be paid from available profits, and within that constraint the rate of dividend is recommended by the directors. In the event of liquidation ordinary shareholders rank last, but they are entitled to the whole of the surplus, if any, remaining after the claims of all creditors and prior ranking preferential shareholders have been met.

Preferential shareholders rank behind all outside creditors in the event of liquidation and are entitled (usually) to repayment at par if there is a sufficient surplus. The dividend on preference shares is fixed and it ranks before the ordinary shareholders' dividend. Preference dividends can be paid only from available profits, and indeed there is no compulsion on the directors to recommend payment of the preferential dividend. However, ordinary shareholders cannot receive any dividend if the preference dividend for the year has not been met.

The higher the ratio of equity capital to loan capital, the lower the gearing ratio. Other things being equal, low-geared companies are less risky than high-geared ones. However, debt finance is usually cheaper than equity because interest is tax deductible whereas dividends are not.

It is a matter of great concern that a company employs the optimal mix of debt and equity finance. If there is too little debt the cost of capital is too high; whereas if there is too much debt, the high gearing ratio causes providers of capital to demand higher returns to compensate for the greater perceived riskiness.

Question 24

(a)   The three broad types of exposure to exchange rate risk are normally classified as:

(i)   transaction risk;

(ii) translation risk;

(iii) economic risk.

Transaction risk arises from normal trading activities when foreign currencies are used in settlement. If an exporter invoices in foreign currency he will lose if the foreign currency has depreciated against the home currency between invoice date and settlement date. The converse applies to an importer who will gain if the foreign currency depreciates against the home currency between invoice date and settlement date.

Translation risk applies whenever there is a mismatch between the mix of currencies in which the assets are denominated and the mix of currencies in which the liabilities are denominated. For balance sheet reporting purposes, the value of the foreign currency-denominated assets and liabilities must be changed (translated) into home currency. Thus, if foreign currency denominated assets exceed foreign currency denominated liabilities, and if the foreign currency has appreciated against the home currency between the previous balance sheet date and the current balance sheet date, there will be a reported translation gain. If foreign-currency-denominated assets exceed foreign currency-denominated liabilities and if the foreign currency has depreciated during this period, the new balance sheet will show a translation loss.

Any translation gain will be matched by an increase in reported net worth, whereas any translation loss will be matched by a reduction in net worth. Changes in net worth affect the reported gearing ratios and thus can affect the attitudes of shareholders, creditors and bankers.

Economic risk is difficult to quantify and cannot be reported in the published accounts. It reflects the extent to which a company can suffer a competitive disadvantage because of adverse movements in exchange rates. For example, a UK company with all its operations and sales within the UK could be at a competitive disadvantage if the currency of the country of a competitor were to depreciate against sterling.

(b)   Interest rate swaps in themselves are not necessarily a means of hedging interest-rate risk. However, they are a mechanism whereby smaller companies can obtain what amounts to, in effect, fixed-rate financing.

Major corporates can borrow at fixed rates if they wish, but smaller companies may not be able to do so or they may have access to fixed-rate funds only at penal rates.

If an interest rate swap is arranged the larger company borrows in the fixed-rate market and the smaller company borrows at floating rates. The maturity dates and principal amounts should be similar for both loans. The companies then swap their interest payment obligations. Thus the smaller company pays a fixed rate to the larger one and receives payment of its floating rate from the larger company. In addition the smaller company must pay a fee to the larger company for the privilege of being able to obtain what amounts to fixed-rate finance. The larger company gains because it obtains floating rates of interest which are effectively reduced by the amount of the fee.

In practice, an intermediary – invariably a bank – is often used so as to guarantee the obligations of both parties to the swap. The bank will charge a fee for this service.

Question 25

(a)   When a company borrows a substantial amount of long-term funds it is taking on a major commitment to service the debt, which will have important implications for its financial position, irrespective of the form of interest rate payable or the currency of denomination of the debt. In particular, if the borrowing is large relative to the scale of the company's operations, the impact on the company of unexpected movements in interest rates or exchange rates may be serious.

(i) If the company borrows at a market-related rate of interest, the main risk that it faces is that of market rates proving to be much higher than expected. The borrower is normally required to service the debt regularly, and hence higher rates of interest mean higher cash outlays. This does not only mean that the company faces possible pressure on its cash flow position, but also it may find itself at a competitive disadvantage if competing companies have raised their borrowed funds at fixed rates or if they have little outstanding debt.

(ii) If the company borrows at a fixed rate it is able to avoid the cash flow risk which arises from unexpected increases in market rates of interest. However, there is still the risk that competing companies might have borrowed funds at market-related rates, and then those rates fall, thus leaving the company with fixed rate debt having to carry relatively expensive debt servicing costs.

The above discussion assumes that the company is committed for a long period to one particular type of interest payment. In reality, it is often possible for borrowers to elect to switch between fixed and floating rates at predetermined times during the loan period. Nevertheless, some commitment has to be made for a certain minimum length of time, and it is likely that levels of fixed rates and margins required over floating rates will be adjusted by the lender to reflect the changing conditions in the financial environment. Consequently, it is most probable that some element of risk will also be present even where switching between commitments is possible. Furthermore, the matter of foreign currency borrowing has been ignored in the above discussion. If the company does in fact raise funds denominated in foreign currencies, it may add to the risks which it faces, unless sufficient of its expected revenues are also denominated in the same foreign currencies. Where expected revenues and interest commitments are denominated in different currencies, any movements in the exchange rates between those currencies may place unforeseen burdens on the borrower (or may lead to unexpected gains), when all flows are converted to a common currency. This exchange rate risk merely compounds the underlying interest rate risk problem, and again may generate implications for the borrower's competitiveness.

(b)   An interest rate swap occurs when borrowers raise funds independently and then swap the associated debt servicing commitments on equal sums.

Borrowers may engage in swap transactions merely because their expectations differ as to future interest rate movements. For example, a borrower with outstanding floating rate debt may believe that interest rates are set to rise substantially, and hence may seek a counterparty with fixed rate debt outstanding who is willing to swap commitments. Clearly, for a swap to be agreed, the counterparty must regard the floating rate commitment as being more attractive than the fixed rate. This may mean that the counterparties have different expectations of interest rate movements; alternatively, it may be that the interest payment pattern associated with the floating rate debt is thought to be more attractive, than that on the fixed rate debt, by the borrower willing to give up the commitment to the latter. Irrespective of the ultimate reason for the counterparties' agreement to swap, the transaction allows the initial holder of the floating rate debt to obtain certainty in respect of the future cash flows required for interest payments, and hence this particular element of risk is avoided. However, the risk is accepted that competing companies with floating rate debt will subsequently be placed at a competitive advantage if market interest rates fall, thus reducing their debt servicing costs. In a similar way, companies may manage their interest rate risk position by swapping different forms of floating rate debt.

It is important to appreciate that the counterparties to a swap transaction maintain their original responsibilities to the lenders of the funds. Therefore, whilst the counterparties may have hedged certain interest rate risks, they must be willing to accept counterparty risk, in the sense that if a counterparty defaults on a commitment to make interest payments, the original borrower is still liable for the debt servicing. Consequently, complex legal problems may arise in respect of swap transactions, which may deter borrowers from becoming involved.

Finally, it should be noted that as a bank will normally be responsible for arranging a swap transaction, the counterparties will have to pay fees to the bank. In addition, in certain circumstances, one of the counterparties will pay a fee to the other in order to bring about the swap. For example, a large company may have access to long term funds at fixed rates of interest, perhaps via the issue of sterling debentures, but a small company may only be able to raise floating rate debt (unless it is willing to pay unduly high fixed rates of interest). Thus, if the small company would like to take on fixed rate debt, it may pay a fee to the large company for the privilege of swapping the servicing commitment on its outstanding floating rate debt for the commitment on an equal amount of fixed rate debt. In effect, the small company gains certainty over its debt servicing, whilst the large company receives compensation (the fee) for taking on the risk of floating rate debt.

Question 26

(a) Within the context of the housing market, negative equity arises where the market value of residential property falls below the outstanding associated mortgage debt. For example, an owner-occupier may have an outstanding mortgage debt of £60,000 relating to a property the market value of which has fallen to £55,000. In this case the negative equity amounts to £5,000. This means that if the owner-occupier wished to sell the property, the proceeds would be insufficient to discharge the debt.

(b) (i) Assuming that a mortgage lender would not normally lend in excess of 100% of the market value of a mortgaged property, the existence of negative equity implies that the owner-occupier has incurred a capital loss, and this may affect the owner-occupier's spending patterns adversely. The reduction in the value of personal wealth may encourage the owner-occupier to raise his/her saving ratio as a means of rebuilding the amount of wealth held.

The main problem for an owner-occupier, arising from negative equity, occurs if there is a desire to sell the property and move elsewhere. By definition, the funds realised from the property sale will be insufficient to discharge the outstanding mortgage loan. This means that the owner-occupier must raise an unsecured loan or run down savings in order to meet the legal commitment of the mortgage loan. If the owner-occupier is unable to call upon savings, the raising of an unsecured loan in such circumstances may be difficult (especially if economic conditions in general are unfavourable, which they are likely to be if the housing market is stagnant). Furthermore, the need for an unsecured loan implies that the owner-occupier will have little, if any, funds to contribute towards the purchase of another property, thus creating substantial difficulties in raising a new mortgage loan. In this case there may be little alternative but to move into rented accommodation.

(b) (ii) An important problem for a mortgage lender, where negative equity arises, is that, by default, it finds itself with a loan outstanding which is partly unsecured. This is particularly awkward for building societies which, in normal circumstances, are limited in the extent to which they are able to make unsecured loans. However, until the borrower wishes to move from the property, the negative equity is not realised, although this does not diminish the risk associated with the mortgage loan for the lender. As indicated above, a borrower may be able to discharge the whole of a mortgage loan upon moving house by using savings. Also, where the borrower is fundamentally creditworthy with a stable income, the risks in making an unsecured loan to cover the negative equity are relatively small. The main difficulty is likely to arise if a borrower with negative equity becomes unemployed or otherwise unable to service the mortgage loan. When this happens there is the serious risk that the borrower will literally walk away from the debt (and the negative equity). The lender then has the expensive task of obtaining possession of the property and attempting to realise as much of its value as possible.

(c) Basically, the price of new houses is determined by the interaction of the supply of and the demand for new houses. However, as existing houses are close substitutes for new houses, supply and demand conditions relating to second-hand houses must be taken into account when considering the determination of the price of new houses. The greater is the supply of new houses coming on to the market, other things being equal, the lower is likely to be the price of new houses. The supply of new houses depends upon the rate of completions by builders, the stock of previously unsold new houses being offered for sale, and the ability of builders to agree sales before houses have been completed. This supply in total is likely to be influenced by factors such as the general state of the economy, and expected trends in unemployment, earnings, inflation and interest rates. Property developers are more likely to invest in construction of residential property if they are optimistic about being able to sell it. Hence supply is likely to rise if real earnings are growing and employment prospects appear good; by contrast, rising unemployment and high interest rates are likely to lead to a reduction in supply.

The total supply of houses on the market will be higher than the number of new houses being made available to the extent that houses are transferred from rental status (where transfers do not involve sitting tenants) and houses are vacated as a result of the owner's death, emigration or move to rented accommodation. The rate of transfer from rental status is likely to increase during periods of buoyancy in the housing market, which in turn will be encouraged by favourable economic conditions. The factors causing the supply of houses on the market to rise for other reasons are unlikely to be linked to shorter-term economic developments, except where houses are vacated due to mortgage loan servicing problems, which is more likely when the economy is depressed and the housing market stagnant. Overall, to the extent that the supply of second-hand houses rises, other things being equal, the price of all houses (including new ones) is likely to be depressed. It is important to note that houses placed on the market by owner-occupiers wishing to move into other owner-occupied houses have no net effect on the supply of houses available, although there may be some impact on the supply of and demand for different types of houses.

As far as a potential purchaser of a house is concerned, new houses and second-hand houses may be very close substitutes. Individual preferences, relative prices and locations of houses will influence the extent of the substitutability. However, as far as the determination of the price of new houses is concerned, the crucial factor is the net demand for houses overall, and this depends upon potential purchasers entering the market for the first time. Existing owner-occupiers moving between houses have no impact on net demand. The factors which affect the demand from first-time buyers at any point in time are those which have been listed above as factors which affect supply. In the longer term, the number of first-time buyers is affected by demographic trends (particularly changes in population and age profiles) and social conventions (including the occurrence of single person households and single parent families). The availability of alternative forms of suitable accommodation is also of importance, and hence government policies in respect of local authority house building, rent levels and private sector rented property developments are of relevance. These longer-term factors are also likely to influence the expectations of future trends in demand held by property developers, and hence will probably affect the supply side of the market. It should also be recognised that changes in government economic policies, in so far as they affect the broad development of the economy and especially the factors listed above as being relevant for the supply of and the demand for houses, are likely to influence the price of new houses. Interest rates affect both the cost of financing the purchase of houses, i.e. the demand, and the costs of building new houses and of 'bridging' the ownership of two houses, i.e. the supply of houses.

As stated above, it is the interaction of the supply of and the demand for new houses that determines their price. Thus, for example, if economic conditions improve, and favourable trends are expected in personal sector earnings and job prospects, it is likely that both demand and supply will be stimulated. But as demand is able to adjust much more quickly than supply, there is likely to be upwards pressure placed on house prices, at least in the short term. The extent of any increase in house prices will depend upon the speed of adjustment of net supply, and ultimately the impact on building costs and land prices. It is possible that the pressure of demand will push up the price of building land, with only a marginal impact on the total supply made available. Consequently, supply may never catch up with demand, and prices of new houses may continue to drift upwards until the trend in demand itself alters. If demand was to fall, perhaps due to the economy moving into a period of recession, the above situation could be reversed with the given supply on the market becoming excessive relative to demand. As property developers do not wish to hold stocks of vacant houses, and as some owner-occupiers with pressing financial problems feel that they have no option but to sell their properties, the pressure on house prices will be downwards. The market price of new houses may then only stabilise once the level of net demand stabilises and the net supply on the market falls to a comparable level.

Question 27

(a) *Building Societies*

These institutions are the dominant providers of mortgage loans, which comprise around 70% of all personal sector financial liabilities, and in recent years deposits (mainly shares) with building societies have formed the largest single element of the sector's liquid asset holdings. Despite the recessionary conditions in the UK during the early 1990s, and in particular the downturn in the housing market, the amount of building society mortgage debt outstanding and the total value of shares and deposits held with building societies continued to grow, although at a slower rate than that experienced during the boom years of the late 1980s.

The increased competition in the personal savings and loans markets, unleashed by the financial deregulation which took place during the 1980s, has tended to erode the building societies' pre-eminence in respect of their specialist financial intermediation roles. The retail banks have shown themselves to be particularly aggressive competitors in certain areas of business. However, it must be recognised that deregulation has opened up new opportunities for building societies to service a wider range of personal sector financial requirements. The major development in this respect was the enactment of the Building Societies Act 1986 (and subsequent amendments), which allowed the building societies for the first time to make unsecured loans and to provide a range of payments and other banking services, including some relating to international transactions.

In addition, many building societies are now active in the provision of facilities designed to meet the longer-term investment needs of the personal sector. For example, it may be possible for individuals to invest in unit trusts, personal equity plans, insurance-based products and personal pension plans through their building societies. The total holdings of these types of investment by the personal sector are huge, although such investments purchased through building societies are still relatively modest. Some building societies also offer share dealing facilities for customers with direct holdings of company shares.

Finally, it should be recognised that as building societies become increasingly like retail banks in the provision of personal sector financial services, their staff are becoming better equipped to offer advice to customers on the management of their finances. Indeed, in 1997, four major societies plan to become retail banks.

(b) *Life assurance companies and pension funds*
Claims on life assurance companies and pension funds are the largest single item amongst the personal sector's financial assets, accounting for around a half of the total of such assets. In recent years the flows of funds into life assurance companies and pension funds, have amounted to approximately 30% of all personal sector uses of funds, and have been of similar magnitude to the amounts of funds spent on the purchase of residential property and other fixed assets by the sector. It is through life assurance companies and pension funds that the personal sector holds the bulk of its claims on the corporate sector, direct shareholdings are relatively small in comparison. Ultimately, the value of company securities depends upon market forces, and hence a boom on the stock market may raise the relative importance of claims on life assurance companies and pension funds without there being corresponding inflows of new funds. By the same token, the importance of such claims may diminish if stock market conditions stagnate.

Investments with life assurance companies and pension funds are long-term in nature. Indeed, the contractual arrangements associated with most of these investments are such that it is not possible for the investor to receive a return until a particular event has occurred. In the case of a pension fund, the retirement of the contributor activates the fund's commitment to pay a pension for the remainder of the contributor's life, and often beyond in respect of dependent relatives. In respect of life assurance, there may be some access to accumulated funds before the maturity of a policy or the death of the person whose life is insured, but the terms are often such that the surrender value represents a poor return on the funds invested. However, a small market in second-hand endowment policies has begun recently. Consequently, whilst investments with life assurance companies and pension funds are of vital importance to the long-term security of members of the personal sector, they cannot be viewed in the same way as deposits with banks and building societies. The latter are generally liquid assets held to meet shorter-term financing requirements and to cover unforeseen demands for funds without excessive transactions costs being incurred.

(c) *Company Securities*
Direct holdings of company securities form an important element of the personal sector's total financial assets (around 10% of the total in recent years), with the bulk of these holdings relating to UK companies. However, of much greater importance for the personal sector are the indirect holdings of company securities represented by investments in life assurance companies, pension funds and unit trusts. Claims on these financial intermediaries amount to over a half of all personal sector financial assets, and company securities comprise around 70% of the assets held by these intermediaries. Therefore, in total, around a half of the personal sector's financial asset holdings ultimately relate to company securities, although about three-quarters of these are effectively locked away in life assurance policies and pension funds, and hence cannot be realised at will (as explained in part (b) above). As the value of company securities is at the mercy of market forces, changes in stock market conditions can have a substantial impact on the value of personal sector wealth. Also, whilst the overall return on investments in company

securities is often greater than that on deposits with banks and building societies, significant risks are associated with the holding of company securities, as was demonstrated by the stock market collapse of October 1987.

In recent years, flows of personal sector funds into company securities via investments in life assurance companies and pension funds have remained at very high levels, despite the depressed economic conditions at the beginning of the 1990s. However, during the late 1980s and at the beginning of the 1990s, the personal sector withdrew substantial amounts of funds from direct holdings of securities. It was only in 1992 that the personal sector again became a direct net purchaser of company securities and the amounts involved were less than half the net deposits placed with building societies, or about one-fifth of the total of funds invested in life assurance companies and pension funds.

Question 28

(a)   The most extreme form of risk faced by any investor is that of default on interest payments or repayment of debt. The most obvious default risk run by the personal sector relates to the granting of trade credit by unincorporated businesses (which are included in the personal sector). Quite simply, debtors may be unable or unwilling to discharge their debt, and hence creditors may be forced to write-off the debt or perhaps initiate expensive legal action. However, the bulk of personal sector financial assets are in the form of claims on financial institutions. There is always some risk that an individual institution will fail, due to inept management or fraud, and hence that depositors/investors will lose the entire value of their deposits/investments. The latter occurrence is rare in the UK, as there are often officially-sponsored depositor/investor protection schemes, which provide at least a limited safety net. There is also the liquidation value of a failed institution, e.g. BCCI, which may allow for some repayment of creditors.

Direct ownership of company securities is inherently risky, although it is rare for well-managed blue-chip companies to go into liquidation. The more likely occurrence is that the trading performance of a company will be eroded, and consequently the level of returns on, and the capital value of, its securities will fall. Government securities, issued by major Western nations, are effectively free of default risk but, if such instruments are to be realised before their maturity dates, investors may incur capital losses if the general level of interest rates has risen since the time that the instruments were purchased.

When an investor purchases a fixed-term asset paying a fixed rate of interest, there is the risk that the rate of inflation may prove to be higher than was expected at the time that the purchase was made, and hence that the real return will be unexpectedly low. Indeed, if the rate of inflation rises above the nominal rate of interest earned, the real return on the investment is negative, as the interest earnings are insufficient even to cover the erosion of the purchasing power of the principal sum lent. In addition, to the extent that inflation generates uncertainty in financial markets, it may undermine business activities, especially at an international level, and this may increase the risk associated with investments in companies susceptible to such effects.

Against a background of economic uncertainty, it is difficult for members of the personal sector to predict with any accuracy their future financial needs, particularly several years in advance. Consequently, decisions on the deployment of financial asset holdings may entail significant risk arising from unanticipated changes in financial or personal circumstances. Investors tend to be faced with a choice between holding relatively low yield liquid assets and holding higher yield illiquid (and more risky) assets. Once a portfolio has been selected, an unanticipated change in financial circumstances may necessitate the forced sale of securities, with the associated risk of capital losses, or the premature withdrawal of deposits from financial institutions, which may incur interest penalties.

As mentioned above, investors holding fixed-term assets which pay fixed rates of interest are at risk from unexpectedly high rates of inflation. They also forgo the opportunity for earning higher returns if market rates of interest should rise. Unfortunately, variable interest rates on assets are equally risky, as the cash earnings on such investments depend upon movements in market rates of interest, and if these rates were to fall, the investor would have been better placed holding fixed-rate assets. Also, interest rate movements are likely to affect the capital value of fixed-interest marketable securities, thus generating a further source of risk for the investor.

Finally, it should be noted that possible changes in government economic policy provide yet another source of risk for the investor. For example, changes in the stance of monetary policy are likely to lead to alterations in the level of interest rates, with the types of effect mentioned above. Again, changes in fiscal policy may affect the tax regimes relating to investments in pension funds, National Savings instruments and Personal Equity Plans, as well as investment earnings in general. Thus the relative benefits attached to particular portfolios of assets may be altered. In fact, the government's economic policy as a whole is likely to be a crucial determinant of the broader economic and financial environment, and hence returns on all forms of investments are potentially vulnerable in one way or another.

(b) Personal sector investors may take a number of actions in order to minimise the financial risks identified in part (a), although it must be recognised at the outset that the sophisticated hedging instruments available to corporate financial managers are largely inappropriate in this context. Rather, prudent management of finances and the application of common sense in financial decision-making are at the root of limiting exposure to risk.

In respect of risk of default, unincorporated businesses should undertake careful screening of the creditworthiness of potential debtors before credit is granted. In fact, there may be a case for curtailing the provision of credit, and instead offering discounts for cash payment as a means of retaining customers.

Investors in financial intermediaries would be well advised to ensure that they only place funds with institutions which have a good reputation and which are part of a sector covered by an investor/depositor protection scheme. Also as most such schemes are designed to protect smaller investors, and hence have strict limits on the cover offered, it may also be advisable for investors to distribute their funds between a number of institutions, so as to spread risk and to maximise the effective insurance coverage. A disadvantage of holding relatively small amounts of funds with a range of institutions is that higher returns might have to be forgone where tiered interest rates are offered.

For investors in marketable securities, the holding of a diversified portfolio of instruments is perhaps the best way of spreading the unsystematic risk, particularly for company equities where performances may vary markedly. Professional advice should also be sought before funds are committed to such uses. The holding of government securities removes the risk of default, but premature realisation may lead to capital losses. Therefore, consideration may be given to the purchase of National Savings instruments, which are the only truly capital-safe instruments. These may be liquidated for their full nominal values either on demand or after a short period of notice, although higher returns might have to be forgone as the price for early redemption. Also National Savings instruments are only available in limited quantities for individual investors.

In order to avoid unexpected transfers of wealth between lender and borrower when inflation rates prove to be higher than expected, lenders may seek to have their interest earnings linked to market rates of interest (which may be expected to move broadly in line with the trend of inflation) or to a suitable price index. The latter approach removes the risk in respect of real returns on loans, but the lender must be willing to accept the uncertainty created in respect of cash receipts. Alternatively, interest-bearing debt may be avoided altogether, and instead funds used to purchase company equity shares, the capital value of which and the income from which tend to rise with inflation, although holdings of such instruments open up other forms of risk for the investor. In a similar way, residential property, land or other real assets may be purchased as a hedge against inflation. However, whilst such assets often prove to be good investments in the longer term, there are often prolonged periods over which their prices fall, and at any time individual purchases may lead to substantial losses.

It is impossible for personal sector investors to hold interest-bearing debt and yet avoid risk. Fixed rate instruments secure cash returns, but these may prove to be relatively poor returns if market rates of interest rise, or if inflation is higher than anticipated. Variable rate debt leads to uncertainty in respect of cash earnings. Movement of funds into other forms of investment bring their own particular risks. Therefore, the investor would be wise to hold a diversified portfolio of instruments, perhaps containing a range of different types of interest-bearing assets, company equities and real property. Within a portfolio it will probably be necessary to forgo some higher return assets in order to maintain a sufficient degree of liquidity. This will give the flexibility of finances to meet unanticipated changes in financial circumstances, and also to respond appropriately to changes in government policy, which may impinge upon the relative returns on financial assets.

Index

439